YHWH in the Wind(s)

"Violet Chiswa Gandiya's close scrutiny of YHWH, the Hebrew Bible's mighty creator god, invigorates the order-from-chaos motifs from traditional biblical studies with a new infusion of ideas drawn from African—in particular, Dogon—mythologies. The resulting inter-reading provides new inspiration and contemplation on ancient and influential sacred texts."
—Johanna Stiebert, Professor of Hebrew Bible, University of Leeds, England

"Violet Chiswa Gandiya writes out of a profound acquaintance with storm theophany and related aspects of the depiction of the God of Israel. In this accomplished monograph she attempts a partial resetting of the study of Israelite creation theology by engaging with traditions from the 'Global South,' represented here by the creation mythology of the Malian Dogon tribe. This energizes her presentation of Israel's God as a God of Wind(s) rather than a Storm Deity and enables other fruitful comparisons that have both religious and societal implications. This perceptive study deals with the biblical texts in depth, is on top of the copious secondary literature, and has the 'exegetical plus' that one always hopes for in a theoretical approach to Old Testament topics."
—Robert P. Gordon, Emeritus Regius Professor of Hebrew, University of Cambridge, England

"Chiswa Gandiya's book, YHWH in the Wind(s), is a literary masterpiece. Situating YHWH's creativity and function in the primordial winds, and deriving support from interdisciplinary African creation mythology, Chiswa Gandiya charts new territory beyond traditional scholarship. The result is a fresh reading of YHWH's role and activity in select biblical texts. I highly recommend this fascinating monograph to students of the Hebrew Bible, interdisciplinary scholars, and readers curious about the nature of divine activity in the scriptures."
—Robert Wafawanaka, Associate Professor of Biblical Studies and Old Testament, Virginia Union University

"Dr. Violet Chiswa Gandiya demonstrates a sound comparative approach to biblical and African myths. Her Afrocentric analysis brings out the unique elements in both myths while highlighting how the elements in the Dogon myth bring more understanding to the obscure elements in the biblical creation myths. This book is a must read to all who are interested in Afrocentric interpretation of ancient creation myths."

—Dora Mbuwayesango, George E. and Iris Battle Professor of Old Testament and Languages, Hood Theological Seminary

"Violet Chiswa Gandiya here presents a masterful piece of work. She has drawn ideas from a vast array of resources and amassed more cogent evidence to produce a well-documented book. Her interdisciplinary and comparative analyses bring new meaning to texts most scholars have grappled with for centuries. By engaging with this insightful study of YHWH's attributes in the chosen texts and those alluded to in the Dogon creation myth, Chiswa Gandiya has opened a new research path."

—Themba Mafico, founder, Mafico Leadership Renewal Institute

YHWH in the Wind(s)

His Creation, Destruction, and Restoration Drama

VIOLET CHISWA GANDIYA

PICKWICK *Publications* • Eugene, Oregon

YHWH IN THE WIND(S)
His Creation, Destruction, and Restoration Drama

Copyright © 2025 Violet Chiswa Gandiya. All rights reserved. Except for brief quotations in critical publications or reviews, no part of this book may be reproduced in any manner without prior written permission from the publisher. Write: Permissions, Wipf and Stock Publishers, 199 W. 8th Ave., Suite 3, Eugene, OR 97401.

Pickwick Publications
An Imprint of Wipf and Stock Publishers
199 W. 8th Ave., Suite 3
Eugene, OR 97401

www.wipfandstock.com

PAPERBACK ISBN: 978-8-3852-0064-1
HARDCOVER ISBN: 978-8-3852-0065-8
EBOOK ISBN: 978-8-3852-0066-5

Cataloguing-in-Publication data:

Names: Chiswa Gandiya, Violet, author.

Title: YHWH in the wind(s): his creation, destruction, and restoration drama / Violet Chiswa Gandiya.

Description: Eugene, OR: Pickwick Publications, 2025. | Includes bibliographical references.

Identifiers: ISBN 978-8-3852-0064-1 (paperback). | ISBN 978-8-3852-0065-8 (hardcover). | ISBN 978-8-3852-0066-5 (epub).

Subjects: LSCH: Bible. OT—Criticism, interpretation, etc. | Bible. OT—Theology. | Creation—Biblical teaching. | African mythology.

Classification: BS1199 C35 2025 (print). | BS1199 (epub).

In Dedication
with deepest affection,
to my mother Rosemary Chiswa
and my late father Miles T. Chiswa
through whom I derive my faith to be formidable in all aspects of life
I put my trust in The Lord
יהוה צבאות

Contents

Preface | xi

Acknowledgments | xiii

Introduction | xvi

Abbreviations | xxiii

1. An Afrocentric and Interdisciplinary Reading of the Cosmogonic Narrative of Genesis 1:1–2, 26–28 in Light of the Dogon Creation Myth | 1
2. YHWH in the Wind as Creator-King | 63
3. YHWH in the Wind as the Savior | 155
4. Proclamation of YHWH as King in the Wind | 212
5. Conclusions | 317

   Bibliography | 355

Preface

THIS MONOGRAPH IS A product of the convergence of overhauled ideas derived from a University of Cambridge doctoral dissertation on the theophany of YHWH with the maturation of ideas from a comparative study on creation myths during my graduate studies. A deeper analysis of the Dogon creation myth of Mali, Africa, brings to bear that the wind is the primary agency at creation, and is the same element by which YHWH manifests his power in ordering chaos both for cosmic and social order. Therefore, the first chapter is comparative from interdisciplinary and intertextual approaches, and aims to establish that YHWH is the creator who appears in the wind for the establishment of cosmic order, and how social organization derives from that conception. The latter forms the rationale for the rest of this book: outlining the function of YHWH as the creator who maintains cosmic order and social order by the same means of the wind in his roles as savior, judge, and universal king.

The first chapter is an expanded version of a paper presented at the Society of Biblical Literature Convention in Denver in November 2022. In the second chapter, a section on Psalm 104 is also a modified and developed version of a paper published in a journal in 2012.[1] The former asserted the long held view of YHWH appearing with storm elements, but, here, the focus is now on the image of YHWH appearing with the phenomenal wind(s). Chapter 3 retains the same texts studied in my University of Cambridge doctoral dissertation but developed with a new trajectory in assertion of the idea on YHWH's self-disclosure in the wind as divine warrior and savior not featuring his storm attributes, as previously held in biblical scholarship. The fourth chapter contains modified and transformed ideas from a paper on Psalm 99 previously presented at the Society of Biblical Literature Annual Meeting in San Diego in November

1. Chiswa Gandiya, "Storm-Theophany and the Portrayal of Yahweh."

PREFACE

2014. However, I have found it appropriate to limit this study to texts drawn from the Psalms, Prophecy (Amos and Jeremiah), and Wisdom Literature (Job), where specific roles of YHWH in the guise of the wind are involved. Yet, there are cases where texts outside the selected literature are referred to on the basis of similarities in motif and detail with the texts under discussion. At the same time, portions or blocks of texts often regarded as editorial additions, foreign or secondary to their contexts have been taken into account in consideration of their originality in their present contexts, and relevance to the subject at hand.

In this monograph, I cite the textual references and the order of biblical Hebrew books according to *BHS*. The equivalent English verse number is given in parenthesis where there is a difference from the Hebrew numbering. The verses quoted in English in this monograph are my own translations. Also, I cite the Ugaritic texts according to the KTU text numbering of Dietrich, Loretz, and Sanmartín's *Die Keilalphabetischen Texte aus Ugarit* (1976) in comparison with the CTA text numbering of Gibson's *Canaanite Myths and Legends* (2004), which is shown in parenthesis. I used the Tyndale Unicode Font for Hebrew, while for Akkadian and Ugaritic terms I have used the Semitic Transliterator in Unicode (Linguist's software). The monographs I refer to frequently appear in abbreviated form, but I use the original or shortened titles for the rest.

The production of a work of this magnitude has involved assistance from a range of people. Therefore, I wish to express my deepest gratitude to Professor Johanna Stiebert, Professor Robert Wafawanaka, and the Distinguished Professor for Old Testament, Professor Temba J. Mafico for their invaluable comments and remarks expressed on my first chapter, which set the tone and rationale for the rest of the book. I am immensely indebted to Mrs. Sheila W. Cockey for her love, support, and professionalism in undertaking the onerous task of editing, and cleaning up my academic mess. Her eye for detail is impeccable and unmatched. She worked tirelessly with graceful dedication to ensure clarity of thought and flawless reading. However, any imperfections, errors, or inaccuracies in the interpretation of material used that may remain in the content of this book are entirely my own.

Acknowledgments

I WANT TO EXPRESS my special gratitude to my former college Peterhouse at the University of Cambridge for awarding me a studentship to conduct research towards my doctoral dissertation, without which this monograph would not have found its nascent form and content. I also endeavor to maintain expertise in writing for a wider audience gained under the wise counsel of the Emeritus Professor Robert P. Gordon. I am also greatly indebted to my first lecturer and mentor, the Distinguished Professor, Temba J. L. Mafico, who spurred me on to pursue academic research in biblical Hebrew. Professor Mafico introduced me to Semitic studies and encouraged me in language study, so that I could study the OT in a comparative way. I also wish to express deep gratitude to the late Professor Frank Moore Cross, formerly Emeritus Professor of Near Eastern and Semitic Languages at Harvard University. I gained immense understanding of the god Baʻal at Ugarit, during Professor Cross's instruction in a course on Israelite Religion and the Ancient Near East. I found his exposition of ideas associated with Baʻal compelling, as he derived meaning from enigmatic biblical texts. Hence, he sowed the seeds for comparative study that blossomed into this work, even though I have deviated from his approach and interpretation, as will be seen in perusing the chapters that follow. My close friend and associate from Peterhouse, University of Cambridge, Dr. Peter Niemann transformed all my German translations of material used in this monograph and ensured accuracy in meaning. He also never tired from helping out when I came across an incomprehensible article, or book chapter needing a clarification of ideas presented, and for that I am immensely grateful.

I am also especially indebted to my family and extended family for their support and encouragement in seeing this work to completion. I owe an incredible debt to my three enchanting children, Nyasha, Tofara

ACKNOWLEDGMENTS

(Toto), and Theo Gandiya, who have withstood, with so much grace and patience, the pressures imposed on them in the process of producing this work. I thank them for their love, financial support, encouragement and constant inquiry about my progress, that enabled me to remain focused on the task. My most profound thanks also go to my siblings particularly my brother Robert (Rob) Chiswa, who financially poured into my efforts, and all my friends, both old and new, too many to enumerate, who have helped financially and in various ways. I owe an irreparable debt to Mrs. Terri Gallagher for creating a quiet space for me to work, and housing my documents and electronic gadgets from decimation, Mrs. Pamela Elis-Aziz and her husband, Mr. Muhammad Aziz for their love and support, and granting me a safe space to think and regurgitate ideas that shaped the first three chapters of this book. I am also grateful to Professor Robert Wafawanaka and his family for housing and supporting me financially for a period of three months, when I needed a pillar to lean on. Without all of them, I would not have seen this work develop from its seminal state to a more mature piece of scholarship. Also, towards the latter, I find it fitting to express my sincerest gratitude to the staff at the Harvard Alumni Association desk for making me aware of online resources I could tap into at Harvard University Libraries. The staff at L. E. Smoot Memorial Library, King George, Virginia, were gracious getting interlibrary loans in a timely manner, thus enabling me to access relevant recent material for updating and developing my ideas. My lifelong mentor, the Distinguished Professor of the Old Testament, Temba J. L. Mafico opened up his cache of resources to aid my quest to expose new meanings to the texts discussed here. Although this applies to the latter stages of the production of this book, I also wish to express my heartfelt gratitude to the staff at the William Smith Morton Library, Union and Presbyterian Seminary, Richmond, Virginia, particularly Ms. Lisa Janes and Christie Bernard Thadikonda for supplying me with much needed research material, and my true-blue friend, Professor Robert Wafawanaka, always adept at providing me with research material beyond my reach, became my link with William Smith Morton Library.

Lastly, but not least, I want to thank my beloved parents, my mother Rosemary Chiswa, and late father, Miles T. Chiswa. I express my deepest gratitude and indebtedness for their unrelenting love and steadfast support over the years. I owe my academic success to their wholehearted sacrifices. I would not have accomplished this work without their firm encouragement and support. My father consistently asked how far I had

ACKNOWLEDGMENTS

progressed with writing this book until his recent passing. Not a moment went by without him making inquiry. His aspiration for my success has sustained me during an extremely challenging period in the production of this book. Hence, as a small token of my love, I dedicate this book in absolute honor of them, and in loving memory of my dear father. May he rest in eternal peace, risen to glory.

Introduction

THIS MONOGRAPH PRESENTS A paradigm shift showing the intersection of epistemologies of the Global North and Global South on the concept of creation, particularly creation-out-of-chaos, as the fundamental theme associated with YHWH's self-disclosure in the wind(s), and the axiom for social organization in the biblical Hebrew tradition. For centuries, biblical scholars have sustained discussions on biblical texts by interacting mostly with the traditions of the ancient Near East (ANE), particularly from Ugarit and Mesopotamia, to the exclusion of others from the Global South that could shed light on some complex biblical Hebrew traditions. There has been an overemphasis on similarities drawn from parallels with the ANE conceptual or linguistic terms on creation[1] deriving from the Semitic background to the point of overlooking plausible comparisons with any other alternative traditions. Therefore, considering the intricacies of the creation myth of the Dogon tribe in Mali, Africa, this monograph is uniquely interdisciplinary, intertextual, and comparative in its approach to insights on elements relating the concept of creation emerging from a wind deity, not a storm god, resulting in social organization, and reflecting similarities with the biblical Hebrew tradition.

---

1. It is noted in this monograph, on the one hand, the ongoing debate on whether the storm or warrior god Ba'al's battle, primarily with Yam (inter alia) in the Ugaritic texts, relates the creation of cosmic order from chaos. On the other hand, though the poetic hymn of the Enuma Elish recites creation of cosmic order in sequel to Marduk's victory over his assailant, Tiamat, some scholars maintain that the Enuma Elish is not a cosmogony, but a composition of how Marduk is elevated to a position of pre-eminence in the Babylonian pantheon. However, these aspects have been thoroughly dealt with in scholarship elsewhere. To that end, comparisons will be drawn only on points of interest in connection with the relevance of the "wind(s)" as the primary factor at the establishment of cosmic order from chaos.

INTRODUCTION

In particular, the Dogon creation myth presents a cosmogony emerging from the supreme god Amma, whose nature is (whirl)wind but before him, nothing existed. All the cosmic elements evolve from Amma's whirling movements reaching a climatic burst and releasing the contents of Amma's creation to form the Dogon cosmology. Amma's creative works involve a first failed attempt at creating the world, and "chaos" ensues in *medias res* at his second attempt in creating the Dogon world. This second attempt involving Amma's fight with the rebellious creature, Ogo, aligns the Dogon creation myth with the idea of creation-out-of-chaos, and positions it as an African, and hence a Global South, version of the *Chaoskampf* myth. These characteristic features of the Dogon creation myth offer close affinity to conceptual ideas on the priestly narrative of Gen 1:1–2 (and related texts) in the biblical Hebrew tradition, as retaining the concept of creation-out-of-chaos, but depicting YHWH[2] as the supreme creator transforming chaos into cosmos by the power of his wind and effectuating world order.

In this monograph, interdisciplinary, intertextual, comparative, and exegetical approaches are utilized. Therefore, the focus is mainly on the literary and theological intentionality of biblical texts that employ ideas from the creation tradition in portrayal of YHWH's appearance with the wind, as he fulfills specific roles in Israel's salvation history. Hence, the preliminary chapter outlines the Dogon creation myth, and deals with the themes and motifs foundational to the comparison of the Dogon god, Amma with YHWH in their function as creator gods employing wind as the primary agency at creation for the establishment of world/social order. Here, the fundamental concepts and formulations presenting these deities as creator gods are explored, and their transformation and control of "chaos" as the axiom for social organization is noted. Comparisons with known parallels with the Egyptian deities, Ugaritic Ba'al, and Babylonian Marduk are only brought into discussion in assertion of the commonality of conceptual ideas on creation. With the informed view of YHWH appearing with the phenomenal wind, as in the case of the Dogon Amma, and transforming chaos into cosmos, other biblical Hebrew texts bearing the same image are reexamined for their meaning and purpose. Consequently, the form and content of the remaining three chapters draw and expand on the conclusions in this preliminary chapter.

---

2. Although the priestly narrative uses the title Elohim, the name YHWH is used here for consistency with other earlier biblical Hebrew texts where the latter occurs.

In chapter two, the focus is on the depiction of YHWH as creator reflecting the common themes and ideas concerning disclosure with the phenomenal wind(s) discussed in chapter one. The prelude to this chapter is devoted to a study of Ps 104. It is noted that this Hebrew psalm, thought to reflect Ugaritic and Mesopotamian antecedents, and often compared with the Egyptian hymn to the god Aten, has more in common with the god Amma of the Dogon creation myth. Noegel's observation[3] on iconographic depictions of hybrid creatures with wings in the ANE, and the conceptual link with winds and cardinal directions further sheds light on the images of YHWH alluding to his appearance in the wind(s), and underscores the parallel with the whirlwind god Amma. Therefore, Ps 104 depicts YHWH appearing with the phenomenal wind(s) to subdue chaos in the manner of a mythological *Chaoskampf*, resulting in creation. As noted by Charles H. Long on the Dogon creation myth as an integration of creation by a supreme deity with other mythological themes, Ps 104 is considered a de facto biblical cosmogony. Ps 104 combines the idea of wisdom and power of YHWH, as the supreme deity, with creation-out-of-chaos and judgment motifs. The latter informs the destruction of the wicked by the same means cosmic chaos is repelled, as an important aspect of YHWH's appearance in the wind, and the establishment of his intended divine order. Accordingly, an exegesis of Ps 104 follows in correlating the motifs of creation, wisdom, and judgment. This close analysis of Ps 104 provides the framework for discussion of other biblical texts with the same themes and motifs considered in this work.

The doxologies of Job in Job 9:4–10 and 26:7–14 relating the wisdom of YHWH to his cosmological activities are considered in view of YHWH's image as the creator, who appears with the phenomenal winds. As in the case of Ps 104, parallels are traced between YHWH's demonstration of power and wisdom against mythical symbols of chaos at creation. But the poet of Job also expresses the same mode of appearance as an expression of YHWH's destructive tendencies. To this point, Job's view that YHWH unleashes his wind(s) against both the "righteous" and the "wicked" is analyzed within the purview of YHWH's cosmological activities. Although Job 38 represents differences in the role played by YHWH's whirlwind, as compared with the preceding texts, it is brought into the discussion inasmuch as it synthesizes elements of creation and wisdom with the idea of judgment. The implication of YHWH's

---

3. Noegel, "Wings," 15–20.

appearance in the "whirlwind" in this text, not to chide Job but to communicate the intricacies of his cosmological activities, is also reevaluated as a paradox on divine justice.

The final section of this second chapter is centered on prophetic passages from the books of Amos and Jeremiah, which derive their form and content from creation, wisdom and judgment motifs. The selected texts from Amos (1:2, 14; 4:12–13; 5:8–9; 9:5–6) and Jeremiah (10:1–16; 25:15–38; 51:15–19) are discussed within their contexts. Therefore, we argue here for the originality of these texts within segments commonly considered to be secondary or erratic blocks that are disruptive of the sequence in their present contexts. Thus, in depiction of YHWH in the wind and language deriving from creation ideology, these texts are analyzed in relation to the themes emphasized in Ps 104 and the texts from Job. In particular, YHWH's control of chaos with the phenomenal winds, as exemplified in Ps 104 and in the doxologies of Job, is represented in Amos and Jeremiah. From the broad contextual background and intertextual analysis of these texts, it is clear that YHWH's phenomenal winds are no longer directed against primeval chaos, but against human wickedness. Hence, as a parody of texts alluding to YHWH's dramaturgical appearance in the wind(s), wisdom and judgment motifs are fused in assertion of YHWH as the creator, whose dispensation of justice and righteousness is a prerogative.

Psalm 18 is the paradigm for chapter three, and intertextual and exegetical approaches are employed to show thematic literary features representing YHWH's appearance in the wind and salvific deeds of YHWH. Psalms 77, 144, and Hab 3 show similar literary features as Ps 18 in expression of YHWH's age-old *modus operandi* in the wind. Here, the aura of YHWH's sight and sound in the wind is described in view of his martial activities against mythic forces recalling primal chaotic waters at creation. But YHWH is featured as the divine warrior appearing with the wind to fight battles for the deliverance of his elected people. This view is a modification of Patrick D. Miller's view on the conception and nature of the divine warrior as deriving from imagery and language[4] drawn from ANE traditions. This discussion also shows the theological implications of the appropriated images of YHWH appearing in the wind(s) in portrayal of YHWH as the savior or redeemer. All the terms and images often associated with the ANE tradition of the storm god,

---

4. Miller, *Divine Warrior*, 170–72.

or said to allude to a mythical battle with the monster(s) of chaos, are defined as representations of the melodramatic appearance of YHWH in the luminous and sonorous sounds of the phenomenal wind(s) as he performs redemptive acts.

The discussion in chapter four is concerned with the proclamation of YHWH's kingship in metaphorical language relating to his theophany in the wind(s). The topical features associated with the kingship of YHWH are discussed apart from the hypothetical enthronement of YHWH, supposedly reflected in the contents of the so-called enthronement psalms, Pss 47, 93, and 96–99. The discussion begins with the exegesis of Ps 97 as paradigmatic for this group of psalms, which contain the YHWH *mālāk* formula. First, the thematic unity of Ps 97 is demonstrated, *contra* the arguments of biblical scholars for its composite nature. Secondly, the imagery used for YHWH in this psalm is discussed in comparison with the characteristics of the wind deities, particularly the Dogon Amma of the epistemologies of the Global South.

The rest of the so-called enthronement psalms are analyzed in relation to Ps 97 with emphasis on the praise of YHWH for salvation deeds at his disclosure in the wind(s), and in critique of the hypothetical enthronement festival, or any views supporting an enthronement of YHWH as king. In particular, terms that are often said to support a cultic enthronement of YHWH are interpreted with respect to their usage in other texts dealing with similar topics on the patent presence of YHWH, as the king in the guise of the wind. Thus, the terms in Ps 47 relating YHWH's ascent and occupation of Zion are discussed in view of the prosaic (2 Sam 5–7) and poetic (Pss 24, 132). The ideas of YHWH's self-expression in the mode of the wind, and alluded to by the Deuteronomistic historian, are considered.

YHWH's guidance of his own people and his dependability are argued for in the light of his eternal kingship asserted by his power over chaotic waters as expressed in Ps 93. His dramaturgical functions of saving, ruling and judging as the ultimate purposes of his theophany in the wind(s) are discussed. As presented in this chapter, similar technical terms and militaristic imagery associated with YHWH's manifestation in the bluster of wind(s) are at issue in Pss 96 and 98 respectively. Other symbolic features: the cherubim, ark, Zion, pillar of cloud, holy mountain, priestly/prophetic figures are discussed as symbolic modes of YHWH's presence in association with his appearance in the wind amid his people. An overview of Ps 99 in relation to YHWH's age-old *modus operandi* in the wind, as alluded to in Deut 33 and other relevant passages from 1 Sam, is also presented. All the elements symbolic of YHWH's appearance in the wind in association with the tradition of the ark are discussed, and the priority of the kingship psalms, including Ps 98 to Deutero-Isaiah, is also emphasized. Any features often deployed for the reconstruction of the hypothetical cultic enthronement of YHWH are reinterpreted to show their purposeful function in light of YHWH's theophany in the phenomenal wind(s) wreaking salvation deeds within the Israelite tradition. Hence, the idea that these psalms portray and laud YHWH as king and judge in Israel's history of salvation is brought to the fore.

The remainder of chapter four focuses on detailed analyses of Pss 29 and 68 where the depiction of YHWH in the wind is more prominent. With that idea in mind, the roles of YHWH as divine warrior, king and judge are thrown into bold relief in these texts. On the one hand, in relation to Ps 29, the formulas and expressions often argued to reflect influence from the Ugaritic tradition of the gods El and Ba'al are reviewed. It is argued that Ps 29 employs a sophisticated image of YHWH appearing with the wind in close affinity with the Dogon (whirl)wind god, Amma. Here, it is pointed out that scholars have overstated ideas akin to Ugaritic and Mesopotamian traditions, to the point of missing that Ps 29 retains exclusively biblical Hebrew features. On the other hand, features cited by biblical critics as ultimately deriving from the Ba'al tradition, and in giving rise to the idea of the enthronement of YHWH, are reconsidered and critiqued. With the evidence for the direct influence from the Ugaritic traditions of El and Ba'al reassessed and discounted, the distinctive images describing the theophany of YHWH in the phenomenal wind is highlighted and the soteriological aspects of the psalm are discussed.

Finally, in chapter 4, Ps 68, considered by scholars as a *crux interpretum*,[5] is reexamined. It is proposed here that the unifying theme of what may seem hard to categorize (Longman),[6] or an anthology of quotations (Albright),[7] or a collection of independent songs (Schmidt)[8] is that of the abiding presence of YHWH in his age-old *modus operandi* in the wind. Ps 68 employs various technical terms and melodramatic images expressing YHWH's manifestation in the wind in Israel's salvation history. Therefore, an exegetical analysis of these technical terms

5. Johnson, *Sacral Kingship*, 77; Jeremias, *Königtum Gottes*, 69.
6. Longman, *Psalms*, 257.
7. See Albright, "Catalogue."
8. See discussion on Ps 68 in Schmidt, *Psalmen*.

representing the phenomenal wind(s) alluding to YHWH's divine presence or deeds of salvation in the wilderness, conquest and settlement traditions is undertaken. The various images used in this psalm to depict YHWH's appearance in the bluster of wind are also given new meaning in light of the comparison with the (whirl)wind god, Amma. This approach also brings into view the expressions relating to YHWH's sights and sounds in the wind, as he accomplishes historic deeds. Moreover, a couple of *hapax legomena*, for instance, בכושרות (Ps 68:7[6]a) and תרצדון (v. 17[16]a),[9] are given a new meaning in view of YHWH's acts of salvation, which evoke this ode of victory. Hence, it becomes clear that the lyric style of Ps 68 does not contain the rudiments of a cultic enthronement procession, but throws into stark relief a celebration of YHWH's judicial roles and sovereignty manifested in the phenomenal winds in dispensation of his divine order.

Thus, we will draw together the various texts to support the proposition that the themes and motifs in the kingship psalms (Pss 47, 93, 96–99) relate YHWH's abiding presence in the guise of the wind asserting his benevolent rule over Israel. These texts inform on the celebration of YHWH as king among his people wielding his power for their salvation in the same manner YHWH vanquishes primal chaos. With Israel as YHWH's chosen nation at the center of his divine rule, a universalistic aspect on YHWH's dominion is brought to bear by the call to the nations, inclusive of the subdued nations, to participate in worship in deference to YHWH's glory revealed in the sight of the nations.

---

9. See pp. 296–99 and 303, respectively.

Abbreviations

AB	Anchor Bible
BASOR	*Bulletin of the American Schools of Oriental Research*
BDB	Francis Brown, S. R. Driver, and Charles A. Briggs, *Hebrew and English Lexicon of the Old Testament*. 1907. Reprint, Oxford: Clarendon, 1951
BHS	*Biblia Hebraica Stuttgartensia*. Edited by Karl Elliger and Wilhelm Rudolph. Stuttgart: Deutsche Bibelgesellschaft, 1983
BZAW	Beihefte zur *Zeitschrift für die Alttestamentliche Wissenschaft*
CTA	Andrée Herdner, *Corpus des Tablettes en Cunéiformes Alphabétiques, Découvertes à Ras Shamra-Ugarit de 1929 à 1939*. 2 vols. Paris: Geuthner, 1963
EE	Enuma Elish
JANER	*Journal of Ancient Near Eastern Religions*
JBL	*Journal of Biblical Literature*
JNES	*Journal of Near Eastern Studies*
JSOT	*Journal for the Study of the Old Testament*
JSOTSup	*Journal for the Study of the Old Testament Supplement Series*
KTU	*Die Keilalphabetischen Texte aus Ugarit: Einschliesslich der Keilaphabetischen Texte auserhalb Ugarits*. Edited by Manfred Dietrich et al. Alter Orient und Altes Testament

	24. Kevelaer: Butzon und Bercker; Neukirchen-Vluyn: Neukirchener, 1976
NCBC	New Century Bible Commentary
NICOT	New International Commentary on the Old Testament
OTL	The Old Testament Library
PEGLMBS	Proceedings of the Eastern Great Lakes and Midwest Biblical Society
TDOT	Theological Dictionary of the Old Testament. Edited by G. Johannes Botterweck and Helmer Ringgren. Translated by John T. Willis et al. 17 vols. Grand Rapids: Eerdmans, 1974–2021
UBC I	The Ugaritic Baal Cycle: Introduction with Text, Translation, and Commentary of KTU 1.1—1.2. Edited by Mark S. Smith. Vol. 1. VTSup 55. Leiden: Brill, 1994
UBC II	The Ugaritic Baal Cycle: Introduction with Text, Translation, and Commentary of KTU/CTA 1.3—1.4. Edited by Mark S. Smith and Wayne T. Pitard. Vol. 2. VTSup 114. Leiden: Brill, 2009
VT	Vetus Testamentum
VTSup	Vetus Testamentum Supplement
WBC	Word Biblical Commentary
ZAW	Zeitschrift für die Alttestamentliche Wissenschaft

General Abbreviations

ANE	ancient Near East
cf.	confer, compare
esp.	especially
ET	English translation
MT	Masoretic Text
OT	Old Testament
v./vv.	verse, verses

1

An Afrocentric and Interdisciplinary Reading of the Cosmogonic Narrative of Genesis 1:1–2, 26–28 in Light of the Dogon Creation Myth

OVERVIEW

THIS DISCUSSION SYNTHESIZES ANTHROPOLOGICAL and ethnographic perspectives on the Dogon creation myth in support of an Afrocentric comparative reading and understanding of the creation account in the priestly narrative, particularly Gen 1:1–2, as retaining the concept of creation-out-of-chaos. Both the Old Testament and the Dogon creation myth have an intentional introductory clause to show that the deities upheld are the sole originator of the respective cosmos and with wind, among other elements, playing a fundamental role at creation. In both cases, the subordination of "chaos" emphasizes the transcendence of the deity over matter: his creativity and transformation of chaos into cosmic order. In view of the Dogon creation myth, and other related texts, it is argued here that Gen 1:1–2 relates YHWH as existing from the beginning, who set out to create and reorganize the transient chaos caused by the rebellious waters into the cosmos. This interpretation comes to bear in comparison with the god Amma's creative activities, which supersede the disruption caused by his primal challenger Ogo, in establishing the

Dogon cosmology. As a paradigm of the epistemologies of the Global South, the Dogon creation myth demonstrates that chaos is not preexistent, but occurs in *medias res* of the divine creative order. Hence, the attempt to read the biblical creation account with an Afrocentric synthesis of parallels expressed in the narrative of the creative activities of the god Amma also showcases affinity with the *Chaoskampf* myth that is common to the ancient Near East (ANE) context. But, in contrast to the commonly held view that the *Chaoskampf* myth legitimizes kingship, it is suggested here that the *Chaoskampf* myth is integral with the concept of creation-from-chaos serving as a charter for social organization. This comparative analysis also evinces that the biblical creation tradition shows similarities in creation concepts from a broad spectrum, but distinctively relational to its own religious and cultural background, so much as to disclaim that it is derivative of any particular cultural tradition.

Conceptual Intersection of Mythological Ideas in the Dogon and Biblical Creation Traditions

This chapter is concerned with analyzing the African anthropological system of beliefs centered on the Dogon creation myth and lines of intersection with mythological ideas on creation in the Old Testament, particularly the priestly narrative of Gen 1:1–2, 26–28. The Dogon are a tribal group occupying cliffs, plateaux, and plains but mostly populated on the Bandiagara escarpment in Mali, West Africa. It is believed that they originated from the Nile Valley of present-day Sudan, then ancient Egypt,[1] around 3200 BCE. They migrated over a period of time around the 1500s CE to avoid conversion to Islam. The French anthropologists Marcel Griaule and Germaine Dieterlen were the first Western scientists to make contact with the Dogon people (in 1931) and conducted ethnological studies, particularly in the Dogon villages of the Sanga region, for three decades. They unraveled the Dogon's complex sacred mythology, rituals, and traditional beliefs in their ancestral descent from the star known as Sirius.[2] The Dogon collaborators also revealed that this knowledge derived from beings known as the Nommo, who descended from the Sirius system. Whatever the Dogon's peregrinations, it appears some

---

1. Diop suggests an Egyptian origin of the Dogon tribes. See Diop, *African Origin*, 179; Martin, "Nature," 84–85; Douny, *Living*, 207.

2. In 1862, scientists discovered the binary star system of Sirius, but for over a century since 1844, they suspected the existence of a companion star known as Sirius B.

resemblances of the Egyptian astronomical, mathematical, and religious elements diffused into the Dogon creation myth.

The Dogon's creation mythology is quite complex, with varied versions showing their different views on the emergence of the cosmos. These variations show that the Dogon are no exception to humankind's relentless searching and grappling with the question of the origin of the universe. However, the focus here is on the version that seems to bear elements also familiar to the biblical Hebrew tradition. Both the Dogon and biblical Hebrew creation traditions relate the idea of a supreme and all-powerful creative god, involvement of natural elements, particularly the "winds" in the creation process, cosmic order emerging from chaos, humanity created in the image of the creator-god, significance of cosmological guardianship conferred on humanity, and how these ultimately define their worldview and social organization. The Dogon creation myth presents an exhaustive cosmogony showing creative processes influencing their thinking on the origin of the world, culture and social organization. The prolific ideas and concepts of the emergence of the Dogon symbolic cosmogonic system will be used in proposition of an alternative interpretation of some enigmatic aspects of the biblical creation tradition.

Humankind feels overwhelmed by the expanse of the cosmos and the marvelous powers imagined to be responsible for its creation. As Skinner[3] points out, cosmogonies arose out of humankind's desire to know how cosmological systems came into existence. Hence, speculative thoughts and imaginations conjured "myths" on the beginning of the cosmos. Before exploring this subject of myths of creation, it is necessary to look at the meaning and function of the term "myth," suggested by scholars pertinent to this discussion.

The Meaning and Function of Myth(s) and Myths of Creation

Several scholars in the fields of anthropology, sociology and history of religions have explained the term "myth" basing their reasons on their observations of different societies in various localities in the world. Although well known for biblical criticism, William Robertson Smith's views on ancient religions as being communal were revolutionary and focused more on practices than beliefs. Smith's propositions emerged

3. Skinner, *Critical and Exegetical*, 6.

from his observation that the religious practices of the Semites centered mainly on the totemic and sacrificial rituals. In his view, the communal performance of religious acts took precedence over individual beliefs in the gods, and these performances were not associated with creeds, or dogma, but with myths. Hence, Smith emphasized that myths were not prominent and consisted of "explanations of rituals," with rituals as obligatory, but myths left at the discretion of the worshiper.[4] In pioneering the myth-ritual theory, Smith proposed that myths emerged in connection with rituals as a rationalization of the deeds of the religious practitioners. Hence, he argued that "myths" derived from "ritual," and not ritual from myth.[5] This idea laid the foundation of what became the known as the "myth and ritual" school.[6] J. G. Frazer subscribed to the same idea on "myth and ritual" early in his career, and expressed in his first edition of *The Golden Bough* that myths are dramatized events in rituals intended for magical effect described in figurative language.[7] Frazer posited this view following his study of totemic "magical" rituals to increase natural/material productivity by native tribes of central Australia. But as scholars[8] note, Frazer's views shifted with the development of his theories on the human mental (and emotional) evolution through three stages: magic through religion to science.[9] The different theoretical statements on myths noted in the editions of *The Golden Bough* illustrate the change in

---

4. Smith, *Lectures*, 17–18, reproduced in Segal, *Religion*, 17–18.

5. Smith, *Lectures*, 18; cf. Von Hendy, *Modern Construction*, 89–90. Von Hendy further comments that Smith added a problem to the complex debate on myth and its relation to ritual by noting the secondary character of myth, and that a myth is not always associated with a ritual.

6. The German philosopher Friedrich Nietzsche's venture into anthropological and folkloristic theory focused attention on the ritual origins of classical Greek tragedy resulting in his publication of *The Birth of Tragedy*. This focus became formative to his influence on the so-called "myth and ritual" school. Nietzsche directly inspired the first generation of leaders of the "myth and ritual" school, such as William Robertson Smith, James G. Frazer, Jane Harrison, and other Cambridge ritualists. However, due to the limitations of this discussion, no chronological development of the myth theories will be followed here, except for key ideas in proposition of a working definition of myth to guide this discussion.

7. See Okpewho, *Myth*, 45.

8. Ackerman, "Frazer," 116, 123, 129; cf. Von Hendy, *Modern Construction*, 92, 97; Okpewho, *Myth*, 45–46.

9. Ackerman, "Frazer," 129. Here, too, Ackerman documents Frazer's disavowal of Smith's view on the primacy of rituals over myths; Von Hendy, *Modern Construction*, 94.

Frazer's thinking.[10] Again, Frazer interpreted myth as "a fiction devised to explain an old custom of which the real meaning and origin had been forgotten."[11] Frazer arrived at this view after studying the reenactment of the myth about the gods and the rise of magic in ancient Italian rituals. He observed that a myth has its counterpart in ritual. Frazer studied the secret cult of the goddess Diana to corroborate his observations. He discovered that the worship of the goddess Diana at Nemi belonged to a wide range of myths devised to explain the origin of a religious ritual, though with no other basis apart from the semblance, real or imaginary, which could be drawn between the myth and some foreign ritual.[12]

Frazer received criticisms, particularly by Robert R. Marett,[13] for the inconsistencies and variations in his theoretical explanations of the origin and function of myth, and the relation of myths to ritual.[14] In a later edition, *Apollodorus: The Library* (1921), Frazer again offered another description of myth: "By myths I understand mistaken explanations of phenomena, whether of human life, or of external nature. Such explanations originate from that instinctive curiosity concerning the causes of things."[15] In analysis of Frazer's change of views on myths and their elusive nature, Ackerman inferred from Frazer's conception of myth as some form of "conscious, purposive mental activity."[16] As Ackerman

---

10. Ackerman, *Selected Letters*, 21; *J. G. Frazer*, 231. Ackerman notes that Frazer developed three different exclusive theories concerning myths: euhemerism, cognitionism and ritualism. The first, euhemerism, comprised Enlightenment philosophies that myths pertained to real events in the lives of real heroes and kings thought to be the precursors of gods. By the second, cognitionism, Frazer embraced E. B. Taylor's thought on myths as attempts by primitive mankind to rationalize and conjure aetiological tales that explain how the world came to be; hence conceiving myths as mistaken efforts at scientific explanations. Ackerman notes that this idea appealed to Frazer, as he expresses it in his second edition contemporaneously with the idea that magic is a precursor of science. The same idea can also be traced in the third edition. The third theory, ritualism, has two assumptions: that religion began with attempts by humankind to control the world by magic, and the second assumption, deriving from Mannhardt and Robertson Smith, asserts that the human, first and foremost, is self-efficacious on what is desirable and that becomes the stories of the gods themselves—myths (Ackerman, *J. G. Frazer*, 231–32).

11. Frazer, *Golden Bough* [1915], 153; *Golden Bough* [1911], 153; Okpewho, *Myth*, 46.

12. Frazer, *Golden Bough* [1917], 72.

13. See Ackerman, *J. G. Frazer*, 229–31.

14. Ackerman, *J. G. Frazer*, 232–34; cf. *Selected Letters*, 307–8.

15. Ackerman, *J. G. Frazer*, 234. See Frazer, *Apollodorus*, 1:xxvii.

16. Ackerman, *J. G. Frazer*, 234.

observed, ambiguities occurred in Frazer's various positions trying to disassociate from Robertson Smith's views concerning the origin and function of myths in relation to myth—and—ritual. Albeit such criticisms existing on the shifting approach to the theoretical explanations of myths, Frazer went on to describe the nature of myths and differentiated between myth, legend, and folktale in studying Greek myths. Hence, in the introduction to *Apollodorus: The Library*, Frazer broadened the scope of myths, beyond ritual, to the subjects of inquiry that concern the origin of the world, humans, the regulation of heavenly bodies, the working of natural phenomena, such as thunder and lightning, beginnings of society,[17] to mention a few fitting the purview of his discussion.

Emile Durkheim, also influenced by Robertson Smith to investigate the origins and nature of religion, developed significant points on the discussion of myths, even though he pointed out that he had no intention to make mythology a subject of his studies.[18] Durkheim's approach concurs with the (post-Comtean) view that myth is a late phenomenon in the development of religion. Although Durkheim held myth as a religious aspect, he considered it a late and secondary mode of collective representation associated with ritual, to which it is generally etiological.[19] However, as Von Hendy notes, Durkheim unintentionally contributed to the discussion on myth by emphasizing the corporate nature of religious thought and behavior in primitive societies.

For Durkheim, as with the Comtean view, religion is a collective representation of beliefs and practices that unites worshiping believers into one moral community. So, Durkheim identified religion as a product of collective thought,[20] invented to justify religious sensations. On this view, he repeated Max Müller's thesis that humans' religious sentiments were aroused by the forms and forces of nature that appeared to them as immense and infinite.[21] Every aspect of nature awakens in humankind an "overwhelming sensation"[22] of its infiniteness and immensity. Durkheim explained that these forces of nature, on which humankind

---

17. Frazer, *Apollodorus*, 1:xxviii.

18. Durkheim, *Elementary*, 121–22. Durkheim analyzed the elementary forms of religion as manifested in Australian totemism, but scarcely deals with myth in relation to the subject of his studies.

19. Von Hendy, *Modern Construction*, 98.

20. Durkheim, *Elementary*, 62; cf. Von Hendy, *Modern Construction*, 99.

21. Durkheim, *Elementary*, 92–93.

22. Durkheim, *Elementary*, 93.

depend, cease to exist as abstract entities, or inanimate elements, when they dominate humanity. Instead, as he further observed, humankind imparts personal characteristics to these forces and perceives them as living beings.[23] Again, as with Müller, the metamorphosis of abstract forms, or religious sensations into personal agents, or living beings, is brought about by language.[24] This metamorphosis of thought into personifications of living or supernatural beings marks the inception of religion. These beings become "spiritual powers or gods; for it is to beings of this sort that the cult is generally addressed."[25]

As with Müller, Durkheim developed his argument further on the role of language in formulating and apprehending forces of nature as real objects. Durkheim realized that the creative work of language and mythology imparted personal characteristics to natural phenomena, which consequently became distinct gods. Therefore myth, as Durkheim demonstrated, is essential to religious life[26] and inseparable from religion. According to Durkheim, myth prescribes the peculiar traits and determines the personalities of the gods.[27] The nature of a rite or cult rendered to these divine beings is determined by the qualities by which the divine beings are believed to make themselves manifest in nature. Durkheim further explained how a belief sanctions the cult, or rite, and how myths are appropriated to give an explanation of the rites that express them. In essence, as Durkheim argued, the myth justifies the rite or cultic practice addressed to the divine beings, and the rite is nothing other than the myth put into action.[28] The African cosmology and biblical cosmogony reflect this connection between belief/myth and ritual. According to this association, the Dogon Sigi (Sigui) festival is celebrated every sixty years by the Dogon to commemorate the renewal of the universe based on their beliefs on the elliptical orbit of Sirius B (*po tolo*) every fifty years

23. Durkheim, *Elementary*, 93.

24. Durkheim, *Elementary*, 93. Durkheim notes that Müller sees this transformation of the inanimate to animate beings as a metamorphosis only made possible through language, which sanctions action upon thoughts.

25. Durkheim, *Elementary*, 93.

26. Durkheim, *Elementary*, 100.

27. Durkheim, *Elementary*, 101.

28. Durkheim, *Elementary*, 101. This statement seems to imply the primacy of myth in determining the peculiar traits of the supernatural beings, and nature of the rite prescribed. Thus, contradicting a view Durkheim expressed in analysis of totemism in Australian aborigines that considered myth to be "modeled after the rite in order to account for it" (Durkheim, *Elementary*, 121).

around Sirius A (*sigi tolo*), and the origins of the universe and humanity. Analogously, the ritual observance of the Sabbath in biblical Hebrew is associated with the priestly etiological beliefs on the emergence of the biblical cosmogony ending with the divine rest.

Also influenced by the sociology of Durkheim and the anthropology of Frazer, Bronislaw Malinowski made a significant contribution to the discussion on myths. Malinowski provided his own conception of myth, aside from the connection between myth and religion already discussed by his predecessors. He explained how myths function as narratives in social and cultural realities among the communities of antiquity into which they diffused.[29] Malinowski studied the function of myths in the lives of the Melanesian society of New Guinea. He intended to show what he considered an innate link "between the word, the myths, and the sacred tales of the tribe, on the one hand, and their ritual acts, their moral deeds, their social organization, and their practical activities, on the other."[30]

Furthermore, Malinowski argued that myth as it exists in communities of antiquity is not merely a story told, but a reality lived.[31] The myth is not recited into words, but given expression in the way the people live, or in a pattern of behavior of clans. So, according to Malinowski, the myth is considered a "living reality" believed to have once occurred in primordial times and continues to influence the cosmos and human destinies. Here Malinowski expressed that the reality of myth to the [primitives];[32] that is communities of antiquity, is comparable to the Christian belief in the biblical story of creation, the Fall and the redemption symbolized by the Cross, reenacted in rituals and morals, as the guiding principle of faith and conduct.[33] Hence, Malinowski emphasized here that myth is not symbolic, or an explanation, but a narration of primeval reality rooted in deep conviction of religious and moral sensibilities.[34] As Malinowski noted, in its indispensable function in social organization, myth "expresses, enhances, and codifies belief; safeguards and enforces

---

29. Malinowski, *Magic*, 111.
30. Malinowski, *Magic*, 96.
31. Malinowski, *Magic*, 100.
32. Malinowski, *Magic*, 100. Malinowski uses the term "primitive," but for its derogatory meaning it is replaced here with communities of antiquity.
33. Malinowski, *Magic*, 100.
34. Malinowski, *Magic*, 101.

morality,"³⁵ thus serving as a "pragmatic charter of primitive faith and moral wisdom."³⁶ Malinowski asserted his viewpoints with analysis of Melanesian myths of origin (among others).

Malinowski discovered that there are a number of myths that the natives of New Guinea recount as the basis of their social organization. He observed that several myths narrated the origin of the clans, and warranted the social stratification of the Melanesian natives.³⁷ Particularly of relevance to this discussion, Malinowski observed in the main myth of origin he studied, that the clan believed they emerged from a hole in the ground, and were accorded rank or superiority of each clan, based on the order of emergence.³⁸ This myth of origin also functions to authorize the clans' claim to the land from which they believed to have emerged.³⁹ As Malinowski noted, the sociological relevance of these accounts becomes apparent in the manner in which the natives grasp their legal rights in realization that their local pursuits have precedence and pattern in the mythological first beginnings in bygone times.⁴⁰ Here, Malinowski made an important observation, bringing to bear some key elements as the basis for understanding the meaning and function of myth. He showed that the myth of origin combined with the conviction of common descent and emergence from the ground, as giving full rights, contains the legal charter of the community.⁴¹ So, in their social function, the myths of origin reinforced social cohesion, patriotism, and kinship in the community within which historical traditions, legal principles and various customs were integrated and welded to manifest native social organization.⁴²

Mircea Eliade, a historian of religion, and generally considered a leading interpreter of myth,⁴³ dealt with myth as a concept rooted in his broader view of religion as a whole. He followed from his theory of religion that [archetypal] myth originated as a narrative expression of the hunger of the homo religious—total [hu]man—for the sacred and search

---

35. Malinowski, *Magic*, 101.

36. Malinowski, *Magic*, 101.

37. On the idea of myths understood as narratives within a context of the community's sociology, religion, customs, and outlook, see Strenski, *Malinowski*, xxi.

38. Malinowski, *Magic*, 112–13.

39. Malinowski, *Magic*, 116–17.

40. Malinowski, *Magic*, 116.

41. Malinowski, *Magic*, 116.

42. Malinowski, *Magic*, 117.

43. Allen, *Myth*, xi, xiii.

for unity with the cosmos.⁴⁴ As much as Eliade was specific about the origin of myth, he also stated with clarity the exact function of the nature of this narrative. For Eliade, myth narrates a sacred history,⁴⁵

> an event that took place in primordial Time... through the deeds of Supernatural Beings, a reality [that] came into existence, be it the whole of reality, the Cosmos, or only a fragment of reality ... a particular kind of human behavior, an institution.⁴⁶

Hence, myth pertains to creation, and relates how things came to existence.⁴⁷ Thus, Eliade incorporated the idea of "creation" to emphasize the function of myth. So, myth, then, is always an account of a creation—a cosmogony—relating how things came to be, and constituting "the paradigms of all significant human acts."⁴⁸

In expression of the purpose of myth as relating something that actually happened, Eliade noted that it is the supernatural beings that are protagonists in myths, and known preeminently for their activities in primordial times. In that view, myths reveal the supernatural beings' activities and the sacredness of their work.⁴⁹ Hence, as Eliade further argued, myths describe the acts of these supernatural beings as "dramatic breakthroughs" by which the world is established, and a human is formed and defined as "a mortal, sexed, and cultural [/societal] being,"⁵⁰ who works according to certain rules.⁵¹ Here, Eliade's views bring to bear that it is the act of the supernatural beings in creating the world which provide a model on which human activities are centered. Ceremonies and rituals are carried out in the manner in which the world was established, and find justification in the existence of the world and the cosmogonic myth

---

44. Allen, *Myth*, 164.
45. Eliade, *Myth and Reality*, 5.
46. Eliade, *Myth and Reality*, 5–6; Allen, *Myth*, 184.
47. Eliade, *Myth and Reality*, 18; Von Hendy, *Modern Construction*, 183. An important point to note here, though, is that Eliade conceived myth to be centered on the creation of the world. According to him, this idea is preeminent. All other myths relating the origin of man, beginning of an institution and other things, as he holds, are subsequent and complement the cosmogonic myth (Eliade, *Myth and Reality*, 21). In studying religion in Africa, Geoffrey Parrinder also subscribed to the view that creation is the primal myth.
48. Eliade, *Myth and Reality*, 6 (see also 18).
49. Eliade, *Myth and Reality*, 6. See Allen, *Myth*, 184–85.
50. Eliade, *Myth and Reality*, 6, 11. See Allen, *Myth*, 185.
51. Eliade, *Myth and Reality*, 11.

pertaining to it. In essence, a myth functions as a paradigm or model for a human's acts, in order to see oneself in that one grand vision of reality of "sacred"[52] time[53]—*in illo tempore* when the "cosmos" emerged from "chaos." So, for Eliade, just as Malinowski, myth provides that one grand vision of reality modeled on the primordial event, which acts as codifier and charter[54] for human societies.

As in the main, scholars define myths and determine their function from the perspective of their respective disciplines, but there is a general consensus that myths account for the origin of both physical and/or social phenomena. But, Malinowski and Eliade's views are significant to this discussion, as they associate the content of myths with origins, or creation, and relate the emergence of physical phenomena to social organization, that is within purview of the Dogon and biblical cosmogonies. Also, Eliade succinctly stated that myth is always related to creation. In his previous work, Eliade considered creation as manifest cosmologically from chaos to cosmos.[55] Accordingly, for Eliade, myth relates to creation and constitutes the paradigms of all human behavior.[56]

This idea is in keeping with Susan Feldman's study[57] of cosmogonic myths of the Dogon of Mali and Bambara tribes of Senegal. In order

---

52. Eliade, *Myth and Reality*, 19; see also Allen, *Myth*, 185–86, 189. Eliade is credited with contributing to the phenomenology of the sacred by insisting that humans experience the sacred by entering the timelessness of the original event through myth and ritual. See Von Hendy, *Modern Construction*, 184.

53. It is in these events imagined to have happened in time immemorial that humans oriented their being. Similarly, Mbiti discussing the concept of time in African traditions in relation to the view on "eschatology," expressed that "time" in traditional African thinking, is related to events in the past, with implications for the present. Mbiti argued that arising from this are myths for the humans to better apprehend the world and their experience of the universe. From the African context, particularly, Mbiti observed that these myths dealing with events in the "past" cover themes such as the creation of the world, explanation of natural phenomena, origin of humankind, various customs and traditions, advent of death in the world, and the evolution of different societies. See Mbiti, *New Testament Eschatology*, 24–25.

54. Eliade, *Myth and Reality*, 19–20. Geoffrey Parrinder, whose view in general is that "creation" is the primal myth, echoes Eliade's conception of myth as a codifier or a charter for human behaviors and institutions. Parrinder noted, "Myth is real and sacred, and serves as an example in providing a pattern for human behavior and explanation of its mysteries" (Parrinder, "Foreword," 12).

55. Eliade, *Myth of the Eternal Return*, xi, 10, 18, 54–56, 60.

56. Eliade, *Myth and Reality*, 18.

57. Feldman studied myths and tales of different African tribes, and discovered that many African myths are formed around various themes. Feldman outlined several myths from a number of African communities. She observed variations in the

to justify their social stratification, these two tribes speculated on the origin of the world and creation of the social order, which they perpetuated. Hence, through the formulation of cosmogonic myths, the tribes explained the beginning of their existing systems by referring to some imaginary divine origin. As they thought their social order to be divinely ordained, they, therefore, held ritual enactment befitting to sustain it. By so doing, the tribes continue to feel that they are living in line with the creator's providential purpose for creating the world.[58] These propositions on myth relating creation, as the manifestation of the cosmos from chaos, and the sociological relevance of beliefs on creation as sanctioning social organization, are central to the close analysis of common concepts between Gen 1:1–2, 26–28 and the Dogon myth of creation.

The Dogon Myth of Creation and the Concept of *Creatio ex nihilo*

Thanks to the extensive ethnographic work of Marcel Griaule and Germaine Dieterlen, the Dogon creation myth is understood to be a complex narrative on the origin of both the world and humankind. Scholarly analyses and interpretations of the Dogon cosmology rely heavily on two major works: *Conversations with Ogotemmêli*[59] and *The Pale Fox*.[60] It is clear from these two major works that there are various versions of creation narratives. One version often referred to by scholars emerges from the conversations with a priest-elder, Ogotemmêli. Ogotemmêli reported that the god Amma created the sun and moon: with an invention not first disclosed to mankind.[61] He postulated that the stars were made from mud pellets flung into space by Amma. Similarly, he recounted the

---

mythic themes on the beginning of things from primeval times, origin of man, gods' withdrawal, lost paradise, and origin of death. In this study, however, she noticed the scarcity of myths in African communities on the origin of the world. Consequently, her discussion focused on the Dogon of Mali and Bambara tribes of Senegal. Feldman pointed out that these cosmogonies are a reflection of the developed states of the Dogon and Bambara people (Feldman, *African Myths*, 23).

58. On Malinowski and Eliade's views, see pp. 8–11.

59. Griaule, *Conversations with Ogotemmêli* was initially published in 1948 under the French title *Dieu d'Eua: entretiens avec Ogotemmêli*. The Dogon priest-elder, Ogotemmêli, supported by informants, delegated esoteric knowledge to Griaule in a period of thirty-three days.

60. Griaule and Dieterlen, *Le Renard Pâle: Tome 1. Le mythe cosmogonique*, translated by Infantino to *The Pale Fox* from Dieterlen's compilation following Griaule's death.

61. Griaule, *Conversations*, 16.

earth as formed from a lump of clay squeezed, thrown and flowed into a fetus shape in the womb with its limbs showing the north—south and east—west orientation.[62] The earth, conceived as feminine, lay flat facing upwards, with the anthill as its sexual organ and the termite hill as its clitoris.[63] The god Amma is said to have been desirous of intercourse with the earth, but the termite hill represented its masculinity and prevented copulation. So Amma, who is considered omnipotent, excised the termite hill and copulated with the earth. This forced union resulted in the birth of a jackal, but not the intended twins. Hence, the act of incision of the earth, and consequent copulation marked the original point of blunder, and primordial "chaos" in the intended order of the universe.

However, as further narrated, Amma again copulated with the earth, "water" entered the womb of the earth, resulting in the birth of two beings, or ancestral spirits called the Nommo, but also conceived as water beings of the divine essence of Amma himself.[64] It should be noted, however, that in this version the idea of the jackal as an agent of disorder, and of the Nommo as adjuncts of Amma's intended order tallies with the idea of the "fox" and Nommo assuming the same roles in the complex version narrated in *The Pale Fox*. The latter is ethnographic material recounting a phenomenal myth, which, as Ray[65] and Heusch[66] correctly observed, unfolds from several levels, but is centered on a supreme creator-god, whose artifice transforms chaos to cosmos and the social organization deriving from it. Although often dismissed as a collection of anomalies[67]

62. Griaule, *Conversations*, 17.

63. Griaule, *Conversations*, 17.

64. Griaule, *Conversations*, 18. See Griaule and Dieterlen, *Pale Fox*, 157, 157n185. Apart from being cast as beings of the same essence as Amma, the Nommo were associated with rain and fresh water and considered masters of the water. Yet, as also noted in the main, there are variations in the depiction of these first beings Amma created, who are also conceived as fish and associated with fire.

65. Ray, *African Religions*, 28–29.

66. Heusch, *Sacrifice*, 125.

67. Beek, "Dogon Restudied," 139–67; "Haunting Griaule," 43–68. Beek, though a specialist in ecology ("Dogon Restudied," 143; "Haunting Griaule," 54), severely critiqued Griaule for indoctrinating the Dogon to come up with such a complex cosmogony. Following his anthropological survey among the Dogon in the 1980s and 1990s, and failing to come up with any similar information, Beek dismissed the existence of the Dogon cosmogonic system as an invention and declared that the Dogon had no creation myths (Beek, "Dogon Restudied," 148–50; "Haunting Griaule," 56, 60; *Dogon*, 103). On the other hand, Sagan argued that the Dogon's astronomic knowledge on Sirius as a binary star system must have been influenced by outside contact (Sagan, *Broca's Brain*, 149, 186–200; reprint [2011], 115, 145–57). However, Sagan's proposition

formulated by an ardent anthropologist, this ethnographic work presents esoteric Dogon cosmogonic and mythopoeic traditions echoing narratives from the ANE and biblical Hebrew traditions to resembling general knowledge of modern science[68] on the origin of the universe. In spite of the denigration by anthropologists and others of Griaule's ethnographic work as fabrication, Griaule reveals esoteric knowledge on an African creation myth with elaborate symbolic and cosmological systems of the epistemologies of the Global South, thus deserving academic debate. However, due to the limitation here, focus is mainly on points of intersection of creative processes and concepts presented both in the Dogon creation myth and the biblical Hebrew tradition in relation to creation from chaos.

As narrated in *The Pale Fox*, the Dogon creation myth unfolds with a theme compatible with the belief in "*creatio ex nihilo.*" The Dogon believe that, "in the beginning," before the formation of all things, the god Amma existed and sat upon "nothing."[69] It is believed that Amma existed in the form of an egg consisting of four clavicles joined together in the form of a ball. From this concept, the term "Amma's egg in a ball,"[70] or "egg of the world" (*aduno tal*) is derived. The four clavicles prefigured the four divine sectors, being Amma's womb of all the world signs that opened up to cast out the world.[71] These four clavicles also contained the harbinger of the four fundamental elements: water, air, fire,[72] and earth,

---

contradicted evidence offered by Germaine Dieterlen of a 400-year-old artifact with representations of the Sirius stars. While other scholars' and anthropologists' criticisms have labeled Griaule's ethnographic work on the Dogon as bricolage of invention, it shows the general reluctance by the West to give precedence, acknowledge erudition, and attribute ingeniousness to African philosophical and cosmological thinking that is inherent with ancient African civilization.

68. The latter view is presented in Scranton, *Science of the Dogon*; *Cosmological Origins*.

69. Griaule and Dieterlen, *Pale Fox*, 81; Ray, *African Religions*, 24. Perhaps herein lies a parallel to the biblical concept of *creatio ex nihilo* that has remained subject to scholarly discourse for centuries. See, for example, EE 1:1–5, expressing that nothing existed except for the comingling waters of Apsu and Tiamat (Heidel, *Babylonian Genesis*, 3, 18; Foster, *Before the Muses*, 439; Lambert, *Babylonian*, 51).

70. Griaule and Dieterlen, *Pale Fox*, 81.

71. Griaule and Dieterlen, *Pale Fox*, 81, 121.

72. Griaule and Dieterlen, *Pale Fox*, 81, 153. It is interesting to note that the existence of fire is not only presaged with the morphology of Amma's egg, which is his existence, but also emerged from Amma's breathing and is consubstantial with Amma, by which he can destroy the universe at will (539).

and each one in its own quarter.⁷³ In essence, all these fundamental elements were out of his very nature. It is said the earth is the discharge from Amma's expectorate, water his saliva, fire emerged from his breathing, and wind from his puffing out.⁷⁴ The bisectors separating the water, air, fire, and earth represented the cardinal directions,⁷⁵ or space. Thus, the future space and fundamental elements were preserved in the formation of Amma's "primordial" egg.

But, at first, Amma designed the cosmos in his thought before creating it, and "signs" manifested his creative thought.⁷⁶ Amma used "water"⁷⁷ as the basic matter to trace his primordial signs in space.⁷⁸ So, Amma's theoretical conception of the cosmos manifested itself in the form of 266 primordial signs⁷⁹ (*bummo*), which are the invisible Amma himself,⁸⁰ and represented his thought. It is held that at the formation of the first world, Amma created the first seed, *sene*, and incorporated the four fundamental elements in it.⁸¹ Then, Amma placed the signs and seed on a disk, and as the elements spun, water dried out causing disorder.⁸² This marked the failure of Amma's initial creative acts. Therefore, not content with the first world, Amma destroyed it, but retained the *sene* seed with its four fundamental elements, and as the first of flora⁸³ for the second genesis.

---

73. Griaule and Dieterlen, *Pale Fox*, 84; Ray, *African Religions*, 25.

74. Griaule and Dieterlen, *Pale Fox*, 110.

75. Griaule and Dieterlen, *Pale Fox*, 81, 159, 186. As narrated in *Pale Fox*, the four clavicles that determine space and cardinal directions opened in the north, a direction particularly linked with Amma as he spun (186).

76. Griaule and Dieterlen, *Pale Fox*, 84–85.

77. Griaule and Dieterlen, *Pale Fox*, 83. Water was the first creation of Amma (230). On water as the prime element in Egyptian and Mesopotamian cosmogonies, see Tsumura, *Creation and Destruction*, 129–30.

78. Griaule and Dieterlen, *Pale Fox*, 84, 155. Signs and words are identified as the same (188), meaning words and water are identical in the Dogon cosmology.

79. Griaule and Dieterlen, *Pale Fox*, 84 (see also 103, 117); Ray, *African Religions*, 25. "Signs" and "words" in the Dogon creation myth are identical (Griaule and Dieterlen, *Pale Fox*, 188). The idea here that words are creative agents is comparable to Mesopotamian, Egyptian, and Asian cosmogonies.

80. Griaule and Dieterlen, *Pale Fox*, 103 (see also 84).

81. Griaule and Dieterlen, *Pale Fox*, 110.

82. Griaule and Dieterlen, *Pale Fox*, 114.

83. Griaule and Dieterlen, *Pale Fox*, 115–16, 123. The importance of the *sene*, as the first creation of all trees, is comparable to that of the Nommo as the first beings (116).

YHWH IN THE WIND(S)

Amma's second genesis proceeded with the creation of the first and most important, yet also the smallest seed, the *po* (*Digitaria exilis*) known in Dogon language as the *kize uzi*,[84] the "little seed." As cited, twenty-two signs (*yala*) represented the *po* seed at the center of the spiral made up of the 266 signs enclosed in Amma's egg.[85] The numerical value of sixty-six signs (*yala*) assigned to the *po* seed is significant in that the *po* comprised the entire universe conceived by Amma's thought. This encompassed six *yala* for the sex of the *po*, also representing the prefiguration of the first animate being (*nommo anagonno*),[86] another sixteen *yala* for the body of the *po*, forty *yala* assigned to the eight seeds (five *yala* per seed) associated with the eight ancestors of humanity,[87] and the final four *yala* of the *sene* bearing the four elements—water, air, fire, and earth—that Amma reserved at the destruction of the first world.[88] The *yala* of the eight seeds and of the *sene* were all bestowed on the *nommo anagonno* and located inside the *po*.[89] All these elements comprising the sixty-six *yala* Amma incorporated into the body of the *po* formed its central spiral. It is often stated that some mysterious "internal vibrations" caused the *po* (*kize uzi*) to burst its enveloping sheath, and emerged releasing matter that reached the uttermost confines of the universe.[90] But, this undefined mysterious "internal" movement may be apprehended as the wind, in view of the description of the god Amma in relation with the *po*, as presented in *The Pale Fox*.

Amma is this "spiraling motion" manifested as "wind" imbedded with the *po*.[91] Just as the *sene* seed was the center of the first creation, the *po* became the "image of the origin of matter"[92] in the second genesis. Of significance here is the symbiotic relationship of the *po* with Amma, where the seed is viewed as the image of the creator.[93] It is clear, though, that in this myth the nature of Amma, as integral with the *po*, was considered esoteric and defied definition. But, the reference to "wind," or

---

84. Griaule and Dieterlen, *Pale Fox*, 131n120. See "Dogon," 84.
85. Griaule and Dieterlen, *Pale Fox*, 117, 121.
86. Griaule and Dieterlen, *Pale Fox*, 122, 139, 159.
87. Griaule and Dieterlen, *Pale Fox*, 123.
88. Griaule and Dieterlen, *Pale Fox*, 123.
89. Griaule and Dieterlen, *Pale Fox*, 159.
90. Griaule and Dieterlen, "Dogon," 84; *Pale Fox*, 122.
91. Griaule and Dieterlen, *Pale Fox*, 130.
92. Griaule and Dieterlen, *Pale Fox*, 130.
93. Griaule and Dieterlen, *Pale Fox*, 130.

GENESIS 1:1–2, 26–28 IN LIGHT OF THE DOGON CREATION MYTH

"whirlwind" seems to be the closest acceptable representation of this sublime nature.[94] Hence, according to this myth, a whirlwind rose representing the god Amma emerging from the egg of the world. The *po*, though the tiniest (thing), contained at its center the invisible wind, as a form of Amma himself and his creative will. It is said, Amma made the *po* to come out first. This central air ball remained inaudible and invisible, but whirled and dispersed the particles of matter in a "sonorous and luminous motion."[95] Undoubtedly, here, and in sequel, natural phenomena played a central role in the formation of the Dogon cosmology. As stated, these primordial movements were agitated by Amma, in the form of a whirlwind or wind, causing the *po* to spiral and reveal all things in formation. As expressed in relation to the Dogon ceremonies celebrating the role of the *po*, the spiral or spinning that released the contents of *po* with a loud sound, representing the creative "word," was also identified as the "voice" of the *po*.[96]

It appears that the *po* was consubstantial with Amma in that the *po*, as the image of the origin of things, was also considered the image of the creator transformed to wind, in order to replace him,[97] who was "whirlwind" himself, as the whirling force that animated the world.[98] This idea also bodes well with the reference to the four winds[99] of the sky as the manifestation of the god Amun, seen as an embodiment of the Egyptian *hermopolitan ogdoad*.[100] As Smith asserts, the four winds merge into one single high wind, which brings the (Egyptian) cosmos into existence.[101] Amun, as the wind,[102] is attributed with the separation of the earth and

---

94. Griaule and Dieterlen, *Pale Fox*, 131.

95. Griaule and Dieterlen, *Pale Fox*, 130.

96. Griaule and Dieterlen, *Pale Fox*, 441 (see also 465, 534). The whirling of the *po* and the release of its contents with a "loud sound" (manifesting the word [423]) is celebrated at ceremonies by the sounds called "voices" of the chief priest, Hogon's horn (441). This idea has implications for the translation of the Hebrew term "voice" often considered as YHWH's thunder, but should be seen as the image of YHWH appearing with the loud sound of whirling winds (Pss 18:14[13]; 29; Job 37:1–5).

97. Griaule and Dieterlen, *Pale Fox*, 130–131 (see also 417).

98. Griaule and Dieterlen, *Pale Fox*, 142, 405.

99. Smith, *Carlsberg*, 57; the four winds are also called Amun's diadem (62–63).

100. Smith, *Carlsberg*, 53, 194.

101. Smith, *Carlsberg*, 194. Smith notes that the god Shu is also associated with the wind, and also attributed with the separating of the sky from the earth (58–59).

102. Smith, *Carlsberg*, 57, 62–63; Frankfort et al., "Myth and Reality," 10.

sky.[103] Fundamentally, it is suggested that Amun is the creator of the egg, who also emerged from it.[104] This Egyptian parallel shows the veracity and prevalence of the wind as deified in a cosmological context. Therefore, the nature of Amma is in keeping with another ancient African context, and shows the primacy of the "wind/whirlwind"[105] as a creative agent in establishing the Dogon cosmic order.

Proceeding with the second genesis, Amma, as the internal spiral,[106] wind,[107] or spiraling motion[108] superposed all the four elements of the *sene* and mixed them inside the *po*. This process caused internal vibrations, as evidence of the motion of the "word" of Amma symbolizing the life of the seed.[109] This force, or vibrations, as hypostases of Amma's creative "word" infused into the seed, caused the seed to vibrate seven times and protrude into seven extensions of increasing length.[110] These seven vibrations metamorphosed into an anthropomorphic shape, as harbinger of the formation of the first animate beings. This process of the creation of humankind by the seven vibrations is fused with the identification of Amma's creative word, or the seven words that *po* articulated[111] and emitted to the first animate beings with the birth of the Dogon universe. These seven articulations were the seven vibrations of the "word," which formed the image of the creative spiral—whirlwind—, which is Amma himself.[112] In this internal movement of life, however, the seventh vibration broke through the sheath of the *po*, like a birth; thus creating a shorter and eighth segment.[113] This eighth segment not only prefigured the formation of the first animate beings, but also the birth of Amma's second universe that emerged from the *po*.[114]

103. Smith, *Carlsberg*, 63.
104. Smith, *Carlsberg*, 63–64.
105. Griaule and Dieterlen, *Pale Fox*, 463.
106. Griaule and Dieterlen, *Pale Fox*, 122–23.
107. Griaule and Dieterlen, *Pale Fox*, 130–31 (see also 142).
108. Griaule and Dieterlen, *Pale Fox*, 136.
109. Griaule and Dieterlen, *Pale Fox*, 136 (see also 122).
110. Griaule and Dieterlen, *Pale Fox*, 138 (see also 140).
111. Griaule and Dieterlen, *Pale Fox*, 165, 167, 338 (see also 441, 534, noted as the "voice" [of po], or articulated "word" that became the "sound").
112. Griaule and Dieterlen, *Pale Fox*, 136–42, 323–24. See pp. 16–17.
113. Griaule and Dieterlen, *Pale Fox*, 138, 374–76, 423. This eighth segment is considered as a birth, and associated with the reproductive organs, as evidence of future production of life.
114. Griaule and Dieterlen, *Pale Fox*, 140. The *po* agitated by the whirling spiral

Amma continued to make eight additional seeds, considered as the "word,"[115] and placed them inside the *po*, including the *emme ya*[116] (female sorghum), as a symbol of the world.[117] Then, Amma transformed his egg into a double placenta to create the first beings, *nommo anagonno*;[118] a term designating their variant forms: rain/water, man or fish.[119] In both placentas Amma formed a pair of androgynous twins,[120] and one pair occupied the upper half and the other the lower half of the placenta, prefiguring the posterior "separation" of the sky and earth. According to the narrative in *The Pale Fox*, this formation of two pairs of male twins, *nommo anagonno*[121] occurred inside *po*.[122] As noted in this narrative, this progression of Amma's creation in the "egg of the world"

---

motion of Amma's wind, eventually broke its sheath and poured all its contents into the "ark" of the Nommo (423, 426).

115. Griaule and Dieterlen, *Pale Fox*, 148.

116. Griaule and Dieterlen, *Pale Fox*, 142–45.

117. Griaule and Dieterlen, *Pale Fox*, 144.

118. Griaule and Dieterlen, *Pale Fox*, 157. The term *ana* means "rain," or "man," and *gonno* "to sinuate" hence the word *anagonno* can mean "sinuous rain" or "male (who walks by) sinuating." As stated in *Pale Fox*, the term *ana* foreshadows the idea that the being created will become man. But this may also imply the formation of aqueous beings, in keeping with the theme of Amma's use of water as the basic substance for his design in creation (155).

119. Griaule and Dieterlen, *Pale Fox*, 157 (see also 162, 330, 335).

120. It may be pointed out at this point, that the Dogon concept of twinness before the creation of the universe proper is similar to the ANE male and female principle marking the transitional stage towards the origin of the world. This notion dominates the organization of the Dogon society and their family structure.

121. Griaule, *Pale Fox*, 180–81, 184. These four primordial ancestors, called the *nommo anagonno*, prefigured roles in the development and organization of creation. The first, *nommo die* (great Nommo), formed and placed in the north (197), stayed in heaven as agent and regulator of Amma's creation, i.e., to issue the rain manifested in storms, lightning, and rainbow (180). The second one, *nommo titiyayne*, placed in the west, would be the guardian and protector of the spiritual principles of the first *nommo*, and executioner of the sacrifice. The third, *o nommo* belonged to the pond, and sacrificed for the purification and organization of the earth following the misdeeds of its twin. At this point *o nommo*, located east, known as *nommo semi*, became Nommo at sacrifice. In sequel, Nommo resurrected in human form and descended to the earth with the first human ancestors on an ark created from Nommo's placenta. Once on earth, Nommo resumed his form and later resided in the waters and multiplied through the birth of offsprings. The fourth, *nommo anagonno* called Ogo, located south, and not represented as fish, rebelled against its creator and brought disorder into the universe. As punishment, Amma eventually transformed Ogo into the pale fox (*Vulpes pallida*), *yurugu*; the image of its downfall for the "chaos" he initiated to Amma's intended universal design (184).

122. Griaule and Dieterlen, *Pale Fox*, 159, 169.

when related in terms of gestation, is comparable to the developments in the "womb of a woman."[123]

So, it is believed that all things came from Amma's placenta,[124] which surrounded the spiraling *po*. It is important to note here, that while in formation inside the *po*, the *nommo anagonno* were imparted the image (*kikinu*) of Amma in the form of spiritual principles, as Amma's eyes.[125] This ascription prefigured the *nommo anagonno*'s function as the guardian and protector of the world created by Amma.[126] It is also said, the seven "signs" (*yala*) of the beginning of the *po*, which were the unarticulated "word," were bestowed by *po* into the *nommo anagonno*,[127] symbolizing their posterior duty in perfecting Amma's creation.[128] Again, as the replica of their creator Amma,[129] the *nommo anagonno*, though endowed with the four fundamental elements—water, air, fire, and earth—"fire"[130] and "flame"[131] feature primarily in their formation, and these beings are also later associated with "fire."[132] Amma proceeded to place the *po* in the northern clavicle and the four *nommo anagonno*: *nommo die*, *nommo semi*, *nommo titiyayne*, and Ogo in the north, east, west, and south clavicles respectively, representing the four cardinal directions.[133] Then, Amma set out to bestow female twins with potential existence for these four primordial ancestors, but a state of maturity was not reached. One of the androgynous twins, Ogo,[134] revolted before the

---

123. Griaule and Dieterlen, *Pale Fox*, 191 (see also 225–26). The imagery of a child coming out of the mother's womb is deployed here to illustrate how all things emerge from the *po*. See Griaule and Dieterlen, *Pale Fox*, 424–25.

124. Griaule and Dieterlen, *Pale Fox*, 190–91 (see also 225–26).

125. Griaule and Dieterlen, *Pale Fox*, 161.

126. Griaule and Dieterlen, *Pale Fox*, 161, 164.

127. Griaule and Dieterlen, *Pale Fox*, 165.

128. Griaule and Dieterlen, *Pale Fox*, 139, 139n140.

129. Griaule and Dieterlen, *Pale Fox*, 139, 14n72.

130. Griaule and Dieterlen, *Pale Fox*, 162, 170, 174–75.

131. Griaule and Dieterlen, *Pale Fox*, 174. This idea of the association of "fire" and "flame" in the formation of the Nommo, who also become guardians and protectors of the world Amma created, provides an interesting parallel with the notion of fire and flame as YHWH's ministers as described in Ps 104:4.

132. Griaule and Dieterlen, *Pale Fox*, 180, 263, 392, 393.

133. Griaule and Dieterlen, *Pale Fox*, 197. But the order is later reversed due to Ogo's theft (see 225).

134. Griaule and Dieterlen, *Pale Fox*, 198. It appears there are several versions on the formation of Ogo, but there is concurrence on the development of his character in opposition to Amma, causing the deviation from the intended order of the universe.

gestation period completed in an attempt to take over Amma's creative work, and disrupted Amma's intended cosmic order.

From Chaos to Cosmos

The male twin Ogo, overcome by incessant restlessness, rebelled and broke out of the lower half of the placenta prematurely, causing the diversification in Amma's work. He tore off a segment of his placenta, leaving the incomplete female counterpart behind. It is said Amma intended to give the female counterpart to the male twin, Ogo at her birth, as previously done to Ogo's brothers following sixty periods of the male twins' formation.[135] Ogo became restless, and desiring to possess Amma's creative work, he revolted and embarked on a search for the female twin. He attempted to acquire the *sene* seed by aggression, intending to make a world of his own to supersede Amma's first one.[136] It is said, "they fought."[137] Undoubtedly, at this point, the Dogon creation myth is in conformity with the pervasive ANE *Chaoskampf* myth. At this combat, Ogo snatched two of the *sene*'s elements, water and fire, and left only air and earth in it. But, Amma deprived the *sene* of its creative function, thus accentuating Ogo's imperfection and incompleteness[138] from his acts of aggression.

As Ogo left his placenta prematurely, he breached his own gestation period and descended with his eyes still closed into primordial darkness.[139] According to the narrative, the "whirlwind"[140] of the *sene*, deemed as the blood of Ogo's placenta, propelled his descent. The piece of the placenta that Ogo tore off and deployed for his descent, Amma turned into dry sandy earth.[141] Ogo thereupon resumed his relentless search for his twin. He dug holes and penetrated the earth; an act resembling an incestuous relation with his mother, the earth—a relic of his placenta.[142] This presumed incestuous act committed with the earth meant that, this

---

135. Griaule and Dieterlen, *Pale Fox*, 198; Ray, *African Religions*, 26.
136. Griaule and Dieterlen, *Pale Fox*, 199; Ray, *African Religions*, 27.
137. Griaule and Dieterlen, *Pale Fox*, 199 (see also 204).
138. Griaule and Dieterlen, *Pale Fox*, 199.
139. Griaule and Dieterlen, *Pale Fox*, 203.
140. Griaule and Dieterlen, *Pale Fox*, 205.
141. Griaule and Dieterlen, *Pale Fox*, 207; Ray, *African Religions*, 27.
142. Griaule and Dieterlen, *Pale Fox*, 209; Ray, *African Religions*, 27.

union like its progenitor, resulted in "incomplete, imperfect and single beings,"[143] showing Ogo's incapability to match Amma's creative prowess.

Frustrated with the failure of his first attempt to equate Amma, Ogo ascended to the sky to resume the futile search for his female twin, causing further transformation in Amma's creative work. At Ogo's revolt, Amma handed over and conferred charge of Ogo's female twin soul to the pair in the other part of the remaining egg. In view of the determination and attempt by Ogo to return, Amma turned the placenta into "sun,"[144] and the blood of the placenta into "rays"[145] to obstruct his approach. With the heat from the sun's rays forming an impassable barrier, Ogo only succeeded in stealing the eight male seeds, and another small piece of his placenta that he employed as his second ark and concealed the stolen seeds at his second descent. But, Amma transformed the "hole" left in his placenta into a "moon," as evidence of Ogo's theft.[146] So, both the sun and moon emerged from Ogo's antagonistic behavior, and as vestiges of his celestial placenta.[147] Meanwhile, the earth produced imperfect and incomplete beings[148] consistent with Ogo's otiose nature. Amma observed the disorder, or "chaos" caused by Ogo in the midst of his intended creative order, and he considered purification, instead of recreation, of the placenta to restore order.[149] Consequently, Amma initiated the sacrifice of Ogo's twin brother[150] as both punishment for shared responsibility[151] in Ogo's revolt, and for the purification and reorganization of the universe. This systemized cosmological reordering from the disorganization caused by Ogo's rebellious acts, shows that the key mythic element of "creation-out-of-chaos" is inherent with the Dogon creation myth.

---

143. Griaule and Dieterlen, *Pale Fox*, 209–10.

144. Griaule and Dieterlen, *Pale Fox*, 218 (see also 222). The earth and the sun are considered twins, as in essence these celestial bodies were made from vestiges of the same placenta.

145. Griaule and Dieterlen, *Pale Fox*, 218.

146. Griaule and Dieterlen, *Pale Fox*, 227.

147. Griaule and Dieterlen, *Pale Fox*, 227. The façades of the Dogon totemic sanctuaries show drawings of the sun and moon, as images of Ogo's placenta.

148. Griaule and Dieterlen, "Dogon," 86; *Pale Fox*, 230.

149. Griaule and Dieterlen, *Pale Fox*, 248.

150. Griaule and Dieterlen, *Pale Fox*, 248. Versions vary on the choice of the victim to be sacrificed (cf. 251), but the essence of the myth is the same; the Nommo is sacrificed to purify the world.

151. Griaule and Dieterlen, *Pale Fox*, 248; Ray, *African Religions*, 27.

The sacrifice of *nommo semi*, who became Nommo,[152] though considered as punishment for causing the disorder in Amma's creation, determined the purification and construction of a viable "cosmos." It should be noted that, just as in the ANE conflicts among deities, here antagonism towards the primordial deity is represented by Nommo's irate personality that motivated the execution of punishment.[153] From his body, all the fundamental elements of the world are created. So, Amma, alongside the executioner, *nommo titiyayne*, proceeded with the sacrifice and emasculated Nommo, severed his umbilical cord from the placenta and at the same time completely cut off his sex organ.[154] In fact, as narrated, the emasculation effectively meant the separation of the Nommo from his placenta. Thus, symbolizing the separation of sexes.[155] The umbilical cord became the *sigi tolo* star—Sirius—; known as "the navel of the world," or the image of the center of the universe.[156] The planet Venus[157] emerged from the blood issuing from the sex organs of the victim.[158] Amma reserved the contents of the sex organs as a posterior essential resource for life on earth issuing as water, seas and rain,[159] and lightning, thunder, and fire were associated with the life force of the sacrificed Nommo.[160] This initial stage of the sacrifice of Nommo marked the beginning of stars, planets, and the reorganization of the universe.

However, Ogo misjudged the completion of the emasculation and reascended to the sky in another attempt to regain his female twin and seeds by stealth. Once again, Ogo became victim to his surreptitious behavior. At his attempt to escape, *nommo titiyayne* grabbed Ogo by the foreskin, thus circumcising him.[161] Hence, the planet Mars emerged from the emission of blood from Ogo's circumcision by the sacrifice.[162] How-

---

152. See 19n121 above; cf. Ray, *African Religions*, 27.
153. Griaule and Dieterlen, *Pale Fox*, 257.
154. Griaule and Dieterlen, *Pale Fox*, 256–57.
155. Griaule and Dieterlen, *Pale Fox*, 259.
156. Griaule and Dieterlen, *Pale Fox*, 257, 349.
157. Griaule and Dieterlen, *Pale Fox*, 259 (see also 514–21). In light of this complex myth, the Dogon observe six positions of the planet Venus in relation to agrarian rites and ceremonies commemorating the mythical events of this sacrifice.
158. Griaule and Dieterlen, *Pale Fox*, 259–60.
159. Griaule and Dieterlen, *Pale Fox*, 260.
160. Griaule and Dieterlen, *Pale Fox*, 260–63.
161. Griaule and Dieterlen, *Pale Fox*, 268.
162. Griaule and Dieterlen, *Pale Fox*, 269–70, 284.

ever, it is clear that *nommo titiyayne* acted hastily in circumcising Ogo without Amma's consent, and his blood penetrated both the celestial and terrestrial placentas. Thus, it became requisite for Amma to proceed with the sacrifice of Nommo for the purification of the cosmos in formation.[163]

However, of significance here too, is that Amma formed the stars and planets that are central to the Dogon cosmology, from the blood issuing from the sacrifice of Nommo. The seeds and stars were strewn with blood flowing like a torrent as Amma seized Nommo with his head down and brought him to the "north,"[164] the same place Amma's egg opened. Among the seeds were the *po pilu*, from which the star *po tolo* emerged, as "the symbol of the beginning of the universe,"[165] and also the *emme ya*, which transformed into the star *emme ya tolo*, that eventually became a companion of the *po tolo* revolving around Sirius.[166] The north—south orientation of the blood flow formed the Milky Way.[167] Amma also transformed Nommo's principal organs into planets and constellations, among them the Pleiades and Orion.[168] A series of plants, as evidence of Nommo's dismembered body, were also brought to life from the blood spewing from the excision of his organs.[169]

---

163. Griaule and Dieterlen, *Pale Fox*, 305–6.

164. Griaule and Dieterlen, *Pale Fox*, 306, 310. The identification of the "north" with Amma, the spinning and opening of his egg (186), and his reorganization of the universe may not be coincidental, as most major deities were associated with a cosmic mount or abode in the north. In Ugaritic literature, El's abode is located in the north. The biblical tradition alludes to the same idea with the term *yarkĕtê Ṣāphōn* in Ps 48:3[2]c. Cross notes that although the term is associated with the holy mountain of YHWH at Zion, elsewhere it is identified with Mount Amanus farther north (see Cross, *Canaanite Myth*, 37–38; Robinson, "Zion and Ṣāphōn," 118–23). Robinson argued that Mount Ṣāphōn of Ugarit is identified with Mount Casios, which is Jebel el Aqra north of Ugarit as the abode of Baʿal. He also noted that Kraus supported the idea that Ṣāphōn was transferred to Zion via the Jebusite cult of El (119).

165. Griaule and Dieterlen, *Pale Fox*, 310.

166. Griaule and Dieterlen, *Pale Fox*, 310–11. Other constellations of Taurus and Venus also formed from the flow of blood.

167. Griaule and Dieterlen, *Pale Fox*, 313.

168. Griaule and Dieterlen, *Pale Fox*, 317–19. It seems here two tripartite clusters of Orion were formed: one named "Orion's belt" (cf. Job 38:31b, "cords of Orion") and the other "sword of Orion." In comparison, the prophet Amos claimed YHWH as the creator of the Pleiades and Orion (Amos 5:8). But, the poet/author of the book of Job mentions the Bear, Orion, the Pleiades (Job 9:9; see 38:31–32) and the constellations (Job 38:32; see Isa 13:10; 40:26). This also indicates biblical knowledge of astronomy, attributing these constellations to YHWH's creation.

169. Griaule and Dieterlen, *Pale Fox*, 320.

Amma's placement of the organs, essentially considered as the "seats" of the articulations of "words,"[170] on the line of Nommo's bloodflow forming the spatial universe, means Amma's creative words[171] diffused throughout space regenerating the universe. Amma proceeded to work with these elements and saved the organs for the resurrection of the Nommo, and regeneration of the world. Upon emptying Nommo's body of his organs, "the seat of all words,"[172] Amma dismembered the body and split it into sixty parts. To this, he added six elements of the contents of the semen (see sex of the *po*)[173] accruing to the total of sixty-six pieces. These pieces corresponded with the "signs" (*yala*) of the "spiraling primordial seeds"[174] central to the formation of the universe,[175] as Amma designed previously in his egg before Ogo's rebellious act. By this means, Amma resumed his creative work. He set into motion the development of the universe as he originally intended. In sequel, Amma put the dismembered body parts of the sacrificed Nommo into seven piles to resemble the creation of the *po* seed with its seven vibrations, or spirals of increasing length. Therefore, the seven piles represented the image of the spiral of the *po*, and symbolized the fundamental notion of the development of life.[176] In essence, at this sacrifice, Amma reorganized and repeated his elementary primordial acts of creating the universe.

Furthermore, Amma's acts of sacrificing Nommo constituted the spatial restructuring of his creative work in its entirety. As symbolic of the purification of the universe, again Nommo's body pieces were split into four parts at the south point, where the flow of blood is thought to have stopped, and ejected to the four cardinal spaces through a hole in the sky.[177] This "opening" in the sky foreshadowed the descent of the ark[178] in the reorganization of the universe. Perhaps, here, the idea echoes Ba'al's opening of a window in the sky[179] to issue thunder, lightning and

170. Griaule and Dieterlen, *Pale Fox*, 319.
171. Griaule and Dieterlen, *Pale Fox*, 122.
172. Griaule and Dieterlen, *Pale Fox*, 319.
173. Griaule and Dieterlen, *Pale Fox*, 121–22.
174. Griaule and Dieterlen, *Pale Fox*, 323 (see also 121).
175. See pp. 18–20.
176. Griaule and Dieterlen, *Pale Fox*, 323–24, 328 (see also 137–38). See pp. 18–20 above.
177. Griaule and Dieterlen, *Pale Fox*, 324.
178. Griaule and Dieterlen, *Pale Fox*, 325.
179. KTU 1.4.VII:17–19, 26–28[=CTA 4.vii:17–19, 26–28]. There is a protracted debate on Ba'al's initial reluctance for the installation of a window in his palace. The

rain for sustenance, or the biblical appeal to YHWH to rend the heavens and come down[180] for the beneficence of the adherents below.

However, upon this purification of the universe, Amma retrieved the dispersed body parts, and kneaded the vital organs, as the symbols bearing the "word," with the earth[181] of the placenta in order to revive Nommo in the form of male and female.[182] Amma endowed the resurrected Nommo with the twenty-two *yala* representing the principles of the body and sex of the *po*, thus conferred upon him the creative "word," which were the image of the *po*, and also corresponded to the development of life.[183] Amma also molded the first eight ancestors of humanity inside the *po* from the substance of the placenta.[184] Each male ancestor and its female twin were created out of the basic elements contained in the placenta and associated with them. *Amma Sérou* became associated with air; *Lébé Sérou* with earth; *Binou Sérou*—water; and *Dyongou Sérou*—fire.[185] With the remaining placenta of the resurrected Nommo, Amma

---

significance of this gesture is that the opening of the "window" in Baʿal's palace is stated in parallelism with the opening of the "rift in the clouds." This symbolic gesture of Baʿal reflects the correspondence between two worlds—the mythical and the natural. As the two spheres converge in this context, Baʿal's character as god of thunder and rain is evidenced. As often noted by biblical scholars, this symbolic gesture also corresponds to the idea of Marduk rending the clouds to give sustenance to people below (EE VII:119–121). Thus, the opening of a "window" in the myth of Baʿal and the uttering of Baʿal's "voice" correspond to the instantaneous "rending of the clouds" at the peal of "thunder" when rain falls to the earth. So, two epithets of Baʿal merge in this window episode. Baʿal asserts himself as the provider of rain, hence a fertility god, and at the same time sends out his "voice"(=thunder) in assertion of his power and authority as king (see *UBC* II 608–9). But, as suggested in this monograph, perhaps what is at issue here, and asserted as Baʿal's thunder, is the loud sound of the wind dispersing the rain bearing clouds.

180. Job 9:8 (see p. 93).

181. Griaule and Dieterlen, *Pale Fox*, 329–330; Amma emasculated and sacrificed Nommo in the form of a hermaphrodite, but resurrected him as a mixed pair of human twins; male and female. Amma achieved resurrecting Nommo by kneading the seven vital organs; the embodiment of the "word," with "earth" (397) collected from the different places associated with the sacrifice, at the point (of Sirius) where the umbilical cord and sex organs were severed. This image of Amma kneading and molding human beings with earth, recalls the biblical Yahwist creation narrative (Gen 2:7).

182. Griaule and Dieterlen, *Pale Fox*, 330 (see also 137, 259).

183. Griaule and Dieterlen, *Pale Fox*, 337; in essence, with the sex of the *po* imbued with Amma's creative word, it means that the Nommo embodied Amma's presence in the universe (122).

184. Griaule and Dieterlen, *Pale Fox*, 390.

185. Griaule and Dieterlen, *Pale Fox*, 392 (see also 62).

created the "ark"[186] that descended with the contents of the *po*; that is everything Amma had created. The ark of the resurrected Nommo, in contrast to Ogo's impure earth, symbolized the pure, fertile and cultivated earth.[187] In correlation with the role of master and ruler[188] conferred on the Nommo, Amma designed the ark to embody that role assigned him: "To organize, direct, and control the whole created universe."[189]

The descent of the ark and its contents shows correspondences with the fundamental elements characterizing the nature of Amma[190] at the beginning of the establishment of this symbolic universe. The ark[191] emerged from Amma's womb filled with the entire world; the resurrected Nommo, and the eight ancestors,[192] as well as the sun, stars, trees, rivers, mountains, animals, reptiles, plant-life, and craftsmanship.[193] As stated in the creation myth, the *po* whirled and unwound. Some internal force, that is, a delineation of Amma as whirlwind,[194] propelled the *po* to pour all that he created into Nommo's ark. This ark descended to the earth through an opening in the sky covered with "clouds,"[195] and swung with a north-south orientation. The descent of the ark with a whirling motion in a double helix, assisted by the whirling breath of the ancestors, reproduced the whirlwind. In this respect, the Dogon concept of the whirling descent of the ark through a rift in the sky resonates with the biblical idea of YHWH, who "parts the heavens," to come down (Ps 18:10[9a]; see Isa 63:19[64:1]) as the "rider on a cherub" (Ps 18:11[10]a; cf. 68:34[33] a; 104:3b; Isa 19:1; Hab 3:8; Deut 33:26),[196] and "soars"/"marches" on the

186. Griaule and Dieterlen, *Pale Fox*, 446 (see also 411).

187. Griaule and Dieterlen, *Pale Fox*, 446 (see also 449).

188. Griaule and Dieterlen, *Pale Fox*, 319 (see also 139n140).

189. Griaule and Dieterlen, *Pale Fox*, 449.

190. See pp. 16-17.

191. Although the Dogon viewed the ark as symbolic of the whole universe, in another version of this myth, due to its shape as a basket, the ark was also conceived as a granary for containing the primordial seeds (see Griaule and Dieterlen, *Pale Fox*, 456).

192. Griaule and Dieterlen, *Pale Fox*, 449-50.

193. Griaule and Dieterlen, *Pale Fox*, 449-456; Ray, *African Religions*, 27.

194. Griaule and Dieterlen, *Pale Fox*, 463. See Amma attested as "wind" (130-31) and "whirlwind" (142, 405). See also pp. 16-17.

195. Griaule and Dieterlen, *Pale Fox*, 461.

196.		
	רכב שמים	He rides the heavens (Deut 33:26)
	לרכב בשמי שמי־קדם	The one who rides the ancient heaven (Ps 68:34[33]a)
	השׂם־עבים רכובו	Who sets the cloud (as) his chariot (Ps 104:3)
	כי תרכב על־סוסיך	When you ride on your horses,
	מרכבתיך	and your chariots (Hab 3:8)
	הנה יהוה רכב על־עב	Behold, YHWH rides on a cloud (Isa 19:1)

YHWH IN THE WIND(S)

wings of the wind (Pss 18:11[10]b; 104:3, respectively); reflecting the biblical idea on YHWH's movements implied by the whirling motion of the wind.

As argued elsewhere,[197] this notion of a riding deity finds resonance in Baʿal as "rider on the clouds" (*rkb ʿrpt*),[198] and Marduk as the "storm charioteer," who employs winds as an arsenal and harnesses a "team of four" for his storm chariot (EE IV:49–51). That the "team of four" here implies the four winds (see EE IV:42) is supported by making reference to the Babylonian version of the flood story, where the storm god Adad is said to harness the south, north, east and west winds as asses to his cloud chariot.[199] Here, too, the phenomenal winds, associated with Amma, are in close attendance with the descending ark.

These references are often used by scholars to show the extent of the influences of ANE sources, as represented in the Ugaritic and Mesopotamian texts, as far as the depiction of a riding deity is concerned. But the descent of the ark of Amma propelled by the centrifugal force of the whirlwinds is compelling in shedding light on the idea of YHWH riding, symbolic of the movement of the wind in the biblical tradition.

197. Chiswa Gandiya, "Storm Theophany in the Hebrew Psalms," 29–40.

198. This epithet of Baʿal occurs sixteen times in the Ugaritic texts (cf. Rahmouni, *Divine Epithets*, 288–90). Rahmouni omits KTU 1.10.III:21, citing only fifteen occurrences of this epithet. There has been much debate on the translation of *rkb ʿrpt* offering variations in translations (Rahmouni, *Divine Epithets*, 289n5): "Charioteer of the clouds" (Wyatt, *Religious Texts*, 65; Olmo Lete and Sanmartín, *Dictionary*, 184; Olmo Lete, *Mitos y leyendas*, 175), "rider of the clouds" (Ginsberg, "Ugaritic Myths," 130), "rider of clouds" (Parker, *Ugaritic*, 69), and also "cloud rider" (Parker, *Ugaritic*, 103; Cross, *Canaanite Myth*, 165n82). Scholars have argued for the reminiscence of Baʿal's epithet in Ps 68:5[4] depicting YHWH as *rkb bʿrbwt*. As Jeremias pointed out, some scholars such as Albright and Ginsberg suggested an emendation of the Hebrew labial *b* to *p* so as to read *rkb bʿrpwt*, thus making the comparison with the Ugaritic *rkb ʿrpt* complete (see Albright, "Catalogue," 18; Ginsberg, "Ugaritic Texts," 112; Jeremias, *Theophanie*, 70n2). In the same vein, Arnold and Strawn attempted to maintain a Ugaritic connection by proposing to read "rider of the clouds" for *rkb bʿrbwt*, "rider of the steppes" in Ps 68:5[4], and even suggested eliminating ביה שמו ("in Yah (is) his name") as a gloss. Arnold and Strawn maintain this view following Vogt, Lipiński, Kraus, et al. (Arnold and Strawn, "*Beyāh šemô*," 429–31). But the natural translation of the Hebrew phrase is "rider of the steppes" (or "wilderness"), as argued by Johnson. He takes *ʿrbwt* as the plural of *ʿrbh*, thus depicting YHWH as riding through the desert. The idea alludes to YHWH's intervention by the power of his winds for the deliverance and victory of his people during the desert wandering as mentioned in Ps 68:8–9[7–8] (Johnson, *Sacral Kingship*, 70; cf. Tate, *Psalms*, 176; Green, *Storm-God*, 240n91). Johnson's idea is in keeping with Loretz, as he also prefers to retain the idea of YHWH as "the rider through the deserts," and profoundly critiques the argument presented by Arnold et al. See Loretz, "Ugaritisch-hebräische Parallelismus," 522–24.

199. Lambert and Millard, *Atraḫasīs*, 123. However, it is plausible that the ferocious mythical beasts, as mentioned in the subsequent description in EE IV:52–53, as part

The "whirlwind," termed the "movement of life,"[200] which caused the first seed to burst, is the same force behind the descent of the ark. Though in this instance, the movement is sustained by the "breath of the ancestors," and is called the "spinning wind" which gives impetus to the spiral of descent.[201] As the ark descended, the Nommo proclaimed the "word,"[202] (divine *logos*) that Amma originally implanted in its internal organs, to the four cardinal spaces, and the same "word," or distinctively termed Nommo's "voice," would be later transmitted to humankind.[203] Again, the fundamental elements associated with Amma are in view. This conflation of the "whirlwind," "spinning wind," "breath" and "word/voice," as hypostasis of Amma, accentuates Amma as the centrifugal force causing the descent of the whirling ark. After all, Amma's wind is also associated with the blast of breath from his mouth.[204] The idea draws parallels with the OT depiction of YHWH's descent from the heavens soaring on the "wings of the wind," with a blast of "breath" from his nostrils, and issuing a thunderous "voice" in accompaniment with other phenomenal elements (Ps 18:11–16[10–15]).

At any rate, during the descent of the Nommo's ark,[205] all beings aboard witness the *sigi tolo*—Sirius—shining, and the first rising of the

---

of Marduk's phenomenal entourage, may be references to theriomorphicized winds, or an allusion to the mythical dragons associated with the storm god, as shown in the iconography from the Old Babylonian period (see Green, *Storm-God*, 27–29).

200. Griaule and Dieterlen, *Pale Fox*, 463.
201. Griaule and Dieterlen, *Pale Fox*, 463.
202. Griaule and Dieterlen, *Pale Fox*, 465 (see also 338).
203. Griaule and Dieterlen, *Pale Fox*, 465; Ray, *African Religions*, 27.
204. Griaule and Dieterlen, *Pale Fox*, 110. See p. 15 above.
205. There are various representations of the ark modeled on the basis of the role and function of the ark in this myth (see Griaule and Dieterlen, *Pale Fox*, 481–84). Despite the variations, the concept of an ark as a "chariot" is symbolic to the Dogon totemic sanctuaries (484). The idea derives from the transformation of Nommo into a horse upon landing, and pulling the ark into the depression (caused at its landing), which filled with the first rain (on Nommo's semen, see p. 23 above) forming the first pond (Griaule and Dieterlen, *Pale Fox*, 471–72, 474). As cited, the image conjured here is that of the ark as "a chariot pulled on ropes by a four-legged creature" (472). Thus, a small statuette of a wooden horse that pulled the "chariot" is found in these sanctuaries. A horseman, a symbol of Amma, is sometimes placed next to, or on the horse, which is the symbol of Nommo. According to one of the Dogon dialects, Wazouba, the term *so*, or *suru*, is a word for a horse, and can also mean "power." So the horse is called *amba suru*, or Amma's power, because of the role played by Nommo, as Amma's viceroy in bringing the ark and "word," thus, demonstrating his strength on the earth. Hence, it is said, "with the chariot, the horse [Nommo] brought forth the word" (485).

sun, as it illuminates the universe.[206] In essence, this allusion to the first rising of the sun also spells out the expulsion of primordial darkness.[207] It is maintained in this myth that the rising and setting of the sun—the remnant of Ogo's placenta—remains as evidence of the arrival of the ark and the Nommo's occupation of the earth of the Fox.[208] These posterior events that originate from the "chaos" caused by Ogo's revolt, and manifest Amma's ordering of the universe, provide the apparatus for social organization in the Dogon cosmology.

Social Organization from the Creation-out-of-Chaos Concept

As Griaule and Dieterlen observed in the Dogon system of myths and symbols, the Dogon correlate their social organization with their world order, as they perceive it. Their social institutions and, in general, all the organized social activities, kinship ties, crafts, arrangements of dwellings and cultivated lands are in accordance with the several aspects of this complex creation myth.[209] So for the Dogon, the world is conceived as a whole entity, thought, manifested and established by one creator.[210] They believe the same principles of world order underlie their social organization, which, by analogy, are built into their symbolic systems that undergird proper ordering of society and the universe,[211] and departure from it means a return to a primeval state of chaos and disorder. However, due to the limitation of space, this discussion focuses on the point of view of creation-out-of-chaos and its implications for the organization of society in the Dogon cosmology. As a system of representations, the emasculation, sacrifice and resurrection of the Nommo, being central to Amma's mythical ordering of the universe,[212] establish the schema for social organization at various levels in the Dogon society. This can be seen in the structure of their tribal system classified by totems and rituals

---

206. Griaule and Dieterlen, *Pale Fox*, 471.

207. Griaule, *Pale Fox*, 509. All of Ogo's acts in diversifying Amma's design into chaos occurred in primordial darkness.

208. Griaule and Dieterlen, *Pale Fox*, 471 (see also 468).

209. Griaule and Dieterlen, *Pale Fox*, 60–67; "Dogon," 92–102; Ray, *African Religions*, 30–31.

210. Griaule and Dieterlen, *Pale Fox*, 57–58.

211. Griaule and Dieterlen, *Pale Fox*, 59–61; "Dogon," 83–84.

212. Griaule and Dieterlen, *Pale Fox*, 66–67; Ray, *African Religions*, 32.

deriving from their beliefs on the primordial organization of the universe. Therefore, societal organization is cosmogonic; the four fundamental elements, cardinal points, and Amma's ordering from chaos to cosmos form the basis for the Dogon societal structures.

It is believed that the four Dogon tribes; *Dyon, Arou, Ono,* and *Domno* are avatars of the first ancestors; *Amma Sérou, Lébé Sérou, Binou Sérou,* and *Dyongou Sérou,* respectively,[213] who each inhabited one of the cardinal points associated with the four fundamental elements.[214] This division into four tribes is not only applicable to the Dogon people as a whole, but is extended to smaller communities for the purposes of fulfilling certain ritual functions. Hence, the four eldest men of a Dogon community,[215] believed to represent the first ancestral beings formed in Amma's womb, are given four body parts of a victim at a sacrifice commemorating Amma's division and ejection of Nommo's four body parts for the purification and ordering the universe.[216] On the other hand, from a social standpoint, the twenty-two body parts of the resurrected Nommo, representing the twenty-two articulations, or words, which resemble the body and sex of the *po* at the center of Amma's womb, underlie the division of the Dogon people into kinship by totemism. The totemic structure of social organization multiplied indefinitely and expanded into territorial groups and lineages. Each new totem within this expansion is linked to one of the twenty-two fundamental parts of the resurrected Nommo, or essentially, the manifestations of the "word."[217] This indicates the stability and protection provided by Nommo for the inhabited territory.[218]

Accordingly, all beliefs, institutions, and rites of the Dogon society are linked with Nommo's dismembered body[219] at the purification and

---

213. See p. 26. Griaule and Dieterlen, *Pale Fox*, 41, 47. There are differences here in the pairing of the four Dogon tribes with the four mythical ancestors with that cited in Griaule and Dieterlen, "Dogon," 89. The tribal lineages and location at the cardinal points mismatch. However, the citations concur on the elements associated with these mythical ancestors.

214. Griaule and Dieterlen, *Pale Fox*, 62. See Griaule and Dieterlen, "Dogon," 89.

215. Griaule and Dieterlen, *Pale Fox*, 325.

216. Griaule and Dieterlen, *Pale Fox*, 325, 329; Ray, *African Religions*, 32.

217. Griaule and Dieterlen, *Pale Fox*, 338–40; Ray, *African Religions*, 32.

218. Griaule and Dieterlen, *Pale Fox*, 341.

219. Griaule and Dieterlen, *Pale Fox*, 389.

reorganization of the universe. A series of altars[220] are set in a "mythical territory" to reenact the sacrifice of Nommo representing the act of reorganizing the universe. Apart from the purposes of reparation and organization of the universe, these altars are also associated with mythical ancestors, totemic clans, and social organization.[221] Wherever feasible, clusters of these altars are arranged in a spiral form within or circulating societal settlements in recollection of the spiral movement of Amma's egg and the force that enlivened it.[222]

Furthermore, in relation to social organization, the four observable solstitial and equinoctial positions of the sun, also known as the "path of blood"[223] are marked by altars and allocated to the four Dogon tribes, as avatars of the four ancestors who descended on the ark. These four tribes perform rites at these sun's positions in commemoration of the chaos initiated by Ogo and the reestablishment of order achieved by the sacrifice of Nommo, his twin brother.[224] From this viewpoint, the Dogon hold this dynamism of a union with the dismembered parts of the Nommo in the reorganization and renewal of the cosmos. They see themselves in integral communion with these body parts in space and time,[225] and its effect on social cohesion of the Dogon people.[226]

A Convergence of Cross-Cultural Elements in Genesis 1:1–2

The synopsis in Gen 1:1–2 is a cosmogonic narrative. It presents YHWH as the sovereign creator, who made heaven and earth "in the beginning" (*bĕrē'šît*) of creation. This Hebrew word *bĕrē'šît*,[227] from the root *rō'š*,[228] indicates an absolute beginning of heaven and earth brought into

220. Griaule and Dieterlen, *Pale Fox*, 249; Ray, *African Religions*, 32.
221. Griaule and Dieterlen, *Pale Fox*, 249.
222. Griaule and Dieterlen, *Pale Fox*, 389.
223. Griaule and Dieterlen, *Pale Fox*, 510.
224. Griaule and Dieterlen, *Pale Fox*, 511.
225. Griaule and Dieterlen, *Pale Fox*, 389.
226. Griaule and Dieterlen, *Pale Fox*, 390.

227. Hamilton, *Book of Genesis*, 103–8, gives a summary of the arguments on whether the statement in Gen 1:1 is an independent or subordinate clause, therefore affecting the interpretation and nuance of this statement.

228. The meaning "head" is conceptually related to the Egyptian root *tp*. The Egyptian word *tpy* is derived from this root, and found in the expression *sp tpy*, referring to primeval time, or the beginning of creation. See Hoffmeier, "Some Thoughts," 42.

existence by an omnipotent deity. On semantics grounds, this statement in Gen 1:1 as an independent clause stating the existence of YHWH before the creation of the world is conceptually comparable to the inception of the Dogon cosmogony by creator-god Amma. As in the case of Amma who created a world first manifested in his thought, the term *bārā'*, "create"[229] only occurs in the Hebrew Bible with YHWH as the subject.[230] In Gen 1:1, the term designates creative activity and emphasizes the deity's efficacy in creating the heaven and earth from nothing, *creatio ex nihilo*,[231] as there is no reference to primordial matter in this construct.

Again, it may be assumed that as Amma's universe commenced in darkness,[232] YHWH's creative acts also began in primordial darkness. Analogously, Ogo's disruption of Amma's creative design corresponds here with the chaos that occurred in the course of the earth's formation. Therefore, the summative statement in Gen 1:1 is followed by an expression of the inchoate earth covered by the watery "deep" (*tĕhôm*) and "darkness" (*hošek*) transposed. As Amma is depicted at his creation as a "wind/whirlwind-deity,"[233] YHWH is acclaimed as the phenomenon, *rûah 'ĕlōhîm*, "wind of God" presiding over the "waters" (*mayim*) before the formation of a viable cosmos suitable for harmonious cohabitation of the first beings (vv. 26–28). Although brief, the full meaning of this cosmogonic narrative, as developing from chaos[234] to cosmic order, is obscured by the enigmatic morphology and syntax of terms in Gen 1:1–2. The terms employed here in description of the chaotic pre-cosmic state may be understood through a thorough comparative analysis. Some

---

229. See Becking and Korpel, "Create," 2–21, who argue for the meaning to "create" in conjunction with other verbs conveying the same meaning in the context of Gen 1. See also Wardlaw, "Meaning of ברא." Wolde argues that the verb ברא in Gen 1:1—2:4a should be translated to mean "separate" and not "create" (Wolde, *Reframing*, esp. 184–200; "Why the Verb," esp. 19–22). Walton concurs with the same view. He argues for the (latent) meaning "to separate" based on the *Piel* form of the root ברא. However, Walton also points out that ברא in other Hebrew contexts refers to bringing cosmic functions into existence (Walton, *Genesis*, 127–33, 139).

230. Day, *Creation*, 5; cf. Walton, *Genesis*, 128.

231. Rad, *Genesis*, 49, 51; cf. Bockmuehl "Introduction," 3–4. Here is a synopsis of arguments put forward suggesting creation from preexistent matter, and even suggesting transformation of chaos into order.

232. On primordial darkness, see pp. 21, 30n207.

233. On Amma as wind/whirlwind, see pp. 16–17.

234. For Rad, *Genesis*, 49–50, the idea of chaos bodes well with the divine creative activity.

scholars have argued to "leave chaos out of it," particularly, Debra Scoggin Ballentine.²³⁵

Ballentine objects to the use of the term "chaos," including *Chaoskampf*, as an inaccurate characterization of the mythological motif of the conflict between a warrior deity and the sea/dragon or antagonistic forces in West Asian myths. She extends the same argument against Hermann Gunkel's proposition of the use of the term(s) in the biblical tradition patterned after the Mesopotamian concept of primordial matter, or a divine enemy such as Tiamat, as representing chaos.²³⁶ Ballentine's view is in line with that of Lambert, who mentions the absence of the term chaos in Sumerian or Babylonian creation material, and neither sees any chaos in the comingling of the waters in the creation of the primordial bisexual gods.²³⁷ Needless to say, the agents of chaos are in view in Gen 1–2. As in the main, the analysis of the Dogon creation myth, representing the epistemologies of the Global South, exposes elements not previously identified as compelling for proposing the cosmogonic narrative of Gen 1:1–2 in its description of creation from chaos. But, first, it is worth exploring scholars' views on chaos in relation with the *Chaoskampf* mythology to date, as these terms come within the purview of interpreting creation-out-of-chaos in Gen 1:1–2.

The *Chaoskampf* myth is known as the battle of the so-called storm god or warrior god vanquishing a sea/water god or chaos monster. This putative myth is considered ancient and too pervasive²³⁸ to trace its origin.²³⁹ Its key motif as a battle to repel chaos in order to establish cosmic order is linked with victory in political terms in the ANE traditions for the purposes of legitimizing kingship.²⁴⁰ Scholars hold that the same idea

---

235. Ballentine, *Conflict Myth*, 186–89. Ballentine follows a few scholars who object to the idea of chaos implied in biblical texts. See Tsumura, *Creation and Destruction*, 1–3, 56–57, 74–75, 143–44, 196–97; Watson, *Chaos*, 1–4, 15–19, 29–30, 58–73; 265–71, 394–99. Tsumura continues to sustain his argument against using the term "chaos" for the conflict in the Enuma Elish as much as in the biblical concept of cosmic origin (Tsumura, "Chaos and *Chaoskampf*," 255 [see also 280–81]).

236. Ballentine, *Conflict Myth*, 186–87.

237. Lambert, "Creation," 44, 46.

238. Kitts, "Near Eastern *Chaoskampf*," 88; Schwemer, "Storm-Gods II," 27.

239. Wyatt, "Arms," 154–55; Jacobsen, "Battle," 106–8; Day, *God's Conflict*, 11–12. These scholars debate on the West Amorite origin of the myth, *contra* Schwemer, suggesting an eastern Mediterranean origin and an early spread, such that individual lines of traditional history are irretraceable (Schwemer, "Storm-Gods II," 27).

240. Wyatt, "Arms," 156–57; Schwemer, "Storm-Gods II," 24–27.

underlies the biblical tradition with some texts drawing on this same legitimizing symbolic meaning of the *Chaoskampf* myth.[241] However, Kitts also observed the versatility of the *Chaoskampf* myth in serving different etiological purposes, that is, cosmogonic, celebrating victory over chaos, celebrating demiurgic feats by kings.[242] Although Wyatt concurs on the use of the *Chaoskampf* tradition for legitimizing claim to royal authority, he also observed the diverse application of this *Chaoskampf* myth in various cultures and their gods.[243] In the same vein, and in analysis of other traditions, Kitts argues that the *Chaoskampf* is versatile and its allomorphs can be modified to suit native culture and purposes. As Kitts notes, the *Chaoskampf* motif is employed to serve a variety of mythic purposes—cosmogonic, reestablishment of order,[244] the institution and maintenance of royal authority, and possibly, for entertainment.[245] Kitt's observation on the diversification of the *Chaoskampf* myth has intrinsic bearing on its symbolic manifestation and early identification in its cosmogonic form in the biblical tradition.

Early in biblical scholarship, T. K. Cheyne and George A. Barton identified the relation between "creation" and "chaos" by showing the relevance of the Mesopotamian Enuma Elish to the idea of divine conflict and creation[246] in the Hebrew Bible. Although it is often assumed that Gunkel benefitted from Barton's work,[247] Gunkel[248] wrote more

---

241. Wyatt, "Arms," 157, 176–80. Regarding the idea of the *Chaoskampf* myth associated with YHWH's kingship, see Day, *God's Conflict*, 19–22.

242. Kitts, "Near Eastern *Chaoskampf*," 88.

243. Wyatt, "Arms," 157–58. More recently, Wyatt associates the *Chaoskampf* tradition with the battle of Marduk against Tiamat leading to creation, although he remarks the latter idea as contended. However, Wyatt also notes the general use of the term by scholars in a broader sense (Wyatt, "Distinguishing," 204). Wyatt sees *Chaoskampf* as a recurrent theme in the category of divine combat myth (244–45) and also holds the Enuma Elish as the primary model of the *Chaoskampf* theme (246).

244. Kitts, "Near Eastern *Chaoskampf*," 95n37. Here, Kitts refers to Isa 51:9 as a petition for the reestablishment of order structured on the *Chaoskampf* motif. Yet, as will be shown in this discussion, this petition is based on YHWH's feats by the power of his wind at creation seen through the prism of the *Chaoskampf* ideology.

245. Kitts, "Near Eastern *Chaoskampf*," 95.

246. Day, *God's Conflict*, 1–2.

247. Day, *God's Conflict*, 2n2.

248. See Gunkel, *Schöpfung und Chaos*. Although "*Chaoskampf*" became a common term, meaning "battle with chaos" or "chaos battle," translator William Whitney Jr. notes that he searched in vain for the use of this term in Gunkel's original edition (Gunkel, *Creation and Chaos*, xxxviin26).

YHWH IN THE WIND(S)

extensively on this idea, and focused on the battle between a storm deity and chaos (sea-god) resulting in creation, as seen in the Marduk/Tiamat[249] conflict in the Enuma Elish. Despite some scholars' objections on the causal relationship between *Chaoskampf* myth and creation, the biblical tradition shows this symbolic ideological association, as does the Dogon creation myth. Therefore, by intertextual analysis and comparison with the Dogon ethnographic material, the attempt is made to further render meaning to images and motifs characteristic of the *Chaoskampf* alluded to in Gen 1:1–2 in narration of creation from chaos. Undoubtedly, the analysis of the Dogon creation myth in the main shows the fundamental notions of a cosmogony emerging from chaos suggesting that similar cross-cultural conceptions underlie Gen 1:1–2.

The Dogon creation myth features some key elements in keeping with a *Chaoskampf*, perhaps showing signs of cultural adaptation (cf. Kitts and Wyatt) to suit this African context. Although the creative activities evolve from Amma's act termed "sacrifice," for purposes of cleansing Ogo's impurity, and reorganization from his misconduct, there are key features in this myth fitting the characteristics of a *Chaoskampf*. As noted in the main, Amma the creator encountered aggression from an assailant intending to possess his creation and a "fight"[250] led to chaos. Chaos ensued, as Ogo emerged from the placenta prematurely, and violated Amma's order of the universe. The Nommo, the male twin of Ogo, who is considered here as an accomplice, and taken as a substitute victim for slaughter for the purging and organization of the universe, is portrayed as aqueous in nature—water/rain.[251] The idea is consistent with the description offered by the Dogon elder, Ogotemmêli, in an alternative creation account referring to the Nommo as [the] water of the seas, coasts, torrents, storms, and of spoonfuls.[252] Even at the castration, Amma reserves the contents of Nommo's sex organs as the source of water for the seas and rain.[253] Yet, Nommo's aqueous nature is also consubstantial with the amphibious, as implied by the dismembering of his

---

249. *Contra* Sonik's suggestion for Tiamat as an antagonist not representative of a cosmogonic chaos associated with creation, but kratogenic chaos in association with the establishment of a divine order, rule, or civilization (Sonik, "Hesiod's Abyss," 1–25).

250. See p. 21.

251. See pp. 19, 19nn118, 121 above.

252. Griaule, *Conversations*, 18. See pp. 19, 19n118 above.

253. See pp. 23, 29n205 above.

body as a fish, but destined to resurrect in human form.²⁵⁴ The protean nature of Nommo recalls the variation in the designation of Tiamat as sea—*tiamtum* etymologically equivalent to the biblical *tĕhôm*,²⁵⁵ though her vertebrate nature is also implied.

As noted by Pitard,²⁵⁶ Tiamat's multiform as oceanic, anthropomorphic, serpentine, or monstrous/dragon-like forms are implied at various points in the Enuma Elish. She is specified as the primordial "waters" of the ocean (EE I:1–4). Yet she is also depicted anthropomorphically as someone agitated by the noise made by the young gods (EE I:27–34).²⁵⁷ In another instance she is identified as a woman (EE II:92), and, moreover in ridicule for pitting herself against a man (lines 143–46).²⁵⁸ But in the single combat with Marduk, Tiamat is depicted like a dragon with a cavernous maw to swallow Marduk, and her subdued carcass is considered as a monstrous lump that is split in two "like a fish for drying"²⁵⁹ (EE IV:90–105, 135–37).²⁶⁰ At this dismemberment, Tiamat's primary form as the primordial waters also pales in the background: Marduk "ordered them not to let her 'waters' escape" (EE IV:140).²⁶¹ There is also reference to her tail that Marduk coils up as the link between heaven and the world (EE V:59).²⁶²

In the same manner, Ba'al's archrival Yam in the Ugaritic texts is identified in various forms. Although the Ba'al epic is not explicitly a creation²⁶³ account, Yam, as Ba'al's challenger to kingship is identified as Sea, and variously personified as Judge River (*ṭpṭ nhr*), the tyrant with

---

254. Griaule and Dieterlen, *Pale Fox*, 181. Griaule, *Conversations*, 18, cites half human and half serpent.

255. For other common cognate terms in the ANE deriving from a common Semitic term *tihām* meaning "ocean," and an attempt to dispel influence from the *Chaoskampf* myth, see Sonik, "Hesiod's Abyss," 3n8.

256. Pitard, "How Many Monsters?," 82–83.

257. Foster, *Before the Muses*, 440; Lambert, *Babylonian*, 51, 53.

258. Foster, *Before the Muses*, 449, 451; Lambert, *Babylonian*, 69, 71.

259. Pitard, "How Many Monsters?," 82; cf. split like "shellfish into two parts" (Speiser, "Creation Epic," 67).

260. Foster, *Before the Muses*, 460–62; cf. Speiser, "Creation Epic," 66–67.

261. Pitard, "How Many Monsters?," 82; Foster, *Before the Muses*, 462; Speiser, "Creation Epic," 67.

262. Pitard, "How Many Monsters?," 82; Foster, *Before the Muses*, 465; cf. Dalley, *Myths*, 257; Grayson, "Additions to Tablet V," 37.

263. Day, *God's Conflict*, 17; Watson, *Chaos*, 20–21, 30.

the seven heads, twisty serpent, Lotan/Leviathan[264] (*ltn*; KTU 1.5.1:1–3), or Tunnan/Tannin[265] (*tnn*; KTU 1.3.III 38–42). Perhaps, at Ugarit, these different designations of Yam are just variations in form[266] of the antagonist as in other traditions cited here, and represent the ancient anathema typical of a *Chaoskampf*. However, in the context of creation emerging from chaos, the Babylonian creation epic is paradigmatic, and a brief look at the commonality of elements in these traditions will counter scholars' dissent on the relationship between creation and chaos in association with the *Chaoskampf* tradition.

It is important to note that Tiamat represents chaos for aligning herself with the rebellious young gods in conflict with the pantheon of older gods and seeks their destruction. Marduk accepts the challenge to confront Tiamat and champion the cause of the pantheon. However,

---

264. In identifying Yam/Nahar in various forms as the arch enemy of Ba'al in the Ugaritic texts, Pitard identifies the description of Lotan in KTU 1.5.1:1–3 as the *btn brḥ* ("fleeing serpent"), *btn ʿqltn* ("twisting serpent") and the "powerful one with seven heads" with Tunnan/Tannin similarly characterized with the latter two epithets in lines 40–41 as a continuation of the poetic description of the destruction of Yam/Nahar in KTU 1.3.III:38–47. The description of Leviathan with similar terms: *nāḥāš ʿăqallātôn* (Isa 27:1) and *nāḥāš bāriaḥ* (Isa 27:1; Job 26:13) is seen as reminiscent of the Ugaritic Lotan and by extension Tunnan equivalent to the Hebrew Tannin. However, Pitard's view on Leviathan occurring in parallelism with Tannin by replacing an MT verb with this epithet in Ps 74:14 is overdrawn (Pitard, "How Many Monsters?," 76–83; cf. Emerton, "Leviathan," 327–31). But in Ps 74:14 Leviathan is paralleled by *yam*. *Yam* appears in parallel with Rahab, Tannin (Job 7:12), and *těhôm* in Isa 51:9–10. Thus, here, this association of Leviathan with Tannin as referring to the same monster is possible. Compare with Ortlund's argument on Leviathan and Behemoth as representations of chaos that YHWH will ultimately vanquish (Ortlund, *Piercing Leviathan*, 114–44).

265. Benz, following Day, sees these characterizations as separate entities (Benz, "Yamm," 127–39, esp. 138; Day, *God's Conflict*, 13–15). But, Pitard argues for the identification of Yam/Nahar with Tannin based on occurrences of appellations in parallelism in these texts describing Anat's acts as part of her campaign for the establishment of Ba'al's kingship: KTU 1.3.III:37–42[=CTA 3.iii:34–39]; KTU 1.83:8–12[=RS 16.266 lines 8–12]. In both texts, Pitard notes the similarity in the occurrence of Yam/Nahar and Tannin in conjugation with the root *šbm* possibly implying the act of "muzzling" by Anat in her destruction of Ba'al's rivals. Furthermore, Pitard argues that if this Ugaritic identification of Yam and the dragons is true, that may have implication of a continuing Canaanite tradition in some biblical Hebrew texts, particularly Ps 74:12–14; Isa 27:1; Job 7:12 (Pitard, "Binding," 279–80; "How Many Monsters?," 77–83). See also Isa 51:9–10 (in table below). Pitard argues that the use of proper names paralleled by epithets is not uncommon in bicolon or tricolon in texts. Hence, he makes a case for identifying Yam/Nahar with Tannin and the other dragon-like epithets (Pitard, "How Many Monsters?," 83).

266. Pitard, "How Many Monsters?," 83, 86.

there is no evidence of a proper contest,[267] apart from Marduk's show of extraordinary potency with his array of irresistible winds that pacify and vanquish Tiamat. The most significant aspect is that the dismembering of Tiamat by Marduk is associated with the organization of the Babylonian cosmogony.[268]

Thanks to recent publications for unveiling further evidence on Marduk's creative acts in support of the statements in EE VII, lines 112 and 116 alluding to the connection between the battle with Tiamat and Marduk's ingenious creativeness resulting in the Babylonian cosmic order: "[Marduk,] who because of the battle with Tiamat can create artful things"[269] (EE VII:116). It is clear from the legible[270] parts of the Enuma Elish tablet V, that Marduk creates the stars, constellations and all the luminaries from Tiamat's carcass (EE V:1–21).[271] Again, according to tablet V, Marduk creates the clouds and makes them scud, raises the winds, causes the rainfall and mist to billow from Tiamat's spittle. He forms the mountains from Tiamat's head and udder, and opens up the deep causing the Tigris and Euphrates to flow from her eyes (EE V:47–59). Marduk also fashions Tiamat's crotch, perhaps as a pedestal,[272] to hoist the heavens in place (EE V:61). Hence, the heaven[273] (=Esharra; cf. EE IV:144–45) and earth[274] are established (EE V:61–62; cf. V:65; VII:86) following the splitting of Tiamat's body in half (EE V:62; see also IV:137–38).

---

267. Sonik, "Hesiod's Abyss," 22.

268. Foster, *Before the Muses*, 436, 463, 465.

269. Foster, *Before the Muses*, 482; Speiser, "Creation Epic," 72; Heidel, *Babylonian Genesis*, 58; Lambert, *Babylonian*, 131.

270. As Grayson notes, lines 25–44 of tablet V are too fragmented for translation, but Marduk is attributed with the establishment of the moon and sun (see Grayson, "Additions to Tablet V," 36). However, the preserved parts of tablet V retain detail on the extensive cosmic creativity of Marduk (Grayson, "Additions to Tablet V," 36–37; Foster, *Before the Muses*, 464–65; Lambert, *Babylonian*, 101).

271. Dalley, *Myths*, 255–56; Foster, *Before the Muses*, 463–64; Speiser, "Creation Epic," 66–67.

272. The idea of pillars as supporting the heavens and earth, as found in the OT (Job 9:6; 26:11; Ps 104:5; Prov 8:29) is analogous to this Babylonian antecedent.

273. Marduk creates the heavens (=Esharra) as the abode for the gods (EE V:120; see also IV:144–46) and Babylon as its terrestrial counterpart (EE V:120–30). See Grayson, "Creation Epic," 502; "Additions to Tablet V," 38; Foster, *Before the Muses*, 467–68; Dalley, *Myths*, 259–60; Lambert, *Babylonian*, 105.

274. Grayson, "Creation Epic," 501–2; Foster, *Before the Muses*, 464–65; Dalley, *Myths*, 256–57; Lambert, *Babylonian*, 101.

Similarly, the whirlwind-deity-Amma, dismembers and sacrifices Nommo, as the substitute for Ogo, in his efforts to reorganize his creative design violated by Ogo's revolt. In this African creation myth, a combat with the main assailant is implied and the dismembering of the victim, Nommo, ensues for shared responsibility[275] in the violation of the intended order by the sole creator-god Amma. Moreover, as in the case of Tiamat, Nommo's carcass and flow of blood are the base materials for Amma's formation of stars and planets, plants, animals and humankind. Also, Amma deploys Nommo's placenta as the ark, propelled by the "whirlwinds," to deliver all the created matter to the earth. These findings show that a combat, however miniscule in these traditions, results in the establishment of a cosmic order, and has implications for a profound interpretation of the cosmogonic narrative in Gen 1:1–2.

Personifications of YHWH's Wind and the Cosmic Forces at Pre-Creation State

As in the Dogon creation narrative, and at par with the Enuma Elish, Gen 1:1–2 shows antecedents to a combat leading to a cosmogony. A comparative analysis of other biblical texts indicates an intrinsic connection between this idea of a battle and creation, as implied in statements lauding YHWH's invincibility. The attribution is rendered owing to YHWH's victory wielded by wind, often personified as the strong arm, or right hand, over the opposing forces, and resulting in cosmic order as outlined below in table 1:

---

275. See p. 22.

Table 1—Comparative Biblical References on the Personification of the Wind in Battle					
Biblical Hebrew text	Natural Phenomena	Arm	Right Hand	Opposing Forces	Creation
Ps 104:3–9	wind, fire (v. 4) thunder= (windblasts, v. 7) waters (těhôm// mayim) rebuked			těhôm// mayim (v. 6)	entire cosmos (vv. 10–25)
Isa 51:9–10	wind implied in drying up yam and the waters of the great těhôm (v. 10)	arm cuts up Rahab and pierces Tannin (v. 9)		Rahab// Tannin (v. 9) yam//těhôm (v. 10; see Job 38:16)	creation and redemption at Yam Suph combined (vv. 9–10)
Ps 89:10–14[9–13]	wind implied in scattering enemies (v. 11[10]b)	arm of might crushes Rahab (v. 11[10], see v. 14[13] a)	right hand (v. 14[13]b)	yam//Rahab (vv. 10[9], 11[10]; see Job 26:12b, 13b)	heaven and earth and its fullness (v. 10[11])
Ps 74:13–15	wind implied in drying up the rivers (v. 15)		right hand (v. 11) implied: it splits yam, crushes the heads of Leviathan and dries up rivers—nahar[ôt]	yam// Leviathan// nahar[ôt] (vv. 13–15)	subterranean waters, luminaries, earth and seasons (vv. 15–17)
Ps 93:1–4	qol=wind[276] subdues the roaring waters (v. 4; see Ps 29:3a, c)			nahar[ôt]// mayim [rabbim]//yam (vv. 3–4)	world established (v. 1)

Data compiled by Violet Chiswa Gandiya, 2023

In these outlined biblical texts, the terms *těhôm*//*yam*//*mayim* [*rabbim*] are employed interchangeably to represent the deep waters, sea, or many waters as the cosmic forces representing chaos. In other texts as shown, *yam* (sea) appears in parallel with Rahab, Tannin, Leviathan, or twisting serpent, in keeping with the aquatic, serpentine, or draconic nature of these inimical forces[277] as attested in the ANE traditions. Perhaps, these draconic terms, as found in the biblical tradition, are entirely mnemonic

---

276. That the term *qol*, meaning "voice" or "sound," alluding to wind, is suggestive of similar phenomena representative of the same essence as Amma. See pp. 16–17.

277. See pp. 37–38, 37–38n264, 38n265 above.

to throw into bold relief the power of YHWH's wind directed against these rival forces at creation.

Therefore, YHWH's arm, or right hand, often symbolizes the natural phenomena, that is wind and/or fire, and combined for synergistic effect in annihilating the forces of chaos. As previously studied,[278] it is possible to see the "arm" of YHWH as corporeal for meteorological elements; cloudburst, rain-storm, and hailstones accompanying YHWH's wind (קול [blast])[279] doing his bidding as described in anticipation of his theophany in Isa 30:30 (see 29:7; Pss 147:15–18; 148:8; Job 37:9–13). In light of this common occurrence of the wind, either personified as the arm or right hand in the Hebrew texts as illustrated in the texts in table 1, the same posture of YHWH as the wind "hovering" over the waters to bring order out of chaos is implied in Gen 1:2. Thus, an intertextual and comparative analysis of biblical texts and other extra-biblical traditions respectively, is imperative for the interpretation of Gen 1:1–2, as relating cosmic order emerging from chaos—namely *tĕhôm*—modeled on the *Chaoskampf* myth,[280] and the enigmatic Hebrew term, *tōhû wābōhû*.

The state of the earth presented as *tōhû wābōhû* in Gen 1:2 in prelude to YHWH's creative acts is difficult to understand in isolation, and has been subjected to extensive debate among biblical scholars. Drawing from other Semitic traditions, Tsumura maintains that *tōhû* means "desert" or "waste" based on its parallel appearance with *'ereṣ midbār*—a desert land—in Deut 32:10.[281] He also supports this interpretation from the Ugaritic cognate *thw*, with a possible feminine, or plural form *thwt* meaning "waste" or "desert," and derived from a common Semitic root *thw*.[282] But, failing to find a Ugaritic cognate for *bōhû*, with only three

---

278. Chiswa Gandiya, "Storm Theophany in the Hebrew Psalms," 149.

279. On the identification of the whirlwind with the "voice," "creative word," spinning, whirling, and the loud sound as the creative movement that brought the Dogon cosmos into being, see pp. 16–17, 17n96 above.

280. See pp. 34–38. Generally, with the pioneering work of Gunkel, Cheyne, and Barton, Gen 1 has often been associated with the Babylonian Enuma Elish, even though others (namely, Tsumura) argue against Gunkel's comparison and correlation of the "deep," *tĕhôm* (Gen 1:2), with the Babylonian Tiamat based on linguistic terms (Tsumura, *Creation and Destruction*, 36–38). In fact, Tsumura argues that the terms *tĕhôm* and *tōhû wābōhû* have nothing to do with chaos ("Chaos and *Chaoskampf*," 255, 280–81). Other scholars, however, proposed Ugaritic and Egyptian parallels (Robin Routledge, "Did God Create Chaos?," 72, 72nn12–13, 15).

281. Tsumura, *Earth*, 17; *Creation and Destruction*, 10; "Chaos and *Chaoskampf*," 261.

282. Tsumura, *Earth*, 18–19; *Creation and Destruction*, 10–12.

occurrences in conjunction with *tōhû* in the Hebrew Bible,[283] Tsumura argues for its etymology from the Semitic root *bhw*, and explains its nuance by the Arabic term *bahiya* meaning "to be empty,"[284] and as he further suggests may definitively imply "nothingness," or "emptiness."[285]

Nonetheless, Tsumura deduces that *tōhû wābōhû* has a morphological correspondence with the Ugaritic *tu-a-bi-ú* of which its original form is *túhwu-wa-bíhwu*, and he supposes the Hebrew term to have developed from the latter.[286] However, in view of other uses of *tōhû* in the Hebrew Bible, with twenty occurrences,[287] Tsumura argues that *tōhû* means "desert," "desert-like place," "a desolate or empty place, an uninhabitable place," and "emptiness."[288] From this analysis, Tsumura infers that *tōhû wābōhû* has a similar meaning and refers to a state of "aridness or unproductiveness," or "desolation" (Jer 4:23; Isa 34:11cd, respectively).[289] Thus, he concludes that *tōhû wābōhû* in Gen 1:2 should be understood as describing a state of "unproductiveness" and "emptiness,"[290] and in essence, Tsumura calls the inchoate earth "desert-like," implying that it is "desolate" and uninhabited, which he sees as fitting the literary structure of the whole chapter.[291] This desert-like state of the earth also resonates with the description in Gen 2:5. In addition, however, the watery deep (*tĕhôm*) covered the earth and the pervasive "darkness" (Gen 1:2bc) further describes the inchoate state of the earth. An intertextual analysis and comparison with extra-biblical traditions shed light on these ambiguous terms relating the rudimentary stage of the earth and the pre-cosmic state described in Gen 1:2.

---

283. Gen 1:2; Isa 34:11cd; Jer 4:23. See Tsumura, *Earth*, 21; *Creation and Destruction*, 13; Day, *Creation*, 8; Walton, *Genesis*, 140.

284. Tsumura, *Earth*, 23; "Chaos and *Chaoskampf*," 261.

285. Tsumura, *Creation and Destruction*, 13.

286. Tsumura, *Earth*, 24; *Creation and Destruction*, 15–17.

287. Tsumura, *Earth*, 30; *Creation and Destruction*, 22.

288. Tsumura, *Earth*, 41; *Creation and Destruction*, 22–23; Day, *Creation*, 8–9.

289. Tsumura, *Earth*, 41; *Creation and Destruction*, 24–32.

290. Tsumura, *Earth*, 41; *Creation and Destruction*, 33–35.

291. Tsumura, "Chaos and *Chaoskampf*," 261; *Creation and Destruction*, 33; Wyatt, "Distinguishing," 230–31.

Tōhû wābōhû—a Chaotic State—and *rûaḥ 'ĕlōhîm* as the Wind [of God] in Light of the Egyptian and Dogon Worldviews

The rudimentary nature of the earth envisaged in Gen 1:2 as *tōhû wābōhû*, meaning desert-like and uninhabitable or unproductive, is comparable to Ogo's infertile, imperfect, incomplete, dry, and sandy earth.[292] The latter is resultant to Ogo's revolt and premature egression from Amma's womb into primordial "darkness."[293] All of Ogo's disruptive activities occur in primordial darkness.[294] In essence, darkness co-exists with Ogo's inhabitable earth in which incomplete beings and offspring of incest are conceived. Also, as Smith points out, the creation of the wind in an ancient Egyptian cosmology is related in a dialogue between Atum and the Ocean, which takes place in darkness.[295] There is also mention of one of the gods of the Egyptian *hermopolitan ogdoad*, Kuk and his consort Kauket as personifications of pre-creation darkness.[296] Hence, in keeping with these African traditions, the biblical priestly account is in conformity in postulating the existence of darkness,[297] as a common pre-creation element in cosmogonies.

Furthermore, the idea of darkness and waters of the "deep" (*tĕhôm*) in close attendance resembles the coexistence in the Egyptian *hermopolitan ogdoad* of the anomalous pre-creation gods; Kuk, darkness and Nun, the primordial waters.[298] They are often considered as part of the quad of cosmic forces and their consorts representing chaos[299] in the Egyptian worldview. The mention of these elements in the priestly account shows that the Hebrew tradition shares similar concepts on the formation of the universe. But, the use of the childbirth imagery[300] employed in relating the Dogon myth of creation, is more alluring and provides a background

---

292. See p. 21.

293. See pp. 21, 30, 30n207.

294. See pp. 21, 30, 30n207.

295. Smith, *Carlsberg*, 58–59.

296. See Frankfort et al., "Myth and Reality," 10; Wilson, "Egypt," 52; Hoffmeier, "Some Thoughts," 43.

297. In the Enuma Elish, darkness also preexisted with the pantheon of gods before Marduk created the luminaries.

298. Wilson, "Egypt," 52.

299. Wilson, "Egypt," 52; Hoffmeier, "Some Thoughts," 43.

300. See pp. 19–21, 20n123.

for a better apprehension of the chaotic state implied by the deep covering the "inchoate" earth as stated in Gen 1:2.

Undoubtedly the waters of the deep, as in the case of Amma's design in creation,[301] represent the waters formed as the first basic substance of YHWH's design. As in the case of Ogo, who disrupted his gestation period and Amma's cosmic order, the waters of the deep mentioned in the biblical tradition breach YHWH's cosmic order before YHWH assigns them a purpose. The poetic narrative of Job 38 is evocative of this image, and suggests the rebelliousness of the waters toward the creator's intended design: "The sea/deep burst forth from the womb" (Job 38:8), causing a state of chaos which underlies the description in Gen 1:2. Thus, chaos erupts as the waters momentarily intercept YHWH's creative activity *in medias res*. Arguably, this chaotic state is apparent in the reference to the deluge in Ps 104:6: the deep (*tĕhôm*) covers the [inchoate] earth, and the raging waters[302] stand above the mountains. It should be noted that, perhaps, the priestly editor not much concerned with how this chaotic state is obtained,[303] effaces that from the priestly narrative in preference to asserting YHWH's sovereignty over the waters. Hence, the statement: *rûaḥ 'ĕlōhîm mĕraḥepet 'al-penê hammayim* ("the wind of God hovered over the waters") in Gen 1:2b alluding to YHWH's posturing in subduing the waters and demarcating its boundaries (Gen 1:9; see Jer 5:22c; Ps 104:9) in the establishment of an orderly cosmos.

There has been a long standing scholarly debate on whether the term *rûaḥ 'ĕlōhîm* means "wind of God," "Spirit of God," or "mighty wind."[304] Walton sees *rûaḥ*, meaning wind/spirit as the only deified, or personified term in Gen 1:2 by the adjoining appellation *'ĕlōhîm*, and finds parallels in Egyptian cosmological texts on the creative potency of the god Amun, rather than Mesopotamian parallels.[305] Therefore, Walton apud Smith's work on Egyptian demotic cosmogony, relates Amun's personification in the single wind, as corresponding to the spirit's relationship with *'ĕlōhîm* in Gen 1:2.[306] Indeed, Walton acknowledges the involvement of Amun's

---

301. See p. 15.

302. Day, *Creation*, 9.

303. The conflict motif seems to be missing in Genesis, such that Gunkel claimed that this is a completely "Judaized" version of the Enuma Elish (Gunkel, *Creation and Chaos*, 82). See Routledge, "Did God Create Chaos?," 72, 72n14.

304. Hoffmeier, "Some Thoughts," 43–44; Day, *Creation*, 9–10.

305. Walton, *Genesis*, 146.

306. Walton, *Genesis*, 147.

wind in fundamental acts of creation; be it as agency in the separation of the earth and sky, or as the egg's consort from which the solar deity, who became the creator, emerges.[307] He sees the possibility of similar creative activity by the wind in Gen 1:2, but objects that it is inherent to this context.

Furthermore, Walton observes possible echoes of the Egyptian background in the participial verb *mĕraḥepet* ("hovering") describing the activity of the *rûaḥ 'ĕlōhîm* that is associated with some bird activity over its nestlings in the biblical tradition (Deut 32:11) and other ANE contexts (Syriac and Ugaritic), as implying either protective brooding, or hovering in preparation for the next movement.[308] Nonetheless, Walton dismisses any reference to an egg, or the act of separating heaven and earth by the *rûaḥ* in Gen 1:2. But, he agrees on the commonality of the shared elements that he considers adapted and made unique to each tradition. To that end, Walton argues that the role ordinarily associated with the wind in a bird-like brooding image, as though preparing for a creative activity, is identified in the Israelite tradition with the spirit, which is exceptionally associated with God.[309] Hence, in support of preceding scholarship on this subject, Walton sees *rûaḥ* as the spirit representing God, and manifesting creative acts through the efficacy of the "word," not only in Gen 1, but as Walton argues, as attested from other biblical texts.[310] Yet, Walton's lack of resolve on whether creation is by the agency of the "wind," or "spirit" resurfaces. Although Walton's view maintains close affinity with Egyptian cosmologies, he relegates the creative role of the wind to the spirit. But, as already noted in the main,[311] Egyptian cosmologies show distinctive characteristics of the creative potentiality of the wind of Amun comparable to that of Amma in the Dogon creation myth. Hence, to understand the crux of the image in Gen 1:2, *rûaḥ* should be translated "wind," and not "spirit," in this context of creative activity in conformity with the Egyptian and Dogon worldviews on the beginning of the universe.

As shown in table 1 in the main,[312] the biblical texts describe YHWH appearing with the phenomenal elements—winds, fire, voice/

---

307. Walton, *Genesis*, 147–48. See also pp. 17–18.
308. Walton, *Genesis*, 148–49. See Scurlock, "Searching for Meaning," 52–53.
309. Walton, *Genesis*, 149.
310. Walton, *Genesis*, 149–50, 149n74.
311. On the idea of Amun as the wind equivalent to Amma, see pp. 17–18.
312. See p. 41.

thunder(=windblasts)—to vanquish the waters, or monsters as mnemonic, showing the superiority of his power at the creation of the cosmos. Thus, in keeping with the same idea, Gen 1:2b states *rûaḥ ʾĕlōhîm*, "wind of God,"[313] hovering over the waters in depiction of YHWH subduing the chaotic waters at the creation of a cosmic habitat (Gen 1:9; see Pss 24:2; 65:8[7]aβ; 93:1, 3–4; 104:5–7; Job 38:4–6), and setting a limit on the destructive waters from engulfing the earth (Gen 1:10; Jer 5:22c; Pss 33:7; 104:9; Prov 8:29; Job 38:10–11). That the term "waters" (*mayim*), paralleled with the "deep" (*tĕhôm*), here also represents the waters subdued by YHWH's ordering command, can be shown by the collocation of terms representing the raging waters expressed in Pss 104:6–7: *tĕhôm//mayim* (deep//waters) and 93:3–4: *naha[rôt]//mayim [rabbîm]//yam* (rivers//many waters//sea).[314] The origin of the term "many waters" (*mayim rabbîm*) and its implication as it appears in the Hebrew tradition cannot be established with precision, but its similarity to the appellation of Yam in an Ugaritic text is quite suggestive.[315] In her role as advocate for the rule of Baʿal, Anat rhetorically claimed to have defeated Yam (*ym*), and put an end to Nahar, *ʾil rbm* (KTU 1.3.III:39 [CTA 3.iii:36]). These wars of Anat against the enemies of Baʿal occur within the Baʿal cycles, and so may be seen to add to the picture of the total defeat of Yam.[316] Smith and Pitard suggest rendering the epithet *ʾil rbm* "great God" or "the God of the Great waters," as plausible epithets referring to Yam in relation to

---

313. Hamilton, *Book of Genesis*, 111, 111n26; Sarna, *Genesis*, 6; Wenham, *Genesis*, 16–17.

314. See table 1.

315. See May, "Cosmic Connotations," 9–21. May observes no direct derivation of "many waters" from the Ugaritic god Yam, though he is certain that the rebellious waters are symbolic of the archrival of the storm god in ancient traditions. He identifies the "many waters" with sea and rivers as representations of YHWH's enemy comparable to Baʿal's enemy Prince Sea and Judge River at Ugarit. May sees the "many waters" in the Hebrew tradition as the resurgent cosmic force that constantly needs to be checked by YHWH. In his survey, May finds that the use of the term "many waters" concerns historical events, persons or nations.

316. This concurs with Miller's view. He sees the warring activities of Anat as associated with the battles of Baʿal (Miller, *Divine Warrior*, 46). See also *UBC I* 10–11; *UBC II* 247, 265; Walls, *Goddess Anat*, 174–86. Murphy supports the assenting voice on the role of Anat as an ally of Baʿal but also emphasizes Anat's independence (Murphy, "Myth, Reality," 533–34). In concurrence with the latter view, Green argues that the battles fought by the goddess Anat should be considered significantly different from the battles of Baʿal (Green, *Storm-God*, 185).

YHWH IN THE WIND(S)

the other epithets mentioned in KTU 1.3.III:38–42.³¹⁷ Therefore, *'il rbm*,³¹⁸ as an epithet, is another mythological variant of Yam who is the sea-god subjugated by the storm god Baʻal, and the term *'il rbm* could be seen as an elliptical for the Hebrew *mayim rabbîm*. Therefore, the parallelism of the "sea" (*yam*) with "many waters"³¹⁹ (*mayim rabbîm*) in Ps 93:4 (see also Ps 77:20[19]; Hab 3:15) echoes the mythological representations of the epithets of Yam and indicates that this symbolism is not far removed from the ancient tradition of the conflict between the so-called storm god and the unruly waters. In keeping with other cultural lore mentioned here, the Hebrew tradition is no exception in using variations³²⁰ in parallelism to refer to the unruly waters. Notwithstanding, if the variant terms *tĕhôm*//*mayim* (deep//waters) in Ps 104:6–7 or *naha[rôt]*//*mayim [rabbîm]*//*yam* (rivers//many waters//sea) in Ps 93:3–4 are used, then the reference is still to the chaotic waters subdued by YHWH's "rebuke" or "roar" (גער, Ps 104:7a), or "voice"³²¹ of thunder (קול רעם, v. 7b; cf. Pss 29:3–9; 93:4).

To-date, biblical scholars have interpreted קול רעם in light of the ANE traditions. YHWH's thunderous voice is related in mythical terms as indicative of his power over the many waters comparable to that of Baʻal as he asserts himself in nature, as the victorious storm god.³²² YHWH's voice is interpreted as such in Ps 29 in symbolism of his sovereignty and authoritative intervention in saving Israel from its enemies. But in purview of YHWH's creative activities and maintenance of the cosmic

---

317. *UBC II* 247–58. On Pitard suggesting an identification of other epithets mentioned in this text as variant forms of Yam/Nahar, see pp. 37–38, esp. 37–38n264, 38n265.

318. Rahmouni, *Divine Epithets*, 239; *UBC II* 248, translate this epithet *'il rbm* to "immense waters" and "great waters," respectively.

319. Jeremias, who noticed the pluralism in the terminology that echoes the personification of the god Yam, interpreted the ideas preserved in Ps 93:3–4 as in keeping with the language of the whole range of Baʻal's battle with the gods at Ugarit. Thus he stated that, "Prince Sea" becomes the primeval sea in v. 4, "Judge River/flood" becomes the primeval floods in v. 3. Jeremias also noted that the "mighty waters" in v. 4 and the "roaring of the waters" in v. 3 retain the idea of the "sons of Asherah" (*rbm*) the destroyer(?) (*dkym*, KTU 1.6.V:2–3 [CTA 6.v:2–3]; Jeremias, *Theophanie*, 21). Be that as it may, it appears the Baʻal and Yam conflict offers closer parallels with terms applicable to YHWH's battle against the unruly waters. But unlike in the Baʻal/Yam battle, YHWH's deployment of winds to subdue the waters is peculiar, and supersedes the variations in the combat myth.

320. On variations in terms/epithets used, see p. 41.

321. Cross, *Canaanite Myth*, 147–69; cf. Habel, *Yahweh versus Baal*, 77–84.

322. Cross, *Canaanite Myth*, 156–62;

order in quelling antithetical forces to his design, the characterization of Amma as wind, or whirlwind, proffers a closer translation of this term קול רעם as representing the sonorous sound of YHWH's wind, which is often personified as YHWH's voice (Pss 18:14[13]; 29:3–9; 104:7; Job 37:2, 4). But this biblical phenomenon should be better understood in comparison with the "voice," loud sound, creative spiral, wind or whirlwind representing god Amma.[323]

Generally, the winds, as the morphology of the creative deity, are associated with creation.[324] Paradoxically, however, Marduk employs the same phenomenal winds as a martial arsenal, including the "seven winds" he creates, to combat his assailant, Tiamat (EE IV:42–48). Marduk deploys the raging winds to roil Tiamat's insides in order to subdue her, and the north wind bear off the blood of Tiamat's arteries, as proof of her deposition leading to the creation of the Babylonian cosmos out of her corpse (EE IV:99, 132).[325] Hence, from these extra-biblical traditions relating the creation of cosmic order, inferences may be drawn on the similar role of the winds at creation in the biblical tradition. Arguably, the occurrence of the term גערה ("rebuke/roar") paralleled with קול רעם ("voice/sound of thunder") in an asyndetic construction in Ps 104:7, implies the deployment of the same phenomenal winds in this context of YHWH appearing with winds (vv. 3c–4a) to repel the chaotic waters (*tĕhôm//mayim*, v. 6), and has connotations for the interpretation of *rûaḥ 'ĕlōhîm*, meaning "wind of God" as the creative agency in Gen 1:2.

The Hebrew גערה Synonymous with רוח/קול רעם for "Winds" in YHWH's Cosmic Design

The term גער[326] and its substantive גערה are part of the theophanic genre describing how YHWH does battle with the watery chaos represented by the seas, rivers and waters: תהום (Ps 104:6), נהרות (Nah 1:4) or נהרים (Hab

---

323. See pp. 16–17, 29.

324. See pp. 16–17.

325. See Foster, *Before the Muses*, 460–61; Dalley, *Myths*, 253–54. The fact that Marduk employs the winds to subdue Tiamat and the north wind bear off her blood as proof of her demise, means the appellative "storm god" is overemphasized than a wind deity, who uses the winds as ploy to bring about cosmic order.

326. Day notes that the term גער, which he translates "roar," occurs specifically in contexts relating YHWH's conflict with the chaotic waters (Day, *God's Conflict*, 102–27).

YHWH IN THE WIND(S)

3:8), and מים (Ps 18:16–17[15–16]) respectively. Thus, when YHWH arrays himself against these unruly waters he rebukes and subdues them. YHWH's fierce pronouncement against the rebellious waters causes the drying up of the seas and rivers (Isa 50:2 [see Ps 106:9]; Nah 1:4), or makes the waters to flee (Pss 18:16[15]; 104:7; cf. Isa 17:13).[327] The verb גער or its substantive גערה is employed in association with רוח in expression of force[328] directed against the waters of chaos. In particular, the close relation of גערה and רוח is seen in the theophany of Ps 18:8–17[7–16]. YHWH's גערה in collocation with the "blast of breath from his nostrils,"[329] נשמת רוח אפו (v. 16[15]c), denotes the emanation of wind exposing the bottom of the sea (Exod 15:8). Hence, גערה and רוח are in tandem in the manifestation of YHWH in the wind (Pss 18:11–16[10–15]; 104:3–7).

As Caquot pointed out, in light of his study of passages reflecting the storm manifestation of YHWH, the religious usage of גער and its derivatives as representing YHWH's anger can hardly be isolated from the phenomenal elements that accompany YHWH's disclosure. Accordingly, he noted that the divine *geʿarah* in Isa 50:2 and Nah 1:4 is associated

---

327. Jeremias, *Theophanie*, 33.

328. Macintosh argues from a philological point of view in comparison with cognates from other languages that the term גער originally described physical reactions expressing anger or fury and in instances where God is the subject. But Macintosh also notes that גער could be interpreted in the normal sense of "moral rebuke" resonating with the Jewish understanding of God (Macintosh, "Consideration," 471–79; Reif, "Comments," 253). Reif, previously in disagreement with Macintosh, argued for the use of גער in the sense of denoting anger in respect to Ps 104:7 and Mal 2:3, as observed by some Jewish scholars. He added that the root גער only expresses moral rebuke in the context of wisdom literature (Prov 13:1, 8; 17:10; Eccl 7:5). Reif further stated that credit was owed to medieval Jewish commentators for their early discovery of the root as implying "destruction" or "deprivation" (Reif, "Note on גער"). However, Reif has since revised his views. He notes that גער has been used widely to denote moral rebuke, and also to express weaker meanings such as rejection, refusal or reprimand. In fact, Reif concedes that Macintosh correctly identified גער to mean "moral rebuke" and "passionate anger" as exposed by some Jewish exegetes (Reif, "Comments," 254–58, 260–67).

329. Kennedy, "Root *gʿr*," 47–64. Kennedy points out that the root גער is not completely compatible with רוח and נשמת though found in collocation. He argues that whereas the terms רוח and נשמת may be used to imply the life-giving force from YHWH as in Gen 2:7 and Job 33:4, גער on the other hand does not designate any life-giving force. As he further points out, גער does not connote a curse as Macintosh holds, but signifies the violent expulsion of divine breath (Ps 18:16[15]). On the basis of similarities in the terms employed in Exod 14 and 15 to refer to the forces that drove the waters, Kennedy sees *geʿarah* in Ps 18 as expressing the same physical force (Kennedy, "Root *gʿr*," 50, 52). The effect brings the total surrender of the forces of chaos or of a human enemy.

with a "hurricane"[330] that dries up the sea. In fact, Nah 1:3–4 declares YHWH's rebuke in close connection with his appearance lodged with the "whirlwind" and "storm-wind." The idea is also perceptible in Ps 104 where the chaotic waters are rebuked (v. 7) in close view of the depiction of YHWH as "riding on the wings of the wind" (v. 3). However, the term גערה (rebuke/roar) in v. 7 is paralleled with קול רעם (voice/sound of thunder, see Ps 77:19[18]) to refer to the forceful expulsion of the same phenomenal winds, directed against the chaotic waters causing them to flee. In light of this גערה, גער, and רוח are terms associated with YHWH's dynamic discharge of some forceful roaring wind(s) directed against the sea, or waters.

In the same vein, Gen 1:2 relates YHWH's wind, perhaps as a "blast of breath from his nostrils," or YHWH "riding on the wings of the wind," purposefully poised to repel and confine the chaotic waters. The raging waters transposed to containment by this creative action shows that the waters are unequivocally in opposition to YHWH's cosmic design (Ps 89:10[9]). To that end, Gen 1:2 presents a relic of the motif of the conflict with the sea,[331] and depicts YHWH's phenomenal wind[332] "hovering" (*mĕraḥepet*) over the waters in preparedness to whip and stir the primordial waters into motion, and setting them in place (Gen 1:9–10). Even prophetic passages extolling YHWH as the creator suggest the movement of the wind stirring up the raging waters (Isa 51:15; Jer 31:35) to show YHWH's mastery over them in ordering creation.

Accordingly, Day suggests reading "wind of God" in connection with the participle *mĕraḥepet*, meaning "sweeping" or "hovering," to relate a birdlike[333] image as implied in Ps 104:3 with the image of YHWH "riding on the wings of the wind,"[334] poised to charge the chaotic waters.[335] This depiction brings to light the subtleties in the biblical tradition of the

---

330. Caquot, "גער," 51.

331. Geller, "God," 432.

332. Scurlock expresses the preference of the Targums to interpret *rûaḥ* as wind but also reflects Geller's view as retention of traces of the motif of YHWH as storm in conflict with the sea, in keeping with the idea from ancient Mesopotamia. See Scurlock, "Searching," 54, 56n31; Day, *God's Conflict*, 52–53, *contra* Scurlock's preference to translate *rûaḥ* as "spirit" in connection with the descent of the spirit at Jesus's baptism in Mark 1:10–11 (Scurlock, "Searching," 55, 61).

333. Day, *God's Conflict*, 53; *Creation*, 10.

334. Day, *Creation*, 9–10.

335. Day also sees these chaotic waters as behind the priestly narrative of Gen 1:1–2 (Day, *Creation*, 9).

dialectical tension between the manifestation of YHWH in the form of wind, or wind as a phenomenon deployed to do YHWH's bidding (Ps 148:8b). For instance, by his wind[336] YHWH made the heavens (šāmāyim) fair (Job 26:13a), and YHWH made his wind pass over the earth and the waters subsided (Gen 8:2b). Nonetheless, the priestly writer, at pains to describe the "numinous,"[337] preferred to present the image of YHWH as wind in Gen 1:2, and imaginatively alluded to the "egg of the world" by linking to the idea of "hovering," in order to express YHWH's unmatched creative potentiality. Arguably, this image of YHWH's wind hovering is comparable to the characterization of god Amma; in whom the concept of the "wind" and "world egg" are compatible. Amma, as the primal being, is conceived as the "egg of the world," out of which the Dogon cosmology emerged. But, Amma is also said to be the "wind/whirlwind"[338] symbolizing the creative whirling that caused the scattering of matter at creation in a "sonorous" and "luminous" motion.[339] Similarly, the "wind of God" (*rûaḥ 'ĕlōhîm*) in Gen 1:2 is the manifestation of YHWH in the pre-creative activity to hold sway over the chaotic waters, and transform chaos to cosmos. Undoubtedly, drawing from this comparative analysis, Gen 1:1–2 is a synopsis of a cosmogony, abounding with cross-cultural concepts, showcasing the creative activity of YHWH manifested in the "wind." The text focuses the generation of a cosmos from chaos caused by the waters breaking out *in medias res* of YHWH's creative order.

Creatio ex nihilo to Cosmic Order with Chaos in *medias res* in Genesis 1:1–2

The synopsis of the biblical cosmogony presented in Gen 1:1–2, puts into perspective the content spelled out in the priestly literary unit of

---

336. See pp. 16–17. Also, as Smith observed in the Egyptian cosmology, the separation of the sky and earth is accomplished by the agency of the wind (Smith, *Carlsberg*, 58).

337. A term first coined by Rudolf Otto in expression of the numinous experience of the "wholly other" (Otto, *Idea of the Holy*, 7, 25, 29).

338. Cf. Foster, *Before the Muses*, 458; Speiser, "Creation Epic," 66; Lambert, *Babylonian*, 89. The elements dispatched also recall Marduk's combat with Tiamat (EE IV:39–50). The Enuma Elish texts evince no definitive evidence of a battle, apart from Marduk's exploitative use of the phenomenal winds to subdue Tiamat. Here, too, Marduk employs various winds: south-north-east-west-winds, whirlwind, cyclone, and the seven winds he made to roil and ensnare Tiamat (lines 42–48).

339. See p. 17.

GENESIS 1:1–2, 26–28 IN LIGHT OF THE DOGON CREATION MYTH

Gen 1—2:4 relating the formation of an orderly macrocosm. Although the priestly account is devoid of complex detail compared to the Dogon creation myth, there are stark similarities in the concepts relating to the creation of a purposeful universal order. However, a reinterpretation of the synopsis in Gen 1:1–2 is possible in consideration of the content in the extant biblical and extra-biblical texts. As stated in the main, the god Amma is presumed the sole deity "in the beginning" who existed and rested upon "nothing." The creative process begins inside Amma's egg, or placenta/womb,[340] which prefigures heaven and earth.[341] Similarly, Gen 1:1 relates the biblical thought of YHWH's preexistence as the sole sovereign creator[342] (Pss 90:2; 93:2), who founded the heaven, earth ([and seas] Pss 24:1–2; 33:6a; 89:12[11]; 121:2b; 146:6) in the beginning (see Ps 102:26[25]). There is no mention in this prelude (Gen 1:1) of preexistent matter from which the heavens and earth are formed. Hence, as in the Dogon creation myth, creation from nothing—*creatio ex nihilo* is implied.[343] But in prelude to this generation of the cosmos, the priestly account focuses on the diversification of YHWH's creative design as the chaotic waters cover the inchoate earth in primordial darkness (Gen 1:2). The priestly author casts this state of chaos *in medias res* of YHWH's creative activity to demonstrate YHWH's potentiality in controlling chaos and incorporating its elements into cosmic order. Both the raging waters and darkness are transformed into cosmic order. Also, the creation of light to dispel darkness before the formation of the luminaries in Gen 1 is distinctively unparalleled in extra-biblical traditions.

Even though Amma's wind is said to be luminous[344] in nature, his first creative acts occur in primordial darkness.[345] On the other hand, in the priestly creation account the emission of light precedes all of YHWH's creative acts (Gen 1:3). In a discussion on the dialectic between YHWH's immanence and transcendence in the traditions of the

---

340. See pp. 19–20.

341. See p. 19.

342. See Geller, "God," 424, 428. Geller alludes to this idea of the sole sovereignty of YHWH in reference to the use of the term "generations" in the Genesis creation narrative as expressing a process of the sexless divine activity of bringing things into existence by speech. Geller sees this as part of an underlying polemic against ANE traditions in which creation developed on the basis of sexual generations by gods giving birth to other gods who represented an aspect of nature.

343. See p. 14, 14n69.

344. See p. 17.

345. See pp. 21, 30, 30n207.

YHWH IN THE WIND(S)

Pentateuch, Geller argued that YHWH is shielded from human and angelic gaze by some divine "glory" (*kābôd*, Isa 6:3), and he imparted some of that supernatural light to his creation.[346] Accordingly, the manifestation of "light" (*'ôr*) in Gen 1:3 relates to the effulgence of YHWH (Isa 2:5; 60:19c), and inevitably in collation with the wind, represents YHWH's immanence at creation. Thus, in this priestly account on creation, the involvement of natural phenomena in representation of YHWH's luminous and sonorous sound, equivalent to the nature of Amma, may not be ruled out.

In sequel, the formation of the sky, as the expanse to separate the chaotic waters into celestial and terrestrial waters (Gen 1:6–8a), by the creative word, or voice personifying the wind (Ps 33:6a), further signifies the doctrine of *creatio ex nihilo*.[347] This statement resonates with the reference to YHWH turning empty space or void into cosmos (Job 26:7; cf. 37:18) by his phenomenal elements, and bringing things to life by his creative word/voice; a metonym for the wind (Ps 33:6, 9; see also 29:3–4). As already noted in the main, the idea of the wind sweeping over the heavens (*šāmayim*) in Job 26:13a,[348] along with the mention of the "thunder of his might" (רעם גבורתו, v. 14c) suggestive of windblasts; fundamentally implies the phenomenal winds in tandem as agency in creation. Analogously characteristic to Amma's "sonorous" sound at the creation and scattering of matter,[349] YHWH's (whirl)wind is imposingly deep and resounds like thunder-peals. Here, too, in Gen 1:9–10, YHWH subdues the waters by means of his thunderous wind (v. 9; see Pss 29:3–4; 93:4; 104:7). Consequently, YHWH's wind,[350] (Gen 1:2b; see Ps 104:3c),

---

346. See Geller, "God," 438–39; Clifford, "*Creatio ex nihilo*," 65.

347. See pp. 14, 33; *contra* Bockmuehl, "Introduction," 4. In interpreting the doctrine of *creatio ex nihilo* in the biblical tradition, Anderson, apud McFarland, Soskice, and Tanner, argues that there is less concern on how the world was formed than on how it is sustained and governed (Anderson, "*Creatio ex nihilo*," 22). Moreover, Soskice gives her working definition of *creatio ex nihilo* that God "created the world out of nothing—really nothing—no preexistent matter, space or time" (Soskice, "Why *Creatio ex nihilo*?," 38) implying "beginnings." Yet, she further gives a contradictory explanation that this doctrine is not about "beginnings" (40–41), as she focuses her argument more on the nature of God rather than the beginning of the world. Following Keller's argument on Genesis, Soskice dispels the *creatio ex nihilo* doctrine from Gen 1–3 except for other biblical and extra canonical texts (48).

348. See p. 52.

349. See p. 17.

350. In Ps 83:14[13], the wind (*rûaḥ*) is mentioned in collation with "tempest" and "storm" (v. 16[15]) as representations of YHWH's power against the enemies, whose plight is synonymous with the chaotic waters.

GENESIS 1:1–2, 26–28 IN LIGHT OF THE DOGON CREATION MYTH

comparable to Amma's whirlwind as the movement that stirs things to life, sends the raging waters pell-mell to their designated place to form the seas[351] (Gen 1:10b; Ps 95:5; Job 38:10–11), and sets its boundaries to demarcate the earth (Gen 1:10a; Ps 104:9; Prov 8:29). With the heavens, earth and sea in place, again YHWH's thunderous wind brings to life all the flora (Gen 1:11–12) and fauna (vv. 20–22) *ex nihilo*. In the same fashion, YHWH's blustery wind engenders the luminaries: sun, moon, and stars (Ps 33:6b), and assigns their solar and lunar functions to purposely mark the periods of "light" and "darkness," respectively (Gen 1:14–18). Hence, as in the case of Amma, YHWH employs the (whirl)wind, alternatively personified as the creative "word," "voice," or "loud sound," and incorporates the elements of chaos to form a viable cosmos.

As noted in Amma's creation, a combination of phenomenon: whirlwind, wind/breath, and word/voice work in tandem[352] in the formation of the Dogon cosmogony. Thus, as in the Dogon creation myth, it is possible to see in this priestly cosmogony the winds as resembling the generative word (*fiat*), or voice as complementary reflexes of YHWH's cosmic activity in the formation of an orderly cosmos, and fitting the axiom *creatio ex nihilo*. However, the creation of male and female, which marks the apex of the divine order, is idiosyncratic. There is no reference to any direct involvement of the phenomenal elements. Instead, YHWH makes a corporate address to heavenly beings[353] in determining the creation of human beings, but that pales in the background, as YHWH imparts his own image—*imago Dei*—to human beings (Gen 1:26–28). Be that as it may, this concept is analogous to the Dogon creation myth in two notable aspects. On the one hand, the human beings' formation in the image of YHWH parallels the creation of the Nommo replicating the image of the creator-god Amma. On the other hand, in both cases, humanity is granted rulership and stewardship over the cosmos.

Yet, quite distinctive in the priestly creation narrative is the reference to the divine "rest" and institution of the Sabbath, as the culmination of the establishment of cosmogonic order. Although the term "Sabbath" is

---

351. The reference to YHWH creating the seas and forming land by "hands" (Ps 95:5) also implies that the role of phenomenal winds at creation is in view.

352. See pp. 17–19, 29.

353. Day summarizes scholarly opinions on the plural address here as referring to gods or God's spirit but also notes that the reference to a heavenly court is the commonly held view (based on Job 38:7 mentioning the "sons of God," and, more closely, Ps 8, where a resemblance between humans and gods is drawn). See Day, *Creation*, 11–13. Yet, the final decision to create human beings rests with YHWH himself.

not specifically mentioned in the priestly account of creation, it is implied in that YHWH "rested" (*šābat*) on the seventh day from all the work he created and sanctified that day (Gen 2:2–3). Arguably, as Levenson observed in the context of the priestly theology of creation in association with the idea of rest in the commemoration of the Sabbath, human beings are no "partner in creation."[354] But, they are granted co-regency in cosmological order by virtue of their creation in the image of God.[355] Thus, human beings are obligated to participate in divine rest through the observation of the Sabbath. By hallowing the Sabbath, human beings (*sic.*, Israel) imitate their creator. Levenson sees here another instance of the priestly theology of *imitatio Dei*.[356] Perhaps this aspect of rest should be understood relative to YHWH's repose upon display of power in disposing chaotic waters to their designated place and generation of order out of chaos.

An Intersection of Ideologies in Genesis 1:2, 26–28 and the Dogon Creation Myth on Cosmic Order through Chaos to Social Organization

The priestly creation account relates the establishment of cosmic order from chaos consistent with the *Chaoskampf* myth, as in the Dogon creation myth. Both cosmogonies show a development of creation out of chaos inclusive of the creation of humanity in the image of the creator culminating in an orderly macrocosm. Amma's design shows that male and female were part of the creative order[357] and charged to organize the earth as emanations of Amma.[358] Similarly, the priestly account portrays the establishment of human culture in the creation of the male and female, as part of YHWH's design. In bearing YHWH's image, humans share the subordinate rule of the earth. This idea aligns with Eliade's definition of myth in relation with the idea of "beginnings" as manifestations of the creativity of supernatural beings by which humans are formed

---

354. Levenson, *Creation*, 117.

355. Levenson, *Creation*, 119. Levenson goes further in linking the observance of dietary laws and the concept of "separation" as an act of creation as having implications on the fundamental idea of Israel being set apart as holy in alignment with YHWH (117–19).

356. Levenson, *Creation*, 119.

357. See pp. 21, 22, 26, 26n181.

358. See pp. 20, 26–27.

as sexed and cultural beings, and function in keeping with particular rules.[359] Thus, in both contexts, humankind is charged with the power to master and rule the earth following the ordering of chaos. A third millennium BCE Egyptian text, "The Instruction for King Meri-ka-Re,"[360] on advice given by a king to his succeeding son, suggests similar ideas.

The Egyptian text, "The Instruction for King Meri-ka-Re," alludes to the creator who creates heaven and earth, and subdues a "water monster."[361] The creator is acclaimed to make breath for the nostrils, and humanity emerges from his body as the images[362] of the creator. The creator is also attributed with the creation of fauna, flora, fowl and marine life for humanity's consumption. It is said he vanquishes their enemies and hedges them in with a shrine of protection, and imparts royalty status "in the egg."[363] As cited in this Egyptian text, it appears the vanquishing of the water monster is in sequel to the formation of heaven and earth, as much as the destruction of enemies follows after the creation of humans. Both the water monster and enemies pose a threat to the deity's creation and are contained for the maintenance of cosmic order. Herein, the association of the creation of the cosmos and human beings endowed with rulership/kingship with the containment of inimical forces—*Chaoskampf*—for proper social organization disclaims scholarship that limits the *Chaoskampf* myth to the legitimization of kingship.[364] Instead, and again, as in "The Instruction for King Meri-ka-Re" text, rulership is simply a role assigned to humanity as a creation event by virtue of the humans being created in the image of the creator.

A pattern emerges therefore, showing a process of creation proceeding with the containment of chaos *in medias res* to a viable cosmos where humanity shares governance in the cosmos indwelt by the creator, who vanquishes enemies, and orders their affairs. Similarly, the Dogon-*nommo anagonno* are imparted Amma's image in the womb/egg and

---

359. See pp. 10–11.

360. Wilson, "Instruction," 414–18.

361. Wilson, "Instruction," 417. See Hoffmeier, "Some Thoughts," 48. Hoffmeier derives the determinative "after" in reading this text and suggests the creation of heaven and earth as subsequent to the vanquishing of the water monster.

362. Levenson, *Creation*, 114–16; Day, *Creation*, 14–15, 14n40.

363. Wilson, "Instruction," 417; lines 131–136. Perhaps this reference to an "egg" here shows belief in a cosmos that emerged from a cosmic egg.

364. See pp. 34–35.

assigned rulership and guardianship of the world Amma creates.[365] Here, too, social organization is structured on the mythical emergence of a cosmos from chaos. As noted in relation to the Dogon societal structures, human beings reorient themselves in relation to the establishment of the original order from the chaos initiated by Ogo. Hence, social organization and institutions for the Dogon are centered on the mythical sacrifice and the division of Nommo's body in commemoration of Amma's purification and ordering of the universe. Therefore, the social communities reenact the mythical sacrifice in their rituals, in order to experience that dynamism of a union in space and time with the body of Nommo, as fundamental to the reorganization of the universe and how it functions.[366] At the altars set up in human societies for the reenactment of the sacrifice and division of the body of Nommo, human beings enter into an integral communion with these body parts enabling social coherence. To that end, the association of creation-from-chaos with social organization identified here in the Dogon creation myth aligns with Malinowski and Eliade's propositions[367] on myth; particularly Malinowski's view on myths of origin as schema for social cohesion,[368] and more cogently, Eliade's idea on creation from chaos, as a codifier and charter for social organization.[369] From that perspective, the Dogon creation myth relates a cosmic pattern featuring creation-chaos-(then)*kampf*-cosmos-social organization. In view of this observation, an intertextual reading of biblical texts exposes that the Davidic-Zion theology is in keeping with this pattern, and shows the link between creation, *Chaoskampf*, humankind's origin and role in the cosmic order and social organization.

The fundamental notions of creation from chaos, creation of humanity in the image of god that are central to the priestly narrative of Gen 1:1–2, 26–28, and supported by other biblical texts, feature in the Davidic-Zion[370] theology bearing resemblance to ideas stated in the Egyptian Meri-ka-Re inscription and the Dogon creation myth. Consistent with these traditions, the priestly author's interests in creation

---

365. See pp. 20, 26–27.

366. See pp. 30–32.

367. For Malinowski, see pp. 8–9. For Eliade, see pp. 9–11.

368. For Malinowski, see pp. 8–9.

369. For Eliade, see pp. 10–11.

370. On the unresolved scholarly debate on the date and origin of the Zion tradition as part of the Davidic royal ideology, see Ollenburger, *Zion*, 17–19.

GENESIS 1:1-2, 26-28 IN LIGHT OF THE DOGON CREATION MYTH

and the sacral symbolism of Zion,[371] deriving from YHWH's presence in Zion, permeates the Davidic-Zion theology. Central to this theology is the House of David's claim for election (Ps 89:21[20]; see 78:70) with its basis in the concept of creation (Ps 8:3-6). In keeping with the creation of humanity in *imago Dei* in Gen 1:26-28, King David emphasized his divine appointment by his claim as created by YHWH (Ps 8:4-5), and made a surrogate[372] ruler of all creation (Ps 8:6-8; see Gen 1:28; Ps 89:5[4], 20[19], 25-30[24-29]). As Levenson notes, here is a thought common to ANE inscriptions where the king is identified as the image of the deity and selected as viceroy.[373] Nonetheless, as Levenson points out, the idea related here in Ps 8, although not entirely dependent on Gen 1:26-28, elucidates the idea of humanity made in the image of god and given dominion over the rest of creation as regent.[374]

Levenson, apud Wildberger, sees evidence from "The Instruction for King Meri-ka-Re" text for all humanity to join in the deification of status in bearing the resemblance of the deity once exclusive to kings. As Levenson further argues, the extension of this royal status to all humanity made in the image of the deity and mandate to share in the governance of the world is a democratization of a royal epithet.[375] Again, Levenson argues for the idea of humanity made in the image of god in Gen 1:26-28, as put into perspective in the cosmogonic narrative of Ps 89, where creation culminates with YHWH's consignment to the humans to have dominion in the world (vv. 27-28[26-27]), as agents in YHWH's name as the creator.[376] Moreover, the role of humanity, as re-

---

371. Ollenburger, *Zion*, 23.

372. Day, *Creation*, 14-15. Day, following Levenson, observed that the royal epithet of vicegerent, only once reserved for rulers and kings seen as the "image" of the creator-god in Egypt and Mesopotamia, is extended to encompass all humanity. This "democratization" of vicegerency for all humanity is also implied in Ps 8:4-8. Notwithstanding the close resemblance to Gen 1:26-28, the democratization is expressed particularly in Ps 8:5-6 in royalty language ("crowned [them] with glory and honor") to clarify humanity's commission to rule as agents over YHWH's creation. Hence, as Levenson argued, the democratization of the role of humanity expressed in royal terms in Ps 8:4-8 compares to the role of the Davidic dynasty in Ps 89, as YHWH's regent over cosmic order (Ps 89:26-27[25-26]). Be that as it may, this divine appointment of humanity over the created world in the biblical tradition is in keeping with "The Instruction for King Meri-Ka-Re" text and Dogon creation myth. See Levenson, *Creation*, 115, 117.

373. Levenson, *Creation*, 114.

374. Levenson, *Creation*, 113-14.

375. Levenson, *Creation*, 115.

376. Levenson, *Creation*, 117.

gents assumed by the House of David in Ps 89, resembles YHWH's power at creation. Thus, the idea of "setting his hand upon the sea, and right hand upon the rivers" (Ps 89:26[25]) implicates David's containment of inimical forces (vv. 23–24[22–23]; see Ps 18:38[37], 41[40]) and recalls YHWH's ordering of the chaotic waters (Ps 89:10[9]). Here, the mythical creation-out-of-chaos is also evoked. The reference to the stilling of the waves paralleled with the destruction of Rahab, the monster of chaos[377] (Ps 89:10–11[9–10]), and the scattering of the enemies "with the arm of [your] might" (בזרוע עזך, v. 11[10]b), implies YHWH's wind is deployed. This is also personified as the mighty "arm" and strong "right hand"[378] (v. 14[13]), which wields order out of chaos. This image of YHWH subduing chaotic forces by his potent wind is drawn to show that the House of David will endure, sustained and undergirded by YHWH's strength (vv. 22–24[21–23]).

Furthermore, the ideas of creation and *Chaoskampf*[379] are incorporated into the Davidic-Zion tradition in association with Zion as a sacral center. Zion as YHWH's choice of abode[380] (Pss 78:68b–69; 132:13–14),[381] and indwelt by YHWH's presence (Ps 2:6b; see 15:1; 46:5b–6[4b–5]; 48:4[3]; 78:68–69), is imbued with creation concepts. Notable here is the declaration of Zion as a sanctuary firmly and securely established just as YHWH founded the earth[382] (Ps 78:69) from chaos (Gen 1:2; Ps 24:1–2). Thus, YHWH's establishment and defense of Zion by quelling inimical forces is comparable to YHWH's subjugation of chaos at the creation of the earth (Ps 78:69; see 65:8[7]). Fundamentally, as already noted, YHWH employs the winds to subdue the chaotic primal forces (Gen 1:2; Ps 104:3, 7–9; Job 26:13). The same language expressing YHWH's founding of the earth from chaos is evoked for the ordering of social welfare among his people, Israel. YHWH, who subdues the sea/deep/mighty waters (Gen 1:2; Ps 104:7; see Pss 65:8[7]ab; 89:10[9]),[383] or sea-dragons/monsters[384] (Ps 89:11[10]; see 74:13b–14; Job 9:13; 26:12b, 13b)

377. See table 1, p. 41 on Job 26:12b, 13b. See also 37–38n264 above.
378. See pp. 41–42.
379. See Ollenberger, *Zion*, 55–58.
380. Ollenberger, *Zion*, 55.
381. Exod 15:17; Ps 48:2–3[1–2]
382. Ollenberger, *Zion*, 55.
383. Pss 74:13a; 93:3–4; 104:6–7; Job 26:12a.
384. Hoffmeier acknowledges the mention of these monsters in the biblical tradition, but denies that there is combat between them and YHWH (Hoffmeier, "Some Thoughts," 48).

in establishing cosmic order (Gen 1:10–11; see Ps 89:12–13[11–12]),[385] has the potentiality to annihilate enemies, comparable to the stilling of roaring sea/waters[386] (Ps 65:8[7]; see 29:3; 93:4), in guaranteeing Israel's social security and stability (Ps 65:9[8]; see 29:11b; 46:9–10[8–9]).[387]

In essence, as noted by Eliade on the belief in myth on the cosmos emerging from chaos and all its permutations as defining social order,[388] Israel's social organization is modeled on YHWH's establishment of cosmogonic order. The Davidic-Zion theology laid out here parallels the Afrocentric orientation of social organization to the origin of the world found in "The Instruction for King Meri-ka-Re" text and the Dogon creation myth. In that respect, the Davidic-Zion theology bears the same ethnocentric marks in proclaiming an origin from a supreme deity, surrogate rulership, and the ordering of social and sacral affairs oriented to the chaos-to-cosmos myth serving as charter for social organization.

Final Reflection

Although certain elements and motifs discussed here are common to ANE traditions, there are more stark similarities in the creation concepts between the Hebrew tradition and the Dogon creation myth. This interdisciplinary and intertextual analysis of these two cosmogonies shows the conflation of the ideas on *creatio ex nihilo*, voice/word/*fiat*, and breath/wind/whirlwind with *Chaoskampf* myth in the establishment of cosmic order for the validation of social organization. Creative order, from "nothing," is accomplished by one primal deity whose fundamental generative power in whirlwind/wind(s), personified[389] as the creative

---

385. See Ps 93:1c; Job 9:8–9; 26:7–10.

386. This idea is significant to the prophet Isaiah. In delivering judgment against nations threatening the existence of Israel, he seizes this idea of creation out of chaos in portraying YHWH as creator and redeemer subjecting inimical forces to "winds" and vanquishing rebellious nations, who are compared to the roaring waters at creation (Isa 17:12) subjected to YHWH's powerful winds (v. 13; see 29:5–6; Ps 83:15–16[14–15]).

387. See Pss 18:41[40]; 89:24[23]; 2 Sam 7:9.

388. See pp. 9–11.

389. It seems the personification of the winds as YHWH's arm, or hand is unparalleled in the Dogon creation myth, although there is reference to Amma [who is identified as wind or whirlwind] using his arms at creation (Griaule and Dieterlen, *Pale Fox*, 194–95, 384).

word/voice, and peculiar to the Hebrew tradition as strong arm or right hand, or rebuke/roar, transforms chaos into cosmos.

Humankind is formed as part of the creative design, as the image of the deity and conferred guardianship, or rulership of the earth. The ideologies on social organization are centered on the deity's repelling of primal chaos, and some form of ritual is observed in commemoration of this primordial act for continual alignment with the cosmic order. Therefore, both the biblical Hebrew tradition and the African Dogon creation myth show that the security and stability of a society is guaranteed in allegiance to the primal and sovereign creator who overcomes chaos. The cosmogonic synopsis of Gen 1:1–2, 26–28, offers a perfect foil to this idea of YHWH vanquishing chaos in ordering a viable cosmos. As proxy of other biblical texts related here, Gen 1:1–2, 26–28 recounts creation accomplished through *Chaoskampf* as symbolic for the ideological purposes of evoking and legitimatizing social organization integral with an orderly cosmos, showing that the idea of creation is not a secondary, or late concept in the biblical Hebrew tradition, as normally presupposed.[390] This and other questions on this fundamental notion of creation call for further exploration.

---

390. Simkins, *Creator and Creation*, 7–11; Flynn, *YHWH Is King*, 43–47, 54, 68–69, 172–73, 175–79.

2

YHWH in the Wind as Creator-King

Creation Motif

THE THEME OF CREATION has attracted the interest of religion and biblical scholars for a long time. Studies have been carried out on creation from different perspectives. In biblical Hebrew, creation is perceived by birth (Ps 90:2; Job 15:7), creation by word of mouth (Gen 1:3; Pss 33:6, 9; 148:5; Job 38:11), or creation from nothing—*creatio ex nihilo*—and creation out of chaos (Pss 65:7–8[6–7]b; 74:13–14; 89:10–11[9–10]; 104:5–9; Job 26:12–13).[1] These different ways in which creation is expressed show that the OT spoke of creation with a different form and meaning that was understood at specific points in time.

The historian of religion Charles H. Long, preferring to use the term "cosmogony,"[2] first identified six types of cosmogonies and treated them under different categories: emergence myths, world-parent myths, creation from chaos myths, creation from cosmic egg myths, creation from nothing myths, and earth diver myths.[3] However, Long, upon following

---

1. See Clifford, *Creation Accounts*, 1–3, who also noted four types of creation identified by Westermann: creation by birth(s), by struggle/victory, by action/activity, and creation through word.

2. Clifford, *Creation Accounts*, 2.

3. Clifford, *Creation Accounts*, 1. Long combined creation from chaos with the idea of creation from the cosmic egg, pointing out that the determination to link these two types of cosmogonies was not based on the frequent concurrence in the same myth,

studies by Scottish folklorist Andrew Lang, later refined his categories of cosmogonic myths to include creation by a supreme being.[4] Long considered creation by a supreme being as a "specific" and prevalent structure. Under this creation type, Long identified the idea of a sky deity, the idea of creation from nothing (the deity preexisting any being, or thing, or the world), and the idea of wisdom and power, among other significant ideas, as essential elements to actualize the world.[5] Although Long noted that the intent of the creator is the creation of a perfect world, he also alluded to "creation from chaos" emanating with a rupture of the supreme being's created order caused by one of the creatures.[6] He cited the Dogon myth as fitting this pattern.[7] As Long stated, this African creation myth not only demonstrates how a "rupture," or chaos occurred within the myth itself, but also focuses on the characteristics of the supreme deity as integral with other mythological themes; such as the symbolism of dualism represented by divine twins, the cosmic egg, and the sacrifice of the other twin to re-establish the supreme deity's created order.[8]

In light of this possible integration of the idea of creation by a supreme being with other mythological themes, Ps 104 is subjected to interrogation. A critical analysis of this psalm as a *de facto* biblical cosmogony, and a paradigm of similar texts, exposes the association of the idea of creation by a supreme deity with pervasive characteristics of wisdom and power, as noted by Long, with the ideas of creation-out-of-chaos, and judgment motifs. YHWH, as the supreme deity, is pictured here with winds, accompanied by other phenomenal elements in manifestation of his wisdom and power at the establishment of cosmic order, and his posture against any forces antithetical to his divine order. Hence, inevitably, Ps 104 portrays the establishment of social organization in the Hebrew

---

but by the intent to show some connection between the two types. Here, Long outlined some myths associating water as symbolic of chaos with the cosmic egg motif (Long, *Alpha*, 113–18).

4. See Long, "Creation," paragraphs 12–13; Griaule and Dieterlen, *Pale Fox*, 75; Pettazzoni, *Essays*, 26–36. Pettazzoni discussed the beliefs of supreme beings as creators in other traditions in relation to affinities between creation myths and myths of beginnings.

5. Long, "Creation," paragraph 13.

6. See Long, "Creation," paragraphs 14–15. See also pp. 20–22 above.

7. Long, "Creation," paragraphs 15–16.

8. Long, "Creation," paragraph 16. Regarding the sacrifice of the *Nommo* in reordering creation, see pp. 22–25.

tradition.⁹ As noted in the previous chapter, the "wind" and "breath,"¹⁰ synonymous elements originating with Amma, play a significant role in the Dogon creation myth. So, too, in Ps 104, the "wind(s)/breath" (רוח) form a chiasmus and represent YHWH's sole involvement in the origin of the cosmogony, and maintenance of that cosmic order in portrayal of YHWH as creator-king and universal judge. This purview deviates from previous scholarship to date on the concept of creation in Ps 104.

Former Scholarship on Psalm 104

P. C. Craigie, writing in 1974 with the intent to suggest the *Sitz im Leben* for Ps 104 within the Hebrew poetic tradition, gave a summary of the comparative work done on the psalm for literary, or aesthetic purposes, or perhaps, even in order to establish literary or religious interrelationships between cultures.¹¹ But, rather than focusing more on pre-nineteenth-century comparative study of the text, Craigie focused on developments of new ideas in the twentieth century with the discovery of archaeological material in the ANE. As Craigie noted, some studies compared Ps 104 with the Egyptian "Hymn to Aten" and considered derivative from it, while other studies compared the text to Gen 1, thereby in association with the Babylonian Enuma Elish, Ugaritic texts, and also intertextually with other Hebrew poetry.¹² Craigie noted these various comparisons, but focused more on the Egyptian and Ugaritic parallels.¹³

First, Craigie mentioned the groundwork laid by Breasted, following Hugo Gressman, on the proposed affinity of Ps 104 with the "Hymn to Aten," though subsequently considered with circumspection. Craigie noted the implications of relating two texts that are chronologically dated four centuries apart, have geographic provenance and linguistic differences. Again, Craigie cautioned on the view of the Hebrew author/poet's insight on this "Hymn to Aten" due to its location. The hymn is known to have been a wall inscription in a sealed tomb at (later known as) Armana, suggesting the difficulties of directly associating Ps 104 with the "Hymn

---

9. Chapter 1 (56–61) set forth the idea of creation-out-of-chaos and related mythological themes serving as a charter for social organization.

10. See pp. 15, 16–17, 29.

11. Craigie, "Comparison," 10.

12. Craigie, "Comparison," 12.

13. Scholarship has expanded on the Ugaritic parallels with Ps 104, and the references to such will only be slight in this analysis.

to Aten."[14] Furthermore, as Craigie observed, the parallels between Ps 104 and the "Hymn to Aten" are not a direct translation of the Egyptian text; therefore, not verbatim. Even the sole formulaic expression: "How manifold are your works, O' YHWH; you made all of them in wisdom" (Ps 104:24) suggested as showing correspondence with "How manifold it is, what [Aten] has made. They are hidden from the face [of man]" ("Hymn to Aten," lines 76–77),[15] is not entirely the same in thought and sequence[16] to enforce any exceptional similarities. Craigie also observed that the formulaic expression is not unique to Ps 104 but is also found in Ps 92:6.[17]

Other general parallels can be drawn between Ps 104 and different Egyptian sun-hymns, and even a Mesopotamian hymn to the sun god Shamash.[18] However, the common element between all these texts is not so much the sun, but creation.[19] The similarities are not cosmogonic, but more on the general cosmological aspect of the relationship between the created order and its creator.[20] With that view, Craigie argued that Ps 104 mentions the sun as part of YHWH's creation and ascribes praise to YHWH as the creator, in contrast to the Egyptian and Mesopotamian sun-hymns lauding praise to the sun itself as a deity.[21] However, Craigie proposed the dedication of the Solomonic temple to YHWH to be the *Sitz im Leben*[22] for Ps 104, to whom, in his transcendence, the temple was built.[23] Notwithstanding this proposition, Craigie argued for the general similarities in the "Hymn to Aten" and Ps 104 on the basis of the same subject matter, as opposed to a direct link, and, perhaps suggesting a common, either Egyptian, or possibly broader ANE background.[24]

---

14. Craigie, "Comparison," 13.
15. Craigie, "Comparison," 13; Day, "Psalm 104," 214.
16. Craigie, "Comparison," 13.
17. Craigie, "Comparison," 13, esp. 13n16.
18. Craigie, "Comparison," 13–14.
19. Craigie, "Comparison," 14.
20. Craigie, "Comparison," 14.
21. Craigie, "Comparison," 20.
22. Craigie, "Comparison," 19, 21. Dion, objecting the dedication of the Solomonic temple as the setting for Ps 104, does not see affirmative parallels with the construction of Ba'al's palace (Dion, "YHWH," 48n18).
23. Craigie, "Comparison," 20.
24. Craigie, "Comparison," 14–15. Here Craigie discusses several viewpoints in scholarship on the parallels noted with Ugaritic, Canaanite/Phoenician backgrounds.

Although Craigie noted Dahood's contribution on the linguistic and grammatical parallels of Ugaritic with elements in Ps 104,[25] he agreed with previous scholarship (of Breasted, Gressman, et al.) that argued for the influence of the Egyptian "Hymn to Aten"[26] through Phoenician[27] literature, of which he saw Ugaritic as a part.[28] Craigie identified terms and motifs deriving from Ugaritic literature, and mostly vestiges of elements related to the Ba'al myth. Therefore, Craigie outlined some general similarities with Ugaritic literature, but for purposes of a cogent argument on the appearance and cosmological activities of YHWH with the winds, a few relevant comparisons are noted here.

For instance, Ba'al's title *rkb 'rpt* ("rider of the clouds"),[29] as echoed in the idea of YHWH riding on the clouds[30] expressed in Ps 104:3, personifies the windblown clouds. Instead, the creation narrative on the idea of the Dogon ark, descending through an opening in the sky with a whirling motion from the whirlwind,[31] resonates with the image of YHWH riding on the clouds as his chariot and marching on the wings of the wind.

The "fire" and "flame"[32] mentioned as refining elements in the construction of Ba'al's palace, appear as personifications of YHWH's lackeys

25. Craigie, "Comparison," 15.
26. Craigie, "Comparison," 15–16.
27. See Smith, *Origins*, 14–18. Smith analyzes the preference by biblical scholars on the use of terms "Ugaritic," "Canaanite," and "Amorite" on linguistic, cultural, and historical grounds in relation to the development of the Israelite culture and religion. Smith suggests using the broader term "West Semitic," dropping the "Canaanite," as he thinks that for the latter, little is known to make it an identifiable and coherent culture from the textual perspective. However, even though no fine lines can be drawn between the terms, the significance of the parallels cannot be diminished, as the biblical tradition shows evidence of mythical material common to people who lived in the coastal lands that the biblical scholars regard as Canaan. Hence, he also seems to suggest the influence from the Phoenician culture via later sources showing reflexes from the Ugaritic materials (Smith, *Origins*, 17).
28. Craigie, "Comparison," 16.
29. See p. 28. For other advocates of the same meaning, "rider of the clouds," see Patton, *Canaanite Parallels*, 20; Vine, *Establishment of Baal*, 82; Dion "YHWH," 51; Tate, *Psalms*, 160, 163, 176 (Tate offers this translation in analysis of similar Hebrew terms in Ps 68); Ginsberg, "Poems," 130, 134, 137–38; Rahmouni, *Divine Epithets*, 288–89. See also Rahmouni, *Divine Epithets*, 289n5, referring to proponents of "rider on the clouds," "cloud-rider," "Charioteer of the clouds," "(Wolkenfahrer=) Cloud-driver," among others, as the preferred meaning for *rkb 'rpt*.
30. Craigie, "Comparison," 16.
31. See pp. 27–28.
32. Craigie, "Comparison," 15. Seeking for Ugaritic parallels, Dahood posed the idea

(Ps 104:4). The association of fire and flame with the formation of the Nommo in the Dogon creation myth, and their function as the guardians and protectors of Amma's world, provides a better correspondence with the Hebrew notion of fire and flame serving as YHWH's ministers.[33]

On the other hand, the idea of thunder mentioned in (Ps 104:7), and compared with Ps 29:3, is often considered as a reflection of the voice[34] of Ba'al. But a closer comparison can be drawn from the "loud sound" emitted by Amma's word, also identified as the "voice," or the seven articulations symbolizing his creative spiral, which is the whirlwind.[35] Thus, bringing to bear the notion of YHWH appearing with the loud sound of the phenomenal winds to subdue the chaotic waters in this context of creation. The concept of Ba'al's window inserted in his palace for the issuing of rain parallels the idea of YHWH watering the mountains from his lofty abode[36] (v. 13; cf. upper chambers in v. 3) bringing into focus YHWH's winds dispersing the rain-bearing clouds (see Job 36:26–29a; 37:9–12aβ). In correspondence to this concept is Amma's reservation of the essential elements of Nommo in the sky to issue as rain.[37]

The idea of wood from Lebanon used to construct Ba'al's palace,[38] is unrelated to the concept of creation. But, in Ps 104:16 the cedars of Lebanon[39] are referenced as established by YHWH. Perhaps, these majestic cedars may find a faint match in the reference to the *sene* considered important as the first of all trees of Amma's creation, and validated as much as the Nommo, the first beings.[40] The trees in general are also specifically mentioned among the creations of Amma that descended in the ark.[41]

---

of fire and flame in Ps 104:4 serving as ministers of YHWH as demythologization of the minor deities initially identified in the Ugaritic pantheon (see *UBC II* 593–94; Gibson, *Canaanite Myths*, 63).

33. See p. 20, 20n131 above.

34. Craigie, "Comparison," 16.

35. See pp. 16–18 above.

36. Craigie, "Comparison," 17; cf. Dion, "YHWH," 52–53, commenting on similarities in the attribution of responsibility to YHWH for issuing rain and fecundity with the characteristics of the storm god in the ANE.

37. See p. 23.

38. Craigie, "Comparison," 17.

39. Craigie, "Comparison," 17.

40. See p. 15, 15n83 above.

41. See p. 27.

YHWH IN THE WIND AS CREATOR-KING

The reference to the Leviathan (Ps 104:26b), often apprehended as a variant of Baʿal's rival,[42] in this Hebrew poetry is a mere creature gamboling[43] with YHWH's marine creation, and mentioned as part of a plethora of elements, and motifs relating to the creativity of YHWH at his disclosure with the winds. However, the question still remains: whether Leviathan[44] is a vestigial representative of the rival monster of the *Chaoskampf* myth in the Ugaritic version of the combat with Baʿal, or mythological overtones of the Egyptian crocodile.[45] Perhaps we find in the biblical tradition Leviathan as the paradigmatic creature fashioned by YHWH equivalent to Ogo created by Amma, the caricature that assumed the rebellious nature,[46] and caused disruption *in medias res* of Amma's cosmic order as delineated in the Dogon cosmogony, and then subdued at the establishment of the cosmic order, a point to return to later.

Following the cosmological/cosmogonic theme on this comparative study of Ps 104 with ANE literature, Craigie linked the establishment of a palace with kingship in sequel to the battle between Baʿal and Yam. As Craigie argued, the Baʿal/Yam conflict and Baʿal's victory were central to the establishment of order with the construction of a palace being monumental to Baʿal's ascension to kingship. Craigie averred, apud Fisher and Cross,[47] that the construction of Baʿal's palace represented some form of a cosmological[48]/cosmogonic[49] concept of order that superseded chaos

---

42. See pp. 37–38, 37–38n264 above.

43. Craigie, "Comparison," 21.

44. On the use and occurrences of this designation in the biblical tradition, see pp. 37–38n264, 41 above.

45. See Pope, *Job*, 330–31; Dahood, *Psalms*, 3:45; Craigie, "Comparison," 15; cf. Uehlinger, "Leviathan לויתן," 513, who sees the provenance of the idea of Leviathan from Egypt as improbable. However, Mettinger sees the Egyptian version of the battle with chaos in Horus harpooning a hippopotamus and crocodile as representations of the evil Seth, as the background for the hippopotamus and crocodile in the book of Job (40–41) resembled by Behemoth and Leviathan, respectively (Mettinger, *Reports*, 247–49).

46. See pp. 21–22.

47. Some scholars argue that the Baʿal/Yam battle should be seen as cosmogonic. See Fisher, "Creation," 316; Cross, *Canaanite Myth*, 43, 113–20; Craigie, "Comparison," 17n32.

48. Craigie, "Comparison," 17.

49. Fisher, "Creation," 316. Fisher upheld the view that the Baʿal/Yam conflict results in kingship, or temple building, while also asserting that the conflict is interconnected with the ordering of chaos, kingship, and temple building. Fisher termed this cosmogonic, reflecting a Baʿal model of creation (Fisher, "Creation," 313–16). Clifford once supported the same view. He saw the conflict, ordering of chaos, kingship of Baʿal,

at the defeat of Yam, hence deemed as creation. Craigie argued that this cosmological theme is paralleled in Ps 104 by YHWH's kingship, and alluded to in his role as creator[50] in Ps 103:19. On that basis, Craigie avowed the connection of Ps 104 with the palace, or temple building analogous to its Canaanite parallel.[51] Regardless of this inostensible parallel with the Baʿal tradition, the mention of the construction of YHWH's abode (Ps 104:2b–3a) precedes the thorough description of his ordering of chaos, providence and sustenance of nature, that is unparalleled in the Baʿal tradition, as will be delineated here. As Craigie rightly noted, no matter what import of the Ugaritic or Egyptian parallels to the psalm, its general tenor is not unusual, if read in the context of other Hebrew texts. Perhaps, any possible external influences were modified and integrated to fit the general Hebrew religious thought,[52] as will be deliberated here.

John Day's[53] extended discussion on the six parallels with the Egyptian hymn to the sun god Aten demonstrates further attempts to strip the authenticity of Ps 104 from the Hebrew corpus. Though Day's study is limited to the latter part of the psalm, the content of the six parallels he drew to show the dependence of Ps 104 on the Egyptian hymn is germane to previous scholarship with similar views. Day compared six parallels between Ps 104:20–30 and the "Hymn to Aten" that he considered to be in identical order. However, these parallels are overdrawn, and the variations in the presumed parallels require exposition to show a tenor in this Hebrew psalm, that is peculiar to its Hebrew tradition.

According to Day, in the first parallel[54] the psalmist celebrates YHWH who makes darkness into night, and in it the beasts of the forest; among them the lions come out to seek food from God (vv. 20–21). But, in the postulated comparison, the Egyptian hymn (lines 27–37) refers to

---

and the building of his palace as cosmogonic in that it is associated with the establishment of order in both heaven and earth; thus facilitating support of human existence (Clifford, "Cosmogonies," 183–201). But Clifford no longer maintains this argument (Clifford, *Creation Accounts*, 132).

50. Craigie, "Comparison," 17.
51. Craigie, "Comparison," 17.
52. Craigie, "Comparison," 18, 21.
53. Day, "Psalm 104," 211–28. Day, apud Lichtheim and Assmann, distinguishes this hymn with what he refers to as a shorter "Hymn to Aten," also found at El-Amarna, formerly known as Akhetaten (Day, "Psalm 104," 211, 211n4). Wilson translates the name of this Egyptian deity Aton, as worshiped by Pharaoh Akh-en-Aton (Wilson, "Hymn," 324).
54. Day, "Psalm 104," 213.

Aten and darkness as two distinct opposing forces, or entities. Aten, as the sun disk, sets and the land is plunged into darkness; humans sleep with heads concealed, so that even goods under their heads are insecure. There is no glimpse of one another. Lions emerge under cover of the dark, and creeping creatures inflict their sting. The darkness is characterized as a death shroud ("Hymn to Aten," line 35). Moreover, in the "Hymn to Aten," there is no specific mention of the purpose of the lion emerging from its den at the setting of the sun.

In the supposed second parallel[55] (Ps 104:22–23), YHWH as the prime mover causes the sun to rise, and the lions to return to their den, and the humans to resume their work until twilight. In contrast, in the "Hymn to Aten," there is emphasis on the darkness expelled by Aten's rays leading to festivity in the lands, humans' daily ablutions, and praise is directed to the rising sun, as the personification of Aten himself. The idea of the world doing their work is appended in the "Hymn to Aten," but there is no reference to the lions' daily routine.

Again, the assumed third parallel[56] is not verbatim. Both the Hebrew psalm and the "Hymn to Aten" refer to the awe and wonder of the deities' multifarious works, attributed to their "wisdom" manifested in creation. But quite distinctive is the psalmist's expression of YHWH's sapiential adroitness displayed in "all" and the fullness of his terrestrial creations (v. 24). In contradistinction, the "Hymn to Aten" alludes to the works of the sole god as inconspicuous to the sight of humans (line 77); but there is an acknowledgement of his creation of humans, cattle, beasts, and all terrestrial creatures, as much as the winged, or volant creatures (lines 76–82). Even Day subtly acknowledges the lack of sequence in the parallels of the Hebrew psalm with the "Hymn to Aten."[57] Instead, Day needlessly implicates relocating the acclamation of YHWH's wisdom in creation in Ps 104:24 after the reference to the sea creatures in vv. 25–26.[58] Yet, in essence, Ps 104:24 buffers two sections. The preceding verses exult YHWH for creating the terrestrial biotic and abiotic systems narrated in vv. 10–18. This is marked off with an interlude in vv. 19–23 expressing YHWH's creation of the orderly ecological cycles of life that are determined and regulated by the celestial luminaries. Therefore, the awe and wonder on YHWH's wisdom expressed in v. 24 interject

---

55. Day, "Psalm 104," 214.
56. Day, "Psalm 104," 214.
57. Day, "Psalm 104," 215.
58. Day, "Psalm 104," 215.

YHWH IN THE WIND(S)

a pause to celebrate YHWH's creative works on the sustainable earth. It also serves as a conjunction to the extension of that awe and wonder in the nautical realm stated in vv. 25–26. But, Day fails to see that this "peroration" is in reference to the "earth" and the abundance of its creatures (see v. 24c), as the focal point of the psalmist's exultation in deep reflective thought on YHWH's creative works on the earth. The earth is described as a habitat abounding with a range of creatures; wild donkeys, birds, cattle, wild goats, and conies mentioned in these verses (vv. 11–18) preceding the perimeters of Day's study. So there is no need to relocate the expression of awe and wonder in v. 24, as Day suggests. The psalmist's reference to YHWH's creation of the nautical realm,[59] represented by the creatures teeming in the sea, including the Leviathan, in vv. 25–26, only further emphasizes the wonder of YHWH's creation. In contrast to the psalmist's eulogy, the expression of Aten's wisdom is preceded by the contemplation on his creative ingenuity focused on the gestation and parturition periods for both humans and fowl (lines 61–75). In sequel, a general reference is made to Aten's creation of his manifold works with a specific mention of the footed creatures that move on the earth, and the winged creatures of the atmosphere (lines 79–82). So these variations in the cause for peroration, or celebration of the deities' creations diminish the case for the psalmist's dependence on the "Hymn to Aten."

Furthermore, in terms of the fourth parallel,[60] the statements on ships and marine creatures are somewhat similar, but in reverse order, and there are significant differences in nuance. In the case of the alleged biblical parallel, vv. 25–26, the psalmist first mentions the vastness of the sea teeming with the innumerable creatures of varying sizes, as an extension of YHWH's creativity attributed to his wisdom (v. 24). The ships and Leviathan appear in an adjunctive statement in illustration of the human and marine activities that occur in the sea that YHWH created. Whereas, in the "Hymn to Aten," the activities of ships and fish are mentioned in emphasis of the effects of Aten's illuminating rays, which enable this orderly function.

The fifth parallel[61] is also superficial. It is apparent that the reference to YHWH's provision of food (vv. 27–28) is an expression of his

---

59. Day, "Psalm 104," 215–16. As with other scholars, Day sees this as another separate (fourth) parallel pivoting on the reference to "ships" in both texts. Day also objects to any suggestions by biblical scholars to amend and read the term ships otherwise.

60. Day, "Psalm 104," 215.

61. Day, "Psalm 104," 217.

YHWH IN THE WIND AS CREATOR-KING

benevolent care to "all" the earthly and marine creatures (cf. vv. 25–28). But in the "Hymn to Aten" (lines 85–86), specific reference is made to setting people in lands and supplying their necessities, including food, with no implication of the same benevolence to the beasts, as Day suggests.[62]

In the sixth and final parallel,[63] as determined by Day, he notes that both deities are identified as the source of life and death. However, the statements on life and death in these two texts are in reverse order. Also of poignancy, are the differences on the significance of the deities' positioning on matters relating to life and death. It is Aten's rays that give life, and death encroaching at sunset. In contrast, and pertinent to the potency of YHWH in creation, is that YHWH's wind/breath (רוח) is the agency in giving life at creation (v. 30), but death occurs with "breath" (רוח) expunged. These distinct differences in details undermine the argument for the complete dependence of the psalmist on the "Hymn to Aten."

The Point of Departure in Nuance for Psalm 104

There are cosmogonic elements occurring in Ps 104 that are totally unparalleled in the Egyptian hymn,[64] but are more in keeping with the Babylonian Enuma Elish and, particularly, the Dogon myth of creation. Ps 104 presents creation in the mythological form of a *Chaoskampf*,[65] and parallels more closely with the Babylonian model and the Dogon creation myth.[66] As Anderson observed, Ps 104 uses the mythopoeic language of the *Chaoskampf* to describe how YHWH overcame chaos

---

62. Day, "Psalm 104," 217.

63. Day, "Psalm 104," 217. As a point of interest, although Day only sees six parallels between Ps 104 and this Egyptian hymn, it may be noted that Wilson previously cited seven parallels, later citing three more in addition. See Wilson, "Hymn," 324–28, 369–71.

64. Craigie, "Comparison," 14. Craigie notes that similarities with the "Hymn to Aten" are specifically cosmological and not cosmogonic.

65. Anderson, apud Eliade and Pettazzoni, also points out the concurrence of the *Chaoskampf* myth everywhere (though he does not see elements of this in the Genesis creation account), not only confined to the ANE traditions, thus making traces of the *Chaoskampf* myth conceivable within the Dogon myth of creation as its African counterpart. See Anderson "Introduction," 2–3, 12, 15. See also pp. 34–36 above.

66. Regarding the Dogon creation myth as an African version of a *Chaoskampf*, see p. 36.

to "depict the order of creation."⁶⁷ As in the Dogon creation myth, the mythopoeic language in Ps 104 delineates the creation of cosmic order out of chaos. This ordering and origination of the world is in keeping with wisdom⁶⁸ thought. Hence, in Ps 104:24 the poet/psalmist breaks out in adoration of the divine wisdom of the supreme creator manifested in cosmic order. YHWH is depicted with winds, and other meteorological forces in attendance, as he appears to subjugate the chaotic cosmic waters; thus, setting boundaries in establishing the earth.⁶⁹ The issue is not just that YHWH founded the world, but that there is emphasis on the display of power, and what is at stake in the maintenance of that order in both the cosmic and social realm.⁷⁰ So, here, too, the psalm involves the language characteristic of wisdom, which is not only concerned with the origin of the orderly universe but *creation continua*, that is, the creation activity in the present and the continual dependence of all creation on YHWH.⁷¹

We noted in the case of the god Amma that the wind is also his breath.⁷² As with Amma's wind whirling and swirling in the formation of the Dogon cosmos,⁷³ so also YHWH is associated with the creative power of the "wind(s)" (רוח) in the origination of an orderly world, and giving life, or breath⁷⁴ to all animate entities. With that depiction of YHWH, the mythopoeic language of Ps 104 expresses the origination of the cosmic order from chaos, the dependence of all creation on the creator—viewed as wisdom—and maintenance of that order.⁷⁵ Hence, the idea of YHWH appearing with the winds, in display of his power, is

---

67. Anderson, "Introduction," 12.

68. Anderson, "Introduction," 12–13; Weiser, *Psalms*, 667; Hermission, "Observations," 123–25. Hermission argued that Ps 104 comprehensively presents the wisdom concept of creation of purposeful ordering and continuous creative activity of the creator that is portrayed in Proverbs. In the same vein, Rad stated that Ps 104 reflects the same awareness of the world raised to orderliness by the wisdom concept as expressed and expanded in Job 28 and Prov 8:22–31 (see Rad, *Wisdom*, 155). On the idea of wisdom in creation as noted by Long in light of the Dogon creation myth, see p. 64 above.

69. Anderson, "Introduction," 13.

70. *Contra* Anderson, who sees the correspondence of YHWH's cosmic order with the social order in other psalms, but not in Ps 104 (Anderson, "Introduction," 10–11).

71. Anderson, "Introduction," 13–14.

72. See pp. 15, 29, 55.

73. See the mention of Amma as wind and the breath of the Nommo at the creation of the Dogon cosmos on pp. 18, 27–29.

74. Luyster, "Wind," 2.

75. Anderson, "Introduction," 12–14.

YHWH IN THE WIND AS CREATOR-KING

linked with the creation-out-of-chaos (*Chaoskampf*), wisdom, and judgment motifs. An analysis, and interpretation of Ps 104 as paradigmatic for other biblical texts, which combine similar motifs in the portrayal of YHWH as creator-king, is in order at this point.

Psalm 104—The Wind(s) as the Creative Agent(s)

It is evident from the introductory part of the psalm that the intention of the psalmist is to praise YHWH for his greatness. The psalmist is not so much concerned with expressing the order of events at creation as with portraying YHWH as the sole creator and sustainer of the orderly cosmos. In contrast with the Genesis account,[76] which presents a sequence of creative acts in six days, Ps 104 is more concerned with describing the origination and the state of created order as it mirrors YHWH's creativity and, consequently, depicts the dependence of all life upon its creator. The psalm, therefore, is oriented towards the nature of YHWH, his creativity and his preservation of the created order.

First and foremost, in this psalm, is the portrayal of YHWH's glory and majesty as they are revealed through phenomenal elements, with the "wind" as the most potent disclosure of his power. Here, the psalmist makes use of ideas and expressions that are often associated with the manifestation of YHWH, and the reverence imposed with it (Pss 29:2a; 96:9b). YHWH is said to be "clothed" (לבש) with "splendor and majesty" (הוד והדר, Ps 104:1c). However, the term "splendor and majesty" does not carry the literal meaning of royal regalia.[77] In Ps 96:6a, the term "splendor" (הדר, see Ps 29:4b) characterizes the presence of YHWH, and the reference to YHWH's "splendor and majesty" suggests the phenomenal winds depicting YHWH's grandiose appearance (Ps 104:1c; Job 40:9–10).

Other references in the Hebrew Bible show that the phrase "splendor and majesty" expresses the grandeur of YHWH's presence (Ps 96:6 [9; Ps 29:4; 1 Chr 16:27, 29; 2 Chr 20:21]). This phrase, on the one hand, is repeated almost verbatim in Job 40:10 (הוד והדר תלבש), appearing in a context emphasizing YHWH's self-disclosure through the power of his

---

76. See Levenson, *Creation*, 53–59; *contra* Humbert, "La relation"; Anderson, *From Creation*, 139, 217–19, who see parallels in the order of creation events.

77. The idea of "being clothed" (לבש) is only metaphorical. On the use of "clothe" (לבש) as a metaphor with abstract nouns in Hebrew, see chapter 4 and Ps 93—YHWH's wind over the waters.

strong arm (זרוע), a metonym for wind.⁷⁸ In this context, the whirlwind (v. 6) serves as a foil of YHWH's manifestation, and Job is challenged to thunder (רעם) with a voice (קול) like YHWH's and deck out himself not only with the "majesty and grandeur" (גאון וגבה), but also with the "splendor and majesty" (הוד והדר) that characterizes YHWH's appearance (v. 10; cf. Ps 104:1c).

In both Ps 104:6-7 and Job 40:9-10 the context shows YHWH's majesty experienced in a (whirl)wind accompanied by its roaring "loud sound"⁷⁹ (רעם/קול, Ps 104:7b; Job 40:9b). On the other hand, in Hab 3:3, Ps 148:13, and Job 37:22 the word "splendor" (הוד) relates to YHWH's appearance in the wind(s), as implied in these contexts. YHWH is said to march from the southern region with his winds causing the earth to shake, mountains to crumble, and nations to tremble (Hab 3:3, 6-7). The winds do his bidding (Ps 148:8b). YHWH's splendor emerges from the north, and the wind sweeps the skies clean (Job 37:21-22; see Job 26:13). Thus, the occurrence of the phrase "splendor and majesty" in Ps 104:1 suggests that the same phenomenal wind is implied. The parallel statement that "he [YHWH] covers himself with light⁸⁰ (אור) as with a garment" (v. 2) is also reflective of an aniconic representation of YHWH's radiant incandescence similar to Amma's luminous appearance.⁸¹

As established in chapter 1, the manifestation of light relates to the effulgence of YHWH, and is a component of YHWH's intrinsic nature (Isa 60:19c).⁸² The substantive אור and its verbal form also occur in contexts referring to YHWH's luminous appearance with the phenomenal elements. For instance, in Job 36:32; 37:3, 11, 15,⁸³ אור means lightning (Hab 3:11). In Pss 77:19[18] and 97:4 the verb אור in its *Hiphil* form

---

78. See pp. 40-42.

79. On the conflation of elements relating to Amma's appearance with (whirl)wind, see pp. 16-17.

80. Some scholars misinterpret YHWH's donning of light as the first act of creation paralleled in Gen 1:3. See Levenson, *Creation*, 55.

81. See p. 17.

82. In relation to the presence of light in Gen 1 before the creation of luminaries, see pp. 53-54.

83. In Job 37:15, אור occurs with a technical term הופיע often used in descriptions of the appearance of YHWH (Deut 33:2; Pss 50:2; 80:2[1]). As Barth noted in analysis of Deut 33:2, הופיע, meaning "shine forth," expresses phenomena that usually involve light. Barth observed that הופיע is not only used synonymously with זרח, meaning "light up," but also characterizes a visible appearance, or coming as implied by other verbs, בא and אתה, meaning "to come," and employed in the immediate context (v. 2). In Ps 50:2, the term הופיע correlates with בא (v. 3). In Ps 80:2[1] הופיע is parallel to הלך ("come") in v. 3[2] to relate the appeal for the appearance of YHWH. See Barth, "יפע," 222-23.

expresses the brilliance or numinous radiance caused by lightning at YHWH's disclosure with the natural elements. The lightning is also a component in the configuration of the image of YHWH, with the thunderous sound emerging from the "whirlwind"[84] (גלגל, Ps 77:19[18]), as described in the events alluding to the exodus in Ps 77. Therefore, the reference to YHWH "enveloped in light" (נאור) in Ps 76:5[4] is also illustrative of the luminous radiance imbedded with YHWH's wind(s), and the context further mentions YHWH's "rebuke/roar," (גערה, v. 7[6]; see Isa 50:2; 106:9) to denote the wind(s) drying up the Red Sea leading to the crossing on dry ground. The idea further illustrated in Ps 76:7[6] by the reference to "both horse and chariot lie still," is reminiscent of the events at the exodus, when YHWH unleashes his wind (Exod 14:21) on the waters that engulf the Egyptians and their chariotry (Exod 15:1, 10; Ps 106:9–11). These same numinous phenomenal elements are at play in Ps 104, as YHWH appears to vanquish the chaotic "waters" (מים, v. 6; see Gen 1:2).

Therefore, the mention of YHWH covered with light in Ps 104:2[85] describes nothing other than the effulgence associated with his appearance, as in the case of the "luminous motion"[86] of the god Amma at creation. In that view, the phrase "splendor and majesty," juxtaposed with the idea of donning light as a garment, describes the celestial splendor of YHWH (Ps 104:1c–2a) manifested in the winds. Thus, with the use of participles, tantamount to epithets, in the initial verses of this paean, the psalmist compliments YHWH who manifests his winds, appears "wrapped in light" (עטה אור); and by these winds "stretches out the heavens" (נטה שמים)[87] and "lays the foundations" (המקרה) of his celestial abode (vv. 2–3a).

---

84. BDB 166. Although Isa 17:13 denotes a simile of YHWH's enemies put to flight, it is instructive for translating גלגל as a phenomenon representing some form of wind, as the term appears here in collation with רוח (wind) and סופה (stormwind).

85. Aalen, "אור," 164. Aalen sees this verse as problematic. Even though he realizes that the noun אור and its synonym, נגה ("brightness," Hab 3:11; Ps 18:13[12]; Ezek 1:4, 27, 28), appear in theophanic texts, he objects to the idea that the word "light" in Ps 104:2 is associated with YHWH's theophany. Instead, he argues that the reference to "light" here should be considered as an attribute of YHWH.

86. See p. 17.

87. As discussed in the main in relation to other theophanic texts (see Jer 10:12=51:15; Job 9:8; 26:7), the creation of the heavens by means of his wind(s) is one other factor that proves YHWH's preeminence in contrast to idols (see Ps 96:5).

YHWH IN THE WIND(S)

The motifs of "stretching out the heavens" and "creating" or "founding" the earth are often connected in texts that emphasize the nature and power of YHWH as creator,[88] and the wind(s) as the creative agent is implied.[89] In assertion of YHWH as the maker, Deutero-Isaiah draws from the *Chaoskampf* myth, and shows a pale form of this tradition. Thus, in Isa 51 the correlation of the theme on YHWH stretching out the heavens, laying the foundations of the earth (v. 13), and stirring the sea with his winds and making its waves roar, is identifiable (vv. 15–16), and relates YHWH's subjugation of the forces of primordial chaos. Similarly, the same correlation of "stretching the north" from the void, hanging the earth from nothing (Job 26:7), quieting the sea with his wind, shattering the forces of chaos (v. 12), piercing the fleeing serpent, and making the heavens fair (v. 13), has the same import of a cosmogony deriving from the wind as YHWH's creative agent. It is apparent that the formula "he who stretches out the heavens" is not isolated in Ps 104:2, and, as Habel notes,[90] functions to identify YHWH as the creator who establishes the heavens like his tent whence he emerges in luminous splendor to create the earth.

In Ps 104, therefore, YHWH's establishment of his heavenly abode serves not only as the backdrop for his emergence and where the winds originate, but also shows YHWH's exclusive authority to create and employ the winds[91] for his mobility and to subdue the primal chaotic waters

88. Habel notices that Deutero-Isaiah incorporates the motif of "stretching out the heavens" seven times (Isa 40:22; 42:5; 44:24; 45:12; 48:13; 51:13, 16) and correlates it with the establishment of the earth in developing the theme of salvation. He notes further that the power of YHWH as creator is the same power at work to redeem his people. See Habel, "He Who Stretches Out," 417–21.

89. In each of the texts identified by Habel with the theme of stretching the heavens and founding the earth, there is mention of the wind in the context. In Isa 40, the wind causes the grass to fade and the flowers wither (v. 24), and YHWH himself metes out the wind (v. 13). It appears in Isa 42:5, where the analogous pairing of "stretching the heavens" and "creating the earth" is associated with giving breath to the humans in it, or walking in (/inhabiting) it (see Isa 45:12, 18). This evokes the idea of the wind as a creative agent, giving breath to animate entities (see the idea of the four winds of heaven giving breath to dead bones [Ezek 37:9]). YHWH alone is said to stretch both the heavens and spread out the earth (Isa 44:24), and the wind is said to dry up the rivers and the deep (v. 27). Isa 45:12 refers to YHWH's hands, that is personification of the wind(s), as the agency at the creation of the heavens (48:13; 51:13bc, 16cd). See pp. 40–42.

90. Habel, "He Who Stretches Out," 422–23.

91. This idea is paralleled in the Enuma Elish with Marduk, who creates (*banû*) all the different types of winds that he employs, as though ammunition, on his mission to exterminate Tiamat (EE IV:45–50). But sharing more closely with the idea in Ps 104:2

(vv. 6–8), in order to establish the earth (vv. 5, 9). Here, YHWH is depicted as the one "who sets clouds (as) his chariot" (הַשָּׂם־עָבִים רְכוּבוֹ), "who walks on the wings of the wind" (הַמְהַלֵּךְ עַל־כַּנְפֵי־רוּחַ, cf. Ps 18:11[10] b) and "makes/creates[92] (עֹשֶׂה) the winds[93] (רוּחוֹת) [as] his messengers" and "flaming fire [as] his ministers" (Ps 104:3b–4). The concurrence of wind and fire here also recalls the morphology of the whirling deity Amma.[94] However, in keeping with other Hebrew texts expressing YHWH's commission of atmospheric paraphernalia (Pss 147:15–18; 148:8; Job 37:1–13), here too, the winds, accompanied with flaming fire,[95] are at YHWH's command to do his bidding (Ps 104:4, 7). In this case, the totality of YHWH's control of the winds takes precedence, in close view of YHWH's depiction as the one "who walks on the wings of the wind," and makes the winds his messengers. But, what is the significance of the psalmist's reference to YHWH walking "on the wings of the wind"? Can winds have wings? Noegel's study[96] on the meaning and function of winged hybrid creatures in the ANE made a conceptual connection between winds, wings and cardinal directions,[97] and sheds light on the use of the term "wings of the wind" in the biblical tradition.

Noegel noted the association of winds and wings in Mesopotamian, Egyptian and biblical texts[98] as deriving from older mythological connections in which the four winds were identified with hybrid creatures

---

in terms of the provenance of the wind(s) is the Egyptian god Amun, who embodies the four winds that came from the four openings in the sky and fertilized the egg (Smith, *Carlsberg*, 62–63); see Amma who is wind himself from whom all of the Dogon cosmos emerges from the egg.

92. For the dual meaning of עשׂה, "do, make/create," see Ringgren, "עָשָׂה," 387–90.

93. As in the case of Marduk, YHWH's power to create and employ the winds (see Amos 4:13) bodes well with the idea of mustering the winds for his own purposes.

94. See p. 14, 14n72 above.

95. See pp. 67–68 above.

96. Noegel, "Wings," 16–20.

97. In fact, Noegel, following Neumann, clarified that in Mesopotamia the cardinal points are not geographic localities but actually represented by the winds: eastwind, westwind, northwind, and southwind (Noegel, "Wings," 16n8).

98. Noegel noticed Hos 4:19a as a perfect biblical example showing cardinal winds associated with wings: "A wind has bound her ([Ephraim, i.e., Northern] Israel) in its wings" (Noegel, "Wings," 20). This verse appears in a context where Hosea condemns male shrine prostitution. Perhaps this statement forebodes the punishment to befall the Israelites, as they will be swept away by the wind (רוּחַ, Ezek 5:10; 12:14) and abased for their shameful sacrifices (Hos 4:19b).

or four mythological beings,[99] and perhaps dating to the third millennium BCE. In Mesopotamian texts, winds are associated with wings. For instance, Gudea relates the northwind as a man with enormous wings,[100] and Adapa torments the southwind with the warning that he would break its wing.[101] In a prophetic oracle to Esarhaddon, Ištar of Arbela rhetorically issues the words of encouragement to the king in divine warfare, and refers to the enemies as wind with wing(s): "What wind has risen against you, whose wing I have not broken?"[102]

On the other hand, as Noegel notes, in the early *Pyramid Texts* of ancient Egypt, the four winds are personified as hybrid creatures with wings, and represent the four cardinal directions.[103] This association of winds with wings is also seen in analogies relating to the flapping of birds to generate winds,[104] as testified in an Egyptian myth depicting a divine falcon beating its wings to create the four winds.[105] In keeping with this avian connection with the wind, Shu, god of air and wind, is depicted with a feather on his head. Also, apropos is the symbolism associated with the appearance of Shu, which represents the four pillars of heaven mounted on the four corners of the earth, from which the four winds are said to originate.[106] Hence, it is not surprising that in the Egyptian *Coffin Texts* the four winds are at the command of Shu, who is declared

---

99. Noegel, "Wings," 15–16; Wiggermann, "Four Winds," 127–29, 133. Wiggermann identifies the four mythological representations of the wind as the southwind, depicted as feminine, and the other three—northwind, eastwind, and westwind—as masculine (Wiggermann, "Four Winds," 127). But Wiggermann also noted at variance that the north and southwinds are considered as feminine, and the east and westwinds as masculine (127n16).

100. Noegel, "Wings," 16; Wiggermann, "Four Winds," 129.

101. Noegel, "Wings," 16.

102. Parpola, *Assyrian Prophecies*, 4; Jong, *Isaiah*, 266.

103. Noegel, "Wings," 17.

104. Noegel, "Wings," 18; Wilkinson, "Horus Names," 98–104; Goedicke, *Unity and Diversity*, 205–6. Goedicke notes the dynamism expressed by Horus traversing the sky.

105. Noegel, "Wings," 18.

106. Noegel, "Wings," 19; Smith, *Carlsberg*, 57, 62–63. Smith, discussing the personification of the Egyptian god Amun and his association with the four winds, also mentions Amun as sharing the same provenance as the winds that emerge from the four openings in the sky. The idea of four winds associated with the heavens, and as its origin, is well attested in some biblical texts. YHWH claims to bring the "four winds" from the four ends of the heavens to scatter the people of Elam (Jer 49:36; cf. Zech 2:6; 6:5), and in Ezek 37:9 the "four winds" are called upon to bring the "breath" of life to revivify the valley of dry bones.

YHWH IN THE WIND AS CREATOR-KING

as the god of wind and light.¹⁰⁷ The latter also recalls the "luminous motion" of Amma.¹⁰⁸ This depiction further sheds light on the concurrence of wind(s) and light in attendance of YHWH's appearance presumably from the heavenly abode that he created, as described in Ps 104:2–3.

At any rate, in both Mesopotamian and Egyptian contexts, the winds are involved in the creation of the universe, as seen when Marduk deploys the winds¹⁰⁹ to vanquish Tiamat, and in the Egyptian context when the four winds unite to become one wind in the creation of heaven and earth.¹¹⁰ Nevertheless, of relevance here is that in both the Mesopotamian and Egyptian cosmogonies the winds form the divine primal force for creative order. Similarly, the Hebrew tradition attests the same creative concept of the agency of wind through use of terms determinative for wind.

The idea of "wings of the wind" in Ps 104 is made clear by Noegel's observation on the association of ANE hybrid creatures with wings, wind, and cardinal directions.¹¹¹ The artistic depictions of the hybrid creatures show variations in the number of wings and iconographic features. These hybrid creatures range from having two to six wings with anthropomorphic, theriomorphic, or avian faces, depending on the cosmological import intended to be conveyed.¹¹² Undoubtedly, as Noegel observed, the "cherub" (כרוב) is identifiable as a biblical representation and conceptual parallel of these winged hybrid creatures.¹¹³ Although there is no mention of wings on the cherub in Ps 18:11[10]a=2 Sam 22:11a, or cherubim in Gen 3:24 (1 Sam 4:4; Pss 80:2[1]; 99:1), there is the implication that the cherub possesses wings, as YHWH is said to "fly" (יעף) in

---

107. Here, too, Shu is attested as claiming the storm as his liquid and the tempest as his outpouring. See Noegel, "Wings," 18; cf. Smith, *Carlsberg*, 58.

108. See p. 17.

109. In EE IV:99 Marduk is described as using the raging winds (šārē) to distend Tiamat's belly. It is apparent that the Israelite tradition reflects similar use of winds (Isa 17:13; Ps 83:16[15]) and storm/(whirl)winds (שערה/סערה/סערה) in its depiction of YHWH's theophany to annihilate the wicked (Jer 23:19–20=30:23–24; Amos 1:14; Nah 1:3; Zech 7:14; see Prov 10:25a). On YHWH's *Deus praesens* in the whirlwind, see Mettinger, *Search of God*, 185–86.

110. Noegel, "Wings," 37; Smith, *Carlsberg*, 62.

111. In view of the panoply of YHWH's appearance in Ezek 1, see Wright, *Message*, 48. However, the focus of this discussion is more on the identity of the wings with wind(s) than relational to the four cardinal directions.

112. Noegel attributes these variations to different periods and the related cosmic aspect in the ANE. See Noegel, "Wings," 23n49, 28–40.

113. Noegel, "Wings," 20–21; cf. Wood, *Of Wings*, 25, 31, 99, 162, 175.

81

YHWH IN THE WIND(S)

Ps 18:11[10]aβ=2 Sam 22:11aβ. The idea resonates with other biblical texts that mention wings in connection with the cherubim (Exod 25:20; 37:7-9; 1 Kgs 6:23-27; Ezek 10:5, 8, 16, 18, 20-22[114] [see 1:4-28]; 2 Chr 3:10-13). At any rate, as noted by Noegel, the iconographic significance of the cherub/cherubim and its wings is its representation of the winds, in keeping with the ANE depictions of winged hybrid creatures.[115] Therefore, Ps 18:11[10](=2 Sam 22:11) employs *hendiadys*,[116] or appositional synonyms, that are syndetic terms, in order to amplify YHWH's cosmic potency to appear with the wind(s): He rode on the "cherub" (="wind"), and he flew; and he soared[117] on the "wings of the wind" (ירכב על־כרוב ויעף וידא על־כנפי־רוח). This representation depicts YHWH coasting and whirling the winds as if with outstretched wings. In fact, the image of a deity riding the winds is well substantiated in the *Atrahasis* epic, which cites the storm god Adad riding the winds as his mules.[118] Hence, this nuance in Ps 18:11[10] has an implication on the meaning of the same term, "wings of the wind" in Ps 104, in expression of YHWH in charge of the brooding winds at the primal creative event (Gen 1:2).[119]

Undoubtedly, the psalmist is consistent in the use of images relating to YHWH's demonstration of mastery over the cosmic elements. As already suggested, the term "rebuke" (גערה, Ps 104:7a) though a synergistic for winds,[120] also denotes an anthropopathic imagery of YHWH's

---

114. The "beings" (החיות) Ezekiel sees in the vision described in Ezek 1:4-28 are identified with the "cherubim" (כרובים) in 10:20-22. As Noegel notes, the visions in Ezekiel are a classic example of the association of wings with the wind, cardinal directions, and, undoubtedly, anthropomorphic, theriomorphic, and avian characteristics (Ezek 1:4-24; 10:9-22). Particularly in Ezek 1:4-24 the four "winged" living creatures (חיות, v. 5)—presumably cherubim (10:20-22)—move with the wind (1:20) towards the four cardinal directions (v. 17). Therefore, it is not coincidental that Ezekiel envisions YHWH's appearance associated with the cherub/cherubim as graphic representations of wind, in a context where the four "winds" (רוחות) are invoked to bring "breath" (רוח) to dead bones (Ezek 37:1-9). See Noegel, "Wings," 21.

115. Noegel, "Wings," 21-22 (see also 15n1, 37-39); Greenberg, *Ezekiel*, 51-58.

116. On the explanation of the use of appositional synonyms that are syndetic in discussion on appositional hendiadys in the Hebrew Bible, see Lillas-Schuil, "Survey," 82-93; Arnold and Choi, *Guide*, 148, 199.

117. BDB 178 translates the root דאה as "fly swiftly" or "dart," from which this term is derived.

118. Noegel, "Wings," 26.

119. See pp. 46-47, 49-51 above.

120. The concurrence of גערה and רוח was previously discussed in chapter 1 (49-51), which suggested that these terms are associated with the manifestation of YHWH and represent some form of winds based on the occurrences in the Hebrew tradition.

expulsion of breath, which is the wind directed against the chaotic waters. Caquot observed that the manifestation of the גערה is barely distinct from those elements that accompany a storm[121] (cf. Ps 18:16[15]). Therefore, Caquot sees similarities with the same occurrence of phenomena in the parallelism of גערה and "thunder" in Ps 104:7. Nevertheless, the close relation of גערה with the demonstration of YHWH's power and anger at the drying of the sea and rivers (Isa 50:2; Nah 1:3-4) by the wind(s) shows that the manifestation of YHWH with the same phenomenal winds is not in question.[122] Thus, the term "rebuke" in Ps 104:7a also relates the roar of the "winds" as the embodiment of YHWH, or ministers (Pss 148:8b; Job 37:21) at YHWH's commission to repel the chaotic waters (Ps 104:7a; see Isa 50:2; Ps 106:9).[123] This portrayal of YHWH employing the cosmic elements is consistent with, and authenticates, his phenomenal repelling of the waters of chaos by his winds with its accompanying sonorous or "loud sound"[124] (קול רעם, Ps 104:7b).

The use of the verbs "flee" (נוס) and "take to flight" (חפז) both suggest commotion, and denote a pale reflection of a cosmogonic battle, in the form of a *Chaoskampf* in Ps 104:7. The verb חפז, when used with animate subjects, often conveys the meaning of haste or hurried flight owing to panic (2 Sam 4:4; 2 Kgs 7:15; Ps 48:6[5]). In a sense, then, the occurrence of חפז ("take to flight") in parallel with[125] נוס ("flee") expresses the disorderly flow of the waters. This image presents a personification of the waters rising and falling helter-skelter in reaction to YHWH's roaring winds. The reference to the waters "going up"[126] (עלה) the mountains and

---

121. Caquot, "גער," 51.

122. Caquot, "גער," 51.

123. It is significant that in both texts, Isa 50:2 and Ps 106:9 (see Nah 1:4), YHWH's "rebuke," which is synonymous with the winds, is the mechanism by which the sea [rivers turn to desert] and Red Sea, respectively, are dried up (Isa 51:10; Exod 14:21).

124. Regarding the loud sound characterizing the whirling of god Amma, see pp. 16–17, 48–49 above.

125. If the *nun paragogicum* (ון-) is peculiar to older forms of verbs (Waltke and O'Connor, *Introduction*, 347), then Ps 104 is an early Hebrew psalm. It is in v. 7, describing the impact of YHWH's winds on the waters, that the paragogic nun makes its first appearance. There are more verses in Ps 104 that retain this feature (vv. 9, 10b, 22, 26a, 27a, 28, 29, 30a). On the other hand, Kautzsch notes that the occurrence of this morphological phenomenon in verbal forms expresses marked emphasis (Kautzsch, *Gesenius*, 128, 47m).

126. This verb is also used with natural phenomena: mist going up from the earth (Gen 2:6), waters going up from the north (Jer 47:2), or as a metaphor of Egypt rising like the Nile (Jer 46:7-8), and land compared to the rising of the Nile (Amos 8:8; 9:5).

YHWH IN THE WIND(S)

"flowing down"[127] (ירד, v. 8) the valleys, figuratively shows the waters[128] blown and tossed up by YHWH's winds (see Ps 107:25–26a). Thus, the waters move pell-mell to the places assigned for them. YHWH directs the springs to flow in the valleys and to go between mountains (Ps 104:10). Consequently, YHWH marks out the confines for the waters, so that they will not return to cover the earth (v. 9).[129] This control of the chaotic waters (see Ps 93:3–4) results in the establishment of the earth; it is firmly secured on its foundation and cannot be moved (Ps 104:5; see Pss 93:1–2; 96:10). The psalmist understands the creation of the earth in terms of the ancient *Chaoskampf* in establishing a cosmogony, and relates it to fit the pattern of creation-out-of-chaos.[130]

The psalmist's portrayal of cosmic order in the rest of the psalm further conforms to the mythic pattern at many points, but also shows the winds deployed for its functionality. In keeping with the mythical tradition of victory over chaos,[131] whereby the subdued waters are assigned a purposeful function, the psalmist explores the theme of divine providence and sustenance. The confined waters of chaos,[132] that YHWH turns into subterranean waters and springs (Ps 74:15a), become a source of life for the beasts and birds. The springs deriving from the chaotic waters give drink to the beasts of the field, and the volant creatures dwell by them (Ps 104:11–12). In addition, the reference to YHWH sending rain from his celestial residence (v. 13a) alludes to the idea of YHWH "riding on the wings of the winds," that is, coasting with the winds as though with outstretched wings and scattering the rain-bearing clouds (Ps 135:7; Job 36:28–29; Jer 10:13), in order to water the trees and mountains. The earth is nurtured by these creative works (Ps 104:13b–16). The trees planted by YHWH become a domain for the birds (v. 17). The mountains that

127. In Deut 9:21 this verb also expresses the idea of a stream flowing down the mountain. See also waters flowing downstream in Josh 3:13; Ezek 47:8b.

128. Cf. Sutcliffe, "Note," 179. We are to read "waters" as the subject of the verbs in v. 8a as there is gender agreement with the masculine plural forms used. There is a suggestion to read "mountains" and "valleys" as the subjects, but there is lack of congruence, with the latter being a feminine substantive. Moreover, the idea of confinement in the parallel phrase (v. 8b) suits the plight of the waters as substantiated by a similar case in the Marduk epic (EE IV:140): he fixed a crossbar, posted guards and commanded them not to let Tiamat's waters escape.

129. Jer 5:22; Ps 148:6; Job 7:12; 38:8–10; Prov 8:29 echo this idea of YHWH setting a limit on the cosmic waters.

130. On *Chaoskampf* and creation-out-of-chaos in Gen 1:2, see pp. 34–36.

131. Gunkel, *Schöpfung*, 91–99.

132. See Weiser, *Psalms*, 668; Kraus, *Psalms 60–150*, 300.

YHWH uncovers from the waters of chaos (v. 6b; v. 8) are fructified by water and become a natural habitat for his creatures (v. 18).

In sequel to this description of YHWH's formation of an orderly cosmos, the psalmist mentions how YHWH stations the sun and moon in order to govern the orderly cycles of life on earth (vv. 19–23; see Jer 31:35ab): at night the beasts prowl in search of food (Ps 104:20-21), and when the sun rises man goes out to his labor (v. 23). Perhaps the emphasis on the regularity of the sun and moon marking the day, night and seasons, respectively, is a polemical statement intended to show YHWH's control as creator of the luminaries (Ps 74:16; cf. 19:5b–6 [4b–5]).[133] Nonetheless, with a profound sense of awe at YHWH's creation, providence and sustenance, the psalmist understands that this wind-generated cosmic order bears witness to divine wisdom.

As the psalmist proclaims, the manifold works of YHWH on earth display his wisdom[134] (Ps 104:24; cf. EE VII:116–17). Undoubtedly, the comprehensive sounding "all of them" (כלם),[135] implies YHWH's creations in the nautical realm, the "sea" (ים) and "Leviathan" (לויתן), and also points to the skill and craftsmanship of the sovereign author of all life-forms. The "sea," and "Leviathan"—which in ancient mythology are symbolic of chaos (Ps 74:13–14; Job 7:12)—are depicted as part of YHWH's design. The psalmist here employs satire to depict Leviathan as an object of YHWH's handiwork frolicking in the sea (Ps 104:26b), and, perhaps, as YHWH's plaything (Job 40:29[41:5]). In Job 40–41, Leviathan is described in sequel to Behemoth, as the first of YHWH's primeval works, though Behemoth as a powerful beast is put under control by the

---

133. From that perspective, the biblical Hebrew tradition vehemently condemned the worship of heavenly bodies with the claim that YHWH created them (see Deut 4:19; 17:3; cf. 2 Kgs 23:5; Isa 47:13; Jer 10:2; Dan 4:7; Amos 5:8a).

134. Marduk is described as [the] "sage" of the gods (EE IV:93), who creates ingenious things upon his battle with Tiamat. Hence, Marduk is upheld as profound in wisdom (EE VII:116–117). It is apparent in both contexts of biblical Hebrew and Enuma Elish, that wisdom, as an element, is integral with both cosmogonies (Ps 104:24; see Job 38:1–6; EE VII:104, 116–117, respectively). However, though the term wisdom is not specifically used in the narrative of the Dogon creation myth, Griaule and Dieterlen perceived wisdom in the consistency of thought and development of the Dogon wisdom in the Dogon society's basing all the aspects of life and social institutions on the cosmogony in all its "phases and permutations" (Griaule and Dieterlen, *Pale Fox*, 15). Regarding Long's idea, see p. 64.

135. The collective word כל also refers to all of creation in Jer 10:16=51:19 and Ps 146:6.

sword (Job 40:19).¹³⁶ There is no mention of Leviathan disrupting the order of YHWH's creation, but the divine discourse in Job rhetorically alludes to YHWH imposing his dominion over this primeval monster. Just like Behemoth, Leviathan is subjected to YHWH's authority at creation, as part of YHWH's primordial acts (40:25–32[41:1–8]). The idea of YHWH subduing Leviathan at the establishment of the cosmic order, alluded to in the rhetorical statements of this divine discourse, not only parallels the sea as a symbol of chaos in Job 38:8–10, and no less in Ps 104:6–7, but recalls Leviathan as a primeval dragon of chaos, as in other biblical Hebrew texts, a point to return to later.

However, Leviathan, as a mythological dragon of chaos, seems to be stripped of its fearsomeness in Ps 104:26 to show that its strength is no match to YHWH,¹³⁷ who, as the creator, subdues it into an acquiescent creature (Job 40:25–26[41:1–2]; 41:1–2[9–10]). Thus, Leviathan's presence in Ps 104:26b among the sea creatures testifies to YHWH's creation of wisdom under his sovereignty. All the living creatures depend on YHWH's providence and are sustained by his continual presence. They look up to YHWH for their food (vv. 27–28). When YHWH hides his face¹³⁸—which is symbolic of the withdrawal of his countenance and presence—all the animate beings are in dismay, and no longer have his life-giving "breath" (רוח). They return to dust (v. 29). But, when YHWH gives them his "breath,"¹³⁹ they are created and renewed (v. 30).

The hark back to creation here also means that at issue is the appearance of YHWH with the creative winds as the source of life-giving force. With these statements, the psalmist expresses the principle of the passing away and coming to life of all animate things through YHWH's continual creative power. In essence, the psalmist emphasizes that all life revolves around YHWH, who orders and sustains creation. Hence, the psalmist deploys the poetic device of *inclusio* to link up the beginning

136. Ansell, "Fantastic Beasts," 109.

137. Kwakkel, "Monster," 87.

138. The idea of YHWH hiding his face is often taken as a sign of divine disfavor (Pss 13:2[1]; 30:8[7]; 44:25[24]; 88:15[14]). By contrast, the idea of YHWH showing his face, or making it shine as in the Aaronic benediction (Num 6:24–26), expresses his presence. This means that deliverance and blessings are assured (Pss 4:7[6]; 31:17[16]; 67:2[1]; 80:4[3], 8[7], 20[9]; 119:135).

139. Gen 2:7; Num 16:22; Job 12:10; 34:14–15. Undoubtedly, in his polemical statement against the worship of idols, Jeremiah intended to emphasize that idols lack this life-giving force, רוח (Jer 10:14b). It is, therefore, futile to depend on idols (see below, Jer 10:14–15=51:17–18).

of the psalm with the end by using the same term רוח—wind/breath—to amplify the dynamism of YHWH's creative winds, and how he creates and animates nature, and sustains all creation. The psalmist shows his ingenuity in expressing awe on YHWH as the creator with this play on words and tenor of the term רוח. With his רוח—wind—YHWH creates an orderly and functional cosmos, and with his רוח—breath—YHWH gives life[140] and sustains all animate things. Here, too, the psalmist incorporates the dialectical opposition between life and death. Hence, if YHWH hides his face, or countenance, all creation sets into quietus without his life-giving wind/breath (רוח).

YHWH's Creative Winds vis-à-vis the Destruction of the Wicked in Psalm 104 as Paradigm

In concluding Psalm 104, the psalmist expresses the wish that the "glory" (כבוד) of YHWH, which is manifested through his works (v. 31; Pss 19:2–5[1–4a]; 97:6), may endure forever. He, therefore, extols YHWH and bids him to rejoice in his creative works. Though the psalmist discerns the purposeful function of YHWH's created order, at the same time he shows how creation is at YHWH's disposal. He restates the idea of theophany in reverse form: YHWH who appears with the winds, accompanied by other phenomenal elements to establish the earth on its foundations, and to confine the waters of chaos, is also "the one who looks"[141] (המביט, cf. Job 28:24) to the earth and causes it to tremble, and touches the mountains and they smoke[142] (Pss 104:32; 144:5; cf. Amos 9:5).

As in the case of the wind-deity Amma, who has the potency to raze his work at will by his fire,[143] so, in this Hebrew psalm is a similar implication. The psalmist's intention is to show that the cosmos is not independent of YHWH's sovereign will. Thus, YHWH's blustery and fiery wind causes the earth to tremble, and his fire (Ps 104:4) causes the mountains to smolder. The cosmic order is susceptible to a return to chaos. With this awareness of YHWH's governance of the cosmos, the

---

140. See Job 33:4; Lévêque, "Argument," 282.

141. Again, the psalmist resumes predicative participles as in other passages that extol YHWH as creator in theophanic language. See Jer 10:12–13=51:15–16; Amos 4:13; 5:8–9; 9:5–6.

142. The idea of YHWH's disclosure causing the earth to tremble and the mountains to smoke replicates his appearance with similar effects at the exodus (Exod 19:18).

143. See 14n72.

psalmist possibly views the continuity of the created order as expressing the creator's faithfulness. Thus, in acknowledgement of YHWH's glory displayed in the created order, the psalmist vows to honor YHWH throughout his life (v. 33), and to act in accordance with YHWH's purpose (v. 34). Again he alludes to "wisdom." Intrinsic in this response of praise is an expression of reverential fear,[144] and trust, and a submission to YHWH's lordship as creator. This reverential trust is characteristic of the conventional principle represented by "the fear of the lord" (יראת אדני) in the sapiential traditions (see Job 28:28; Prov 1:7; 9:10). Also, in accordance with the intended harmony of the created order, the psalmist petitions for the "wicked"[145] or the "sinners" to be annihilated (v. 35).[146]

Although the psalmist does not suggest how the wicked should be blotted out, an answer may be found in the divine discourse in Job 40:1–10. In response to Job's accusation that the wicked are allowed to prosper, YHWH does not give a definitive response. Instead, he challenges Job as to whether he has a "strong arm" like his, or can thunder with his "voice" in an outburst of anger and fury, in order to "scatter" and crush the haughty and the wicked (Job 40:9–13). As implied by the rhetorical statements in this text, YHWH, with his "arm" (v. 9; see Isa 50:2–3; 51:9–10), depicting the wind(s)[147] and accompanied by the sonorous[148] sound, unleashes his wrath against the insolent. As noted in the previous chapter, Isa 30:30 is instructive in showing the wind, in collation with other phenomenal elements, as symbolic of the punitive arm of YHWH. He shows impartiality in his exercise of justice in relation to the

---

144. Crenshaw defines "fear of the lord" as a distinctive feature in theological wisdom indicating religious devotion. As he states, this implies the vital essence of a relationship with the creator (Crenshaw, *OT Wisdom*, 85). It is apparent in the biblical Hebrew tradition, however, that the expression of reverential fear is also in keeping with the intended response from the worshipers at YHWH's theophany (Exod 20:18–20; 1 Sam 12:13–18).

145. *Contra* Buttenwieser, who sees the idea of the wicked as foreign to the theme of the whole psalm. Instead, he sees the idea as belonging to Ps 103. See Buttenwieser, *Psalms*, 158.

146. This idea of vanquishing the wicked, or any power not compliant with the created order, is not unfamiliar to creation traditions. Statements in praise of Marduk's cosmological activities illustrate this view. Marduk is acclaimed with vanquishing the evil doers, disobedient, or wicked, and silencing the rebellious by frustrating their plans and scattering them to the winds (EE VII:34, 36, 38, 41, 44–45). See Dalley, *Myths*, 269; Lambert, "Mesopotamian," 56; *Babylonian*, 127.

147. On the arm as synecdoche, or metonymy for wind, see pp. 41–42 above.

148. Regarding god Amma, see p. 17.

wicked (Pss 18:27–28[26–27]; 68:2–3[1–2]; 97:2a–3, 10; Hab 3:13–14). Therefore, the psalmist expresses the desire for the earth to be purged of sinners and the wicked (Ps 104:35), who represent "chaos" and threaten the created order. In essence, the psalmist wishes YHWH to shatter the wicked, and calls for YHWH to banish the insolent to the destructive winds in a similar way YHWH vanquished primal chaos (Isa 17:12–13; Isa 29:5–6; Jer 4:11–13).

Undoubtedly, the poet in Ps 104 combines motifs familiar from other ancient traditions in order to enrich the portrayal of the Israelite monotheistic idea of YHWH as the sovereign creator. Motifs from the mythological tradition of the *Chaoskampf* shine through: the wielding of wind(s) over the chaotic waters and, ultimately, the creation of order is expressed as a function of wisdom. Cosmic order, therefore, is established and is sustained by the deity's acts of wisdom. The will to follow the design of the sovereign creator is inculcated by reverential "fear." By contrast, any dissidence about the creator's design disrupts the created order, and is equivalent to returning creation to primeval chaos. Therefore, the profound wisdom and power of YHWH at creation, manifested through the phenomenal winds (Ps 104:1–4), are also reactivated in order to restore order in the mundane realm, as the subsequent discussion on wisdom and prophetic literature will show. Although there is no uniformity in the language used to describe YHWH's disclosure in the selected texts, the commonality is in the praise of YHWH as the sovereign creator at primal creation, and whose continual appearance in destruction of forces inimical to his cosmic order is featured by means of his phenomenal winds.

CREATION BY THE WINDS AS YHWH'S ACT OF WISDOM IN THE BOOK OF JOB AND TRENDSETTER FOR DIVINE JUSTICE

YHWH in the Wind at "Creation" and "Destruction" in Job 9:4–10

The first two hymns, Job 9:4–10[149] and 26:7–14, lauding the greatness of YHWH[150] as creator, appear in discourses that the poet attributes to Job.

---

149. On the literary structure of Job 9, Habel (*Book of Job*, 189–95) and Hartley (*Book of Job*, 165–66) point out that this hymn is framed with material characteristic of the *rîb* (lawsuit) pattern and lamentation genre. See also Vicchio, *Book of Job*, 82.

150. Even though the poet of Job uses other names—*El, Eloah, Shadday*—for YHWH, the latter will be retained here for consistency. The name YHWH, however,

YHWH IN THE WIND(S)

In a broader context, these texts are Job's rejoinder in response to undeserved suffering, especially in view of the traditional OT teaching on theodicy, which implies that righteousness procures prosperity, and that wickedness incurs suffering. Job attempts to arraign YHWH for injustice (9:3). But Job realizes that in a contest of strength he cannot challenge God, which evokes the hymn of praise (vv. 4–10). As a result of the delayed response from YHWH, Job states his case and echoes the psalms of lament (vv. 22–26). In this case, Job, who defends his innocence, accuses YHWH of inflicting unlawful suffering and sees himself denied justice (vv. 20–21; see 34:5–6). According to Job, the justice of YHWH has become a paradox; the "blameless" (תם) and the "wicked" (רשע) are both destroyed (9:22). Yet, in all this, Job is aware that YHWH is "wise of mind" (חכם לבב) and "mighty in strength" (אמיץ כח, v. 4a). Thus, Job realizes that it is impossible to contend with YHWH and remain sound or unscathed (v. 4b), because YHWH possesses profound wisdom and power. With this recognition, that in a contest of strength YHWH prevails, Job resorts to praise of YHWH for his might displayed in creation.

It is apparent in Job 9:5–13 that the poet draws imagery from the theophanic tradition to describe the invincible power of YHWH demonstrated in cosmic phenomena. Here, as in Ps 104, the poet expresses YHWH's majesty with epithets deriving from his activities effected by his phenomenal winds in creation: "Who removes" (מעתיק) mountains in his anger and turns them over (הפכם, Job 9:5), and "who shakes" (מרגיז)[151] the "pillars of the earth" and causes them to shudder (יתפלצון, v. 6). Undoubtedly, the poet here points out the effects of the wind at the source from which the winds originate.[152] Although the poet uses unusual verbs and a *hapax legomenon* (פלץ) to express the effects of YHWH's powerful winds on nature, the idea of mountains convulsing and the earth trembling is often noted for the impact of YHWH's self-disclosure, as described in texts where the effects of the (whirl)winds accompanied by other natural phenomena are not in question (Ps 77:19[18]; Nah 1:3–5;

---

occurs in contexts mentioning his appearance in the (whirl)winds (Job 38:1; 40:6), as YHWH's *modus operandi*.

151. The verb רגז, from which the participle מרגיז is derived, occurs in Hab 3:7 as *Qal* imperfect with the paragogic nun, but Job 9:6 retains that form of the verbal ending in the second stich. However, in the other texts where רגז occurs it also describes the effects of YHWH's phenomenal appearance. The same verb is used to describe the shaking of the tents of Cushan (Hab 3:7), the foundations of the mountains (Ps 18:8[7]), the deeps and the earth (Ps 77:17[16], 19[18]).

152. See p. 80.

cf. Isa 5:25 [hand=wind]; Ps 114:4). Moreover, as Job states, YHWH is "the one who commands" (האמר, cf. Ps 68:12[11]) the sun not to rise and seals up the stars (Job 9:7). With his "winds" YHWH scuds the clouds to overshadow the luminaries. However, that the concealing of the sun and the stars in Job 9:7 (see Isa 24:21–23)[153] allude to the effect of the winds, is supported by the occurrence of similar meteorological elements in Ps 18:11–13[10–12],[154] where the winds appear stirring the dark rain clouds[155] (cf. Nah 1:3), and advancing the hailstones and bolts of lightning. Undoubtedly, then, the idea of the sun and stars not fulfilling their proper function in Job 9:7 alludes to cosmic darkness caused by YHWH's appearance in the blustery winds.[156] Here Job lauds YHWH as the creator, whose wisdom is profound and greatness encompasses his cosmic creativity and dispensation of ordering in human affairs (Job 9:4). Again, Job points out the earth-shattering effects of YHWH's appearance with the winds, causing both the sun and stars to cease to shine, as much as YHWH spreads out the heavens, and tramples the sea in subjection (vv. 5–7).

Subsequently, the poet acclaims YHWH as creator with epithets that emphasize his cosmogonic activities (Job 9:8–10). In some scholarship, these verses mentioning the creativity of YHWH have been omitted as an editorial insertion.[157] But, these verses that extol YHWH as creator,

153. Day, *God's Conflict*, 147–48. From Day's observation on the effects of Ba'al's theophany described in KTU 1.4.VII:52–60, he notes that the fading of the sun and moon occurs following Ba'al's theophany in the storm when daylight is intercepted by the elements linked with the storm, and he argues for similar occurrences in Isa 24:21–23. Day mentions that similar cosmic effects are attested in Josh 10:12b–13 and Hab 3:11a in association with storm elements. But all this roiling of elements is the result of the winds.

154. See Day, *God's Conflict*, 108–9.

155. Similarly, the mention of luminaries and constellations not giving light and the quaking of the heavens and earth (Isa 13:10, 13) is suggestive of the cosmic darkness and shaking that are associated with YHWH's "sonorous" winds. The same idea of cosmic darkness brought about by an overlay of thick clouds is expressed in Joel 2:2a. Moreover, the veiling of the sun, moon, and stars is connected with YHWH issuing his "loud sound" (נתן קולו, Ps 68:34b[33b]; Joel 2:10–11), hence alluding to bursts of wind.

156. With most scholars, these cosmic effects—often linked with theophanies—are mistaken for an eclipse and earthquake (see Dhorme, *Commentary*, 128–29; Hartley, *Book of Job*, 170–71, esp. nn15–16, citing scholars in support of this misconstrued interpretation). For the earth shattering effects considered as volcanic or seismic, see Andersen, *Job*, 157. For an overview on scholars' interpretation of the poetic verses as referring to an earthquake, or as just as YHWH's mighty acts in nature, see Vicchio, *Book of Job*, 83.

157. For example, Duhm, Delitzsch, and Torczyner. See Dhorme, *Commentary*, 130;

are original and have thematic relevance in their context. It is clear that Job, though driven to despair in search of justice for his undeserved suffering, calls to mind the incomparable and mysterious works of YHWH in the cosmos. Therefore, the poet places on the lips of Job epithets derived from YHWH's creation of the cosmos as prognostic, in anticipation of the claims of YHWH as creator and dispensation of justice in the discourse in Job 38.

Furthermore, it is apparent, as Dhorme notes, the poet of Job employs the same formula in Job 9:8 as that found in Isa 44:24 to express YHWH's exclusive claim to cosmic creativity: "He alone stretches out the heavens, and treads the high places (or 'back') of the sea."[158] Here the parallelism of the creating of the heavens and treading on the waves of the sea is the crescendo recalling YHWH's creative activity by his wind(s) as found in Gen 1:2[159] (see Ps 104:3-9). Arguably as portrayed in the book of Isaiah, the arm/right hand of YHWH (Isa 48:13; 51:9) is figurative of his winds by which he, "alone," creates the heavens (Job 9:8a) and earth (Isa 44:24) and subdues the sea (Job 9:8b; 51:9-10; 15-16). Therefore, the expression "he alone" (לבדו) in Job 9:8 throws into bold relief the monotheistic belief of the poet that Job is dealing with this one deity, whose cosmological activities are unchallenged. Also, the titles ascribed to YHWH in view of his creative acts, though loosely connected, may be given fuller meaning by other references in the text of Job. YHWH "stretches" (נטה) out the heavens (Job 26:7; Jer 10:12; Ps 104:2) as his abode; there he establishes his throne (Job 26:9; see Isa 66:1; Ps 2:4), covers himself with clouds (Job 22:14a; 26:8-9; see Pss 97:2; 104:3b), and with his winds traverses the circuit of the heavens (Job 22:14c; cf. Isa 40:22).

Yet, YHWH does not limit himself to the skies. In view of the alternative meaning of "bend"[160] for the verb נטה (Ps 18:10[9]; see Isa 63:19c[64:1a]), and as Dhorme suggests,[161] YHWH can lower the heav-

---

Vicchio, Book of Job, 84.

158. Even though Dhorme points out that these verses found on the lips of Job are considered by other scholars as interpolations and appropriate to issue from Eliphaz, they are adapted here to fit a new context. See Dhorme, Commentary, 130.

159. See pp. 49-51.

160. BDB 639-40.

161. Dhorme, Commentary, 130. The author may concur with Dhorme on the other meaning of "lower" (נטה), to imply the idea of YHWH coming down from the heavens, thus warranting the idea of "treading the back of the 'sea.'" However, Dhorme assumes that the poet was inspired by Amos 4:13 or Mic 1:3 and replaced the accusative "earth"

ens to reveal himself, in order to tread on the high places of the earth (Amos 4:13; Mic 1:3).[162] To that end, a double meaning is implied in the use of נטה in Job 9:8: by his winds: YHWH stretches out the heavens like a tent as a creative act and also bends, or rends, the heavens like a tent curtain, and comes down, in order to tread on the high places, that is, the waves of the sea, making it roar. It is clear that the poet's expression about treading the surging waters, as though a monster, is not totally removed from the world of mythology. Similar eulogies are found in Enuma Elish; Marduk is praised as the one who crosses the sea in his wrath (EE VII:74), the sea functioning as the craft[163] upon which he rides (line 77). Although the idea of controlling the boisterous sea as expressed in Job 9:8 may be in keeping with mythical thinking, the main point of the poet's language is to demonstrate YHWH's incomparable dominion and command of his winds. Job is awed by the grandeur of YHWH's incomprehensible manifestation with his winds at creation, subjugation of the chaotic sea, and no less of the wicked at YHWH's maintenance of that order in the natural realm.

Apart from the mythical terminology describing YHWH's control of chaos, his uniqueness is emphasized by his creation of the constellations and the southwinds (Job 9:9). In Job 9:9, as in 38:32 and Amos 5:8, the constellations are identified by the names; Bear, Orion and Pleiades. These heavenly bodies are personified with the intention of expressing a polemic against the worship of starry hosts, which YHWH called by name as part of his own creation (cf. Deut 4:19; 17:3; 2 Kgs 23:5; Jer 8:2; 10:2). Along with these constellations, YHWH creates the chambers of the southwinds. Scholars often see here a reference to the chambers of the south from whence the constellations came forth. However, Job 37:9 also mentions the idea of the storm bearing winds that proceed from chambers (תוצא, Jer 10:13=51:16; Ps 135:7c). As Pope correctly observes, the

---

in the expression at issue with "sea." But the idea of YHWH traversing the sea is not lacking in an immediate reference. In Job 38:16b, YHWH questions Job whether, like him, he has walked about the "range of the deeps" (חקר תהום). See the similar idea of YHWH treading the sea in connection with the crossing of the Red Sea in Hab 3:15. Nonetheless, we may argue that the reference to treading the "sea" relates to YHWH's mastery by the power of his wind at creation, whereas the treading of the "earth" is in association with YHWH's theophany in, and dominion over, the mundane sphere. See discussion on Amos 4:13.

162. Dhorme, *Commentary*, 130.

163. Cf. Dalley (*Myths*, 270), who translates this as "barque," and Lambert ("Mesopotamian Creation Stories," 57; *Babylonian*, 129), who renders it as "boat."

noun תמן in Job 9:9 also means southwind.¹⁶⁴ So, in the view that the poet marvels at YHWH's creation, he also focuses on YHWH's creation of the chambers of the "southwind" to bring to bear the "whirlwind" (שְׂעָרָה, Job 9:17), "tempest/storm wind," or "eastwind" (סופה//קדים, 27:20b–23; cf. Job 38:24b) as the means by which YHWH accomplishes his purposes against the wicked. Hence, Job deems his predicament as relational to the plight of the wicked (see Pss 1:4; 11:6). Even an assertive statement from the lips of Job's friend, Eliphaz the Temanite, that the wicked perish from the "breath" (נשמת) of God, and by the wrath of his "wind" (רוח, Job 4:9) is in conformity with this diction.

So, in relation to his own situation, Job uses technical terms that are often associated with the movement of natural phenomena to describe YHWH's invisible and elusive presence. Job says that, if YHWH "passes by" (עבר) him, YHWH is elusive and cannot see him. When YHWH "moves on"¹⁶⁵ (חלף), even then he does not perceive him (Job 9:11). It is apparent that in other wisdom texts these two verbs, חלף and עבר, are associated with the natural phenomena. The verb עבר¹⁶⁶ describes the "passing by" of a "storm wind" (סופה) in Prov 10:25 and of the "wind" (רוח) in Job 37:21. In view of the use of these verbs¹⁶⁷ associated with the natural elements in expression of his fate comparable to that of the wicked, Job refers to YHWH's presence as being attended by natural phenomena. As Job grapples for a solution to his problem of suffering and implores an answer from YHWH, he throws his lot in with the wicked, and relates with premonition that YHWH will only crush him with a

---

164. See "eastwind"//"southwind" (קדים//תימן, Ps 78:26); "northwind"//"southwind" (צפון//תימן, Cant 4:16).

165. Tengströme ("חָלַף," 432–35) notes that the verbs חלף and עבר (as its synonym) express movement involving approach: to "come upon" or "come over" someone. He states that the verb חלף may express the movement of violent natural phenomena and catastrophes. For instance, in Isa 21:1 the armies of the Medes and Elamites are compared to the storms that "sweep" (חלף) through the desert in the Negev (434). Although YHWH's presence is not associated with the wind in 1 Kgs 19:11, the verb עבר is employed to express the movement of the wind tearing the mountains apart, and shattering rocks. In Hab 1:11 the verbs חלף and עבר occur in parallel and express the movement of the wind with which the raiding Chaldeans are equated. However, Hartley also observes that the verbs חלף and עבר are not unfamiliar to theophanic passages describing YHWH's self-disclosure to Moses (Exod 33:18–23) and Elijah (1 Kgs 19:11–13). See Hartley, *Book of Job*, 172n25.

166. Cf. Job 30:15 where the verb עבר occurs in a simile expressing the passing away of salvation like a cloud.

167. In Cant 2:11 the two verbs in parallel describe the "passing away" of "rain" (גשם).

"whirlwind"[168] (שְׂעָרָה, Job 9:17; see 30:22), elsewhere a trope of YHWH's judgment of the wicked (Nah 1:3; see Ps 83:16[15]; Job 27:20–21; Prov 10:25). Job's own seven sons and three daughters (Job 1:2) perish in the "mighty wind" (רוּחַ גְּדוֹלָה) blowing from the desert (1:19; see Jer 4:11, 12; 13:24). Perhaps with melancholy, as Job further muses, YHWH's unfathomable aniconic presence in the wind(s) can "snatch away," but no one can halt him (Job 9:12).

Consequently, Job alludes to YHWH's feat at the primordial events, at which YHWH deploys his invincible mighty winds and makes the cohorts[169] of Rahab to cower beneath him (Job 9:13; cf. 26:12; Isa 51:9). Thereby, Job emphasizes that it is futile in his situation to challenge the invincible power of YHWH. In that respect, Job is concerned with presenting the attributes of YHWH and commending him for his wisdom and might displayed through his mastery of the winds at primal creation and continual governance.[170] Job therefore, depicts YHWH as the creator, who can subdue him with his "whirlwind" (Job 9:17), and deprive him of his human "breath" (רוּחַ, v. 18); a reversal of YHWH's revivifying winds at creation (Ps 104:29–30). Job contends, therefore, that as much as YHWH is exalted in power, and his nature is beyond understanding, so it is impossible to discern YHWH's way of establishing "justice" and "righteousness" (Job 9:19–24; cf. Job 37:23).

YHWH's Creative Power in the Winds Deemed as Wisdom in Job 26:7–14

Before Job's encounter with YHWH in the "whirlwind" (סְעָרָה, Job 38:1), in the rejoinder to sneering Bildad's pretentious knowledge of divine order (Job 25:2–6), Job resumes praise in Job 26:7–14 in hymnic style comparable to Job 9:4–10. Job attributes to YHWH cosmological acts

---

168. The Targum and Syriac versions repoint this word to mean "hair," but the meaning becomes obscure. In light of the manifestation of YHWH through the winds referred to in this text, it is likely that here Job muses on YHWH intervening in similar ways; שְׂעָרָה=סְעָרָה, Isa 29:6.

169. Though Rahab is a chaos monster identified with Leviathan in the Ugaritic conflict myth, the allies of Rahab mentioned here are often equated with the auxiliaries who marched with Tiamat in battle against Marduk. See Dhorme, *Commentary*, 134; Vicchio, *Book of Job*, 84–85.

170. *Contra* Perdue, *Wisdom*, 134–35, who argues for this shift in meaning of YHWH's theophany from a metaphor normally intended to bring about cosmic order or redemption, but now referring to destructive effects on creation.

that parallel rhetorical statements in the divine discourse (Job 38). Job's response, culminating in the doxology in Job 26:7–14, is a reprise of Bildad's statement of human sinfulness before YHWH (Job 25:4–6). Bildad's statement is as persuasive as Eliphaz's contention (Job 4:17–18; 15:14–16)[171] that all humans are not righteous, and that YHWH has the right to punish them. Without responding to the issue of divine justice advocated by his comforters, Job sarcastically questions Bildad as to whether he has counseled anyone without wisdom or saved anyone without strength (Job 26:2–3). By questioning Bildad's source of counsel or divine revelation (v. 4), Job brings to the fore the idea of the council of the LORD (see Jer 23:18), which is an essential factor in determining true or false prophetic messages (see 1 Kgs 22:19–22; Job 15:8–10).

According to Jeremiah, false prophets who did not sit in YHWH's council would experience YHWH's wrath in a "whirlwind" and "tempest" (סערה/סער, Jer 23:19–20=30:23–24). In the same vein, in Job 26:4, Job censures Bildad for lack of discernment of divine revelation to inform his counsel. Hence, with an element of satire, Job outlines the vastness of the power of YHWH and its effect in both the natural and supernatural regions (Job 26:5–6). He mentions that the infernal regions experience the power of YHWH, and that in Rephaim (the shades) the inhabitants writhe below the waters, while Sheol and Abaddon lie exposed before YHWH (vv. 5–6; cf. Job 28:24), whose wisdom they can only conceive and witness as a rumor (28:20–22). Therefore, Job rebukes Bildad for lack of wisdom. By contrast, Job refers to the incomprehensible power of YHWH manifested in cosmological activities, with the intent to emphasize that YHWH's wisdom beheld in creation is not fully conspicuous, but only amounts to a rumor (Job 26:12–14). So, here again, in awe of YHWH's power and wisdom, Job lauds YHWH's enigmatic acts of creation by his wind, and invokes YHWH's epithets in as much as they are reflective of his creative acts (Job 26:7–14).

The doxology in Job 26:7–14 is presented in language asserting YHWH's wisdom in his cosmogonic activities. In addition to the reference to YHWH's creation of the heavens in Job 9:8, YHWH, in Job 26:7, is praised as the creator of the "north" (צפון). Job not only alludes to the mythological abode[172] of the Canaanite god Ba'al but sees in its establishment, as Habel suggests, an alternative expression of YHWH stretching

---

171. See Lévêque, "Argument," 268–69; Smick, "Job," 965.
172. cf. Isa 14:13 and Ps 48:3[2].

out the heavens as his tent,¹⁷³ which is also inaugural to YHWH's theophany. However, the association of the north with the emergence of the world from god Amma's creative work is significant to the biblical interpretation. So, Amma whirled and his egg (which is Amma himself as the spinning wind) opened up in the north¹⁷⁴ to produce his own creation. Arguably, whether YHWH stretches the heavens, or the north, both are locales associated with the provenance of the winds,¹⁷⁵ and not less with creation.

Yet, more spectacular, and in contrast with other texts in which YHWH stretches out the heavens at the time of his founding of the earth,¹⁷⁶ is the emphasis on YHWH "stretching" (נטה) the north over the "void" (תהו), and "suspending" (תלה) the earth over "nothing" (בלי־מה, Job 26:7). This creativity figuratively alludes to the idea of *tōhû wābōhû* ("formless and void"), as mentioned in Gen 1:2.¹⁷⁷ The notion of spreading the "north" on "formlessness," and suspending the earth on "nothingness" is no more than a poetic hyperbole on the notion of *creatio ex nihilo*, but, also, not exclusive of the heavens being supported by pillars. It is not unusual in the OT, however, that both the heavens (Job 26:11; cf. 2 Sam 22:8) and earth (Job 9:6; Ps 75:4 [3]; cf. Ps 104:5; Prov 8:29) are thought to be supported by "pillars" (עמדים). In the Enuma Elish, Marduk fashions Tiamat's crotch, perhaps as a pedestal, to hoist the heavens in place (EE v:61).¹⁷⁸ Therefore, the OT concept of the heavens and perhaps the earth, having pillars for suspension is analogous to this Babylonian antecedent. Nonetheless, the Egyptian symbolism of the god Shu in association with the four pillars of heaven as the provenance for the winds¹⁷⁹ proffers a closer meaning related in Job 26:11. Here, these pillars of the heavens are mentioned in connection with the cosmic

---

173. Habel, "He Who Stretches Out," 421–22.

174. Griaule and Dieterlen, *Pale Fox*, 186. See 15n75, p. 24, 24n164 above.

175. The mention of YHWH coming from the "north" in golden splendor and awe-inspiring majesty (נורא הוד)—see discussion on Ps 104:1—assumes the northern skies as the setting for YHWH's emergence with the winds (Job 37:22). Regarding Amma beginning his creation by spinning and opening up at the north, see 15n75 above.

176. See Isa 42:5; 44:24; Jer 10:12=51:15; Zech 12:1.

177. Kravitz and Olitzk, *Book of Job*, 155.

178. Foster translates: "He set her crotch as the 'brace' of heaven" (*Before the Muses*, 465). Lambert translates: "[He set up] her crotch—it wedged up the heavens" (*Babylonian*, 101).

179. See p. 80 above.

reactions caused by the efficacy of YHWH's rebuke, or roar (גערה): being the wind causing such agitation.

Moreover, Job's mention of the earth's pillars trembling at YHWH's presence in his previous doxology (Job 9:6) shows that the metaphor of the earth resting on a foundation is not dispensed with in Job 26:7-14. The question then is, whether it is the heavens and their pillars or the earth and its pedestals: on what are they supported? The rhetorical question by YHWH in Job 38:6 as to whether the earth's pedestals were sunk (טבע) on anything further points to the mystery surrounding the cosmic structure. Therefore, the thrust of this statement in Job 26:7 is that the earth stands firm and is reinforced by its pedestals, though the latter are not borne by anything.[180] Job's metaphor of the earth resting on nothing, corresponds with the implication of the divine question in Job 38:6. By referring to the images of empty space, or void (26:7), Job wants to express the profound wisdom with which YHWH creates and sustains the cosmos, and alludes to the efficacy of YHWH's winds in expression of the sovereignty, power, and subtlety of YHWH at creation.

Thus, Job further lauds YHWH as the one who, with the winds in circuit, causes the clouds to "bind" (צרר) the waters,[181] and the clouds do not burst open under the weight (v. 8; cf. Prov 30:4), showing YHWH's ingenuity in his cosmological activities. In addition, the association of the wind-tossed clouds[182] with YHWH's throne (Job 26:9; see 22:14) implicates his appearance with the winds in dispersing the clouds; an idea that is corollary to the clouds functioning as YHWH's chariot (Pss 18:12[11]; 104:3) or his covering (Exod 19:16; Pss 97:2; 99:7) in theophanic texts. Subsequently, in the remainder of the doxology in Job 26, Job amplifies

180. See Lévêque, "Argument," 268-70 (though Lévêque wrongly attributes the discourse in Job 26 to Bildad).

181. A similar idea comes as a rhetorical question in Prov 30:4c in expression of YHWH's greatness in creation and control of the winds (see Ps 135:7). For the idea of the clouds covering YHWH's throne (Job 26:9) and his walking under cover of the clouds (Job 22:14) see discussion on Job 9:7. This may be compared with Marduk who creates the clouds above the waters (EE VII:83; V:49-50).

182. Habel cites other functions of the clouds as attested in the OT, such as veiling YHWH's presence at Sinai (Exod 19:16; 24:15-16), in the tabernacle (40:34-38), and in the Solomonic temple (1 Kgs 8:10-11). The cloud also veiled YHWH's essential being, i.e., his glory or his face (Exod 33:17-23). It is relevant to Job's situation, as Habel points out, that Job finds himself distanced from catching a glimpse of YHWH's face (Job 23:3-4; see 13:24), and is thus hindered from arguing his case. Most significant, however, is that Habel observes a parallel between the traditional motif of the ark covered with a cloud and that of the clouds covering YHWH's throne in the celestial abode, as described in Job (Habel, *Book of Job*, 372).

the power of YHWH's winds in recital of YHWH's deeds at primeval creation.

Undoubtedly, in Job 26:7–14, as in the first hymn (Job 9:4–10), Job alludes to ancient mythological motifs as he describes YHWH's feats of wisdom in creating the earth with the winds in close attendance. The statement in Job 26:10, "he prescribed a boundary upon the face of the waters" refers to the creation of the earth. The latter is the boundary between light and darkness, as supported by evidence from other wisdom texts. In Prov 8:27, 29 the verb "mark out"[183] (הקק), with personified wisdom in attendance, refers to both the prescribing of a "horizon"[184] (חוג, see Isa 40:22) upon the face of the "deep" (תהום, Prov 8:27) and the establishing of the foundations of the earth (v. 29). Here the earth is not just a terrestrial dome; it is set as a border of the subterranean waters (Gen 7:11; Ps 24:2; Prov 8:28b; cf. Job 38:10–11). According to Job 28; a poem about the search for wisdom, the sources of the rivers are underneath the earth. In essence, the idea of humans blocking off subterranean waters in their search for precious stones, as stated in Job 28:11, relates to the securing of the fountains of the deep by YHWH at creation. As Job 28 further suggests, this region below the earth is engulfed with darkness, such that light is invented to eliminate it[185] (Job 28:3). It is evident, then, that the earth marks the boundary between light above and darkness beneath it. In which case, the mention of marking a "prescribed limit" (חק) on the face of the waters, and an "end" ([= boundary] תכלית) between light and darkness in Job 26:10, implies the creation of the earth attributed to YHWH's acts of wisdom.

In keeping with Ps 104, this hymnic section of Job (26:10–14) alludes to YHWH's creativity through the power of his rebuke or roar, a personification of the wind(s). So vast is its effect that the pillars of the heavens quake (Job 26:11; cf. 2 Sam 22:8b), and the force of it "stirs" the sea[186] (Job 26:12a). Undoubtedly, here, too, Job alludes to YHWH

---

183. In both vv. 27 and 29 this verb occurs in the infinitive with "horizon" and "foundations of the earth," respectively, as accusatives.

184. In Isa 40:22 the word חוג refers to the realm of the earth; here YHWH is said to dwell above the horizon of the earth.

185. The irony of this poem is that, even though mankind may penetrate the depths of the earth to mine metals, wisdom cannot be mined, or exchanged for precious metals (Job 28:16–19). Yet, as the poet adds, wisdom belongs to the deity who understands its way and where it dwells (v. 23).

186. The same idea is expressed in prophetic passages, where YHWH declares himself as creator and as the one "who stirs" (רגע) the sea (Isa 51:15; Jer 31:35), thus

YHWH IN THE WIND(S)

roiling the sea at the primal creation of the earth (see Ps 104:7). However, in Job's doxology, the stirring of the sea is paralleled with the slaying of the mythical monster, Rahab (Job 26:12b). Admittedly, even though the reference to the primeval dragon, Rahab, and the act of "smiting" (מחץ, Isa 51:9) find immediate parallels with Ugaritic, or Babylonian myths, as pointed out in connection with Job 9:13, the ultimate act of creating the earth by the wind is in keeping with the Dogon creation myth of the whirlwind-deity[187] Amma,[188] who is also said to be the image of the visible elements.[189] In light of the emphasis on the use of the phenomenal winds by which YHWH accomplishes his creative acts in Ps 104, and which reflect his wisdom, the same is implied by the statement that he smote Rahab by his "understanding"[190] (תבנה, Job 26:12b). Again the idea alludes to YHWH's destruction of Rahab by his arm[191] (see Ps 89:11[10]); analogous to his winds,[192] and consequential to YHWH's creative feats manifested at the establishment of the world. So, YHWH's mastery and power in the winds is deemed as wisdom. Even the idea of the wind sweeping over the heavens in Job 26:13a, along with the mention of the "thunderous 'sound' of his might" (רעם גבורתו, v. 14c), echoing Amma's "sonorous sound," fundamentally implies the wind playing a part in creation. Arguably, the reference to the thunderous sound is onomatopoeic for the wind bursts emerging from YHWH's storehouses (Jer 10:13; Ps 135:7; cf. Job 38:22). Therefore, in Job 26:7–14, as in Ps

---

causing its waves to roar. Whereas in Isa 51:16 YHWH claims to set the heavens in place and create the foundations of the earth, in Jer 31:35 the appointing of the sun, moon and stars is ascribed to him too, as YHWH Ṣebāʾôth who agitates the sea/waves by his winds causing it to roar.

187. See pp. 16–17; Griaule and Dieterlen, *Pale Fox*, 130, 142.

188. Regarding the creativity of god Amma, see chapter 1.

189. Griaule and Dieterlen, *Pale Fox*, 131.

190. The word "understanding" (תבנה) is analogous to "wisdom" (חכמה). It may be noted here that this substantive when used in association with acts of creation often refers to the process of creation (Jer 10:12=51:15; Ps 136:5; Prov 3:19). With the exception of Ps 136:5, חכמה and תבנה in the mentioned texts occur in parallelism.

191. See Ps 89:11[10]b, 14[13]. On the arm/hand as analogous to winds, see pp. 41–42, 60.

192. The ideas expressed here are also a pale reflection of the battle of Marduk deploying the winds to roil Tiamat to subjugation (EE IV:95–100; see also lines 41–47). In the same context of this single combat, Marduk is distinguished as the sage of the gods (EE IV:93). In this epic, there is also emphasis on Marduk's attribute of wisdom that is manifested by his acts of creation (EE VII:116–17).

104, YHWH in his infinite wisdom (Job 9:4; Prov 8:22–30a) engages in cosmological activities by means of his winds.

Evidently, in Job 26:7–14 YHWH is depicted as the creator-king. He spreads the northern skies as his abode wherein he is enthroned and shrouds himself with clouds. At the same time, he reveals himself with the thunderous (whirl)wind (see Ps 77:19[18])[193] of his might to destroy cosmic foes and set the cosmos in order. However, as Job testifies, these cosmological activities represent the outer limits of his ways, amounting to no more than a "whisper" about him (Job 26:14a). As Job further confesses, the full extent of YHWH's cosmic potency is incomprehensible (v. 14b). This conclusion to the doxology[194] seems to support all the more Job's view in 9:10 concerning the innumerable and unfathomable wonders of YHWH as creator. Again, Job's thinking becomes poignant; if one cannot comprehend the works of YHWH, the one wise of heart and robust in power, how can one justify himself before the creator?

YHWH's Disclosure in the Whirlwind as Creator in Job 38— A Paradox on Divine Justice

Eventually, with the contest of words between Job and his comforters irreconcilable, concerning the mysterious governance of YHWH, Job is finally silenced by the divine speech in Job 38 focusing on YHWH's feats of strength and wisdom. The long-awaited encounter with the divine, however, does not offer answers to Job's concerns on divine justice. Instead, it proffers a paradox of YHWH's design of the cosmos. Here, just as the perplexity that Job expresses in the doxologies at the incomprehensible manifestation of YHWH's power in nature, the discourse emphasizes the limits of human understanding of YHWH's governance, as much as the complexity of his deeds at creation. Thus, while the question of YHWH perverting justice is dismissed, the divine discourse offers a context for interpreting divine cosmological activities.

---

193. In Ps 77:19[18] the onomatopoeic "thunderous sound" (קול רעם) is conflated with the "whirlwind" (גלגל), in recollection of YHWH's *modus operandi* at the exodus. Also, in Ps 83:14[13] גלגל translating whirlwind (see BDB 165) appears in parallel with רוח showing emphasis on the winds as central to YHWH's form of disclosure.

194. Cf. Lévêque, "Argument," 268–69; Perdue, *Wisdom*, 85, 174–76, who attribute Job 26:4–14 to Bildad. The view expressed here does justice to the affinity with the doxology in Job 9:4–10, thus it is appropriate to assign this doxology to the lips of Job.

The irony of Job's encounter with YHWH, therefore, is that YHWH does not appear in the whirlwind (Job 38:1) to punish Job, as is the expected fate of the wicked[195] (Job 27:13, 20-23). There is no unleashing of the elements by YHWH's winds against him, as a rod of correction (Job 37:13a), but instead a revelation of the extraordinary that emphasizes YHWH's absolute hegemony in creation. In sustained rhetoric, YHWH challenges Job with his wisdom in creation and his sustenance and governance of his created order. Here is a description of YHWH's incomprehensible cosmic design. And so, after questioning and criticizing YHWH's governing actions in the universe, Job is chided for obscuring that "design" (עצה, v. 2), because of his lack of knowledge. YHWH exposes Job to the complexities of his cosmic design crafted with wisdom to a pattern of governing and regulating principles, in order to keep in check, and contain the potential forces of chaos.[196]

Even though Job credits YHWH with the cosmological activities recounted in the doxologies in Job 9:4-10 and 26:7-14, the charge is that he may not understand how YHWH operates since he was not there at the beginning of creation (Job 38:4-5). With rhetorical statements, YHWH pronounces his primordial activities when he functioned as the wise architect designing the structure of the cosmos. Again, there is allusion to YHWH's control of the boisterous sea by his winds when it burst forth[197] from the womb (v. 8). As in the case of Amma, YHWH initiates order by his winds on the chaotic waters, and sets its boundaries (vv. 10-11). The earth is declared to be firmly fixed and secured on its foundation (vv. 4a, 6; see Pss 93:1c; 96:10b; 104:5), while the sea is described in figurative language as swaddled with thick darkness and having its barriers set up (Job 38:8-9; see Jer 5:22; Ps 104:6-9). Here, as Habel notes, the designer of the cosmos does not eliminate the destructive forces of the sea. Instead, the sea is governed by a prescribed law (חק, Job 38:10), which limits and keeps its destructive tendency in check.

It is clear from the divine discourse of Job 38 that even the constraint, and punishment of the wicked, is mentioned among YHWH's functional decrees of the grand cosmic structure[198] (vv. 12-15). The morning, or

---

195. Job himself subscribes to the same ideology that the wicked suffer YHWH's wrath through the wind/tempest. Thus, in his predicament, Job anticipates punitive measures to take the same form (Job 9:17). See pp. 94-95.

196. Habel, "Defence," 34-35.

197. See p. 45.

198. Habel, "Defence," 34-36. No wonder the prophet Jeremiah, who predicts

dawn, is personified as though it would seize the earth by its "wings," that is, its four corners representing the cardinal points, and shake the wicked out of it. But, as Noegel noted on the correlation between winds, wings and cardinal points,[199] the idea of the winds dispersing the wicked is also implicated here (v. 13). Moreover, the notion of the dawn casting its light on the wicked alludes to YHWH's regulation of night and day to limit the works of the wicked from becoming a dominating force over his cosmic design. The wicked, who commit their deeds in darkness (Job 24:14–17), as though it is in the light of day (v. 17), their arms will go limp (38:15), when YHWH appears in wrath (see Isa 13:6–13) with his outstretched arm—symbolic of the thunderous (whirl)winds—to uproot the wicked. Ironically, *contra* to YHWH's outstretched arm, the arm of the wicked is broken (Job 38:15; see Ps 37:17). With the break of dawn, the wicked are left scampering for cover (Job 24:16), their strength is weakened, and they are cut off in judgment (vv. 22–24). To that end, the idea of keeping the malevolence of the wicked in check is also integral with YHWH's activities in establishing cosmic order, as also declared in the divine discourse from within the whirlwind in Job 40:6–13. Here, in sequel, and with the same kind of irony as in Job 38, YHWH challenges Job to display an "arm" (זרוע) like his with a thunderous sound (Job 40:9) and assume his "majestic appearance" (הוד והדר, v. 10; see Ps 104:1c), in order to unleash his wrath to humiliate the proud and crush the wicked (Job 40:11–12). Undoubtedly, the emphasis is on YHWH's theophany with the whirling winds (v. 6) to manifest both his acts of creation of the universal order from primeval chaos, as much as abolish the wicked from his intended cosmic order (Job 38:6–12, 15–19). Therefore, the two facets of "creation" and "destruction" are in discourse synchronously, in order to assert YHWH's establishment and maintenance of his cosmic design.

Yet, not far from the idea of the phenomenal winds as YHWH's instrument of judgment, as often predicted by the prophets (Isa 29:6c; 30:28; Ezek 13:13), is the reference to YHWH's winds dispersing the celestial arsenal of snow and hail in Job 38:22 (Isa 30:30; cf. 28:17c). YHWH himself declares that he reserves these elements[200] for the time

---

YHWH's judgment upon the nations in terms of the universe reverting to its primordial chaos, uses the metaphor of the roaring waves of the sea rising up against Babylon (Jer 51:42).

199. See pp. 79–80.

200. Indeed, in consideration of similar occurrences, YHWH manifested his might

of trouble and the day of war and battle (Job 38:23). Even more profound to the numinous sublimity of YHWH, is the allusion to the force of winds, which disseminate these meteorological phenomena (vv. 24–30, 34–37). Admittedly, the irony in these questions is intended to challenge Job whether he has any knowledge of the place where the (east)winds are scattered, or the light is dispersed, or (knowledge of) who paves the channel for the torrents of rain or the way for the lightning bolts (vv. 24–25), or if he is capable of raising his voice to the clouds, in order to cover himself with a flood of water (v. 34), or summon the lightning,[201] as lackeys, to do his bidding (Job 38:35; cf. Ps 148:8). YHWH says all this to show that power resides in him, and so does the dispensation of his phenomenal elements.

But, key to the function of all this phenomena is the allusion to the provenance of the winds, and the place where they are dispensed (Job 38:24b). This revelation draws attention to certain marvelous actions of the wind highlighted in the Elihu speeches; perhaps deliberately inserted by the poet of Job as a foil to introduce YHWH's appearance in the whirlwind and the mystery of his creative works. On one hand, as Elihu states, the winds emerge from chambers created by YHWH (Job 37:9a; see 9:9b), and on the other, the cold winds that produce ice (Job 38:29; see 37:9b) originate as YHWH's "breath" (נשמת, Job 37:10; see 2 Sam 22:16c=Ps 18:16[15c]). However, the sharp focus here is on YHWH's winds blowing and distilling rain in the clouds, causing them to swirl and release rain (Job 38:24–26; see 36:27–29a; 37:11–12).[202] Hence, YHWH challenges Job whether he has wisdom to count the clouds, in order to tip them and cause a downpour (Job 38:36–37). In essence, the point is YHWH himself embodies wisdom and understanding (v. 36). As a corollary to this idea, YHWH's discernment and transcendent wisdom is embodied

---

through hailstones at the exodus (Exod 9:26) and conquest (Josh 10:11). YHWH is able to do all this because, in accordance with his wisdom, he establishes the course for the rain and lightning bolts (Job 28:26). He also begets and precipitates dew, ice and hoarfrost (Job 38:28–29), which he disperses by his winds (Pss 147:18b; 148:8; Job 37:9–12).

201. The idea echoes Elihu's depiction of YHWH with the palm of his hands figuratively filled with lightning, which he commands to strike the mark (Job 36:32).

202. Noegel observed the use of polysemous parallelism (wordplay, as conventional to wisdom literature) on the dual root פוץ (I & II) meaning "scatter, disperse," or "flow, overflow" as employed in the Elihu and YHWH speeches (Job 37:11; 38:24–25, respectively), and argues that the root is used here to refer to the winds scattering, or dispersing other meteorological elements, hence causing rain/water to flow (Noegel, *Janus*, 124–26). Kravitz and Olitzk note a similar observation on the winds serving the same purpose (Kravitz and Olitzk, *Book of Job*, 216).

in the weighting of the clouds and measuring out of the waters of heaven when the earth is parched (Job 38:37b–38). So, even here in Job 38, these rhetorical statements further emphasize YHWH's sovereign power and the effectiveness of his sonorous winds in nature in distilling rain (Job 36:27—37:6). Thus, whether YHWH's decrees relating to the natural elements (Job 28:25–26) operate in providence or punishment, his display of wisdom and might through the force of his winds, is in focus.

In Job 38, unlike the doxologies in 9:4–10 and 26:7–14 where the sonorous winds play an active role at creation (Ps 104:3–9), these complex elements are presented as products of YHWH's creative acts, as much as instruments for his sovereign governance. In this divine discourse, YHWH impresses Job with how he formed the natural elements and appointed their regular function. Paradoxically, however, and in display of his predominance over the meteorological elements, the whirlwind here functions as the setting from which YHWH intimates to Job his sovereignty as creator. YHWH declares how he designed the mysterious order in the celestial and terrestrial realms that also has its counterpart in the extreme infernal regions. Moreover, not only does he know the governing principles of the cosmos, but he decrees them. The wisdom by which YHWH designed the universe or appraised the clouds also enables him to regulate and direct the meteorological phenomena in order to accomplish his own purposes. Thus, in Job 38 elements of creation, wisdom, and judgment are integrated. YHWH, who is capable of raising his voice to the clouds, causes a flood of water and commands the lightning bolts to execute his will and purpose, and exercises his power in eliminating forces that conflict with his divine plan and design. In essence, YHWH's appearance in the whirlwind to exercise his will in the mundane realm supersedes the similar wielding of his power at creation (Ps 104:7–9; Job 9:8, 10, 13; 26:11–13).[203] Therefore, this speech enriches the depiction of YHWH as the sovereign creator whose wisdom is mediated through cosmic order. The profundity of his wisdom and might reaches beyond and nullifies any forces that militate against his divine order. Hence, the idea of YHWH's sonorous winds, as the precise *modus operandi* by which YHWH asserts his dominance over primeval cosmic chaos, as portrayed in Ps 104 and the doxologies of Job, expresses, and also focuses, the idea of his tempestuous winds charging against the wicked. Therefore, YHWH is portrayed as the sovereign creator, who reveals his power, and

---

203. See foregoing discussion on the references cited.

combats idolatry by means of his winds, as expressed in prophetic texts such as Amos and Jeremiah.

Contextual Background of Amos 1:2, 14; 4:12–13; 5:8–9; 9:5–6

According to the ascription in Amos 1:1, the prophet Amos appeared on the scene during the reigns of Uzziah king of Judah (ca. 792–740 BCE) and Jeroboam II king of Israel (ca. 793–753 BCE). However, the dates given by scholars for the overlapping regnal periods of these two kings vary greatly. For instance, Andersen and Freedman estimate Jeroboam II's reign as 793/2–753/2, or 786–746 BCE, quoting Thiele and Albright, respectively, and that of Uzziah as 792–740 BCE.[204] In view of the long duration both these kings were in power, and in spite of the brief mention of their achievements in biblical sources; II Kings and the Chronicler, Andersen and Freedman suggest locating Amos's prophetic activities in the period between 765 and 755 BCE.[205] On the other hand, Paul gives the dates for the reign of Uzziah as 785–733, and for Jeroboam II as 789–748 BCE.[206] Both kingdoms were experiencing relative peace and prosperity politically and economically, with a territorial expansion perhaps comparable to the era of David and Solomon.[207] So, Paul suggests that Amos' prophetic ministry would have come to completion before 745 BCE,[208] as there is no mention in Amos's oracles of the reversal of domestic political affairs following Jeroboam's death, or any reference to the Assyrian territorial expansion westward during the reign of Tiglath-Pileser III.[209]

With a similar approach in analysis of the political context, Carroll R. presents an overview of the range of dates offered for the reigns of Uzziah and Jeroboam II: 785–760 and 788–748 BCE, respectively, quoting Hayes and Hooker, and also mentions Coogan, who suggests 785–733 and 788–747 BCE.[210] From this general overview of the regnal years that these two kings overlapped, Carroll R. suggests that Amos's ministry

204. Anderson and Freedman, *Amos*, 19.
205. Anderson and Freedman, *Amos* 19; Radine, *Book of Amos*, 53.
206. Paul, *Amos*, 1n3. For an overview of dates offered by scholars, see Carroll R., *Book of Amos*, 6. The dates cited here are approximate.
207. Paul, *Amos*, 1, 2; Carroll R., *Book of Amos*, 11–15.
208. Paul, *Amos*, 1.
209. Paul, *Amos*, 1; Radine, *Book of Amos*, 54; Carroll R., *Book of Amos*, 10.
210. Carroll R., *Book of Amos*, 6.

spanned from the mid 780s to approximately 750 BCE.[211] Also, Carroll R. sees the reference to the occurrence of an earthquake, dated to 760 BCE by Yadin from his research at Hazor (Stratum VI), as significant in locating Amos's prophecies to around 760 BCE.[212] As Carroll R. further notes, the lack of mention of Israel and Judah in external sources, particularly in Assyrian inscriptions, obstructs locating Amos's ministry to a definitive historical background during the Assyrian domination under Tiglath-Pilezer III in the eighth century BCE. Assyria is not mentioned in Amos's prophecies, apart from a nation that remains anonymous (Amos 3:11; 6:14) as YHWH's agent for punishment.[213] Thus, based on the lack of reference to the chaotic political atmosphere that followed the reign of Jeroboam II, and the resurgence of the Assyrian political campaigns under Tiglath-Pilezer III, Carroll R. suggests Amos's ministry to span more broadly between 765 and 750 BCE.[214]

The absence of Assyria on the world stage during a period of political weakness (782–745 BCE) due to domestic problems in the reigns of the three sons of Adad-nirari III,[215] left the international stage devoid of imminent threats. Assyria under Adad-nirari III had also dealt a deathblow to Damascus (=Syria), hence allowing Israel's territorial expansion (2 Kgs 14:25, 28) and economic growth.[216] During this time of relative peace, international trade grew, and with no conflict between the two kingdoms, commerce developed.[217] Israel and Judah prospered economically and their political strength fostered their security. But the political and economic successes were coupled with socio-economic inequalities causing social stratification.[218] As Carroll R. points out, attempts have been made in the past three decades through interdisciplinary studies based on archaeological finds and social sciences to shed light on the nature of the socio-economic realities that Amos critiqued.[219] A few of

---

211. Carroll R., *Book of Amos*, 6, 9.

212. Carroll R., *Book of Amos*, 6–7.

213. Carroll R., *Book of Amos*, 7–9, *contra* scholars who see an allusion to the Assyrian threat for exile. Even the agent of YHWH's wrath against his people (Amos 3:11; 6:14) remains anonymous (see Rosenbaum, *Amos*, 22, 24–25; Paul, *Amos*, 1–2).

214. Carroll R., *Book of Amos*, 10.

215. Carroll R., *Book of Amos*, 11–12.

216. Carroll R., *Book of Amos*, 14–17.

217. Carroll R., *Book of Amos*, 18.

218. Carroll R., *Book of Amos*, 15–16.

219. Carroll R., *Book of Amos*, 16–20.

these approaches are presented here to give background to Amos's ire on the socio-economic inequalities.

As noted by Carroll R., one of these approaches is "rental capitalism," whereby the peasants are reliant on moneylenders and merchants to own land. This scheme, depending on natural or family disasters, could lead the peasants into debt slavery, while the landowners and merchants prospered. However, this scheme is critiqued and lacks theoretical and archaeological evidence to support its basis, compared to other proposed approaches on the socio-economic and political structures at the time. Possibly, key to the system that generated the prophecies of Amos is the social-scientific theory called the "tributary form of production" proposed by Gottwald,[220] which created wealth in the hands of landowners to the detriment of the peasants. But Carroll R. adds caution to this clear-cut tributary hypothesis, in that, corruption was woven into the fabric of Israelite society from the range of social groups to individuals in these social groups exploiting those similarly disadvantaged, or less than they. So for instance, the struggle to survive set in motion the exploitation of the weaker persons at different levels; this means the merchants and landowners, the elders who were supposed to dispense justice at the gate, or heartless kinsmen took advantage of the weaker.[221]

Although Carroll R. sees this model as fitting the descriptions of socioeconomic inequalities that Amos deplored, he suggests the patronage system[222] as underlying the imbalances in the socioeconomic realities of the situation compelling prophetic critique. Carroll R. argues that under this model, the patron provided the needs and protection of the client within the agricultural, village and kinship-based societies. He adds that this system characterized with benevolence and justice might have continued, and became popular as Israel developed into a monarchical system, thus extending to the king as the patron of all people. Hence, following Houston, Carroll R. contends that the unethical practices and injustices against the poor stemmed from the abuse of this patronage system.[223]

Whether it was the theoretical tributary, or the patronage system, designed for the socioeconomic situation that prompted prophetic denouncement of the oppression of the poor, one element is certainly clear.

---

220. Carroll R., *Book of Amos*, 20–21.
221. Carroll R., *Book of Amos*, 22–23.
222. Carroll R., *Book of Amos*, 24–25.
223. Carroll R., *Book of Amos*, 24–25.

That is; social injustice permeates Amos's prophetic message. The moral corruption of the privileged, religious leaders, and those in roles of power caused a lack of concern for the decay of the religious and social structure of the nation. From Amos's prophetic perspective, these moral and social ills were reflective of the distorted religious beliefs and practices, and were magnified in apostasy (Amos 2:4). The nation rejected YHWH's laws and corrupted the worship of YHWH, which was supposed to be the basic tenet of their religion and central to the identity of the people of Israel. Little wonder that Amos denounced the empty religious practices at Israel's chief religious centers (Amos 5:5; 8:14).

Israel's syncretistic worship of idols resulted in religious decline leading to the violation of the basic tenets of Yahwism. The main thrust of Amos's indictments against both Israel and Judah (Amos 3:1) was their acts of apostasy, or the falsehood[224] of following after other gods[225] (Amos 2:4; 5:26; 8:14). The sanctuaries at the centers of worship were infiltrated with idolatry evident in its characteristic ritual prostitution[226] (Amos 2:7c), thus desecrating the places of worship. The mention of a father and son entering the same girl, and lying down on garments taken as pledge, and beside "every altar" "in the house of their god" (v. 8), shows that this practice, in all its forms of profanity, occurred in sacred precincts (see Hos 4:14–15) and was undeniably prevalent (Gen 38:21–22; 1 Kgs 14:24; 15:12; 2 Kgs 23:7; Job 36:14). Hosea's condemnation of the same cultic practice (Hos 4:10, 18; 5:3–4) sheds light on the existence of the male-shrine prostitution and adultery associated with the Canaanite Ba'al fertility cult, and singles out the male counterparts for such reproof (Hos 4:14). The Mosaic laws also forewarned and condemned such

---

224. *Contra* Carroll R., who sees the term כזבים as a reference to the falsehood proceeding from other prophets, or misguiding leaders, and situated in the socio-political and religious setting with nothing to do with religious apostasy (Carroll R., *Book of Amos*, 176).

225. It is not unusual for OT prophets to use derogatory terms to refer to idolatry. There are similar denigrating terms in line with the word "falsehood" (כזבים, Isa 28:15, 17) used by Amos in Amos 2:4 to refer to idolatry. For instance, "worthlessness" (הבל, Jer 2:5) and "not profitable" (לא־יועלו, hence "worthless," Jer 2:8, 11) are the terms used by Jeremiah to expose existing apostasy in his time (Jer 2:2–37). Scholars who fail to recognize idolatry as the cardinal transgression causing the neglect of the covenant argue that Amos 2:4 is a later addition by a redactor. Wolff even suggests omitting Amos 5:26 and 8:14, which allude to idolatry, as late additions to the texts (Wolff, *Joel and Amos*, 259–60, 265–66, 325–26).

226. Some scholars dispute any reference to cultic prostitution in this verse. See Rosenbaum, *Amos*, 63; Carroll R., *Book of Amos*, 188, 188n220.

practices (Deut 23:17–18). As Amos denounced, these practices were coupled with the breach of recognized ethical requirements entrenched in bribery, exploitation and oppression of the poor (Amos 2:6–7aβ; 4:1; 5:11; 8:4, 6). So, the people of both Israel and Judah were culpable for the ethical infringement of YHWH's law regarding the welfare of the poor (Deut 15:7–11).

This breach of the society's ethical obligations aggravated the economic imbalance between the rich and the poor. The rich boosted their success by unjust methods; thus perverted justice and so, deliberately oppressed the poor (Amos 2:6; 5:12). They bribed the judicial system to the detriment of the poor, or righteous, who were sold for paltry debt (Amos 2:6–7b; 8:4, 6). Here Amos uses graphic images to emphasize the perversion of justice against the oppressed: the poor sold for a pair of sandals, or their heads trampled on. Generally, scholars see here debt-slavery[227] reflected in the legal and social practices in the society of Israel at the time. As Shveka argues, in Amos 2:6 the charge is against all of Israel for selling, or extraditing the run-away-slaves for a charge as low as a pair of shoes.[228] By such means the poor were cheated, exploited and oppressed, and were denied justice (Amos 2:7aβ). Similar cruelty and injustices against the poor occurred at the marketplace. These perverts of justice, the rich merchants, increased profits from the sale of grain, even including wheat refuse (Amos 8:6), by using false balances (v. 5). According to Amos's indictment, more exploitative acts against the poor and needy were in the form of maladministration of justice at the "gate"[229] (שַׁעַר, Amos 5:10). The gate was traditionally the place where YHWH's will for Israel's social order had been implemented and differences redressed. But, as the statement in Amos 5:10 implies, the "gate" no longer functioned as the locale for the administration of justice (Deut 21:19; cf. Prov 22:22; Isa 29:20–21). With the arbiter compromised, the poor

---

227. Carroll R., *Book of Amos*, 183, 183n203.

228. Here Shveka sees similarities with the Hittite law 22a stating that a captor of a fleeing slave be rewarded a pair of shoes. However, Shveka suggests that Amos condemns debt-slavery as a form of social injustice both at the national level as a whole (Amos 2:6) and at the merchandise level by slave owners and rich merchants (8:6). See Shveka, "Pair of Shoes," 96, 104–12.

229. Paul notes here the similarity with the Ugaritic *ṯgr* ("gate") as a place of assembly and judgment (Paul, *Amos*, 170n115). Carroll R. cites references from the Hebrew Bible to show that the gate is a place in a town or city where justice was administered, business transactions took place, or local people assembled (Carroll R., *Book of Amos*, 314).

had taxes exacted from them to finance the indulgent luxury of the rich (Amos 5:11). Moreover, injustice became prevalent and institutionalized with the judges' taking of bribes, and so the needy were turned aside (v. 12). Not only did these treacherous acts of bribery deny impartial justice to the poor, or needy, but this also meant violation of the *torah* (Exod 23:1–3, 6–8; Deut 16:18–20).[230]

Again, Amos critiqued the self-reliance and misconceived preeminence in the leadership positions of those in Zion and at Mount Samaria (Amos 6:1). In essence, Amos decried the self-complacency of the elite, laying judgment equally at the feet of the centers of power in the southern and northern kingdoms. He condemned their indulgent opulence. They sprawled on beds inlaid with ivory, dined on fine lambs and tender calves, and showed no concern for the decay in the fabric of the nation (v. 6). Their comfort and revelry in idle songs and debauchery in drinking (vv. 4–6) acted as a mirror image to the existing social injustice. Amos's satiric attack on the women of Samaria as "cows of Bashan"[231] pestering their husbands to bring them more to drink and so promote their lavish entertainment at the expense of the poor (Amos 4:1), emphasizes the rampant opulence without sensibilities to the welfare of the poor and needy (see Amos 2:8; 6:6).

Koch's suggestion, as noticed by Jacobs,[232] to view the women of Samaria as cows in light of their participation in the syncretistic bull cult at Samaria (Hos 8:5) is of relevance here too. In essence, Amos's rancor is double edged; as the thrust of his condemnations is idolatry. He alludes to the calf worship at Samaria as inextricably linked with the exploitative women who egged on their husbands, perhaps the nobles, or ruling elite, to bring them more at the expense of the poor and needy. Arguably, these women of the elite classes were the feminine (cows) counterparts of the worship of the bull cult at Samaria[233] (Amos 8:13–14; Hos 8:5; Mic

---

230. See Carroll R., *Book of Amos*, 319.

231. The fertile pastures of Bashan were known for their sleek and strong bulls/animals (Ps 22:13 [12]; see Deut 32:14; Ezek 39:18). The term "cows of Bashan" has been considered by womanist interpreters as derisive of women. But Carroll R. critiques this as confusing sexism with striking socio-economic parody (Carroll R., *Book of Amos*, 249–50). Undoubtedly, Amos uses the term "cows of Bashan" as a metaphor in emphasis of another aspect of the particulars of the endemic practices of social injustice in which the women of Samaria participated, overbearing on the poor and needy, to whom their husbands were masters.

232. Jacobs, "Cows," 109–10.

233. Jacobs, "Cows," 110.

1:5). They persisted in pagan idolatry (Amos 8:14a; Hos 8:6), and at the same time, their incessant demands, in order to satisfy their inebriation, etched the socio-economic imbalances (Amos 4:1).

Thus, YHWH's law on social responsibility, as it applied to the care and protection of the underprivileged[234] (see Exod 23:6–8), was subverted. Although these inebriated women had roamed sleek and freely like the cows of Bashan, and perpetrated social injustice, they would be caught like fish, and expelled from their natural habitat into exile with their nostrils bridled with fishhooks[235] (Amos 4:2–3; cf. 2 Kgs 19:28; Isa 37:29; Ezek 38:4). Not only are these perpetrators of social injustice displaced from their land in this humiliating manner, but Amos's prediction of the punishment to follow, evokes the prophecies of Hosea underscoring the idea of YHWH unleashing the whirlwind (Hos 8:7; see 4:19a) in judgment for their evil deeds compounded by idolatry.

Amos 1:2, 14—The Roaring Winds in Destruction

It is apparent, from the listing of oracles against the nations in Amos 1:3—2:16, that Amos condemns Israel and Judah for disobeying the law of YHWH, as much as other neighboring nations are indicted for breaking the rule of YHWH,[236] and acting against common humanity.[237] From

---

234. The importance of justice in Israelite society regarding the care of the underprivileged is made explicit by its prominence in the covenant code. Exod 22:21–24 forbids the oppression of the widow and orphan. A breach of this law would entail severe punishment. But, the idea of social justice is not unique to the Hebrew tradition. In the ANE, the judging and protection of the poor, orphan and widow was the concern of the king. However, the exercising of judgment is YHWH's prerogative. As stated in Deut 10:17–18, YHWH is regarded as LORD over all other gods, as well as judge and protector of the widow, orphan, and foreigner. The same thought is developed in Ps 82 where YHWH is depicted as the supreme deity and judge. He imposes judgment on the other gods for failing to dispense justice for the underprivileged. See Fensham, "Widow," 129–39.

235. Nwaoru, "Fresh Look," 472–73.

236. Andersen and Freedman, *Amos*, 26.

237. Shveka proposes a new meaning for the idea of buying or selling the poor for a pair of sandals as relating to debt slavery, and as a matter of social injustice that Amos critiqued at two levels. At one level, although matters are internal, Shveka argues that it is the highest classes that are condemned for the oppression of the poor, and at the second level; the entire people are held accountable for allowing such injustice in their norms and equally condemned like the surrounding nations who, on the international scene, delivered a whole people into slavery. See Shveka, "Pair of Shoes," 108–12.

the outset, Amos alludes to YHWH's sovereign rule[238] over the surrounding nations, and his mastery of the forces of nature he unleashes upon them as punishment. As Amos predicts, the nations of Damascus, Gaza, Tyre, Edom, Ammon, and Moab are destined to experience the wrath of YHWH in the destructive force of fire. Moreover, as Amos warns in the rebuke on Ammon, YHWH would manifest his wrath by "tempest" (סער) and "storm wind" (סופה, Amos 1:14).[239] Here, also, YHWH's appearance with the winds is in view.

The two terms סער and סופה appear in parallel in Ps 83:16[15] (see Isa 29:6)[240] in an appeal by the nation of Israel to YHWH to destroy his enemies with these tempestuous winds; showing a conventional diction for YHWH's disclosure in the Hebrew tradition. Hence, with the associated elements of the sonorous sound (Amos 1:2b), fire[241] (אש, vv. 4, 7, 10, 12, 14), and the tempestuous winds (סופה//סער, v. 14), nothing other than YHWH's intervention with his entourage of natural phenomena is pivotal in this context. Not only does Amos use a numerical formula, "for three transgressions and for four," similar to numerical expressions in wisdom literature[242] (cf. Job 5:19; 33:29; Prov 6:16; 30:15–31; Qoh 11:2), to indict Judah and Israel as much as other nations, but the same ominous judgment is pronounced upon them. With the word "roar" (שאג, Amos 1:2=Joel 4:16[3:16]; see Jer 25:30b; Job 37:4) and the expression "gives his voice" (יתן קולו), typical of YHWH's appearance with the phenomenal elements (Pss 18:14[13]b; 68:34[33]b; Jer 25:30b; Joel 4:16[3:16]; cf. Job 37:4–5a), Amos draws from the dictum common to other texts relating YHWH's appearance with the winds. In both Ps 18 and Joel 4[3], the expression "gives his voice" (יתן קולו), implying the issuing of the sonorous sound, is complemented with the trembling and shaking of the heavens and earth (Ps 18:8[7]; Joel 4:16[3:16]).[243] The darkening of the sky, or

---

238. Andersen and Freedman, *Amos*, 90–91.

239. Carroll R., *Book of Amos*, 167; cf. McComiskey, "Amos," 289, who objects to the view that these elements connote YHWH's theophany.

240. See Farr, "Language," 316–17; Carroll R., *Book of Amos*, 167, 167n153.

241. Weinfeld points to the use of fire and lightning as elements of divine judgment found both in the OT and the ANE. See Weinfeld, "Divine Intervention," 136–40.

242. See Wolff, *Joel and Amos*, 138; Terrien, "Amos," 449–51; McComiskey, "Amos," 282.

243. Farr, "Language," 313–14. The notion of heavens trembling and the earth quaking is clearly associated with the goddess Inanna (also identified as the Babylonian Ištar), whose appearance (either in storms, or extreme heat) is pictured in the accompaniment of a thundering storm, rain and lightning. See Kinsley, *Goddesses' Mirror*,

YHWH IN THE WIND(S)

concealing of the heavenly luminaries (Ps 18:12[11]; Joel 4:15[3:15]) is integral with the roar of YHWH's voice[244] emanating from his prevalent winds (see Job 26:8–11).

But Amos 1:2 omits the cosmic shaking and darkening of the luminaries, and only makes reference to the "pastures of the shepherds" mourning (אבל, see Hosea 4:3; Jer 4:28; 12:4, 11), and the "top of Carmel" withering (יבש, Amos 1:2). Scholars identify the Hebrew אבל as an etymological equivalent to *abālu* in Akkadian meaning "dry up."[245] This translation is fitting in a merism showing that there would be complete devastation manifested in drying up, or withering extending from the low lying pastures to the top of Carmel.[246] Even though YHWH is said to "roar,"[247] and "give his voice" in this context, his appearance portends devastation, not by a thunderstorm bringing rain, but experienced in the (*sirocco*-like) winds effecting drought.[248] Arguably, we should anticipate here, that by the term "roar" (Amos 1:2a), Amos makes reference to YHWH emitting the winds that dried up the sea to wreak the creation and salvation of the people of Israel. This marks an overture to YHWH's forthcoming judgment by the same winds, leading to the destruction of his elected people and the surrounding nations.

Indeed, as though serving as an *inclusio* to this first chapter, Amos mentions the tempestuous winds in a statement foreboding YHWH's indictment and devastation of Ammon (Amos 1:14). Perhaps, the goddess

---

131; Wolkstein and Kramer, *Inanna*, 95.

244. Andersen and Freedman, *Amos*, 220.

245. Paul, *Amos*, 39–40, 40n65; Carroll R., *Book of Amos*, 122, 122n26.

246. Paul, *Amos*, 40; Carroll R., *Book of Amos*, 123–24.

247. Strawn discusses the broad association of gods with lions in the ANE dating back to the sixth or seventh millennium BCE (Strawn, *What Is Stronger*, 190, 200). He also notes that the lion was more frequently associated with the female than the male deities (252) and singles out Ištar as the lion goddess depicted standing/stepping over a lion (194–95, 208, 258), and other male deities enthroned on lions (199). Strawn also points out that the god as lion, occurred in a context of violent war imagery (207). Although Strawn cautions on a simplistic identification, or separation of the aspects of storm and war, nowhere else does he see that these aspects are integral except in the characterization of the Anzû bird, Umdugud (207). He sees its leonine character as an extension of the thunderous roar and martial connotations (208). However, Strawn also notes that the storm gods are found with composites: either winged lion-griffin/eagle, or winged lion-dragon (253). But Strawn views the leonine depictions of YHWH in the Hebrew tradition (255), as the leonine antecedent of the goddesses, particularly Ištar and her martial attributes (258), and also probably the goddess Sekhmet (262–67).

248. See Paul, *Amos*, 39–41; Carroll R., *Book of Amos*, 122.

Innana's association with a lion,[249] her most famous epithet as the queen of heaven and earth, and her other dominant characteristics, particularly her manifestation with stormy winds in nature and battle,[250] shed light on the aspects of YHWH's appearance described in Amos. As cited in the excerpts from the hymn of Enheduanna, priestess of Inanna, a collation of similar characteristics features in the identification of this Akkadian goddess Inanna (Ištar). The consecutive lines[251] in this hymn portray Inanna as roaring at the earth,[252] propelled by "wings,"[253] charging a storm, thundering, and exhaling evil winds,[254] thus avowing Inanna's tempestuous nature. Inanna is acclaimed with the propensity to roar resembling thunder, so that no vegetation can withstand her.[255] She is said to fan fire against people. Her tempestuous radiance is said to cause fear and trembling in humankind. Undoubtedly, the idea of "wings" bestowed on Inanna by the storm, and flying about the nation, alludes to her soaring on the winds causing devastation on the lands compounded by the "evil winds" she vents out. Nothing other than the effect of the winds is pertinent to this nature. In light of this, the idea of YHWH's roar, and the giving of his voice mentioned in Amos 1:2 relates the rumbling of

---

249. Strawn, *What Is Stronger*, 208–9.

250. Kinsley, *Goddesses' Mirror*, 124–33. Kinsley notes that Inanna played a central role in Sumerian mythology, theology, and cult. Inanna was worshiped in Sumer in the third to first millennium BCE and in the form of the Babylonian Ištar until the end of the first millennium BCE (113). In one story, it is narrated that Inanna acquired her powers from her father, Enki, the god of wisdom, upon inebriation (124–26). So Inanna sailed off in a heavenly boat and held sway over nature, culture, life and death. In a celebration hymn, Inanna lauded herself for the possession of heaven and earth, lordship, and queenship, battle and combat, including possession of the flood and tempest (127). See also Strawn, *What Is Stronger*, 209.

251. See Hallo and Van Dijk, *Exaltation of Inanna*, 15–19, esp. lines 10, 12–13, 17–18, 21–22, 27–31; Kinsley, *Goddesses' Mirror*, 130; Black et al., *Literature*, 316–17.

252. In another hymn, the goddess Inanna is said to manifest in the "dark breezes" (wind) causing the quaking of the earth. See Kinsley, *Goddesses' Mirror*, 131; Wolkstein and Kramer, *Inanna*, 95; Strawn, *What Is Stronger*, 209.

253. On the association of wings and wind, see pp. 79–80. Hallo and Dijk see Inanna viewed as a bird and, by extension, compared with the storm or even the storm god Iškur (Hallo and Dijk, *Exaltation of Inanna*, 51). The idea of a storm or storm cloud compared with a bird with outstretched wings was not uncommon in Sumerian iconography. Perhaps this idea corresponds with Noegel's observation of wings associated with winds, as the winds are predominantly the bearers of storm phenomena.

254. Kinsley, *Goddesses' Mirror*, 130; Hallo and Dijk, *Exaltation of Inanna*, 18–19, lines 27–31.

255. Kinsley, *Goddesses' Mirror*, 130; Hallo and Dijk, *Exaltation of Inanna*, 15 line 10; Strawn, *What Is Stronger*, 209n481.

tempestuous winds,[256] causing nature to mourn, thus evoking images of dryness. Hence, the fruitful pastures dry up, and the top of Carmel withers from the pervasive tempestuous winds at YHWH's disclosure.

Quite significant, perhaps, is the primacy accorded to Zion,[257] or Jerusalem, as the appropriate locus of YHWH's disclosure with cosmic phenomena, in order to reinforce YHWH's direct involvement in the events of history, and execution of judgment in the historical arena. To that end, YHWH manifests himself from Zion, in order to exercise his lordship over the nations, and no less on Judah and Israel. So, here, in the oracles of Amos, is an allusion to the preexilic idea of YHWH's universal dominion. It is on the basis of this sovereignty of YHWH that Amos appropriates the language of creation and gives impetus to the message of judgment announced in the oracles. Amos uses the language conventional to YHWH's self-disclosure with the winds in depiction of YHWH as both the sovereign creator and the judge[258] of his own people. This theme is hymned in the doxologies in Am 4:13, 5:8–9 and 9:5–6,[259] where the rudiments of a theophanic tradition are introduced and integrated with creation ideology in the portrait of YHWH, who is the creator and universal judge.

Amos 4:12–13—Prepare to Meet Your God!

It is evident that the theme of the inescapable divine presence of YHWH is central to Amos's denunciation of various acts of profanity and injustice.

256. Andersen and Freedman, *Amos*, 227, mention the effects of the hot desert winds causing the pastures to wither, though misinterpreting the image of the roar of a lion.

257. See Cross, *Canaanite Myth*, 38; Robinson, "Zion," 122. Just as the temple at Zion is considered to be a microcosm of its heavenly counterpart, so also the metaphor of YHWH manifesting himself from his celestial abode is transferred to this terrestrial replica. In terms of creation, as accentuated here, perhaps the close identification of Zion with the far north—*yarkĕtê ṣāpōn*—is relational to the provenance of the winds and origination of creation as in the case of the whirlwind-deity Amma. See p. 24, 24n164.

258. In view of the doxologies in Amos, Crenshaw sees a link between creation theology and retribution (Crenshaw, "Prolegomenon," 34–35; *Hymnic Affirmation*, 120–21).

259. Although these doxologies are often considered late insertions by a redactor or intrusive to their current context (see Mays, *Amos*, 84–85, 95, 155; Crenshaw, *Hymnic Affirmation*, 123, 128–29, 131; Paul, *Amos*, 152; Andersen and Freedman, *Amos*, 453–55; Carroll R., *Book of Amos*, 282), it is argued here for their originality in assertion of their purposeful function in the prophecies of Amos.

Though he announces that YHWH's judgment reaches beyond the confines of Israel and Judah, partly to emphasize the transcendent power and might of YHWH, the rest of Amos's message focuses on the chastisement of YHWH's own people. Amos points out to both Israel and Judah, as to one nation[260] (Amos 3:1), and their special privileges: "You only have I known of all the families of the earth" (v. 2). But Israel's privileged status also calls forth severe punishment for its rampant acts of oppression. As Amos declares, using a wisdom term, the chosen people do not know how to do "right"[261] (נכחה, Amos 3:10). Wolff noticed that the term נכחה occurs frequently in wisdom literature to mean what is "right."[262] Quite instructive here is the use of the term in Prov 8:8–9 where the term צדק ("righteous") is used in parallel with the term נכחה. The words of wisdom are said to issue with rightness[263] without anything tortuous or twisted, and are right and upright to the discerning and those who find knowledge. As Wolff observed, Amos also employs the intransitive verb "know" (ידע) to predicate the term right as the object of discernment.[264] Thus, the term right used in Amos 3:10 fits the connotation implied in Amos's indictment, as the antonym of the perverse and crooked nature of Israel's oppressive conduct. Conduct marked by oppression and the acquiring of wealth by violence and robbery (Amos 3:9–10; see 2:6–8; 5:11–12; 8:4) shows lack of concern for social responsibility and justice

---

260. Henceforth, the term Israel will be used to represent this nation. See Amos 6:1, using the cities Zion and Samaria to represent the whole nation, showing that they were both heedless to the call of justice as demanded by the law of YHWH, and Amos 3:13, in which the whole twelve tribes are referred to as the house of Jacob (Israel).

261. Wolff, *Amos*, 56–59; Terrien, "Amos," 452–53; Jeremias, *Book of Amos*, 58.

262. Wolff, *Amos*, 57. Sandoval notes that although Wolff mentions the frequent appearance of the term נכחה, it occurs only twice in Proverbs (Prov 8:9; 24:26) and once in Sirach (11:21), wisdom contexts (Isa 30:10), and exilic and post exilic texts (Isa 26:10; 57:2; 59:14). Sandoval admits that the term נכחה belongs to wisdom rhetoric, but sees its function more in distinguishing the discourses Amos relates than in showing the impact of wisdom on Amos's prophecy. See Sandoval, "Prophetic," 145. This terminology from sapiential literature is appropriate to Amos's discourses with thought and style common to the wisdom tradition (Terrien, "Amos," 448–55). McLaughlin not only questions the nuance of נכחה in Amos 3:10 in relation to its identification with wisdom literature (McLaughlin, "Amos (Still)?," 293–94) but also challenges this notion of Amos using thought and literary devices with affinity to wisdom literature (281–303). Arguably, it is asserted that Amos's discourses entail the intersection of wisdom and creation; hence, the similarities with some texts from the book of Job mentioning creation and wisdom.

263. BDB 841.

264. Wolff, *Amos*, 57.

as demanded by YHWH.²⁶⁵ For these acts of disobedience, Amos announces the judgment to fall upon Israel at the hands of an enemy (Amos 3:11). Their fortresses and the altars of Bethel, along with their horns that provide a false sense of religious security (Amos 3:14; cf. Exod 27:2; 1 Kgs 1:50–53), will be destroyed. The destruction at the center of their religious system will show the futility of their symbols of refuge, as the destruction will be widespread.²⁶⁶ Also the expensively decorated homes, indicating the lavish lifestyle of the rich, will be demolished (Amos 3:15).

In chapter 4, Amos continues to expand on the accusations introduced in chapter 3 concerning the infringement of YHWH's law and provoking YHWH's judgment. The metaphor of fish caught on hooks employed here (Amos 4:2; cf. Hab 1:14–15) to symbolize judgment, was common in the ANE since the third millennium BCE, and featured in Mesopotamian literature.²⁶⁷ The idea is evoked here to compare people to fish caught from water, extracted from their ill-forged affluence through breaches in the wall (cf. Jer 52:7; Ezek 12:5), and banished to an undisclosed location (Amos 4:3).²⁶⁸ Again, in sustained satiric rhetoric, Amos exhorts the people to attend their historic religious sanctuaries, Bethel and Gilgal, to perform their meaningless rituals for self-aggrandizement in fulfilling their false religious impulses (vv. 4–5).²⁶⁹

In spite of YHWH's persistent use of natural catastrophes to warn and punish his people, in order for them to return to him, they sustain their wayward practices. YHWH withholds the rains; drought ensues causing scarcity of food. Gardens and vineyards are blighted, and, as may be implied by the proverbial saying about the total destruction of Sodom and Gomorrah (cf. Isa 1:9–10; Jer 20:16; 23:14), the rebellious people suffer near destruction (Amos 4:6–11). Even though their narrow escape is compared with that of a "fire brand plucked from burning," they still fail to heed the divine caution and so finally call inescapable destruction upon themselves. Thus, the finality of an encounter with YHWH, in which the offending nation will fully experience the might of this deity, is summed up in the command: "Prepare to meet your God, O Israel" (Amos 4:12). Undoubtedly, this imperative²⁷⁰ suggests a theophany, as

---

265. See p. 112, 112n234.
266. Carroll R., *Book of Amos*, 244–45.
267. Yoder, *Fishers of Fish*, 60.
268. Yoder, *Fishers of Fish*, 69–70,
269. See Carroll R., *Book of Amos*, 258–63.
270. When discussing the use of the expression "be ready" (הכון, Amos 4:12; cf.

is implied by the expression, "to meet your God"²⁷¹ (לקראת־אלהיך), which recalls the account of the events leading to YHWH's theophany at Sinai (Exod 19:17). However, in contrast with the Sinai incident, this pronouncement does not relate the making or renewal of the covenant, or an event intended to warn Israel to repent.²⁷² In this case, following the specified events to bring Israel to repentance that go unheeded (Amos 4:6–11), the formula summons Israel to face its final calamity: to meet YHWH in judgment.

Although the nature of the impending judgment is not expressed, Amos identifies the nature of this deity who is capable of executing judgment. Thus, in a hymnic verse (Amos 4:13), he portrays the power and majesty of YHWH in language deriving from his creative acts. This verse is the first of the hymnic texts introducing YHWH as the creator. What is in a name? YHWH is described as "the one who forms" (יוצר) the mountains (see Ps 65:7[6]) and the "creator" (ברא) of the winds (cf. Ps 135:7). The collocation of these participial appellations that allude to aspects of YHWH's power as creator, and the reference to his declaring (מגיד) his thoughts to humans (Dan 2:28), indicates that such a deity reveals his thoughts to mankind, as much as he manifests his cosmic power in nature. The juxtaposition of creative acts showing YHWH's power as creator with his intervening in the mundane realm shows that here Amos relates the creative power of YHWH that brought order out of primordial chaos to his mighty acts performed in the historical arena.

Moreover, as the remainder of Amos 4:13 spells out, YHWH also exercises his power over natural phenomena that he created. YHWH creates the winds (Job 9:9b) and employs them for his own purposes (Job 37:9–12; Ps 148:8b). Thus, in keeping with YHWH's appearance with the winds that he formed, the idea of "making" (עשׂה) dawn into darkness

---

Ezek 38:7), Wolff notes that the Sinai pericope (Exod 19:11, 15) employs the same root in the participle to express the readiness of Israel to meet YHWH. He argues that the summons "to meet God" is a liturgical call upon those assembled at the destroyed altar of Bethel to give themselves over to YHWH (Wolff, *Joel and Amos*, 222). Brueggemann, on the other hand, sees similarities in the use of the imperatives "prepare/meet" (Exod 19:11, 15, 17; 34:2) but links to a call to obedience and covenant renewal (Brueggemann, "Amos," 5–10). Jeremias argues that the imperative "prepare" implies a time of reckoning for Israel either to encounter death, or compassion of the one passing by (Jeremias, *Book of Amos*, 75).

271. Paul thinks the encounter is of God himself in person (Paul, *Amos*, 152).
272. *Contra* Paul, *Amos*, 151n119.

(עיפה)²⁷³ heralds the majestic power of his wind²⁷⁴ dispersing the clouds and intercepting daylight (see Amos 5:8; see Job 9:7).²⁷⁵ This clause, as in other contexts relating YHWH's impending judgment, forebodes the darkness of the day of YHWH coming to execute judgment (Jer 4:28; Joel 2:2, 10, 31[3:4]; 4:15[3:15]; Ezek 32:7; Zech 14:6; Zeph 1:15), and order chaos. The basis of this image is the [earthshaking] winds dispersing the ominous clouds touching the high places of the earth, possibly the mountains²⁷⁶ mentioned in the poetic parallelism (Amos 4:13aβ), and turning the dawn into darkness.

Consecutively, the idiom expressing the idea of YHWH "treading" (דרך) the high places²⁷⁷ of the earth (Mic 1:3), implying the exercise of his dominion on earth, is a parody of the metaphor of YHWH's theophany

---

273. Paul, *Amos*, 155; Jeremias, *Book of Amos*, 66; Whitley, "עיפה," 128–32. Whitley notes that the term עיפה (derived from the Semitic root עיף ["to be dark"]) is frequently translated "darkness," and relates to the ominous image of YHWH "who makes dawn into darkness," though he sees this meaning as misplaced in a context relating YHWH's role as creator. Instead, Whitley proffers a new meaning for the term עיפה deriving from the root עיף meaning "to fly," and compares with cognates such as the Egyptian ˁpy commonly held to be a Semitic term designating the solar winged disk also known as "the flying thing." Whitley also observed similarities with the Phoenician עפת and Aramaic עפתא, particularly the Phoenician Yeḥawmilk stele with a scene in its upper section depicting King Yeḥawmilk making an offering to the lady of Byblos, flanked with an image of the winged sun disk. On that basis, Whitley sees a bearing of this scene to the Semitic term עפת given to the winged sun disk. Hence, he suggests the term עיפה designates winged sun disk, and translates the clause in Amos 4:13 as "the one who makes the winged disk at dawn." He views this not as solar imagery in description of YHWH, but as a couplet showing YHWH's total control of ordered creation paralleling Ps 19:5b–7[4b–6], and pointedly pairing with the idea of YHWH creating the wind in the chiastic structure of Amos 4:13. Also, Whitley sees in Amos 4:13 a juxtaposition of the imagery of a deity associated with mountains and the winged sun disk common to the ANE texts and iconography (Whitley, "עיפה,"132–38). However, Whitley's proposition focuses more on creation and dismisses the reference to YHWH's control and maintenance of that created order, as the crucial note intended in Amos's message on the impending judgment.

274. Paas, *Creation and Judgement*, 272.

275. See p. 91.

276. Linville mentions the mountains of Samaria—or possibly Mount Rimmon—as subject to YHWH's mastery of the high places (Linville, *Amos*, 96).

277. Linville states that *bāmôt* not only designates hills or mountains but also the shrines built upon them (Linville, *Amos*, 96). Emerton offered various meanings for *bāmôt* but also remarked that there were many sanctuaries in ancient Israel and Judah called *bāmôt* and often constructed on hills, though not always. However, Emerton asserted that the term *bāmôt* does not always need to be rendered to imply an elevated position. See Emerton, "Biblical High Place," 116–32.

YHWH IN THE WIND AS CREATOR-KING

to tread the "backs" of the sea in the primeval battle[278] (Job 9:8b; Hab 3:15). The image recalls YHWH's mastery of the winds in subjection of the chaotic waters, and the same portends the inevitable desolation of the "high places" of Isaac, the sanctuaries of Israel (Amos 4:4; 5:5; Mic 1:5), including the destruction of the house of Jeroboam (Amos 7:9).[279] By the same means of the wind by which YHWH shapes cosmic creation, he is able to destroy the syncretistic high places.

In echoing YHWH's creative acts in the doxology in Amos 4:13, Amos demonstrates not only YHWH's supremacy in creation, but also his power to overturn creation,[280] as shown in the images presaging his intervention in human affairs for judgment.[281] Indeed, Amos portrays YHWH the creator, as the one who has the right to appear with the power of his "roaring" winds (Amos 1:2, 14; 3:8; Jer 4:11-12; 13:24; 49:32, 36; Ezek 5:10, 12), and bring order back to a chaotic state. This is an appropriate revelatory depiction for the appellation YHWH 'ĕlōhê Ṣebā'ôth meaning YHWH the God of hosts,[282] and connotes the divine

---

278. Andersen and Freedman, *Amos*, 456-57.

279. Linville, *Amos*, 97.

280. Jeremias, *Book of Amos*, 77. Linville, apud Jeremias, cites Job 5:9-10 as the closest parallel to the doxologies in Amos, pointing out that it is no accident that creation themes are connected with judgmental passages (Linville, *Amos*, 93).

281. Jeremias, *Book of Amos*, 76-78.

282. Zobel notes that 1 Sam 17:45 is the only reference that interprets Ṣebā'ôth, a feminine plural of the noun Ṣābā', as "army, host" in association with the militaristic nature of YHWH, though this interpretation is met with scholars' dissenting voice (Zobel, "צְבָאוֹת," 218-20). However, Zobel argues that the term Ṣebā'ôth appears frequently as one of the shortest and most employed divine epithets of YHWH in the OT tradition. The first occurrence of the epithet with the Shiloh tradition in association with the ark places its provenance with the temple cult at Shiloh (1 Sam 1:3, 11; 4:4), and links with the nominal term "the one who is enthroned on the cherubim" (1 Sam 4:4); a title also transferred to the temple tradition in Jerusalem (2 Sam 6:2, 18; Zobel, "צְבָאוֹת," 222-23). Mettinger argues for the origination of Ṣebā'ôth from the Canaanite god El, designated as El Ṣebā'ôth, thus, denoting him as the king of the gods presiding over a heavenly council. He also sees the nominal formula of YHWH sitting on the cherubim throne linked with the Ṣebā'ôth epithet as belonging to, and deriving from the El iconography and tradition of the Shiloh temple cult, that were adapted for YHWH and later transferred to the Solomonic temple tradition (Mettinger, "YHWH Sabaoth," 112, 128-36; cf. Cross, *Canaanite Myth*, 69-70). But, Wood dispels Mettinger's views as lacking supportive evidence, and too conjectural (Wood, *Of Wings*, 14-18). Nonetheless, suggestions by biblical scholars for the meaning of the epithet Ṣebā'ôth have varied from an assertion of YHWH's militaristic nature in connection with the ark as a martial dais, or as a formula relational to the sovereignty of YHWH among heavenly beings/hosts (divine council), or his comprehensive power and majesty (Zobel, "צְבָאוֹת," 224-25). In view of YHWH's feat at creation in the passages in

militaristic nature of YHWH (1 Sam 17:45; cf. 1 Kgs 22:19). However, the designation of YHWH in Amos 4:13 is employed in the context of creation to show his cosmic potency (cf. Isa 40:26), and, at the same time, his propensity to break into the social realm by the power of his winds. Hence the injunction: "Prepare to meet your God, O Israel," foreboding the ominousness of the encounter with the God whose power and majesty in nature is incomparable. The image portrayed of "the one who creates the wind," whose presence is manifested in the historical arena by his roaring winds, provides the framework within which Amos pictures YHWH as creator, and explains his prerogative to intervene and execute his rule. It is clear, as in the case of Amos 4:12-13, that the other doxologies in Amos 5:8-9 and 9:5-6 are directed against Israel's self-incriminating acts of idolatry and social injustice, and set the tone for the climactic theophanic encounter with YHWH as the creator and judge.

The One Who Flashes "Destruction": An Elegy in Amos 5:8-9

The second doxology in Amos 5:8-9[283] occurs in the series of woes (Amos 5-6) that are subsequent to the warning in Amos 4:13. It is apparent in Amos 5:1-2 that Amos pronounces the demise of Israel with such certainty that he prefaces his message on the impending judgment with a dirge over a fallen state. The desecrated cultic places at Bethel, Gilgal and the Judean sanctuary of Beersheba (Amos 5:5) were the epitome of Israel's religious decay. These prominent places of worship in Israel, as may be judged from 1 Kgs 12:26-33,[284] were infiltrated by idolatry and for that reason were destined for destruction.

---

discussion, the appellative Ṣebā'ôth should be interpreted in the purview of YHWH's display of his all-comprehensive power and majesty manifested in the winds against forces of chaos, both in the cosmic and social realm.

283. Although generally regarded as intrusive and disruptive to the flow of Amos's denunciation of those perverting justice, beginning in Amos 5:7 and continuing in vv. 10-13, this doxology is purposely placed here to emphasize the nature of the deity to be met in judgment. Also, it serves to confirm the destruction that Amos predicts and views with such certainty as to warrant an elegy in Amos 5:1-2. Among the critics arguing for the intrusive nature of this doxology, see Mays, *Amos*, 83-84, 95; Crenshaw, *Hymnic Affirmation*, 124, 127; McComiskey, "Hymnic Elements," 144, esp. 140-41n7. For comments by scholars on the intrusiveness of this hymnic element, see Hadjiev, *Joel and Amos*, 139.

284. Note the pagan worship centered on bull images instituted by Jeroboam at Bethel and Dan.

YHWH IN THE WIND AS CREATOR-KING

Undoubtedly, Amos's apparent lampoon on the astral deities that Israel would carry into exile, as in Amos 5:26, further suggests that idolatry corrupted the religious significance of Israel's centers of worship (Amos 8:14). More fundamentally, idolatry distanced Israel from YHWH, thus leading to the neglect in administering the law, and, as a consequence, impropriety in despising justice (Amos 5:7, 10–12). Accordingly, Amos levels the accusation of turning "justice" into wormwood and thrusting "righteousness" to the ground (Amos 5:7; cf. 6:12). Therefore, as a counterpoint, the ode in Amos 5:8–9 following the charge in v. 7 is intended to show the contrast between those who perpetrate injustice and YHWH, whose reign is founded on "justice" and "righteousness" (Pss 89:15[14]; 97:2), as the basis of his rule for social order. The prophet Amos also stresses that these elements: "Justice" and "righteousness" (Amos 5:24), should characterize the life of YHWH's people as devotees of this deity who "roars" from Zion.

As observed by Wolff,[285] by referring to the word pair "justice" and "righteousness," Amos, here, also appeals to the sapiential tradition to emphasize the gravity of violating YHWH's ethos of governance in defense of the poor and defenseless. As Amos shows, those concerned with administering justice at the "gate" (cf. Amos 5:12d, 15aβ) subvert their normal judicial protocol (vv. 10, 12). These perverts of justice acquire mansions and vineyards at the expense of the poor (v. 11). Thus, those who overturn YHWH's social order face the threat of confronting the one who solely creates and governs the universe. This idea accounts for the emphasis that all creation originates with YHWH, and those who neglect his law (Amos 2:4) by following idols, face the creator, who "turns" nature to accomplish his own ends.

Here, in a *double entendre* against astral worship coupled with injustice, Amos objectifies the idea in Amos 5:8–9 by eulogizing YHWH as the "creator" (עֹשֵׂה) of Pleiades and Orion[286] (see Job 9:9; 38:31), "who turns" (הֹפֵךְ) deep darkness to morning and darkens day to night (Amos 5:8aβ), and "who calls" (הַקּוֹרֵא) on the waters of the sea and pours them

---

285. For comment on Amos's use of this pair of terms, "justice and righteousness," that is resonant with wisdom sayings (cf. Prov 2:6–9; 15:8–9; 21:3), to indicate the real basis for the royal throne, see Wolff, *Joel and Amos*, 245–46. The same pair of terms is also used as the measuring standard for the proper function of the expected judicial procedures at the "gate" (Amos 5:12, 15).

286. It is possible that the prophet Amos derived this idea from wisdom sources, from which he inferred that YHWH created the constellations, with the intent to denounce and deter the worship of astral deities.

over the face of the earth (Amos 5:8cd=9:6cd). Not only is YHWH described as the creator and regulator of day and night, but he can also change the light of day to darkness (Amos 5:18, 20; 8:9; see Job 9:7) for his own purposes. This latter idea, in combination with the allusion to a deluge, in the remaining part of Amos 5:8, further suggests the appearance of YHWH with meteorological phenomena, particularly the billowing winds roiling the rain clouds from the sea, eclipsing the daylight, and causing a downpour on the surface of the earth. Even here, there is allusion to the ancients' insight on the essential water cycle of evaporation, condensation and precipitation. Nonetheless, at creation, YHWH employs the winds to form dry ground. Perhaps, too, the reference to YHWH "calling" (הקורא) on the waters of the sea and pouring on the land implies the revoking of the statute, or boundary applied to the sea at creation (Amos 5:8; cf. Jer 5:22; Ps 104:9; Job 38:8–11; Prov 8:29) to cause a flood.[287]

As much as the first doxology (Amos 4:13), the hymnic verse in Amos 5:8 underscores the power of YHWH to revert creation into chaos. By his phenomenal winds, YHWH summons the waters of the sea to cause devastation on the land.[288] Though Carroll R. notes the use of the term "pour out" (špk, Amos 5:8e) as abrupt, it appears in prophetic literature with YHWH dispensing his spirit[289] (רוח, Isa 32:15; 44:3; see Ezek 39:29), which also possibly translates to YHWH pouring out his rain-bearing-wind to fructify parched lands in the Isaianic texts cited. But, as Carroll R. further notes, the term špk is particularly employed in connection with YHWH unleashing his wrath (Jer 6:11; 42:18; 44:6; Ezek 7:8; Hos 5:10; Zeph 3:8).[290] In the same vein, the hymnic description in Amos 5:8 relates YHWH's indisputable prerogative to hold sway over the chaotic waters as at the primordial creation. In this case, YHWH commands the waters to do his bidding in desolation of those who turn justice into wormwood. Thus, this hymn celebrating YHWH's cosmological activities associates the theme of creation and judgment within a context in which the sinfulness of the people is juxtaposed with the inevitable divine intervention.

In that case, the emphasis on the "darkness" (חשך) and "gloom" (אפל), exclusive of "light" (אור) and "brightness" (נגה, Amos 5:18, 20; cf.

287. See Linville, *Amos*, 106; Hadjiev, *Joel and Amos*, 140.
288. Hadjiev, *Joel and Amos*, 140.
289. Carroll R., *Book of Amos*, 311.
290. Carroll R., *Book of Amos*, 311.

2 Sam 22:13=Ps 18:13[12]; Ezek 10:4; Hab 3:4, 11), often associated with YHWH's theophany, expresses the inescapability of the forthcoming judgment. This anticipates the expected day of YHWH, which appears as a reversal of creation with light turning to darkness (Jer 4:23, 28b). This gloom spells doom in the historic arena (Amos 5:18-20). The emphasis is on the name YHWH (Amos 5:8d), who is featured here as the creator-god, and as "the one who bursts or flashes forth"[291] (המבליג, Amos 5:9a); thus expressing his violent destructive tendencies. So, YHWH will "pass by"[292] (עבר, Amos 5:17; see Job 9:11) in the imperceptible roaring winds to impose destruction with his phenomenal meteorological elements (see Job 9:17; 37:2-12; Prov 10:25) intercepting light and turning it into darkness (Amos 5:18, 20; Isa 24:21-23).[293] YHWH appears in order to mete out judgment and inflict destruction on the ones spurning his rule of "justice" and "righteousness." Consequently, in his sovereignty and exercise of his rule, YHWH with his formidable power as creator will "burst forth" with destruction on the mighty transgressors and their fortresses (Amos 5:9). It is little wonder; therefore, in consideration of the robust power of YHWH, that Amos views the destruction of Israel with such certainty that he utters an elegy as though the event has already occurred (Amos 5:1-2). The inevitability of this event, and its imminence, moreover, is the subject of the vision of YHWH poised by the altar, prefacing the final hymn in Amos 9.

Amos 9:5-6—YHWH the Lord Almighty Poised for Destruction

The power and majesty of YHWH expressed in the final hymn in Amos 9:5-6 affirms the inescapability of the impending divine judgment. As a matter of fact, this hymn fits the context describing the imminence of

---

291. This participle from the root בלג has posed problems in translation for most scholars. In some texts, the term bears the meaning "to smile" or "to be cheerful" (Ps 39:14[13]; Job 9:27; 10:20). Some scholars suggest amending a few terms in Amos 5:9, in order to continue the string of astral references in verse 8 (see Carroll R., *Book of Amos*, 311-12, 312n438). But the preferable meaning of to "burst," or "flash" (BDB 114) makes more sense in this context showing the incomparable power of YHWH, who holds sway over creation and is capable of turning its elements and flashing violence against the transgressors, who spurn justice and righteousness, which are the foundations of his rule (see Pss 89:15[14]; 97:2).

292. Regarding the implied elusive presence of YHWH in the wind(s), see pp. 94-95; cf. Crenshaw, "Amos," 206.

293. Regarding Day's discussion on Isa 24:21-23, see p. 91.

YHWH IN THE WIND(S)

YHWH's final judgment. As stated in Amos 9:1, the vision of YHWH's command to Amos to strike the capitals, in order to cause the threshold to shake, is the epitome of the total destruction of Israel for their vain religious practices owing to idolatry (Amos 2:4; 4:4–5; 5:5, 21–26; 8:14). The reference to YHWH at the altar and the command to strike the "top of the capitals" in Amos 9:1, harks back to the idea of YHWH roaring from Zion in Amos 1:2, and together form a chiastic structure framing YHWH's manifestation in his acts of judgment. The vision of YHWH at the altar, and possibly at the sanctuary in Zion,[294] demonstrates the inevitability of this judgment. It is clear, that the presaged destruction and exile (Amos 5:5–6) is imminent with YHWH initiating judgment at the very center of worship, where Israel had a sense of security (Amos 3:14; 5:5) and practiced empty religion.

In Amos 9:2–4, the prophet Amos describes the lengths to which the looming and inescapable judgment will be carried out. Amos eliminates any hope of escape from this final divine calamity with conditional statements listing antithetical parallelisms of locations where the Israelites might find refuge (cf. Ps 139:8–10). But, there, YHWH will pursue them. Neither Sheol nor the heavens, nor the top of Mount Carmel, nor the depths of the sea, nor even captivity, will provide refuge beyond the reach of YHWH.[295] Indeed, as implied in Job 38:16–18, these locations were inaccessible to humans, but not to YHWH. He is avowed with the appellative the "lord God Almighty"[296] (*'Adōnāy YHWH Ṣebā'ôth*); hence, the creator, who set these extremities in place. Again, these images of the cosmic recesses throw into bold relief the extent of YHWH's unrivalled domain. His gaze asserts that YHWH's theophany is not in question: YHWH's eyes are fixated on the House of Israel for harm and not for good (Amos 9:4c; cf. v. 8; Ps 104:32). Thus, with the hymnic participles in Amos 9:5–6, Amos affirms the scale of YHWH's power to execute retributive measures, and, further, reminds Israel that YHWH is the sovereign creator.

---

294. In the Hebrew Bible tradition, the theophany of YHWH was inextricably linked with the temple of Jerusalem, as the microcosm of YHWH's celestial abode and the same idea carries here.

295. See discussion on Ps 68:23[22] regarding Bashan in a *merism* with the depths of the sea. Therefore, in Amos 9:2–3, Sheol, heavens, Mount Carmel, and the depths of the sea are antithetical parallelisms representing contrasting recesses of the universe and expressing the extent to which YHWH pursues the wicked.

296. According to Zobel, this appellative occurs only five times in the OT tradition (Zobel, "צְבָאוֹת," 218).

YHWH IN THE WIND AS CREATOR-KING

Therefore, in the doxology in Amos 9:5-6, Amos recapitulates terminology familiar from the theophanic tradition to emphasize YHWH's cosmic power. As Crenshaw also observes, the idea of YHWH as the one "who touches" (הנוגע) the earth and causes it to melt (מוג) is in harmony with other theophanic texts.[297] There is allusion here to the effects of the wind with striking resemblance to the doxologies in Job lauding YHWH as the one who shakes the earth/heaven and the pillars tremble/quake by the power of his winds (Job 9:6; 26:11). As already established in view of the tempestuous goddess Inanna, who causes the earth to quake,[298] YHWH causes the whole earth to shake by his roaring winds, and the same idea is localized and focused on the land of Israel in judgment (Amos 9:8-9a). In this case, Amos correlates the collateral effects of YHWH's touch by his arm—that is the wind.[299] In essence, the reference to YHWH's roaring winds that cause the pastures to "dry up" in Amos 1:2 corresponds with his touch that causes the earth to melt, and the people give out sighing sounds through terror, expressed as mourning in Amos 9:5c.

The idea of the earth melting from YHWH's touch again in Amos 9:5aβ compares with the similar effects expressed in Ps 46:7[6]b: he (YHWH) gave his voice (נתן בקולו) and the earth melted (תמוג). As noted for Amos 1:2 the phrase נתן בקולו appears as merism along with the term "roar" to represent the grandeur of YHWH's roaring and fiery winds, and the corollary effect on the "earth melting" to figuratively express the winds blowing out, or eroding the earth. On the other hand, this impact of YHWH's touch on the people is corresponded with the reaction in nature, such as the mountains smoking,[300] as attested in other theophanic contexts (Pss 104:32; 144:5) with fire in the mix. Furthermore, the symbolism of the land "rising" and "subsiding" in comparison with the Nile

---

297. Crenshaw, *Hymnic Affirmation*, 134-35. However, Crenshaw sees the theophany of YHWH as causing an earthquake, thus maintaining the same view as in his article (Crenshaw, "Amos," 210). By contrast, it should be emphasized here that the shaking of the earth, often mistaken for an earthquake, is consequent to YHWH's appearance with the violent winds. It is surprising, though, that Crenshaw sees parallels to this effect in the doxologies of Amos and Job; where in fact the trembling of the earth and its pillars in Job 9:6 and the pillars of heaven in Job 26:11 are undoubtedly effects of YHWH's winds (see pp. 90-91, 99 above, respectively).

298. See 115, 115n252 above; Wolff, *Joel and Amos*, 342.

299. See pp. 40-42.

300. The reaction of the mountains smoking at YHWH's manifestation echo a similar effect on Mount Sinai, as a result of his theophanic descent (Exod 19:18a).

of Egypt suggests the overwhelming scourge of floodwaters brought about by YHWH's ferocious cloud-bearing winds.³⁰¹ Admittedly, Amos shows the correlation of YHWH's sovereignty as creator, his mastery and command of nature, particularly the winds causing agitation in the earth, and put the wind up in the transgressors for judgment purposes.

As with the other hymnic elements, here, too, Amos further brings into sharp focus his acclamation of YHWH as the creator in the face of his desolation of sinful people at his disclosure (Amos 9:2-4). Hence, he extols YHWH as "the builder" (הבונה) of his upper chambers in the heavens (see Ps 104:3) and the founder of its vaults³⁰² (אגדתו) over the earth (cf. Isa 40:22; Job 22:14). So, in this hymnic verse, Amos subtly recalls the creation of the heavens and earth, and the effects of the winds at YHWH's disposal. In that respect, Amos underscores the sovereignty of YHWH as the creator, a characteristic that permeates the theme of judgment as he sets it forth. By the same token, the idea of YHWH "calling" on the waters of the sea and pouring them on the face of the earth, not only predicts the inevitable destruction of Israel, but alludes to YHWH's predominance in manipulating the winds (of his own creation; Amos 4:13aβ) to unleash the cosmic waters that he once contained, to cause a deluge on the land (Amos 9:6 as in 5:8-9).

Undoubtedly, the hymnic sections are placed strategically in Amos's contexts of judgment purposely to portray the nature of the deity who is capable of restoring his order of justice when his will is subverted. Although Amos's portrayal of YHWH with the appellatives *YHWH Ṣebā'ôth*, or *'Adōnāy YHWH Ṣebā'ôth* as creator is not explicitly in wisdom terms, his use of phraseology and ideas relating to creation, and the characterization of YHWH's intended rule on the basis of wisdom terms "justice" and "righteousness," reflect influence from the sapiential tradition. Thus, Amos's message on the idea of YHWH manipulating the elements within his creative order, as punitive measures to restore his

---

301. Cf. Amos 5:8. See pp. 123-24. The idea of waters rising up from the north has a double meaning; that is, expressing literally, a windblown downpour of YHWH's destructive waters, but also as a metaphor for the enemy coming up from the north to devastate the nations (Isa 28:17b; Jer 46:7-8; 47:2). However, the conflation of natural phenomena and human force(s), in order to achieve YHWH's divine purposes is not unfamiliar, as portrayed by Jeremiah in his messages of impending doom (Jer 25:14-32; see 10:12-22; 51:15-29). In the same way, before the tables were turned, YHWH thundered in pursuit of his elected people routing their enemies (1 Sam 7:10-11; cf. 2 Sam 22:14-15, 37-41=Ps 18:14-15[13-14], 38-41[37-40]).

302. On the idea of "vaults" or "pillars" as supporting structures for the heavens and association with the winds and the effect, see pp. 97-98; cf. 80.

rule of justice, is also resonant with the wisdom tradition familiar from Job 9:4–9. Hence, the rhapsodic integration of the ideas of creation and judgment in the doxologies enriches the depiction of YHWH as creator and judge. Here, the wisdom and power of YHWH is celebrated in the manifestation of the force of his winds for cosmic creativity, and the establishment of his divine will. In light of Amos's prophetic doxologies, YHWH, who has the power to create cosmic order, is also able to appear with the phenomenal winds to judge the wicked, who disrupt his intended social order. The prophecies of Jeremiah attain similar dialectical ideas in description of YHWH as the creator, whose sovereignty is highlighted by his power to "create" and "destroy" by holding sway over the phenomenal winds.

Jeremiah on YHWH's Charge against Idolatry— A Contextual Background

The prophet Jeremiah is no exception in framing his message in similar terms as those developed in the prophecies of Amos. Jeremiah also incorporates the theme of creation integral with YHWH's sovereign monopoly over the winds, as proof of YHWH's power to judge the idolatrous Israel, as well as other nations. A brief recourse to a contextual background underscores the purpose of YHWH's intervention, and the predestined cosmic effects by the power of his winds to chide Israel for its continual apostasy. In no uncertain terms, the prophet Jeremiah exposes idolatry as the principal sin leading Israel to forsake YHWH (Jer 1:16; 2:5–28; 4:1; 11:10–13 [cf. 10:2–5]; 25:6–7; 32:30–35; 44:3; 2 Kgs 17:7–16). As expressed in the divine instruction to Jeremiah to enter the prophetic office, YHWH appoints Jeremiah to pronounce his "judgment" (משפט) on the people because of their "wickedness" (רעתם). The practice of burning incense to other gods, and "prostrating" themselves (שחה) at the "works of their own hands" (מעשי ידיהם, Jer 1:16; see 25:6–7; 32:30) indicate the people's rebellious state. The recurrent theme then is Israel's violation of the covenant that requires judgment.

In his messages, therefore, Jeremiah sets forth YHWH's covenantal faithfulness in antithesis to Israel's rebellion. As is said in Jer 2:5–8, Israel first violated her covenant relationship with YHWH generations ago. Their infidelity is expressed by a pun on the substantive "worthlessness" (הבל) and its denominative "become worthless" (יהבל, Jer 2:5), to show

YHWH IN THE WIND(S)

the extent to which Israel has defiled the covenant with YHWH. That the word "worthlessness"[303] here alludes to idols may be substantiated by its occurrence in parallel with the word "idol" (פסל) in Jer 8:19. The people of YHWH are as worthless as the gods they serve. Even the representatives of YHWH, the priests, prophets, and "shepherds" (הרעים), that is rulers who are supposed to lead and guide the people, fail to fulfill their tasks (Jer 2:8; 3:15; 23:1; 25:34). The priests neglect the law (cf. Deut 31:9–11); the rulers rebel, and the prophets abandon YHWH and prophesy by Baʻal in the course of their defection to "the unprofitable" (לא־יועלו, Jer 2:8). Consequently, YHWH threatens his people with a lawsuit and pronounces judgment upon them (Jer 2:9) for their unfaithfulness.

The language Jeremiah employs, which is suggestive of a legal case,[304] is so apropos to state YHWH's readiness to "bring charges" (ריב) against his own people (Jer 2:9). As shown in Jer 2:10–13, YHWH charges his people with a unique, but appalling, commitment to idolatry. So the subject of the case is presented: exchanging the "glory" (כבוד) of YHWH for ("worthless") idolatry. Israel is compelled to survey the scene from, Kittim to Kedar, the western to the eastern regions. So, Jeremiah challenges the people to see whether any nations have given up their gods, even though they are not gods at all. The emphasis is on the incredibility of Judah's unsurpassed apostasy represented in their substituting "worthlessness" for YHWH's glory (Jer 2:10–11; cf. Ps 106:19–20). As the divine plaintiff continues and the accusations are leveled against them, it becomes clear that the people of Israel are condemned for committing two sins. Here, also, Jeremiah uses two symbolic images: Israel's disobedience to YHWH compares to forsaking the spring of living water, and, secondly, for turning to idolatry, which is equivalent to digging cisterns that do not hold water (Jer 2:13). Furthermore, overtures familiar from the *rîb* pattern[305] are employed to express the futility of Israel's allegiance to Egypt and Assyria. Jeremiah uses the figure of failing water resources to express the apostasy of the people in their political fealty to Egypt and Assyria, whose waters they drink. Their dependence on these two

---

303. See 2 Kgs 17:15. This worthless form of worship is derived from imitating other nations contrary to YHWH's command. In Jer 10:15=51:18, however, the substantive הבל represents products of humans' craftsmanship; hence the delusions that characterize their worship. In Jer 14:22 the same word implies the "vanities of the nations" who are challenged to produce rain.

304. Thompson, *Book of Jeremiah*, 159–60; Brueggemann, *Pluck Up*, 32.

305. Thompson, *Book of Jeremiah*, 174.

political powers, Egypt and Assyria, compares to quenching thirst from the waters of Shihor (a branch of the Nile), or the river (Euphrates?), respectively (Jer 2:18). So, along with the reliance on foreign political power and idolatry, go Israel's detestable practices.

Jeremiah captures Israel's idolatry in picturesque images. He describes Israel's resort to other gods as prostitution conducted under every hill and leafy green tree (Jer 2:20; 5:7-8; cf. Amos 2:7-8; Hos 4:10-14). Israel's lust for other gods is compared with wild animals cravingly searching to mate (Jer 2:23-24). In stark satire, Jeremiah pronounces that Israel and its failed leadership are to be disgraced like a thief caught in its tracks for their practices and reliability on gods fashioned by human hands (vv. 26-27). They kill the prophets YHWH sends for their correction (Jer 2:30c; see 26:20-23; 2 Kgs 21:16), and their human sacrifices (Jer 7:30-33; 19:4-6; see 2 Kgs 17:17) characterize their pagan religious rites.

Jeremiah decries apostasy similar to the situation against which Amos preaches. The religious decline of Judah corresponds with the oppression of the poor (Jer 2:34; 7:6a; 22:17 [cf. v. 2-3]; Amos 2:7aβ; 4:1; 5:11-12; 6:1-6), though now escalated with a new facet involving the shedding of innocent blood (Jer 2:34; 7:6b; 22:3). Despite all this wickedness, the people declare their innocence (Jer 2:35). Yet, with YHWH's judgment impending, even their political alliances are futile and will become their shame (Jer 2:36-37; cf. vv. 15-19). However, YHWH's punitive measures designed to stir the people towards repentance (Jer 2:30; 5:3) are the warnings preceding doom, as similarly pronounced by the prophet Amos. By YHWH withholding the rains (Jer 3:3aβ; see 14:1-6; Amos 4:7-8); although a means of his providence (see Ps 104:13; Job 36:27-28; 37:11, 13b; 38:28a), YHWH reverses his creative acts. Yet, undeterred, the people continue in their unfaithfulness (Jer 3:3b; 14:10; see Hos 9:9). Therefore, with YHWH relentless, and under divine command, Jeremiah announces disaster looming from the north, for which purpose he appeals to creation theology.

Images of creation in correspondence with YHWH's appearance with the winds abound in Jeremiah's message, as he warns the people of the impending predicament (chapter 4). As noted in the case of the prophet Amos, here YHWH offers to Israel the opportunity to repent by putting away its "detestable things" (שקוצים, Jer 4:1; cf. Hos 9:10). The requirements of true repentance, and not pretense, are stated: to swear in "truth," "justice" and "righteousness" that YHWH lives (Jer 4:2). In keeping with this idea of sincere repentance, Jeremiah implores the nation to circumcise their hearts, that is, figuratively the act of repentance, and thereby avert YHWH's wrath that would otherwise break out like fire (Jer 4:4; see Amos 5:6). On that same note, Jeremiah warns the unrepentant people of the imminent disaster from the north (Jer 4:6).

Again, as in the case of Amos (Amos 5:1–2), Jeremiah pronounces the judgment of YHWH in the perfect tense to heighten the inevitable events described (Jer 4:7–8). Jeremiah envisages YHWH's judgment in the form of the wind/tempest comparable to a lion (Jer 25:38; Amos 3:8), and identified as the "destroyer of nations" (משחית גוים, Jer 4:7b). This epithet expresses the purpose of this agent of wrath, that is, YHWH's destructive wind. Its purpose is in keeping with Jeremiah's message of judgment upon all nations; "to uproot, and to tear down, to destroy, and to throw down" (Jer 1:10)—terms describing the destructive force of the potent winds. Hence, as in the doxologies of Amos, the image of YHWH likened to a lion (see Amos 1:2a) and called the destroyer of nations (Jer 4:7), is nothing other than the destructive and tempestuous winds. In accordance with this universal perspective, Jeremiah resorts to figurative use of the phenomenal winds in expression of YHWH's imminent judgment.

However, with immediacy, the forecast of the divine judgment is pictured in the form of a hot "wind" (רוח, Jer 4:11) sent at YHWH's bidding (v. 12) to sweep down on Judah in judgment. In addition, the idea of the impeding destructive hot "wind" is paralleled with the agent destined for YHWH's utter ruin, whose movements are compared to the cosmic phenomenal elements. The agent is said to rise like the clouds, whose chariots' devastating effect is comparable to that of a "storm wind" (סופה), and the charging steed is swifter than eagles (v. 13). Jeremiah pronounces that a "voice" is declaring that the enemy to besiege the cities of Judah is advancing from the north to surround these cities for rebelling against YHWH (vv. 14–17). This destruction is coming upon the people for its appalling conduct (v. 18).

As the weeping prophet, Jeremiah forebodes agony as he envisages the desolation of the land (Jer 4:16–21). With premonition on the destruction YHWH's wind will inflict, Jeremiah's bowels "writhe" (חול), and the walls of his heart "murmur" (המה) as he envisages the "sound of the *shôfār*" (קול שופר) and the "shout"[306] (תרועה) of a battle (Jer 4:19).

---

306. See discussion on Ps 47 mentioning the "sound of the *shôfār*" and "shout" as metonyms representing the sonorous sound of YHWH's wind.

YHWH IN THE WIND AS CREATOR-KING

Unquestionably, Jeremiah shows familiarity with the diction of YHWH's theophany with the wind(s) as shown in this language framing his personal anguish and expressing the predicted destruction as he sets it forth. This weeping prophet envisions the whole land devastated, and his tents ruined (v. 20). So, Jeremiah immediately interposes his personal agony and agitation with a rhetorical question on how much longer he has to bear hearing the sound of the *shôfār* (v. 21). Subsequently, Jeremiah reverts to expressing the necessity of YHWH's involvement for retribution due to the unethical conduct of the covenanted people (v. 22). Somewhat echoing the injustices manifested in oppression, and robbery that Amos decries in Amos 3:10, Jeremiah inflects his expression of personal grief with a divine complaint about the wickedness of the people. Indeed, the people's lack of discernment between good and evil is noted in wisdom terms. According to the satire in the divine utterance, the people are "the wise ones" (חכמים, Jer 4:22) in doing evil. But, in contrast, they do not know how "to do good." This situation, therefore, demands YHWH's manifestation with the destructive winds for judgment, which Jeremiah envisions as though creation has returned to chaos.

Jeremiah's prediction of the imminent devastation sets the stage for the effects of the roiling wind expressed in Jeremiah's vision of the earth as though reverted to primeval chaos[307] (Jer 4:23–25, 28). The once potent inventive winds of primal creation are now instrumental to destruction, to the point that the desolation of the whole land attains a state of primal chaos. In that sense, Jeremiah sees the earth now "formless and void" (תהו ובהו, see Gen 1:1–2) and the heavens without their luminaries (Jer 4:23). Indeed in collocation, and suggestive of YHWH's appearance with the agitating winds for judicial purposes in this context, is the concomitant idea of the mountains "shaking"[308] (רעשים), paralleled with the hills "swiftly shifting themselves" (התקלקלו, v. 24; cf. Ps 114:4, 6). Again, in terms of the reversal of creation, the land is deserted: without humans and birds (Jer 4:25), thus implying the earth's pre-creation state. The divine utterance in Jer 4:27–28 unequivocally confirms the inevitable disaster: the land will mourn (see Amos 1:2; 8:8aβ; 9:5) and, here also, in concomitance, the heavens grow dark (Jer 4:23, 28b; see Amos 5:8, 20;

---

307. Thompson, *Book of Jeremiah*, 230.
308. Regarding characteristics of the tempestuous goddess Inanna in the main, see p. 115.

YHWH IN THE WIND(S)

Job 9:7), thus portending YHWH's winds for destruction. Hereinafter, Jeremiah envisages the land lying in desolation.[309]

In sequel, Jeremiah's prophecy on the inescapable judgment by YHWH is replete with images from creation theology to give form and content to the wickedness of the unrepentant people and the ethical ramifications. In this text, chapter 5, the challenge in the initial verses (Jer 5:1-2) to go and find even one person who is upright, sums up the extent and seriousness of the transgressions committed. The leaders and the people alike do not know the ordinances of YHWH. Their apostasy, as in previous addresses, is exposed: idolatry, prostitution/adultery (vv. 7-8), robbery (v. 26), amassing wealth through deceit (v. 27), and social injustice by the infringement of the law on the protection of the needy and fatherless (v. 28), all signal their disobedience.[310] Again, Jeremiah appeals to the creation tradition to highlight the disobedience of Judah in antithesis to nature, which, though the sea may roar cannot cross the sand boundary as the statute laid down at creation (Jer 5:22-24). Here, too, in sustained rhetoric, Jeremiah alludes to the profound effect of YHWH's face, that is, his gaze personifying his presence in the winds, which often causes the trembling[311] at his disclosure (Jer 5:22b). But the people are unrelenting in the brazenness of their idolatry (v. 23).

The people's rebelliousness is cast in sharp contrast to nature in obeisance to YHWH's set rules at primal creation. Thus, in assertion of YHWH's cosmic power at primal events, Jeremiah harks back to YHWH's roiling of the chaotic waters by his winds, which commands them to their designated space. By this means, YHWH's declaration of the "sand" appointed as an eternal boundary for the sea is heightened. Although the emphasis is on the sea not crossing its set limit, though its waves may roar, in essence, the idea underscores the unsurpassed roaring winds of YHWH (see Ps 93:4) that establish that barrier (Jer 5:22; Ps 104:7-9; Job 38:10-11). But, conversely, YHWH's people, in the stubbornness of their hearts, transgress his statutes and go astray (Jer 5:23).

---

309. Also instructive for the understanding of YHWH's judgment envisaged here is the form of an enemy (Jer 4:29) accompanied by the winds of YHWH (see Isa 5:25-30). Deriving from the same thought, the prophet Isaiah presents the idea of the enemy equipped with weapons, horses and chariots with wheels whose movements are compared with "storm winds" (Isa 5:26-29). Their invasion is conflated with the manifestation of YHWH with winds causing the mountains to "shake" (v. 25) and dispersing the clouds to "darken" the light (v. 30; see Amos 5:8; Job 9:7; pp. 91, 123-25, 133-34).

310. See Jer 2:2-37; pp. 129-31 above; Ps 106:35-39.

311. See goddess Inanna's effects on nature (cf. Ps 99:1).

They have no reverential fear[312] of YHWH, or commitment to do the will of the one "who gives rain" (הנתן גשם, Jer 5:24; Job 5:10) in season. The latter appellation declares YHWH as the true God with the intention to deter the people from going after gods, who are not gods at all (Jer 5:7; 10:1–11; Deut 32:21).

These gods, or rather molten images, are essentially labeled nonentities with no breath in them (Jer 10:14; Hab 2:19; Ps 135:17). Therefore, they are incapable of producing the rain-bearing winds (cf. Ps 135:7; Job 36:28–29). In support of this view, the rhetorical expression in Jer 14:22 states in the affirmative that it is not the "vanities of the nations" that send rain, or the heavens that issue showers at their own accord, but YHWH (Ps 104:13). By his winds, syntagmatic of his breath, YHWH sheds the waters abroad (Jer 10:13; Job 37:10–13; see 1 Kgs 18:45; Ps 135:7). It may be noted at this point that the penalty of rainfall being withheld in Zech 14:16–17 is meant to show YHWH's power to bestow, and no less to withdraw, rain; hence his cosmic kingship[313] is asserted. As such, Jeremiah employs these themes and ideas on creation to lay a charge against YHWH's people, and formulate a polemic against the worship of idols in favor of the one true deity, whom he portrays as the creator-king and judge.

The theme of judgment in Jeremiah is paralleled with that of the sovereignty of YHWH over all the nations. Although the punishment of Judah is the primary focus, the neighboring nations are not exempt from the divine verdict[314] (Jer 25:8–38; 46–51). The reason for the punishment of the neighboring "wicked" (הרעים, Jer 12:14) nations is clear. They are to be uprooted from their heritage and punished for attacking YHWH's inheritance, and instructing the elect people to go after an alien religion

---

312. See 88n144 above.

313. In fact, considering the historical events determined by YHWH, it is evident that Zech 14:16–17 is a command to worship YHWH as the universal king without any idea of investing him with royal status. Therefore, the idea that we have here the rubric of an Israelite New Year festival at which YHWH was enthroned, as some scholars would like to argue, is arbitrary, *contra* Day, who supports this hypothetical enthronement festival (Day, *Psalms*, 70–71). By contrast, Zech 10:1 supports the idea of YHWH giving rain (as the maker of the lightning bolts; see Job 28:26; 38:35), and the herbage of the field in his role as creator. Therefore, to those failing to obey the command in Zech 14:16, YHWH withholds his rain (v. 17). He is the creator-king who comes with the "tempestuous winds" of the south (Zech 9:14).

314. Jeremiah's call and ministry involve all the nations (Jer 1:5, 10; see 25:15–26), as with other prophets like Isaiah (Isa 13–23), Ezekiel (Ezek 25–32) and Amos (Amos 1–2).

YHWH IN THE WIND(S)

(Jer 12:14–16). Undoubtedly, here lies the overarching theme of YHWH's governance of all the nations. YHWH will reprimand Judah, and all the surrounding nations (Jer 25:9, 11) for their deeds and for worshiping "the work of their hands" (vv. 6–7) through his agent Babylon (vv. 9–13). YHWH is the creator of the earth and all that is in it (Jer 27:5; 32:17): therefore, he has the authority to hand over the nations to whomever he wishes. Yet, ultimately, YHWH will also chastise Babylon for its deeds (Jer 25:14; see 50:15, 29; 51:24) and its idolatry (Jer 51:44, 52), and will take vengeance for Zion (vv. 24, 49).

Unquestionably, within this dominant theme of divine judgment provoked by idolatry thriving within preexilic Judah, and also in the surrounding nations, the prophet Jeremiah appeals to the creation tradition. By this idea, he shows that YHWH is not only the lord of nature, but sovereign in history. In that view, the relevance and significance of Jer 10:12–16=51:15–19 and Jer 25:30–32, as sections often alleged to be intrusive or irrelevant to the content of the message of Jeremiah, is apparent. Here Jeremiah presents YHWH, the creator-king, who manifests himself in the cosmos (Jer 10:12–16=51:15–19) by the force of his phenomenal winds in execution of his will (Jer 25:30–32). As in the case of the prophet Amos, Jeremiah appeals to the creation tradition in assertion of YHWH's sway over the phenomenal winds at both "creation" and "destruction" of his universe. In essence, Jeremiah's message throws into bold relief the intersection of the creation tradition with the judgment motif and elements from the wisdom tradition in depiction of YHWH as the creator-king and judge.

Jeremiah 10:1–16: YHWH's Wind—Mighty in Power over Idols

In view of the elements relating to the nature of charges on Israel for disobedience to YHWH in succumbing to idols, and the predicted judgment thereof, Jer 10:1–16[315] appears to be a crucible of the themes dealt with so far in Jeremiah's message. Jer 10:1–16 integrates elements of

---

315. The provenance of this text, however, is often questioned. Proposals are even made to omit this text on the basis of its contents. Disputing the authenticity of Jer 10:1–16, see Bright, *Jeremiah*, 79; Nicholson, *Book of the Prophet*, 100; Holladay, *Jeremiah*, 324; Andrew, "Authorship," 128–30; McKane, *Jeremiah*, 219; Jones, *Jeremiah*, 171; Carroll, *Jeremiah*, 254–59; Allen, *Jeremiah*, 124–29. For a dissenting voice (including this author's), attributing Jer 10:1–16 to prophet Jeremiah, see Weiser, Overholt, Margaliot, Thompson, Lundbom.

YHWH IN THE WIND AS CREATOR-KING

wisdom thought, creation, and theophanic traditions within a context of judgment. In this context, Jeremiah depicts YHWH as the sole creator with profound wisdom. On that basis, YHWH expresses his right to judge and restore his rule against the injustices incited by idolatry. The message in this text is addressed to the entire house of Israel (Jer 10:1; see 4:1), as Jeremiah deals with the problems associated with following religious practices of other nations. These religious practices of the nations also involve worship of astral bodies, to which Jeremiah is totally opposed. He therefore elaborates on the polemic against idolatry already found in Jer 2:5–37,[316] and shows the distinctive features identifying and separating YHWH, the true deity, from idols.

In the poetic exposition (Jer 10:1–16), Jeremiah sets forth the falsehood of a religion based on astral bodies (v. 2), that YHWH himself made, and on the images made by human hands (v. 3). Jeremiah deals at length with the aspect of objects fashioned with human hands, and shows in detail that the impotence of idols is inherent in their manufacture. With a note of irony, he describes how a tree from the forest is cut down and modeled with an axe (v. 3; cf. Isa 44:14), then ornamented with gold and silver (Jer 10:4a, 9; see Isa 30:22; 31:7), and finally fastened with nails so that it will not totter (Jer 10:4bc; Isa 40:19–20). In their state of impotence, idols have no speech and cannot move. Therefore, Jeremiah describes them "as a post of hammered work"[317] (כתמר מקשה, Jer 10:5). As a result of this state of inertness, they are incapable of doing any good deeds, or inflicting harm. In fact, by these bold statements, the immobility of the idols is herein pronounced, and represents the kernel of Jeremiah's message on their worthlessness. But to counterbalance, Jeremiah emphasizes the incomparability of YHWH and extols him for his unparalleled greatness (v. 6a). He praises him for his might and power that characterizes his name (v. 6b), in order to throw into bold relief the futility of adhering to objects incapable of speech, or motion.

At the same time, Jeremiah draws on terminology familiar from sapiential traditions to emphasize the character and nature of YHWH in contrast to idols. Thus, by a rhetorical question implying the reverential fear[318] to be accorded YHWH as "king of the nations" (מלך הגוים, Jer 10:7a), Jeremiah emphasizes the commitment to true religion and the

---

316. For verses from Jer 2 on the contextual background to Jeremiah, see pp. 129–31.

317. For this expression some biblical critics prefer to translate to "a scarecrow in a cucumber field," see Holladay, *Jeremiah*, 323.

318. See 88n144 above.

expression of reverential trust that is due to a deity who manifests his might (vv. 6b–7a), and, who, above all, is superior to all the "wise ones of the nations" (חכמי הגוים, v. 7b). Implicit in this statement is that all wisdom derives ultimately from YHWH, which underscores the senselessness and idiocy enshrouding idolatry. Jeremiah derisively calls "both" (באחת) the worshippers and their idols, which represent falsehood, the "wise ones." The stupidity and foolishness of the worshippers emanates from their wooden idols, whose inanimate nature cannot afford them any "counsel" (מוסר, v. 8), as that is not inherent with them. Even though skilled artisans—craftsmen and goldsmiths—manufacture these idols using beaten silver and gold, they are still a product (see Ps 135:15), and the "work of the wise men" (מעשה חכמים, Jer 10:9). In contrast, however, Jeremiah emphasizes that YHWH embodies "truth" as the "living" and "eternal king" (מלך עולם) in affirmation of YHWH's power. Unlike the idols, YHWH manifests his "wrath" (קצף) causing the earth to "tremble" (רעש, Jer 10:10c; see Pss 18:8[7]; 68:9[8]a) in the convulsion of the winds, and the nations cannot withstand YHWH's "indignation" (זעם, Jer 10:10d; cf. Isa 30:27; Nah 1:6; Hab 3:12).

The expression of YHWH's wrath not only buttresses YHWH's authority over the earth deriving from his predominance as the creator. Also, the manifestation of YHWH's wrath implies that his divine plan and purpose are at stake (Jer 10:10). Again, at this point in Jer 10, Jeremiah appeals to the creation tradition. He describes YHWH's activities at creation, echoing primal events familiar from similar biblical texts on creation. YHWH is attributed with the formation of the heaven and earth, such that he has the prerogative to dispel the idols from the earth, and under the heavens (Jer 10:11). Thus, Jeremiah depicts YHWH in bold contrast to idols. Most significant here, too, is the echo of sapiential thought reinforcing the distinctiveness of YHWH from the nonentities. Jeremiah asserts the profound "wisdom," "discernment," and "power" of YHWH displayed at the founding (עשה/כון) of the earth (Jer 10:12ab; Prov 3:19), and his "stretching out" (נטה, Jer 10:12c; see Isa 40:22; 42:5; Ps 104:2; Job 9:8; 26:7) of the heavens. These terms allude to the pervasiveness of YHWH's power in the wind in establishing the cosmos. No wonder, therefore, there is the inclusion of a verse in Aramaic (Jer 10:11), a language of diplomacy in the ANE in the general period (2 Kgs 18:26; see Isa 36:11), in recognition of YHWH as the creator of the heavens and earth—thus guaranteeing his power to abolish the idols from the face of the earth and from below the heavens. Jeremiah employs this Aramaic

YHWH IN THE WIND AS CREATOR-KING

verse to affirm YHWH's sovereignty and throws into bold relief YHWH's mastery at creation, as hymned in the doxology in Jer 10:12–16. By this means, Jeremiah points to the inevitability of judgment and YHWH unleashing his wrath against the idolaters. To that end, Jeremiah alludes to YHWH's sway over natural phenomena, particularly the wielding of the wind (v. 13), as he recounts YHWH's creation of the cosmos.

As in general, Jeremiah also adopts the participial style to allude to YHWH's creative acts, in keeping with the hymnic pattern lauding YHWH as the creator (Jer 10:12; Amos 4:13; Job 9:9). Hence, YHWH is the "creator" (עשׂה) of the earth by his "power" (כח) and "establisher" (מכין) of the world by his "wisdom" (חכמה, Jer 10:12). The reference to the earth founded by YHWH's "power" and "wisdom" recollects his appearance with the wind;[319] a nuance that cannot be denied in view of the reference to the earthshaking[320] experience (Jer 10:10c). Furthermore, the reference to the "sound of his (YHWH's) utterance" (קול תתו, Jer 10:13=51:6; see 25:30c; Pss 18:14[13]; 46:7[6]b; 68:34[33]b) equivalent to the issuing of his blustery breath,[321] echoes his roaring wind affecting the "tumult of the waters" in the heavens. Here, Jeremiah alludes to nothing other than the outburst of YHWH's winds. The emphasis is also on the rainmaking act of YHWH deriving from the correlated wind cycle originating from YHWH, and not from idols (Ps 135:6–7).[322] Thus, by mentioning the clouds rising from the extremities of the earth, and YHWH releasing the "wind" from the storehouses, Jeremiah highlights the power of the winds at YHWH's disposal in dispersing the rain-bearing-clouds (Jer 10:13cd; Job 36:27–29; 37:9–11; 38:24, 34–35). In that sense, YHWH's effectiveness is expressed through the phenomenal winds and, by contrast, the ineffectiveness and worthlessness of idols is heightened by the fact that they lack "breath" (Jer 10:14c; Ps 135:17b).

Yet, what is more poignant and decisive for Jeremiah's polemical thinking is the statement that all humans are brutish, because they lack knowledge owing to their void and empty objects of worship (Jer 10:14aβ; Ps 135:18). At the appointed time, YHWH will punish these vain idols

---

319. See in the main, on Ps 104:6–9, 24; Job 9:4–10; 26:7–14.

320. See goddess Inanna's effects on nature.

321. See pp. 15, 29.

322. It is clear in Ps 135, where the contrast between YHWH and idols is also evident (vv. 15–18), that other than having the natural phenomena at his disposal, YHWH acts according to his own will in the heavens, earth and the seas (v. 6). Therefore, the same idea is set forth in this psalm as well that YHWH commands the elements either to benefit or punish humans (vv. 5–7; see also Job 37:9–13).

and idolaters, and they will soon perish (Jer 10:15). Again, YHWH, as the benefactor par excellence of Israel, is brought into stark focus, and distinctively designated with the all-comprehensive appellation YHWH Ṣebā'ôth, in expression of his power and majesty as the "Potter"[323] (יוצר) of all things (הכל), that is, including the phenomenal winds (Jer 10:16; Amos 4:13). No wonder, YHWH's sway on all the cosmic elements is unrivalled.

So, in this short poetic section (Jer 10:1–16), elements of the wisdom tradition and creation and judgment motifs are drawn together. By this means, Jeremiah emphasizes the role of YHWH as the sovereign creator with unparalleled power to restrain evil, in this case idolatry. It is in view of this latter aspect that Jeremiah throws into stark relief YHWH's preponderance over the wind or tempest. Therefore, YHWH's dominance manifested by the phenomenal winds becomes a subject which occupies Jer 25:15–29 and vv. 30–32, 38. The interpretation of these verses mentioning the cup of YHWH's wrath, and his anger compared to a young lion emerging from its den, is crucial in determining Jeremiah's portrait of YHWH, as the creator-king disclosing himself with the phenomenal winds, for the destruction of forces arrayed against his will and purpose.

Jeremiah 25:15–29—The Wind as the Cup of YHWH's Wrath and Destruction

Jeremiah mentions "the work of (human) hands" to clarify that idolatry is the root cause of YHWH's rage, particularly in this case, against Judah, and the surrounding nations (Jer 25:6–7, 14). As Jeremiah states, the people of Judah pay no heed to all the persistent signals (vv. 4–5) cautioning them not to defer to other gods and bow down to the work of their own hands. Thereby, they provoke YHWH's anger that will cause them harm (vv. 6–7). But, YHWH's retributive measures take on a universal dimension. YHWH will summon the nations of the north and raise Babylon as his agent of judgment to "exterminate" (חרם)[324] all the surrounding nations, including Judah (Jer 25:9–11). Even though Babylon serves as

---

323. BDB 427.

324. The term חרם is often used in the OT to mean "put under ban" or "devote" to destruction, as in the case of the Israelite destruction of cities at the conquest of Canaan (Josh 6:17, 21) in keeping with the Deuteronomic command (Deut 20:16–18; see Num 21:2–3). In expression of the meaning "exterminate" or "totally destroy" as implied here, see also Wood, "חרם," 324; Lohfink, "חרם," 181–83.

YHWH's agent of wrath, it is not free from the guilt for which the other nations are indicted. Upon completion of YHWH's purposes, Babylon, too, will be requited not only for bringing Zion to ruin (Jer 50:28–29; 51:6, 11, 24; cf. 50:15), but also for its idols (Jer 25:13–14; see 51:52). Babylon and its regions will suffer the same fate, and will be consigned to perpetual ruin (Jer 25:12; 50:21, 26; 51:2–3). Here Jeremiah envisages the universal scope of YHWH's judgment, and affirms YHWH's universal lordship by virtue of being the creator.

Undoubtedly, the universal scope of judgment that Jeremiah envisions calls for an all-embracing and comprehensive measure against all the nations. Therefore, Jeremiah develops the theme of YHWH's universal judgment using the image of a cup filled with YHWH's wrath that all the nations, according to the divine command, have to drink (Jer 25:15–29). The cup of wrath, however, is only symbolic of the fate to be experienced by the nations. This image of a chalice of wrath, by which the people are subjected to inebriation, logically relates the idea of "staggering" from inebriety to "quaking" from the effects of the winds (see Isa 51:17–21). This is recounted as the punitive wrath experienced by the remnant of YHWH's people during the exile to Babylon. However, the idea is set in tension with YHWH's deeds in the past. Unquestionably, in this Deutero-Isaiah text, Isa 51, there is a clear correspondence of the portrait of YHWH as the creator, who employs the winds at primal creation, destroys the chaos monsters: he cuts up Rahab and pierces Tannin (Isa 51:9). He dries up the "sea/great deep" for the redemption of his own people (v. 10). This symbolism of YHWH's power is set in tension with the insignificance of constant fear inflicted by the oppressor disposed towards destruction. Hence, YHWH's people are admonished for overlooking their Maker, who is also described as the one who stretches out the heavens and lays the foundations of the earth (v. 13). YHWH's past deeds guarantee his potency to surpass the wrath of the [mortal] oppressor (v. 14). Again, YHWH is idiosyncratically celebrated with the nominal epithet YHWH Ṣebā'ôth (v. 15c), as the one who dries up and churns the sea so that its waves roar by the force of his winds (v. 15aβ). This image of YHWH is cast in recalling his creative deeds in the past, as much as it is set forth in YHWH dispensing his cup of wrath in acts of judgment on his people (v. 17). This is the same deity bent on destruction, who metes out the cup of wrath, not filled with wine (v. 21), but his "rebuke" (v. 20); a metonym for YHWH's winds, which cause the staggering from its whirling force.

Similarly, as pronounced by Jeremiah, the nations will not become drunk with wine, but the divine judgment inflicted by YHWH's winds, which will cause the people to reel (cf. Jer 25:27),³²⁵ and will be comparable to their religious stupor. Accordingly, this image of the "goblet" of wrath represents YHWH's onslaught mediated by his agent of judgment (Babylon) accompanied by the tempestuous winds (Jer 25:30–32). Then again, the ominous verdict featuring a great whirlwind is also delivered not only on Jerusalem, the city that bears YHWH's name, but also against the unruly nations, who dwell on the earth (Jer 25:29).

Jeremiah 25:30–32, 38—YHWH's Wind as a (Young) Lion Emerging from Its Lair

Familiar terminology from the prophecies of Amos also features in Jer 25:30–32, 38 to heighten the impact of YHWH's winds. Jeremiah describes YHWH's appearance from his holy "abode" (מרום//מעון, Jer 25:30cd; cf. Ps 68:6[5b], 19[18]a) in order to pass judgment. Hence, Jeremiah foreshadows YHWH in the image of a young lion emerging from its lair (Jer 25:38a; see 49:19a=50:44a;), as "he roars"³²⁶ (שאג, Jer 25:30bd; see Amos 1:2a=Joel 4:16[3:16]a; Job 37:4a) and "(he) gives his voice" (יתן קולו, Jer 25:30c; see Amos 1:2b=Joel 4:16[3:16]b; Pss 18:14[13]b; 68:34[33]b), to emphasize the sound of the howling winds. In view of the universal aspect of YHWH's judgment, the winds are the fitting gambit for the punitive wrath on all the nations.

So as Jeremiah states, and echoing the poetic imagery as expressed by Amos, YHWH's "roar" reaches to the extremities of the earth, thus indicating his far-reaching cosmic judgment effected through the swirling whirlwind (Jer 25:31–32; 23:19; cf. רוח מדבר, Jer 13:24). YHWH's purposes for this phenomenal self-disclosure are explicitly stated: in order to bring a "lawsuit" (ריב) against all the "nations" (גוים), impose judgment on all flesh, and commit "the wicked" (הרשעים), to the sword (Jer 25:31). Once again, YHWH is identified with the same appellative,

---

325. See Isa 51:17–22. The image of Jerusalem being drunk from the cup of YHWH's wrath is associated with his "rebuke" (גערה, Isa 51:20) representing YHWH's roaring wind.

326. These expressions—"he roars" (ישאג) and "he gives his voice" (יתן קולו), occurring in Job 37:4 and Ps 18:14[13] respectively—are both in parallel with the phrase "he thunders" (ירעם) in representing the sonorous winds; see Amma's loud sound from his whirlwind also called the "voice." See also pp. 16–17, 29.

YHWH Ṣebā'ôth in anticipation of the predicted judgment dispensed by a mighty "whirlwind," (סער, v. 32). YHWH will stir the whirlwind from the ends of the earth to go up from one nation to another, perhaps marshaled along with the sword of "the oppressor" (היונה, v. 38c). Thus, the universal nature of YHWH's reach is emphasized by the idea of the whirlwind stirring from the extremities of the earth (v. 32c), and so will be the extent of the slain to the ends of the earth (v. 33).

Of significance, too, is the fact that the devastating effects of the whirling winds intended for "the shepherds" (הרעים, Jer 23:1, 19–20; see 22:22a) of Israel, here are turned against "the shepherds"[327] of all the nations. There is no escape for the shepherds, or leaders of YHWH's flock, as they too will experience the full extent of YHWH's tempestuous winds (Jer 25:34–37; see 30:23). As pronounced by Amos, Jeremiah echoes the devastation caused by the ravaging winds. Even the shepherds' pastures will be laid to waste, and the meadows become a desolation (Jer 25:36–37; see Amos 1:2). However, in contrast to Amos, who pictures YHWH roaring from Zion (Amos 1:2; 3:8), in Jeremiah YHWH roars from his heavenly abode (Jer 25:30, 38; Ps 104:2b–3) to reach the farthest bounds of the earth. Hence, by this image Jeremiah portrays YHWH's roaring winds accompanying the sword of the oppressor, possibly Babylon, in causing destruction and meting out judgment to "all the nations" of the earth (Jer 25:29, 31–32, 38) to underscore his all-encompassing might as YHWH Ṣebā'ôth (Jer 25:8, 27, 29, 32).

Jeremiah 51:15–19—YHWH Ṣebā'ôth: The Creator-King and Judge against Babylon

In due time, with YHWH's purposes for divine retribution accomplished, Jeremiah pictures in similar terms the punishment intended against Babylon for its destruction of the wicked, and no doubt for idolatry too (Jer 25:12–14). As much as Jeremiah envisions YHWH's tempestuous winds directed against the nations, so fitting is the appellation the "wind of destruction" (רוח משחית) reserved for the devastation of Babylon (Jer 51:1). Babylon's desolation is due to YHWH's vengeance for its impetuous deeds in the destruction of the earth (Jer 25:12; 50:28–29; 51:25, 44) and

---

327. Perhaps, here, there is a deliberate allusion to YHWH as the arch shepherd (see Jer 23:1–4; 50:44), intending to chastise his surrogates (see Jer 23:1–2, 19–20[=30:23–24]; 25:34–36) with the whirling wind for submitting to idolatry, and, thereby, failing to tend his flock.

the worship of "the work of its hands" (Jer 25:14b; cf. 50:2, 38). Moreover, Jeremiah announces YHWH's injunction to attack Babylon for its sins in vengeance for its destruction of other nations (Jer 50:14–15; 51:25) and the temple of Jerusalem (Jer 50:28; cf. 51:24). Whereas, Babylon as "the oppressor" from the north is stirred up to invade a whole host of nations, but for its own predicament, YHWH prepares an alliance of nations[328] to bring about Babylon's demise.

Here, too, YHWH's sovereignty is thrown into bold relief by reference to the predicted capture of Babylon and subjection of its prime god, Bel-Marduk to shame and terror (Jer 50:2). This nature of defeat signals the helplessness of Babylon's gods or idols. The futility of worshiping these images and idols is exposed through a presaged confrontation with YHWH's unrivalled might, and the inevitable devastation of Babylon. The extremity of Babylon's destruction, as predicted, is comparable to the decimation of the cities of Sodom and Gomorrah (Jer 50:40; Isa 13:19–20; cf. Amos 4:11). Even so, the severity of the attack will cause Babylon itself and the earth to tremble (רעשׁה, Jer 50:46; 51:29). This sordid sentimental statement expresses musing on the anticipated appearance of YHWH in the historical arena. Therefore the mention of the trembling and writhing of the earth in Jer 51:29a foreordains the convulsing effects of the whirling "wind(s) of destruction" (see Jer 51:1) at the prospect of Babylon's utter desolation (v. 29cd).

In keeping with the characteristics of YHWH's appearance with the winds, and his involvement in the historical arena, the band of foreigners (Jer 51:2) emerging from the north to devastate Babylon, is said to be accompanied by this "wind of destruction" (v. 1; see Jer 4:11, 12)[329] aroused by YHWH for his vengeance. The reference to the "wind of destruction" bodes well with Jeremiah's commission to pronounce a message foreshadowing YHWH's cataclysmic destruction: "Uprooting, tearing down, destroying and overthrowing" (Jer 1:10; cf. 12:14–15, 17). As the creator of the earth and heavens, YHWH has the prerogative, and is able, to stir the "four winds"[330] (ארבע רוחות, cf. Jer 49:36; Zech 2:10[6]) from the

---

328. The invaders are identified as the Medes in Jer 51:11 who are in alliance with other kings (50:9, 41) subject to them (Jer 51:28; see Isa 13:17; 21:2; Dan 5:28, 31). YHWH now marshals them in mediation of his vengeance on Babylon. However, Allen notes that though Babylon is said to fall to the Medes (Jer 51:11, 27–28), it falls to king Cyrus of Persia from the east (Allen, *Jeremiah*, 508).

329. See p. 132.

330. See pp. 77–79.

YHWH IN THE WIND AS CREATOR-KING

heavens for his own purposes. Arguably, here, too, the wind of destruction corresponds with the human element, as the sword of YHWH's wrath to wield YHWH's judgment (Jer 51:1-2; see 25:15-16, 30-38; cf. Ezek 5:12; see also v. 2; 12:14) for the desolation of Babylon.

In allusion to the effects of the winds as in Jer 25:15-29, Jeremiah takes up again the image of the cup of wrath[331] as a symbol of divine punishment, but now turned against the Babylonian leaders, officials and wise men (Jer 51:57; cf. 13:12-14). YHWH intends to vanquish this nation that lives by "many waters," and is endowed with treasures by deceitful means (Jer 51:13). YHWH's response to carry out his purposes is in no uncertain terms, as he has sworn by himself (v. 14) to bring destruction on Babylon. At this point, in verses 15-19, YHWH's identity is made explicit: he is the creator (vv. 15, 19) differentiated from the idols sarcastically labeled as the "breathless" molten images (vv. 17c-18a). By contrast, nothing other than the power of YHWH's wind, a synonym of his "breath"[332] (see Exod 15:8a, 10a; Ps 18:16[15]c), is implied here to be at work at creation. To that end, it is right and proper to summon the same power of the wind for the destruction of Babylon. In essence, Jeremiah appropriately inserts the doxology in Jer 51:15-19 (=10:12-16), often alleged to be an erratic block[333] without relation to its contextual background, in order to set up a contrast between YHWH and idols. As much as Jeremiah pictures the creative power of the deity threatening Babylon with its nemesis, as is the case against Judah in Jer 10:1-16, the thrust of this hymnic element is that YHWH's power, in the guise of the winds, prevails over the Babylonian breathless and impotent idols.

In actual fact, the brief view of the nature and character of YHWH Ṣebā'ôth (Jer 51:19) presented in this segment (vv. 15-19, as in Jer 10:12-16), evinces a better use of images familiar from the creation and sapiential traditions. Therefore, the depiction of YHWH, whose wisdom is manifested in the creation of the earth and heavens in Jer 51:15, underscores his sway over creation. As in Jer 10:12-16, the reference to

---

331. Perhaps the initial reference to Babylon as the golden cup of wrath (Jer 51:7) is an ironic conflation of Babylon with YHWH's tempestuous winds, symbolized as the cup of wrath but now turned against Babylon and identified as the "wind of destruction" (v. 1).

332. See pp. 65, 74.

333. Bellis sees this as a later addition to Jer 51 (Bellis, *Structure and Composition*, 136-37). Similarly, Lundbom refers to Jer 51:15-19 as an interpolation and proposes changes to it (Lundbom, *Jeremiah*, 450-52). Allen also considers the text as a late composition and a recycle of material from Jer 10:12-16 (Allen, *Jeremiah*, 509).

"bringing up the clouds from the ends of the earth" (Jer 51:16b) implies the winds dispersing the rain-bearing clouds[334] accompanied by the luminous (=lightning) and the sonorous sound[335] (v. 16c; cf. Job 28:26) to mete out YHWH's wrath (cf. Job 37:9–13a) against Babylon. Accordingly, Jeremiah declares that the one who is able to bring out the "wind" (רוח) from its storehouses (Jer 51:16d), is the one stirring the "wind of destruction" (v. 1aβ) against Babylon. Therefore, Jeremiah ridicules Babylon's submission to the powerless and breathless idols as folly. YHWH has already predetermined their utter destruction (v. 18b; cf. Ps 97:7) as proof of their worthlessness (Jer 51:18a; cf. Ps 96:5).

Hereinafter, Jeremiah also uses images suggestive of YHWH's command of the winds, and *Chaoskampf* in his message of doom, to further challenge the impotence of idols, as he forecasts the desolation of Babylon in the face of YHWH's might. In creation texts, mountains are mentioned as part of the cosmic features expressing the stable and durable cosmic creativity of YHWH (Amos 4:13; Pss 65:7[6]). But the reference to Babylon as a "destroying mountain, who destroys the whole earth" (Jer 51:25) is a satiric overture to primal creation. Though Babylon, as the figurative mountain, might seem an enduring symbol of YHWH's creation, YHWH will stretch out his hand, a metonym for his winds,[336] and shatter its rocks (vv. 25–26).[337] Its desolation will be so thorough to the point that no rock from it can be used as a cornerstone, or any stone for a foundation (Jer 51:26). The effects of YHWH's winds are further affirmed by the reference to the "shaking" (רעשׁ, Jer 51:29)[338] and "writhing" (חול)[339] of the earth, resulting from YHWH's intervention with his winds at Babylon's capture (Jer 51:29–32).[340]

Furthermore, with recourse to the creation tradition, Jeremiah espouses YHWH as the creator, who has sole governance,[341] and so, deals with nature at will. Here, the satire is heightened by the use of contrasting

---

334. See 1 Kgs 18:45; Ps 147:18b, showing the close association of the winds rising to cause a downpour of rain.

335. See pp. 16–17.

336. See 1 Kgs 19:11 expressing YHWH's potent winds tearing into the mountains and shattering rocks.

337. See 1 Kgs 19:11; Job 9:5.

338. See Judg 5:4; Pss 18:8[7]; 68:9[8]; 77:19[18].

339. Pss 29:8; 97:4.

340. Jer 50:46.

341. Pss 95:4–5; 104:24.

images that YHWH will dry up the sea and springs (Jer 51:36; cf. Isa 51:10), as much as he will also let the roaring sea deluge Babylon, as though returning creation to primeval chaos[342] (Jer 51:42; see 4:23). Therefore, in avenging Babylon for its wickedness, YHWH will dry up its seas and desiccate its springs, thus making the land uninhabitable (Jer 51:36–37, 43). As though in a contest of power, YHWH will close up the springs that Marduk, as creator, is acclaimed to have opened up and regulated the subterranean waters,[343] in order to apportion water in abundance.[344]

Also, in parody with Judah in Jer 4:23,[345] where creation is described as though it had returned to chaos, here, too, the circumstances threatening Babylon are comparable to the pre-creation state. The mention of the sea rising up; churned by YHWH's winds, in order to cover Babylon as stated in Jer 51:42, implies a repeal of the limits set by YHWH on the sea at creation[346] (Ps 104:9; Jer 5:22). Undoubtedly, this polemical statement is in line with the idea of YHWH as the incomparable creator, who has absolute hegemony to reverse the order in creation to its primeval state. Perhaps with that intentional ironic turn of events, this means of identifying YHWH's supremacy in stark contrast to the inertness of idols, accentuates the peculiarity of YHWH. Here, in particular, the specificity of the idol in contention, though revered in Babylon, to whom the signal for destruction is raised, is intentional. So, Babylon's chief god Bel, is purposely identified as Marduk[347] (Jer 50:2), the creator-god of Babylon, who also fashioned winds to annihilate Tiamat (EE IV:45–47). But he is ill fated, as he is no rival before YHWH. Thus, the prediction of the sea surging over Babylon depicts YHWH exercising his unrivalled power over the winds against the creative ingeniousness of Marduk (EE VII:116–17), by unleashing the chaotic sea (=Tiamat) that Marduk is acclaimed to annihilate and confine[348] (EE IV:137–40). Hence, YHWH

---

342. See pp. 45, 102, 102–3n198.

343. The land of Babylon is described as with many waters (Jer 51:13), but will be left with a drought and disgraced idols.

344. See EE V:54–55; 7:59–60; Foster, *Before the Muses*, 465, 479; Dalley, *Myths*, 257, 269; Lambert, *Babylonian*, 101, 127.

345. See pp. 133–34.

346. See pp. 83–84, 134.

347. Thompson, *Book of Jeremiah*, 732.

348. EE IV:128–32, 139–40: Marduk vanquished Tiamat and ordered her waters not to escape (Kessler, *Battle of the Gods*, 131).

will stir up the sea to rise over Babylon, and the land will lie desolate as though a reversal to pre-creation chaos (Jer 51:42–43).

Besides, just as YHWH punishes the nations for their idolatry, so will he vanquish Babylon's chief god, Bel (Marduk), and all its images (Jer 51:44, 47, 52). As stated in Jer 50:38, Babylon's pride in idolatry is described as acting madly over the worship of idols, but they will be abased. In addition, the image of punishing Bel by making him regurgitate all that he ingested (Jer 51:44), though symbolic of YHWH causing Babylon to spew out articles of plunder in vengeance on Babylon for destroying the nations, and especially in revenge for the ruin of Zion (see v. 11), carries mythological overtones of a primeval battle with the dragon.[349] Jeremiah employs the ideas of a battle and YHWH's mustering of winds drawn from the creation and *Chaoskampf* traditions to give form and content to his message presaging judgment against Babylon.

There are features in Jeremiah's message that indicate that the images of creation no longer relate to a primeval battle with chaos, but are transposed to a historical plane. So, in Jeremiah's forecast of events, creation is personified in its involvement with accomplishing YHWH's divine purposes. Pointedly, since YHWH is the creator-king, even the heavens, earth and all that occupies them will witness with jubilation the judgment imposed on Babylon (Jer 51:48). Even if Babylon is elevated and attempts to fortify a lofty stronghold reaching up to the heavens, YHWH will still stir destruction (v. 53; see vv. 48, 56). There will be no escape; showing the extremities of YHWH's reach,[350] and again alluding to YHWH's limitless bounds of his winds stirring from the heavens (Jer 25:30–32).[351]

Yet, more significant is the idea of YHWH laying waste and silencing Babylon's din as being comparable to the subjugation of the "many waters"[352] (מים רבם, Jer 51:55) at primal creation. Babylon is pictured here as the resurgent waters, whose waves roar and raise a tumult (שׁאון

---

349. Bellis, *Structure and Composition*, 194–95.

350. See Amos 9:3–4, 6a; Ps 139:8.

351. See Jer 10:13=51:16d.

352. The term מים רבם, though reminiscent of the symbol of the archenemy in the mythical battle with the warrior god, particularly Ba'al and Yam, should also be viewed as representing historical foe(s) (see the discussion on Pss 18, 77, and Hab 3 in chapter 3).

YHWH IN THE WIND AS CREATOR-KING

קולם).³⁵³ But, in the face of YHWH's unmatched "roaring" winds,³⁵⁴ YHWH will vanquish the "great sound" (קול גדול) in Babylon. YHWH will silence Babylon's din. This image expresses the finality of Babylon's demise initiated by YHWH's destruction. YHWH will chastise its idols and the inhabitants will lie slain (Jer 51:47, 52). At this point, the collateral identity of YHWH Ṣebā'ôth as the creator (vv. 15, 19) is also made explicit: he is "the king" (המלך, v. 57d),³⁵⁵ and, therefore, recompenses in full as God of retribution (Jer 51:56d).³⁵⁶ Therefore, as the ultimate true king, with winds at his disposal, YHWH Ṣebā'ôth will smite Babylon's officials, wise men, and warriors such that they will stagger and fall to their complete demise, comparable to a sleep-drunken death (Jer 51:57). In view of all these correlated features, it is clear that Jeremiah pertinently places in context the doxology in Jer 51:15–19(=Jer 10:12–16), in order to express the nature of YHWH as "the king," who can break into the historical arena with his winds against Babylon to assert his judicial power, as the sovereign creator-king and judge.

A Note of Hope for the Remnant of Israel

Overall in this context (Jer 50–51), Jeremiah's ominous message on Babylon's predicament is also punctuated with a note of hope.³⁵⁷ The destruction of Babylon is counterbalanced with the redemption of its captives (Jer 51:45; see v. 6). In the midst of this crisis, the captives are urged to flee to their native lands³⁵⁸ with a pledge from YHWH to restore Israel (as a whole nation, Jer 50:19), purge its sins and recompense its remnant (v. 20). Yet, in contrast, Babylon will be disgraced (v. 18),³⁵⁹ desolated and left without a remnant (Jer 50:22–26). Instead, YHWH will defend Israel's

---

353. Cf. Ps 93:4.
354. See Amos 1:2; Jer 25:30–32, 38. See also pp. 114–16, 121, 126–27, 132–33, 142–43, 148.
355. See Ps 97:9.
356. See Ps 97:10.
357. Cf. Amos 9:11–15.
358. Jer 50:8, 16.
359. Jer 51:47.

cause, and avow himself as its redeemer³⁶⁰ (גאל, v. 34).³⁶¹ Moreover, the rhetorical question³⁶² of "what shepherd can stand against YHWH?" purposely asserts him as their unrivalled shepherd³⁶³ in ridicule of the same epithet applied to Marduk in the Babylonian tradition. Marduk's battle with Tiamat is linked with the salvation of the gods (EE VI:49), and, consequently, he is entreated to "shepherd" the gods like "sheep"³⁶⁴ (ṣēnu) with the subjugation of Tiamat in check (EE VII:132). Marduk's valiant nature accords him hegemony and recognition as the shepherd (rēʾû), not only of the gods, but also of humankind in acknowledgement of his provision and protection of them (EE VI:107, 124–26). Accordingly, he is proclaimed as the establisher of pastures and watering places (EE VI:124), or guardian of the land as (the) faithful shepherd (EE VII:72).

The idea of protection and provision bodes well with the Hebrew conceptual idea of YHWH as shepherd—an epithet in conformity with similar usage in the Babylonian tradition. The allusion to YHWH as the "shepherd" (רֹעֶה) of the descendants of Jacob and Joseph, Ps 77:16[15])³⁶⁵ can be traced in the subtle expression of him "guiding his people like 'sheep'" (צֹאן, Ps 77:21[20]), upon YHWH's subjugation of the rebellious waters by means of his "arm" (=wind, v. 16[15]), or (whirl)wind (v. 19[18]).³⁶⁶ Certainly, in Ps 80, another psalm of lament as Ps 77, the idea of YHWH as the shepherd (Ps 80:2[1]) of Israel is evoked with overtones of his theophanic experience. YHWH, who is depicted as the dweller of the cherubim, symbolic of YHWH's winds,³⁶⁷ is implored to "shine forth"

---

360. YHWH is portrayed here as a kinsman-redeemer (cf. Lev 25:47–49; Ruth 2:20), whose interest is to protect and redeem Israel as his inheritance. However, the foreshadowed event will be like a new exodus (cf. Exod 6:6; 15:13), though in this case, from the Babylonian exile.

361. Isa 41:14.

362. *Contra* Lundbom stating that there are no rhetorical questions in the Babylonian oracles (Lundbom, *Jeremiah*, 367).

363. Jer 50:44[=49:19]; cf. Ps 80:2[1].

364. EE VII:131. See Talon, *Standard*, 75; Lambert, *Imagining Creation*, 59; *Babylonian*, 131; Dalley, *Myths*, 273; Foster, *Before the Muses*, 483; Heidel, *Babylonian Genesis*, 59.

365. See Ps 80:2[1].

366. See Exod 14:21–22; 15:8, 10.

367. See pp. 81–82. It has been established that the cherubim symbolize YHWH's winds. However, not all the Hebrew texts that refer to YHWH as a shepherd relate the idea in conjunction with YHWH's appearance with the winds. In some texts, YHWH is explicitly depicted as shepherd (Gen 48:15; 49:24; Pss 23:1; 80:2[1]), but in other cases the idea is merely implied (2 Sam 5:2; 7:7; Isa 40:11; Jer 23:1–4; 25:34–36; 31:9[10];

YHWH IN THE WIND AS CREATOR-KING

(הופיע). In essence, here, too, the psalmist lodges YHWH's identity with the winds, and invokes YHWH to arouse himself as avenger to wreak salvation on behalf of the tribes of Ephraim, Benjamin, and Manasseh (vv. 2-4[1-3]). Therefore, in recollection of YHWH's deeds in the past, the psalmist petitions YHWH to renew his restorative acts, whilst he lauds YHWH's shepherding ideals of protection, provision, and guidance. He acclaims metaphorically YHWH's acts of "pasturing" (רעה), as he sets forth the ideals of benefactor and protector of his people, in recollection of him "guiding" (נהג, v. 2[1]) his people like a flock,[368] and, subsequently, "driving out" (גרש) the nations for their establishment (Ps 80:9[8]; see 78:55), and "planting" (נטע) the tribes of Israel like a vine (Ps 80:9[8]).[369] It seems, then, that the same conceptual function of shepherding a flock, underlies the satiric attack expressed in Jer 50:45. In essence, YHWH's predestined desolation of the pastures of Babylon further implies ridicule on the proclamation of Marduk's shepherding ideals.

In this context (Jer 50:44-46),[370] therefore, the implication is that YHWH, in rhetoric, is championed as the prime shepherd. YHWH is poised to overthrow Babylon, destroy its pastures, and free YHWH's people. Again, in this oracle, as in Jer 25:38, the image of a lion, emerging (עלה) from the thickets of Jordan (Jer 50:44), is symbolic of YHWH's roaring winds surging to snatch the young flock. At the same time, the swirling winds will cause the total destruction of Babylon's pastures (v. 45)[371] with the collateral quaking of the earth portending the fall of Babylon (Jer 50:46).[372] Again, the idea of the earth quaking throws into bold relief the manifestation of YHWH's unrivalled power in the winds in contest of Marduk's shepherding ideals. Hence, the reference to the "wind of destruction" in Jer 51:1, brings to bear YHWH's impending

---

49:19-20=50:44-45; Ezek 34:8-14; Hos 13:5-6; Amos 3:12; Pss 74:1; 77:21[20]; 78:52-53). However, in most, if not all of these Hebrew texts, the image of YHWH as shepherd shines through within contexts alluding to YHWH's appearance with the winds (Jer 23:1-4; 25:34-36; 49:19-20=50:44-45; Ezek 34:8-14; Hos 13:5-6; Amos 3:12; Pss 77:21[20]; 78:52-53; 80:2[1], in view of Jer 23:19; 25:30-32; 49:19a=50:44a; Ezek 34:12; Hos 13:15; Amos 3:8; Pss 77:16[15], 19[18]; 78:13; and 80:2-4[1-3], respectively).

368. See Pss 77:21[20]; 78:52.

369. Jer 2:21; cf. 11:17; Exod 15:17.

370. The same verses occur almost verbatim in Jer 49:19-21 in an oracle against Edom.

371. Cf. Amos 1:2; Jer 49:19-20.

372. Cf. Jer 49:21.

phenomenal devastation of the pastures of Babylon and the land as a whole (50:44–46).

Unequivocally, however, the fall of Babylon also means that the redemption of the remnant[373] of YHWH's flock is achieved, and culminates with the restoration to its pastures[374] on Mount Carmel and Bashan (Jer 50:19; cf. Amos 1:2). Perhaps, the message of Jeremiah is quite instructive for the importance and relevance of this element of "destruction" as counterbalanced with the idea of "restoration" recalling the essence of Jeremiah's commission to pronounce a message of judgment: "To uproot, and to tear down, to destroy, and to throw down, but also to build and to plant" (Jer 1:10), respectively. This thematic prophetic commission corresponds with the image of YHWH appearing with the roaring winds to frame his dispensation of judgment not only for the demise of Babylon (cf. Jer 30:23–24), but also for the restoration of Israel (Jer 31:10–13). As predicted in Jer 33:6–13, Jeremiah's message summarizes the restorative acts of YHWH Ṣebā'ôth, which reassert his nature as creator, as much as they resonate with his manifestation in the wind. YHWH promises to bring back the captives from captivity and "rebuild" Israel and Judah (v. 7). As stated, when YHWH restores his people to wealth, health, peace and stability, the nations will hear, and "tremble" (רגז, cf. Hab 3:7) with awe at YHWH's renown (Jer 33:9). Instead of the sounds of desolation, as though nature has been reverted to chaos (v. 10), sounds of jubilation will be heard all over again in the towns of Judah, including the streets of Jerusalem as a result of YHWH's phenomenal intervention (v. 11). Moreover, the idea of restoring the pastures for the flocks implies that YHWH, here underscored as YHWH Ṣebā'ôth (v. 12), in his rainmaking act, will affect a tumult of waters in the heavens and bring his [rain-bearing] winds from the storehouses (Jer 10:13=51:6) to fructify the desolate pastures of all of Israel's towns, villages, and foothills (Jer 33:12–13; see vv. 6–7; 14).

In like manner, Amos's final message of hope is congruous with the depiction of YHWH's creative and destructive tendencies with the winds, as evident in the doxologies (Amos 4:13; 5:8–9; 9:5–6), and which even prefaces his message of judgment (Amos 1:2; see v. 14). The book of Amos, therefore, counterbalances the message of destruction of the

---

373. YHWH will also bind himself to both the remnant of the people of Israel and Judah with an eternal covenant that will not be broken. See Jer 30–33 (often referred to by commentators as the book of "consolation" or "comfort"), esp. 31:30–32[31–33].

374. See Ps 80; pp. 150–51, 203; Kessler, *Battle of the Gods*, 85.

idolaters and the perverts of social justice with a note of hope for the restoration of Israel. Amos's final words of hope in Amos 9:11–15, in such contrast with his message of judgment on the sinful kingdom, have often been treated as the work of a later redactor. The form and content of Amos's message of restoration echoes Jeremiah's prophecies at key points. Amos predicts that YHWH will bring the exiled people to "rebuild" ruined cities, and "plant" vineyards and gardens (Amos 9:14–15). In this message of restoration, YHWH solemnly vows in antithesis to the destructive tendencies of his phenomenal winds, which "pluck up" or "uproot" (נתש),[375] that he will "plant" (נטע, Amos 9:15a)[376] but "not uproot" (לא נתש, v. 15b)[377] his people, and enable them to "build" (בנה, v. 14b),[378] in emphasis of the certainty of the restoration of the Davidic remnant. Therefore, as much as Jeremiah, Amos's significant musing on YHWH's sway on cosmic winds influences the format of his message regarding YHWH's judgment, and the restoration of the fallen booth of David (=Israel).

Final Reflection

Images of creation and YHWH appearing with the winds abound in the biblical Hebrew texts explored, showing YHWH's involvement at primal creation, the establishment of the cosmos, and maintenance of the cosmic order. YHWH's disclosure with the winds in ordering the universe by transforming chaos to cosmos is praised as an expression of YHWH's wisdom. The cosmic waters and chaotic monsters are subdued by YHWH's potent winds at this establishment of the cosmic order. The poet of Job is adroit at employing poetic drama to explore this idea of YHWH appearing in the guise of the (whirl)wind to turn primal chaos into cosmos, and juxtaposes that with Job's apprehension that YHWH might break out against him with the same phenomena, as he throws his suffering with the lot of the wicked. Job's view of his predicament is used as ploy to relate the idea that YHWH unleashes his wind(s) against both the "righteous" and the "wicked" within the purview of YHWH's cosmological activities. Although the paradox of YHWH's divine justice

---

375. Cf. Jer 1:10; 31:27[28]a.
376. Jer 1:10d; 24:6d.
377. Jer 24:6e.
378. See Jer 1:10d; 24:6c; 31:27[28]c.

YHWH IN THE WIND(S)

is presented with subtleties, it becomes clear that Job is not considered a (wicked/)sinner when YHWH appears in the whirlwind, not to chide Job, but to reveal the intricacies of his power and wisdom manifested in creation and his maintenance of the cosmic order (Job 38). Here, too, YHWH interrogatively presents to Job his cosmogonic activities accomplished by his potent winds integrated with his control of the wicked by the same means (Job 38:12–15; 40:6–13)—an idea previously alluded to by Elihu (see Job 36:29–37:13). Thus, YHWH's cosmogonic activities wreaked by his potent winds become the trendsetter for his involvement in both the cosmic and social realm.

Accordingly, YHWH breaks through into the historical arena. YHWH's phenomenal winds are no longer directed against cosmic chaos, but against human insolence. Indeed, the petition for the annihilation of the wicked and sinners from YHWH's created order in Ps 104:35, and other related texts, is brought into historical focus in the prophecies of Amos and Jeremiah. These prophecies give the impression that YHWH, whose profound wisdom and power are manifested in the creation of the heavens and the earth, has on that basis alone, the right to intervene in the historical arena and restore just order. The notion of YHWH's appearance with winds at creation is employed, and correlated with elements from wisdom thought and judgment motifs, in order to enrich the idea that YHWH, who created the cosmos with wisdom, also asserts his power in the historical arena to quell any forces antithetical to his divine will and cosmic design, as he fulfills his roles as the creator, shepherd-king and judge. Similar correspondences of the creation motif with images of YHWH appearing with the winds to expunge the wicked[379] abound in contexts where the concern is the maintenance of social order in YHWH's role as savior and redeemer, and calls for further exploration.

---

379. See chapter 3 on Pss 18, 77 and Hab 3 recounting the salvation procured by YHWH for his anointed/elected people, as a result of the subjugation of the wicked by the power of his winds.

3

YHWH in the Wind as the Savior

An Overture to YHWH in the Wind as Divine Warrior *Contra* Previous Scholarship

It is clear from the superscription of the Hebrew Psalm 18(=2 Sam 22)[1] that it originated from the mouth of King David upon divine deliverance from all his enemies, and from the hand of Saul. The Psalmist, that is King David, outlines detailed thanksgiving[2] as he exalts and attributes appellations to YHWH (Ps 18:1–4[1–3]; 47–51[46–50]) recalling YHWH's evocative appearance, or theophany (8–16[7–15]) culminating in the saving deeds (vv. 17–20[16–19]). King David qualifies his righteousness by his personal avowal to the observance of the "ways of YHWH" (vv. 21–31[20–30]). Thus, he sees himself earning divine intervention from the perilous encounters (vv. 5–7[4–6]), and the consequential empowerment to become invincible in battle against other nations or foreigners (vv. 32–46[31–45]). The flow of this psalm shows unity of literary

---

1. Previous scholarship devoted such extensive analysis and comparison of these two poems that no attempts are made here for a thorough textual analysis of this archaic variant, or recension. See Cross and Freedman, "Royal Psalm," 15–34; Schmuttermayr, *Psalm 18*; Chisholm, "Exegetical"; Vesco, "Psaume 18," 5–62; Kraus, *Psalms 1–59*, 252–66; Gray, *Psalm 18*.

2. Generally scholars agree on this poem as a thanksgiving psalm by King David, although scholars offer variant *Sitz im Leben* for its form and suspected origin. See Gray, *Psalm 18*, 44–49.

thought and content to dispel suggestions on two distinct compositions[3] superimposed and conflated to form a unified whole.[4] Nonetheless, at stake in the arguments on the partitioning of this psalm is the lack of the correct identification of the image described, and the relevance in meaning of this unit (vv. 8–16[7–15]) often thought to be intrusive.[5] Not so. This unit describing the theophany of YHWH has relevance to the rest of the psalm. To that end, the solution to the dilemma of the composite nature of Ps 18 lies in the unequivocal identification of the Psalmist's artistic portrait of YHWH coming with the winds described in the unit in question, in order to posit the unity in composition.

As already established in the anterior discussions,[6] Ps 18 is in keeping with other Hebrew texts with images recalling YHWH appearing with the winds at the primal creation. Therefore, it is proffered here that Ps 18 is a unified text, and employs graphic language reaching over to the tradition of a *Chaoskampf* relating the origin of the earth in depiction of YHWH's theophany in the blustery winds, as he intervenes to destroy the forces of chaos.[7] This identification of the form of YHWH manifesting his martial deeds on behalf of the Psalmist also brings to bear YHWH's cosmological activities at the creation of the earth, thus showing the significance of the theophany to the present context and the Hebrew tradition at large. So, the predominance and efficaciousness of YHWH's winds in this theophanic disclosure render a portrait of YHWH's warring activities with a background from creation and *Chaoskampf*. This portrait supersedes and departs from previous scholarship presenting with Canaanite mythic antecedents focusing attention particularly on the conceptual notion of YHWH as the divine warrior. This point of departure asserting YHWH's *modus operandi* in the winds in fulfillment of the same role, calls for a preliminary review of biblical scholarship on Ps 18 before an extensive exposition of the theophanic disclosure incorporated into this psalm.

---

3. Kraus, *Psalms 1–59*, 256; Kuntz, "Psalm 18," 19; Green, *Storm-God*, 269.

4. Weiser sees unity of thought in the two parts (Weiser, *Psalms*, 186–87). On the arguments for the categorization of the structural units in the psalm, and the presumed dissonance in the unity of the psalm, see Gray, *Psalm 18*, 40–44.

5. Cross thought this unit is not original to the text, and saw it as an insertion from an older source (Cross, *Canaanite Myth*, 158; cf. Kraus, *Psalms 1–59*, 256).

6. See pp. 27–28, 48–49, 79, 81–82.

7. Kraus, *Psalms 1–59*, 260; Kuntz, "Psalm 18," 18.

In his monograph *The Divine Warrior in Early Israel* (1973), Miller discusses the wars of YHWH and his hosts in relation to Canaanite mythology and other ANE traditions. His thesis is that the gods of Canaanite mythology, as well as in the ANE lore, fought wars for the deliverance or punishment of people in order to maintain or enhance order in their universe. The warring activities of the gods determined fundamental matters of kingship, salvation, creation, and temple building.[8] In keeping with ancient traditions, Israel came to understand YHWH as the divine warrior. Thus, in his survey of the divine warrior motif in pentateuchal poems, historical writings, and psalms, Miller observes general features relating to the war tradition of YHWH when YHWH and his heavenly armies or hosts (cosmic forces) fight historical battles. In that vein, and focusing on drawing close parallels with both Canaanite and Mesopotamian antecedents, Miller sees "plague" and "pestilence"[9] as the personification of deities, who are part of YHWH's retinue in battle.[10] Miller finds that the idea of YHWH as a warrior gives definition to the concept of deliverance, and relates to Israel's self-understanding as a nation. As Miller states in connection with YHWH's battle in Hab 3:8–15, the act of deliverance of his people is a significant aspect of YHWH's warfare and is without parallel in the myths of Ba'al[11] or El.[12]

At any rate, Miller points out that the image of YHWH as divine warrior attended by his cosmic hosts introduces the theme of salvation.[13] Miller sees the main image of YHWH related in the theophany in 2 Sam 22:7–18=Ps 18:7–18 as that of the divine warrior. He identifies in this image that the clouds are mentioned as a feature at YHWH's feet but not his chariot as in other texts he analyzes. Instead, Miller remarks that the

---

8. Miller, *Divine Warrior*, 64.

9. Miller sees the latter as the equivalent of *Resheph*, the god of pestilence (Hab 3:5) with a Canaanite provenance (Miller, *Divine Warrior*, 119). See Green, *Storm-God*, 245, 245n106, 266.

10. Miller, *Divine Warrior*, 119.

11. Miller acknowledges the close parallels between the tradition of Ba'al and Marduk. His preference to limit his survey of the divine warrior motif to Canaanite mythology is largely due to the work of Jacobsen conferred by the influence of his mentor, Frank Moore Cross. Jacobsen argues for Ba'al's combat with Yam to be the primary source of the conflict myth. However, Miller sees the Ba'al/Yam battle as a reflex of that between Marduk and Tiamat, though he also notes that the myths developed in different respects, and with no indicators of which myth preceded the other. See Miller, *Divine Warrior*, 25–28.

12. Miller, *Divine Warrior*, 120–21.

13. Miller, *Divine Warrior*, 173 (see also 121–22).

cherubim on the ark functioned as YHWH's "palladium of holy war,"[14] as it were, a locomotive YHWH rode into battle. However, without further clarity on this point, Miller also states that the cherubim represented members of YHWH's court. At any rate, Miller notes correctly that the violent epiphany of YHWH is associated with the defeat of the Psalmist's foes and his deliverance.[15] Also, Miller identifies the idea of YHWH soaring on the wings of the wind. But he overlooks the pale reflection of YHWH's battle in the guise of the wind against mythological forces of chaos that is recalled and juxtaposed with the description of his battle and consequent victory on behalf of the Psalmist. Hence, Miller misses the point, on account of the overdrawn comparison with the thundering voice of the storm god Ba'al,[16] that it is YHWH's phenomenal winds, which dispelled the forces of chaos at creation, that are wielded against the Psalmist's enemies.

Nonetheless, Miller's thesis is that YHWH fights wars for the liberation of his people and the destruction of their enemies. Hence, the theme of salvation is merged with YHWH's role as divine warrior. Miller sees theophany as central to YHWH's wars but places excessive emphasis on YHWH accompanied by cosmic hosts or various forces,[17] thus matching other ANE traditions asserting the same idea. Therefore, he divests the texts of speaking for themselves. So, in modification of Miller's view, this exposition seeks to show the centrality of winds to YHWH's theophany accompanied by other meteorological elements, and not by some mythological heavenly armies or cosmic hosts as Miller espouses.

It has been established that YHWH's *modus operandi* in the winds appertains to YHWH's manifestation against the forces of chaos at creation, and the same conceptual idea focuses YHWH's divine intervention, or theophany, in the historical plane.[18] So, YHWH fights Israel's

14. Miller, *Divine Warrior*, 122.

15. Miller, *Divine Warrior*, 122.

16. Miller, *Divine Warrior*, 122.

17. Miller emphasizes this view in light of the various Hebrew texts (Exod 15; Pss 29, 18, 68; Deut 33; Judg 5; Hab 3; *inter alia*) as he sees the portrayal of YHWH's theophany going to war for the aid of the people of Israel. See Miller, *Divine Warrior*, 5–6, 69, 75, 85–87, 91, 104–5, 107, 118–21. It is interesting to note that Miller sees YHWH's theophany, heavenly hosts—although an element Miller remarks as lacking in Exod 15 (Miller, *Divine Warrior*, 113)—and holy war inextricably linked in the description in Ps 68:1–5[1–4]. The latter echoes the song of the ark in Num 10:35–36, which presents an exhortation to YHWH to fight the wars of Israel against its foes, while the role of Israel in these wars is minimized (Miller, *Divine Warrior*, 104–5).

18. On YHWH's involvement in the historical arena as the creator and universal

battles as the "man of war" (Exod 15:3), or divine warrior to save his people. Indeed, as Miller asserts, YHWH avails strength and defense to his people and becomes their salvation.[19] If the divine warrior motif is integral to the theophany[20] of YHWH in the Hebrew traditions, then, in view of Miller's thesis that the theme of salvation is central to the motif, or vice versa, then the depiction of YHWH as savior in theophanic traditions where the winds are prevalent, as retained in Ps 18 and the related Hebrew texts, is in order.

To date, scholarship has concentrated on the literary form and style of theophanic hymns in the Hebrew tradition with an overt emphasis on parallels with the storm god in the ANE.[21] In the same vein, Green focuses on the identification of YHWH, as he perceives a transformation of his martial image. Green's characterization of YHWH derives from his proposition on the changing nature of the storm god in the ANE. In his book *The Storm-God in the Ancient Near East*, Green presents a survey of the storm god starting in Mesopotamia, Anatolia, Syria, through to coastal Canaan. In each of these geographic regions, Green explores the iconography, mythology, history, religion and political environs to investigate the various factors that determine the changing perceptions of the storm god. With that foreground, Green outlines the goal of his project. His focus is on the ideological and social functions of the storm god and its attendants in each of the cultural environments. From this aspect of inquiry, Green proposes a broader meaning and function of

---

judge, see pp. 112–16, 136–39 above.

19. Miller, *Divine Warrior*, 173.

20. As is evident in texts from the psalms, the description of YHWH's manifestation in battle reflects language and imagery in keeping with other gods of non-Israelite tradition, that are associated with the winds.

21. Cross discusses theophanic structures as a complex genre represented by two major features: the storm god preparing and waging war, and then his return and display of power at his mountain-abode (Cross, *Canaanite Myth*, 147–77). Jeremias, on the other hand, is concerned with the development of the theophanic form from a simple to a more complex genre. He argues that the original form is expressed in two parts: YHWH coming to war and the effect his appearance has on nature (Jeremias, *Theophanie*, 100–111). He finds the Song of Deborah (Judg 5:4–5) to be the prototype from which other elaborated texts derive (Jeremias, *Theophanie*, 15). Berry, on the other hand, using different literary methods—textual, form-critical, rhetorical, and reader-oriented approaches to the study of Ps 18—states that the psalm "shows clearer relationships with non-biblical Near Eastern literature." Here, however, Berry mentions parallels with the Babylonian and Ugaritic deities, particularly in the manner, as he deems, of YHWH descending on a cloud echoing Ba'al as "Rider of Clouds," and Marduk mounting the "storm-chariot" to confront Tiamat. See Berry, *Psalms*, 63–64.

the storm god throughout the ANE.[22] As Green points out, he achieves this by considering the presence of the semi-divine attendants associated with the storm god as a key element in deciphering the importance and function of the storm god motif.[23] This is critical to Green's investigation, as he analyzes both iconographic and textual evidence in different regional and socio-cultural contexts. In this survey moving from the east to the west, Green proposes an evolutionary development of the storm god. He applies the same thesis as influential in the early formative stages of Yahwism. That is, he sees the development of Yahwism from a synthesis of YHWH with the Canaanite El in the patriarchal age[24] to an integration of YHWH/El/Ba'al elements leading to the conception of YHWH as "Israel's incomparable storm god"[25] at the time of settlement of the people of Israel in Canaan.

From the outset, however, Green admits that there are inevitable challenges to this comparative study of the conceptual function of the storm god as perceived from region to region.[26] Based on the iconographic evidence in Mesopotamia, Green states that the impact of the storm god is undeniably obvious. He sees the concept of this deity evolving with the changing cultural and political processes, and perceptible in the characteristics of the mythical semi-divine attendants, which progressively combine the earlier forms through each succeeding period.[27] This is the background that leads Green to consider that YHWH emerges as a storm god and derives his meaning from the same environment. Therefore, Green espouses the emergence of YHWH from southwest Syria. From that perspective, Green states forthright the dearth of variety of sources for the storm god YHWH,[28] comparable to the iconographic, epigraphic, architectural, and artifactual evidence for the storm god in Mesopotamia, Anatolia and Syria.

However, Green's investigation largely focuses on the biblical texts in establishing the nature and function of YHWH as a storm god. At first, Green argues that the description of the evolving nature of YHWH appears with the characteristics of the Canaanite El based on evidence

22. Green, *Storm-God*, 3–4.
23. Green, *Storm-God*, 4–5.
24. Green, *Storm-God*, 246.
25. Green, *Storm-God*, 257.
26. Green, *Storm-God*, 6–7.
27. Green, *Storm-God*, 33–34.
28. Green, *Storm-God*, 219.

drawn from the earliest poetic sources (Judg 5:4–5; Deut 33:2–3; Ps 68:2, 4–8, 11–24; Hab 3:3–6).[29] Green notes that the style, language, and vocabulary in each of these texts show affinities with Canaanite mythology, in particular the god El,[30] and, to a lesser extent, some commonality with the imagery of the storm god Baʻal alluded to in storm theophany.[31] Green sees in these texts the historic triumphant march of YHWH as a warrior from the southern region, and he argues for the identity of YHWH with the god El[32] based on Ps 68:20–21[19–20], 25[24]. Also, Green identifies YHWH with the Canaanite god El as a warrior, in view of the epithet *Ṣebāʼôth* mentioned in Ps 68:13[12]. Hence, Green, apud Cross, argues that the title associates YHWH with El, who creates the heavenly hosts or armies (vv. 12–13[11–12]). These warriors are called *Ṣbʼwt* and Green sees both heavenly and earthly armies as YHWH's attendants fitting the epithet of YHWH as YHWH *Ṣebāʼôth*[33] mentioned in Ps 68. So, according to Green, YHWH and his entourage are responsible for the victories of his people, as they march from the south.[34]

Green argues that the same idea of YHWH's hosts as warriors is more pronounced in the hymn in Habakkuk 3.[35] Then, based on the poetry, Green adduces provenance to the twelfth to tenth century BCE, and he argues that YHWH's character progressively assimilated characteristics that are associated with the storm god Baʻal.[36] But, the occurrences of storm characteristics commonly associated with Baʻal in the portrait of YHWH/El in these early texts pose a problem, to which Green attempts to offer suggestions to support the significance of these occurrences. In his analysis of a selection of texts (Exod 15; Deut 33; Judg 5; Hab 3; Pss

---

29. Green, *Storm-God*, 236–53. Furthermore, Green sees similar references in epithets and function of YHWH as the patriarchal god El in Gen 49 and other prose sections in Genesis as evidence of the El's attributes associated with YHWH in early patriarchal Yahwism. In that view, Green infers that the martial characteristics of YHWH portrayed in these early texts, indicate early influence of the tradition of the Ugaritic El. Therefore, Green thinks that the prosaic texts, Gen 32:29; 33:18–20; 35:10, which refer to YHWH as *ʼēl ʼĕlōhê yiśrāʼēl*—El the God of Israel—are further proof of the synthesis of YHWH with El (Green, *Storm-God*, 246–56).

30. Green, *Storm-God*, 243–44, 246.

31. Green, *Storm-God*, 246.

32. Green, *Storm-God*, 243.

33. Green, *Storm-God*, 244.

34. Green, *Storm-God*, 243, 253.

35. Green, *Storm-God*, 244–45.

36. Green, *Storm-God*, 256–57.

18, 29, 68, 77, 89) that he assigns provenance ranging between twelfth to tenth century BCE, Green argues for the progressive evolution of YHWH as a storm god retained in these texts. To that end, Green sees the martial characteristics of YHWH, commonly associated with El, assimilating Baʿal's attributes[37] as a storm god, and focusing his mythical battle against cosmic forces causing mythical cosmic reactions.[38] In light of the latter, Green argues that Ps 18 employs the same language in the description of YHWH's theophany as in Exod 15 and Hab 3. He states that Ps 77 reflects the mythical pattern of YHWH's theophany in Hab 3, though consistent with the imagery associated with the mythical elements of the storm god Baʿal.[39] But Green overemphasizes the similarities with the mythopoeic language of the storm god Baʿal and overlooks the reference to the events surrounding the exodus, particularly to the crossing of the *Yam Suph* (Red Sea) as uniting Hab 3 with Ps 77.

Even Green's notion of the semi-divine attendants[40] in YHWH's entourage in the theophanic march from the southern regions has historical antecedents in the exodus tradition to be discussed here. However, in his exposition, Green either mentions vaguely, or overlooks entirely, the implications of the storm imagery (as he identifies it as such)[41] on the functionality of YHWH within the respective historical contexts.[42] Therefore, Green's thesis continues the trend of scholarship overstating parallels with the storm attributes of Baʿal, and/or an amalgamation of the El/Baʿal attributes, to the point of missing the correct identification of the theophany, as an ellipsis of YHWH's presence in the "wind(s)," not the "storm." This chapter, therefore, seeks to show the concept of YHWH as savior, or deliverer, that is in view in YHWH's theophany in the winds. The idea derives from the creation-out-of-chaos tradition with the theological intentionality of portraying YHWH's divine intervention for the salvation of the chosen one(s).

On the other hand, Gray's approach in studying metaphors in Ps 18 attempts to uncover the theological intentionality of the imagery in the

---

37. Green, *Storm-God*, 258–73.
38. Green, *Storm-God*, 270–71.
39. Green, *Storm-God*, 271–72.
40. On fire and Resheph, see p. 182 below.
41. This is in keeping with previous scholarship linking the idea of a theophany with the storm god tradition. See (amongst others referenced in this volume) Jeremias, *Theophanie*; Cross, *Canaanite Myth*.
42. Green, *Storm-God*, 259–74.

theophanic unit in this psalm. In a revised version of a thesis[43] submitted to the University of Cambridge, Gray analyzes words and (mind)pictures[44] to explore the themes and messages conveyed by the metaphors she identifies in Ps 18. Upon reflection on previous scholarship on this psalm, Gray notes that the focus has been on the theophanic unit,[45] or on its parallel version in 2 Sam 22, its *Sitz im Leben* and association to the cult, the presumed irregularities in form and structure leading to dissonance over the psalm's unity, composition, dating and authorship.[46] But, again, as with previous scholarship on Ps 18, Gray derives the meaning of the theophanic unit from the storm imagery, and attributes her analytic undertaking of some of the grammatical, stylistic, or pictorial aspects of the psalm to the work of R. B. Chisholm in an unpublished dissertation.[47] Gray sees a "storm god warrior"[48] in the midst of what she observes in the theophany as an array of dazzling images depicting YHWH's appearance. Furthermore, in analysis of the metaphors in the theophany described in Ps 18, Gray sees word-pictures reflecting a blending of ANE conceptions of the "storm" and "battle" to mirror an ultimate depiction of YHWH as a warrior-king and storm-deity.[49] At this, too, Gray also misses the correct identification of the image presented in this theophany relating YHWH's appearance in the winds, as in the creation tradition, and lending meaning to this psalm as a composite whole.

The creation-out-of-chaos tradition and the appearance of YHWH with the winds, as established in the previous chapters, provide the basis for the attribution of the role of savior/deliverer to YHWH in Pss 18 (A Psalm of Royal Thanksgiving), 77 (Lament), 144 (Royal Lament) and in Hab 3 (Lamentational Prayer). This variety of texts shows the fluidity of the tradition of the creation-out-of-chaos and the collateral image of YHWH with the winds in literary texts describing YHWH's actions for the deliverance of his elected king and people. Although the concept of

---

43. Gray, *Psalm 18*.

44. Gray, *Psalm 18*, 3.

45. Here, Gray refers to Jeremias, [Chiswa] Gandiya, Hunter, and Maré. See Gray, *Psalm 18*, 3n16.

46. Gray, *Psalm 18*, 4.

47. Chisholm, "Exegetical."

48. Gray, *Psalm 18*, 79. See also Day, who sees a theophany of a storm described in vv. 5–18[4–17], and even argues for its *Sitz im Leben* in the hypothetical autumnal festival in anticipation of the rainy season, where there is allusion to the deliverance of the king within the cultic celebration (Day, *God's Conflict*, 122–25).

49. Gray, *Psalm 18*, 83 (see also 196).

YHWH as savior is not as explicit in Pss 77 and 144, as in Ps 18 and Hab 3, these have elements and ideas that are also suggestive of this motif. All the literary features involved are discussed with respect to Ps 18 as the paradigmatic structure within which YHWH's deeds of salvation are manifested. The main focus is on those features alluding to the tradition of creation-out-of-chaos and YHWH appearing with the winds as the savior of his surrogate king and his chosen people. YHWH's appearance is heralded by the sonorous winds[50] and the discharge of other natural elements[51]—clouds,[52] lightning,[53] fire,[54] hail,[55] and rain[56]—causing the agitation in the cosmic order.[57] This theophany of YHWH with the winds dispersing phenomenal elements is characterized as divine intervention for deliverance from, or through, the "many waters" in Ps 18:17[16] (see 144:7) and Ps 77:20[19] (see Hab 3:15) respectively.

A Portrait of YHWH in the Wind as Savior in Psalm 18

Ps 18 originated from the royal circles of the Davidic dynasty, as is indicated by the inscription (v. 1 [Eng. superscription]) and a specific reference to David (v. 51[50]), may imply the psalm's period of provenance.[58] It is clear from the tone of the psalm that the Psalmist, King David, celebrates a past victory and the divine protection bestowed on him. Throughout the psalm the language employed is oriented towards the inception and progression of the theme of deliverance. The Psalmist sets the scene by

50. Pss 18:11[10], 14[13]b, 16[15]c; 77:19[18]a; Hab 3:15–16. See pp. 81–82, 113–14 above.

51. Not all the natural elements are regularly represented in each psalm under discussion, but the mention or allusion to the phenomenal wind(s) is crucial to the depiction of YHWH as savior.

52. Pss 18:12–13[11b–12a]; 77:18[17]a; cf. Hab 3:11a.

53. Pss 18:13[12]b; 77:19[18]b; Hab 3:11bc.

54. Ps 18:9[8]; Hab 3:5b; cf. Ps 77:18[17]c.

55. Ps 18:13[12]b.

56. Ps 77:18[17]a; Hab 3:10b; cf. Ps 18:12[11]b.

57. Pss 18:8[7], 16[15]; 77:17[16], 19[18]c; Hab 3:6, 10a. See p. 113.

58. See p. 155, 155n2. It is appropriate then, that a tenth century BCE date of composition for this psalm as proposed by most scholars is upheld. For proposals on this date for Ps 18, following the pioneering study by Cross and Freedman, and others suggesting a date between tenth to ninth century BCE, see Green, *Storm-God*, 270n209. Also, for a debate on a postexilic date, or provenance antedating the fall of Samaria in 722 BCE on this psalm, though untenable based on the evidence presented in this discussion, see Green, *Storm-God*, 269–70.

narrating the circumstances that motivated divine intervention. He portrays his plight in metaphors representing cosmic forces of chaos. These forces of chaos are represented by torrents of perdition (נחלי בליעל, v. 5[4]), Sheol (שאול), death (מות, v. 6[5]), and many waters (מים רבים, v. 17[16]). Although the Psalmist mentions all these elements, the actual forces threatening to engulf him are the waters, in particular the "many waters" (מים רבים). The other representations of chaos are exclusively chthonic; the torrents of perdition, cords of Sheol and death, are most likely to be associated with the foundations of the mountains and the depths of the sea. These latter two are euphemistic for the underworld that YHWH uncovers upon his approach (v. 16[15]).

The identification of the foundations of the mountains and the depths of the sea with the underworld is not unknown in ancient traditions. In the Ugaritic texts the domain of Mot, the god of death, is located below the "two hills bounding the earth" (KTU 1.4.VIII:4–7 [=CTA 4.viii:4–7]) and at the "limits of the waters" (KTU 1.5.VI:4–5 [=CTA 5.VI:4–5]). This is the realm where the "cords of Sheol and death" are the ruling forces. The occurrence of these destructive forces in association with "torrents of perdition"[59] (Ps 18:5[4]), even though the latter expression cannot be rendered with certainty, is primarily to emphasize the engulfing capacity of the "many waters" foreboding the Psalmist's peril, and possibly death. On the whole, therefore, the term "many waters" embodies the antagonistic forces mentioned in this psalm, threatening the Psalmist's demise, which compel YHWH's divine intervention.

As already noted, the origin of the term "many waters"[60] (מים רבים) in the Hebrew tradition cannot be established with certainty, apart from

---

59. The etymology of this term poses problems. Cross and Freedman construe the term as *balī ya'lê* with the meaning "place from which none arises," as euphemism for Sheol or the underworld (Cross and Freedman, "Royal Psalm," 22n6). Yet, the translation of the root *bl'* to "entangle," "confuse," and "swallow" based on the Arabic root is suggestive for the dire situation portrayed by the Psalmist (Otzen, "*bĕliyya'al*," 133–34). The term בליעל in Ps 18:5[4] is found in parallel with מות and שאול, which are terms relating to death. Similar usage of בליעל for the manifestation of chaos, possibly symbolic of death, is found in Ps 41:9[8], a psalm of lament as a result of sickness. Although the etymology of this compound term from עלה and בלע defies definition, the Psalmist uses this term in the phrase נחלי בליעל to express mythological connotations of the engorging capacity of the waters—his enemies—as the "torrents" entangling him for his demise (see Gray, *Psalm 18*, 70–71).

60. See pp. 47–48 above. May argues for the lack of connection between the Hebrew term מים רבים ("many waters") and the Ugaritic appellation of the god Yam. Of significance to this discussion, however, is the symbolism of "many waters" as the chaotic forces that YHWH pits with his potent winds at his appearance as savior.

its similarity to the appellation of Yam, who is the subdued antagonist in an Ugaritic text:

> lmḫšt. mdd ʾil ym
> "Did I not destroy Yam the darling of El?"
> lklt. nhr. ʾil rbm
> "Did I not make an end of Nahar the great god?"
> (KTU 1.3.III:39[=CTA 3.iii:36])[61]

In the sequence of Ugaritic texts, Anat's boastful outburst about her annihilation of Yam follows a text, KTU 1.3.II [=CTA 3.ii], recounting Anat's blood bath as a result of her frenzied slaughter of human warriors. Apparently, Anat's violent efforts are not limited to the slaughter of these warriors. She mentions that she dispatched all the foes threatening to drive Baʿal from the heights of Ṣāphōn.[62] In her role as advocate for the rule of Baʿal, Anat claims to have defeated Yam, ʾil rbm.[63] Whereas the term ʾil rb is applied to other gods, this is the only occurrence of ʾil rbm[64] as an epithet of Yam. The reference to Anat's violent rage, directed against Yam (ʾil rbm) and other opponents of Baʿal, leads to events culminating in the establishment of the rule of Baʿal as the storm god in the cosmic realm.

As mentioned in view of Miller's observation,[65] Anat's feat against Yam is seen as advocacy towards Baʿal's quest for triumph over his archrival, Yam. In light of that, ʾil rbm, as an epithet, is a mythological variant of Yam who is the sea god subjugated by the storm god Baʿal. Therefore, the representation of the "sea" and the "many waters" as the mythological symbol of chaos, in these Hebrew psalms, echoes the symbolism of the

---

61. See p. 47.

62. KTU 1.3.III:39–47 [=CTA 3.iii:36–44].

63. Kloos suggests that the "*m*" must be a case of mimation. Kloos states that in the Ugaritic texts, Yam is not referred to as *mym rbm*, and, yet, in her analysis of Ps 29, she is convinced that the epithet *mym rbm* signifies Yam. See Kloos, *Yhwh's Combat*, 52.

64. According to Whitaker's concordance of Ugaritic, the only other attestation of *rbm* relates to the gods, called the sons of Athirat, whom Baʿal smites (KTU 1.6.V:2 [=CTA 6.v:2]). Rahmouni cites the many scholarly interpretations of the epithet ʾil rbm. She also notes that there is a general consensus on *nhr* as a proper name for Yam, but not on the meaning of the syntactical relationship of ʾil and *rbm* (Rahmouni, *Divine Epithets*, 238n2). At any rate, the epithet is associated with Yam/Nahar and is seen as an elliptical for the Hebrew מים רבים, "many waters." Rahmouni and Smith and Pitard translate this epithet ʾil rbm to "immense waters" and "great waters," respectively (Rahmouni, *Divine Epithets*, 239; *UBC II* 248). See pp. 47–48, 48n318 above.

65. See p. 47, 47n316 above.

assailant in the tradition of the conflict between the storm god and the mythic waters. Arguably, the parallelism of the "sea" (ים) with "many waters" (מים רבים) in Ps 77:20[19] and in Hab 3:15 indicates that this symbolism is not far removed from the ancient tradition of the *Chaoskampf*, and no less relates to the subjugation of chaos. The point is, in spite of the elliptical term *'il rbm* shedding light on the occurrence of the term *mym rbm* (מים רבים, "many waters") in the Hebrew tradition, and recalling Baʿal's arch rival Yam, there is no mention of Baʿal, or Anat, wielding winds, or any meteorological elements in the fight against Yam. But, in the Hebrew tradition, this symbolism reminiscent of the ancient conflict myth is subjected to YHWH's sway over the phenomenal elements, and juxtaposed with the monumental historical event at the crossing of the Red Sea:

> Your way was through the sea [ים],
> Your path through the many waters [מים רבים].
> (Ps 77:20[19])
> You trampled the sea [ים] with your horses,
> the surging of the mighty waters [מים רבים].
> (Hab 3:15)

Here, the idea of YHWH's theophany *vis-à-vis* the "many waters," which are symbolic of his archrival, recalls the mythic battle from the non-Israelite tradition. Yet, in the context of salvation in Ps 18 and related psalms (Pss 77, 144 and Hab 3), as shown in the discussion below, the imagery is used primarily to enhance YHWH's purposeful acts of deliverance in relation to either the elected king or the people, rather than as a mere recital of a mythical battle. The use of such imagery, in connection with other elements relating to Israel's salvation history, is meant to import the far-reaching implications of YHWH's redemptive acts. As Weiser[66] notes in relation to Ps 18, there is a conflation of elements from the Sinai theophany and events at the *Yam Suph*, that are refined and integrated in this text in description of YHWH's theophany at his salvific acts. Therefore, in Ps 18 (with Ps 144 in affinity) there is an amalgamation of features that relate to those two significant events in Israel's history of salvation, but then are linked with other elements familiar from the creation-out-of-chaos tradition, in depiction of YHWH's disclosure to do battle against the chaotic "many waters":

---

66. Weiser, *Psalms*, 190–91.

YHWH IN THE WIND(S)

8 The earth quaked (תגעש) and shook (תרעש);
and the foundations of the mountains quaked (ירגזו)
and reeled to and fro (יתגעשו) because of his anger.
9 Smoke (עשן) went up from his nostrils and a devouring fire
(אש) from his mouth;[67]
coals kindled from him.
10 And he bent[68] (נטה) down the heavens and descended,
and a heavy cloud (ערפל) under his feet.
11 And he rode on the cherub (כרוב) and flew.
And he soared on the "wings of the wind" (כנפי־רוח).
12 He set darkness (as) his covering; his booth (of) masses of water surrounding him, (and) masses of clouds.[69]
13 From the brightness (נגה) of his presence, his clouds issued forth hailstones and coals of fire.
14 And YHWH thundered (ירעם) from the heavens;
and the Most high, his voice(/loud sound, קל) gave forth hail (ברד) and coals of fire (גחלי־אש).
15 And he sent forth his arrows, and scattered them (יפיצם),
and many flashes of lightning (ברקים), and confounded them.
16 And the channels of the waters [אפיקי מים] were seen, and the foundations of the world exposed,
at your rebuke [גערתך] O YHWH and from the blast of wind[70] (נשמת רוח) of your nostrils.
17 He stretched out from on high and took me,
and drew me out of the many waters (מים רבים)
(Ps 18:8–17[7–16]).[71]

Even though YHWH's disclosure, here, is marked by elaborate phenomenal elements not attested in the Sinai theophany, other characteristics compel a comparison with the latter. YHWH's theophany is defined by the idea of the "earth"[72] and "mountains"[73] "quaking" along

---

67. See pp. 14–15, 14n72 above. Fire is one of the fundamental elements of the morphology of the wind god Amma. But at Amma's first attempt at the creation of the first world, it is said Amma breathed (out) fire, and "blew" hard to release wind (Griaule and Dieterlen, *Pale Fox*, 110). The goddess Inanna has the same propensity with fire in her fanfare announced by the evil winds she releases, alongside other meteorological phenomena. See p. 115.

68. See pp. 92–93.

69. BDB 728.

70. BDB 675.

71. The translation from the MT is the author's.

72. Ps 18:8[7]a; 77:19[18]c; cf. Hab 3:7.

73. Ps 18:8[7]b. See Exod 19:18c; Hab 3:10a.

with the emission of "smoke"[74] and "fire."[75] Undoubtedly, as was already established, wind, fire, and, inevitably, smoke, are hallmarks of the appearance of a wind deity.[76] In sequel, the reference to YHWH bending down (נטה, Ps 18:10[9]) the heavens for his descent,[77] reaches out to the creation tradition (see Job 9:8), in order to relate the confrontation of the chaotic "many waters" (מים רבים, Ps 18:17[16]). Thus, YHWH's graphic descent is characterized with outbursts of the "sonorous sound"[78] from the wind and "luminous" sight or "lightning"[79] (Ps 18:14–15[13–14]; see Exod 19:16b; 20:18a; Hab 3:11, 16; Pss 77:19[18]b; 144:6). As already noted, the emphasis on YHWH's theophany in the wind in the discussion on Ps 104,[80] the Psalmist uses *hendiadyses* or appositional synonyms in Ps 18:11–12[10–11] to throw into bold relief the quintessence of the deity causing convulsions in nature.

The Sight and Sound of YHWH in the Wind(s)

In light of Noegel's observation,[81] the Psalmist employs appositional synonyms from iconographic representations to amplify YHWH's theophany in the winds. Thus, YHWH is said to ride on a "cherub" (כרוב) and fly, and soar on the "wings of the wind" (כנפי־רוח) in expression of his appearance with the winds (v. 11[10]), and the heavy/dark "clouds" attending his presence[82] (v. 12[11]; see v. 10[9]b; Ps 77:18[17] aβ). The Psalmist, however, sets in tension the idea of the *Deus praesens* with *Deus absconditus* by referring to YHWH appearing enveloped in heavy/dark clouds (v. 12[11]). In essence, the elements representing the

---

74. Ps 18:9[8]a; see Exod 19:18a; Ps 144:5.

75. Ps 18:9[8]b, 13; see Exod 19:18b; Hab 3:5.

76. See p. 168n67.

77. See pp. 92–93.

78. Here the same term יתן קולו appears in parallel with ירעם to refer to the outbursts of YHWH's blustery winds. See pp. 113–14, 142, 142n326. In Jer 25:30, the term יתן קולו appears in parallel with ישאג to relate the same idea of YHWH releasing outbursts of the loud winds.

79. This conceptual idea of lightning (Ps 18:13[12]aβ; 15[14]b) attending the winds is nothing other than the Psalmist attempting to apprehend the splendor of the glinting and forceful winds causing the cosmic convulsions and his enemies to "scatter" (v. 15[14]bβ). See pp. 170–72 below.

80. See p. 82.

81. See pp. 81–82.

82. On clouds as YHWH's covering, see p. 98, 98n182.

phenomenal disclosure of YHWH in Ps 18 echo his theophany at Mount Sinai (Exod 19:9, 16b, 18; 20:21). At the same time, however, the mention of the "brightness" (נגה) of YHWH's presence in Ps 18:13[12]a, not only parallels the "luminous" nature of the wind-deity Amma at creation,[83] but also throws into bold relief YHWH's numinous image in association with the clouds issuing forth hailstones, and coals of fire (Ps 18:13[12]b). The latter recalls the idea of the fiery cloud that lit the path for the escapees at the exodus (Exod 14:20b; see Pss 78:14b; 105:39b). So, the Psalmist purposely depicts YHWH surrounded by masses of clouds in contradistinction; showing darkness on one hand (Ps 18:10[9]b, 12[11]), and light on the other (v. 13[12]). This image is drawn from the narrative of the events at the exodus expressing cloud(s) being darkness to the foe (Egyptians, see Josh 24:7) but giving light to the fugitives (Israelites, Exod 14:19–20).

All the phenomenal elements associated with the winds, heavy/dark clouds, darkness and light, hailstones and fire, are drawn from the creation tradition, Sinai theophany, and the crossing at the *Yam Suph*. These elements are conflated with the swirling winds in Ps 18 in portrayal of YHWH's theophany, and directed for a divine purpose against the mythical "many waters" for the deliverance of YHWH's chosen. The Psalmist subtly implies that YHWH is the provenance of the phenomenal elements aligned with his presence, which are also at his disposal. Hence, in Ps 18 the God of creation, whose blast of wind produces ice,[84] binds up frozen waters—hailstones—in the clouds, and causes the clouds to swirl by his winds, as highlighted by the poet of Job (Job 37:11a, 12–13), is featured here unleashing hailstones as a weapon (v. 12aβ; see Job 38:22–23).

The Psalmist also depicts YHWH's power and majesty in his blustery luminous wind gleaming like (metal) arrows, or lightning,[85] assailing the chaotic many waters (Ps 18:15[14]). Unquestionably, the Psalmist employs the synonymous[86] terms: your "rebuke" (גערתך) and "blast[87] of wind" (נשמת רוח, v. 15[16]) to focus attention on YHWH's potent winds

83. See pp. 17, 75–77.

84. Job 37:9b–10; cf. 38:29; Ps 147:17.

85. See 169n79; on the idea of YHWH's resplendent presence noted in Ps 18:13[12]a, 15[14]b.

86. On גערה and רוח as synoynmous terms and used interchangebly for winds, see pp. 49–50, 82n120.

87. BDB 675 renders the translation of נשמת as breath, which means the phrase נשמת רוח would translate breath of wind. This again relates to the mythological idea of deities breathing out fiery wind (see p. 168n67 above).

directed against the chaotic waters, as at the primal creation[88] (Ps 104:7a), and at the *Yam Suph* crossing (Exod 15:8, 10a). The blustery winds cause the channels of the waters to be exposed (Ps 18:16[15]; see Exod 15:8; Ps 77:20[19]), also recalling YHWH's control of the waters at the establishment of the cosmic order. Nonetheless, this image also focuses the idea of YHWH's blast of wind(s) drying up of the channels of the *Yam Suph*, as YHWH performs liberation acts for the Israelite fugitives at the exodus. Hence, once more, at the Psalmist's crisis, the undeniable impact of the "blast of wind" from YHWH's nostrils in exposure of his might against the "many waters" (Ps 18:16[15]; see Exod 15:8, 10), effects the deliverance of YHWH's elect.[89] All these ideas collated in Ps 18 deriving from events relating to the mythological battle at primal creation, the crossing of the *Yam Suph*, and theophany at Mount Sinai, give form and content to YHWH's involvement with the winds for divine intervention for the Psalmist. Hence, Ps 18 is paradigmatic, and provides an elaborate link of various themes and motifs in description of YHWH's theophany with the sight and sound of the luminous and sonorous winds, as he directs his power against the "many waters," symbolizing the Psalmist's historical foes.

YHWH's Wind against the "Many Waters"— A Symbol of Historical Enemies

Arguably, in the description of YHWH's theophany as savior, the Psalmist uses terms alluding to divine intervention against historical foes, rather than a mere recital of diction familiar from a mythological battle against the many waters. It is clear from the outset, that the Psalmist relates YHWH's intervention for his deliverance from his "enemies" (איבי, Ps 18:4[3]). But, there is no specific reference to the human foes within the theophanic unit itself (vv. 8–17[7–16]) other than the pronominal objects in v. 15[14]. Even though it is stated that the arrows of YHWH "scattered them" and his luminous sight, or lightning, "confounded them" (v. 15[14]aβ) it is the "channels of the waters"[90] (אפיקי מים, v. 16[15]) and

---

88. See 82–83 above.

89. Pss 18:16[15], 17[16]. See Exod 15:8; Hab 3:15; Pss 77:17[16]; 144:7.

90. Some scholars argue for the emendation of the phrase to "channels of the sea" (אפיקי ים), as it appears in 2 Sam 22:16 (Cross, *Studies*, 147; Dahood, *Psalms*, 1:109). In fact, the suggestion to emend the text brings it closer to the parallelism of "sea" (ים) and "many waters" (מים רבים) as in Ps 77:20[19] and Hab 3:15, but it is suggested here to retain the term as in the MT.

the "many waters"⁹¹ (מים רבים, v. 17[16]) that are central objects of the wrath of YHWH. The allusion to human foes is slight to the point of being overshadowed by the representation of YHWH's confrontation of the "waters."

The identity of YHWH's foes becomes clear as the imagery of his battle extends to the realm of nature. Indeed, the Psalmist proclaims that the "channels of the sea" are exposed at YHWH's rebuke (גערה) and at the "blast of wind" from his nostrils (נשמת רוח אפו, v. 16[15]). Then, in this theophanic descent, with his blustery winds dispersing other meteorological elements⁹² (vv. 9–15[8–14]), YHWH reaches from on high and "draws out" (משה) the Psalmist from the "many waters" (v. 17[16]). The enemies of the Psalmist are conflated with the many waters for purposes of focusing attention on the theophany of YHWH comparable to primal creation, and the deliverance that YHWH executes. To that end, the victory achieved for the Psalmist is presented primarily as a conquest of the many waters against which divine intervention is involved.

Once YHWH's purposeful intervention is consummated, the narration of events shifts, with the substitution of victory over human enemies. Some terms expressed in Ps 18:18[17] and the latter part of the psalm (vv. 19–51[20–50]), show that the Psalmist boasts of a victory over entities that are variously identified as "my enemy" (איבי, v. 18[17]) or "my enemies,"⁹³ the "ones who hate me" (משנאי, vv. 18[17], 41[40]) or "sons of foreigners" (בני־נכר, vv. 45[44], 46[45]). In fact, the identification of victories over the many waters with the human foes whom they symbolize, is brought to bear by the Psalmist's petition for deliverance from many waters, occurring in apposition with the "sons of foreigners," a variant designation of the Psalmist's opponents, as presented in Ps 144:7:

---

91. YHWH's conflict with the waters is in keeping with the imagery of the battle of Ba'al against Yam and of Marduk against Tiamat. But, unlike Ba'al's, the battles of Marduk against Tiamat, and of YHWH against the waters represent the *Chaoskampf* tradition and stand apart in their use of the winds as the main phenomenal element deployed for repelling the chaotic waters. In the Hebrew tradition, the chaotic waters also represent historical enemies.

92. In the book of Job, Elihu declares YHWH's winds as the provenance for ice and the force behind the scattering and swirling of the clouds (Job 37:9–12). See also the discussion on the heavy-rain-laden clouds scudding along with YHWH's winds, and the force of the wind disseminating meteorological elements at YHWH's command for his purposes in chapter 2.

93. Ps 18:4[3], 38[37], 41[40], 49[48].

YHWH IN THE WIND AS THE SAVIOR

Send your hand from on high, set me free and deliver me from the "many waters" [מים רבים] and from the hand of the "sons of foreigners" [בני־נכר].

Hence, the sons of foreigners are symbolic of chaos as much as the primal many waters. In which case, the victory of YHWH is extended beyond the mythical waters to the Psalmist's anthropomorphic, or historical inimical forces. Arguably, the reference to the sons of foreigners implies nothing other than the kings and nations King David subdues with the help of YHWH, as mentioned in 2 Sam 8:5–15. This means that the notion of YHWH's arrows scattering them (יפיצם, Ps 18:15[14]a) is a figurative representation of nothing other than the luminous and sonorous winds sending these sons of foreigners helter-skelter at YHWH's graphic intervention. Indeed, the Psalmist juxtaposes the idea of YHWH's triumph over and against the historical foes with the many waters to show that YHWH's winds repel any forces antithetical to his divine design, as at the primal creation (see Ps 104:7).[94] Consequently, the Psalmist's enemies are consigned to the fate of the wicked, and scattered by the winds in keeping with YHWH's maintenance of cosmic order. Therefore, in triumphant exultation of YHWH, the Psalmist states that YHWH delivered him from enemies stronger than he (vv. 18–20[17–19]) and set him on a broad place (מרחב, v. 20[19]; cf. v. 37[36]). Here, too, the Psalmist's deliverance to a "broad place" is couched in terms echoing the events surrounding the exodus.

The Psalmist uses language patterned after the events relating to the redemption of Israel at YHWH's intervention, and the ultimate victory at the exodus. The language employed here in depiction of YHWH's response to the Psalmist's "cry," as represented by his "descent" for emancipation, and the deliverance to a broad place, is familiar from the events pertaining to the exodus:

The lord said, "Indeed I have seen the affliction of my people who are in Egypt and I have heard (שמע)[95] their cry (צעק)[96] before their oppressors, for I know their suffering.

---

94. See pp. 82–83.
95. Cf. Ps 18:7[6].
96. Cf. שוע Ps 18:7[6].

Therefore I am coming down (ירד)⁹⁷ to deliver them (נצל)⁹⁸
from the hand of the Egyptians,
and to bring them up from that land to a good and broad land
(רחבה, Exod 3:7–8).⁹⁹

In the same manner, YHWH's descent, or coming down for intervention with his blustery winds, accords the Psalmist salvation and security from the inimical forces. YHWH's triumph over these forces, that is the band of kings and foreign nations, is essential to his portrayal as savior of his anointed.

YHWH's Presence in the Winds at the Exodus Revisited in Psalm 77

The description of YHWH's theophany in Ps 77,¹⁰⁰ as he leads his elected people through the "many waters," indicates the significance of the psalm for the portrayal of YHWH as savior. YHWH's appearance, as in Ps 18, is accompanied by disruptions in the natural order signified by the shaking of the world, and paralleled with the earth quaking (Ps 77:19[18]c)¹⁰¹ resulting from the blustery winds.¹⁰² YHWH's presence with the sonorous winds impacts the waters and makes them "writhe" (חול, Ps 77:17[16]b)¹⁰³ and the deeps "quake" (רגז, Ps 77:17[16]c), while the clouds, swirled by these winds, "pour forth floods" (זרם, v. 18[17]a). These upheavals in the cosmic order in conjunction with the wielding of phenomenal natural

---

97. Cf. Ps 18:10[9].

98. Cf. Ps 18:18[17].

99. Cf. Ps 18:20[19]. As with other textual verses, the translation from the MT is the author's.

100. This psalm is postulated as a tenth century BCE composition by Dahood (*Psalms*, 2:224–25, 231) and Cross (*Canaanite Myth*, 136–37), but others have assigned this psalm to late eighth century BCE, or even the postexilic era (Tate, *Psalms*, 274; Green, *Storm-God*, 271, 271n217). Nonetheless, the unity of this psalm, consisting of a lament (vv. 1–10[1–9]) and a hymn (vv. 14–21[13–20]), which incorporates the theophany tradition (vv. 17–21[16–20]), is argued for elsewhere (Kselman, "Psalm 77," 51–58). Though the nature of the Psalmist's misery is not specified, the Psalmist is driven by despair and questions the deity's care and justice (vv. 8–10[7–9]). He recalls YHWH's past acts of deliverance as a motive to renew his power to save (vv. 17–21[16–20]).

101. Ps 18:8[7]a; Hab 3:6, 9b–10a.

102. See pp. 168–69, 169n78.

103. Hab 3:10a.

elements (vv. 18–19[17–18])¹⁰⁴ culminate with the deliverance of YHWH's people (v. 21[20]).

Although the Psalmist's recollection of YHWH's redemptive acts narrated in Ps 77 is couched in terms familiar from the exodus tradition, the Psalmist also employs mythopoeic language of a Chaoskampf associated with the creation tradition we find in the book of Job.¹⁰⁵ In spite of his despair driven by YHWH's elusiveness, Job calls to mind the incomparable and the mysterious wonders of YHWH's cosmogonic activities (Job 9:10).¹⁰⁶ Job is awed with YHWH's mastery of the chaotic sea, and enumerates YHWH's control of the sea among his wonderful primal deeds (Job 9:8b). Similarly, the Psalmist in Ps 77 harks back to YHWH's subjugation of the primal chaotic waters as the basis to evoke hope that YHWH will act again (v. 6[5]). As noted by most scholars, the Psalmist makes reference to YHWH performing wonders¹⁰⁷ (עשׂה פלא, Ps 77:15[14]a).¹⁰⁸ The Psalmist focuses the idea of YHWH's emancipation of his people by means of his "arm" (זרוע) at the crossing of the Red Sea (Ps 77:15b–16[14b–15]; see Isa 51:9–10); an event which inflicts an undeniable imprint of fear and dread¹⁰⁹ on the minds of the surrounding nations.¹¹⁰ So, the Psalmist recites YHWH deploying his arm¹¹¹—symbolizing the whirlwind (Ps 77:19[18] cf. Exod 15:10)—for shattering the enemy.

---

104. Ps 18:12–15[11–14].

105. See Kselman, "Psalm 77," 54n10.

106. See pp. 92–93.

107. Kselman, "Psalm 77," 51; Ross, *Commentary*, 2:636–37; *contra* Brueggemann and Bellinger, *Psalms*, 334, who link the wonders of the past with the storm god, an idea that is dissented here in assertion of a theophany in the wind, as in the age-old ways at creation.

108. Ps 77:12–13[11–12]; Exod 15:11.

109. See Watson, *Chaos*, 148–49; Brueggemann and Bellinger, *Psalms*, 334.

110. Exod 15:13–16. See Deut 26:8.

111. See table 1. The "hand" (יד) and "arm" (זרוע) are used synonymously to refer to the winds. Jer 32:21 states the mighty hand in conjunction with outstretched arm in reference to YHWH's acts of deliverance for Israel (Deut 11:2–4), causing terror for the onlookers (Exod 15:14–16; see Deut 26:8). The recital of events in Exod 15 (the Song of the Sea) conjures images of the wonders performed by YHWH at the crossing of the Red Sea. Thus, in this Song of the Sea, YHWH's act of drying the sea with his winds, that is, the blast of breath from his nostrils (v. 10; see v. 8), is recited and celebrated as a show of the power of his right hand (v. 6) and the greatness of his arm (v. 16; see Deut 4:34 referencing taking a nation from another nation). It is evident, therefore, that the (right) hand, or arm of YHWH is synecdoche for YHWH's winds.

YHWH IN THE WIND(S)

It seems not uncommon, however, that in other biblical texts, the "arm" (זרוע) of YHWH is mentioned in contexts where YHWH's power is wielded by the winds. In Num 11:23, 31, YHWH rhetorically poses the question whether his "hand"[112] (יד) is cut short (cf. Isa 50:2; 59:1) But, the immediate response is the manifestation of a wind of YHWH from the sea demonstrating YHWH's potency in the provision of quails to the famished multitude wandering through the desert (Num 11:31). On the other hand, the description in Isa 30:30 is instructive on the association and identification of YHWH's arm with the phenomenal winds to the point of being indistinct. Hence, the descent of YHWH's "arm" (זרוע) is blended with the sounding forth of YHWH's majestic "voice" (קול), which is the sonorous sound of YHWH's wind in expression of his raging anger (זעף אף), manifested by "consuming fire" (להב אש), "cloud burst" (נפץ) and "rain storm"[113] (זרם) for judgment. Also, as was already established in Job 40, the significance of the arm of YHWH as symbolic for the potent winds is expressed with a rhetorical question (v. 9). YHWH challenges Job about whether he possesses an "arm" comparable to his, or has potency to "thunder" (רעם) with his "voice." There is a greater immediacy of response to this interrogative posed to Job within the context of YHWH's manifestation in the sonorous whirlwind (v. 6). In the same vein, Ps 18:10[9]a depicts YHWH stretching out from the heavens, as though unveiling his arm, to draw out (v. 17[16]a; cf. v. 36[35]) the Psalmist from the waters. But, it is in fact YHWH's wind, personified as the hand (144:7), which wields deliverance for the Psalmist.

YHWH's deliverance [of his people] through the "many waters" is described by the Psalmist collaterally with the wielding of YHWH's winds in subjugation of these waters (Ps 77:19–20[18–19]). Yet, in Josh 4:23–24, the crossing of the Jordan is compared with the crossing of the Red Sea, as two significant events where nothing other than YHWH's powerful "hand" (יד, v. 24), symbolizing the winds, paves the path in the Red Sea for salvation. In light of that, YHWH's hand is the image of the winds personified as YHWH's agency involved at the drying of the waters. No wonder the Psalmist in Ps 77 expresses exuberant confidence in recollection of the great deeds performed by the age-old right "hand" of the Most High (v. 11[10]). Again, the Psalmist proclaims the strength of YHWH's "arm" in display at the redemption of YHWH's people

---

112. The nouns יד ("hand") and זרוע ("arm") appear in parallel in Ps 89:14[13], 22[21] and is instructive to the reference of the same metonymy here.

113. For the discussion on Isa 30:30, see p. 42.

manifested by the phenomenal elements causing the convulsions in nature (vv. 16–19[15–18]). Thus, the Psalmist's recital retains the same image of YHWH subduing the waters with YHWH's "arm" (זרוע, v. 16[15]) used figuratively for the "whirlwind" (v. 19[18]), as the weapon deployed against the many waters for the deliverance of YHWH's elected people and the destruction of their Egyptian foes in pursuit.[114]

Furthermore, Ps 77 reflects the exodus typology by use of the play on words linking the lamentation in the first part of the psalm (vv. 1–13[1–12]) with the latter hymnic section (vv. 14–21[13–20]). As the Psalmist muses over the circumstances that require divine intervention, he expresses his outcry (צעק, Ps 77:2[3]) for YHWH to intervene and he reminisces about the predicament of the people of Israel in bondage (see Exod 3:7). So, to bolster his faith in anticipation of YHWH's response to his voice, the Psalmist refers to his "voice" (קול) "crying out" with an outstretched hand to YHWH in petition for deliverance from his dire straits. Accordingly, he refers to YHWH's "voice" (קול) conflating that with his "thunder" (רעם, v. 19[18]a), as the means of his self-disclosure for salvation in anticipation of a response to the petition.

The Psalmist's allusion to "thunder" recalls divine diction (Ps 81:8[7]), in another lamentational psalm, expressing YHWH declaring his response to Israel's pleas for deliverance from oppression in Egypt out of the "secret place of thunder"[115] (סתר רעם). Undoubtedly, as already noted, YHWH's disclosure in the winds is double-edged. He wields the winds to pave a way in the Red Sea for the oppressed to escape from slavery while contemporaneously executing judgment on their Egyptian oppressors in pursuit (Exod 14:21–22, 28; see 15:4–5, 8,10). It has already been established in this monograph, that the term "rebuke," implying YHWH's roaring wind, appears in parallel with the sound of thunder (קול רעם), or loud sound in Ps 104:7, and unquestionably personifying the winds causing the chaotic primal waters to take to flight. The Psalmist in Ps 77:18[17], 19[18] employs the same terms (קול/קול רעם), to relate the sonorous wind(s)—the whirlwind. Hence, the Psalmist associates terms from the mundane with the mytho-historical to depict YHWH's voice,

---

114. See Ps 76:7[6]; Exod 15:1. Even in Ps 76:6[5] there is an allusion to the hands of the mighty men of Egypt found to be no match to the "hand" of the Most High God. His hand, that is the winds, termed "rebuke" in this psalm, cast the charioteer and horse into the sea (v. 7[6]). On "rebuke" as also representing the winds, see the discussion on pp. 49–51, 82–83.

115. BDB 712.

YHWH IN THE WIND(S)

as the whirlwind subduing the waters and annihilating the enemies for the redemption of his people. Therefore, the substantive קול רעם denotes the sonorous outbursts of the winds (v. 19[18]) discharging the clouds[116] pouring forth rain (v. 18[17]a), and causing the uproar of nature (17[16] bc, 19[18]c). In essence, the Psalmist cannot help but proclaim that the sound of YHWH's thunder is in the whirlwind; thus, bringing to bear that the "secret place of thunder" (Ps 81:8[7]) is lodged with the (whirl) winds, also personified as the (right) hand, or arm wielding salvation.

However, despite all the uproar of nature, there is no mention of a direct combat with any other elements beyond what is affected by YHWH's appearance. When the "waters" (מים) and the "deeps" (תהמות) see YHWH's winds they writhe and quake with fear (Ps 77:17[16]). So, here is only a subtle allusion to YHWH's battle with forces of chaos in the mention of waters "writhing" and the deeps "quaking" at the sight of YHWH.[117] The account of this warlike intervention of YHWH, as though to destroy the tempestuous waters, reaches its height with him making a path in the "sea" and a way in the "many waters" (v. 20[19]aβ). In spite of the uproar in nature, YHWH remains the *Deus absconditus* as he marches with his people through the "many waters." The Psalmist is at great pains to emphasize the invincibility, as much as invisibility of YHWH, by remarking on the elusiveness of YHWH's presence. Again, as in Ps 18, the Psalmist presents the *Deus praesens* in tension with *Deus absconditus*. As the Psalmist exclaims, YHWH's "footprints" (עקבות, v. 20[19]c) are not seen on the path he paves in the sea by his whirlwind (cf. Job 9:11), though YHWH's immanence is comprehended in his guidance of his people like a flock through the mediation of Moses and Aaron (Ps 77:21[20]).

Nonetheless, the climatic element of this exodus event with YHWH leading his people like a shepherd, and guiding them like a flock (v. 21[20]

---

116. See Deut 33:26; Ps 68:35[34], as a symbol indicating YHWH's numinous presence. In Ps 18:10[9] and 12[11], ערפל and שחקים respectively, are used as substantives expressing YHWH's covering, and echoing the visible elements representing YHWH's theophany at Sinai (Exod 20:18; see 19:9, 16). Solomon also confirms the continuity of YHWH's presence: "YHWH has said that he will dwell in the thick cloud (ערפל)" (1 Kgs 8:12). Therefore, it may not be coincidental, however, that the "thick cloud" (ערפל), 'cloud' (ענן) and YHWH's "glory" (כבוד), in conflation with other meteorological elements dispersed by the phenomenal winds, become part of the stock language in description of YHWH's theophany.

117. Cf. Tiamat's body shaking in reaction to the sight of Marduk armed with the raging winds for the single combat: EE IV:90–100. See Lambert, *Babylonian*, 91.

a)[118] carries overtones of an appeal to YHWH's continual abiding presence, as the shepherd. Ps 80:2[1] reflects this idea and implores YHWH as the shepherd, "dweller of the cherubim" (ישב הכרובים), to "shine forth" (הופיע, see Pss 50:2; 94:1) in recollection of his majestic manifestation as in the Sinai tradition (Deut 33:2). The appeal directly to the "dweller of the cherubim" to shine forth evokes the sight and sound of YHWH's manifestation with the luminous and sonorous winds.[119] Perhaps, by this means, the Psalmist here entreats YHWH for the restoration of his blessing and protection that is ushered by his presence, as represented in the cryptic language: "Let your face shine" (Ps 80:4[3], 8[7], 20[19]; see Num 6:25–26). Therefore, the Psalmist in Ps 77 intentionally appeals to the exodus tradition by recalling the shepherding element of YHWH. The historical intentionality of the reference is indicated by the mention of historical figures in the verses framing the theophany: Jacob and Joseph are the ancestors of the liberated people (v. 16[15]b; cf. Ps 80:2[1]aβ), and Moses and Aaron are the mediators (Ps 77:21[20]b) of YHWH's hand of deliverance (v. 16[15]a). These historical references show that the theophanic intervention of YHWH relates to the events at the exodus. Yet, as the redemptive acts are recited in Ps 77 they are reinterpreted with a mythic flavor. YHWH's power to guide his people through the "many waters," that he renders impotent by his whirlwind, represent YHWH's acts of salvation and throws into bold relief his roles as savior and shepherd lodged with his old ways of acting by the power of his wind.

YHWH's Age-Old *modus operandi* in the Winds in Habakkuk 3

The same motif of the exodus appears more elaborately in mythic terms in the theophanic text of Hab 3. This text recounts in detail the salvation procured by YHWH as a result of his conquest of the "wicked" in combination with the subjection of the "rivers," "sea," and "many waters" at his appearance with the phenomenal winds. The parallelism of the sea with many waters (v. 15) in this account of YHWH's acts of deliverance, as in Pss 18 and 77, recalls the ancient conflict with the mythic waters at primal creation. The ideology is expressed in the rhetorical question of

---

118. See Ps 80:2[1]aβ. On YHWH as the shepherd, see pp. 150–51.
119. See p. 17.

YHWH IN THE WIND(S)

v. 8 which refers to YHWH, in his wrath, raging against the "rivers" or the "sea:"[120]

> Is it against the rivers it is kindled, O YHWH, against the rivers [נהרים] your anger, or against the sea [ים] your wrath; as you rode on your horses,
> on your chariots of salvation [ישועה]? (Hab 3:8)

Tsumura notes that in Ugaritic texts the titles ym//nhr occur in conflict scenes referring to Baʻal's archenemy, the god Sea or (Judge) River. The plural form "rivers" (נהרים) paralleled with "sea" (ים) in the Hebrew text corresponds to the Ugaritic word pair ym//nhrm, though in reverse order in the latter, where it occurs in a damaged text, which describes a non-conflict scene.[121] However, the poet-prophet's use of these terms is exceptional in that he adopts these ideas to represent YHWH's enemy in his description of YHWH's battles to bring about salvation. The portrayal of YHWH's rage against the rivers/sea/waters is compounded with features familiar from YHWH's ordering of chaos at creation. Here, the poet-prophet blends elements of the primal creation with the historical event of crossing the Red Sea and the conquest to give form and content to YHWH's deeds at the deliverance of his people.

In the description of YHWH's triumphant march from the south (Hab 3:3), the poet-prophet echoes the Sinai tradition wherein YHWH's majestic manifestation "shines forth" (הופיע, Deut 33:2c; cf. Ps 50:2), and proceeds with the "southwind"[122] (תימן, Hab 3:3) from Mount Paran.[123] Yet, the poet-prophet also recalls the "splendor" (הוד, Hab 3:3c) and luminous[124] appearance (נגה, v. 4a, 11c) familiar from the appearance of YHWH at creation to subdue the chaotic waters (see Ps 104:1–2). But, here, too, the poet-prophet goes further in alluding to the strength of YHWH lodged in the natural phenomena, as he states that "horns"[125] be-

---

120. The identification of the river/s with the sea is well represented in the text of Anat's bloodbath (KTU 1.3.III:39 [=CTA 3.iii:36]).

121. KTU 1.3.VI:5–6=CTA 3.vi:5–6; Tsumura, "Ugaritic Poetry," 30; *Creation and Destruction*, 165–66; *UBC* II 360, 365, 370–72.

122. BDB 412; see Ps 78:26b.

123. Deut 33:2c.

124. See pp. 75–77.

125. Horns are characteristic features of deities in ANE iconography (Dalley, *Myths*, 262, 262n37), *contra* scholars who propose the idea of horns as belonging to the temple tower in the ascendancy of Marduk to kingship (Heidel, *Babylonian Genesis*, 49n128; Horowitz, *Mesopotamian*, 123). According to Wallis, a horned headdress is one of the

YHWH IN THE WIND AS THE SAVIOR

long to his hand (Hab 3:4b). The poet-prophet also uses the term "hand"[126] figuratively as the place where YHWH's horns are embedded to refer to the numinous winds as the means by which YHWH's strength, or power is manifested (v. 4c). With that identification of the nature of YHWH, the poet-prophet subsequently enumerates the different phenomena associated with YHWH's appearance.

The poet-prophet pronounces his recollection of the manifestation of YHWH at the exodus with a historical tenor. In Exod 9, YHWH declares that he would unleash "hail" to demonstrate his sovereign power and for his own renown (vv. 14, 16, 18). Arguably, then, the reference to thunder, hail, and fire issuing from heaven, implies the roaring wind manifested by the luminous sight from the fire and "sonorous sounds"[127] (קלת) accompanied by the discharge of hail (Exod 9:23). This unleashing of the phenomenal elements causes extensive devastation leaving an undeniable imprint in memory since Egypt became a nation (9:24), so much as to deserve a mention in the Habakkuk poet-prophet's recollection. Therefore, the poet-prophet's reference to the plague[128] (דבר), named in Hab 3:5a as preceding YHWH's appearance, is evocative of the worst plague[129] YHWH performs by the power of his "hand" (יד).[130] Here, too, in Hab 3:4b, the hand is synecdoche for the phenomenal wind, and is also identified as such by the reference to it as the "hiding place" (חביון)[131] of YHWH's might (cf. Ps 81:8[7]).

---

elements of a shepherd's insignia (Wallis, "רָעָה," 548). Lambert also published a Babylonian text, "Hymn to Gula," that makes reference to Marduk's horns. There is mention of Marduk's head covered with a turban, like a crown, of superb horns (Lambert, "Gula Hymn," 127 line 171; see Reiner, *Assyrian Dictionary*, 139n5d). Also, Kedar-Kopfstein notes Marduk as one of the Akkadian gods, amongst Enlil and Ramman, depicted with a horned crown (Kedar-Kopfstein, "קֶרֶן,"169). For other references on Marduk as decked with a horned crown, see Buren, "Concerning the Horned Cap," 321; Coudert, "Horns," 4130. However, in the Hebrew tradition, as noted by Kedar-Kopfstein, horns are used as a symbol of power and victory bestowed on YHWH's people (cf. 1 Kgs 22:11[=2Chr 18:10]; Pss 132:17; 148:14). See Kedar-Kopfstein, "קֶרֶן" 173.

126. "Arm." See p. 175, 175n111.

127. On יתן קולו meaning issuing sonorous sound symbolic of the roaring winds, see p. 113. On the association of sonorous sound with hand/arm to represent the thunderous wind, see the use of the Hebrew terms קול//זרוע in Job 40:9, as discussed on p. 88.

128. See Exod 9:15b; *contra* Bekkum, who sees Deber and Resheph as counterparts of the storm god Ba'al's entourage. He sees similar occurrences with the storm god Marduk (Bekkum, "Your Rage," 56–57, 68–69).

129. See Exod 9:24.

130. Exod 9:15a.

131. See Bekkum, "Your Rage," 57; Robertson, *Books of Nahum*, 221, 225. Some

YHWH IN THE WIND(S)

Furthermore, the report of "fire" (רשף),[132] as coming forth from YHWH's feet or footsteps (Hab 3:5b) relates fire to YHWH's natural elements characterizing his theophany with the powerful winds at creation (Ps 104:4). Yet, fire also features in the event of the indelible memories of the plague of hail. It is described as flashing amid the excessive hail (Exod 9:24). But more pertinent to the events the poet-prophet Habakkuk muses over, is, perhaps, the appearance of the combination of a cloud and fire at the Red Sea. Hence, the poet-prophet intentionally recalls and presents here an image with historical import on YHWH's theophany with fire in attendance giving light to the redeemed people at the exodus (Ps 105:39) in keeping with the context he ponders over. Undoubtedly, the poet-prophet Habakkuk describes the blending of the gloomy and luminous in the pillar of cloud forming a buffer between the pursuing Egyptians and the people of Israel at the exodus (Exod 14:19–20). The cloud appears as a bulwark of darkness to the Egyptians in the rear, but on the other side, emits light emanating from the fiery manifestation of YHWH guiding the people of Israel at the crossing of the Red Sea (v. 20).[133] In sequel, YHWH's frontal presence divides the sea to form dry ground (Exod 14:21). Pointedly, fire is associated with the incandescent wind(s) in representation of YHWH's dominant presence for both his creative and destructive potency.[134] Thus, the poet-prophet of Habakkuk shows familiarity with the descriptions of the luminous and sonorous appearance of YHWH in the wind implied by the mention of the "brightness" of YHWH's presence paralleled by his might lodged with the sonorous wind (Hab 3:4). As may be implied in the poet-prophet's recital,

---

scholars see this term as reminiscent of an Ugaritic deity ḥby (see Bekkum, "Your Rage," 68; Xella, "HABY," 377). Xella even goes as far as highlighting that ḥby, as an Ugaritic deity, is depicted with horns and a tail in expression of its bovine form but now deployed at YHWH's service in Hab 3:4 (Xella, "HABY," 377).

132. BDB 958 translates "firebolt" in parallel with "pestilence" (דבר). Fire is symbolic of YHWH's luminous presence, but there is no smoke without fire. No wonder there is often reference to smoke in descriptions of YHWH's theophany with—or without—the mention of fire, respectively (Exod 19:18; 20:18; Ps 104:32; Isa 6:4). See Andersen, *Habakkuk*, 306, *contra* scholars who see here a mythical figure of Resheph, the god of pestilences, as one of the attendants associated with a deity in the ANE (Andersen, *Habakkuk*, 300, 305–6; Day, *God's Conflict*, 105–6; Tsumura, *Creation and Destruction*, 179–80). Miller even mentions *Resheph* as a warrior deity of Canaanite origin (Miller, *Divine Warrior*, 119); while Green states that *Resheph* is an attendant in the storm god Baʻal's retinue (Green, *Storm-God*, 245, 245n106).

133. Pss 78:14; 105:39.

134. See god Amma's creation of fire as one of the fundamental elements of his creation. But Amma can also use fire for destructive purposes. See 14n72 above.

YHWH IN THE WIND AS THE SAVIOR

the destruction[135] of one nation, Egypt, paves the way for the creation of another, Israel. The brilliant and luminous light emanating from the fiery cloud illuminates the path paved by the eastwind for the creation of Israel as a nation. In any case, the reference to fire in the poet-prophet's recital of the dominant motif on YHWH's presence in his age-old modus operandi in the wind pales into the effects of YHWH's march from the south.

However, there is no direct mention of the winds in the poet-prophet's recital, apart from the expression of YHWH's wrath causing the agitation in the earth, age-old mountains, and hills (Hab 3:6acd), and the dread inflicted on the nations (v. 6b). These reactions are conventional to the effects of YHWH's phenomenal winds. Despite this subtlety, the poet-prophet alludes to YHWH's disclosure with the winds, and specifically identifies this mode as YHWH's "ancient ways" (הליכות עולם, Hab 3:6e), to evoke the enduring winds as YHWH's modus operandi. Thus, the poet-prophet recalls YHWH's deeds manifested by the power of his winds in the past causing convulsions in the most durable symbols in creation, and terror to the tent dwellers in YHWH's path. The earth trembles,[136] nations become disquieted in consternation at YHWH's gaze,[137] the everlasting mountains shatter,[138] and eternal hills bow down,[139] in essence, tremble (vv. 6–7). Undoubtedly, YHWH breaks into the historical arena by the same means: the wind. But the adversary is no longer the cosmic primal chaotic waters but historical entities: that is, the tent dwellers of Cushan and Midian (v. 7).

YHWH's Winds as Horses and Chariots and the Bow and Shafts

Although the poet-prophet in Hab 3 maintains his focus on historicity, he reverts to the mythical in sustained rhetoric on YHWH's wrath vented towards the rivers and sea (v. 8). Here he makes a subtle reference to the

---

135. Israel, though covenanted to YHWH, is not exempt from YHWH's destruction for wickedness at YHWH's disclosure by fire and whirlwind (Ps 50:3). On YHWH's people scattered by the wind, see Jer 31:9[10]; Ezek 5:10; 12:14.

136. Ps 104:32; Job 9:6.

137. On people mourning in Amos 9:5, see p. 127.

138. Hab 3:6c; cf. 1 Kgs 19:11; Nah 1:6d; Job 9:5. See also pp. 90, 133, 146, 146nn337–38 above. Gray (*Psalm 18*, 82) notes that the mountains are considered ancient (Gen 49:26; Deut 33:15). In the same context, it may be added that the hills are considered everlasting or eternal.

139. Hab 3:6d; cf. Ps 114:4, 6.

mythical battle of Ba'al against his archenemy Yam also designated as Judge River, though with elision by using the plural term "rivers." The term rivers paralleled by the sea in v. 8 (נהרים//ים), distinctively recall the Kishon[140] (Judg 5:21; see Ps 83:10[9]), and Jordan rivers, and the Red Sea (cf. Ps 114:3, 5), where YHWH manifests his power in the wind for the salvation of his people at the respective events. As narrated in Judg 4 on the event led by Deborah and Barak against the army of the Canaanite King Jabin, YHWH's wind brings a scourge of a torrential downpour: the heavens droop, and the clouds drip water (Judg 5:4cd), which causes the "age-old" Kishon River to swell up (4:4–7, 12–13; 5:19–22). So, just as YHWH's wind stirs up the Red Sea to engulf the Egyptians, the heavily running Kishon River floods the Canaanite army led by Sisera (5:19–22). Correspondingly, the destructive reaction of the ancient Kishon River resonates with the events at the Red Sea, and is consistent with the violent commotion conventional to YHWH's appearance with his raging winds to raze the enemy. There is no mention of shattering the enemy at the crossing of the Jordan, but YHWH's wind roils the waters to form dry ground replicating the crossing at the Red Sea. Hence, the poet-prophet juxtaposes the rivers and sea to allude to YHWH's power wielded in his eternal ways in the wind causing the common reaction of the waters, by which the salvation of his people is accomplished.

The poet-prophet figuratively portrays the raging of the wind against the rivers and sea as YHWH riding on his horses and chariots of victory. As pointed out in chapter 1, this imagery of riding on horses and chariots, or harnessing steed, denotes the graphic movement of the wind. Thus, the poet-prophet employs the same image, and further elaborates on the militaristic characteristics of YHWH by referring to the horses and chariots[141] of salvation (Hab 3:8). He pictures militaristic parapher-

---

140. Robertson, *Books of Nahum*, 231.

141. Day, who argues for the Ugaritic mythology as underlying the mythological allusions in Hab 3, assumes that the idea of YHWH riding on the horse-drawn (cloud-)chariot compares with Ba'al's horse-drawn chariot. As there is no explicit reference to Ba'al and his horse-drawn chariot in the Ugaritic texts, Day appeals to the myth of Zeus. He argues that the god Zeus appears in a chariot drawn by winged horses and fights at Mount Casius, identified with Ba'al's Mount Ṣāphōn, thus prompting an association of this tradition with the myth of Ba'al. Day conjectures that Ba'al, like his counterpart Zeus, had a cloud chariot drawn by winged horses. Consequently, he sees the tradition of the chariot of Ba'al and his winged horses reflected in Hab 3:8, 15 (Day, *God's Conflict*, 107). However, Day observes correctly that the idea of the riding deity is prevalent in both Hebrew and Ugaritic traditions, but is probably incorrect in arguing for an exclusive parallelism of mythological allusions in Hab 3:8, 15 with Ba'al

nalia in representation of the (whirl)wind to assert YHWH's warrior motif in recollection, though with subtleties, of the events at the Kishon/Jordan Rivers and the Red Sea. In any case, this image the poet-prophet employs of horses and chariots resonates with a similar depiction in Judg 5:22 of "horses treading and galloping" in animation of the presence of YHWH in the rushing sound of the wind.[142]

The narrative on the ascension of Elijah to heaven in 2 Kgs 2:11 is instructive in shedding more light on the symbolism of horses and chariots as representing natural phenomena associated with fire and the whirlwind. Also, the prophet Isaiah relates a similar idea on horses and chariots as representing natural phenomena in his satiric pronouncement on the futility of relying on Egypt for political help in Isa 31:1. In this text, he announces that, even though Egypt is said to possess a multitude of horses and chariots, its horses are "flesh" and not wind (v. 3b). Furthermore, he mentions the idea of YHWH "stretching out his arm," figurative of YHWH wielding his winds (v. 3c) in collocation with YHWH's foreboding disclosure in the wind. However, the implication is that Isaiah employs horses and an arm synonymously as metaphors for YHWH's wind. Therefore, YHWH's horses, which are not flesh but wind, will make both the helper to stumble and the assisted to topple. That means, Egypt and Israel will stagger and fall together to their demise at YHWH's disclosure with the razing wind (v. 3deβ).

Nonetheless, the poet-prophet in Hab 3 uses the same symbolic idea and metamorphosizes the horses and chariots to represent the wind(s),[143] as he reflects on YHWH's subjugation of the waters in Hab 3:15: "You tread the sea with your horses, the surging of the many waters" recalling YHWH's involvement with the wind(s) in the mythical battle with chaos. Undoubtedly, the poet-prophet appeals to the creation-out-of-chaos tradition to relate the image of YHWH treading on the sea with the idea of YHWH subduing the waters by his potent winds (see Job 9:8b).[144] At the

---

mythology (Day, *God's Conflict*, 109). There is no explicit reference to Ba'al's cloud-chariot as having winged horses. The evidence for Ba'al as a riding deity is drawn from his epithet "rider on the clouds" *rkb ʿrpt*. See Tsumura, "Ugaritic Poetry," 31; *Creation and Destruction*, 166.

142. See 7 Kgs 7:6. The Arameans misinterpret the sound of gusts of wind for chariots and horses. They abandon camp assuming that the king of Israel had formed an alliance with the kings of the Hittites and Egyptians to attack them.

143. See also Day (*God's Conflict*, 107) suggesting the winds as represented by the winged horses and cloud-chariots (see Tsumura, *Creation and Destruction*, 167).

144. See Job 9:8. See also pp. 92–93 above.

same time, the poet-prophet throws into bold relief YHWH's mastery of the chaotic waters by his sonorous winds, as described in Ps 104:3–9,[145] while focusing attention on the acts of YHWH, not only as warrior, but as deliverer.[146] Here, too, sarcasm underlies the allusion to the superiority of YHWH's horses and chariots representing the roiling winds. YHWH treads and churns the waters of the Red Sea for the destruction of the Egyptian army. Its chariots and horses are tossed to complete destruction by the waters of the Red Sea, while YHWH accomplishes the deliverance of the people of Israel.[147]

Overall, the poet-prophet of Habakkuk conflates mythical motifs associated with the creation tradition and *Chaoskampf* myth to allude to the presence of YHWH in the winds in recital of historical battles for the redemption of his people. YHWH's redemption is reviewed here through a hyperbolized conquest of the "sea" or "many waters" in connection with a defeat of, or deliverance from, mortal enemies with mythical weapons:

> 9Your bow [קשתך] laid bare, the shafts [מטות] (were) oaths of your word[148] ...
>
> 12You strode the earth in anger, in wrath you trampled the nations.

145. See Ps 18:11–16[10–15].

146. Hab 3:8e; see v. 13.

147. Deut 11:2b–4; see Exod 14:26–28.

148. This colon proves to be the most difficult part of v. 9, as evident from the different interpretations proposed for it:

"You sated the shafts of your quiver" (Hiebert, *God*, 6).
"You were satisfied with the club which you commanded" (Patterson, "Psalm," 165).
"En-chanted (your) shafts I see" (Haak, *Habakkuk*, 27).
"Seven clubs thou didst bring to view" (Andersen, *Habakkuk*, 312).
"You will say (that) you have satisfied your bowstring" (Thomas, *Habakkuk*, 140)
"Oaths are the rods, a word" (Renz, *Books*, 371).

In the case of Hiebert and Patterson, the interpretation of this verse is based on textual emendation. Hiebert suggests that the first word of this colon be read as the verb שׂבע ("be sated"). He justifies this interpretation from the occurrence of this root in Jer 46:10 where it expresses the idea of satisfying a weapon. Coincidentally, the same verb describes the satisfaction (KTU 1.3.II:29–30) that the goddess Anat derives from her frenzied slaughter of the warriors with her bow and arrows (KTU 1.3.II:15–16). See Hiebert, *God*, 26–27. Patterson, following Albright, also supports the emendation of the colon to yield a reading similar to that found in the account of the battle of Anat (Patterson, "Psalm," 172). By contrast, Haak for the most part retains the original root שבע in the sense "to swear." He finds the meaning to conform to the idea of empowering a weapon by incantation before a battle. But he revocalizes the word אמר and proposes the translation "to see" on the basis of the Ugaritic meaning (Haak, *Habakkuk*, 94–95). Haak's viewpoint contrasts Cassuto's suggestion of an allusion to Baʿal's club in

13 You went forth to save [יֵשַׁע] your people, to save [יֵשַׁע] your anointed.
You crushed [מָחַצְתָּ] the head of the house of the wicked, laying bare fundament [יְסוֹד]¹⁴⁹ to the neck.
14 You pierced [נָקַבְתָּ] with his staff [מַטָּיו], the head of the warriors (as) they were tempestuous...
15 You trampled the sea [יָם] with your horses, the surging of the many waters [מַיִם רַבִּים]
(Hab 3:9, 12–15).

Day proposes to translate the phrase שְׁבֻעוֹת מַטּוֹת ("oaths of shafts") in v. 9 by altering "oaths" (שְׁבֻעוֹת) to "seven" (שִׁבְעַת) to refer to YHWH's seven shafts or arrows of lightning. Day argues that the seven lightnings of Hab 3:9 are comparable with the seven thunders that he finds depicted in Ps 29.¹⁵⁰ He further points out that the "seven lightnings and thunder" of Hab 3:9 and Ps 29 find a parallel in the myth of Baʿal.¹⁵¹ It should be noted that there is no number parallelism in the "seven thunders and lightnings" conjectured by Day for Hab 3:9 and Ps 29, corresponding to Baʿal's "seven lightnings" and "eight storehouses of thunder." Arguably, as

---

the word אמר (ʾaymr, Cassuto, *Biblical*, 2:11). There are several other interpretations for this colon not outlined here that have been suggested (see Tsumura, *Creation and Destruction*, 169; Renz, *Books*, 373, 382–83). However, the translation suggested for the mythopoeic weaponry mentioned here attempts to offer a meaning in keeping with the mode of YHWH's appearance with the winds, and represents as best as possible the MT unaltered.

149. This phrase has also posed a challenge to scholars in translation. Some scholars translate the phrase as, "Laying him out from tailend to neck." The interpretation is based on an underlying idea of YHWH's conflict with a mythical dragon (Eaton, "Origin," 145, 155; Hiebert, *God*, 40–41). In other cases, as Avishur notes, textual emendations either to read מות ("Mot"), or בהמות ("Behemoth") in place of מבית ("from the house") have been suggested in view of the respective conflicts of Baʿal/Mot and Marduk/Tiamat (Avishur, *Studies*, 186). Renz translates this last part of v. 13 as, "Laying bare the foundation to the neck," and gives alternative meanings with reference to the destruction of architectural structures (Renz, *Books*, 372, 374–75, 389).

150. Day, *God's Conflict*, 106. In his discussion on this view, Tsumura criticizes Day for taking the seven occurrences of the phrase "the voice of YHWH" in Ps 29 as representing seven thunders (Tsumura, "Ugaritic Poetry," 40). However, what makes Day's suggestion untenable is that he emends Hab 3:9 in order to link it with an idea expressed in a different text (Ps 29). Though without much numerical correspondence of the texts under discussion, he creates an expression "seven thunders and lightnings" to suit his idea of Baʿal's seven thunders and lightnings.

151. Day states:
šbʿt. brqm. [yr]   Seven lightning bolts [he cast],
ṯmnt. [ʾi]ṣr rʿt   eight storehouses of thunder
(KTU 1.101:3b–4 [Ugaritica 5.3.1: 3b–4]; Day, *God's Conflict*, 107).

asserted in this monograph, the reference to thunder is a representation of YHWH's sonorous wind. The same applies to the seven thunders as onomatopoeia for YHWH's winds comparable to Amma's seven words, or voices, or articulations forming the spiral, which is his whirlwind.[152] But the phenomenon Day interprets as thunder in v. 9, is in fact the sonorous sound of YHWH's whirling wind, which causes the does to calve, while stripping the forests bare.

Moreover, the word מטות in Hab 3:9, which Day translates as "lightning," does not occur in KTU 1.101:3b–4 [Ugaritica. 5.3.1:3b–4]. Instead, *brqm* is used for "lightning." In Hab 3:9, מטות, often translated as "shafts,"[153] appears in conjunction with קשת ("bow"), and the two elements are strongly suggestive of the weapons of the goddess Anat. Moreover, a more significant parallel with the latter tradition occurs in the reference to YHWH's battle: he crushes (מחץ) the head of the house of the wicked and bores with his shaft (מטה) the head of the "tempestuous" warriors (Hab 3:13–14). Traditionally, the language employed exhibits the characteristics of the blood bath of the warrior goddess Anat presented in KTU 1.3.II:6–16 [=CTA 3.ii:6–16]. This blood bath episode depicts Anat armed with her "shafts" (*mṭm*) and "bow" (*qšt*) in a massacre of warriors. She smites (*tmḫṣ*) and then adorns herself with the heads of those whom she slaughters.[154]

However, Hiebert, reiterating Irwin, points to the association of *miṭṭu*[155] and *qaštu* as weapons used by Marduk in his combat with Tiamat.[156] In this Akkadian myth, the bow and arrow are associated with natural elements—lightning, blazing fire, rain-flood, storm-chariot, winds—that Marduk employs as weapons in his battle against Tiamat (EE IV:35–50). As Irwin notes, the arming of YHWH to do battle reflects

---

152. See pp. 16–18, 17n96 above and the discussion on Ps 29 in chapter 4.

153. On Hiebert and Haak's translation of this verse, see 186n148 above. See also Tsumura, "Ugaritic Poetry," 35–37; *Creation and Destruction*, 168–69.

154. This scene of Anat's bloodbath comes before the events leading to the building of Ba'al's palace. The trend of events seems to be more of a modest attempt to show the interconnectedness of the imagery of Anat as warrior-goddess with the role of Ba'al contesting for kingship.

155. Tsumura argues that the Akkadian cognate for "mace" is distinguished from "arrow" or "shaft" and, as a divine weapon, is sometimes mentioned as a fifty-headed mace. On the basis of this observation, Tsumura finds it possible for the Hebrew מטות to refer to a mace or staff (Tsumura, "Ugaritic Poetry," 37).

156. Hiebert, *God*, 26–27; see Irwin, "Psalm," 24. Lambert translates "bow" and "club" (Lambert, *Babylonian*, 88, 89).

YHWH IN THE WIND AS THE SAVIOR

this Babylonian pattern.[157] It is therefore possible to retain the translation "shaft" in its mythopoeic pairing with "bow" in Hab 3:9, as well as in conjunction with other natural phenomena in keeping with the Babylonian tradition. But in the Hebrew tradition these mythical weapons are more than mere martial ordnance.

Perhaps, the apparition that Ezekiel beholds is instructive on the idea of the bow in Hab 3:9 as referring to natural phenomena in the Hebrew tradition. In this grand vision, Ezekiel beholds the dazzling apparition with glorious splendor resembling a "bow"[158] (קֶשֶׁת) lodged with the appearance of the rain-bearing cloud (Ezek 1:4). Fire and "brightness"[159] (נגה) are part and parcel of the paraphernalia of the whirling wind from the north (רוח סערה, v. 4). Similarly, fire and brightness, or luminous intensity are attributes associated with the whirlwind god, Amma. Undoubtedly, in Hab 3:9, the poet-prophet uses similar mental pictures of YHWH armed with his bow and shafts as metaphors for the natural elements imbedded with the splendor of YHWH's wind poised here to represent YHWH's promise of divine deliverance put into action.

Although the bow and shafts, equivalent to the warring deities in the ANE, are mentioned in Hab 3:9, they pale into the background as the poet-prophet focuses attention on YHWH's age-old ways in the winds. Presumably, the phrase "the shafts (were) oaths of your word" shifts to a metaphor expressing YHWH fulfilling his promise of divine deliverance. Unquestionably, the reference to the shafts as "oaths of your word" underscores the idea of YHWH acting in remembrance of his covenant to the patriarchs for deliverance and settlement in the promised land by conquest.[160] Hence, YHWH's promise is put into effect. The shafts mentioned in v. 9 are recalled in vv. 13b–14, where YHWH uses weapons to destroy the wicked. As already mentioned, though the mythical ordnance is paralleled by Marduk's bow and arrow in his battle against Tiamat (EE IV:35–37),[161] their significance as YHWH's martial weapons transitions into YHWH's natural phenomenal elements, achieving the same effect of smiting, and piercing the wicked, as well as cleaving rivers, and treading the sea. This martial feat implies nothing other than

---

157. Irwin, "Psalm," 12–14.
158. Ezek 1:28. Some scholars translate this to "rainbow" (Clements, *Ezekiel*, 11; Block, *Book of Ezekiel*, 105).
159. Ezek 1:27–28; see Ps 18:9[8]b, 13[12]a.
160. Ps 105:8–11; see vv. 42–43.
161. See Hiebert, *God*, 27.

YHWH deploying his phenomenal winds to traverse the earth and raze the wicked, but also tread the waters, and cause them to foam and surge. Therefore, Habakkuk uses the terms the bow and shafts only as literary device to relate YHWH's preparedness to attack, as he bares the phenomenal wind as his (age-old) mythological weaponry. The idea corresponds with the expression of his wrath in v. 8, and brings to the fore the warring activity of YHWH in the splendor of his presence in the wind.

The poet-prophet heretofore focuses the historic deliverance wielded by YHWH's potent winds vanquishing the enemy,[162] and, in sequel, the cleaving of the rivers represents the miraculous provision of drinking water for the fugitives during the desert wandering. Thus, the idea of YHWH cleaving the earth with rivers (Hab 3:9c),[163] recalls YHWH's miraculous provision of water that gushed from a rock in the wilderness.[164] This idea bodes well with the recital of YHWH's wondrous deeds of provision in assertion of his presence in relation to his acts of deliverance marking his fame (Hab 3:2). Thus, the poet-prophet resumes the narration of the effects of YHWH's manifestation in the pyrotechnic blustery winds that are in evidence in the midst of his people.

In sequel, the cosmic reactions mentioned in v. 10 expressing the mountains writhing, floodwaters passing, and waters rising up, point to nothing other than the effects of YHWH's age-old ways in the winds. The mountains "writhe"[165] (חיל) because of YHWH's earth-shattering winds (Ha. 3:10a). As in other texts that relate YHWH's march from the south accompanied with torrents of rain from heaven,[166] or the clouds bursting with water,[167] the poet-prophet in Hab 3 recalls the same idea, and describes the event as a "downpour" (זֶרֶם)[168] of water "passing by"[169] (עבר, Hab 3:10b). Again, the poet-prophet brings YHWH's disclosure with the swirling winds to the fore. The collateral idea of the deep (תהם) giving

---

162. Vv. 13–14; see Exod 14:21; 15:8, 10; cf. Isa 50:2; Ps 106:9.

163. See Pss 78:15–16, 20aβ; 105:41; 114:8.

164. Exod 17:1–7; Num 20:11; Isa 48:21.

165. Cf. in Ps 77:17[16] waters writhe, and in Ps 114:7 an alternate root חול denotes the earth reacting in a similar way at the presence of YHWH appearing in the wind at the exodus.

166. Ps 68:9[8]b; Judg 5:4c.

167. Ps 77:18[17].

168. Cf. Isa 28:2.

169. Job uses the same term "passing by" (עבר) to describe the elusive presence of YHWH in the wind (Job 9:11; cf. Amos 5:17b). See p. 94.

up its voice, is figurative of the waters roaring,[170] and causing its waves to lift up comparatively to hands, as though in surrender and submission to the agitation by YHWH's powerful winds.

Also, the cosmic terrestrial disruptions caused by YHWH's winds are paralleled with an overcast of the celestial luminaries (Hab 3:11a). The cloud-bearing winds (bringing the scourge of rain) intercept daylight. As the poet-prophet of Habakkuk states: the sun and moon stand still (Hab 3:11a),[171] in keeping with other texts describing YHWH appearing with the winds charging the clouds, and intercepting the light given off by the luminaries.[172] Again, the poet-prophet alludes here to the dark cloud that comes between the Egyptians and the people of Israel at the crossing of the Red Sea.[173] Hence, in the same verse, the poet-prophet relates this idea of darkness in association with the brightness or glistening[174] like arrows (אור//נגה, Hab 3:11bc), as he recalls the cloud that brings darkness for the Egyptians but light to the elected people. At the same time, however, the poet-prophet focuses attention on the same phenomenon of the rain cloud surrounded by brightness in assertion of the subtleties of elements relating YHWH's *Deus praesens* with the winds[175] in Israel's salvation history.

A Mytho-Historical Depiction of YHWH as Warrior and Savior in Habakkuk 3:3–15

YHWH is depicted in Hab 3:3–15 marching with the southwind as the warrior and savior of Israel. In light of YHWH's display of wrath and mythological weaponry recited in vv. 8–9, Habakkuk depicts YHWH vested with his natural phenomenal wind in preparation for war. To that end, vv. 10–12 relate YHWH's manifestation with the might of his wind, and his success is presented in vv. 13–15. The description of YHWH's anger against the Kishon/Jordan Rivers and the Red Sea, as he charges

---

170. See Ps 93:3b; Isa 51:15.

171. Josh 10:12, 13a,b. It is possible that the prophet Habakkuk also alludes here to the successful battle led by Joshua narrated in Josh 9–13 in assertion of YHWH's fame on display in the guise of his phenomenal wind.

172. See Amos 5:8; Job 9:7.

173. Exod 14:20; cf. Josh 24:7.

174. On the association of wind and light in the personification of the Egyptian god Shu and Dogon Amma, see pp. 80–81.

175. See Ps 18:10–13[9–12]; Ezek 1:4, 28.

on his horses and chariots of salvation in v. 8, corresponds to vv. 13 and 15, which mention the salvation procured by YHWH against the wicked. The asyndetic phrase in v. 9: "Your bow [קשתך] laid bare, the shafts [מטות] (were) oaths of your word," refers to the wind, by which YHWH vanquishes the wicked. Thus, Habakkuk brings to the fore the notion that, by the same means YHWH treads and subdues the sea and many waters (ים//מים רבים), he also vanquishes the enemies. In fact, YHWH's wind churns the waters to bring about the creation of Israel but the destruction of its enemies.[176]

To that end, in Hab 3:12, the poet-prophet mentions yet another parody familiar from the *Chaoskampf* myth in depiction of YHWH treading the earth culminating in the destruction of the wicked. Again, Habakkuk alludes to YHWH wielding the winds but the image is now transferred to the historical plane in expression of YHWH's indignation and anger. In that sense, the poet-prophet sees YHWH deploying the wind on the earth, and putting nations to rout, figuratively comparable to striding the earth and treading over the nations.[177] In sequel, the poet-prophet describes the destruction of the wicked with mytho-historical elements (vv. 13–14). Hiebert thinks that these verses allude to the myth of the dragon fight.[178] He opts for an alteration of במטיו ("with his shafts") to read במת[179] ("back") in order to create the picture of YHWH striking the "back" of the wicked one. Hiebert considers the term the "wicked one" to refer to Tiamat, whose destruction is echoed in the remaining colon: "You laid him bare tail end to neck." But Tiamat is represented as feminine. Moreover, it is implausible to picture YHWH's fight with the dragon in its entirety as proposed by Hiebert, since his interpretation is based on an extensive alteration of the text.

The MT retains conventional terms describing YHWH's onslaught on the wicked in the manner of Marduk's annihilation of Tiamat. YHWH

---

176. Pharaoh and his cavalry (Exod 14:28; 15:1, 4; Pss 76:7[6]; 106:9–11; Isa 43:16–17). On the destruction of the army led by the Canaanite Sisera, see Judg 5:20–21.

177. See pp. 92–93, 120–21.

178. Hiebert, *God*, 36–43, 101–6; see Eaton, "Origin," 161.

179. Hiebert finds Albright's emendation of this word to read מות ("death") an alternative translation that reflects Ba'al's combat of one of his rivals, Mot the god of death. The alternative reading "death" seems to fit the context describing YHWH's enemy river(s)/sea (vv. 8, 15) that is comparable to the cosmic foe of the storm god Ba'al. But Hiebert, in defense of the conflict myth interpretation, advances the idea of the slaying of the dragon in v. 13. He views the mythological allusions in the preceding verses (vv. 8–11) as in parallelism with the conflict of Marduk and Tiamat (Hiebert, *God*, 37–38).

YHWH IN THE WIND AS THE SAVIOR

shatters the head of the house of the enemy and exposes the body (Hab 3:13b). This imagery recalls the valiant Marduk subduing Tiamat and splitting her skull (EE IV:129–30). Though the similarities are evident, the motive of the Psalmist is not to advance a myth on YHWH's conflict with a literal dragon, but to muse on a significant historical event. The word "wicked" (רשע) in Hab 3:13, which Hiebert reads as a personification of the dragon, represents an enemy, though unspecified, of YHWH and his people. In Hab 1:4, 13 the word "wicked" is used as the direct opposite of "righteous." Again in 3:13, the term רשע is in antithesis to terms designating YHWH's people or his anointed, thus representing the two groups with whom the theophany of YHWH is involved, as in other psalms.[180] Therefore, it is possible to link a historical reference to the poet-prophet's recital of YHWH's warrior motif in this blending of mythological and historical elements to show the connection between YHWH's victory over cosmic foes with the victory over Israel's enemies.

In contrast to Hiebert's view, Day[181] observes the destruction of a hostile political power in vv. 12–14 and 16. Day points out correctly the similarity of the description of the deliverance of YHWH's anointed people brought by his victory (v. 13) with that depicted in Pss 18 and 144. It is plausible to argue that the Hebrew tradition reflects ideas, metaphors, and images familiar from non-Israelite traditions in its description of YHWH's deeds of salvation. However, the Psalmist's use of mythological language in the recital of the historical victories of YHWH in Hab 3:13b–14 conforms with the conceptual idea of YHWH as warrior seen in other biblical Hebrew texts, rather than merely preserving wholesale the dragon myth, as Hiebert suggests.

Therefore, as in other psalms,[182] the poet-prophet in Hab 3 employs the mythological language of the dragon fight to symbolize YHWH's decisive subjection of the cosmic waters and the destruction of the "wicked" by the hurtling winds.[183] The poet-prophet recalls YHWH's destruction of the Egyptians, particularly Pharaoh, along with his cavalry and chariotry (Hab 3:13cd).[184] Hence, he refers to the "head" of the wicked, that is, Pharaoh laid bare from "bottom"[185] up to the neck (v. 13d). This phrase

180. Pss 11:4-6; 18:21-27[20-26].
181. Day, *God's Conflict*, 105.
182. Pss 18, 144.
183. Exod 15:1cd, 4–5, 7, 10, 12.
184. See Exod 14:27-28; 15:1cd, 4.
185. BDB 414 gives "base/bottom" as alternate meanings for יְסוֹד. Therefore, since

YHWH IN THE WIND(S)

is in keeping with the theme of the destruction of the wicked, and relates the idea of the wicked exposed to the destructive force of the winds. In Nah 1:3–4, the prophet declares YHWH's age-old *modus operandi* in the wind (v. 3), and manifested in the drying of the sea and rivers (v. 4). To that end, YHWH is predicted to show his force in punishing Nineveh for attacking other nations by the same means. Then, YHWH is anticipated to twirl and lift up the skirts over the faces of the people of Nineveh by his winds and expose their nakedness (3:5) in punishment of their atrocities (vv. 1–5). Unquestionably, Pharaoh and his horsemen suffer the same fate. Again, with subtlety, the poet-prophet alludes to the roiling winds of YHWH,[186] which twirl the garments of Pharaoh and his army as they are hurtled into the sea, and the "churned" waters bare them from the buttocks[187] to the neck (Hab 3:13cd), as their bodies are scattered on the shore of the Red Sea.[188]

Furthermore, the poet-prophet turns the tables over the wicked by employing metaphorical language to refer to the head of the warriors storming to "scatter" them, as he recalls YHWH's winds raging to scatter the enemy causing such panic that he turns his own shaft or "staff" (מטיו) (Hab 3:14a) as weaponry for self-destruction.[189] Perhaps, here, the poet-prophet has in mind the staff borne by Pharaoh in pursuit of YHWH's fugitives. In that view, the poet-prophet throws into bold contrast the storming of the foe as incomparable to the indomitable power of YHWH manifested in the wind-tossed sea causing the complete annihilation of the horse and its rider. So, the one (i.e., Pharaoh) who storms to destroy is destined for destruction at YHWH's theophany in the wind.[190] The winds roil the waters causing them to foam, surge, and throw Pharaoh, the head of the wicked, and his choice horsemen into the sea.[191] Hence, the poet-

---

the reference here is to human anatomy, the "bottom," that is the "fundament," is an appropriate meaning in this context.

186. See Exod 15:8, 10.

187. See Isa 20:4. As predicted on YHWH's disclosure with the winds in Isa 18:3–7 and 19:1 against Cush (Ethiopia) and Egypt, respectively, the captives from Cush and Egypt will be led into exile by the Assyrians in barefoot, naked and with buttocks bared to their shame (cf. Jer 13:26).

188. Exod 14:30–31. This narrative mentions YHWH's great hand, figurative of the wind, with which YHWH saves the people of Israel but destroys Pharaoh and his army (v. 31).

189. See Judg 7:22; 2 Chr 20:23.

190. Exod 14:21; see 15:8, 10.

191. Exod 15:1, 4, 10; see vv. 19, 21.

prophet in Habakkuk asserts with heightened satire that the staff of the wicked (Pharaoh) by its very nature, has no power to save him, and his Egyptian horsemen are incomparable to YHWH's bow and shafts (Hab 3:9), figuratively representing the devastating winds. With sustained subtle irony, the poet-prophet throws the horses of the Egyptians into bold contrast with the might of YHWH's horses (Hab 3:15), which are not flesh but wind (cf. Isa 31:3), and are indestructible. Hence, the reference to YHWH's horses symbolizes the force of the wind animated in the foaming and surging of the waters, as the scourge for the Egyptians at the Red Sea.[192]

Upon musing on YHWH's past deeds of salvation, the poet-prophet waits expectantly for the "sonorous sound" (קוֹל) of YHWH's wind. In keeping with the reaction of the cosmic elements, his body quivers as he forebodes the distress to be inflicted by the winds (cf. Jer 4:19) awaiting the assailants at YHWH's intervention (Hab 3:16). Here, too, the poet-prophet expresses mindful apprehension about the devastation that YHWH's wind impels: the fig tree is stripped of its bud, the vines bear no produce, and the olive tree fails (v. 17abc). Fundamentally, as the prophet Amos pronounces in prospect of YHWH's theophany in the wind, the poet-prophet of Habakkuk echoes the same sentiments with foreboding dread about the flocks to be exterminated (v. 17de), as the pastures are devastated[193] by YHWH's ominous whirling winds[194] on the invading enemy. However, in spite of the devastation of the poet-prophet's current situation, he expresses a note of hope in anticipation of YHWH's disclosure for deliverance by means of his "age-old ways" in the wind as the "savior" (vv. 18–19).

YHWH's Descent and/or Advance and the Nature of His Presence

One of the key elements in the context of deliverance is the pattern of YHWH's manifestation in initiating the act that brings about deliverance. In Ps 18, YHWH's descent from his heavenly abode is couched in phrases suggestive of both Ugaritic and Babylonian literary traditions. He is said to "bend the heavens" and "come down" (Ps 18:10[9]). The same idea is represented in other Hebrew texts in which YHWH's descent from the

---

192. Exod 15:10, 19, 21.
193. See pp. 114–16.
194. See Amos 1:2; Jer 4:23–26.

heavens forms the basis of a plea for him to appear for the welfare of his people. In accordance with this view, the Psalmist pleads in anguish to YHWH to reveal himself (Ps 144:5). Probably in keeping with the same conception, a poet-prophet, on behalf of his distressed people, petitions YHWH to tear open the heavens and come down to deliver them from oppression (Isa 63:19 [64:1]).

Previous scholarship argued for the idea of tearing open the heavens as having its counterpart in the tradition of Ba'al who inserts a "rift in the clouds" and Marduk who is requested to "rend the clouds with his thunder."[195] But, a closer parallel can be seen in the idea of the ark of the god Amma, descending from an "opening in the sky," and propelled by the whirlwind and the breath of the Nommo.[196] This idea is in affinity to the Egyptian four winds with provenance from an opening in the sky.[197] The Egyptian gods Shu[198] and Amun[199] are particularly of relevance in highlighting this idea, as they are associated with the four winds originating from the four pillars of heaven, and four openings in the sky, respectively. Undoubtedly, the occurrence of the same idea in the Hebrew tradition shows that it is still part of the repertoire of the same cosmological import as in the non-Israelite tradition. But, there is an adaptation of the idea in the Hebrew tradition that has been transposed to suit descriptions of YHWH's divine intervention focusing his descent with the winds. Thus, the idea of "a rift in the clouds" is connected with YHWH's approach as he rides on the cherub, which is symbolic of the "(whirl)wind" as his war locomotive. The echoes of an image of a cherub, or chariot in Ps 18 help to portray the deity in riding motion, though figurative of the wind, in order to affirm his presence in the actual act of deliverance.

In Ps 77:17–21[16–20] and Hab 3:3–15 the arrival of YHWH to save the elected people appears more of a "march" rather than the "descent" depicted in Ps 18:10–11[9–10], but the reality of YHWH's approach to intervene is asserted. Nonetheless, the conception of a "march" is in harmony in particular with the tradition of Marduk[200] who is said to embark

195. See pp. 27–28.
196. See p. 29.
197. Noegel, "Wings," 18.
198. Noegel, "Wings," 19.
199. See p. 80, 80n106 above.
200. Speiser, "Creation Epic," 29, 30; Foster, *Before the Muses*, 458; Lambert, *Babylonian*, 87, 89, 91.

on the road to "success and attainment," as the assembly of the Babylonian gods facilitate his marching towards his goal (EE IV:34–35, 69). Marduk employs the various winds in this combat (EE IV:42–47). Thus, YHWH's march for the liberation of his people as recounted in these theophanic hymns has affinity with this mythic tradition. Ps 77:19[18], which is an abbreviated account of the exodus, ambiguously alludes to this idea of YHWH appearing with the "sonorous sound" aforementioned for Amma in the "whirlwind" (גלגל). Presumably the whirlwind, as a meteorological element also associated with the riding deity of ancient traditions, represents the deity's cherub or chariot in this context, an equation which is helped by the fact that גלגל can also be used for the wheel or chariot. As Weinfeld points out in relation to the description of the chariot in Ezekiel,[201] the word גלגל[202] is mentioned in parallelism with אופן to mean "wheels."[203] But in Ezek 10:13, the wheels are explicitly called "the whirling wheels" (הגלגל) for stark emphasis to focus attention on the mobility of the resplendent phenomenon representing YHWH's (four) winds. The significance of "the whirling wheels" is that they are part of the numinous image of YHWH's "windstorm" (רוח סערה, Ezek 1:4) emerging from the "north"[204] (צפון). In essence, there is also an emphasis on the versatility and universal mobility of the wind implied by the descent, and, then, traversing space.

As Noegel observed, Ezekiel's vision combines the cosmological features with the winged hybrid creatures common to the ANE iconography representing the association of wings, winds and the four cardinal directions.[205] The prophet Ezekiel identifies the hybrid creatures,[206] consisting of the initial apparition he beholds on the banks of the Kebar River in Babylon, as cherubim.[207] Thus, here, the prophet Ezekiel denotes YHWH's winds figuratively as cherubim. Apart from the unparalleled

---

201. Ezek 10:2, 6, 13.

202. Cf. Dan 7:9.

203. Weinfeld, "Divine Intervention," 142–43.

204. See pp. 96–97, 97n175 above; Block, *Book of Ezekiel*, 92.

205. Noegel, "Wings," 20–22. See also Wright, *Message*, 48; Block, *Book of Ezekiel*, 97–98, 97n53.

206. Although there are variations in the characteristics of the hybrid creatures, initially called the "living creatures" (חיות, Ezek 1:5), but later identified as the "cherubim" (כרובים, 10:1, 20), their significance is in the phenomenal elements they represent, or are associated with, that is, the winds, and the [blazing] fire portending YHWH's judgment (5:2, 10; 12:14; 17:21 and 5:2, 4; 15:7; 21:4[20:47], respectively).

207. Ezek 1:1–4; see 10:20, 22; Wright, *Message*, 120.

YHWH IN THE WIND(S)

graphic description of the appearance of these cherubim, or hybrid creatures in the Hebrew tradition, and the semblance of the glory of YHWH forming, and, at the same time, embodying this vision, this splendid panoply is the phenomenal wind. Also, as Noegel observed, the wings of the cherubim symbolize the wind[208] in keeping with the ANE conceptual association of wings and winds. Therefore, the reference to the sound of the wings of the cherubim in Ezek 10:5 creating the wind comparable to YHWH's "voice," underscores nothing other than the prevalence of the wind. Again, this identification of the wind with the voice of YHWH echoes the hypostasis of the wind-deity Amma,[209] and highlights the significance of the wind(s) in this biblical context.

As stated in Ezekiel's vision, the mobility of the four cherubim is in total concert with the four wheels showing freedom of movement[210] in all four directions (10:11, 16–17). The wheels are set in motion by the wind of the cherubim (vv. 19–20). Nevertheless, the origination of the wind(s) from the heavens, also identified with the north in Ezek 1:4, along with the specificity of this entire apparition, that is transformed into the locomotive motion of the wheels and cherubim, indicates the significance of YHWH's wind, and its limitless movement. Thus, Ezekiel's vision of the glorious radiance of YHWH focusing the motion of the wind, demonstrates the freedom in mobility of the winds to traverse the entire universe in all the four directions (1:4–28; 10:3–22). In that view, Ezekiel throws into bold relief the significance of YHWH's winds transporting[211] him to the temple of Jerusalem (Ezek 8:1–4), and the

---

208. Noegel, "Wings," 21. See pp. 81–82 above.

209. See pp. 16–17.

210. Perhaps portent to the purposeful role of the winds as the means by which YHWH executes judgment resulting with the scattering of the sinful nation (Ezek 5:2, 10; 12:14; 17:21) the vain prophets (13:11; see Jer 23:16–22), and the destruction of the wall of Jerusalem (Ezek 13:13). But, also, the four winds feature in reviving the dry bones (37:9), thus taking a new form of a re-creation (cf. Ps 104:30).

211. The luminous nature of the apparition (Ezek 8:2) and the juxtaposition of a form resembling a hand and *rûaḥ* ("wind") that picks Ezekiel up (v. 3) refers to nothing other than the wind that transports Ezekiel.

YHWH IN THE WIND AS THE SAVIOR

prospect of the wicked scattered[212] by the winds to the four corners of the earth in judgment.[213]

The versatility of movement in the apparition in Ezekiel's vision sheds light on the mobility of YHWH in the wind from any cardinal direction. In Hab 3:3–15 the notion of YHWH's movement is more graphic. YHWH proceeds from a southern mountainous region[214] (v. 3) in the deserts of Sinai and Paran (Num 10:12) identified as Mount Sinai and Mount Paran in Deut 33:2, from where YHWH departs and advances[215] for the salvation of his people. He proceeds from the region where he initially manifested himself with natural effects.[216] YHWH's "splendor" (הוד) covers the heavens, while "brightness" (נגה) like light represents his luminous nature (Hab 3:3–4). Henceforth, he advances for the victory

---

212. Gile discusses Ezekiel's use of the idea of "scattering" from the Holiness Code (Lev 26:33) and Deuteronomy in relation to the destruction of the land of Israel and the dispersion of its people for idolatry. However, Gile discusses this conceptual idea of scattering without emphasis on the agency of YHWH's winds for this judgment (Gile, *Ezekiel*, 140–63).

213. See Ezek 5:10, 12; 12:14; 13:13; 17:21.

214. Different explanations of this geographical information are given. Some critics consider YHWH's march to begin either from a sea area, or a mountain region in the south (Haak, *Habakkuk*, 83–84). A movement from the southern area is indicated by use of variant names—Teman, Edom, Paran—that refer to the wilderness of Sinai. But on the idea of YHWH coming from the south in connection with the Israel's wilderness wandering, see Miller, *Divine Warrior*, 76, 86, 118, 118n162. In contrast, Pfeiffer argues that the idea of YHWH coming from the south is late, as a result of later redaction of the texts in discussion. So, he also sees the reference to YHWH as the "one of Sinai" (Judg 5:5; Ps 68:9[8]) to be a later addition. Hence, Pfeiffer dismisses the idea of the origin of YHWH from the south. Instead, he proposes for an unpersuasive view that YHWH came from the north with a character fitting that of a storm god thereof. See Pfeiffer, *Jahwes Kommen*.

215. As observed by Miller, the roots יצא and צעד, often in tandem, are technical terms that describe the advance of YHWH as a divine warrior with his host to fight for his people (Judg 5:4; Ps 68:8; Miller, *Divine Warrior*, 132; see Avishur, *Studies*, 184n202).

216. As already established in this discussion, the historical period involved in these verses is that of the exodus, YHWH's revelation on Mount Sinai (Exod 19:16–19) and, subsequently, the wilderness march (Deut 33:1–2; Judg 5:4). As in some verses (Hab 3:8, 15), the historical period also frames the miraculous crossing of the Red Sea (Exod 15:8) and the Jordan River (cf. Ps 114:3, 5). It may be pointed out, however, that the psalm of Habakkuk is not so much concerned with preserving the historical data, as much as highlighting YHWH's command of nature, and his guidance and deliverance of Israel. In particular, as in other traditions (Deut 33:1–2; Judg 5:4–5; Ps 18:9–12[8–11]), this psalm calls to attention the splendor of YHWH's appearance (Hab 3:3–4), the convulsion of nature (vv. 10, 12a), and the effect of his theophanic disclosure with winds on the inhabitants of the earth (vv. 6–7).

of his people, and both nature and the nations along his pathway experience his wrath with devastating effect. The eternal mountains and hills are shattered, and the tent dwellers of Cushan and Midian "tremble" (רגז) due to the disruptive forces signifying YHWH's frontal movement. Regardless of the direction the wind progresses, this graphic march is described as his procession, and the poet-prophet lays claim to YHWH's "age-old ways" (הליכות עולם, Hab 3:6e). Nonetheless, the idea evokes the power and dominion of YHWH manifested in the winds reaching far back to creation. YHWH's manifestation in the winds causing agitation in the ancient mountains and hills is the same phenomena pictured as chariots and horses deployed for the salvation of YHWH's "people" (עם) and his "anointed" ones (משיח, v. 13). This portrayal of YHWH's saving works is achieved through the blending of motifs from the creation and exodus-conquest traditions with non-Israelite mythic elements, but all the while maintaining a historical perspective. Herein lies the fusion of myth and history in the depiction of YHWH as the savior of his anointed.

The idea of YHWH's "chariots" (מרכבת), termed the "chariots of salvation" in Hab 3:8e, is analogous to the "cherub" of Ps 18:12[11]a, and the "whirlwind" in Ps 77:19[18]a symbolic of YHWH's swirling winds. Furthermore, the idea of the torrents of water "sweeping by" (עבר), and the "deep" (תהום) lifting up its voice (Hab 3:10b; Ps 77:18[17]a; 17[16], respectively) corresponds to the descriptions of YHWH appearing with the winds. The prevalence of YHWH's wind is brought into focus by the mention of the sun and moon failing to give light in Hab 3:11. This idea is also paralleled in Ps 18 by the reference to the heavy cloud under YHWH's feet, the darkness and thick clouds that surround him (vv. 10[9], 12[11]), and the rain-bearing clouds in Ps 77 (v. 18[17]); a feature not uncommon in traditions alluding to the winds dispersing the phenomenal elements.[217]

In view of the preceding description relating the images of YHWH's disclosure in the wind, either as a dramatic approach, "descent,"[218] "march," or "procession,"[219] they all represent the idea central to the conception of YHWH's *modus operandi* in the winds, as he engages in battle against the "waters," or mortal enemies. In any case, either form of approach underscores YHWH's mobility in the winds to focus his disclosure directed against antagonistic forces, in order to bring about a new state of affairs for his elected people. It is appropriate, therefore,

---

217. Josh 10:10–11. See Day, *God's Conflict*, 147; Avishur, *Studies*, 183.
218. Ps 18:10[9]; 144:5.
219. Hab 3:13; cf. Ps 77:20[19].

to observe the mortal foes, called the "sons of foreigners,"[220] or the "wicked,"[221] as a thematic element in the interpretation of divine self-disclosure for deliverance.

Thematic Literary Features and Motifs Relating YHWH's Involvement in the Wind(s)

There are other literary features and styles utilized in Ps 18 to describe the accomplishment of divine deliverance by the potent winds. It is not coincidental, that the Psalmist subtly integrates in this psalm of deliverance and victory, the idea of the reverential fear of YHWH implied in his compliance with the "ways of YHWH" (דרכי יהוה, v. 22[21]),[222] that is the observance of YHWH's commands (מצוות).[223] Therefore, the Psalmist affirms his worthiness for divine intervention in his situation of anguish in contrasting terms. Upon YHWH's response to the distressful situation, the Psalmist presents his faithful relationship with YHWH as a reason for divine intervention over and against his foes. He accomplishes this by asserting his righteousness (צדק, Ps 18:21[20]), attained by abstaining from any form of wickedness (רשעה, v. 22[21]) to fit YHWH's cosmic design.[224] The Psalmist emphasizes his observance of YHWH's judgments (משפטים, Ps 18:23[22]) and attributes the divine favor bestowed on him to his loyalty to the divine judgments. Thus, his righteousness underlies the basic motivation for YHWH's help. This is counterpoised by the reference to YHWH's relationship with those who are perverse (vv. 21–27[20–26]). The manner in which the Psalmist's righteousness is asserted as a prerequisite for divine rescue suggests that his foes are perverse and, implicitly, that they are the wicked and so deserving retribution:

> 27With the pure you show yourself pure,
> but with the perverse you prove yourself tortuous.
> 28For you save poor people,
> but humble the eyes of the haughty ones
> (vv. 27–28[26–27]).

220. Ps 18:45[44], 46[45]; 144:5.
221. Hab 3:13; see 1:4, 13.
222. Cf. Ps 18:25[24]; 81:14[13].
223. Deut 10:12–13; 26:17; Eccl 12:13b. In the revealed law, walking in the ways of YHWH means observance of the "statutes" (חקים), "commandments" (מצוות), and "judgments" (משפטים), cf. Deut 26:17).
224. Ps 104:33–35.

The contrast between the two parties is reinforced by the change of roles as the situation is reversed. The once afflicted becomes the suppressor (vv. 38–46[37–45]). This reversal of roles is seen in the Psalmist's cry for help (שׁועה, v. 7[6]), to which YHWH responds and brings deliverance (vv. 4[3], 7[6]), whereas the Psalmist's enemies utter an unavailing plea for help (אין מושׁיע, v. 42[41]). Instead, as with the plight fitting for the wicked, YHWH routs and "scatters them" (פיצם, v. 15[14]) with his phenomenal winds.[225]

YHWH even girds his elected king with strength and aids him in subduing his opponents (v. 33[32], 40[39]). Here, too, the Psalmist employs the language reminiscent of the Chaoskampf reflecting YHWH's cosmological activities as he treads the back of the sea and subdues the chaos monsters by his winds at creation.[226] Similarly, the Psalmist is enabled to "smite" (מחץ)[227] and tread on his assailants, who have fallen under his feet in the face of the wind (vv. 39[38], 43[42]). YHWH strengthens and makes the Psalmist valiant (v. 40[39]) over those who rise up against him, so much so that the Psalmist finds reason to extol YHWH, not only as his shield, but as the "horn of (his) salvation" (קרן־ישׁעי, v. 3[2]c).

The reference to YHWH as the "horn of salvation" conjures images of YHWH protecting and guiding as the shepherd. This poetic metaphor alludes to an ancient symbol of strength, and subtly refers to YHWH's shepherd epithet, perhaps with antecedence in the symbolism of Baʿal as a bull[228] in representation of the variant attribute of the storm god Hadad. In the Ugaritic text KTU 1.101:1–9=Ugaritica 5.3.1:1–9, where Baʿal is depicted as the valiant Hadad the shepherd, Baʿal is said to have "horns" (*qrn*) upon him.[229] But, the idea in the Hebrew tradition may have more resonance with Marduk also depicted enthroned in his sanctuary, the Esagila, and seated with "his horns" (*qarnāšu*) facing the base of the Esharra (the abode of Enlil, the high god). Probably, the mention of Marduk's "horns" along with his unsparing "bow" (*qaštu*) in this same text (EE vi:65–66, 82–90, respectively), correlates the representation of his insignia in expression of his supremacy as the "shepherd," as enunciated

---

225. See pp. 173, 199, 199n212 above.

226. See Job 9:8; 26:12–13.

227. Cf. Job 26:12b; Isa 51:9.

228. See Green, *Storm-God*, 60, 162, 165, 204, 291; Schwemer, "Storm-Gods I," 160; "Storm-Gods II," 33–36.

229. Ugaritic text KTU 1.101=Ugaritica 5.3.1 line 7.

in subsequent lines (EE vi:105–7). Marduk's heroism over his assailant Tiamat to liberate the Babylonian gods, accords him the conceptual ideals of a shepherd[230] for both the gods and humankind.

However, it is possible that in abstaining from any visible representation of YHWH[231] with "horns," as an emblem on his head like in the case of Baʿal-Hadad or Marduk,[232] the term is used in the Hebrew tradition metaphorically with reference to YHWH as a symbol of strength.[233] The latter bodes well with the Hebrew conception of YHWH as shepherd, as expressed in the lament in Ps 80,[234] invoking YHWH's shepherd epithet (Ps 80:2[1]; Gen 49:24c) for the restoration of Joseph's flock. The appeal to the shepherding appellation of YHWH in Ps 80 is associated with the blessings on Joseph, who is bequeathed by YHWH with the "bow"[235] and horns[236] as symbols of his strength. These traditions of Joseph emphasize YHWH as the shepherd and rock, the source of defense who bestows power and strength. Hence, the Psalmist appeals to YHWH, the shepherd, to "shine forth"[237] evoking YHWH's disclosure in the luminous winds, and show strength to save, and bestow power on his chosen one (Ps 80:2–3[1–2], 18[17]).

Therefore, by referring to YHWH as the "horn of salvation," the Psalmist in Ps 18 casts into bold relief YHWH's power to save. In fact, here, the Psalmist draws from the conceptual idea of divine empowerment and protection deriving from the shepherd epithet, an idea that depicts YHWH as the shepherd, not only of Israel as a whole (80:2[1]), but for King David (23:1). In light of that, the reference to YHWH as the shepherd leading beside the "quiet waters" (מי מנחות, v. 2), carries overtones of the mythological chaotic waters representing King David's enemies subdued by YHWH.[238] YHWH gives rest upon their defeat, as recited and celebrated in Ps 18. Thus, the Psalmist's expression of YHWH's theophanic effulgence (v. 13[12]a), which lights up[239] his dark-

---

230. See p. 150 above.
231. Exod 20:4.
232. KTU 1.101:7 [=Ugaritica 5.3.1:7]; EE vi:66, respectively.
233. Ps 18:3[2]=2 Sam 22:3.
234. See pp. 150–51.
235. Gen 49:24.
236. Deut 33:17.
237. See pp. 150–51.
238. See Ps 18:17–18[16–17].
239. No wonder King David praises YHWH as the "light of (his) salvation" (Ps 27:1).

ness (v. 29[28]), recalls YHWH's guiding, leading, and protecting ideals of the shepherd who "shines forth,"[240] as he manifests his power in the luminous winds, in order to rescue the Psalmist from the brink of destruction and death (18:5–6[4–5]). Such divine intervention in the Psalmist's time of crisis evokes an exuberant outburst of trust in YHWH's firm defense:

> 32For who is God, but the lord?
> And who is a rock,[241] except our God?
> 33The God who girds me with strength …
> 34He makes my feet like the hinds' feet,
> and sets me secure on the heights.
> (Ps 18:32–34[31–33]).[242]

In light of all these considerations, Ps 18 displays a development of the theme of salvation from a grim situation, which evokes the plea for help to the point where YHWH responds with his winds for deliverance. The latter is interpreted as a dual deliverance from the "many waters" and/or from "enemies." The Psalmist links up these motifs to his confession of righteousness as the motive for YHWH's readiness to save. Whereas YHWH's disposition towards the perverse is clear from the fate that befalls the Psalmist's enemies, the polarity of YHWH's dealings with the two parties is evidenced by the different terminology applied. Other than the terms "my enemy" (איבי) and "the ones hating me" (שנאי, v. 18[17]) or "men of violence" (איש חמס, v. 49[48]) designating the foes, the Psalmist also calls them "sons of foreigners"[243] (בני־נכר). By contrast, he identifies himself as YHWH's "anointed" (משיח, v. 51[50]). It is evident therefore, that the Psalmist uses various figures and expressions in the description of his interaction with his deity and his foes. Yet, central to the Psalmist's portrayal of this relationship is his declaration of deliverance from the "many waters" and from the "sons of foreigners." Thus, inasmuch as YHWH his savior (v. 3[2]) and shepherd has mastery over the winds, the Psalmist sees himself empowered by YHWH in his involvement to put all his enemies to rout and crush them "like dust before the wind" (v. 43[42]).

---

240. Ps 80:2[1]; cf. 77:19[18]b; 21[20]a.

241. Hab 1:12. The rock is an ancient designation of YHWH expressing the stability and integrity of his ways. The metaphor is not uncommon in the recital of YHWH's saving deeds (Ps 18:3[2]; see Deut 32:4, 15, 18; Ps 92:16[15]) and in theophanic texts (Ps 144:1; Isa 30:29).

242. Deut 32:13; 33:29; Hab 3:19.

243. Ps 18:45–46[44–45]; 144:7, 11. See pp. 172–73, 200–201.

The Relevance of the Thematic Literary Features to the Meaning of the Theophany in Habakkuk 3:3–15

The theme of deliverance is also developed in opposing terms in the psalm of Hab 3. As in Ps 18, the interaction of YHWH with his "anointed" and his enemies is part of the literary masterpiece of the theophanic text of Hab 3. The contrast is presented in v. 13 where the deliverance of YHWH's "people" or his "anointed" is in antithesis to the destruction of the enemy specified as the "wicked" (רשע). Nevertheless, the significance of these literary features in the psalm of Habakkuk hinges on its interpretation in relation to the literary composition of all the texts on the prophecies of Habakkuk.

The distinction between the "righteous" (צדיק) and the "wicked" (רשע) comes to a head in Hab 3, but these two opposites feature already in the references to the national crisis in Hab 1–2. The account of YHWH's past saving works in Hab 3:3–15 looks forward to the deliverance, or judgment of the respective parties. The presence of these two groups in the psalm of Habakkuk makes possible a comparison with Ps 18. Such a comparison permits a reassessment of the theological intent of the theophanic hymn of Hab 3, not only in respect to its relationship to the preceding chapters, but in relationship to other psalms expressing YHWH's age-old *modus operandi* in the winds as he appears for the deliverance of his people.

Although the type of situation reflected in Habakkuk differs from that in Ps 18, the language employed makes for a closer correspondence. In Hab 1:2 the prophet cries out for help (שוע)[244] and implores YHWH to rectify a situation in which no divine help is forthcoming. The rampant state of violence compels the prophet to question "how long" YHWH will be tolerant of moral corruption. The prophet sees the existing situation as the perversion of "justice" (משפט) by the "wicked" (רשע), as indicated by their oppression of the "righteous" (צדיק, Hab 1:2–4).[245]

In contrast with Ps 18 where YHWH's response is immediate, the suffering in Habakkuk is prolonged. Even though YHWH responds to the prophet's first complaint, the response is not a remedy of the existing

---

244. See Ps 18:7[6], 42[41].

245. These verses assume the form of a complaint characteristic of a cultic lament. The prophet also mentions other features—"violence" (חמס), "strife" (ריב), "contention" (מדון)—that are characteristic of the lament genre. However, all these forms of evil show that justice is spurned.

injustice. Instead, the prophet is instructed to look for the great "deed" (פֹּעַל, Hab 1:5) that YHWH is about to perform among the people. The term used here to refer to YHWH's great deed recurs in Hab 3:2.[246] Paradoxically, in the former text (Hab 1:5) this deed is specified as the establishment of the Chaldeans, who are assigned as YHWH's agent of judgment, to dispossess lands not belonging to them (vv. 6, 12). Moreover, their purpose, which is to exercise violence[247] (חמס), is not an answer to the prophet's complaint, but serves to exacerbate the prevailing situation of injustice,[248] and wickedness is perpetuated.

A succession of oracles in Hab 2 points to YHWH's intolerance of wickedness. The destiny of the opposed groups is announced. The "ones with inflated souls"[249] (עפלה, v. 4), who are arrogant when they plunder nations, are destined for destruction. This is YHWH's retribution on the wicked, but the righteous shall live "by their faith" (v. 4). The subsequent verses emphasize the distinction of destinies, and the theological intent of the poet's affirmation of divine intervention. The turning point is marked by v. 5, which intensifies the description of the corruption of the arrogant. This verse, in a manner that recalls the chaotic images of Sheol and death associated with the "torrents of perdition" in Ps 18, expresses the violent and destructive nature of the wicked. Their avarice is compared to the engorging capacity of Sheol (שאול) and to the insatiable greed of death (מות). This metaphor, implying the "swallowing" or "devouring" of the righteous by the wicked, emphasizes the total destruction of the righteous by the wicked as mentioned in the preceding chapter.[250]

---

246. The word פעל refers to YHWH's past acts of deliverance. Presumably the use of the term in Hab 1:5 and 3:2 is purposely to contrast the present crisis and the ultimate divine judgment signifying YHWH's involvement in history by his potent winds.

247. Cf. Ps 18:49[48].

248. Hab 2:9–11. Even though it is difficult to identify the source of the problem causing the prophet's first complaint, a resolution to the prevailing injustice is offered in Hab 3. According to YHWH's past deeds, he appears for the salvation of his chosen people, designated as the anointed (משיח, v. 13). Therefore the "righteous" may well represent the people of Judah in contrast to the "wicked" who are the Chaldeans for whom judgment, though held back for a while, is imminent (Hab 2:2–20).

249. Emerton considers the use of this term as problematic. No other similar uses are found in the Hebrew tradition (Emerton, "Textual," 11–18). However, the meaning of "inflated" is appropriate considering the syntax of v. 5 where the soul of the wicked is mentioned and compared to the pride of Sheol in its capacity to consume lives. Such a comparison emphasizes the evil intention of the wicked and the intensity of the destruction that they cause.

250. Hab 1:13 (see also v. 8).

With this picture of total annihilation of the righteous, Hab 2 shifts to an envisioned retribution on the wicked. The predestined divine judgment is expressed in the form of woe oracles (vv. 6–17). The wicked, that is the Chaldeans,[251] who plunder nations by violence, build towns with blood, degrade surrounding nations, and trust in idols, have a decree of judgment passed on them in accordance with each of these evils. Finally, a "woe" is pronounced on the wicked, who trust in graven images of their own creation, as over and above YHWH. But, YHWH resides in his holy temple: he is not a product of stone, gold or silver created by mortal beings.[252]

The denunciation of those who trust in idols points to the ineffectiveness of these graven images (vv. 18–19; see Jer 10:3–5).[253] By contrast, YHWH's effectiveness is asserted as he calls the whole earth to be silent before his presence in his holy temple (Hab 2:20; Ps 11:4a). The reference to YHWH residing in his temple in Hab 2:20 reflects the David-Zion theology of YHWH's presence in the temple and the conceptual idea of YHWH's constant defense,[254] and the locale[255] from which YHWH emerges to subdue any forces antithetical to his grand cosmic design. The implication of YHWH's presence is also that YHWH can see,[256] and it is only a matter of time until the wicked, who puff up in their wicked schemes, will soon perish. YHWH is sure to bring judgment upon the perpetrators of violence, and unleash his phenomenal winds (Ps 11:6bc; cf. Hab 3:6e), which will make them totter, comparable to the inebriation from YHWH's cup[257] of wrath.

Therefore, underlying this exhortation in Hab 2:20 is that, unlike graven images, YHWH does not need to be aroused to manifest himself. He is capable of acting in any situation. Though some scholars suggest v. 20 echoes the cultic formula that prepares for YHWH's theophany,[258] it may well represent a call for allegiance to this deity who makes his power

---

251. Hab 1:6.

252. On idols as products of craftsmen and goldsmiths, see pp. 137–38 above.

253. On Jer 10:1–16; 51:15–19, see chapter 2.

254. On the idea of the temple in Zion established as stable as YHWH founded the earth, see p. 60.

255. See Amos 1:2; Ps 99:1–2.

256. Ps 11:4c.

257. Hab 2:16; cf. Jer 25:15–17; Ps 11:6c. See Jer 25:15–29—The Wind as the Cup of YHWH's Wrath and Destruction.

258. Zeph 1:7; Zech 2:17[13]; see Eaton, "Origin," 166.

manifest, and also foreshadows YHWH's imminent theophany. His way is in the winds.²⁵⁹ Hence, the reference to the cup in YHWH's right hand, invokes images of the anticipated divine retribution by means of the whirling winds, in keeping with the prophecies of the prophet Jeremiah.

It is unquestionable then, that, the contents of Hab 2:2–20 provide the context for the interpretation of the psalm in Hab 3. The essence of the matter in Hab 2:2–20 is that it anticipates the reversal of fortunes between the "righteous" and the "wicked." Even though YHWH's answer is inflected with a note of delay as regards the vision to be fulfilled at the appointed time, the text assumes the central idea of Ps 18 where the deliverance of the "righteous" is central to the text. In any event, the delayed response to the poet-prophet's petition makes him plead with YHWH to revive his deeds of deliverance in the poet-prophet's own days (Hab 3:2bc; see vv. 16–17). Thus, he rehearses YHWH's past acts, as he looks for deliverance from the contemporary situation.²⁶⁰ The poet-prophet's petition for divine intervention is projected in the theophanic section of Hab 3:3–15 which provides a basis for hope for the future manifestation of YHWH.

In a detailed reference to the exodus and conquest events, as in the traditional mythic pattern, the poet-prophet contemplates YHWH's theophany (vv. 3–15),²⁶¹ and from it pictures a future act of deliverance. The poet-prophet's reaction of deep awe inspired by what he heard of YHWH's past deeds (v. 2) and the expression of hope for salvation (vv. 16–19), precipitated by the recital of YHWH's deeds, indicates that he has faith in the god of the history of salvation. It is evident that the poet-prophet's contemplation of YHWH's redemption of Israel is sufficient

---

259. See Hab 3:6e, 8–15.

260. See Ps 77.

261. Cf. Exod 15:1–16; Deut 33:1–3. Generally, critics agree on the bipartite structure of YHWH's theophany in Hab 3. Vv. 3–7 are said to present YHWH's advance to do battle, and his victory is mentioned in vv. 8–15 (see Sweeney, "Structure," 79–80; Prinsloo, "Reading Habakkuk," 2). But it is proposed here that the poet-prophet in Habakkuk employs mythical elements in description of YHWH's theophany, to give form and content to his recital of YHWH's deeds of deliverance in Israel's history by the power of his winds. Thus, the poet-prophet reflects on YHWH's age-old *modus operandi* in the winds in relating the events at the exodus and settlement in Hab 3:3–7, and, again, the exodus in vv. 8–15. In the latter, the poet-prophet employs mythopoeic language subtly alluding to YHWH's winds subduing the chaotic waters at creation in vv. 8 and 15. Vv. 8 and 15 form an *inclusio* to the verses describing the cosmic impact and effects of YHWH's winds on the natural elements, nations, and the destruction of the wicked in YHWH's southeasterly frontal path at the exodus and settlement.

to inspire confidence and trust that his divine intervention, as at the exodus, would be repeated in resolution of the national crisis in the poet-prophet's days. His consideration of the divine self-disclosure at the exodus serves to ensure that the "wicked" will experience divine wrath. In anger YHWH "strides" (צעד) the earth and in wrath "tramples" (דוש) the nations (v. 12) in order to save his people (v. 13). These acts of judgment that YHWH executed in the past inspire the poet-prophet to trust YHWH to deliver his people from the present crisis. His account of the judgment of the "wicked" in the events of the past reassures him that the contemporary oppressive power would not go unpunished. This is expressed by the poet-prophet's confidence in YHWH as indicated by his agitated reaction in anticipation of the day of distress coming upon the oppressors (v. 16). This brings into perspective the promise given to the poet-prophet that although divine justice delays, it is certainly inexorable (2:1–5).

In that regard, though the idea is expressed in mythological language, YHWH rescued his people in the past and may still revive his deeds. YHWH's deliverance of his people in the past is indicative of his power to save. The past deeds compel the poet-prophet's confidence in YHWH's potent power to inflict divine judgment on the invaders. In affirmation of the poet-prophet's own steadfastness, in face of the devastating circumstances, he resorts to the exaltation of YHWH in acknowledgement of him as his "savior" (vv. 18–19). Such an expression of faith corresponds to the statement in 2:4: the righteous will live by faith while the "puffed up" and those whose soul is not "upright" are destined for punishment. Therefore, the poet-prophet in Habakkuk revives faith in YHWH as savior, as experienced in his former deeds.

The theophanic text of Hab 3, therefore, may be viewed as a recapitulation of varied but interconnected motifs associated with the theme of deliverance. The elaborate account of the exodus-conquest motif may be considered as part of a theophanic structure not uncommon in the lamentational genre, in light of its occurrence in the theophanic poem of Ps 77:17–21[16–20].[262] The portrayal of YHWH's dealing with the "righteous" and silencing of the "wicked" in connection with his subjection of the "many waters," as in Ps 18, are other features exhibited in this psalm of Habakkuk. Yet, as these motifs are reproduced in Hab 3:3–15, they assert YHWH's power to save, and suggest a clear thematic link for the

---

262. Cf. Ps 80:9–10[8–9].

whole book²⁶³ insofar as they mark the high point of the development of the theme of salvation. The climax of the poem of Hab 3 is marked by the poet-prophet's celebration of YHWH's salvation. He is assured of the security and stability granted therewith (vv. 18–19), as witnessed by other traditions relating to salvation. The metaphorical expression summarizing the strength gained in YHWH and the ultimate stability in YHWH is couched as the domination of the "high places" (במות), and expressed almost verbatim as in Ps 18:34[33].

This review of Hab 3 within the wider context of the whole corpus of the prophetic lament and oracles of Habakkuk provides an overall view of YHWH's deliverance of his people from any form of oppression. In light of the consideration of the general literary features—"many waters," evoking the *Chaoskampf* motif at creation, the righteous *vis-à-vis* the wicked in YHWH's cosmic design, and the exodus motif—familiar from other theophanic texts, Hab 3 presents YHWH as savior of his anointed people. In the main, these features are central to the identification of YHWH's salvific acts. The exact purpose of Hab 3, therefore, in relation to the whole book, is to depict the salvific acts of YHWH accomplished by his phenomenal winds in anticipation of the imminent deliverance from the wicked. YHWH is here conceived as savior, as in Pss 18 (see 144) and 77 with similar thematic content.

Final Reflection

Israelite thought, in keeping with ancient mythology encountered within its cultural milieu, depicted YHWH as the divine deliverer coming with the sonorous wind(s): YHWH fights against enemies, or the wicked, and this is pictured in mythical terms as a battle against the "waters" (ים, נהר, מים רבים),²⁶⁴ for the salvation of his people. In YHWH's warfare, the divine warrior motif and the theme of salvation are integrated with

---

263. Markl defends the unity of the book of Habakkuk in view of Hab 3. Though he views the latter as an independent unit with its own heading, he sees the psalm linked to the preceding chapters in many ways, and fulfilling a complex role in the entire context of the book (Markl, "Hab 3," 104). Andersen mentions the unity of Hab 1–3 showing distinctive literary genres: dialogues in 1:1—2:6a, woe oracles 2:6–20, and the psalm of Hab 3:1–19 (Andersen, *Habakkuk*, 14, 16, 49, 53–54, 261–64; Renz, *Books*, 415).

264. May observes the fusion of YHWH's defeat of Israel's enemies with the idea of primeval chaos (May, "Cosmic Connotations," 11–12). The historical and the cosmic planes merge in the Hebrew tradition.

elements from the creation-out-of-chaos tradition to throw into bold relief the idea of YHWH appearing with the winds to accomplish his purposes as at primal creation. Yet, all in all, YHWH's theophany with his blustery winds in the psalms discussed depict YHWH as the divine warrior, and, ultimately, as the savior. As Miller, correctly asserted, in the Hebrew tradition the warring activities of YHWH are not merely ideological but historical.[265]

YHWH fights for the deliverance of his elected people, which also implies the punishment, or judgment, of the enemies, also designated as the wicked. That means, YHWH's dominion is inextricably linked with his martial deeds and the victories over and against Israel's enemies or the wicked by which YHWH's kingship is lodged and affirmed. Therefore, this intertextual analysis presents a modification of Miller's views, and shows that the mythopoeic language of YHWH's battle against the forces of chaos at the primal creation is employed. This mythopoeic language gives form and content to the image of YHWH, as the divine warrior and savior appearing with the sight and sound of the wind(s) to fight historical foes, as presented in Ps 18 and the related Hebrew texts. It is the winds dispersing other meteorological elements that are central to YHWH's battle, and not some mythological heavenly armies or hosts, with which YHWH fights and defeats inimical forces both in the cosmic and historical spheres. In this display of power, YHWH is exalted with fervor as the "strength," "horn of salvation," or shepherd, whose path or "footprints are not seen." But YHWH is assuredly anticipated to appear in his "age-old ways"—the winds. In essence, the wars in which YHWH wields his phenomenal winds against Israel's foes bear the victory by which YHWH is conceived as the divine warrior, and, ultimately, savior. The elect of YHWH are brought to the conviction that YHWH fights their wars, saves them, and asserts his dominion. Additionally, they see YHWH as their strength and defense bringing to bear the fundamental conceptual idea of YHWH's dominion as king.

---

265. Miller, *Divine Warrior*, 173–74.

4

Proclamation of YHWH as King in the Wind

Former Scholarship on YHWH Mālāk (יהוה מלך) Psalms and a Departure

ALL THE THEMES AND motifs dealt with in the preceding chapters relating YHWH in the guise of the wind as the creator, who subdues chaos, and his subsidiary functions of saving and judging, appear scattered in this group of psalms called the YHWH *mālāk* hymns (Pss 47, 93, 96–99). A body of scholarship exists on these psalms, especially the debate on their form, content, and *Sitz im Leben* in the Israelite religious history. But the various interpretations of the kingship psalms by scholars, due to the mistaken identity of the nature of YHWH's disclosure depicted in these psalms, merit a brief cursory glance.

Gunkel's initial observation of the significance of the formula יהוה מלך, which he translates "YHWH has become king"[1] in acknowledgement of the kingship of YHWH in the psalms, led to the classification of Pss 47, 93, 96–99 as enthronement psalms. Gunkel sees in the content of these psalms not only a proclamation of YHWH as king over Israel but also an anticipation of YHWH's overthrow of nations, and his future governance of the world, as already proclaimed in prophetic passages.[2]

1. Gunkel, *Introduction*, 66.
2. Gunkel, *Introduction*, 68–69.

However, Gunkel interprets these psalms as late and eschatologically oriented, as they appear to predict or anticipate YHWH's future reign. Gunkel, therefore, considers them dependent on the prophecies of Deutero-Isaiah[3] (Isa 52:7-10).

In contrast, Gunkel's protégé, Mowinckel, proceeds with this idea of classification of the enthronement psalms to establish a cultic enthronement festival of YHWH, which he reconstructs in view of similar material from ANE traditions, particularly the Babylonian New Year's festival. Therefore, Mowinckel argues for the priority of the psalms and constructs from them a cultic enthronement of YHWH by which his sovereignty is acclaimed and cultically reenacted. Though Mowinckel initially leaves out the eschatological aspect of these psalms, he reconsiders the eschatological concept as rooted in the enthronement cultic festival,[4] to which he assigns his own classification of enthronement psalms (Pss 47, 93, 95-100).[5] Mowinckel sees the idea of a creation battle alluded to in these psalms. Thus, according to him, the past, present and future are fused together, and realized in the cultic festival of YHWH's enthronement.[6] Therefore, Mowinckel suggests the cultic festival, which marks the dramatic epiphany and enthronement of YHWH becoming king, as supporting the true essence of Gunkel's eschatological explanation of the psalms. But Mowinckel vaguely objects to an eschatological interpretation of the actual enthronement psalms.[7] At the same time, he seems to argue for the dependence of Deutero-Isaiah on the enthronement psalms.[8] Thus, in principle, he gives priority to the latter.[9]

However, Mowinckel elaborates the idea of YHWH's enthronement by analogy with the Babylonian New Year festival at which the

---

3. Gunkel, *Introduction*, 79-81; *Einleitung*, 80-81, 94-116. Jeremias also maintains this eschatological view and sees the psalms as reflecting YHWH's ultimate triumph over worldly wickedness. In particular, he finds the formulations and message of Pss 96 and 98 to be typical of Deutero-Isaiah (see Jeremias, *Königtum Gottes*, 133).

4. Mowinckel, *Psalm Studies*, 1:175-79, 479-81. Mowinckel's views on the cultic enthronement festival received acceptance by Hempel, Volz, Hooke, Oesterley, H. Schimdt, Johnson, Engnell, Kapelrud, Lindbloom, Leslie, Loretz, and, with slight modifications, Gerhard von Rad, Weiser, Gaster, Miller, Roberts, Day, but were opposed by Snaith, Eerdmanns, Nötscher, Buttenweiser, Eissfeldt, Kraus, Westermann, to name a few.

5. Mowinckel, *Psalm Studies*, 1:179-80, 183. See Mowinckel, *Psalms in Israel*, 106.

6. Mowinckel, *Psalms in Israel*, 110-13.

7. Mowinckel, *Psalms in Israel*, 110-11, 143.

8. Mowinckel, *Psalms in Israel*, 116, 117, 189-91.

9. Mowinckel, *Psalms in Israel*, 189-90.

establishment of Marduk's cosmic kingship upon the vanquishing of Tiamat is ritually enacted and celebrated. In view of that, Mowinckel sees the enthronement psalms as alluding to an Israelite autumn festival at which the kingship of YHWH is observed and renewed. He maintains that the autumn festival involves a reenacting of the creative activity (which originally followed a battle against a primeval dragon), celebrating the victory over all the gods, judgment of the gods and their nations considered as representatives of primal chaos, the triumphal procession of the ark as YHWH's palladium[10] (as the visible symbol of YHWH's presence), and entry into the sanctuary where YHWH is acclaimed anew as the universal king.[11] All these elements influence Mowinckel's interpretation of the formula יהוה מלך in Pss 93:1, 96:10, 97:1, 99:1 (cf. 47:9[8]). According to him, and in agreement with Gunkel's translation, the expression refers to a situation that has just occurred, hence the translation "YHWH has become king."[12] In light of that, the controversy on this subject involves the interpretation of יהוה מלך, a recurrent feature in the so-called enthronement psalms, and the origin and nature[13] of the latter.

Mowinckel states the topical aspects of the hypothetical autumn festival that underlie the enthronement psalms as the celebration of the kingship of YHWH, the defeat of chaos, creation, the subjugation of Israel's enemies, the giving of fertility associated with the harvest festival (cf. Ps 65), and the beginning of the new year. Other than finding these elements in the nuclei of the enthronement psalms (Pss 47, 93, 96–99), Mowinckel mentions Pss 95 and 100 as having the same features in expression of the theme of YHWH's kingship. He also extends the concept of enthronement to other psalms that he considers their interpretation to be in relationship with the limited group in his classification of enthronement psalms. Thus, Mowinckel adds Pss 8, 15, 24, 29, 33, 46, 48, 50, 66A, 74, 75, 76, 81, 82, 84, 87, 114, 118, 132, 149; Exod 15:1–18, and, later, Ps 68 as relating the enthronement[14] concept with the theme of kingship

---

10. Mowinckel, *Psalm Studies*, 1:175–76, 184; *Psalms in Israel*, 169–70; cf. Flynn, *YHWH Is King*, 66–67, 69.

11. Here, Mowinckel outlines what he refers to as the important liturgical items of the enthronement psalms. See Mowinckel, *Psalms in Israel*, 106–9.

12. Mowinckel, *Psalms in Israel*, 107.

13. Eaton, *Psalms*, 79–107.

14. Mowinckel, *Psalm Studies*, 1:183–84 (see also 179–80); *Psalms in Israel*, 106–92, 243–48.

of YHWH, even though the elements he sees mentioned in the limited group of enthronement psalms are lacking in these psalms.

Weiser (1962)[15] accepts evidence for the enthronement hypothesis[16] but modifies Mowinckel's thesis on an enthronement festival by suggesting the *Sitz im Leben* of the psalms as the covenant renewal ceremony.[17] He states that the psalms (Pss 47, 93, 96–99) retain the theophany elements that he considers central to the covenant festival celebrated at the New Year festival in the autumn. He sees the importance of the ark representing YHWH associated with the theophany, proclamation of YHWH's name, and ideas on creation, salvation deeds, and judgment. As Weiser argues, all these elements are also embodied with rituals from the royal tradition, yet, integral with the matrix of the covenant renewal.[18] From that standpoint, Weiser argues that the psalms in question, and others besides, are only a reflection of the theophany at Mount Sinai as the prototype. Thus, he views the enthronement of YHWH not in its own right, but as a part of the covenant festival tradition. However, other than Pss 50 and 81, which allude to a theophany, and also presuppose a covenant renewal, Weiser includes several psalms in which the covenant idea is lacking. Thus, with the view on the cultic covenant renewal as the *Sitz im Leben* of these psalms, Weiser translates יהוה מלך as a liturgical formula (ungrammatically) meaning "The Lord is become king."[19]

According to Ulrichsen (1977) the argument about the sequence of "verb" and "subject" depends on the context to determine the meaning of יהוה מלך. He points out that the verb may imply ingressive or durative meaning without regard to the word order. He therefore concludes that the word order is of no importance considering 1 Kgs 16:29 and 2 Kgs 15:13 where the noun precedes the verb and in 1 Kgs 15:1 and verse 9 with the verb preceding the noun and yet in either case the translation "he has become king" is deduced.[20] However, there is no scholarly consensus on the translation of יהוה מלך in the so-called enthronement psalms.

Scholars offer various translations of the formula יהוה מלך based on the syntactical structure of the phrase and with reference to similar

15. Weiser, *Psalms*.
16. Weiser, *Psalms*, 62–63.
17. Weiser, *Psalms*, 62; cf. 35–52; Roberts, "Mowinckel's," 99–100.
18. Weiser, *Psalms*, 62–63.
19. Weiser, *Psalms*, 617, 628, 630, 640; cf. 374: "God is become king."
20. Ulrichsen "Jhwh," 361–74.

usages outside the psalms. Kraus (1978) claims that the verb appears after the subject, and, therefore, the meaning is durative. He solves the syntactical problem by emphasizing the resulting state or condition (being king) implied by the verb, rather than the act (of becoming king). He sees 1 Kgs 1:18 as providing a similar word order as the formula יהוה מלך, and suggesting a solution: ועתה הנה אדניה מלך—"And now behold Adonijah is king."[21] Equally, Kraus sees the reverse order in the phrase in 2 Sam 15:10: מלך אבשלום—Absalom is king with the accompanying musical sound of the trumpet as suggesting the immediacy of becoming king or an accomplished state of being king. In that view, Kraus suggests the same implied by יהוה מלך, YHWH is king expressed as a state or condition in the kingship psalms (Pss 93:1; 96:10; 97:1; 99:1).[22] To that point, Kraus proposes to eliminate the cultic enthronement of YHWH, as he sees the act of enthroning YHWH inconceivable without any image symbolizing YHWH raised up to a throne.[23] Also, he argues that the OT shows no basis of a presumption of the rhythmic rising and dying idea of YHWH (cf. H. Schmidt following Mowinckel), and Ps 93:2 emphasizing the eternality of YHWH's kingship poses a problem to the idea.[24] Kraus's proposal focuses on the cultic royal Zion festival based on YHWH's election of King David and choice of Zion as his sanctuary.[25] However, Kraus acknowledges previous influence by Gunkel's ideas to subscribe to the cultic enthronement from an eschatological perspective emanating from the message of Deutero-Isaiah. But Kraus alters his views and corrects the misconceptions and translates יהוה מלך as "YHWH is king" with the broad understanding of the ageless God-King tradition.[26]

Gray (1979) discusses the different interpretations offered for this formula, "YHWH has become king,"[27] and "YHWH is king," as propounded by Kraus with the assumption of a correspondence to the permanent state implied by the Akkadian formula *Marduk ma šarru*[28] (Marduk has become king). However, Gray, supporting Mowinckel, finds in Pss 24, 29, 48, 68, 74, 84, 89, 149 and Exod 15 explicit reference to the

---

21. Kraus, *Königsherrschaft Gottes*, 15–20; see *Psalms 1–59*, 86–87.
22. Kraus, *Psalms 1–59*, 86.
23. Kraus, *Psalms 1–59*, 87.
24. Kraus, *Psalms 1–59*, 87.
25. Kraus, *Psalms 1–59*, 84–86.
26. Kraus, *Psalms 1–59*, 46, 87.
27. Loretz, Lipiński, Kapelrud; cf. Mowinckel.
28. Gray, *Biblical*, 20–24.

kingship of YHWH over and above unruly waters, or mythical monsters or historical enemies, and the judgment imposed by the divine king. Gray, however, on one hand, acknowledges and points out that not all these leading motifs relating to the kingship of YHWH appear in each psalm; in some cases, only one or two of the motifs are found, or, in certain instances, are merely implied.

In his book *God Is King*[29] (1989), Brettler opposes Mowinckel's hypothesis of a cultic enthronement festival[30] of YHWH, and takes on a different approach to studying the so-called enthronement psalms. Brettler explores the idea of YHWH as king as a metaphor. He sees the idea of YHWH's kingship modeled on the rituals relating the coronation of a human royal king in the Israelite tradition. Although Brettler notes that the idea is fraught with problems given that the latter is also a reconstruction based on ANE materials, which may have different coronation rituals, he makes propositions without full or extant texts showing a description of the Israelite coronation rituals. Nonetheless, Brettler also points out the problem of using the narratives on the royal rituals in the OT, as they either come from different sources or show variations in their descriptions.[31] However, he explores historiographic references on royal rituals for the coronations of Saul, David, Absalom, Adonijah, Solomon, Jehu, Joash, and others. Brettler notes that the formula X מלך, "X is king / has become king" means previous kingship has ceded.[32]

Brettler explores various elements from the Israelite human coronation ceremony that are incorporated into the themes of the enthronement psalms in description of YHWH with the king metaphor. To that end, Brettler argues that the rituals relating the coronation of a human king: joy, noise (from musical instruments and clapping), assembly of people, ascent to the throne, and/or declaration of the formula for accession of kingship are projected onto the coronation of YHWH, as the newly enthroned deity. Brettler endeavors to trace all these elements in the kingship psalms,[33] and also incorporates Pss 95 and 98,[34] as he explores the

---

29. Brettler, *God Is King*. A short review of Brettler's study on YHWH as king, as metaphor, is limited to his final chapter (chapter 6), since that deals with the so-called enthronement psalms discussed here.

30. Brettler, *God Is King*, 146–55, 157–58, 167.

31. Brettler, *God Is King*, 126–33.

32. Brettler, *God Is King*, 132.

33. Brettler, *God Is King*, 146–52.

34. Brettler, *God Is King*, 152–53.

best possible translation of the formula יהוה מלך. Brettler sees most of the elements associated with the human ritual coronation projected on the enthronement of YHWH in Ps 47[35] from the Elohistic psalter isolated from Pss 93–99, which belong to group four of the five groupings of the psalter. He argues that Ps 47 addresses to the nations (v. 1), and suggests rendering the phrase in v. 9 *mālak ʾĕlōhîm ʿal gôyim*: "God has (now) shown himself as king over the nations."[36] In light of that, Brettler sees no basis for a cultic enthronement of YHWH. Instead, he views this as the recognition of YHWH's kingship by the nations.[37] However, Brettler explains this oxymoron on the meaning of the formula "YHWH is, or has become king" to mean the celebration of YHWH as the eternal god to Israel, as well as the newly enthroned king newly recognized by the nations or foreigners.[38]

Nonetheless, this conclusion makes Brettler's argument mute. How do his references on the human coronation of the Israelite kings[39] give reason for the nations or foreigners to recognize and celebrate YHWH as the newly enthroned king? Moreover, Brettler does not extend the same injunction on similar imperatives to all nature to join in the jubilation of the reality of YHWH's kingship expressed in Pss 96 and 98. In fact, in these kingship psalms, the people of Israel are enjoined to declare the salvation deeds of YHWH among the nations in expression of the sovereignty of YHWH (Ps 96:2–3, 10; see 98:1–2). Unquestionably, the nations are compelled to resound the jubilation on account of YHWH wreaking salvation for his people in fulfillment of his promise of the covenanted land.[40] In essence, these nations are called upon as witnesses to YHWH's saving deeds in expression of his covenantal faithfulness, and his status as king in antecedence, as declared in these psalms (Ps 98:3, 6a; cf. 47:7a). Therefore, Brettler's claim that the formula "YHWH has become king" pertains to the foreigners' acknowledgment of YHWH's universal sovereignty is null and void. Also, Brettler's alternative approach to

---

35. Brettler, *God Is King*, 154–55, 157.
36. Brettler, *God Is King*, 155.
37. Brettler, *God Is King*, 155–56.
38. Brettler, *God Is King*, 151, 153, 157, 167; cf. Roberts gives a review of the translations of יהוה מלך depending on the understanding of the group of psalms assigned to this cultic enthronement festival of YHWH (Roberts, "Mowinckel's Enthronement," 98, 100–106, 114).
39. Brettler, *God Is King*, 142, 145.
40. Exod 15:14–17; 32:13, 34a; Josh 11:16–12:8; 2 Sam 7:22–24; Ps 105:8–10, 42–44.

analyzing the conceptual idea of YHWH as king, as a metaphor in these kingship psalms, misses the tenor of these psalms on the historical reality of YHWH's deeds as the eternal king, who flexes his political muscles (in the guise of the wind) as the creator, warrior, and judge.

Flynn (2014) notes that Gray's study[41] goes beyond the enthronement psalms, and sees the warrior and creation motifs present in biblical texts expressing YHWH's kingship. On the one hand, Flynn outlines Mowinckel's hypothetical enthronement festival[42] and the influence on scholars,[43] who subscribe to the idea of enthronement of YHWH, though not necessarily advancing the cultic enactment of Mowinckel's theory. On the other hand, Flynn states that the corpus of psalms he classifies as the psalms of kingship (Pss 29, 47, 93, 96–99) are in critique and modification of Mowinckel's original group of psalms (Pss 47, 93, 95–100).[44] But, the central point of Flynn's thesis on the kingship of YHWH expressed in his selected group of psalms (Pss 93, 95–99) is limited.[45] He sees the creation motif, without the warrior motif, as the basis of the idea of YHWH as king in these kingship psalms.[46] Flynn calls this change of focus on the motifs a product of "cultural translation" (CT). Thus, he explains the changes from what he calls earlier material in Exod 15:1–18, Num 23:18–24, Deut 33:5 and Ps 29 emphasizing the warrior motif similar to the Canaanite Baʻal transitioning to depictions of YHWH as the universal creator deity of the Marduk model in Pss 93, 96–99.[47] He considers the latter group as a composition in reaction to the political changes influenced by the rise of Neo-Assyrian imperialism in the ANE. Flynn's separation of these motifs in the divine nature of YHWH and

41. On the development of Gray's views, see Flynn, *YHWH Is King*, 9–10.

42. Flynn, *YHWH Is King*, 3, 6–9, 36.

43. Flynn mentions Miller, Roberts, Day, and others as maintaining the idea of the enthronement of YHWH, showing Mowinckel's influence, albeit with emphasis on other aspects of YHWH's kingship in the psalms studied (Flynn, *YHWH Is King*, 8–10, 37, 45–46); cf. Tate's summary of scholars' views on the preference to use the terms either "enthronement" or "kingship of YHWH" psalms. Tate presents the various views by scholars on the form, structure, language, and *Sitz im Leben* of the psalms considered in advancing the concept of YHWH's kingship (Tate, *Psalms*, 475, 498–500, 505–9).

44. Flynn, *YHWH Is King*, 38–39.

45. Flynn, *YHWH Is King*, 39.

46. Flynn, *YHWH Is King*, 4, 15, 35, 43–46, 175. Hence, Flynn links the rise of the Babylonian Marduk, as the creator in assertion of his sovereign rule to counter the rise of Neo-Assyrian imperialism. Therefore, Flynn sees the superiority projected on Marduk influencing the image of YHWH as king expressed in the selected group of psalms.

47. Flynn, *YHWH Is King*, 175–78.

Marduk's kingship is problematic. Although he sees similarities in the abstract terms describing YHWH's radiance and Marduk's *melammu*, he argues that this element connotes fear and is associated with the warrior aspects of Marduk, and not YHWH.[48]

Furthermore, Flynn observes the warrior motif alluded to in Ps 97:3 in the phrase referring to YHWH's fire routing his adversaries. He also identifies the warrior motif in Ps 98:1–2 in view as the hand of YHWH associated with his victory. Nonetheless, Flynn dismisses the allusion to the warrior tradition in Ps 97 as slight and lacking emphasis. Therefore, he advocates for recontextualizing this psalm as relating YHWH's creative acts. Also, he considers the reference to YHWH's hand in Ps 98 to be far removed from the imagery of YHWH demonstrating his strength against enemies similar to Exod 15:6, 12, 16. Instead, at pains to mute the warrior motif in these psalms in assertion of a simplified creation model, Flynn argues that the reference to YHWH's hand is linked with aspects of YHWH's universal kingship deriving from creation theology. Here, he states that YHWH's hand mentioned in Ps 98, though resonating with the warrior tradition, is now connected with creation to assert YHWH's role in creation. Generally, Flynn claims that there is a reorientation of the imagery of YHWH's hand relating to creation in the kingship psalms akin to the idea expressed in Ps 95:5.[49] And, yet, as averred here, the creation and battle or warrior motifs are closely linked with other themes and motifs relating the lock, stock, and barrel of YHWH's eternal kingship, which is manifested in his incandescent age-old *modus operandi* in the wind, and alluded to in these so-called enthronement psalms and other related texts.

Fundamentally, as already pointed out by some biblical critics, there is no evidence at all in the Hebrew texts to support the hypothetical cultic enthronement of YHWH apart from themes and motifs common from ANE traditions. The conquest of the mythical creatures or the rebellious waters is central to the idea of the establishment of kingship in the Mesopotamian and Ugaritic traditions. These traditions have Marduk and Baʿal, respectively, as warriors, whose victories against an archrival relate to their kingship. In the case of Marduk, he attains lordship by vanquishing Tiamat by means of various phenomenal elements. As alluded to in chapter 1 of this monograph, Marduk deploys natural phenomena

---

48. Flynn, *YHWH Is King*, 129–31.
49. Flynn, *YHWH Is King*, 138–40.

to combat Tiamat. He covers his body with blazing fire, mounts a storm wind as his chariot, and deploys various raging winds to roil and distend Tiamat's belly. Yet, in contrast, for Baʿal, the natural elements play no part in his battle for kingship. Only the essence of Baʿal's function in the maintenance of cosmic order is expressed in meteorological elements.

Similar phenomenal elements relating to both cases of Marduk and Baʿal characterizing the kingship of YHWH, as presented by the aforesaid critics, underlie the mythopoeic language employed in texts that declare YHWH as king. But, as pointed out in the preceding chapters, scholars have overlooked the primacy of the winds in the descriptions of YHWH's disclosure. This idea of YHWH's theophany in the wind is combined with other themes and motifs in assertion of YHWH's kingship both in the cosmic (that is, at primal creation) and historical realm; thus, affecting the celebratory tenor of the kingship psalms. The (whirl)wind deity Amma, who releases all of creation with a "luminous" and "sonorous" motion, perhaps drawing from the Egyptian background of gods who emerge and create with the wind, offer a closer parallel to YHWH's manifestation in the wind, as pictured in the psalms discussed in this chapter.

Of significance in this regard are Pss 29, 68, 97, and prophetic passages mentioned in association, viz. Isa 30:27–33; Nah 1:3–5, which have elements, or in some cases graphic depictions of YHWH's appearance in the winds, and dispersing natural elements, in assertion of his sovereignty. In other words, the texts mentioned incorporate imagery familiar from the creation-out-of-chaos tradition, to emphasize YHWH's intervention in bringing about the victories experienced by Israel in judgment of the nations and their gods. These saving acts constitute the basis for the proclamation of YHWH as king, as he discloses his potent power with the phenomenal winds. So, in view of the description of YHWH appearing in the winds in Ps 97, judgment of the wicked, and the salvation wielded thereof, it is improper to categorize this psalm as an enthronement psalm, or merely eschatological[50] in orientation, as much as all the other psalms set in that rubric. In that regard, interpreting YHWH's theophany as depicting an enthronement procession of YHWH, or proclamation of him as king at an enthronement festival,[51] is unjustified.

---

50. Mowinckel, *Psalm Studies*, 1:183, 192–94; Waltke and Houston, *Psalms*, 208.

51. Mowinckel, *Psalmenstudien*, 56, 215, 234, 236, 250; see Petersen, *Royal God*, 15–17; Brueggemann, *Whom No Secrets*, 49–50, 52–54.

Psalm 97 Declares: YHWH is King in the Wind, and Fire Goes before Him

Among the so-called enthronement psalms (Pss 47, 93, 96–99), elements associated with the theophany of YHWH in the winds are evident mainly in Ps 97. YHWH as king appears shrouded in clouds[52] and thick darkness (v. 2), comparable to other theophanic texts depicting YHWH's *modus operandi* in the wind.[53] In fact, this image of YHWH recalls YHWH's appearance at creation as presented in Ps 104:1–3, where clouds and fire are in attendance. As with the wind and creator god Amma, who bore fire from his breath, and has it at his disposal to destroy the universe,[54] YHWH's fire goes before him and inflicts destruction on all his surrounding enemies (v. 3).[55] Here, too, the Psalmist couches the brightness of YHWH's luminous, or fiery winds as lightning that lights up the world (v. 4a)[56] and causes the earth to tremble (v. 4b)[57] while the mountains, that are a symbol of all that is stable and durable, melt (מסס)[58] like wax before YHWH's blazing presence (v. 5).[59]

Several views on the literary structure of Ps 97 have been put forward[60] in establishing the meaning and purpose of this psalm. The ar-

---

52. Jeremias, *Theophanie*, 28–31. Jeremias notes that the clouds here function as a shield of YHWH (cf. Job 26:9) as distinct from other earlier texts where the clouds symbolize YHWH's war chariot (Pss 18:10[9]; 104:3; cf. Isa 19:1). The association of clouds with darkness in this psalm possibly alludes to YHWH's complementary role as rain-bringer. But the mention of fire that devours YHWH's enemies suggests a battle event rather than the giving of fertility. There is no doubt, however, that the fire and lightning, or rather brilliance, represent YHWH's luminous presence, as in other theophanic texts (see Pss 18:15[14]; 77:19[18]b; 144:6; Hab 3:4, 11bc).

53. Pss 18:10[9], 12[11]; 77:18[17].

54. See pp. 14–15, 14n72 above.

55. Pss 18:9[8]; 68:3[2].

56. See Ps 77:19[18]b.

57. Pss 18:8[7]a; 77:19[18]c; Hab 3:6a.

58. Jeremias points out that the term "melt" is figuratively used here to indicate the graphic destruction of the firmest parts of the earth on YHWH's arrival (cf. Mic 1:4; Jeremias, *Theophanie*, 31). A similar image is expressed in Amos 9:5 of the earth figuratively melting at YHWH's touch by his fiery winds. See p. 127. The idea resonates with the quaking, shattering, and writhing of the mountains in Ps 18:8[7]b, Hab 3:6c, 10a, respectively, caused by YHWH's raging winds. Therefore, the idea of a volcanic eruption in association with a theophany in a thunderstorm, as some critics claim, is dubious (Kraus, *Psalms 60–150*, 259; cf. Tate, *Psalms*, 518; Amzallag, *Psalm 29*, 160).

59. Cf. Amos 9:5.

60. Loretz, *Ugarit-Texte*, 334–43. Loretz gives an overview of scholars' interpretations of Ps 97 up to 1988. He points out that Lipiński concentrates on the literary

guments concern the correlation between the proclamation of YHWH's kingship (v. 1), the theophany description (vv. 2–6) and the relationship of YHWH and his people (vv. 7–12).[61] Gray argues for vv. 1–6 as a separate unit with traditional elements characteristic of a preexilic depiction of YHWH, but interprets vv. 7–12 as a postexilic expansion of the psalm.[62] In the same vein, Loretz divides the verses in this psalm into cola and undertakes a colometric analysis as a basis for the interpretation of the literary structure of the psalm. He considers vv. 2–5 as an interpolation from a text about the storm god and vv. 7–12 as a series of glosses

---

correlation of the psalm and concludes that it is an anthological composition. Lipiński considers the antithesis between the "righteous" (צדיקים) and the "wicked" (רשעים) to be a late motif, and thus finds a basis for the late dating of the psalm (Lipiński, *Royauté*, 215–18). Though Lipiński sees vv. 2–5 as an earlier composition with elements from the storm god tradition, he assigns the psalm to 164 BCE, as he sees it as a song for the temple consecration of that period (*Royauté*, 270). However, Lipiński arrives at the same conclusion as Westermann that the description of a theophany in vv. 2–5 was taken from another context (Westermann, *Praise and Lament*, 149). Howard, on the other hand, sees Ps 97 structurally, thematically, and literarily interlinked with the kingship of YHWH psalms he classifies as Pss 93–100. Howard finds issues with the internal structure of Ps 97 and divides it into two main units but with further subsections in units A (vv. 1–9) a hymn celebrating YHWH's kingship and unit B (vv. 10–12) an exhortation, and he considers the latter part a late composition (Howard, *Structure*, 73–74, 75). Ortlund builds further on Howard's approach and undertakes an intertextual analysis of Ps 97 at three levels: within the broader context of books three and four of the psalter, the theophany unit as an individual composition, and the psalm placed within its immediate context—that is, in Pss 96–99 (Ortlund, "Intertextual," 276, 279). Unfortunately, Ortlund's analysis obtains the same view on the theophanic unit as describing YHWH's appearance in storm elements, which is counterintuitive to the emphasis in this monograph on YHWH's age-old *modus operandi* in the wind (cf. Ortlund, "Intertextual," 277–78; Gerstenberger, *Psalms 2*, 192–93; Waltke and Houston, *Psalms*, 193–98).

61. Not all biblical critics subscribe to the same structural analysis of Ps 97. Kraus regards vv. 1–2 as describing YHWH enthroned, vv. 3–6 the theophany, vv. 7–9 the effects of theophany, and vv. 10–12 the relationship of YHWH and the "righteous" (צדיקים, Kraus, *Psalms 60–150*, 257). In support of the cultic tradition of the feast of Tabernacles as associated with the covenant tradition, Kraus views vv. 10–12 as representing the effects of YHWH's theophany on the righteous traditionally admitted to the sanctuary for a cultic festival (Ps 24). Howard sees problems with the internal coherence of Ps 97. He finds in vv. 1–9 (unit A) the description of YHWH's sovereignty, and exhortation in wisdom terms to the faithful in vv. 10–12 (unit B). However, Howard further breaks up unit A into four units based on the prefixing and suffixing of verb forms to end up with five units of the psalm in total (Howard, *Structure*, 73–75). Waltke and Houston initially divide Ps 97 into two stanzas: Stanza I—the theophany in vv. 1–9—and then Stanza II—admonitions to the faithful to hate evil and rejoice in vv. 10–12. These two stanzas are further split into two strophes each with verses placed under varying sub-units (Waltke and Houston, *Psalms*, 193).

62. Gray, *Biblical*, 69.

and supplements.⁶³ Nonetheless, Loretz maintains that v. 2 connects vv. 1–6 with vv. 7–12, possibly through (several) subsequent redactional phases. Though it is not explicitly stated, the connection Loretz observes is facilitated by the judicial terms mentioned in v. 2.⁶⁴ However, from the colometric perspective, Loretz argues that initially the kingship of YHWH is associated, though obscurely, with the hoped-for rain. But he assumes that the subsequent connection of vv. 7–12 by means of v. 2 further links YHWH's kingship to his judicial function against idol worshipers and the wicked in Israel.⁶⁵

Howard takes a structural analysis to studying Ps 97, focusing on the keywords, themes and syntax of Pss 93–100 as a group. He divides Ps 97 into two main sections: a hymn (vv. 1–9) celebrating the kingship of YHWH divided into four units, and the second section (vv. 10–12) as exhortatory to the people considered to be in a faithful relationship with YHWH. But Howard classifies Ps 97 as a kingship/enthronement psalm.⁶⁶ He relates its structure in sequence with the other psalms in book 4 of the psalter.⁶⁷ He sees Ps 97:1 with the formula יהוה מלך and the earth rejoicing as sharing the same ideas in Ps 96:10–11. According to him, the theophany unit in Ps 97:2–6 asserts YHWH's awe-inspiring nature emerging from Zion, where YHWH reigns. Howard argues that vv. 10–12 is exhortative, and shares a note of wisdom on YHWH's dealings with the wicked and faithful ones expressed in Ps 94:12–15.⁶⁸ But he also notes that other wisdom terms regarding YHWH's judgments based

---

63. Loretz outlines the colometric pattern of the psalm and sees it as composite but does not discuss this at length from that perspective. Instead, he concentrates more on the views of other critics, and leaves his own interpretation of the psalm in obscurity. He appears, however, to concur with the view that vv. 7–12 are a later addition to vv. 1–6 (see Loretz, *Ugarit-Texte*, 334–42). In general, Loretz's intent is to propose an early date for Ps 97 and assert its connection with the Canaanite tradition of the enthronement of Ba'al. Thus, he sees vv. 2a, 3–5 as unaltered linguistic elements of a preexilic enthronement festival comparable to that of the Ugaritic Ba'al (*Ugarit-Texte*, 345–46). Overall, in his analysis of the psalms, Loretz finds evidence that supports the enthronement festival. Thus, he concludes that the Israelites adopted a Canaanite tradition and transformed it into a festival that proclaimed YHWH as a universal and eternal deity (*Ugarit-Texte*, 495).

64. Cf. vv. 8, 11, 12.

65. Loretz, *Ugarit-Texte*, 342–43.

66. Howard, *Structure*, 41, 87.

67. Howard, *Structure*, 177–78.

68. Howard, *Structure*, 124–25; cf. 177.

on justice and righteousness are found apart from wisdom sections in Ps 97:2.[69]

Flynn also analyses Ps 97 within the group of kingship psalms (Pss 93, 96–99), though focusing on the universalistic orientation of the psalms through the lens of the creation motif.[70] But first, Flynn notes that Ps 97:5b, which expresses YHWH as the LORD of all the earth, introduces YHWH's universal kingship echoed in v. 9. Thus, Flynn argues that the reference to the "many islands" (איים רבים) implies the distant coastlands of the known world, paralleled by the "earth," called to jubilation in Ps 97:1, and indicates YHWH's far-reaching dominion.[71] From that perspective of YHWH's universal kingship in Ps 97, Flynn argues that Ps 98 resumes the ideas stated in Ps 96 on YHWH's kingship not confined to Israel but made known to the nations (Ps 98:2). He sees the same universal idea apparent in Ps 99, though Zion is held as the primary locale for YHWH's sphere of influence of his kingship. At any rate, Flynn's view is that these psalms lack the warrior tradition[72] but employ the creation motif as the counterpoint for the ineffectiveness of other gods. According to him, Ps 96:5 emphasizes this new form of YHWH's kingship by emphasizing his potency in creating the heavens in contrast to the people's gods that are idols. To that end, Flynn deploys Ps 93 to show the superiority of YHWH's kingship in creation demonstrated by his establishment of the world.[73] But Flynn states that the creation motif is not as ostensible in Ps 97.[74] Instead, for this missing idea, Flynn substitutes the reactions of all of creation: the many coastlands (v. 1) and the earth (v. 4b), as implicating the creation motif he avers.[75]

Despite these differences in interpretation of Ps 97, there is a definite unity of thought and pattern in the development of the theme of YHWH's kingship throughout this psalm in relation to the theophany unit in vv. 2–6. This continuity of thought is indicated by the occurrence

---

69. Howard, *Structure*, 125.

70. Flynn, *YHWH Is King*, 41–43.

71. Flynn, *YHWH Is King*, 42.

72. Flynn, *YHWH Is King*, 42–44.

73. Flynn, *YHWH Is King*, 42. Though Ps 95 is not included in Flynn's group of psalms (Pss 93, 96–99) for cultural translation, he includes Ps 95 in this analysis and uses vv. 4–5 to emphasize YHWH's kingship in display, not only at creating but controlling all he created (Flynn, *YHWH Is King*, 40–41).

74. Flynn, *YHWH Is King*, 43.

75. Flynn, *YHWH Is King*, 43.

of the same verbal and nominal terms deriving from the same roots. The substantives "righteousness" and "justice" (צדק ומשפט) introduced in v. 2, as the foundation of YHWH's throne,[76] are the key terms that assert the reality of the kingship of YHWH[77] from time immemorial.[78] These two terms—"righteousness" and "justice"—indicate that YHWH's kingship is inextricably linked with the world order. It is fitting then that world order is promulgated at YHWH's theophany. Hence, the word righteousness is reiterated in v. 6. As a characteristic of YHWH and manifestation of his appearance, righteousness is here the subject of proclamation by the heavens. And, ultimately, those who are in accord with YHWH's righteousness by abstaining from evil are referred to as the "righteous" (/צדיק צדיקים, vv. 11, 12) By the same token, the element of justice is echoed in v. 8 in relation to YHWH's execution of judgments (משפטים) expressive of his righteousness[79] that causes joy in Zion.

The thought sequence of YHWH's righteous rule, resulting in the establishment of world/social order, is further given expression by the repetition of the same verbal terms: "Rejoice"//"be glad" (גיל//שמח) used in v. 1 in connection with the worldwide joy at the proclamation of YHWH as king. Though appearing in reverse order in v. 8, the same verbs (שמח//גיל) are employed to express the jubilation in Zion affected by YHWH's judgments, and the cause for the exhortation of the righteous to rejoice in YHWH (שמח, v. 12; cf. v. 11). This correlation of nominal and verbal terms shows the continuity in the development of the theme of YHWH's kingship in vv. 1–6 linked with his acts of judgment in vv. 7–12. Therefore, the manifestation of YHWH in the phenomenal winds bearing other natural elements, as described in vv. 2–6, heralds his judicial role in the exercise of his judgments in vv. 7–9.[80]

As YHWH appears at his judgments, the earth's trembling,[81] and mountains melting,[82] point to nothing other than the force of YHWH's potent blazing winds (vv. 3a, 4–5). Thus, the Psalmist in Ps 97 alludes to YHWH's age-old *modus operandi* in the winds. The heavens, which

---

76. See Ps 89:15[14].

77. Jeremias, *Königtum Gottes*, 138.

78. Ps 93:2.

79. The same association of YHWH's righteousness and exercise of judgment is shown in Ps 99:4–9. See Bullock, *Encountering*, 185.

80. Cf. Jer 25:30–32.

81. See Pss 18:8[7]a; 104:32a.

82. Cf. Ps 46:7[6]b.

PROCLAMATION OF YHWH AS KING IN THE WIND

YHWH creates[83] as his celestial abode,[84] function as the foreground in display of his righteousness, and all the people see his "glory" (כבוד, v. 6). That is YHWH's renown filling up the skies and causing convulsions in the most durable symbols of creation. As may be cited in view of v. 6 in that regard, the focus in the literary structure of Ps 97 is more on YHWH's arrival, as defined by his self-disclosure with the winds,[85] and the effects of YHWH's austere grandeur on nature and all the peoples. As Jeremias notes, YHWH's earth-shattering self-disclosure in judgment produces different reactions.[86] In contrast with the traditional reaction of fear[87] caused by YHWH's appearance,[88] the people behold his glory: Zion and the daughters of Judah rejoice (Ps 97:8). But the idols are overthrown, and their worshipers are humiliated (v. 7). Therefore, these occurrences herald an already "enthroned" or exalted deity, who discloses himself from the heavenly realm, to mete out destruction against enemies and idol worshipers not aligned with his divine mandate (vv. 3b, 7). YHWH asserts his kingship with his acts of judgments by employing phenomenal winds to complement his might against all the worshipers of idols whom YHWH debases along with their worthless gods.[89] These acts of judgment are the cause for jubilation in Zion[90] (Ps 97:8). So, YHWH's majestic appearance appropriately invokes a cause to celebrate his kingship in recognition of his glory and invincible power against idolatrous

---

83. Ps 96:5b.

84. See Ps 104:2b-3; Isa 40:22.

85. Despite the varying tenses used in this text, the language resembles that of other theophany depictions (Pss 18:9-13[8-12]; 77:18-19[17-18]).

86. Jeremias, *Königtum Gottes*, 138-39.

87. The element of fear is in keeping with the effects inflicted by the goddess Inanna's tempestuous nature. She is said to fan fire against people, and her tempestuous radiance causes fear and trembling in humankind. See p. 115 above.

88. Cf. Hab 3:7.

89. Jer 10:14-15=51:17-18.

90. Ps 97 expresses features that seem to reflect ideas and motifs relating to YHWH's intervention on the historical plane, as predicted in Jeremiah's message of doom on Babylon in Jer 51. In this latter text, the prophet Jeremiah declares the power and might of YHWH manifested by the phenomenal acts associated with creation at YHWH's disclosure in the winds (Jer 51:15-16=10:12-13). Jeremiah predicts YHWH's degradation of worthless objects and termination of worship of idols through his judgment (51:17-18; cf. v. 52) in vengeance for the destruction of Zion (vv. 6, 11, 49). Yet, Jeremiah also points to the vindication of Zion through YHWH's judgment (vv. 9-10) with the ultimate declaration of him as king (v. 57).

forces. Thus, vv. 2–6 describe the nature of the deity poised for judgment in his age-old *modus operandi* in the wind, and not for an enthronement.

The appearance of YHWH with clouds, thick darkness, fire, and luminescence comparable to lightning, recalls the phenomenal elements at the exodus. The fiery cloud brings darkness to the pursuing Egyptians but light to YHWH's fugitives. Similarly, these elements manifest YHWH's judicial role in Ps 97, and assert the same counterpoint: YHWH's radiance or glory yields light and brings joy to his people. Yet, the idolaters are put to shame, and their gods are debased and satirically called to total obeisance. Hence, the Psalmist proclaims: "Light is 'sown'" (זרע) to represent the idea of light dawning to the righteous (v. 11a).[91] Here, some scholars[92] read "shine forth" (זרח) instead of "is sown." But the Psalmist intentionally employs the term "sown" metaphorically to refer to YHWH as the source scattering light or radiance yielding only to the righteous amid wickedness for their deliverance (v. 10).[93] By this idea, the Psalmist also recalls the creation tradition. As declared rhetorically in Job 38:18–19, YHWH knows the path to light and the abode of darkness; howbeit his supernatural presence at creation is depicted as garbed with light (Ps 104:2; see Gen 1:3). Moreover, YHWH rules and has sway over all creation. So, he can shed light for the righteous (Ps 89:16[15]b) but deny that light to the wicked (Job 38:15a). Therefore, the climactic element of the rule inaugurated by YHWH's appearance with the luminous wind in Ps 97 is that of the deliverance and guidance of his righteous ones from the schemes of the wicked.

With these aspects of YHWH's kingship in view, the thematic unity of the composite nature of Ps 97 is evident. Most critics, in support of the enthronement hypothesis, concentrate more on the YHWH *mālāk* formula[94] in Ps 97:1a, and its possible implication in a cultic enthronement setting without mention of its connection with the phenomenal manifestation of YHWH in vv. 2–6. The martial nature of YHWH expressed in vv. 3–5 ascertains the cosmic reactions as the consequence of

---

91. Brueggemann translates "light dawns for the righteous" (Brueggemann, *Whom No Secrets*, 52). See Kidner, *Psalms*, 384, Howard, *Structure*, 72–73). See זרח in Ps 112:4 referring to light rising in the darkness for the upright.

92. Loretz, *Ugarit-Texte*, 337; Jeremias, *Königtum Gottes*, 137. At any rate, the word "sown" is metaphorical in this context of judgment and correlates YHWH's theophany with the luminous winds emitting light to the righteous but bringing clouds/thick darkness to the wicked.

93. Cf. Ps 18:29[28]b.

94. Brueggemann, *Whom No Secrets*, 50; Magonet, "Reading," 175–76.

PROCLAMATION OF YHWH AS KING IN THE WIND

YHWH's theophany, and, therefore, fosters the thematic link between his self-revelation and his execution of judgment, that is fundamental to the proclamation of YHWH's kingship among his own people. Undoubtedly, the theophany section in vv. 2–6 throws into bold relief YHWH's disclosure in the phenomenal winds as king dispensing his righteous rule. Hence, it is clear from vv. 2–6 that the evidence for an investiture ritual is lacking. The movement of thought in this psalm asserts the view that YHWH breaks through to the earth (including the coastlands) with his wind and raging fire to rout his enemies in exercise of his sovereign rule. Here, though with subtleties, the Psalmist resounds the lyrics: earth, wind and fire in his declaration of YHWH as the king of the whole earth, who discloses himself dramatically with the phenomenal wind and fire. This means that the fundamental idea expressed in this psalm is the proclamation of YHWH's kingship made manifest by his deeds among his people, rather than a representation of a coronation ceremony.[95] To that end, the Psalmist employs the YHWH *mālāk* formula with the perfect tense verb to express a continuous state, and translates "YHWH reigns,"[96] which in essence means, "YHWH is king." In that sense, the implication is that YHWH shapes and directs the course of Israel's history. The idea is consistent with YHWH's role as creator, who appears with the fiery wind at creation, and by the same means wields great saving acts causing the exultant jubilation expressed in the kingship psalms.

The thematic unity of Ps 97 may be further supported by comparison with Ps 29,[97] another theophany text asserting YHWH's kingship and

---

95. Cf. Bullock, *Encountering*, 183.

96. See BDB 573–74.

97. Ps 29 is argued to have originated as an ancient Canaanite psalm to Baʻal which is adapted for purposes of Israel's worship of YHWH. Ginsberg initiated the proposition that Ps 29 is an adapted Phoenician hymn to Baʻal that is altered slightly to suit the Israelite tradition. He maintains this view without drawing his ideas from a single text on Baʻal, but from isolated references (Ginsberg, "Phoenician Hymn," 472–76). Yet, his view is followed by a majority of scholars (see, among others, Cross, "Notes," 19–21; *Canaanite Myth*, 151–56; Fitzgerald, "Note," 61–63; Gray, *Biblical*, 42; Jeremias, *Königtum Gottes*, 42–43; Avishur, *Studies*, 41–44; Kraus, *Psalms 1–59*, 346; Kloos, *YHWH's Combat*, 98–112). Kloos argues for Ps 29 as an original Hebrew composition but with similar contents, which suggest dependency on Canaanite literal forms (Kloos, *YHWH's Combat*, 107–8; cf. Longman, *Psalms*, 155–57). Yet, more recently, Amzallag presents a brief scholars' purview on the provenance, structure, and composition of Ps 29 (Amzallag, *Psalm 29*, 8–9). However, Amzallag's propositions on YHWH's voice associated with thunderstorm, volcanic, and metallurgy images is a bit amorphous. For the possible Israelite provenance, composition, and thematic structure of Ps 29 focusing YHWH's voice as wind, see pp. 276–90 below.

YHWH IN THE WIND(S)

the effects of his potent winds. Both psalms have distinct features relating to the nature of YHWH's kingship and relationship with his people. The "prominence" of YHWH among the gods,[98] the majesty of his "glory"[99] and his relationship with his people[100] are the principal ideas common to these psalms as they make their assertion of YHWH's universal rule. As stated in Ps 97:9, YHWH is the Most High (עליון) over all the earth and is highly exalted (עלה) above all gods, so much so that even the gods "bow down" (השתחוו) before YHWH (v. 7).

In like manner, in Ps 29:2 the same verb occurs in an imperative addressed to all the (sons of) gods to pay homage to YHWH.[101] While these psalms assert the sovereignty of YHWH, the superiority of his power is further emphasized by the glory and might with which he manifests himself in the natural elements. So, in Ps 29:3 "the god of glory[102] (אל־הכבוד) thunders (הרעים)" over forces threatening his cosmic order. But the sublimity of YHWH's self-disclosure with the potent wind(s) is extended to nature (vv. 4-9). Here, too, YHWH's phenomenal wind hews out with flames of fire (v. 7),[103] presumably for the destruction of enemies as in Ps 97:3b. Indeed, as the postlude of the psalm affirms, the power and glory of YHWH are transmitted to his people as strength and peace, and these qualities are auspiciously guaranteed by his eternal kingship (29:10-11). We may compare this view with Mettinger's[104] observation on the conjunction of YHWH's "glory" (כבוד),[105] theophany and

---

98. Ps 97:9; cf. 29:1. Weiser points out correctly that the polytheistic nature of the religion of the ancient traditions is here converted and portrayed positively in terms of a celestial court purposely to pay homage to YHWH (Weiser, *Psalms*, 262).

99. Ps 97:6; cf. 29:2-3.

100. Ps 97:10-12; cf. 29:11.

101. Here, too, Ps 29 is parallel to Ps 96. Ps 96:7-8a, 9a appear to have been plucked verbatim from Ps 29:1-2. The only difference is that the clans of nations, in substitution of the gods, are compelled to acknowledge the supremacy of YHWH's rule in Ps 96.

102. In tracing the sequence battle-kingship-temple motif, Mettinger finds that Ps 24 demonstrates the connection between "glory" (כבוד), kingship and theophany as YHWH makes his triumphal entry into the temple as the king of glory (מלך הכבוד, 24:7-10; see Mettinger, *Dethronement*, 120-21). However, YHWH's kingship is beyond conformity with this pattern. YHWH's kingship is from of old (Ps 93:2), and not determined by a victory in battle (see discussion on Ps 93).

103. See discussion on Ps 29 on p. 286 below.

104. Mettinger, *Dethronement*, 117-21.

105. Cross points out that the term *kābôd* is often compared with the Akkadian *melammu*, which applies to the aureole of gods, demons, and kings. He states that the earliest attestation of the term *kābôd* in Hebrew refers to the bright aureole surrounding YHWH (Exod 33:17-23). But he further suggests that the idea of *kābôd* may have

kingship in this psalm. The same movement of thought as in Ps 29 is evident in Ps 97 in the portrayal of YHWH's relationship with his people. Whereas in Ps 29:10-11 YHWH's rule is expressed in general terms as that of strength and peace, in Ps 97:7-12 YHWH's kingship is depicted in terms of judicial activity, and the deliverance of the righteous from the wicked (vv. 7-8, 10-12).[106]

Images of YHWH as Warrior-King in Psalm 97 and the Theme of Salvation

An analytical comparison of Ps 97 with the thought content of the Song of the Sea (Exod 15) shows the purport of this psalm in the biblical Hebrew tradition. It is possible that Ps 97 develops a Davidic-Zion kingship and temple theology with its roots in Exod 15:1-18. The latter hymn recounts YHWH's warrior exploits, resulting in the conquest of Canaan. As noted in this monograph, YHWH's martial traits in the wind are no longer confined to the confrontation of the primal waters of chaos but also directed against human foes.[107] YHWH blows his wind to churn the waters of the *Yam Suph* in orchestrating the destruction of the Egyptians (Exod 15:8, 10; see 14:21). YHWH shatters the enemy as his wind causes the waters to cover Pharaoh's chariots and his army for the deliverance of his people (vv. 1, 4-10). The wind, pictured here as his "right hand" (v. 6), wields victory for the fugitives, who deem YHWH as a warrior and eternal king,[108] who dwells in his sanctuary[109] within their

---

originated from the dark and fiery storm cloud in association with the theophany of the storm god. Cross makes clear, however, that *kābôd* is not exclusively a feature of the storm god, though a characteristic of storm theophany (Cross, *Canaanite Myth*, 153, 165-67).

106. Such an antithetical relationship of YHWH with the righteous *vis-à-vis* the wicked, in expression of his divine purpose, is a common feature in other theophany, as seen in Pss 18:18-43[17-42]; 68:2-4[1-3]; Hab 3:12-14.

107. On the idea of human inimical forces quelled under the model of primal creation-out-of-chaos, see pp. 60-61. The conflation of elements from the creation and exodus traditions in depiction of YHWH as savior in his age-old *modus operandi* in the winds clearly demonstrates this conceptual thought. Although the essence is YHWH's appearance in the wind, there are variations in the description of the phenomenal elements relating the idea in the relevant texts. See pp. 170-71.

108. See Roberts's analysis of an early conception of YHWH as king in the Israelite tradition in Roberts, "Zion," 332-33.

109. See p. 60 above. The reference to the mountain of inheritance, or sanctuary where YHWH chooses to dwell in Exod 15:17 reflects the Davidic-Zion theology

midst (vv. 3, 17–18). This image depicted in Exod 15:1–18 reflects, the composite theme, though in reverse order, of the kingship-*Chaoskampf*-(Zion) temple guaranteeing social order for his people.[110] Though Zion is not designated as YHWH's temple in Exod 15, the terms "mountain of your inheritance"//"your abode" (בהר נחלתך/מכון לשבתך, Exod 15:17) mentioned in parallelism are suggestive. However, the temple or abode motif is linked to YHWH's eternal divine kingship, which is asserted by the verse concluding this hymn: "May YHWH reign forever" (יהוה ימלך לעלם ועד, Exod 15:18) in corollary to the kingship-temple theme.

Although inflected with a plethora of motifs, Ps 97 expresses the composite kingship-*Chaoskampf*-temple theme. Vv. 1–2, 3–5 and 7a relate to YHWH's appearance as king with the wind-driven phenomenal elements—clouds, thick darkness, and fire[111]—to combat and debase the wicked, or idol worshipers. Subsequently, the reference in v. 8 to the joy that sweeps Zion, in essence, alludes to the idea of celebration of the rule of YHWH at his temple. Moreover, the immediate connection of the kingship of YHWH (יהוה מלך) in v. 1, his "throne" (כסא) in v. 2, and Zion in v. 8 represent the kingship-temple theme. Despite lack of sequence, the parallelism of Ps 97:1 and 2 and/or v. 8, that is, YHWH reigns//throne and/or Zion (יהוה מלך//כסא and/or ציון) reflects the divine kingship-temple theme found in Exod 15. Therefore Ps 97 assumes a theological thrust, which emerges with Israel's preexilic history, as it is preserved in Exod 15:1–18. But Ps 97 goes beyond in expressing righteousness inflecting the rule YHWH establishes to guarantee "social order," in keeping with the elements of righteousness and justice, as the basis of the foundation of his throne.

In the light of the above, Ps 97 definitively outlines the interrelation of the three roles of YHWH as warrior, king and judge marked by his appearance with the phenomenal effects of the wind, in emphasis of his insurmountable position in Israel's history of salvation. YHWH's conquest of inimical forces (v. 3), and the subjection of the image-worshipers and their idols (v. 7) reflect his role as warrior.[112] The acclamation of his sovereignty (v. 1; cf. v. 5b) and the subservience of all the gods[113] in-

---

expressing the tension between YHWH's establishment of his temple oriented towards YHWH's founding of the earth to guarantee social organization.

110. See pp. 60–61.

111. See pp. 169–70.

112. See p. 232.

113. As already pointed out by biblical commentators, Israel absorbed ideas about

dicate his role as the sovereign king. Though subordinate to the latter, YHWH's image as judge is substantiated by reference to "righteousness" and "justice,"[114] which form the basis of his rule and inform his just judgments. As implied in the text, the realization of YHWH's rule and judgments evokes joy in Zion, and causes the cities of Judah to celebrate.[115] The phrase "Zion hears and rejoices" (v. 8), in its preterit form, emphasizes that the cause of celebration is an accomplished act, but one that is in fact contemporized: the hostile powers are overthrown, thus Zion remains secure and attests to YHWH's power to save. Unquestionably, the theme echoed here is the inviolability of Zion. Its establishment is as firm and secure as YHWH's creation of the earth.[116] YHWH employs the winds to subdue the primal chaotic forces at the creation of the earth, and notable here in Ps 97:2–3, the phenomenal winds with the accompanying natural elements are wielded for judgment on inimical forces militant to YHWH's rule among his people and in Zion.[117] So, YHWH founded Zion and remains its protector and guide in dispensing judgments (vv. 7, 10b).[118] The assurance of divine protection is elaborated as deliverance of the "righteous" from the "wicked" (v. 10c). Again, in view of such feats, it is appropriate, therefore, to translate definitively the formula YHWH *mālāk*, "YHWH is king," as an affirmation and confession of the perpetual saving activities of the divine warrior, judge and king who is exalted "above all the earth and all the gods."

Based on this analysis, it is evident that the fundamental theme of Ps 97 is that of salvation in connection with YHWH's images as warrior, judge and king. Unquestionably, Ps 97 unveils the deity, who not only controls nature but also reveals himself in history through the phenomenal effects of his potent winds. The subjugation of enemies by the

---

the existence of other gods. However, it is significant that in Ps 97 the existence of other gods is expressed in the context of YHWH's ability to dispense justice, thus giving an impression of his chief position among the gods in the divine council as presented in Ps 82 (cf. Deut 32:8; Ps 29:1).

114. The prophet Amos also stresses that these elements (Amos 5:24) should characterize the life of YHWH's people as devotees of this deity who "roars" from Zion (1:2).

115. See Ps 48:12[11].

116. See p. 60.

117. See p. 60. YHWH unleashes the winds deployed to subdue chaos at the creation of the earth for the destruction of inimical forces in establishing social order among his people.

118. See Ps 48:11–15[10–14].

fire-hewing winds, and, consequently, the jubilation in Zion are proof of YHWH's kingship, and evidence of the unfolding plan of salvation for his people. Therefore, this psalm, which begins with the proclamation of YHWH as king, with a theophany and subjugation of inimical entities in sequel, and concludes with an exhortation to praise as a result of YHWH's intervention, may only be classified as "proclamation of salvation"[119] and not as "enthronement."[120] This suggests that the background of Ps 97 is the celebration of YHWH's imperial rule based upon victories achieved for Israel amid the nations and their deities. Hence, Ps 97 asserts the kingship of YHWH above other gods, and ridicules the latter as they cannot move, and are nonentities. But YHWH is capable of motion by his potent winds, and the heavens declare his might and majesty in theophanic radiance, as the lord of all the earth (vv. 4–5b).[121] In that respect, it is imperative to consider the true nature and purpose of Pss 47, 93, 96, 98–99, in dismissing any conjecture of an enthronement of YHWH, based on the evidence presented in Ps 97.

Psalm 97 in Relation to Psalms 47, 93, 96, 98–99 in Celebrating YHWH's Kingship *contra* a Cultic Enthronement of YHWH

Psalm 47—YHWH Arises to and from His Throne

Among the so-called enthronement psalms, Ps 47 is claimed to reflect cultic acts that are interpreted in support of the hypothesis of a yearly renewal of YHWH's kingship, as previously postulated by Mowinckel. However, the inconsistency of the enthronement hypothesis is indicated by the divergent interpretations offered by its proponents. Mowinckel also bases the idea of YHWH's enthronement on the comparison with Baʿal's victories against Mot and his subsequent assumption of kingship, the renewal of which is represented by Baʿal's dying and rising cycle.[122]

---

119. The message of salvation implied in Ps 97 (among others) has led some critics to assume a dependence on Deutero-Isaiah, since the theme of salvation for Israel is central to his prophecies.

120. The idea of "enthronement" implies the accession to a throne of one who previously has not been king, or at least (according to the cultic-mythical drama) the reinstitution of kingship occasionally lost (see Janowski, "Königtum Gottes," 426–27). As is evident in Ps 93:2, YHWH's kingship is of old and is eternal. That implies that there has not been a time YHWH ceased to be king to call for his reinstitution.

121. See Jer 10:10–16.

122. Mowinckel, *Psalms in Israel*, 118–25. In contrast, Gaster emphasizes that the

PROCLAMATION OF YHWH AS KING IN THE WIND

Loretz, on the other hand, sees YHWH's enthronement as illuminated by the Baʻal/Yam fight which ends with Baʻal's victory and accession to power. Thus, Loretz regards the proclamation *Yhwh mlk* as parallel with the Ugaritic *ym lmt bʻlm ymlk* (KTU 1.2.IV:32 [=CTA 2.iv:32]).[123] As is clear in the Ugaritic texts, this formula appears in the context of Baʻal's victory over his rival, the sea-god, Yam. Moreover, Loretz considers the parallelism of *ʻlh* and *ytb* in the Baʻal text KTU 1.10.III:11–14[=CTA 10.iii:12–15] as relating to Baʻal's "ascent" to his throne, and his "sitting down" as indicating the beginning of his kingship at the New Year festival.[124]

Yet, it seems from the text in question that only Baʻal's procreational activity, as another aspect of his kingship, accentuated by the epithet Baʻal son of Dagan (*bʻl bn dgn*), is at issue. In this text (KTU 1.6.1:50–52[=CTA 6.1:50–52]), the god El insinuates a god of fertility, or rain, for a substitute ruler in place of Baʻal, as one possessed of strength and capable of controlling the wind and lightning. Nonetheless, Loretz deduces from the Ugaritic evidence that the use of *yšb* or *šbt* in the Hebrew tradition is

---

events described in Ps 47, though attenuated, assume the result of a victory of the sea over the dragon (Gaster, *Thespis*, 451), meaning the triumph of Baʻal over Yam. Jeremias, on the other hand, considers Ps 47 an "enthronement psalm," although not expressing the beginning of the dominion of YHWH nor an investiture act. Instead, he sees its depiction of events as celebrating YHWH's seizure of Zion and therewith the beginning of his sovereignty as the universal king (Jeremias, *Königtum Gottes*, 65).

123. Loretz also finds the proclamation *Yhwh mlk*, in parallel to *ymlk ʻṯtr ʻrẓ*, a declaration of the rule of the god Athtar when he is appointed king at the death of Baʻal (KTU 1.6. I:55[=CTA 6.i:55]; Loretz, *Ugarit-Texte*, 13–14). If this is a possible parallel which indicates proclamation of lordship and is, as Loretz conjectures, an enthronement formula, then that would suggest that there was more than one enthronement festival celebrated at Ugarit. It may also be pointed out that the terminology Loretz mentions as peculiar to the enthronement of Baʻal also occurs in the Ugaritic text relating to Athtar's assumption of power after the death of Baʻal:

ymlk ʻṯtr ʻrẓ
'Let Athtar the terrible be king!'
ʼapnk. ʻṯtr ʻrẓ
Thereupon Athtar the terrible
yʻl. bṣrrt. Ṣpn
went up into the recesses of Zaphon;
ytb. lkḥṯ [.]
he sat on the seat of
ʼalʼiyn bʻl
mightiest Baʻal
(KTU 1.6.I:55–58[=CTA 6.i:55–58]).

See Gibson, *Canaanite Myths*, 75–76.

124. Loretz, *Ugarit-Texte*, 11.

also connected with being "enthroned."¹²⁵ He further modifies and elaborates his interpretation of the enthronement hypothesis by drawing on Mowinckel's thesis of the myth of the dying and rising deity in explication of the terms that occur in Ps 47. Therefore, Loretz projects into this psalm features similar to the dying and rising of Ba'al symbolized in his conflict with the god of death, Mot.¹²⁶ Hence Loretz states that the cultic myth alluded to in Ps 47:6[5], 9[8] is the return of YHWH, like Ba'al, the rain-bringer, to his throne-seat. Loretz, however, assumes too much influence from external sources in his analysis of Ps 47. There is no indication of YHWH returning from the underworld, nor any mention of his alleged struggle with the god of death, as Loretz maintains. Undoubtedly, all these variations in the interpretation of the psalm merely indicate attempts to reconstruct an enthronement of YHWH, though such an idea is lacking in the Hebrew tradition. Most biblical scholars abandon Mowinckel's hypothesis of an enthronement festival for lack of evidence in support of this idea in the biblical texts. However, an anomaly still lingers in the interpretation of YHWH's enthronement in Ps 47.¹²⁷

Advocates of an enthronement¹²⁸ of YHWH consider Ps 47:2[1], 6[5] and 9[8] to embody cultic notions, which are thought to be illustrative of the cultic enthronement of YHWH at the New Year festival. It is argued that the terms "ascend" (עלה),¹²⁹ the "shout of exultation" (תרועה) and "sound of the ram's horn" (קול שופר) together suggest an enthronement festival. Moreover, the collation of the terms "sit" or "be enthroned" (ישב) and the assumption of royal dominion or "rule" (מלך) in v. 9[8] is thought to indicate the process of YHWH's enthronement. Therefore, it is supposed that a possible cultic act envisaged by the psalm is the enthronement of YHWH, accompanied by festival jubilation. Instead, these

---

125. Loretz, *Ugarit-Texte*, 11.

126. Loretz, *Ugarit-Texte*, 59; see Mowinckel, *Psalms in Israel*, 125, 132–34.

127. Longman still talks of an enthronement but claims not in the same sense suggested by Mowinckel. He argues for the enthronement idea as a figurative celebration of YHWH's greatness and dominion (Longman, *Psalms*, 208–9). DeClaissé-Walford points out that there is no evidence in the OT for an enthronement festival but classifies Ps 47 as an enthronement psalm. DeClaissé-Walford sees this psalm as celebrating the kingship of YHWH as the great king over all the earth similar to the portrayal of Marduk in the Enuma Elish (see DeClaissé-Walford, "Psalm 47," 956–65; *Psalms*, 19).

128. Loretz, Lipiński, Day, Brueggemann, DeClaissé-Walford, et al.

129. According to Mowinckel, YHWH's "ascent" implies his royal ascent or procession in the enthronement festival. Thus, Mowinckel regards the ascent of YHWH to the temple as the focus of this festival (Mowinckel, *Psalmenstudien*, 3–4; *Psalms in Israel*, 171–72).

PROCLAMATION OF YHWH AS KING IN THE WIND

terms have connotations of the movement of winds focusing YHWH's presence, his rule, and the acts of deliverance. For instance, the term עלה[130] can mean "go up, rise" in reference to natural phenomena: cloud,[131] fire,[132] and smoke.[133] In this case, the term עלה implicates YHWH's invisible presence rising in the form of the wind symbolized by the cherubim-throne associated with the ark.[134]

As averred in the main, the cherubim image on the ark is the graphic personification of YHWH's wind.[135] So with the term "going up" (עלה), the same phenomenal element is implied in expression of YHWH's presence in his sanctuary in Zion. Invariably, the *Niphal* form of the verb עלה implies the cloud lifting from above the tabernacle[136] enshrining the ark. YHWH's wind, as the agent propelling the cloud,[137] marks the ensemble of YHWH's invisible presence.[138] Hence, the *Hiphil* form of עלה relates YHWH's act wielded by his potent winds in bringing up the people of Israel out of Egypt at the exodus,[139] which is foundational to YHWH's demonstration of power. Therefore, the Psalmist recites the people's call of distress,[140] to which YHWH responds in the "secret place of thunder" for the deliverance of the captives (Ps 81:7–8[6–7]c). It has been established that the reference to thunder in this context alludes to YHWH's appearance with the sonorous wind[141] to break the bondage of captivity. To that end, YHWH appears with his potent winds in demonstration of

---

130. BDB 748. The same term is employed to express a figurative image of YHWH's potent roaring winds as a lion going up from its thicket to attack Babylon for the deliverance of Israel (Jer 49:19a=50:44a). See Fuhs, "עָלָה," 83. See also p. 151 above.

131. See 1 Kgs 18:44; Jer 4:13.

132. See Judg 6:21.

133. See Exod 19:18.

134. Exod 25:18–22; see Ps 99:1, 5b.

135. See pp. 81–82 above.

136. Exod 40:36; Num 9:17; 10:11; cf. Exod 40:37; Num 9:21–22. Also, Fuhs discusses scholars' views on the use of formulas involving the verbs ʿālâ and yāṣāʾ alluding to the event of deliverance at the exodus. He observes the association of the formula obtaining the *Hiphil* form of ʿālâ with the tabernacle in expression of the deliverance from captivity and the occupation of the promised land (Fuhs, "עָלָה," 85–86).

137. Jer 10:13b; Job 36:29a. See pp. 84, 104–5 above. YHWH causes the clouds to rise and scatters them by his winds. Hence, YHWH is contrasted with the idols that cannot bring rain (see Ps 135:7).

138. Ps 105:39; Exod 13:21.

139. Lev 11:45; Josh 24:17; Judg 6:8; Ps 81:11[10].

140. Cf. Exod 3:7–10.

141. See p. 177.

his power in bringing up (הַמַּעֲלְךָ, Ps 81:11[10]) the captives from the land of Egypt.

Undoubtedly, the reference to YHWH's ascent to Zion using the same verbal root in Ps 47:6[5]a recalls YHWH's age-old *modus operandi* in the wind,[142] in consummation of his promise of deliverance and settlement in the promised land (Ps 105:8–11; see vv. 42–43). Accordingly, YHWH ascends and brings up his people amid jubilant shouts of joy (47:6[5]aβ; see 105:43). The accompanying "sound of the ram's 'horn'" (קוֹל שׁוֹפָר, 47:6[5]b) symbolizes the presence of YHWH's sonorous wind. This idea resonates with the sounds of the Hogon's horn, called "voices," which represent the presence of Amma, and reenact the creative "word" of the whirling *po*, as the sonorous sound of the whirlwind, which brought things into existence in the Dogon cosmology.[143] Similarly, in the biblical Hebrew tradition the sounding of the "*shôfār*" symbolizes the presence of YHWH in the wind (Josh 6:4–5; Zech 9:14).[144] The reference in Zech 9:14 is particularly instructive in that the *shôfār* is associated with "the windstorms of the south wind" (בְּסַעֲרוֹת תֵּימָן) in assertion of the anticipated theophany of YHWH in the potent winds.

Therefore, the shouts of joy accompanying the sound of the *shôfār* in Ps 47, echo the sonorous sound of YHWH's wind,[145] marking his presence and rousing the jubilation of the worshipers in sight of YHWH's victories before the nations (Ps 47:9[8]a; see 105:43–44). Therefore, the idea of YHWH ascending and sitting on his throne as mentioned in Ps 47:6[5]a, 9[8]b, respectively, do not relate an act of investiture. These verses refer to YHWH's occupation of Zion in consummation of his promise for the settlement of his people Israel. Moreover, there is direct evidence in the Hebrew tradition, which shows that the ascent of the ark, representing the invisible enthroned deity, symbolizes YHWH's conquest and occupation of Zion (2 Sam 6).[146] That Ps 47:6[5] is reminiscent of the ascent of YHWH and the occupation of Zion as recounted in 2 Sam 6:15 is indicated by the similar phrasing in the two references:

---

142. Hab 3:6e. See p. 183.
143. See p. 17, 17n96.
144. Cf. 2 Sam 6:15; 1 Chr 15:28.
145. See 2 Sam 5:24, where the rustling of the wind at the top of the balsam trees compares to the sound of "marching" alluding to horses. Horses are symbolic of YHWH's winds, as noted in Hab 3:8, 15.
146. Pss 24:7–10; 68; 132:8–14; see 1 Chr 15; 16.

PROCLAMATION OF YHWH AS KING IN THE WIND

עלה אלהים בתרועה יהוה בקול שופר
God has gone up with shouting (of exaltation),
YHWH with the sound of the ram's horn
(Ps 47:6[5]).
ודוד וכל־בית ישראל מעלים את־ארון
יהוה בתרועה ובקול שופר
David and all the house of Israel brought the ark of
YHWH with shouting (of exaltation) and the sound of the ram's horn
(2 Sam 6:15).

Whereas the latter deals specifically with the bringing up of the ark (*maʿălîm*)[147] to the city of David, Ps 47 appears to combine two ideas, which represent the "ascent" to an earthly abode in Zion and to the heavenly dwelling of YHWH. Here, the Hebrew tradition holds in tension the conceptual idea of the earthly temple as a microcosm of the celestial temple.[148] The two are inseparably connected: YHWH's subjugation of the nations[149] and the giving of the land (נחלה, as the pride of Jacob, Ps 47:5[4]), which is consummated by YHWH's occupation of Zion, indicate the earthly orientation of events.[150]

Yet, at the same time, the heavenly perspective is evident in that YHWH has vindicated his power over the nations by subduing them and asserting his universal dominion, as the "great king over the whole earth" (Ps 47:3[2], 8[7]). YHWH's title "great king over the whole earth" is in recognition of the boundless power of his winds. Therefore, YHWH is not confined to a singular or specific locality. The gathering of the "princes of the nations" emphasizes this universal dominion of YHWH in acknowledgement of YHWH's imperialistic domination (v. 10[9]a). Thus, both ideas are expositions of YHWH's title *ʿelyôn* ("Most High," v. 3[2]), as

---

147. Seow defines the difference as consisting in the use of the *Hiphil* (causative) of ʿlh in 2 Sam 6 to imply the act of bringing up since the ark represents the deity, whereas in Ps 47, as in Akkadian representations of the deities by divine images, the deity is referred to by name. Thus in Ps 47 it is not specifically the ascent of the ark that is mentioned, but that of YHWH himself (see Seow, *Myth*, 121-23).

148. The idea is asserted more distinctly in Ps 68, where a description of the procession of the ark shows YHWH ascending to his earthly mount of abode (vv. 18-19[17-18]), while at the same time his ascendancy and presence in the heavenly abode, from where he demonstrates his power, is acknowledged (v. 34[33]).

149. It appears impossible to reconcile Schaper's interpretation of Ps 46:4[3] as "the battle of nations" with what the text clearly depicts as YHWH's conquest or more exactly "subjugation" (דבר) of nations for the benefit of Israel (Schaper, "Psalm 47," 267). On the meaning of דבר as "subjugate," see Emerton, "Interpretation," 168-69.

150. Cf. Exod 32:13; Ps 105:44.

being the deity who subdues nations (v. 4[3]), and the king of the whole earth who is "highly exalted" (נַעֲלָה, v. 10[9]b). The idea is in direct correspondence with Ps 97:9 where the conjunction of the title "Most High" over all the earth, and the verb "be highly exalted" expresses the preeminence of YHWH, who in the form of his winds is not localized, and therewith, in a subtle manner, emphasizes the heavenly perspective of YHWH's theophany.[151] Hence, in light of the evidence adduced in Ps 97, the "ascent" of YHWH in Ps 47:6[5] not only personifies his occupation of Zion as his seat of dominion, but also depicts his "ascending to" and (mystical) "sitting down" on his heavenly throne (v. 9[8]) supported by "justice and righteousness" (Ps 97:2).[152] Yet, this conflation of the earthly and heavenly temples holds in tension the boundless nature of YHWH's presence in the guise of the wind in assertion of his universal dominion as the king of the whole earth.

YHWH as Great King over All the Earth in Psalm 47 in View of Other Texts

The liturgical section in Ps 24:7–10 reflects the ark procession underlying the ark narrative of 2 Sam 6:12–19,[153] and throws into bold relief the image of YHWH as king of the whole earth alluded to in Ps 47:3[2],

---

151. See Pss 18:10–12[9–11]; 104:2–4.

152. The two possible meanings of "ascent" to an earthly or to a heavenly abode reflect the interchangeability of the two locations of YHWH's throne. Levenson sees this as one being the counterpart of the other (Levenson, *Sinai and Zion*, 123). Again, on the identification of the heavenly and earthly temple, Mettinger states that the temple marks the place where heaven and earth intersect. He, therefore, asserts that Ps 11:4 is to be understood in light of this background (Mettinger, *Search of God*, 131–33). Moreover, the interchangeability of the two may further be supported by the idea of YHWH's theophany from the heavens (Isa 63:19[64:1]; Pss 18:7–14[6–13]; 97:2–6) or Zion (Amos 1:2; Ps 50:2) as no less identical spheres of his demonstration of power in the winds.

153. The details of the jubilation accompanying the procession of the ark that the redactor of 2 Sam 6 expresses, are recaptured by the Chronicler (1 Chr 16) in his attempt to reconstruct, as Kleinig states, the liturgical act of thanksgiving inaugurated by King David (Kleinig, *Lord's Song*, 135, 142). What appears as the synopsis of the material from different sources of the Hebrew tradition in 1 Chr 16 suggests the exact original historical settings which gave rise to the composition of most of the sources mentioned. In particular, the references to the transportation of the ark under King David (1 Chr 16:1–3 cf. 2 Sam 6:17–19a; 1 Chr 16:43 cf. 2 Sam 6:19b–20a) in addition to a psalm, bearing statements reminiscent to the psalms in discussion and recited during the musical worship, indicate the close connection of the occurrences preserved in these prosaic and poetic narratives.

6–9[5–8]. The terminology used in Ps 24:7–10 suggests the dramatic arrival of the triumphant deity, which makes this liturgical psalm more suitable to David's transfer of the ark. But the key to the interpretation of what Ps 24 presents on the nature of YHWH, is provided by the events surrounding the return of the ark by the Philistines leading to the Kiriath-jearim episode. The question: "Who is this King of Glory?" (vv. 8, 10) finds its resolution in the return of the ark by the Philistines to its people, and YHWH's occupation of the city of David. To begin with, YHWH shows the power of his hand by wreaking havoc among the Philistines. Apart from YHWH's power decapitating the Philistine Dagon, the series of outbreaks of tumors in the Philistine cities bring awareness to the Philistines of the power of YHWH associated with the ark prompting them to send it back. But even upon return to its own people, the ark of YHWH causes distress. YHWH strikes down seventy men of Beth Shemesh for looking inside the ark (1 Sam 6:19). Unquestionably, the point at issue is the ark as signet of YHWH's presence, and the manifestation of YHWH's power associated with it. Again, as with the Philistines, the questions asked by the people of Beth Shemesh in v. 20: "Who can stand before YHWH this holy God? And to whom shall he go up (עלה) away from us?" point beyond this event to that of the nature, and effect, of YHWH's presence among his own people.

Yet, even with YHWH's people, the question of requisite morals still pervades the mind of the Israelite community: "Who can go up (עלה) the mountain of YHWH, and who can stand in the place of his holiness?" as expressed in Ps 24:3. Also, subtly implied here is the idea of right living as the prerequisite to be in the presence of YHWH (Ps 15; cf. Isa 33:14–17a). The tension, however, seems to be resolved by the fact that the Davidic dynasty finds favor in the sight of YHWH. Ps 24:5–6 mirrors the fact that David's daring search and bringing of the ark to Jerusalem incurs favor for him and indicates the return of YHWH's blessing and splendor as savior upon his people. Again, the question as to who can "ascend the mountain of the lord" in Ps 24:3a finds a solution in David's undertaking of the transfer and restoration of the ark to a place of prominence amid YHWH's own people.

It is not coincidental that the battle against the Philistines cited in 2 Sam 5:17–24[154] breaks the narrative and precedes David's transfer of the ark to Zion. The ark is not within sight at this encounter. However,

---

154. Cf. 1 Chr 14:8–17.

this account on the battle against the Philistines mentions YHWH manifesting his presence with the "sound of marching"[155] (את־קול צעדה, 2 Sam 5:24) figurative of the sound of the wind rustling on the top of the balsam trees,[156] in expression of YHWH continuing his involvement in battle, as the savior guaranteeing victory for his people. Notably, this idea throws into sharp relief the conceptual disclosure of YHWH marching ahead of his people and scattering the enemies with his winds.[157] Here, in 2 Sam 5:24, with YHWH in the vanguard, he gives the order to strike the Philistines in battle, and the victory is on account of YHWH's presence in the wind.

In sequel, the notion of YHWH's presence is in fact recapitulated by the "ascent" of the ark of YHWH to the city of David[158] upon the victory against the Philistines. The recital of the discovery of the ark and the procession that brings the ark to Zion in Ps 132:6–8, brings to bear YHWH's occupation of Zion referred to in vv. 13–14.[159] And, at the same time, the text focuses the key element relating the presence of YHWH in the wind. The ark is referred to as the "ark of his might"[160] (132:8b; see 78:61), as the focal point of YHWH's power in the wind. Thus, YHWH is invoked to arise, though not to stir up a battle,[161] but in this case, to occupy Zion, the locale designated as YHWH's "resting place"[162] (מנוחה, Ps 132:8a, 13–14).

---

155. See pp. 199, 199n215, 209 above; Hab 3:12a. The term צעד is used here in reference to YHWH striding the earth in his march in the south wind (see Judg 5:4; Ps 68:8[7]).

156. See 1 Chr 14:14–15.

157. Num 10:35; Ps 68:2[1–2].

158. 2 Sam 6:12–19; 1 Chr 15:25—16:3. The Chronicler gives a more detailed account on King David's preparations, assignment of duties, sacrifices, musical instruments, and psalms/songs for the procession of the ark to Zion.

159. Pss 47:6[5]; 48:3[2].

160. See Day, "Ark," 71.

161. Ps 132:8a; cf. Num 10:35; Ps 68:2–3[1–2].

162. Seow argues that the imperative קומה, which occurs in the traditional formula (Num 10:35) used to summon the ark to battle as a palladium for war, and which reappears in Ps 132:8: קומה יהוה למנוחתך, ought not to be translated as "arise," but as in "come, YHWH to your rest." Seow's proposal is based on the comparison with other uses of this verb in texts where it is translated as an interjection (Exod 32:1; Num 23:18; Judg 18:9). Further, *contra* Hillers who maintains that the preposition ל in Ps 132:8 should be translated "from" in accordance with its usage in Ugaritic, and in agreement with the imperative קומה, which indicates the departure of the divine warrior for battle, and not denoting the deity's return as Hillers suggests. Seow contends that the preposition should be translated "to" since "resting place" (מנוחה) in the Hebrew tradition

PROCLAMATION OF YHWH AS KING IN THE WIND

The significance of the possession of Zion is emphasized by the identification of the nature of the deity: YHWH Ṣebā'ôth "enthroned on the cherubim" (2 Sam 6:2; see Ps 99:1). In accord, YHWH is proclaimed the king of glory, strong and mighty in battle (24:8). Thus, the call for the "gates"[163] to lift their heads and the "ancient doors" to open (24:7, 9), highlights the defensive structures that are part of the ancient Jebusite fortress, which David captures and reinforces its defensive structure as his own city (2 Sam 5:9). Furthermore, the call for the gates to raise their heads figuratively emphasizes the grandeur of YHWH's luminous and sonorous wind, which towers over and cannot be confined to the highest heavens, and much less by the structures of the fortified city.[164] Hence, YHWH is acclaimed YHWH *elyôn*,[165] great king over all the earth and highly exalted (Ps 47:3[2], 8[7], 10[9]c).

In addition, the use of the title, YHWH Ṣ*ebā*'ôth ("the lord of hosts") in Ps 24:10 echoes the name of the triumphant warrior-king mentioned in 2 Sam 6:2. Here, YHWH is nominally identified as YHWH Ṣebā'ôth who sits or is enthroned upon the cherubim. With this nominal phrase, the essence of YHWH's potency as the creator,[166] whose power is manifested in the winds, is asserted no less than his martial traits. In

---

often refers to a destination or goal, and not a locale for departure. Thus, Seow proposes to read the phrase as "come, YHWH to your rest" (Seow, *Myth*, 169–71). In contrast to Seow's view, and considering that Num 10:35 implies the scattering of enemies, it is suggested here to translate the imperative קומה to "arise" in connection with a "resting place." The idea implies compelling YHWH, depicted as wind, to move on as the vanguard to the place of settlement (cf. 1 Chr 28:2).

163. In contrast, Cross offers a mythological interpretation in reflection of the battles of Baʻal. Cross states that the phrase, "Lift up, O gates, your heads," as it occurs in Ps 24:7 and 9, may refer to the time when the warrior god returned in victory from war. Therefore, he interprets the "gates" in the Hebrew context as a personification of gate towers, which like the council of the elders or the divine assembly await the return of the divine warrior from war (Cross, *Canaanite Myth*, 97–99).

164. Even before and after the existence of the temple in Zion, the Hebrew tradition holds in tension the idea of confining YHWH in an architectural structure. King David is posed with the challenge whether YHWH desires to dwell in a "house of cedar" (2 Sam 7:5–7). Isa 66:1 expresses the subtleties of YHWH's magnificence that cannot be confined: heaven is YHWH's throne, and the earth his footstool. At that, even King Solomon acknowledges the magnificence of the temple he builds for YHWH but paralleled with the oxymoron that the man-made temple will not contain YHWH's presence (1 Kgs 8:27). See Keel, *Symbolism*, 171–72.

165. See pp. 240–41 above.

166. See pp. 121–22, 121–22n282. It is not coincidental that YHWH Ṣebā'ôth is identified with the same title as that of the Ugaritic El, who is known as creator, though the latter has no attestation of disclosure in the winds.

fact, the title YHWH Ṣebā'ôth expresses YHWH's martial characteristics implied in Ps 24:8 and enriches the concept of YHWH as both the creator of the earth and king as celebrated in the prelude (vv. 1–2), and postlude (vv. 7c–10) of the psalm, respectively. Here, too, the Psalmist's rhetorical questions in v. 3 bring into sharp focus YHWH's choice of abode at Zion in apposition with the conditions requisite for ascending YHWH's holy hill (vv. 4–6).[167] However, the rhetorical questions in the remaining verses allude to YHWH's achievements in battle as warrior-king (Ps 24:8ab). The idea relates YHWH's subjugation of chaos[168] at primal creation (vv. 1–2), as much as his overpowering of nations at the establishment of the people of Israel (v. 8c; Ps 47:4[3]).[169] Accordingly, as the creator, everything on earth is YHWH's possession (Ps 24:1), and he has the overarching power and authority to subdue inimical forces not in keeping with his rule (132:18a). Thereby, YHWH exercises his sovereign power over the earth and its inhabitants (Ps 47:8–9[7–8]) lending him victory in warfare over the kings of the earth (v. 10[9]). Perhaps here, too, the Psalmist has in mind YHWH's demonstration of his renown as YHWH Ṣebā'ôth at the shattering of an alliance of kings by the east wind[170] (Ps 48:5–9[4–8]). Consequently, YHWH Ṣebā'ôth is declared the king of "glory," who is mighty in battle (Ps 24:8, 10). In the confessional prayer in 2 Sam 7:18–27, King David muses over YHWH's victories in acknowledgement of YHWH's warrior traits. He identifies YHWH with the title Ṣebā'ôth (2 Sam 7:26–27a) to throw into bold relief the incomparability of YHWH as the God performing "wonders"[171] at the rescue of his elected people as one nation (2 Sam 7:22–23), and settlement in the land of other nations (Ps 47:3–4[2–3]).[172]

In that regard, the ideas presented in the prose narratives of 2 Sam 5, 6 and 7 are generally retained in the liturgical psalms (Pss 24; 47; 132) and form the tenor for their composition. So, Ps 47, often mistaken for relating an enthronement festival of YHWH, expresses an acknowledgement

---

167. See 2 Sam 6:11–12, perhaps indicating the moral uprightness of the household of Obed-Edom (cf. Ps 15).

168. See Longman, *Psalms*, 141.

169. 2 Sam 7:22–24.

170. See DeClaissé-Walford "Psalm 48," 980. It is specifically the east wind, which roils the waters at the exodus (Exod 14:21).

171. See Ps 77:12–13[11–12], 15[14]. The idea of YHWH performing wonders is associated with his acts of deliverance at his disclosure with the winds.

172. Exod 32:13; 2 Sam 7:23; Pss 105:44a; 135:12; 136:21–22.

of YHWH's presence as the king, who performs deeds by his phenomenal winds for the salvation of his people, and takes up his rightful place at Zion, which he has chosen. YHWH's indomitable presence and accession of a choice abode (Ps 47:5–6[4–5]), as implied in the notion of Zion as a "resting place" (Ps 132:8), further undermines the idea of a royal investment or enthronement of YHWH as reenacted by the "ascent" or procession of the ark. Instead, Ps 47 celebrates the kingship of YHWH in light of his saving deeds in favor of Israel, and preserves the tradition of YHWH's all-time establishment of his throne,[173] as the king of the whole earth (v. 10[9]). This idea undermines the depiction of an enthronement of YHWH with the procession of the ark enacting accession to kingship, which conforms to the worship of idols that the Hebrew tradition holds in tension to defy. A close analysis of the group of psalms claimed for the reconstruction of the enthronement of YHWH further indicates the different thrust of these psalms. Undoubtedly, Ps 47 is classified among these psalms on the kingship of YHWH, and relates the liturgical worship of YHWH in acknowledgement of the victories YHWH wreaks by the power of his wind, as he asserts his perpetual kingship among his people.

Psalm 93—King-YHWH's Wind Mightier Than the Waters

Ps 93 throws into stark relief the warrior aspects of YHWH and his preeminence without any allusion to royal investment, or suchlike idea. Right at the outset, this psalm highlights the martial characteristics of YHWH in the grandeur of his winds:

יהוה מלך גאות לבש לבש יהוה עז התאזר
YHWH reigns, he is clothed with majesty,
YHWH indeed is clothed; he girds himself with strength (Ps 93:1).

The verbs "put on" or "clothe" (לבש) and "gird" (אזר) are often used figuratively with abstract nouns in the Hebrew tradition; that is, "majesty" (גאות),[174] "glory" and "splendor" (הוד והדר),[175] "strength" (אז),[176] and

---

173. *Contra* Mowinckel's view (*Psalm Studies*, 1:180, 183–4, 191, 221; *Psalms in Israel*, 171) as well as other biblical scholars (e.g., Brueggemann, Day, DeClaissé-Walford) in support of an enthronement of YHWH.

174. Ps 93:1b; Job 40:10a.

175. Ps 104:1c; Job 40:10b.

176. Isa 51:9a; see Ps 93:1c where the substantive אז occurs with the verb אזר for

"righteousness" (צדקה),[177] as representing garments. Although the Hebrew texts using these terms are of different provenance, they bear the same common theme on the appearance of YHWH in the magnificence of the wind(s). For instance, as already noted for Ps 104:1, YHWH is depicted clothed (לבש) in "majesty" and "splendor," as he appears to subdue the waters of chaos at primal creation. In Isa 51:9–10, the same verb "clothe" (לבש) is employed in conjugation with language influenced by the mythical conflict with the symbols of chaos that are hostile to YHWH's rule. In this context, the prophet entreats YHWH to intervene, using conventional Hebrew terminology expressing YHWH's primeval combat with the chaos monsters. Accordingly, the prophet appeals for YHWH's arm[178] to put on strength (לבשי־עז זרוע יהוה, Isa 51:9) to ensure victory, as in YHWH's redemptive acts of the olden days. Here, the prophet muses over YHWH's age-old *modus operandi* in the winds at the drying up of the Red Sea, and the routing and destruction of Pharaoh symbolized as Rahab,[179] and his army at the exodus (Isa 51:9–10).

Furthermore, in relating a martial setting, Tarazi[180] observes that the verb "clothe" occurs twice in Isa 59:17[181] in a description of YHWH's military apparel at his intervention. YHWH is described as "putting on" righteousness as a breastplate, with a helmet of salvation, and being "clothed" in garments of vengeance. In essence, this militaristic garb represents nothing other than the overwhelming scourge of "YHWH's wind" (רוח יהוה, v. 19). The context anticipates retribution for the wicked

---

emphasis on the power of YHWH. See Ps 65:7[6] identifying YHWH as synonymously "girded with might" (נאזר בגבורה) at the establishment of the mountains, silencing of the roaring of the chaotic seas, and the tumult of the nations.

177. Isa 59:17a.

178. In other biblical references, the "arm of YHWH" is also depicted as a symbol of strength (Job 40:9), and an instrument of deliverance or victory (Ps 98:1). Similarly, YHWH's right hand (ימני, Exod 15:6, 12), which is acclaimed as glorious in power (v. 6), personifies the wind that dries up the Red Sea, and churns the waters causing the Egyptian army to perish in pursuit of the Israelites (v. 10).

179. In Ps 89:11[10], where the significance of YHWH's holy arm is stressed, the victory that YHWH achieves with his "mighty arm" (עז זרוע) is explicitly stated as the crushing of the chaos monster, Rahab, and the scattering of his enemies. The latter effectively alludes to the winds as the inherent force that puts YHWH's enemies to rout.

180. Tarazi, "Exegesis," 140.

181. In this poetic text foreshadowing YHWH's intervention, YHWH's people are rebuked for a plethora of iniquities in spurning justice and righteousness (Isa 59:9, 14), and chided for turning their backs on YHWH (v. 12). Although the events are future oriented, YHWH will punish his people for their deeds of violence (vv. 6–7), and YHWH's vengeance is cast in figures of speech resembling a battle.

PROCLAMATION OF YHWH AS KING IN THE WIND

but redemption for the repentant (vv. 18–20; cf. 11:4). In a similar manner, the use of the verb "gird" (אזר)[182] in Ps 65:7[6] suggests martial connotations in conditions presupposing a battle with primeval chaos. The use of such terminology in Ps 65 indicates that YHWH is girded with "strength" (כח) and "might" (גבורה) representing his potent winds. Consequently, YHWH is equipped with his winds to subdue the roaring sea, the roar of its waves, and, therewith, the tumult of the people comparable to the latter (v. 8[7]).

Furthermore, the same nominal terms employed in Ps 93 to represent YHWH's winds are found in other Hebrew texts expressing a similar notion. In Deut 33:26 the noun "majesty" (גאות) occurs in the context where YHWH's mastery in the winds for the protection of Israel is acclaimed in conjunction with the appellative "rider of the heavens."[183] YHWH is said to appear in "majesty" for the succor and protection of Israel. Here, too, YHWH's ability to protect Israel is attributed to his "ancient arms" (זרעת עולם), symbolic of the winds[184] by which YHWH takes charge in thrusting enemies to demonstrate his power lodged with his eternality (Deut 33:27).

On the other hand, in Ps 68:35[34], both nouns "majesty" (גאות) and "strength" (עז) occur in conjunction with an imperative statement to acknowledge YHWH's power and majesty displayed in the clouds (שחקם). This idea is expressed as a corollary to the triumphant declaration on YHWH's potentiality to give his thunderous (יתן בקולו) and powerful voice (קול עז, v. 34[33]b) in expression of his appearance with the winds.[185] Undoubtedly, the terms "majesty" and "strength" in Ps 68:35[34]b refer to nothing other than YHWH's sonorous winds representative of his magnificence and potent power on display in the skies, which wields victory for his people (v. 36[35]b).

These texts therefore provide the key to the interpretation of the verbs as they appear in Ps 93:1. The verbs "clothe" and "gird" in Ps 93:1, used in conjunction with the abstract nouns "majesty" (גאות) and "strength" (עז) respectively, metaphorically imply that YHWH is clothed

---

182. In the same vein, the Psalmist acknowledges that it is YHWH who "girds" him with might for battle against his foes (Ps 18:40[39]), as YHWH's wind enables him to rout the enemies (v. 43[42]). See pp. 204–5 above.

183. See pp. 27–28, 27–28n196 above.

184. Cf. "ancient ways" (הליכות עולם, Hab 3:6e).

185. See p. 113.

or girded with the potent winds[186] (Ps 104:1–2), as though kitted out in military attire. Indeed, on the basis of his adornment with "majesty" and "strength," that is the winds, YHWH proves his superiority over all the forces of chaos. Therefore, YHWH owns unrivalled power to subdue and bring chaos into order. This idea is appraised by the conjunction of the verbs "rule/reign," "clothe," and "gird" (Ps 93:1), which associate YHWH's age-old dominion (v. 2)[187] with his rendering impotent all forms of the chaotic forces (ים, מים רבים, נהרות,[188] Ps 93:3–4).

Jeremias, who notices the pluralism in the terminology that echoes the personification of the god Yam, interprets the ideas preserved in Ps 93:3–4 in keeping with the language of the whole range of Ba'al's battle with the gods at Ugarit. Thus, Jeremias states that, "Prince Sea" becomes the primeval sea in v. 4; "Judge River/Flood" becomes the primeval floods in v. 3. Jeremias also notes that the "mighty waters" in v. 4 and the "roaring of the waters" in v. 3 retain the idea of the "sons of Asherah" (rbm) the destroyer(?) (dkym, KTU 1.6.V:2–3 [CTA 6.v:2–3]).[189] However, Jeremias' comparison with the sons of Asherah, as rbm, destroys the parallelism of YHWH's battle against the unruly waters with that of Ba'al and Yam. Arguably, as already pointed out in this monograph, the parallelism of the biblical מים רבים ("many waters") with ים ("sea") echoes the mythological representations of the epithets of Yam as ym and 'il rbm (KTU 1.3.III:39 [CTA 3.iii:36]).[190] At the same time, Jeremias' misconception of the Hebrew expression "their pounding" (דכים) as an allusion to the "sons of Asherah," as dkym; possibly translated "pounder of the sea" in Ugaritic, again, destroys the parallelism with the Ba'al/Yam battle he suggests here. So, these terms in Ps 93, echoing the Ugaritic tradition, are employed as a poetic device to emphasize YHWH's greatness over chaotic forces, that YHWH renders impotent for the establishment of

---

186. See pp. 75–76.

187. Cf. Exod 15:18; Jer 10:10ab.

188. All these terms are derivatives reminiscent of the *Chaoskampf* often used in the Hebrew tradition to represent power in opposition to YHWH's rule (Kraus, *Psalms 60–150*, 235; Weiser, *Psalms*, 620). In Ps 24:1–2, however, YHWH is extolled as creator and the world is profoundly established upon these chaotic waters (ימים) and rivers (נהרות).

189. Jeremias, *Königtum Gottes*, 21–22. Here, too, Dahood's interpretation of *rbm* and *dkym* in KTU 1.6.V:2–3 [CTA 6.v:2–3] as epithets of Ba'al, and, consequently, his identification of the biblical counterpart רבים as an adjective referring to YHWH is erroneous. Dahood also objects to the identification of "many waters" in v. 4 with a similar occurrence in Ps 18:17[16] (Dahood, *Psalms*, 2:341).

190. See pp. 166–67.

the cosmos (vv. 3–4; see Pss 24:2; 104:6–9). Therefore, the primary reference in Ps 93 is YHWH's ageless indomitable dominion manifested by the power of his winds against all forms of chaos. So, the poetic tenor of Ps 93 no longer puts emphasis on the battle-kingship-temple theme to reflect the mythical Baʻal/Yam conflict, which leads to victory, kingship and the construction of a palace.[191]

Instead, Ps 93 from the outset acclaims YHWH as king girded with majesty and strength in the guise of the wind. So, YHWH is portrayed poised with his winds against the chaotic waters. Here, the Psalmist mentions the waters "lifting up" their voice and "pounding" (vv. 3–4a) in personification of the sound of the roaring waves of the sea emanating from the raging chaotic waters, which threaten YHWH's cosmic order.[192] However, the lifting up, or roaring of the chaotic waters cannot compare with the commanding and thundering voice of YHWH symbolized by his sonorous wind (Ps 93:4; see 104:7). Therefore, the waters lift up,[193]

---

191. A temple/house is constructed to mark the kingship of Baʻal (KTU 1.4.IV:43–46, 50–51, 62; V:3–9 [=CTA 4.iv:43–46, 50–51, 62; v:65–71]), following the approval of the high god of the pantheon, El. In Babylon a decree for the construction of a temple for Marduk is sequel to his defeat of Tiamat. The sanctuary is the sign of the gods' gratitude to Marduk for alleviating their oppression and the threats imposed upon them by Tiamat (EE VI:49–52, 57–62). See Heidel, *Babylonian Genesis*, 48; Foster, *Before the Muses*, 470–71; Dalley, *Myths*, 262; Thury and Devinney, *Introduction*, 75; Lambert, "Mesopotamian," 53; *Babylonian*, 113; Speiser, "Creation Epic," 34.

192. Reif notes that the primal waters threatened to overpower YHWH's creation, but he set a limit on them (Reif, "Psalm 93," 202). The idea resonates with YHWH's winds setting a boundary on the chaotic waters in Ps 104:3–9.

193. Sylva, "Rising," 475–77. Sylva misses the point by misinterpreting נהרות as a paradoxical hue of YHWH. The נהרות is familiar from the *Chaoskampf* tradition of the ANE but employed as a poetic device to throw into bold relief YHWH's manifestation of power against primal chaos in establishing cosmic order. The lifting up of the נהרות—rivers or waters—is the result of YHWH's winds roiling the waters and causing the pounding and crashing of the waves. Therefore, the comparative *min* prefixed to the thundering or sound[s] (קולת) of waters brings to bear that YHWH's sonorous winds on the waters are mightier and cause this dramatic din. The comparison of the breakers of the sea, meaning its waves that lift up, with YHWH's winds that originate from "on high" (v. 4c; see Pss 18:7c–11[6c–10]; 104:1–3) puts into perspective the antithesis on the thundering from on high causing the thundering and pounding of the waves, which lift up with potentiality to cause chaos. But the sound of YHWH's majestic wind surpasses the sounds of pounding and the breakers (waves) of the sea (93:4). *Contra* Sylva ("Rising," 479–80), Ps 93 appeals to the *Chaoskampf* myth with implication on YHWH subduing chaos by his winds in *medias res* of primal creation. Thus, Sylva's identification of YHWH with the "rivers"—נהרות—and let alone the latter as the "garb" of YHWH, is an exegetical misnomer. See Sylva, "Rising," 479, 481.

impelled by the force of the wind.[194] Even though the "pounding," and the crashing sound of the sea "breakers" (משברי) or waves is pronounced majestic (Ps 93:3–4b), YHWH's majestic (אדיר) sound of the wind on high (v. 4c), affirmatively in the skies,[195] is unsurpassed. Hence, YHWH's wind hovering in the heights transcends the pounding and crashing sounds of the sea waves.[196]

The image presented here reaches over to the cosmogonic conception of primeval chaos or chaotic waters, which YHWH subdues and renders impotent by his winds at the founding of the earth. As already pointed out, this conceptual establishment of the earth is also given definition in Ps 24:1–2. The primeval waters upon which YHWH establishes the earth are identified as the "seas" (ימים, v. 2a; cf. ים, 93:4b) and the "rivers" (נהרות, 24:2b; cf. 93:3). But YHWH subdues these chaotic waters (מים) with his luminous and sonorous wind (104:6–7). The same idea is also preserved in Ps 89, where a protracted comparison of the majesty of the waves is expressed in stark contrast with the power of YHWH's mighty arm. Even though the noun "majesty" (גאות) refers to the raging sea and its waves lifting up (נשא), YHWH's strong arm[197] (v. 14[13]), personifying the wind, is pronounced more majestic and overpowers the roaring waves to a quietus (vv. 10–11[9–10]). That is to say, the establishment of the world is corollary to YHWH's subjugation of the chaotic forces by the might of his wind (vv. 12–13[11–12]).[198]

Likewise, Ps 93:1–5 has recourse to the same theme of YHWH's conquest of the watery chaos by his wind to guarantee the stability of his creation. YHWH's pre-eminence and invincible power over chaos makes the cosmos secure.[199] Hence, the cosmos is firmly established (v. 1c),[200] because of YHWH's overpowering winds alluded to as "strength" and "majesty" lodged with his throne that is established to eternity (93:1b, 2, 4c). YHWH's strength in the wind is unmatched and prevents the surging waters from becoming forces opposing him (vv. 3–4). Hence, in this short poetic hymn, the description of YHWH's triumph over chaotic waters by his phenomenal wind at primal creation is fused with his

---

194. Cf. Reif, "Psalm 93," 209.
195. Pss 68:34[33]; 104:2–3.
196. Cf. Reif, "Psalm 93," 210.
197. See table 1.
198. See p. 60.
199. Cf. Tate, *Psalms*, 479–80.
200. See Ps 96:10b.

victory and continual check of the uproar of (Israel's) historical enemies represented here by the surge of the mythical waters. Perhaps, YHWH's subjugation of the Philistines recounted in 2 Sam 5:20–21[201] resonates with this idea. David describes YHWH's wrath against the Philistines as "breaking out" (פרץ [of YHWH's wind], v. 20) like an outburst of water,[202] and the Philistines flee helter-skelter, abandoning their idols (v. 21). This demonstrates the incontestable outburst of YHWH's rage manifested in the wind compared to the raging Philistines. In this case, by the same means of the wind, YHWH firmly establishes the world to be as secure as is his eternal throne (Ps 93:1), he also subdues the roar or raging of historical foes (2 Sam 5:20). Thus, in keeping with Jeremias's view, although the terminology and ideas transmitted in Ps 93 compare with Canaanite myth, the rehearsal is not about how YHWH obtains kingship over the world, but how his kingship continuously holds up before the threatening power of the rebellious forces since primeval time.

The kingship of YHWH, therefore, is not determined by, or corollary to, his victory over mythological powers as in the other ancient traditions.[203] It follows, then, that the thematic statement *Yhwh mlk* in Ps 93:1 combined with the connotations of "clothe" and "gird" that metaphorically characterize his warrior traits, without any implications of enthronement regalia, emphasize YHWH's eternal kingship and the constant incontestable power of his winds over potentially threatening forces (v. 4). Thus, the throne mentioned in v. 2 and the reference to the "high locale" in v. 4c, suggest YHWH's ancient celestial sphere of dominion, and at the same time reinforces the idea of his enduring transcendence. YHWH's eternal reign, from on high, guarantees the destruction of chaotic forces or scattering of enemies (see Ps 92:9–10[8–9]). However, YHWH's transcendence is held in tension with his presence

---

201. 2 Sam 5:20–21=1 Chr 14:11. This place of contest between YHWH and the Philistine gods becomes of significance to King David, who calls the site Ba'al Perazim (cf. Isa 28:21a), meaning the "Lord who breaks out" (see Gordon, *1 & 2 Samuel*, 229).

202. See Gray, *Psalm 18*, 71.

203. In contrast, Loretz maintains that YHWH's battle with the gods forms the basis of kingship. He further misinterprets the rivers and the sea as demythologized forces that are no longer a threat to YHWH's sovereignty. Instead, Loretz sees the rivers and the sea in a new state where an invitation is extended to give praise to YHWH, as in Ps 98:7–8. Accordingly, Loretz assumes that there has been remodeling of Canaanite vocabulary in Ps 93:1a, b–4 to suit a description of the (reconstructed) preexilic festival of the enthronement of YHWH. He also sees in vv. 2 and 5 an additional postexilic gloss that he thinks serves to express the glorification of the eternal kingship of the world-creator YHWH. See Loretz, *Ugarit-Texte*, 289–92.

and dominion within the terrestrial realm, as implied by the idea of an earthly temple or holy abode. The Hebrew word "house" (בית) mentioned in Ps 93:5b may denote an ordinary house, temple, or palace.[204] Hence, the reference to both YHWH's celestial throne and his earthly temple in vv. 2 and 5 respectively, indicates that spatial dimensions are surpassed as his indivisible presence broadly conceived in the celestial realm is at the same time embodied in the earthly temple.[205] The assertion that "holiness befits your house" in v. 5, links the idea of the earthly throne and abiding presence of YHWH with the temple gate liturgy, which expresses the demands for "holiness" on the part of all who enter the sanctuary to participate in mystical worship in acknowledgement of YHWH's divine presence (Pss 15; 24:3–6).

The main theme of Ps 93, therefore, is the praise of the eternal king YHWH, who is transcendent, yet immanent, and sustains the universal order by keeping all the chaotic forces at bay by his overpowering winds (vv. 3–4). This eternal king, who is enthroned on high from primeval time, comes close to humanity through his "testimonies" (עדות, v. 5).[206] Even though the meaning of "testimonies" for עדות is considered late,[207] the interpretation proposed here, implying YHWH's revealed will and therewith the governing principle of the moral structure of the world,[208] fits well in this context where the kingship of YHWH is expressed in his

---

204. Anderson, *Psalms 73–150*, 669.

205. Pss 5:8[7]; 11:4. See Mettinger, *Search of God*, 131.

206. Kraus holds that עדות refers to law, and on that basis proposes the cultic tradition of the Feast of Tabernacles as the *Sitz im Leben* of Ps 93 (Kraus, *Psalms 60–150*, 236). In contrast, Shenkel, like Dahood (*Psalms*, 2:342), proposes that 'dt be read as a lexical variant 'd (=Ugaritic "dais") for which the meaning "throne" is suggested based on the parallelism of 'd//ks' in KTU 1.16.VI:22–23 [CTA 16.vi:22–23]. This conjecture is only incited by attempts to promote the enthronement hypothesis. It is clear from Shenkel's suggestion that his proposed reading of v. 5a: "Your throne has been firmly established," is intended to repeat the reference to its heavenly counterpart mentioned in v. 2 and, as he asserts, their corresponding stability should be considered as the basis of confidence in celebrating YHWH's victory (Shenkel, "Interpretation," 408–9). Cross translates this term "covenant" and considers it to be archaic (*Canaanite Myth*, 300, 312). The fact that in Ps 93, where the kingship of YHWH is asserted by the means of his power vested in the wind to subdue chaos in establishing cosmic order, the reading of עדות for testimonies is imperative to refer to YHWH's law also revealed at his theophany (Exod 19:16–18) with the phenomenal winds for establishing social order. See Longman, *Psalms*, 335; Ross, *Commentary*, 3:87.

207. Shenkel, "Interpretation," 404. By contrast, Cross points out the use of עדות in traditions considered to be preexilic (Exod 32:15; Pss 78:56; 132:12; Cross, *Canaanite Myth*, 322).

208. Ross, *Commentary*, 3:85.

sustaining of the universal order. So, the sovereign king YHWH gives his people dependable testimonies. The revelation of the law by the sovereign king brings to bear YHWH's kingship linked with YHWH's involvement in the welfare of his people, and the manifestation of salvation deeds by means of the winds. The "testimonies," as YHWH's solemn directives, enable his people to seek sanctity that is in keeping with YHWH's essence of his being, and the demands for entering his holy abode (cf. Ps 24:3–6). It suffices that עֵדוֹת refers to YHWH's self-expression in the social/moral order, which further affirms the essence of his being and the totality of his control of the universe. YHWH's winds keep chaotic forces in check, while his testimonies are dependable for social/moral directives. These "testimonies," which are the medium of YHWH's self-disclosure and the essence of his very being and purpose, offer guidance to prevent social chaos, and the people continuously experience YHWH's salvation in worship at his earthly abode. Hence, holiness ascribed to YHWH befits his invincible kingship for establishing cosmic order for endless days (Ps 93:5). Thus, neither the eschatological interpretation of YHWH's end-time kingship as proposed by Gunkel, nor that of the ritual enactment of the enthronement[209] of YHWH, as Mowinckel, and others[210] purport to find in Ps 93, has any foundation in this psalm. Undoubtedly, Ps 93 celebrates YHWH in mystical worship as the eternal king in view of his potent power manifested in the wind over the chaotic waters, as much as in the social realm in his establishment of a stable cosmic order.

Psalm 96—YHWH the Creator-King in the Wind Distinct from Idols

There are elements in Ps 96 leading to its interpretation as a psalm praising YHWH for his works of salvation as the goal of his intervention, rather than as an expression of an enthronement ritual, as Mowinckel and advocates of the enthronement of YHWH claim. As is clear in the first segment of the psalm, the Psalmist calls for the praise of YHWH for his victory and glorious deeds (vv. 2b, 3b). YHWH's marvelous deeds illustrate the superiority of his power, in contrast with the ineffectiveness of the other gods (vv. 4–5). The Psalmist, therefore, declares that YHWH is to be feared and exalted above all other gods, inasmuch as

---

209. Weiser detects both elements in this psalm (Weiser, *Psalms*, 617–20).

210. E.g., Loretz, Gerstenberger, Brueggemann, Day, DeClaissé-Walford, Tanner.

they are "worthless" gods or mere idols (vv. 4b, 5; cf. 97:7, 9). Once more, YHWH's image as the creator of the heavens is cast in stark contrast with the worthlessness of idols (96:5).[211]

Moreover, YHWH's glory and majesty are displayed in the heavens, as much as his might and beauty in the earthly sanctuary (96:6). Again, YHWH's celestial and terrestrial sanctuaries are alluded to as two sides of the same coin. The Psalmist, here, too, employs terms alluding to YHWH's glory in the wind as in other psalms to show the boundless nature of YHWH's presence beheld in fullness in the skies, yet, at the same time, dwelling in his terrestrial abode. Thus, the latter segment of Ps 96 (vv. 7–13) summons the people and the nations to worship and ascribe "glory" and "strength" to YHWH, bring gifts to his earthly courts (vv. 7–8), and prostrate before his luminous presence (בהדרת־קדש, v. 9). The people are also enjoined to proclaim YHWH's kingship by virtue of his founding the world with an enduring order. Corollary to this, and inextricably linked, are YHWH's fair judgments manifested in his rule of "equity" (v. 10). Even all nature is personified and exhorted to burst into jubilation in acknowledgement of the dawn of YHWH's rule of righteousness and faithfulness: in essence fair judgment (vv. 11–13).

Generally, critics argue that Ps 96 is dependent on Deutero-Isaiah (Isa 40–55) for its formulations and expressions.[212] For instance, the expression "sing to YHWH a new song" (v. 1a),[213] the exhortation to declare the saving deeds of YHWH (v. 2),[214] and the call to nature to praise

---

211. It should be noted that the Chronicler's author places the episode of YHWH breaking out with the winds to route the Philistines, and causing them to abandon their idols (1 Chr 14:11–12; 2 Sam 5:20–21) prequel to the celebratory worship service that King David institutes. Undoubtedly, the Chronicler alludes to the profound experience of YHWH's dramatic intervention with the winds leading to the scattering of the Philistines, and, subsequently, to King David giving the order for the incinerating of the idols the Philistines abandon (Deut 7:5, 25; 2 Sam 5:21, reporting King David and his men collecting the idols, perhaps, as booty). So apropos is a version of Ps 96 (almost verbatim) integrated in King David's psalm/song (1 Chr 16:23–33) expressing the superiority of YHWH over the Philistines's gods. With a note of irony, King David derides the gods of other nations as idols (v. 26a).

212. Kraus even draws parallels between Ps 96:11–13 and Isa 59:19–20; 60:1; 62:11 (Kraus, *Psalms 60–150*, 252). These parallels are, however, based on similar ideas rather than on actual wording (see Ollenburger, *Zion*, 35). Watson lists a number of scholars arguing for the dependence of both Pss 96 and 98 on Deutero-Isaiah (Watson, *Chaos*, 195–96).

213. Cf. Isa 42:10a.

214. See Isa 40:9; 52:7–10.

YHWH as he comes to judge (v. 11)²¹⁵ are held to show affinity with the message and content of Deutero-Isaiah.²¹⁶ For Kraus, this supposed influence from the tradition of Deutero-Isaiah justifies an eschatological background as the basis of the interpretation of Ps 96, and hence the postulation of a postexilic dating for this psalm. However, apart from the one identical parallel in Ps 96:1a and Isa 42:10a, the rest of the citations in Ps 96 only express a similarity of ideas with Deutero-Isaiah. These suggested connections with Deutero-Isaiah are not precisely verbatim to the point of preventing an alternative interpretation of Ps 96, as preexilic from being considered. There are elements in Ps 96:1–2, 4, 6–10 common to texts that scholars generally consider as older poetic traditions. The idea of a "new song" in Ps 96:1a, thought to be typical of Deutero-Isaiah (Isa 42:10a), is also found in the royal lament in Ps 144 where King David expresses his praise to YHWH for renewing his acts of deliverance (Ps 144:9–10). On one hand, the verb "declare" or "bring good news" (בשר, 96:2), also ascribed to Isaianic influence, occurs in narrative texts referring to the victories wrought by YHWH in the Davidic era.²¹⁷ The verb בשר is a common one in Ugaritic²¹⁸ where it also expresses the meaning "bring news" (cf. KTU 1.10.III:33–34 [=CTA 10.iii:34–35]; KTU 1.19. II:37 [CTA 19.ii:86]).

Furthermore, with the exception of the conjunction כי at the beginning of Ps 96:4a, the idea of the eminence of YHWH, that inspires reverence, or his worthiness to be praised, seems to have been taken verbatim from Ps 48:2[1]aß. The "fearsomeness" of YHWH in comparison with all other gods, stated in the next clause of Ps 96:4, implies the existence of other gods in keeping with earlier traditions, and that is in stark contrast to the exclusive monotheism of Deutero-Isaiah.²¹⁹ On the other hand, the apposition of nouns "strength and glory" (עז ותפארת) in v. 6b alludes to the ark²²⁰ as implied by the occurrence of terms in Ps 78 in the depiction of the ark going into captivity (vv. 60–61; see 1 Sam 4:4–11). The

---

215. See Isa 44:23; 49:13; for Ps 96:12; cf. Isa 44:23; 55:12; Ps 96:13; cf. Isa 40:10.

216. Jeremias observes these connections for both Pss 96 and 98, but asserts that for Ps 98 parallels may no longer be taken as coincidental; thus he points out that Ps 98 adopts the message of this exilic prophet (Jeremias, *Königtum Gottes*, 126).

217. See 2 Sam 18:19.

218. Dahood, *Psalms*, 2:357.

219. See Day, *Psalms*, 72.

220. The idea suggests a preexilic provenance of Ps 96 (Day, *Psalms*, 72–73; "Ark," 71).

same terms appear in Ps 132:8(=2 Chr 6:41aß) in relation to the transfer of the ark to Jerusalem. Therefore, the allusion to the ark in Ps 96:6b has implications for the ark enshrined in the sanctuary.[221] Also, the term "splendor" (הדר) employed in Ps 96:6a, characterizing the presence of YHWH, recalls in part the reference to the splendor of YHWH's "voice" in Ps 29:4b, which is another text assigned early provenance.[222] Yet, as a whole, the reference to YHWH's "splendor and majesty" (הוד־והדר) in Ps 96:6, suggests the elements familiar from earlier traditions depicting YHWH's grandiose appearance with the winds (Ps 104:1c; Job 40:9-10).[223]

Furthermore, Ps 96 bears elements common from older traditions exalting YHWH in his greatness displayed at his theophany. The command to praise in Ps 96:7 compares with Ps 29:1, with the exception that the "tribes of the nations," who are summoned to extol YHWH (96:7a), replace the "sons of the gods" (Ps 29:1a). The ascription of glory to "his name" in the first half of Ps 96:8 echoes Ps 29:2a verbatim. But the second half Ps 96:8 mentions the act of "bringing offering" (נשא מנחה) and reflects the expression of allegiance of pacified nations as in 2 Sam 8:2, 10–12. The call to pay homage to YHWH on account of "the splendor of (his) holiness" (בהדרת־קדש) in Ps 96:9a reiterates verbatim the depiction of YHWH's theophany in Ps 29:2b. As Cross states in relation to the occurrence in Ps 29, the Hebrew *hdrt* has a parallel in Ugaritic where it is used synonymously with the word "vision" (*ḥlm*; KTU 1.14.III:155 [CTA 14.iii:155]).[224] In light of that context, Cross proposes a meaning "apparition" or "revelation" to express the idea of YHWH's presence in Ps 29. Thus, he sees the proper rendering of the Hebrew phrase *bhdrt qdš* in Ps 29:2b as "in (the presence of) his holy splendor," and as indicating a theophany.[225]

---

221. In light of the Chronicler's account, the reference here might be to the tent King David pitched for the ark (1 Chr 16:1).

222. Most scholars (e.g., Cross, Freedman, Tate, Watson) date Ps 29 to the preexilic period. Cross subscribes to the tenth century BCE for the provenance of this psalm (Cross, *Canaanite Myth*, 152). Tate argues for a preexilic date along with other kingship psalms (Tate, *Psalms*, 505–6). Watson discusses the preexilic provenance of the psalm in light of other biblical texts (Watson, *Chaos*, 38–43).

223. In this context of YHWH's theophany, Job is challenged to deck himself not only with "majesty and grandeur" (גאון וגבה), but also with "splendor and majesty" (הוד והדר) that characterizes YHWH's appearance in the (whirl)wind. See pp. 75–76.

224. In this text the god El appears to Keret in a "dream" and "vision," and in a sense both words indicate that the deity has revealed himself (Cross, *Canaanite Myth*, 152–53n28).

225. Cross, *Canaanite Myth*, 153; Ackroyd, "Notes," 395. Along the same line of

PROCLAMATION OF YHWH AS KING IN THE WIND

In the Chroniclers account[226] of King David's transfer of the ark to Zion,[227] the entire colon occurring verbatim in Pss 29:2b and 96:9a, and bearing the phrase "in his holy splendor," also occurs in King David's psalm[228] of thanksgiving as an imperative to worship YHWH (1 Chr 16:29c). This exhortatory call to worship YHWH follows the placement of the ark in a tent King David pitched in Zion (1 Chr 16:1–2). Therefore, the occurrence of the same phrase in Ps 96:9a, as well as in Ps 29:2b appropriately refers to the visible representation of YHWH's presence associated with the ark as found in 1 Chr 16. The subsequent directive on the earth to tremble before YHWH (Ps 96:9b=1 Chr 16:30a) recalls the common reaction of animate and inanimate nature at the impact of YHWH's wind (cf. Exod 15:14; Pss 99:1; 114:7). Accordingly, the "writhing" or "whirling" (חיל) of the whole earth echoes the traditional reaction caused by YHWH's theophany in the wind(s) as in Pss 29:8,[229] 77:17[16]b,[230] 97:4b, and Hab 3:10a.[231] Undoubtedly, the call on the whole earth to writhe in Ps 96:9b[232] in sequel to the mention of the splendor of (his) holiness brings into sharp focus YHWH's power manifested in the wind symbolized by the ark. Furthermore, the series of imperatives on

---

thought as Cross, Ackroyd argues that the terms with the verbal root הדר mean splendor or glory, and sees the terms כבד and הוד appearing in the same context to imply majesty. Therefore, Ackroyd objects to a meaning that suggests actual garments or ornament, on the basis of his survey of the use of the Hebrew הדר and its derivative, הדרה. Ackroyd argues on the basis of the Keret text, which refers to the revelation of a god, and is expressive of divine presence and evoking awe. The Hebrew terms are expressive of the same sense of a realization of presence. Therefore, Ackroyd notes that it is more plausible that the terms imply "holy splendor" with reference to YHWH, whose presence, as implied by the verb "bow down" (שחה, v. 9a), demands reverence and awe on the whole world. See Ackroyd, "Notes," 394–95. Hamilton also argues for the meaning "presence" implied by the word *hdrt* (Hamilton, "Hādār," 208). In that case, the preference for the translation "adornment, ornament, array" maintained by advocates of an enthronement festival is an anomaly (see Warmuth, "הָדָר," 340).

226. Begg discusses the Chronicler's account focusing the prominence of the ark, its dependence on the Ark narrative of 2 Sam 6 for the account of the transfer of the ark from Keriath-jearim to Jerusalem, its omission, and inclusion of content on King David's rulership (Begg, "Ark," 133–45).

227. See Begg, "Ark," 135–37.

228. Nielsen discusses the composite nature of 1 Chr 16 from portions of verses from Pss 96, 105, and 106 (Nielsen, "Whose Song?," 329, 330).

229. See pp. 286–87.

230. See pp. 178, 190, 190n165.

231. See p. 190.

232. Ps 96:9b=1 Chr 16:30a; *contra* DeClaissé-Walford, who translates writhing in relation to YHWH's birthing of the earth (DeClaissé-Walford, *Psalms*, 29).

the animate and inanimate constituents to react to YHWH's presence in the latter part of both Ps 96 and 1 Chr 16 imply YHWH's dramatic self-disclosure in the wind. That YHWH's wind is not in question may be suggested by the note of commotion in nature in the imperatives in Ps 96:11–12 and 1 Chr 16:31–32 for the sea and its fullness to thunder or roar, and the forests to give a ringing cry, howling sound or sing from the aeolian waves.

There are only slight differences in the subject of the imperatives. In the Chronicler's psalm, the call is on the heavens and earth to join in the jubilation (1 Chr 16:31a). This occurs upon the declaration of YHWH's establishment of the world and his guarantee for its stability (v. 30b). So the heavens and the earth are subject to the subsequent imperatives, and are personified to declare YHWH's kingship among the nations (v. 31b). But, in Ps 96 the call is on Israel and the clans of the nations to declare YHWH's firm establishment of the world (v. 10ab). The declaration about YHWH's stable world in Ps 96, is followed by an additional statement on the nature of YHWH's inaugurated rule of equity (v. 10c). Also, the Psalmist's imperative call on the heavens and earth to burst into a joyful din is juxtaposed with that to the sea and its fullness (v. 11). The injunction to the fields and forest to join the jubilation follows later (v. 12). In the Chronicler's psalm the objective for YHWH's appearance for judicial purposes is a truncated version of Ps 96:13[233] but appended to the idea of the joyful din of the fields and trees of the forest as its causal nexus (1 Chr 16:33). Albeit these subtle differences in the Chronicler's psalm and Ps 96, the exhortatory call to declare the kingship of YHWH is linked to the affirmative statement on YHWH's establishment of the world, which is firm and secure. So, in essence, YHWH's creative power in the wind, by which he subdues chaos at creation, is evoked as the means by which YHWH ushers in his rule of equity. To this, the whole of nature, as though animate, is enjoined to resound YHWH's power made manifest, as he institutes this new world/social order as the king among the nations.

It is evident that the leitmotif of Ps 96 is YHWH's self-manifestation for judgment resulting in salvation, which is the cause for exhortation to praise YHWH as the king, as seen in the case of the theophany text in Ps 97. As pointed out, the elements of a theophany with the wind are quite distinct in Ps 96:6 and 9, and analogous to YHWH's phenomenal

---

233. Ps 96:13 expands on the nature of YHWH's rule characterized with righteousness and faithfulness.

disclosure in the winds as described in Pss 104 and 29,[234] respectively. The Psalmist depicts the nature of the king who comes for judgment by juxtaposing the same terms "splendor and majesty" employed in Ps 104:1–2 to represent YHWH's image in the guise of the wind with the founding of the heavens (Ps 96:6a and 5b, respectively). Again, YHWH's potentiality to judge the people with equity is asserted and guaranteed by the stability of the world order that YHWH himself firmly establishes (v. 10). The idea is corollary to the injunction to worship YHWH "in the splendor of (his) holiness" (v. 9a). This nominal phrase evokes YHWH's theophany in the winds as implied by the trembling of the whole earth before him (v. 9b).[235] Ironically, this deity, who shakes [the foundation of] the earth at his self-disclosure in the winds (Ps 96:9b; 97:4b), also maintains world order (Ps 96:10c, 13cd). Hence, this description of the disruption of nature is concomitant with a declaration of YHWH as the king (יהוה מלך), who safeguards the stability of the world, and ensures universal order by imposing his rule of "equity" (מישרים, v. 10c).[236]

The subsequent call for worldwide jubilation in recognition of YHWH's reinstitution of social order in Ps 96:10–13 is expressed in terminology also found in Ps 97. The verbs "be glad" (גיל) and "rejoice" (שמח) in Ps 97:1 appear in conjunction in Ps 96:11 to underscore the effectiveness of YHWH's fair judgment that evokes jubilation even from inanimate constituents. The sea resounds by lifting its waves in response to YHWH's roiling winds, while the fields and trees of the forest rustle comparative to jubilant singing (see 1 Chr 16:33). The call to personified nature in Ps 96:11b–12, purports to exalt YHWH not only as the creator in acknowledgement of his creatorship in vv. 5b and 10b, but also throws into bold relief the certainty of YHWH's presence in the guise of the wind in assertion of his sovereignty as king and judge.[237]

YHWH's sovereignty as king and judge is substantiated by reverting to the idea of the exercise of YHWH's rule (שפט, Ps 96:13), which

234. See pp. 75–76 above 285 below, respectively.
235. See Pss 18:8[7]a; 104:32a.
236. See Ps 99:4.

237. Gray sees the connection of YHWH's kingship with creation and judgment as the distinguishing feature of Ps 96 as an enthronement psalm (Gray, *Biblical*, 68). But the worldwide perspective of this psalm calling families of nations to worship YHWH in desertion of their gods, ridiculed as idols, deters any suggestions of an enthronement festival of YHWH. The latter would essentially place the ark alluded to here, as the central artifact of a ritual replicating the practices of the religions the Hebrew tradition polemicizes.

corresponds to YHWH's performance of juridical acts (ידין) in v. 10.²³⁸ Hence YHWH's governance ushers in "righteousness" (צדק) and "truth" (אמונה, v. 13), of which the former is metaphorically a supporting feature of his throne (see Ps 97:2). The institution of just order in Ps 96:13, if read in the preterit and interpreted along with v. 10, as sequel to YHWH's self-disclosure in v. 9, indicates that the execution of judicial acts is already realized. As a matter of fact, YHWH's intervention and judgment should be deemed as the acts of salvation that the Psalmist wishes to be the subject of his proclamation in vv. 2–3, in acknowledgment of YHWH's universal dominion. The nature of this inaugurated state of justice that occasions this exaltation of YHWH is not immediately apparent in this psalm.

At any rate, it may be presumed on the basis of other psalms (Ps 144:9-10; cf. 33:3; 40:3) that the "victory" (ישועה, 96:2) or "wondrous deeds" (נפלאות, v. 3) accomplished in the sight of other nations, which mark the renewal of salvific deeds, overtly incite this "new song" in praise of YHWH.²³⁹ In any case, the terminology associated with the ark representing YHWH's "strength and glory" (עז ותפארת)²⁴⁰ and "the splendor of (his) holiness" (בהדרת־קדש) mentioned in Ps 96:6b and 9a evokes an occasion linked with the ark tradition, and, therewith, alludes to a period before the exile. The Chronicler's citation of this psalm in his narrative

---

238. Mafico points out that the roots *dyn* and *špṭ* as synonyms in Hebrew correspond to the parallel use of *dyn* and *ṭpṭ* in Ugaritic texts (e.g., KTU 1.16.IV:33–34 [CTA 16.iv:33–34]; KTU 1.17.V:7–8 [CTA 17.v:6–8]; Mafico, "Judge," 1105). The biblical meaning, however, is determined by the context, though the general implication is the dispensation of justice.

239. The liturgical function of this psalm is assumed by the Chronicler's attempt to reconstruct and incorporate this psalm into an account of the transfer, installation of the ark, and the subsequent liturgical worship (1 Chr 16). The content of Ps 96 and 1 Chr 16 is comparable, and in some cases stated verbatim: for 1 Chr 16:23 cf. Ps 96:1b, 2b; 1 Chr 16:24 cf. Ps 96:3; 1 Chr 16:25 cf. Ps 96:4; 1 Chr 16:26 cf. Ps 96:5; 1 Chr 16:27a cf. Ps 96:6a; 1 Chr 16:28 cf. Ps 96:7; 1 Chr 16:29aβ cf. Ps 96:8aβ; 1 Chr 16:29c cf. Ps 96:9a; 1 Chr 16:30 cf. Ps 96:9b, 10b; 1 Chr 16:31aβ cf. Ps 96:11aβ; 1 Chr 16:31c cf. Ps 96:10a; 1 Chr 16:32a cf. Ps 96:11c; 1 Chr 16:32b cf. Ps 96:12aβ; 1 Chr 16:33a cf. Ps 96:12c; 1 Chr 16:33bc cf. Ps 96:13aβ. Kleinig argues for the composite psalm in 1 Chr 16:8-33 of which a version of Ps 96 is a part (1 Chr 16:23–33), as designed for liturgical praise or thanksgiving to YHWH (Kleinig, *Lord's Song*, 144–48). There is no similar psalm embedded in the ark narratives in 2 Sam. But its use for (celebratory) worship at King David's installation of the ark in Zion suggests that the Chronicler's composition of this psalm precedes the exilic period, and preserves the narrative on the establishment of the elect in the land of promise.

240. Day translates "splendor" (Day, "Ark," 72).

suggests the context of daily liturgical praise of YHWH for the victories[241] won in the Davidic period[242] (1 Chr 16:37–41; cf. Ps 96:2). Here, the acknowledgement of YHWH's presence represented by the ark in his sanctuary, presumably Zion,[243] is expressed in one breath with his universal rule of all the people in the world YHWH established. Thus, in Ps 96, YHWH's universalistic manifestation in the wind is asserted by the call to all families of the nations of the debased idols (see Ps 97:7) to worship YHWH as the creator-king. This inauguration of YHWH's imperialistic rule is complemented with the cosmic jubilation evoked with images of the heaven and earth called to whistle; comparable to singing, the sea, and everything in it to resound with the roaring wind, and the fields and trees of the forest to rustle in response to YHWH, in the guise of the wind, appearing to establish his rule of righteousness and social order. Ps 98 echoes the same themes, and exhorts praise for YHWH, who discloses himself through righteous deeds in the face of the nations.

Psalm 98—King YHWH's Wind Wrought Salvation

The introductory stitch in Ps 98, inscribed in jussive form, compels for a declaration of YHWH's marvelous deeds that are already accomplished, in fulfillment of "his faithfulness" (אמונתו, v. 3; cf. 96:13cd). These deeds are attributed to the might of his right hand and holy arm, as personifications of YHWH's wind. Therefore, Ps 98, like Ps 96, is an imperative hymn, and both begin with the exhortation to sing a "new song" to YHWH. Despite phrases that are seen to be literally identical on the invocation to sing a new song,[244] and compelling the sea and its fullness,

---

241. See 1 Chr 14; 8–17; 2 Sam 5:6–25.

242. Nielsen, "Whose Song?," 335.

243. Although the Psalmist prescribes day-to-day worship (see Ps 96:2; 1 Chr 16:23), it is also possible that this celebration of YHWH's deeds of salvation takes place at the three festivals: the Passover, festivals of Weeks or Harvest, and Tabernacles ordained by YHWH (Deut 16:1–17; Lev 23:4–8, 15–21, 33–43; Num 28:16–25, 26—29:39). Here, YHWH gives an injunction to "rejoice" (שמח, Deut 16:11; Lev 23:40) in celebration of the festivals commemorating YHWH's salvation deeds at the place designated for YHWH's name, where the worshipping community is inclusive of foreigners (Deut 16:11, 14). Ps 96 consists of the same ideas as seen in the imperative to sing and let the earth be glad (שיר/גיל, vv. 1, 11) inclusive of all nations called to worship (v. 7) before the presence of YHWH in his sanctuary in acclamation of his strength (v. 6b) and marvelous deeds (v. 3).

244. Ps 98:1a//96:1a.

the world and its inhabitants to roar[245] on account of the presence of YHWH and his rule of fair judgments,[246] other elements are decisive in showing interpretational differences between these two psalms.

As Jeremias points out, Ps 96:4, 6, 7–9 and 10a have no parallels[247] in Ps 98. Ps 98 no longer speaks of YHWH in comparison with other deities,[248] has no specific phrases alluding to the ark[249] and shows no recourse to the conventional language typical of theophanies (cf. Ps 96:9). Apart from these differences with Ps 96, Ps 98 is further isolated from Pss 47, 93, 97, and 99. As established in biblical scholarship, Gray[250] correctly observes that the proclamation יהוה מלך ("YHWH reigns"), as the distinguishing feature of these kingship psalms, is lacking in Ps 98. Instead, the declaration of YHWH's lordship is expressed by the phrase המלך יהוה ([before] "the king [who is] YHWH," Ps 98:6b). Despite these differences, Ps 98 is linked with the group and with other Hebrew texts[251] on the basis of its content and focus on the saving acts of YHWH wielded by his wind for the House of Israel.

The main emphasis of Ps 98, as already seen by Weiser,[252] is on "salvation" (ישועה, vv. 2, 3) wrought by YHWH for his people, and asserted as the revelation of his "righteousness" (צדקה) to the nations. YHWH's victory or salvation wielded by his "right hand" (ימין) and "holy arm" (זרוע קדש), and the disclosure of his righteousness are expressions of his

---

245. Ps 98:7a//96:11c.

246. Ps 98:9//96:13. However, these concluding verses in Pss 98 and 96 have very slight differences. Ps 96 repeats "for he comes" (בא כי) in the second clause, and both psalms end with different substantives. Ps 98:9 concludes with "equity" (מישרים) and 96:13 with "truth" (אמונה) in relating the nature of YHWH's judgment.

247. Jeremias, *Königtum Gottes*, 133. Perhaps Jeremias should have mentioned that Ps 96:5 is also unparalleled, as there is no allusion to YHWH as creator *vis-à-vis* the worthlessness of idols in Ps 98. As there is no ascription to King David on Ps 98, probably the lack of repetition of the same material indicates similar use of the psalm as part of an integral collection of psalms/songs of worship, as exemplified by the Chronicler's author in 1 Chr 16.

248. Cf. Ps 96:4.

249. Cf. Ps 96:6, 9.

250. Gray, *Biblical*, 68. Attempting to follow Mowinckel's enthronement hypothesis, Gray further states that there is no reference in Ps 98 to the chaos conflict, which he considers to be a feature typical of enthronement psalms. Nevertheless, Gray notes the response of the rivers and sea in v. 8 as a possible obscure reference to chaos conflict. Gray sees the psalm as post-exilic, and, following Loretz, also suggests an eschatological orientation of the psalm.

251. Exod 15; 1 Chr 16; 17; and in Deutero-Isaiah.

252. Weiser, *Psalms*, 638.

PROCLAMATION OF YHWH AS KING IN THE WIND

roles as divine warrior and judge, respectively. These roles are the form, which his kingship takes in this psalm. As noted in previous studies, Ps 98 adopts the same imagery employed in Exod 15[253] in description of YHWH as a "man of war" (Exod 15:3), that is, a "divine warrior,"[254] who performs salvific acts. In the same manner, Ps 98 praises YHWH because he has done wonderful things (נפלאות עשׂה, v. 1)[255] by means of his "right hand"[256] and "holy arm,"[257] symbolizing the wind. Hence, the Psalmist in Ps 98 muses over YHWH's age-old *modus operandi* in the wind in performing wonders for the salvation of his people.[258] In Ps 77 YHWH's victory is attributed to his right hand and arm (vv. 11[10], 16[15]), synonymously recalled with reference to YHWH's theophany in the phenomenal winds for the deliverance of Israel at the exodus (vv. 15–20[14–19]). Similarly, Ps 98 echoes the same terms in expression of YHWH's renewed saving deeds in the "sight of the nations" (vv. 1–3). On this point, Jeremias argues that Ps 98 adopts more directly the proclamation of Deutero-Isaiah on YHWH bearing his arm to save his people in the eyes of the nations (Isa 52:10).[259]

Therefore, Jeremias maintains that this expression in Ps 98:1 is adopted from Isa 52:10, since he argues for the priority of Deutero-Isaiah to this psalm. Jeremias seems to be quite inconsistent on the literary relationship of Ps 98 and Deutero-Isaiah, as he also holds the literary interdependence of the two.[260] However, he notes that Ps 98:1 mentions the "holy arm" of YHWH, which only occurs in Isa 52:10a, while Ps 98:3b, referring to "all the ends of the earth" witnessing "YHWH's salvation," occurs verbatim in Isa 52:10b. Though Ps 98:2 lacks much correlation

---

253. Even though the language employed here is so close to that used to confess YHWH's saving deeds at the exodus, it is not clear which event motivated the emergence of Ps 98. Longman points out that though some critics find the exodus as the background, others see the linguistic similarities with Deutero-Isaiah as indicating post-exilic events which motivated the composition of this psalm (Longman, "Psalm 98," 269; cf. Jeremias, *Königtum Gottes*, 133). But the similarities with Ps 96 and other elements relating to the worship instituted by King David following the installation of the ark suggest King David's victories surrounding the transfer of the ark to Zion as the background.

254. Cf. גבור מלחמה, Ps 24:8.

255. See Exod 15:11 [Exod 3:20]; 1 Chr 16:9b, 12a.

256. See Exod 15:6.

257. Cf. Exod 15:16.

258. See Ps 77:11–12[10–11], 15[14].

259. Jeremias, *Königtum Gottes*, 133.

260. Jeremias, *Königtum Gottes*, 133–34.

with Isa 52:10, Jeremias adds that the phrase "in the eyes of (all) the nations" in Ps 98:2 follows the final part of Isa 52:10a. It should be pointed out that despite the lack of uniformity in the sequence of verses in Ps 98:1–3 and Isa 52:10, the verses are similar ideologically on YHWH's involvement in salvation deeds manifested by the power of his wind.

Ps 98 emphasizes accomplished acts of vindication (v. 2b; cf. v. 3), whereas Isa 52:10 is extrapolative of acts relating to YHWH's acts of salvation in the future. But in both contexts, a universal perspective on YHWH's acts of salvation is thrown into bold relief by the reference to YHWH bringing to bear his holy arm in the sight of the nations (Isa 52:10aβ; cf. Ps 98:1c–2). This image personifies YHWH unleashing his powerful winds reaching to the ends of the whole earth, and wielding salvation deeds in the eyes of the nations (Isa 52:10:bc; cf. Ps 98:2, 3c). In any case, Ps 98 celebrates salvation deeds wrought by YHWH's phenomenal winds, and his rule of righteousness seen in his faithfulness to the House of Israel unfolds before all the nations (v. 3). Here, the Psalmist recalls YHWH's deeds on display in all the earth in fulfillment of his covenant of faithfulness, as recited in the Chronicler's thanksgiving psalm[261] attributed to King David.

The universal perspective of YHWH's righteous deeds in Ps 98 is even more elaborated by the extent of the jubilation effected by YHWH's theophany. As in Ps 96, the cosmic jubilation involves every sphere in creation: all the earth or the world and its dwellers, and the sea and its fullness (Ps 98:4, 7). This is marked by the exhortation to all the earth to burst into song,[262] the world and its inhabitants, the sea, fields and all their fullness to resound this worldwide joy[263] in response to the aeolian movement of the wind. Hence, the earth is personified and enjoined to shout (רוע) for joy with the accompaniment of musical instruments at the presence of King YHWH (Ps 98:5–6). The *Hiphil* imperative [264]הריעו ("shout [in joy]") employed in vv. 4a, 6b to summon all the earth to raise a "shout" in acclamation of King YHWH, resonates with the תרועה ("shout" [of joy]) at the ascension of the ark described by the Psalmist

---

261. See 1 Chr 16:14–18.
262. See 1 Chr 16:23a.
263. See 1 Chr 16:32.

264. BDB 929 translates רוע "shout" meaning raise a shout to God in a context of religious worship and cites; Pss 47:2[1]; 66:1; 81:2[1]; 95:1, 2; 98:4, 6. The substantive תרועה ("shout" [of joy]) derives from this root and occurs in Ps 47:6[5] in celebration of the ascension of the ark (see 1 Sam 4:4, 5; 2 Sam 6:15).

in Ps 47:6[5]a,²⁶⁵ and also recalled by the Chronicler's author²⁶⁶ in the account of the ascension of the ark to its restful place.

Of significance is the Psalmist's interest in the ensemble of instruments employed at the celebratory worship that are not mentioned in the ark narratives (2 Sam 6:14–15). As stated in Ps 98:5–6, harps (כנור), trumpets (חצצרות), and ram's horn (שופר), though the latter is only implied by the reference to its sound (קול שופר, v. 6), parallel some of the instruments played at the ascension of the ark to the city of King David, as explained in the Chronicler's account (1 Chr 15:28–29). The Chronicler's account highlights the instruments used in worship by mentioning the sounds. It seems the elision of the instrument producing the sound is intentional. Perhaps, this occasion of worship is filled with commemorations of YHWH's recent theophany when he breaks out against the Philistines at the locale King David venerates as Baʿal Perazim (1 Chr 14:11–12).²⁶⁷ So, here, too, the mention of the "sound of the ram's horn" is a deliberate foil to resound the manifestation of YHWH's awesome power in the wind against the Philistines. Thus, the author intentionally states in 1 Chr 15:28 Israel bringing up the covenantal ark with a "shout" and the "sound of the ram's horn," to underscore the grandiloquent representation of YHWH's theophany in the wind—an idea that is comparable to the sound of the Hogon's horn echoing Amma's whirling sound at creation. Therefore, it is not coincidental that in Ps 98:6 the "sound of the ram's horn" (קול שופר), and not the horn itself, is distinctively mentioned among the genre of the musical instruments played before King YHWH. The specificity of the "sound of the ram's horn," throws into bold relief the sound of the wind, symbolizing YHWH's invisible presence, and echoes the theatrical musical din at the transfer of the ark of YHWH alluded to in Ps 47:6[5].

Arguably, it is this sonorous sound of YHWH's wind that is identified as the "'shout' (תרועה) of the king" in Baʿalam's prophetic declaration of YHWH's presence among the people of Israel.²⁶⁸ Also, the Psalmist's use of the term רעם in the summons to animate nature to "thunder" is intentional (Ps 98:7) and resonates with YHWH's thunderous outburst of wind against inimical forces, as similarly alluded to in 1 Sam 2:10 and 1 Sam 7:10. Moreover, King David is no stranger to experiences of

265. See 2 Sam 6:15.
266. 1 Chr 15:28.
267. See 2 Sam 5:20–21.
268. Num 23:21cd; cf. Ps 98:6.

YHWH's phenomenal disclosure in the wind, as seen in the theophany unit in Ps 18. And, as pointed out in analysis of Ps 47, YHWH's appearance in the wind, expressed figuratively as the sound of "marching"[269] in the balsam trees at the battle with the Philistines, prior to King David's installation of the ark, is probably one of the most contemporary events which incites this new song in celebration of YHWH's victories in covenantal faithfulness (1 Chr 14:15–17; 16:14–18). As the Psalmist declares in Ps 98:3, YHWH's acts of salvation in faithfulness to the house of Israel are performed in sight of the extremities of the whole earth. Therefore, the whole earth is behooved to "shout" out in song, and break forth in exultation (v. 4) to resonate with the "shout" of King YHWH, who breaks out with the wind in performing deeds of salvation. Hence, the injunction on the sea and its fullness to "roar,"[270] and the world[271] and its inhabitants to "thunder [in praise]"[272] (רעם) in Ps 98:7, compels an expression of reverential awe at YHWH's presence, and no less the reaction in nature at YHWH's effervescence in the wind.

YHWH's wind churns the waters of the sea and causes its waves to roar.[273] But, here in Ps 98:7a, as much as in Ps 96:11b, the sea is implored to roar in jubilation of YHWH's judgments.[274] Therefore, this note of celebration in Ps 98 is even more pronounced by the summons to personified nature to join the musical din in exaltation of YHWH because of his salvation deeds (vv. 8–9). Nothing in nature escapes the power of YHWH's winds. The rivers[275] are enjoined to "clap their hands" (ימחאו־כף), while

---

269. 2 Sam 5:24=1 Chr 14:15; cf. Hab 3:12a.

270. See Ps 96:11c; 1 Chr 16:32a.

271. The Chronicler's account of King David's thanksgiving cites the call to nature to rejoice expressing the same idea but employs different terms. It replaces the term "world" in Ps 98:7b with the "fields" and its fullness in conjugation with a different verb "exult" (עלץ, 1 Chr 16:32b).

272. See BDB 947.

273. See Ps 93:3; Isa 51:15. YHWH subdues the roar of the seas with his wind.

274. See 1 Chr 16:31b–32a.

275. Cf. "Trees" (Isa 55:12d; 1 Chr 16:33). Again, the Chronicler's account shows slight variations. But the theme on inanimate nature bursting into jubilation for YHWH's judgments, as king, is the same. Instead of the mountains summoned to sing as in the case of Ps 98:8b, it is the trees of the forest called to exuberant exaltation of YHWH coming to judge (1 Chr 16:33). Therefore, the idea of the trees of the forest singing is metaphorical for the whistling or rustling sound of the wind blowing in the trees, and brings to bear the conceptual notion of YHWH's presence in the sonorous wind causing this commotion in nature.

the mountains burst into song.[276] This jubilant clamor personifying the swirling or rippling sound of water in rivers, and whistling sounds of wind rushing through the mountains, respectively, points to nothing other than the aeolian movements of King YHWH over and above the elements of nature as he appears in his age-old *modus operandi* in the wind in fulfillment of his judicial role (vv. 6-9).

Undoubtedly, Ps 98, in its terminology and description of YHWH's salvation, obtains close affinity with the historical events on Israel's victories, the celebration of the transfer of the ark to the city of King David, and the musical worship service (1 Chr 16:4-7, 37) instituted in celebration of YHWH's faithful deeds (Ps 98:3; cf. 1 Chr 16:8-9, 15). The universal scope of the Psalmist's celebrations of Israel's victories is not unique to the psalm, but echoes King David's thanksgiving in declaration of YHWH's salvation revealed to the nations[277] and mirrored by all nature called to celebrate King YHWH for his judgments.[278] Thus, in Ps 98, YHWH's functions of saving, ruling, and judging are revealed. In essence, the poetic-historical orientation of the psalm dispels any association with the myth of a cultic enthronement of YHWH.

As noted, the allusion to the ark narratives and the Chronicler's account in Ps 98 shows the significance of the power of YHWH in the wind objectivized in the ark,[279] and performing wonderful deeds of salvation in the eyes of the surrounding nations.[280] Like King David's recital of YHWH's covenantal faithfulness in the Chronicler's psalm (1 Chr 16:15-24), YHWH's acts of salvation lend the Psalmist, perhaps King David himself, the confession on YHWH's steadfast divine protection, that ultimately invokes a ringing shout of jubilant praise for his unrelenting faithfulness (Ps 98:3-4). As portrayed in both the Chronicler's psalm of thanksgiving as much as in Ps 98, YHWH's presence among his people also relates a durative import on the fulfillment of YHWH's judgments. For Israel, therefore, the inaugurated universal salvation is celebrated in anticipation of YHWH's consummation of the establishment of justice (Ps 98:9b; 96:13aβ; 1 Chr 16:33c). The Psalmist's positive view on the inaugural fair and just rule of YHWH aligns with King David's claim on

---

276. See Isa 44:23c; 55:12c.

277. 2 Sam 7:23; 1 Chr 14:17; 16:8, 14, 24; cf. Ps 98:2.

278. See 1 Chr 16:32-33.

279. It should be noted however, that there is no involvement of the ark in the victories against the Philistines preceding its transfer to the city of King David.

280. Ps 98:2; 2 Sam 7:23; cf. 1 Chr 16:14-16, 24.

YHWH's promise of protection for generations, with its root in the everlasting covenant decreed to Israel (2 Sam 7:28; 1 Chr 16:14–17). Hence the success and certainty of YHWH's fair judgments, which begin with Israel, and witnessed by the nations, point to the universal dimension of YHWH's execution of judicial acts into the future (Ps 98:9; 1 Chr 16:33c). This hope for YHWH's continual rule, characterized by "righteousness" and "equity" (Ps 98:9b), is forged and sustained by the knowledge of YHWH's deeds of vindication already accomplished in the eyes of the nations. Therefore, the Psalmist finds the cause to celebrate YHWH for his marvelous deeds of salvation, and indomitable presence among the people as king, whose strength is manifested in the wind.

Psalm 99—Tremble before the King of the Nations

Right from the outset, Ps 99 throws into bold relief YHWH's sovereignty over the nations and his divine presence in the wind, which evokes reverential fear. The reference to YHWH, who dwells on the "cherubim" and the imperatives on the nations to "tremble" (רגז)[281] and the earth to "shake" (נוט, v. 1), brings to bear YHWH's presence in the phenomenal winds. The thrust of the psalm, however, is not so much of YHWH's dealings with the nations but with Israel's personal encounter with YHWH and the relationship derived therefrom. The Psalmist concentrates on the symbolic features of YHWH's presence amid his people in two sections (Ps 99:1–5, 6–9). The focus is on the cherubim,[282] Zion, the ark(=footstool) in vv. 1–5, and then the prophetic/priestly figures of Moses, Aaron, and Samuel, the pillar of cloud, and the holy mountain in vv. 6–9, as the different modes associated with YHWH's manifestation in the wind among his people. YHWH's transcendence, yet also immanent nature, is brought to the fore by use of these different symbolic elements representing YHWH's presence.

Initially, in Ps 99, the idea of YHWH's immanence is developed by associating the invisible presence of YHWH as king in Zion with the cherubim (v. 1), Zion (v. 2) and the footstool[283] (= ark; v. 5) that are known traditionally as elements of the Zion tradition. YHWH's power

---

281. See Exod 15:14a.

282. The idea of the wind enshrined with the cherubim enthroned above the ark highlights the image of the ark conceived as YHWH's footstool (Pss 99:1–2, 5; 132:7; cf. Exod 25:20–22; Num 7:89).

283. Ps 132:7.

emanates from Zion as the center of his dominion. Zion, as YHWH's choice of abode[284] is given primacy as the place where YHWH roars in disclosure with his sonorous winds.[285] YHWH's greatness is discernible through his establishment of "equity"[286] and execution of "justice" and "righteousness" with regard to his people (v. 4; Jacob=Israel). Here, too, the Psalmist emphasizes the nature of YHWH's rule as king by linking his divine presence with the deeds of salvation for Israel. On account of the display of these ethical qualities characterizing YHWH's rule, the Psalmist summons the people to prostrate themselves before YHWH in his holiness (v. 5).

The relationship of Ps 99:1–5 and vv. 6–9 is not at first apparent because of the precise historical references in the latter. But the two sections are connected in that vv. 6–9 take up again the idea of YHWH's presence through mediation and the exercise of YHWH's ethical righteousness as seen through past traditions (v. 8). The Psalmist emphasizes here the intercessory role of the priestly/prophetic figures as a different mode of YHWH's revelation, or mediation of his presence. The Psalmist highlights this mode of disclosure by reference to Moses, Aaron, and Samuel, esteemed mediators (v. 6),[287] through whom YHWH's royal prerogatives are made known and exercised. In their priestly/prophetic function they call on YHWH and he answers them (vv. 6, 8). The Psalmist mentions in this connection the "pillar of cloud" (עמוד ענן) as a sign of the presence of the invisible and inaccessible God.[288]

The inclusion of Samuel with Moses and Aaron in the experience of the presence of YHWH in the "pillar of cloud" is due to the past traditions on the manifestation of YHWH's power, a point to be returned to below. As is stated, these intercessory figures observed YHWH's "statutes" and "laws" (עדות וחק, Ps 99:7),[289] and so deserved YHWH's positive response. Thus, in a subtle manner, the Psalmist proclaims here that there is salvation in keeping YHWH's ordinances, as indicated by repeated references

---

284. Exod 15:17; Ps 68:17–18[16–17], 30[29].

285. See Amos 1:2. In the prophetic message by Amos on the impending judgment against Israel, Judah and the surrounding nations, Zion is marked as the appropriate locus for YHWH to manifest his winds against the nations.

286. See Pss 96:10c; 98:9.

287. 1 Sam 12:6–8; Jer 15:1.

288. Exod 13:21; 33:9–10.

289. Ringgren, "חָקַק," 145. As Ringgren observes, both terms are used here indiscriminately to refer to the revealed will of YHWH or the Torah, as is also the case in the parenetic sections of Deuteronomy (Deut 4:45; 6:20).

to "calling out" (קרא) and YHWH's "answering"[290] (vv. 6, 8). But the Psalmist lays emphasis on Samuel "among those who called on the name" (v. 6b) of YHWH as intercessor. Here, the Psalmist unequivocally recalls the Philistine crisis at a time Samuel gathers the House of Israel at Mizpah for intercession following the Israelites' contrition from worshipping the Ashtoreths and foreign deities (1 Sam 7:2–12). The Philistines hear of this gathering, and their rulers plan an assault on the Israelites. The Israelites implore Samuel to intercede and cry out to YHWH on their behalf for deliverance. Indeed, Samuel cries out, and YHWH answers him (1 Sam 7:9). Accordingly, the idea that YHWH thunders (רעם) with a great voice (בקול־גדול) in response, throws into bold relief the bluster of YHWH's sonorous winds causing the Philistines to panic to their peril (vv. 10–11; see 2 Sam 5:19–21). For the Israelites, the victory is proof of the dependability of YHWH as their strength and helper (1 Sam 7:12).[291] YHWH's response is in keeping with his covenantal promise to protect Israel for obeying YHWH's statutes.[292] However, with that brief recollection on YHWH's response implied in Ps 99:6b–8a, immediately the context shifts in Ps 99:8b from YHWH's gracious response to his intercessors, to his mercy and judgment in his dealings with Israel. These principles of mercy and judgment are couched in the language of "forgiveness" and "chastisement," respectively.

The reference to YHWH as a "forgiving" and at the same time "chastising" deity resembles the Deuteronomistic theology with its unfolding fourfold pattern of Israel's apostasy: when Israel sinned, YHWH raised an oppressive power over them, and when Israel repented, the oppression was terminated.[293] Even Samuel himself, as portrayed in 1 Sam 12,[294] recounts Israel's history of apostasy extending from the period of Moses and Aaron to the time of Israel's demands for a human king. Samuel also emphasizes YHWH's righteous acts towards Jacob in contrast to the people of Israel's recurring apostasy by reflecting on this theme of sin/judgment and deliverance (1 Sam 12:7–11). Similarly, the Psalmist in Ps 99:8–9 takes up this theme of grace and judgment in view of YHWH's

---

290. The Psalmist presents the crux of Israel's salvation history: Israel "cries" and YHWH hearkens to its voice (Exod 3:7; cf. 2:23–24). In a profound sense, YHWH's relentless mercy is depicted here.

291. Deut 33:29c.

292. Exod 19:5; 23:20–22.

293. Judg 2:11–23. See Eslinger, *Hands*, 64–79; Niditch, *Judges*, 10–11, 48–50.

294. 1 Sam 12:6–9; cf. Deut 31:27–29; Ps 78:8, 40–42.

covenant faithfulness. Though YHWH chastises, his righteousness endures as it is experienced in "forgiveness." Hence, the Psalmist calls for the glorification of the just and merciful deity, who not only reveals himself in the scheme of grace and judgment (v. 8),[295] but also makes himself known in the power of the wind (v. 1; 1 Sam 7:10; 12:18).

By appealing to past traditions, the Psalmist presents the schema of YHWH's saving acts in which his righteous reign is disclosed. These further garner evidence showing that Mowinckel's thesis of cultic enthronement, and the subsequent advocates of the tradition of an enthronement of YHWH are in error to ascribe Ps 99 to the group of psalms suggested as supporting the idea of YHWH's enthronement as king. The dual mention of YHWH "answering them" in vv. 6 and 8 in reference to his responses to Moses, Aaron, and Samuel further highlights the Psalmist's allusion to the dynamics of YHWH's theophany at the dispensation of his righteous rule. YHWH's responses to these mediators fit the theme on the mode of YHWH's appearance in the winds that pervades this psalm.

YHWH's disclosure in the midst of the cloud is expressed in relation to all the three intercessory figures: Moses, Aaron, and Samuel in Ps 99. Yet, no such explicit encounter is attested to in the episodes involving Samuel,[296] but only for Moses[297] and Aaron.[298] However, considering the avowal on their "calling out" and YHWH "answering"[299] in Ps 99:6 (see v. 8a), the Psalmist places stress on the appearances of YHWH responding in much more than a pillar of cloud. In essence, the Psalmist harks back to YHWH's appearance in the wind. YHWH "descends" on Mount Sinai with "fire" accompanying the phenomenal winds depicted as thunder (קלת), lightning (ברקים), thick cloud (ענן כבד)[300] and the sound of the ram's horn (קל שפר). Here, too, the latter symbolizes the sound of the

---

295. Exod 34:5–7.

296. Weiser, however, assumes that the Psalmist may have understood YHWH, when speaking to Samuel from above the ark (1 Sam 3:3–4), as "speaking out of a 'pillar of cloud'" (Weiser, *Psalms*, 644).

297. Exod 33:9; Num 12:5; 14:13–19; cf. Exod 19:9; 20:21.

298. Num 12:5; 17:7[16:42].

299. In both cases of Moses and Samuel, there is an invocation for YHWH to appear, as they defer to the covenant conditions. Perhaps this balancing order of "calling out" and YHWH "answering," emanates from the fact that Moses (along with Aaron; Exod 19:24) and Samuel are advocates of the covenant (Exod 19:5, 7; 1 Sam 12:14, 24, respectively) and demand fear and obedience as requisite dispositions towards covenantal obligations. Therefore, YHWH responds to them in their undertaking of the divine sanction.

300. Apart from the reference to "sound of the ram's horn," all the other elements

wind of YHWH causing the people to tremble and the mountain to convulse.³⁰¹ Moses speaks (דבר) and YHWH responds with his voice (קול) personifying his wind on the mountain covered with smoke.

As Moses himself comments on this experience, YHWH intends to instill fear (ירא), for Israel to abstain from sinning (חטא, Exod 20:20), or at best, to maintain covenantal fidelity. Likewise, in the case of Samuel, YHWH's appearance in the phenomenal wind at Samuel's invocation, following Israel's demand for a king, is meant to instill reverential fear in the people of Israel (1 Sam 12:13–14, 16–18). At this point, Samuel tries to bring Israel in conformity with the covenantal regulations, as the request for an earthly king implies rejection of YHWH's kingship, essentially revoking the "shout[=bluster of wind] of [the] King YHWH" among them. Therefore, despite setting up a (human) king in response to Israel's request, Samuel reminds the people of Israel of the consequences associated with disobedience and divine retribution. That is, by either experiencing a form of blessing or curse: meaning goodwill incurred from reverential fear by following YHWH's commands, or experiencing YHWH's wrath for violating covenantal conditions (1 Sam 12:14–15). So, Samuel ratifies his word by "calling out" (קרא) to YHWH, and YHWH gives a loud sound (יתן יהוה קלת) in bursts of wind with a downpour of rain (מטר), causing Israel to express awe and reverence for both YHWH and Samuel (v. 18). Ironically, YHWH's appearance with the bluster of wind and rain is also an expression of his displeasure to Israel for demanding a human king (1 Sam 12:17–19). Therefore, while YHWH's response in the sonorous sound of the wind parenthetically sanctions and validates Samuel's role as YHWH's mouthpiece,³⁰² at the same time YHWH's kingship, which the prophet insists on preserving, is also declared.

Inasmuch as Moses(, Aaron) and Samuel, as intercessory figures are connected by the fact that YHWH answers them, the peculiarity and strength of linking Moses and Samuel in this psalm proclaiming YHWH's kingship lie in the fact that YHWH discloses his power in the wind, as Israel's king at their mediation. As mediators, they channel divine protection and blessing to Israel. Moses,³⁰³ as the promulgator of

---

appear in the description of YHWH's descent with the phenomenal winds in Ps 18:8–15[7–14].

301. Exod 19:16, 18; 20:18.

302. Gordon, *1 & 2 Samuel*, 129.

303. Deut 33:4 also asserts Moses as lawgiver in defense of the Torah as a possession of Jacob(=Israel).

the law, declares YHWH as the king[304] of Jeshurun[305] ([=Israel]; Deut 33:5), who attests his spectacular appearances in acts of providence. The succor and protection of YHWH as king is couched in language characteristic of the theophany tradition expressing YHWH's movements in the winds. YHWH is portrayed as "riding the heavens" (רכב שמים)[306] and the "clouds" (שחקים) in his "majesty" (בגאות), as he comes to Israel's help (Deut 33:26, 29).

Similarly, YHWH also discloses himself as the divine protector in response to Samuel's intercessory prayer and offering during the crisis imposed by the Philistines. Samuel's intercession, in sequel to Israel's confession, provides the backdrop to YHWH's exonerative response. This context also has affinity with the confession in Ps 99:8b that YHWH is the forgiving deity. A demonstration of YHWH's forgiveness is illustrated through acts of vindication against the Philistines (1 Sam 7:5-11). Samuel "cries out" (זעק) to YHWH and "he answers" with a thunderous sound (רעם, v. 10)[307] of the wind and confounds the Philistines to utter annihilation.[308] Even so, here, the declaration of YHWH as a source of help, as attested in Deut 33:26, 29c, is also affirmed. To that end, Samuel sets up a stone to commemorate YHWH's mediation of his divine protection against the Philistines (1 Sam 7:12-13) in remembrance of his love and faithfulness to the house of Israel (Ps 99:3).

In light of the intertextual evidence from other biblical texts with subtle connections with Ps 99, it is clear that the Psalmist draws variant ideas from past traditions in portrait of the incessant presence of YHWH among his people. Therefore, the terminology used in Ps 99:1 goes back to the tradition of YHWH's age-old self-disclosure in the wind. The verb "quake" or "tremble" (רגז), indicating the reaction of the nations, is part of the language of theophany traditions.[309] The reference to YHWH by

---

304. In light of this early tradition, among others (Exod 15:18; Num 23:21; Ps 68:25[24]), Cross points out that the argument which sees the concept of YHWH as king as a relatively late development in Israelite thought is unfounded (Cross, *Canaanite Myth*, 99n30).

305. BDB 449. A poetic name for Israel meaning "upright one" (see Deut 32:15; 33:5, 26; Isa 44:2).

306. Cf. Pss 18:11[10]; 68:34[33].

307. See Ps 18:14-15[13-14].

308. 1 Sam 2:10. Here, too, Hannah's prophetic word on YHWH's roar of the wind from the heavens, against inimical forces striving against him, is realized.

309. See Pss 18:8[7]; 77:17[16]; Hab 3:7.

the appellative "the one sitting on the cherubim" (ישב כרבים) in Ps 99:1, further calls to attention that YHWH's theophany in the wind is in view.[310] In light of this tradition, the imperative on the people to "tremble" and the earth to "shake," in the presence of the one dwelling on the cherubim in Ps 99:1, underscores musing on YHWH's presence in the potent wind in demonstration of his sovereign power over the nations. By this means, YHWH rouses the sense of awe and reverence that behooves his people to glorify his name.

This overview on Ps 99 dispels any evidence of elements deployed for the reconstruction of a cultic enthronement of YHWH in Ps 99. Instead, the Psalmist focuses on the ideas of YHWH's enduring presence and the exercise and establishment of divine justice. By reflecting the Deuteronomistic interpretation of YHWH's grace and judgment in Israel's salvation history (vv. 6–8), the Psalmist bears in mind the deeds of righteousness performed by YHWH in covenant faithfulness. This is achieved by emphasizing the integral key features—"cherubim," Zion, ark, "pillar of cloud," and the "holy mountain"—symbolic of YHWH's close communion with his people as he ordains "justice" and "righteousness" as the sovereign king and judge, the one who loves "justice" (v. 4). In that case, Ps 99 neither shows indications of a covenant renewal, as Kraus[311] maintains, nor of a ritual of YHWH's enthronement. Instead, Ps 99 presents a religio-historical tradition based on the divine liberation as witnessed in YHWH's deeds of righteousness, which call forth the act of worship at his footstool in Zion—the holy mountain. At this locus, YHWH is exalted as king over all the nations (v. 2), and beams forth his power with the sonorous and luminous winds (v. 1)[312] in display of his holiness (vv. 3b, 5c, 9c) and kingship. YHWH's rule of justice is instituted in Zion, and spreads out to the nations (vv. 1a, 4). Ineluctably, all the nations are exhorted to respond with trembling in awe of YHWH as king, who shines forth with his phenomenal winds in, and, from Zion.

So, we can state with certainty that the contents of Pss 47, 93, 96–99 do not warrant a theory of an enthronement festival of YHWH. In all cases, the elements deployed for the reconstruction of an enthronement festival express nothing other than YHWH's redeeming activities wielded by the power of his wind, that occasion the liturgical praise and proclamation of his unrivalled sovereign rule. All of these psalms bear themes

310. See pp. 81–82 above.
311. Kraus, *Psalms 60–150*, 269.
312. Pss 50:2–3[1–3]; 96:6; Amos 1:2, 14.

and motifs alluding to historical antecedents associated with King David's victories,[313] and Israel's experiences of YHWH's disclosure with the wind for their deliverance. Therefore, it is evident that in this group of psalms, and the related texts, various elements relate to YHWH's presence in the phenomenal wind in his role of saving, judging, and ruling. The symbolic features of YHWH's divine presence, the demonstration of his power above all gods, his conquest of chaos, creation, the subjugation of nations, the establishment of his throne in Israel and the declaration of his kingship are the various motifs connected with his judicial acts and salvation of Israel, as the common focus. The following discourse in analysis of Pss 29 and 68 further highlights the contexts of YHWH's theophany in his age-old *modus operandi* in the wind proper, as the unchallenged divine warrior-king, and shows the theme of Israel's welfare at the center of YHWH's salvation deeds among the nations.

The Roaring Wind as the "Voice" of the King in Psalm 29

Ps 29 has received a diversity of interpretations from scholars.[314] It is compared with Babylonian texts,[315] and Canaanite myths,[316] in an attempt to prove a non-Israelite origin of the psalm on the one hand, while, on the other, it is claimed that the psalm is an Israelite composition.[317] In most

---

313. This suggestion calls for a review of the group of psalms (Pss 93; 96—99) assigned to book four of the psalter, labeled enthronement psalms and set in the exilic period (see DeClaissé-Walford, *Psalms*, 41), and argued as the basis for Israel seeking the kingship of YHWH following the presumed failure of the monarchical reign after the Babylonian exile. Pss 93; 96—99 lack titles, perhaps to indicate that they were used collectively for liturgical communal temple worship instituted by King David, as may be intimated by the Chronicler's account in 1 Chr 16.

314. Loretz gives a comprehensive presentation of remarks made by biblical critics on Ps 29, and a brief recourse more recently by Amzallag, such that a recount of the variations in the interpretations of Ps 29 is unnecessary. See Loretz, *Ugarit-Texte*, 76–97; Amzallag, *Psalm 29*, 8–9. See also p. 230, 230n97 above.

315. Gunkel, *Einleitung*, 52–53; Gaster, "Psalm 29," 55–65. Gaster, however, compares Ps 29 with both the Babylonian Enuma Elish, and Ba'al texts. He presupposes the common elements to be drawn from a primitive Ritual Pattern: the weather-god defeats a rebellious monster, attains kingship, and consequently acquires a new temple/palace (Gaster, "Psalm 29," 55–65; *Thespis*, 443–46).

316. See 230n97 above.

317. Schmidt, *Königtum Gottes*, 57–58; cf. Margulis, "Canaanite," 332–48; Kloos, *Yhwh's Combat*, 107–12; cf. Craigie, *Psalms 1–50*, 245–49. Even though Craigie acknowledges some Canaanite elements in Ps 29, he challenges the view that this psalm originated as a Canaanite/Phoenician hymn. On the other hand, Tsumura sees

cases, the arguments for the comparison of the psalm with either Babylonian or Ugaritic traditions are based on style and common religious ideas and expressions. Thus, direct literary dependence or adaptation of foreign material is often assumed. Many biblical critics continue to support the theory that the psalm is an original hymn to Baʿal[318] that has been adapted and modified for the worship of YHWH. It is imperative therefore, to show that despite the use of ideas and expressions familiar from non-Israelite traditions, the Psalmist retains an image of YHWH that is still consistent with Israel's theological heritage. The ideas presented here show that Ps 29 does not present any new concepts and beliefs on the character of YHWH.

The idea of YHWH as king and of his supremacy among other gods is well attested in the psalms discussed, but Ps 29 compliments the image of YHWH with its sophisticated use of the image of YHWH's appearance in the wind with close affinity to the Dogon god, Amma. The wind god Amma is the phenomenal wind, which is the primordial internal movement, or vibrations forming a spiral that releases with a loud sound all the things Amma creates. The whirling of matter ending with the loud sound, which distributes all things Amma creates, is also called the manifestation of his word, or the seven articulations identified as the "voice."[319] The same idea of a voice representing the loud sound resulting from the whirling movement of wind bodes well with the Psalmist's image of YHWH, who manifests his power in the wind. No other theophanic text expresses the strength and effect of the "wind of YHWH," personified here as the "voice,"[320] with such mythical allusions as in other Hebrew texts discussed. Yet, a similar figure of the seven voices mentioned in the psalm is employed with clear intent to portray the prominence of YHWH's power in the wind, which undergirds his

---

the association of Ps 29 with the Canaanite tradition as overstated, though he supports the use of storm language in both Pss 29 and 18 as metaphor (Tsumura, *Creation and Destruction*, 155). Although elements resembling other ancient traditions are discernible in Ps 29, an Israelite origin of the psalm is tenable with emphasis on the view that this psalm depicts YHWH distinctively in his age-old *modus operandi* in the wind(s) for the salvation of Israel in the eyes of the nations.

318. See Day, "Echoes," 143–45; Pardee and Pardee, "Gods," 121–24; Flynn, *YHWH Is King*, 66–67, 69.

319. See pp. 16–18 above.

320. On the voice as the whirling winds, or word of Amma, see pp. 16–18, 17n96 above. On the conflation of whirlwind, spinning wind, breath, word/voice as hypostasis of the wind-deity Amma, see p. 29.

kingship. Scholars have overstated the Baʿalistic tendencies retained in Ps 29, or similarities with the elements relating the battle and victory of Marduk, to the point of missing the evocation of YHWH's age-old *modus operandi* in the wind in this psalm.

In relation to the use of complex images throughout Ps 29, biblical scholars have seen evidence of mythical motifs that are associated with creation and kingship. The combination of these motifs, however, is thought to be a result of the integration of ideas derived from the traditions associated with the Ugaritic El and Baʿal. Some scholars consider this integration of ideas from the tradition of El with that of Baʿal as indicating its Israelite composition. On the other hand, some aspects are traced to Mesopotamian myths about Marduk. Be that as it may, an analysis of the ideas and expressions in common shows that the Psalmist appropriated non-Israelite ideas, yet adequately portrayed the kingship of YHWH without compromising its characteristic features in the biblical Hebrew tradition.

First, the argument must be dealt with that Ps 29 reflects traditions about the Ugaritic El. The expression "sons of (the) gods"[321] (בני אלים) and the idea of ascribing "glory" (כבוד) are considered evidence for the influence of the El-tradition on Hebrew thought. But the Psalmist aims to express the majesty of YHWH in Ps 29. Therefore, he employs the image of a divine assembly as no more than a backdrop for the portrayal of the preeminence of YHWH in that contemporary polytheistic world. The Psalmist incorporates this polytheistic notion, and, yet at the same time, dismisses the idea as he depicts a single transcendent deity, only peculiar to the Hebrew tradition, who embodies all power and awesome glory. Even if the expression בני אלים is an indication of familiarity with the El tradition, the Psalmist's objective is to portray the superiority of

---

321. This expression is often considered as originating from the tradition of the Ugaritic El. The different interpretations for this term offered by scholars indicate the problems associated with its precise meaning. In some cases, the term is thought to be a construct state with a genitive case ending in addition to an enclitic *mem*; thus translated "sons of El" (Freedman and Hyland, "Psalm 29," 242; Cross, *Canaanite Myth*, 152). The interpretation "sons of God" is also suggested in spite of what appears as a double plural construction (Craigie, *Psalm 1–50*, 243; Jacobson, "Psalm 29," 655). See Pardee and Pardee translating the double plural construction: "Heavenly beings [sons of the gods]," (Pardee and Pardee, "Gods," 123). Other scholars interpret the expression as "gods=angels" in an attempt to suppress polytheistic beliefs in the Hebrew tradition. See Fensham, "Psalm 29," 88; Anderson, *Psalms 1–72*, 234; Barbiero, "Two Structures," 384–85.

YHWH IN THE WIND(S)

YHWH over the gods.³²² Nevertheless, the idea of a pantheon is too pervasive in Near Eastern traditions, to limit exclusive claim for influence from just the Ugaritic tradition of El.

Accordingly, in the course of rejecting the idea of a special relationship between YHWH and El traditions, Kloos points out that the concept of a god-king surrounded by a court of subordinate heavenly beings is not peculiar to the Ugaritic El. She further notes that the image of a supreme deity amidst other gods who pay homage is a familiar feature in Near Eastern hymns.³²³ The pantheon of gods called upon to proclaim the praise of Marduk is referred to as the "sons of (the) gods" (*ilāni mārê-šunu*; literally "gods their sons," EE VI:158).³²⁴ Therefore, the reference to "sons of gods" (בני אלים) in Ps 29:1 only indicates the proximity of the Hebrew tradition to forms and expressions current in its religio-cultural environment. Yet, at the same time, the mention of this court of the gods exhorted to give exclusive homage to YHWH, effectively indicates the supremacy of YHWH in a way that contrasts Israelite belief with that of its contemporaries.

Furthermore, the lack of precise formal parallels to the use of *kbwd* undermines the case for the influence of the El-tradition on the kingship of YHWH in Ps 29. Kloos offers important points in distinguishing the kingship of El from that of YHWH. Although there is a common formula expressing the idea of paying homage in both traditions, she argues that at Ugarit honor is not only due to El, but also to other gods. Secondly, the term occurs in its verbal form "to honor" (*kbd*) in association with other verbs: "Bow down" (*hbr*), "fall down" (*ql*) and "prostrate oneself" (*šḥw*).³²⁵ In contrast, apart from Ps 86:9 and v. 12, which retain the verbal form "to honor," the Hebrew tradition employs a formula that contains "glory/honor" as a substantive, sometimes in connection with the verb

---

322. Cf. Ps 82:1, 6. Ps 82 depicts YHWH in the assembly of gods. He calls on the gods, as his deputies, to account for their administration of justice. Again, in Ps 89:8[7] YHWH's superiority based on his covenantal faithfulness is used as the basis to express how his awesomeness supersedes all in the assembly of the heavenly council.

323. Kloos, following Gunkel, mentions Marduk, Sin, and Amon-Re as gods given honor by other gods (Kloos, *Yhwh's Combat*, 23).

324. Heidel, *Babylonian Genesis*, 53; cf. Dalley, *Myths*, 266; Foster, *Before the Muses*, 475; Lambert, *Babylonian*, 119.

325. The formula, in association with the stated verbs, occurs in Ba'al's instruction to his messengers to do obeisance to Anat (KTU 1.3.III:7 [=CTA 3.iii:7]), Kôthar-wa-Ḥasīs (KTU 1.3.VI:19–20 [=CTA 3.vi:19–20]), and Mot (KTU 1.4.VIII:28–29 [=CTA 4.viii:28–29]; see Kloos, *Yhwh's Combat*, 26).

"prostrate oneself" (שחה).[326] Given this difference of terminology in the Hebrew tradition, in addition to the fact that honor is exclusively due to YHWH, it follows that the giving of "honor," "strength," and "glory" to the name of YHWH may not derive from the tradition of El.

Jeremias argues that the references to YHWH's glory do not suggest close affinity between YHWH and El. Although he argues that this *leitwort* of the *kabod*-theology is an element in the El-tradition, he observes that the expression, "the god of (the) glory thunders"[327] (אל־הכבוד הרעים) in Ps 29:3, has no counterpart in the Ugaritic tradition.[328] That indicates, therefore, that there is no expression of honor exclusive to El that justifies a comparison of the attribution of honor to YHWH in Ps 29:1-2 and 9c with the Ugaritic El. These verses retain expressions proclaiming YHWH's glory as he reveals his power through the winds in conformity with the Hebrew religio-cultural tradition. On this point, a consideration of some of the elements that converge in the composition of Ps 29 is in order.

The term *kābôd* here in Ps 29 bears the same nuance of the luminous wind, as in other biblical texts alluding to YHWH's presence in the wind (Deut 5:22-26[19-23, ET 22-26]).[329] The concurrence of *kābôd*, in association with the voice (=wind) and fire in the Hebrew tradition is demonstrated at the promulgation of the ten commandments at Mount Sinai. Moses declares that YHWH issues the decree of the ten commandments with a "loud voice" (קול גדול, Deut 5:22[19, ET 22])[330] from the

326. Pss 29:1-2; 96:7-9; cf. 1 Chr 16:28-29. In Ps 66:1-4 "glory/honor" occurs in a call to "praise" (זמר) the name of YHWH, but the verb "bow down" is not part of the imperative. Elsewhere only the verbs "give" (נתן, Jer 13:16) and "set/render" (שׂים// נתן, Josh 7:19) in association with the substantive "glory/honor" are used in the call to praise YHWH.

327. On the association of *kābôd* and theophanies, see discussion on Ps 97. Some biblical scholars link *kābôd* with theophanies in view of the tradition of Baʿal (Cross, *Canaanite Myth*, 153, though he says not exclusively, 167), while others see this as characteristic of El (Margulis, "Canaanite Origin," 348; Mettinger, *Dethronement*, 117). Jeremias sees the *kbd* of El as displayed in the temple, while that of Baʿal is in the sense of display of power in nature, and he argues that the two former traditions are fused in the Yahwistic tradition (Jeremias, *Königtum Gottes*, 35, 43). By contrast, Kloos disputes any connection of *kābôd* with either El or Baʿal (Kloos, *Yhwh's Combat*, 23, 58).

328. Jeremias, *Königtum Gottes*, 35.

329. The English translation here is the same as the MT, though the latter has two sets of numbering. However, the elements accompanying YHWH's disclosure in the wind are the same as in the references to similar occurrences of YHWH's theophany (see Exod 19:16-19; 33:19-22; 34:6).

330. See Exod 19:19; 20:18.

YHWH IN THE WIND(S)

mountain engulfed with "fire," cloud, and deep darkness.[331] In response, the people of Israel acknowledge the magnitude of beholding the sight of YHWH's "glory" (כבד) and majesty from this phenomenon involving the sound of YHWH's "voice"[332] (קול) from the "fire" (אש, Deut 5:24[21, ET 24]). With a sense of foreboding dread, the people express their desire to refrain from hearing the "voice" of YHWH for fear of perishing in the great fire (v. 25[22, ET 25]). The people's deference to the sight and sound of YHWH also shows the conflation of fire and wind in the phenomenon encountered representing YHWH's presence.

At the same time, however, the people express the enigmatic rhetoric statement about who of mortal flesh can live upon hearing the "voice" of the living God emerging from the fire (Deut 5:26[23, ET 26]). This rhetorical statement brings into tension the people's claim of YHWH showing them his "glory" and "majesty," and the conundrum in the divine declaration to Moses that no one can sight the nature of YHWH, and live. YHWH makes this declaration in reference to the overpowering effulgence of his *kābôd* upon Moses's inquiry on the guarantee of YHWH's presence in guiding the nation of Israel (Exod 33:20). Indeed, the nature of the *kābôd*[333] revealed here should be viewed as the luminous appearance of YHWH's wind (symbolized as the voice) accompanied with the [flaming] fire (see Deut 5:22[19, ET 22]),[334] comparable to the characteristics of the wind-deities, Amma and, possibly, Inanna.

---

331. Deut 5:22-24[19-21, ET 22-24]; see Exod 19:16-19. This apparition is also consistent with the dazzling radiance, or light of YHWH emanating from a combination of natural phenomena—clouds, thick darkness, and fire—as in other theophanic hymns emphasizing the "glory" (כבד, Ps 97:6b) and splendor of YHWH's appearance in the wind (Ps 97:1-6; see 50:2-3; 104:1c-2a, 31a; Hab 3:3c-4). The nuance is also in keeping with the image of the apparition Ezekiel beholds of the כבוד־יהוה resembling fire and light (Ezek 1:28; see 10:4-6).

332. The phenomenon the people of Israel experience at the decree of the ten commandments, that causes dread on them, is the luminous and sonorous wind of YHWH emitting the same effulgence Moses experiences, as stated in Exod 33:19-22 (cf. 34:29-30). Here, YHWH causes his *kābôd* to "pass" (עבר, 33:19, 22; see 34:6), as wind before Moses to reassure his presence on the journey through the wilderness.

333. On Geller's view on *kābôd* in Isa 6:3 as relating the light of YHWH to illuminate his nature at creation (cf. Isa 60:19), see pp. 53–54 above. On Shu as god of wind and light, see pp. 80–81. However, that light or the luminous wind is identified with YHWH's countenance, or face can be seen in the lamentational petition to YHWH, who is seated between the cherubim, to "shine forth" (הופיע, Ps 80:2-4[1-3]) as the shepherd of Israel. Here, the Psalmist evokes YHWH's past acts of blessing and protection recalled with the cryptic language: "Let your face shine." See p. 179.

334. See Exod 20:18; 24:16-17; Ps 29:7.

PROCLAMATION OF YHWH AS KING IN THE WIND

In due course following the revelation at Mount Sinai, YHWH's voice(=wind), a personification of YHWH's glory, emanates from the cherubim seated on the atonement cover of the covenantal ark (Num 7:89). This idea further sheds light on the significance of the ark in association with the phenomenon representing YHWH's glory and presence in the wind. For instance, there is an intersection of elements: the voice, cherubim, and arm/hand embodied in the symbol of the ark. All these elements represent YHWH's holy presence in the guise of the wind, and are welded together in the narrative on the crossing of the River Jordan. According to the divine injunction mediated through Joshua, the Levites carry the ark and stand in the River Jordan until the people cross on dry ground (Josh 3:7–4:24). The water stops flowing as soon as the priests carrying the ark come to the edge of the River Jordan (3:13–16). As stated, the ark of "the lord of all the earth" (3:11, 13) is positioned in the center of the Jordan, and the waters upstream stop flowing to allow the people to cross on dry ground (v. 17). This safe passage on dry ground at the River Jordan alludes to YHWH wielding his power in the wind embedded with the symbol of the ark. Moreover, in commemoration of this event, the power of YHWH at the crossing of this river is personified as the wielding of his powerful "hand" (יד, 4:24)[335] over the waters. That the event is recalled by the Deuteronomistic historian as undeniably comparable to the crossing of the Red Sea[336] further indicates that the involvement of YHWH's phenomenal wind is not in question.

In the account of the crossing of the River Jordan, the Deuteronomistic historian juxtaposes the powerful hand of YHWH with the ark to allude to the potent wind of YHWH, as the force behind the drying up of the waters. Therefore, the phenomena associated with the ark and personified as YHWH's "hand" (ימין, Josh 4:24),[337] or "voice" (Deut 5:23[20, ET 23], 24[21, ET 24]) denote YHWH's powerful wind. As noted, the voice is identified with YHWH's "glory" and embodied with the ark that bears YHWH's name (2 Sam 6:2; 1 Chr 13:6). No wonder, the Deuteronomistic historian accounts for the defeat of the Israelites by the Philistines, and stresses on the capture of the ark of the covenant with an expression of acquiescence, as the "departure" of YHWH's "glory" from Israel (1 Sam 4:7). But in contrast, and also in affirmation of the association of the ark with YHWH's presence, the Psalmist proclaims the return of YHWH

---

335. See Exod 14:31.
336. Josh 4:23–24; Exod 14:21–22; cf. 15:8; Ps 114:3, 5.
337. See Exod 15:6, 12 [זרוע], 16 [ימין]; cf. 14:31.

from battle, as the king of glory (Ps 24:10), who is the victorious warrior (vv. 7–9). As already stated in relation to Ps 24, YHWH's might in battle is stated in sequel to YHWH's founding of the earth in emphasis of his power over the waters (vv. 1–2; see Ps 93:1–4). The idea evokes images of YHWH girded with might, as demonstrated by his mighty arm and strong hand (יד//זרוע) personifying YHWH's wind at work at primal creation (89:14[13]; see v. 11[10]).

As already pointed out, a more specific reference to YHWH's might manifested in the wind is lodged with the cherubim enthroned above the ark, lending the latter the appellative: "The ark of your [YHWH's] might." The invocation to YHWH, but directed at the ark to "arise"[338] to its resting place, indicates the Psalmist's reference to YHWH manifested in the wind. As one of the compositions attributed to King David, Ps 29, therefore, is no exception in recalling the same ideas alluding to YHWH's glorious might or power depicted in the sevenfold intonation of the wind personified as the "voice." All these features and symbolisms point to King David's recognition of the significance of YHWH's presence among the people of Israel and YHWH's manifestation of his might in the winds (see Ps 18). Here, too, in Ps 29, King David incorporates all the various symbolic features familiar from the Hebrew religio-cultural tradition into this short song in praise of YHWH's deeds of salvation. Thus, the thrust of Ps 29 as one of the songs associated with the musical worship before the ark (1 Chr 16:28–29; cf. Ps 29:1–2), comes to light in view of the symbolic elements relating the presence of YHWH and his might manifested in the wind.

As already pointed out in the main, the "sons of gods"[339] (בני אלים) mentioned in the prelude of Ps 29, are called upon to render praise to

---

338. *Contra* Day, who sees in this formula a reference to the reenactment of the cultic enthronement festival. He supports this idea in view of other biblical texts mentioning the procession of the ark accompanied with the "shout" and going up at the sound of the horn (Day, "Ark," 67–71). Day misses the point on these elements representing YHWH's age-old *modus operandi* in the wind.

339. The translation "gods" for אלים, as opposed to an appellation for YHWH, is preferable here, since nowhere else in the Hebrew texts is YHWH referred to by that nominal expression. It is also possible that King David used this term "sons of gods" as a satiric reference to the kings of the nations he defeated in keeping with the ANE notion of the father-son relationships between kings and their respective gods (cf. Ps 2:7; 2 Sam 7:14; Gordon, *1 & 2 Samuel*, 239). Perhaps Ps 68:13[12]a attests to this idea of the hosts of kings who flee at their defeat. In that sense, then these defeated kings of the nations are enjoined by King David to give homage to YHWH in recognition of the superiority of his power.

YHWH. In this respect, the psalm includes an acknowledgement of the existence of other gods[340] to whom YHWH's power is unrivalled in defeat of the nations.[341] Also, as in other texts, which reflect the idea of a pantheon, the heavenly beings are portrayed as subordinate to YHWH. This is also the case in another psalm of King David, Ps 89:8[7],[342] where, with the only other occurrence of the term בני אלים, YHWH's indisputable sovereignty above other gods[343] is expressed. Ps 29:1, therefore, assumes the same poetic tenor and relegates the "(sons of) gods" to the status of paying homage to YHWH. The comparison recalls the gods of the nations subdued by YHWH, and serves as a counterpoint of their nature as non-entities. This idea is identical to that represented in the context of YHWH's manifestation in the wind in Ps 97:7. Yet, in bold contrast, YHWH is acclaimed the creator of the heavens,[344] where he displays his glory.[345] Thus, in comparison to other gods, be it the heavenly council of the holy ones, or the gods of the defeated nations ridiculed as non-entities, YHWH embodies all power, and deserves honor. Taking that into account, the summons to the sons of the gods to ascribe "glory/honor" (כבד), "strength" (עז, v. 1), and to "bow down" (שחה, v. 2)[346] in Ps 29, is not meant to invest YHWH with these qualities. Instead, the summons calls for obeisance to the one for whom demonstration of these attributes, as mentioned elsewhere in the biblical tradition[347] is a prerogative. As Ps 29 shows, these are the fundamental attributes that YHWH displays in his power invested in the wind.

---

340. See Pss 96:4b–5; 97:9.

341. Pss 47:4[3], 8–9[7–8]; 96:3–4; 97:7.

342. It is of significance to some biblical scholars who interpret Ps 29 in terms of its affinity to a mythological battle with the sea, that in Ps 89, "the sons of (the) gods" are mentioned in the context of YHWH's defeat of the sea monster, personified as Rahab (Ginsberg, "Phoenician Hymn," 472).

343. Other references acknowledge the supremacy of YHWH in a council or court of gods, as attested by these terms: בני האלהים (Gen 6:2, 4; Job 1:6; 2:1; cf. Job 38:7) and בני עליון (Ps 82:6). Cf. 1 Kgs 22:19 attesting to an existence of a celestial constitution, צבא השמים—host of the heavens—that stands before YHWH's throne (כסא).

344. Ps 96:5; see 1 Chr 16:26.

345. Ps 97:6.

346. See Ps 96:9.

347. See Ps 93:1; Isa 51:9.

YHWH IN THE WIND(S)

Undoubtedly, the complimentary expression "splendor of (his) holiness"³⁴⁸ (הדרת־קדש)³⁴⁹ in Ps 29:2, as noted for Ps 96, suggests the grandeur of YHWH's luminous wind that is central to YHWH's entitlement to such praise. That the idea of wind implied by the phrase "splendor of (his) holiness" is not in question. It is supported by the occurrence of the same verse in Ps 96:9 and 1 Chr 16:29c–30a recited in the liturgical worship instituted by King David at the transfer of the ark.³⁵⁰ This imperative to worship YHWH occurring in Ps 96:9a and 1 Chr 16:29c, undoubtedly, as regimen from "day after day,"³⁵¹ is followed by the same subjunctive clause in Ps 96:9b and 1 Chr 16:30a compelling the earth to "writhe"³⁵² (חיל), befitting the reaction to YHWH's manifestation in the wind.³⁵³ This reaction is evoked in light of YHWH's indisputable presence and glorious power revealed before the nations and beheld in the stable creation, as presented in both Ps 96:1–10 and 1 Chr 16:23–30. It is evident that Ps 29 focuses on the same theme, and lauds YHWH whose glory is manifested in the powerful wind through all creation, as YHWH appears to execute his unchallenged rule (vv. 3–9).

First and foremost is YHWH's control of the insurgent forces that are metaphorically represented as "waters" (מים) or "many waters" (מים רבים, v. 3). In this context of Ps 29, as in other Hebrew texts, the "waters" (מים)³⁵⁴ or the "many waters" (מים רבים)³⁵⁵ are mentioned here to represent the chaotic waters, historical opponents, the wicked, insolent people, or indeed Israel's enemies. Hence, here King David recalls the appearance of YHWH in the roaring wind over the waters at primal creation, and transposes the same idea on the mundane plane as YHWH directs

---

348. The meaning proposed here becomes more apparent in light of YHWH's wind by which YHWH makes his majesty known.

349. See Ps 96:9; 1 Chr 16:29c.

350. 1 Chr 16:4–6; see vv. 37–42. Although 1 Chr 16 is an expansion of the ark narrative in 2 Sam 6, this element of continuous worship is missing in the latter Deuteronomistic text.

351. 1 Chr 16:23b; see Ps 96:2b. This imperative to proclaim YHWH's salvation, as routine from day to day, compels for regular liturgical or mystical worship, and does not relate to a reenactment of the cultic enthronement, as some scholars in support of Mowinckel's enthronement theory would suggest.

352. On the verb חיל, expressing the effect of YHWH's appearance with the wind, see pp. 174, 190 above.

353. See Exod 15:14b; חול, as the alternative term is employed in Ps 114:7a.

354. Pss 69:2–3[1–2], 15–16[14–15]; 104:6b–7; 124:4–5.

355. Pss 18:17[16]; 144:7; Hab 3:15.

the course of historical events. The magnitude of YHWH's "strength" (כח) and "splendor" (הדר) in the wind (v. 4) is not only signified by his control of the chaotic waters (v. 3)[356] resulting in the establishment of the world, but underscores YHWH's superiority in subduing the "many waters," representing historical enemies,[357] for the establishment of peace to the benefit of his people, as Ps 29:11 indicates.

But the supremacy of YHWH's power in the wind is also discernible in nature. YHWH's self-disclosure to impose his rule is seen in its devastating effects on elements thought to be strong and durable. The specificity of names suggests historical incidents producing the marked impression of YHWH's audible and loud sounds emanating from his manifestation in the wind and leaving the undeniable imprint on nature. Thus, the cedars of Lebanon, despite their loftiness (Isa 2:13a), rip and shatter from the force of YHWH's wind (Ps 29:5). Again, as attested in other biblical texts, YHWH's wind causes the mountains to quake (v. 6).[358] Compared to Amma's breath that hews out fire, YHWH's wind bursts out with flames of fire (Ps 29:7). But here, King David mentions specifically the mountains of Lebanon and Sirion(=Mount Hermon[359]) skipping[360] like a calf and a young wild ox[361] respectively, while the desert of Qadesh "writhes" from the force of YHWH's wind (v. 8). He relates the image of the hinds[362] calving while the forests are stripped bare, as an epic eyewitness account of the force of impact of YHWH's bluster of wind (v. 9aβ; cf. v. 5).

---

356. See Pss 24:1–2; 93:4; 104:6–7.

357. See Pss 18:17–18[16–17]; 144:7.

358. See Pss 18:8[7]b; 114:6; Job 9:5a; Hab 3:6c, 10a.

359. See Deut 3:8–9; Judg 3:3 with the latter indicating reference to the same mountain range.

360. The imagery of mountains "skipping" is rooted in theophanies in the Hebrew tradition (Ps 114:4, 6). Jeremias interprets these disruptions as a consequence of an earthquake (Jeremias, *Königtum Gottes*, 33). Instead, this image is only a hyperbole on the massive impact of YHWH's self-manifestation with the phenomenal winds causing the convulsions in nature.

361. This is stated literally in the MT as "young one of a wild oxen" (Ps 29:6b).

362. Some scholars propose to read here "oaks" (אילות) as in the MT to maintain a parallel with "trees/forests" (יערות) in the following stich. Therefore, the reference to "hinds" appears to be inappropriate. But since King David is describing the effects of YHWH's power in nature, he introduces the idea of "hinds calving" (חלל אילות; cf. Job 39:1) with the intent to show that YHWH not only has control over the waters (v. 3), but also animate creation (see Job 39:1–4).

YHWH IN THE WIND(S)

King David incorporates ideas that derive from other Hebrew sources with this series of otherwise unparalleled images in the Hebrew tradition to relate different contexts of YHWH's theophanies, and throw into bold relief YHWH's power through the wind. YHWH's sway over the cedars of Lebanon, as represented by his sonorous wind breaking them, recalls his creative power. YHWH creates the cedars of Lebanon (Ps 104:16); but despite their loftiness,[363] the cedars of Lebanon[364] cannot withstand YHWH's forceful wind or his wrath (Ps 29:5).[365] Moreover, YHWH's sonorous wind causes the mountain ranges of Lebanon and Sirion to skip. Although the image is a hyperbolic interpretation of the effect of the aeolian movement of YHWH's roaring wind on natural features, the image recalls the conventional idea of mountains "skipping" at YHWH's disclosure in the wind at the conquest of the promised land (see Ps 114:4, 6). Unquestionably, the mention of the wilderness of Qadesh[366] "writhing" is King David's attempt to link the experience of YHWH's manifestation in the wind with historical antecedents relating to the tradition of the ark (Num 10:33–35), though, perhaps, lost to this poetic interpretation in Ps 29.

By the same token, the idea of YHWH cleaving or emitting a flame of fire, though characteristic of paraphernalia associated with wind deities, alludes to the Mount Sinai experience. Here, YHWH discloses his "glory" (כבוד), "greatness" (גדול) and sonorous "sound" (קול) of the wind accompanied by "fire" (אש).[367] But the similarities of the elements mentioned here to the theophany in Ps 18, point to the same sight and sound of YHWH in the wind retained in Ps 29, as articulated by King David, and, perhaps, indicating the provenance of Ps 29 from a similar event. Yet, of further significance, is the effect of YHWH's roaring wind that causes hinds to calve indicating not only YHWH's infinite power over animate nature, but also King David's firsthand account of the impression of the divine theophany in the wind. However, the majesty of YHWH in

---

363. Isa 2:13; cf. Ps 92:13[12]b; cf. Isa 10:34.

364. The cedars of Lebanon were durable and widely sought after for the construction of royal courts and temples in the ANE (1 Kgs 5:6, 13; cf. 2 Chr 2:3, 8–9). But, as King David implies in their tearing up and shattering in Ps 29, it means their durability would not bear up the force of YHWH's wind.

365. Cf. Isa 10:33–34.

366. The desert of Qadesh is mentioned a few times, as one of the locales of sojourn for the people of Israel during their wilderness experiences (Num 13:26; 20:1, 14, 22; 33:36; Deut 1:46).

367. Deut 5:22–24[19–21, ET 22–24]; see Exod 19:18.

the wind is revealed with this combination of a plethora of phenomena in Ps 29, to quell inimical forces (v. 3), and therewith, empower and give succor to his people (vv. 10–11). In response to this intervention of the supreme deity in the mundane realm, the worshipers ascribe praise to YHWH in his temple (v. 9c), which resonates with the proclamation of his glory among the heavenly beings (vv. 1–2).[368]

In view of other Hebrew texts alluding to YHWH's appearance in the wind, Ps 29 employs imagery that is familiar from other traditions, in a most peculiar manner, in connection with Hebrew thought forms and traditions, in order to present the principal theme of YHWH's presence and kingship. YHWH's rule is not only recognized by his power to manipulate cosmic forces, but by his control of events in the historical arena. In fact, what King David relates in mythical terms about the power of YHWH's thunderous voice over the "(many) waters" ([רבים] מים) is nothing other than his subjugation of Israel's enemies and, arguably, the foreign nations subjected to YHWH's blustery wind (see Pss 18:8–18[7–17], 43[42]a; 144:7). Thus, the sevenfold intonation of the wind of YHWH, personified as the "voice," alludes to a liturgical or mystical worship of YHWH, as the mighty and exalted king, who is glorious in power and wields victories for his people, Israel. YHWH stoops down in the guise of the wind to intervene for his people as the divine warrior in assertion of his eternal kingship (Ps 29:10b).

Moreover, in sharp contrast to YHWH's authoritative intervention that affects and convulses nature or repulses enemies(=[many] waters), something of the tranquility of YHWH is also apparent. He instills "strength" (עז), and grants his people "peace" (שלום, v. 11). Here, Ps 29:11 in part recalls the Aaronic benediction with reference to YHWH exposing his countenance of favor to Israel, in order to usher in peace[369] as the absolute state of well-being and security procured by YHWH's constant presence. At the same time, this notion of YHWH granting his people peace implies his face shining upon them (Num 6:25–26a). The idea evokes YHWH's disclosure in the wind destroying Israel's enemies.[370]

---

368. By neglecting the boundaries between the earthly and heavenly temple (1 Kgs 8:27–30), the Psalmist, here, too, intends to show the contemporaneousness of praise in the earthly and heavenly realm. But the earthly orientation of the praise could be maintained if the exhortatory call to the sons of the gods in Ps 29:1 is directed to the kings of the defeated nations.

369. Num 6:26b.

370. Pss 47:4[3]; 96:3; 97:3, 10; 98:1–3.

YHWH IN THE WIND(S)

Hence, it follows that the term "many waters" (מים רבים) in Ps 29:3, as much as in Ps 18, symbolizes historical opponents lending the interpretation of Ps 29 as soteriological, in view of YHWH's wind subduing them (v. 3), like the chaotic waters at creation. And, with the realization of historical salvation, there is YHWH's empowerment of his people, thereby tranquility in social order is affirmed (v. 11). As a result, the heavenly enthroned YHWH (v. 1), who intervenes as divine warrior to determine his people's destiny, is praised as the eternal king (v. 10). Accordingly, YHWH is "enthroned (as) at the flood" (למבול ישב).[371] Here, too, at this epoch, YHWH routs the wicked by his flood. But, in sequel, YHWH's "wind" (רוח) causes the waters to recede (Gen 8:1). Once, again, the idea resonates with YHWH's potentiality to repel the waters, as at primal creation[372] in keeping with YHWH's prerogative as "king to eternity" (מלך לעולם, Ps 29:10b). With all these elements and traditions considered relating YHWH appearing in the phenomenal winds, this rendition of Ps 29 by King David is apropos:

> 1 Ascribe to YHWH, sons of gods; ascribe to YHWH glory and strength.
> 2 Ascribe to YHWH glory of his name; bow down to YHWH in the splendor of his holiness.
> 3 The wind of YHWH is over the waters; the God of glory roars, YHWH over the many waters.
> 4 The wind of YHWH [is] with power, the wind of YHWH with splendor.
> 5 The wind of YHWH breaks the cedars; and YHWH breaks the cedars of Lebanon.
> 6 And He makes them skip like a calf; Lebanon and Sirion like a young one of wild oxen.
> 7 The wind of YHWH hews out flames of fire.

---

371. Tsumura also proposes not to associate this term with the *Chaoskampf* tradition, and not as a "locative" but as "temporal" in keeping with the usage in the Mesopotamian tradition (Tsumura, *Creation and Destruction*, 155). But, for views associated with the ANE *Chaoskampf* myth and suggestions on YHWH's enthronement over the flood, see Longman, *Psalms*, 155, 157; Weiser, *Psalms*, 260–61; Craigie, *Psalms 1–50*, 248–49. Cross even suggests translating this phrase in Ps 29:10: "Over the Flood-dragon," in view of Ba'al's enthronement stated in KTU 1.101:1–2[=RS 24.245:1–2] (Cross, *Canaanite Myth*, 147n4). Similarly, Day objects any reference to the flood of Noah in preference to the cosmic waters he considers alluded to in Ps 29:3. Therefore, he sees both vv. 3 and 10 relating YHWH's dominion over the cosmic waters in close connection with the myths of Ba'al (Day, *God's Conflict*, 59).

372. Gen 1:2; Ps 104:1c–9.

PROCLAMATION OF YHWH AS KING IN THE WIND

8 The wind of YHWH writhes the wilderness; YHWH writhes the wilderness of Kadesh.
9 The wind of YHWH causes hinds to calve, and strips the forests bare, and in His temple they all cry "glory."
10 YHWH sat at the flood, and He sits as king to eternity.
11 YHWH gives strength to His people;
YHWH blesses His people with peace (Ps 29:1–11).

Fundamentally, the Psalmist, in Ps 29, takes up an old theme on YHWH's *modus operandi* in the wind, but in an artistic manner, which incorporates various images to enrich his ideas and expressions of the kingship of YHWH. Therefore, the interpretation of the psalm proposed here suggests a different meaning for the primary statements of vv. 3 and 10. YHWH's wind is over the waters, the God of "glory" roars over[373] the many waters/enemies (v. 3). This acclamation sums up YHWH's act in subduing the chaotic waters by his phenomenal wind at primal creation, and by the same means, YHWH asserts his power over the many waters representing historical foes.[374] Also, YHWH demonstrates his power in the guise of the wind, when his divine design is subverted, as at the historical flood. Hence, the Psalmist avers: YHWH sat[375] [enthroned] at the flood, and YHWH remains[376] king to eternity (v. 10),[377] as he continuously works salvation for the welfare of his elected people (v. 11). To that end, these statements in Ps 29:3 and 10 are not mythical allusions relating to a cultic enthronement of a victorious deity over some mythical flood. Instead, they present the kingship of YHWH asserted in acts of destruction of inimical forces. Therefore, Ps 29 bears the same content as Ps 97, and not less of other theophanic texts (see Ps 96), that is, YHWH's theophany in the wind, kingship and welfare of the people are the dominant motifs. Although the ideas and expressions incorporate elements with mythic flavor, Ps 29 is original to the Hebrew tradition, and uses dramatic images common to other texts alluding to YHWH's disclosure in the winds in the course of presenting the fundamental character of YHWH as divine warrior and king.

373. See Pss 93:4; 104:6–7.
374. See Pss 18:17[16]; 144:7.
375. BDB 442 offers three meanings for the verb root ישב: "sit," "remain," and "dwell."
376. Opting here to translate the *Qal* imperfect of the root ישב to "remain," in order to assert the idea of the eternality of YHWH's reign, as attested in other biblical Hebrew texts.
377. See Pss 93:1.

YHWH IN THE WIND(S)

Psalm 68—YHWH's Victorious March in the Phenomenal Winds

The connection of YHWH's intervention with the occurrence of the phenomenal wind deployed for Israel's deliverance is more evident in Ps 68. It is along these lines that the original meaning of the psalm is likely to be found.[378] As already noted in the course of this discussion on YHWH's theophany in the winds, the Psalmist in Ps 68 uses two distinct appellatives: "Rider of the steppes" (רכב בערבות, v. 5[4]) and "rider of the ancient heavens" (רכב בשמי שמי־קדם, v. 34[33]) to give his message on YHWH's divine presence its form and content. These two appellations are purposely placed in the prelude and postlude segments of the psalm. Though the terms may seem to have different meanings, the Psalmist uses them complementarily to express YHWH's role in relation to the deliverance of his people. First, it is proper, therefore, to elucidate the meaning that is pertinent to the title ascribed to YHWH in the prelude of the psalm (v. 5[4]).

As already pointed out,[379] most biblical scholars generally argue that the epithet, רכב בערבות, in v. 5[4] should be translated "rider on the clouds," or "rider of the clouds" in view of the Ugaritic title for Ba'al, *rkb 'rpt*. Yet, the Hebrew context favors the translation "rider of the steppes." This title is compatible with the description of the appearance of YHWH in the wilderness tradition, as he "marches" (צעד) through the "wasteland" (ישימון)[380] ahead of his people (Ps 68:8[7]). The title also resonates with the references to Sinai (vv. 9[8], 18[17]) in relation to the record of YHWH's theophany and intervention in the wilderness tradition.

Although vv. 9[8] and 18[17] employ the title Elohim with reference to the Sinai tradition, in place of the appellative YHWH, which occurs more frequently in the description of the Sinai theophany proper,[381] the

---

378. It goes without saying that Ps 68 has been considered a *crux interpretum* (see Buttenwieser, *Psalms*, 30; Johnson, *Sacral Kingship*, 77; Dahood, *Psalms*, 2:133; Jeremias, *Königtum Gottes*, 69). Albright calls it the most difficult psalm, and "a catalogue of lyric poems" (Albright, "Catalogue," 7). The psalm has undergone several emendations at the hands of critics in attempts to make sense of the text. Several works are devoted to the analysis of this psalm (see Olmo Lete, "Ps 68," 191–92).

379. See 28, 28n198 above.

380. Other references to the wilderness traditions show that מדבר, ישימון, and ערבה are synonymous terms that often occur in parallel: ישימון//מדבר (Deut 32:10; Isa 43:19, 20; Pss 78:40; 106:14); ערבה//מדבר (Isa 40:3; 41:19; Jer 2:6; 17:6; 50:12; Job 24:5; 39:6).

381. Exod 19:16–19; 20:18–19; see Deut 5:19–24[22–27, ET 19–24].

PROCLAMATION OF YHWH AS KING IN THE WIND

Psalmist emphasizes on the name of "Yah(weh)"[382] as seen in Ps 68:5[4].[383] In the latter verse, this title "Yah" appears in collocation with the designation "rider of the steppes." This designation alludes to the wilderness tradition, and throws into bold relief the identity of the deity, whose presence in the wind wields salvation for Israel. In addition, the imperative for YHWH to "arise" in the prelude to this psalm, points to nothing other than the tradition of the ark as YHWH's war armor in the vanguard. Therefore, the reference to the truncated name of YHWH is appropriate in this context alluding to the ark as one of the symbols associated with his name, and, therewith, self-disclosure in the wind.[384] These references to the identity of YHWH, and the terms associated with the ark and wilderness traditions, therefore, do not warrant the Hebrew appellative, רכב בערבות interpreted in accordance with the Ugaritic meaning. Again, King David is at pains to depict YHWH demonstrating his power in nature by his potent wind, as he moves along with his people through the wilderness. Here, too, in Ps 68, as is typical of the reactions to YHWH's sonorous wind, the earth "shakes" (רעש), and the heavens "drip" (נטף, v. 9[8])[385] stirred by YHWH's wind.

Moreover, it is implied in Ps 68 that YHWH's appearance in the wind has two purposes. He intervenes for the redemption and establishment of his people, and, at the same time, brings the existence of the wicked to an end.[386] This twofold aspect of YHWH's saving deeds, prominent in the theophany texts discussed, recurs in this psalm in connection with the

---

382. *Contra* Arnold and Strawn, who suggest eliminating this title by maintaining that ביה שמו ("in Yah (is) his name") in Ps 68:5[4] is a gloss (Arnold and Strawn, "*Beyāh šemô*," 430).

383. The prophet Isaiah pictures a theophany against Assyria in terms of the "name of YHWH" (שם־יהוה, Isa 30:27) in association with the "arm of YHWH," personifying the wind, by which YHWH achieves victory against his enemies; in this context set to chastise Assyria (v. 30b; cf. Exod 15:16 [see v. 6]; Isa 51:9; 52:10; Ps 98:1).

384. Ps 29:2; see 96:6–8a, 9; 1 Chr 16:29.

385. Cf. water, Judg 5:4cd.

386. See Prov 10:25a; the Psalmist employs proverbial wisdom to show the stark contrast on the fate of the wicked in the face of a tempest. Even though not in favor of Cassuto's proposal to render the epithet by רכב בערבות, "who rides upon the clouds" in light of Ugaritic evidence (Cassuto, *Biblical*, 1:243–44), the other designations of YHWH that imply riding on the cloud(s) (Deut 33:26–29; Isa 19:1; Hab 3:8; Pss 18:11[10]; cf. Ps 68:34[33]); in allusion to YHWH's winds dispersing the clouds, are connected with the idea of retribution for the wicked and salvation for the righteous (Cassuto, *Biblical*, 244–45).

theme of divine presence.³⁸⁷ The Psalmist deliberately appeals to some earlier OT traditions on YHWH's appearance and triumphant march (Ps 68:2–3[1–2])³⁸⁸ that are bound up with the idea of the patent presence of YHWH in the wind, and emphasize YHWH's deeds of salvation in history. Therefore, YHWH's age-old *modus operandi* in the wind is the unifying element for what may seem unrelated traditions in this psalm.³⁸⁹

The statement at the beginning of the psalm invoking YHWH to arise (Ps 68:2[1]), and echoing the sacramental "shout" when the ark is taken out for battle (Num 10:35), expresses the assurance that YHWH saves, and, at the same time, embodies the sentiments of the theme of YHWH's indisputable presence that recurs throughout the psalm. Alongside the descriptions of YHWH's appearance, the Psalmist highlights his active involvement in warfare. The idea that YHWH's warfare is centered on divine intervention in the guise of the phenomenal wind, is suggested by the figurative language that describes the destruction of the wicked; notably the images of "blowing" like smoke or "melting" like wax before the fire (Ps 68:3[2]). The concepts of blowing and melting conjure up images and paraphernalia associated with the wind deities. The imagery of "melting" is not uncommon in depiction of YHWH's disclosure in the fiery wind.³⁹⁰ Therefore, this idea of "melting" like wax, in conjunction with that of smoke (עשן) "driven about" (נדף [by wind]), amplifies the description of the wicked in helter-skelter at YHWH's melodramatic appearance with the fiery wind. Thus, when YHWH arises (קום) his enemies scatter and flee "from his presence" (מפניו). In contrast to the plight of the wicked, however, the righteous are liberated "at his

---

387. The psalm presents the three major traditions in the history of Israel: wilderness (Ps 68:2–5[1–4], 8–9[7–8]), conquest (vv. 10–16[9–15]) and settlement traditions (vv. 17–36[16–35]), each of which involves the destruction of the wicked (vv. 2–3[1–2], 7[6]c, 13[12], 15[14], 22–24[21–23], 31[30]) in contrast with the salvation of the righteous or YHWH's people (vv. 4[3], 6–7[5–6]b, 10–11[9–10], 20–21[19–20], 35–36[34–35]). As mentioned considering other texts, the theophany of YHWH involves the destruction of inimical forces, and the creation and protection of Israel.

388. See Num 10:35; Ps 68:9[8]; Judg 5:4–5.

389. Albright proposed that the psalm is an anthology of quotations because of its allusion to various traditions in Israelite history (Albright, "Catalogue," 1–39); cf. Schmidt, who saw the psalm as a collection of independent songs (Schmidt, *Psalmen*, 125). Olmo Lete sees a combination of Canaanite and Yahwistic elements in two songs blended together (Olmo Lete, "Ps 68," 192).

390. See pp. 127, 223 above. In Ps 97:5 and Mic 1:4 it is the mountains and hills respectively, that figuratively melt (cf. Ps 46:7[6]; Nah 1:5) showing the force of impact from the aeolian movement of YHWH's potent fiery winds on these natural symbols of stability and permanence.

PROCLAMATION OF YHWH AS KING IN THE WIND

presence" (לפניו, Ps 68:4[3]). In response, they rejoice before YHWH, for whom the Psalmist solicits praise as "rider of the steppes" (v. 5[4]), in symbolism of his immanence. The praise is offered in return for YHWH's care and sustenance of his people during the "march" in his age-old *modus operandi* in the wind.

YHWH's presence and guidance during the triumphant procession is expressed as a "going forth" (יצא) and a "march"[391] (צעד, Ps 68:8[7]) through the wilderness. The collocation of these two verbs[392] in expression of divine deliverance is exclusive to theophany texts. The idea may be drawn from the only other occurrences of the same word pair in Judg 5:4 and Hab 3:12-13, which also recall the victorious march through the wilderness in connection with YHWH's theophany in the wind for deliverance. Moreover, it is significant that, of all the occurrences[393] of the verb צעד, YHWH appears as subject only in these theophany texts. The intervention of YHWH in the wind during the wilderness march causes the earth to "shake" (רעש). Some scholars see the "shaking" of the earth as the effect of an earthquake.[394] But, in light of other similar occurrences, it is certain that YHWH's disclosure in the wind causes the convulsions in the most durable and stable features of the natural order.[395] Therefore, the reference to the "shaking" of the earth in Ps 68:9[8]a is in keeping with the conventional effects of YHWH's theophany in the winds. Moreover,

---

391. As Seow notes, the root צעד is employed in 2 Sam 6:13 in connection with the procession of the ark. Thus, with the use of the same verb in Ps 68, Seow suggests that the psalm is associated with the procession of the ark (Seow, *Myth*, 104-7). In any case, as already noted in King David's contest against the Philistines, the term צעד is employed in the phrase "the sound of marching," heard at the top of the balsam trees, as the signal of YHWH's divine intervention in the guise of the wind (2 Sam 5:24). However, the allusion to the procession of the ark is one other aspect in Ps 68 indicating intimation of YHWH's presence in the wind. Therefore, it is appropriate to conclude that the psalm is liturgical and used in celebration of YHWH's victories in the wilderness.

392. Avishur argues that יצא//צעד are a word pair appearing in theophany descriptions. In view of Hab 3:12, he criticizes Tur-Sinai for emending תצעד ארץ ("you march upon the earth") to תערץ ארץ ("you cause the earth to tremble"). He notes that צעד is one of the principal elements in theophany descriptions; see Judg 5:4 (Avishur, *Studies*, 184n202).

393. Gen 49:22; Judg 5:4; 2 Sam 6:13; Jer 10:5; Hab 3:12; Ps 68:8[7]; Prov 7:8; Job 18:14.

394. Among others, Tate, Johnson, and Olmo Lete associate the shaking of the earth with an earthquake (Tate, *Psalms*, 177; Johnson, *Sacral Kingship*, 79; Olmo Lete, "Ps 68," 201).

395. Pss 18:8[7]a; 77:19[18]c; cf. Hab 3:7bc.

YHWH IN THE WIND(S)

YHWH's sonorous wind gives rise to the natural phenomena mentioned in this psalm: the winds mete out the clouds releasing the bounteous rain (vv. 9–10[8–9]a). The image presented here is also consistent with other texts recalling YHWH asserting his presence in the skies with torrents of rain during the wilderness march.[396] The idea is further elaborated by the concluding part of Ps 68, where the Psalmist relates the greatness of YHWH displayed by the power of his "voice," that is, the wind in the heavens (vv. 34–35[33–34]).

Undoubtedly, YHWH's thunderous or blustery wind underlies the reactions seen in nature.[397] This effect is further supported by the identity of YHWH expressed in this psalm as the "One of Sinai" in relation to the wilderness tradition (Ps 68:9[8]). Indeed, as the God of Israel, YHWH discloses himself with the loud sound of his luminous wind, fire and smoke, on a mountain covered with a thick cloud. In a sense, these elements associated with the wind motion, and recalled in Ps 68, signal divine judgment as YHWH comes to save the afflicted and destroy the wicked (vv. 4–7[3–6]ab; vv. 2–3, 7[1–2, 6]c, respectively). The idea of the heavens pouring rain, in part as an agent of deliverance (v. 9[8]), anticipates and guarantees the gift of bounteous rain at the settlement (v. 10[9]). By the same elements with which YHWH chastises, he also benefits[398] the poor. So the Psalmist connects the idea of the "march of victory"[399] with the unleashing of meteorological elements and the meting out of divine justice. With this idea in view, it is therefore appropriate to conclude that Ps 68 is a hymn on the "march of victory." The victories achieved by YHWH are also manifested in his people's welfare and settlement. So, the welfare for the solitary, poor or afflicted—weary inheritance—is vouchsafed, but the rebellious ones are consigned to parched land[400] (vv. 6–11[5–10]). Inasmuch as YHWH is depicted here as divine

---

396. See Judg 5:4; Ps 77:18[17]aβ; Hab 3:10b.

397. Exod 19:16–18; cf. 20:18, 21; Deut 5:22–24[19–21, ET 22–24]. Although rain is not mentioned explicitly in the Sinai tradition, we may presume that the rain is issued from the thick cloud, as the former is also often a part of the multifarious elements doled out by the blustery wind (see 1 Sam 12:18; Hab 3:10b; Job 37:11–13).

398. Job 37:13.

399. See Mann, *Divine Presence*, 177–78. Mann correctly identifies this as referring to the march in the wilderness. But our views differ in his suggestion to link this to cultic processions similar to the ANE traditions.

400. See Ps 68:10–11[9–10] in contrast to v. 7[6]c. In keeping with the Psalmists' style of using contrasts, the ones vindicated by YHWH, as his treasured possession(=inheritance: נחלה), though "weary" (נלאה, v. 10[9]), are replenished with bounteous rain, and welfare is established (v. 11[10]), but the rebellious are banished

warrior, he is also the father for the orphans, supreme judge for the widows (vv. 6–7[5–6]),[401] and fertility giver for the poor or afflicted (vv. 10–11[9–10]), as he safeguards divine justice for the underprivileged.

It should be noted at this point that the biblical *hapax legomenon* בכושרות[402] in Ps 68:7[6]b can be satisfactorily interpreted within its context. The Psalmist points out that YHWH "in his holy dwelling"[403] (במעון קדשו, v. 6[5]b) takes up the cause of the afflicted and solitary, and appears for their redemption. Undoubtedly, YHWH's concern is to vindicate those deprived of life's basic necessities. This occasions YHWH's appearing for their protection. The Psalmist uses locatives "in a home" (ביתה), and "in a scorched land" (צחיחה) in parallel with בכושרות to represent the different conditions into which YHWH brings the underprivileged *vis-à-vis* the rebellious. As Kraus notes,[404] צחיחה means "barrenness," therefore כושרות, in antithesis, should be "fruitfulness."[405] The deity who

to scorched land (v. 7[6]c).

401. See Ps 82. As stated in Deut 10:17–18, YHWH is regarded as lord over all other gods, as well as judge and protector of the widow, orphan, and foreigner.

402. Several suggestions are offered regarding the interpretation of this word in terms of the Ugaritic *ktrt*. A few translations are suggested: "Professional singers," on the basis of the Nikkal text and Aqhat epic; "matrimonial goddesses," who assist at birth; or "skillful" on the basis of *ktr* (as in the name *ktr-w-ḥss*). See Jeremias, *Königtum Gottes*, 70n4; Strawn, "*kwšrwt*," 631–48.

403. See Deut 26:15 expressing a plea to YHWH to look down from heaven. Certainly, the Psalmist in Ps 68, intends to emphasize the heavenly abode of YHWH as the place whence he appears for divine judgment (Jer 25:30; Zech. 2:17[13]; see Ps 18:6[5]b).

404. Kraus, *Psalms 60–150*, 46.

405. In contrast, Strawn seeks to resolve the enigmatic meaning behind this biblical Hebrew *hapax legomenon*, כושרות with a translation implying "skillfulness" (Strawn, "*kwšrwt*," 637–38). First, Strawn gives evidence of the different translations presented in various manuscripts and versions. Then, he presents translations suggested by some scholars (e.g., Buhl, Waltke and O'Connor, Albright, Dahood) via different methods, which as Strawn comments, also attest to the variation, if not confusion on the meaning of this term (635). However, he discusses and critiques Albright's approach in associating this *hapax* with either male singers or *kôṯarātu*—divine midwives or midwife goddesses. Strawn also opposes Dahood's view on linking כושרות with the skillful Kôṯar-wa-Ḥasīs, thus deriving the meaning as bringing prisoners forth from chains. Strawn sees nothing of Albright or Dahood's suggestions as applicable to the context of Ps 68:7[6]. Therefore, he dismisses the suggested interpretations either relating to prisoners set free with/or the accompaniment of music. Strawn also dispels any association of the term with *kôṯarātu*—divine midwives or midwife goddesses (Strawn, "*kwšrwt*," 634n24). Nonetheless, he continues to suggest a connection of the Hebrew כושרות with the Ugaritic root *ktr* as represented by the divine name Kôṯar-wa-Ḥasīs. Thus, he proposes the translation "skilled and wise" (641). Furthermore, in view of Smith's analysis of important cognates *kšr/ktr* from other Semitic languages, Strawn

appears to disperse the rain-bearing clouds, and drenches the earth, is the same deity who brings his people into "fruitfulness" or "prosperity."

In Eccl 11:6 the root כשר ("succeed/prosper") is used in relation to sown seed. So, the idea of "prosperity" implied by the term כושרות is in order. Therefore, just as YHWH causes the "solitary" to dwell "in a home" (יחידים ביתה, Ps 68:7[6]a), he also brings forth "prisoners into prosperity"[406] (אסירים בכושרות, Ps 68:7[6]b) alluding to the settlement in the fertile land of promise. By contrast, but in line with YHWH's act of judgment on the wicked, the "rebellious" (סוררים) dwell in sterility, hence abandoned in "scorched land" (צחיחה, v. 7[6]c). Nonetheless, the reference to the welfare of YHWH's people in v. 7[6]aβ, may, in turn, be interpreted along with vv. 10b–11[9b–10]. In the latter verses, the Psalmist resumes the idea of YHWH securing provision for the elect. He expresses this as YHWH's act of establishing his "property" or "inheritance" (נחלה, v. 10[9]b). Although it is parched or "weary"[407] (נלאה), YHWH drenches

---

notes that Smith concludes that the basic meaning of the root seems to denote "skill" or "labor," which, as he quotes, has developed analogical meanings: "To be proper" or "to prosper." Subsequently, Strawn suggests that the basic meaning of "skill" for the root *ktr* makes good sense with inference on *bkwšrwt* in Ps 68:7b. Hence he translates:

"God ‹returns› the lonely to a house;
He brings forth prisoners with skill (*bkwšrwt*)
But the rebellious dwell in an arid land" (Strawn, "kwšrwt," 642–43).

Besides, Strawn also discusses morphological issues associated with the Hebrew feminine plural ending ôt (ות–) in justifying the relation with the Ugaritic root *ktr*. He therefore suggests analyzing this as a morphological feature not uncommon with abstract nouns in biblical Hebrew and other Semitic languages, including Ugaritic. The latter attests abstract forms with feminine plural and/or -(ū)t endings. At any rate, in conclusion, Strawn proffers the translation "with skillfulness" meaning "with skill" or "skillfully." He also deems the Ugaritic root *ktr* as offering an appropriate meaning for בכושרות, though he perceives בכושרות as stripped from any association with goddesses of birth or some hypothetical musical procession from bondage. Within its context, therefore, Strawn derives the meaning "skillfully" from his presumption of some dynamics of divine activity that is restorative for both the "lonely persons" and "prisoners" (644). Although Strawn's proposal is attractive and meaningful, it neither retains the idea of contrasts, in keeping with the nuance in this psalm, nor shows the different statuses to which YHWH consigns the righteous *vis-à-vis* the wicked, as manifested through YHWH's presence in the wind.

406. See BDB 507. Moreover, this outcome is quite appropriate in the view that the people of Israel were brought forth from slavery into a land metaphorically described as "a land flowing with milk and honey" (Exod 3:8; Deut 6:3; 26:15; 31:20; cf. 32:13–14).

407. The key to understanding the possible meaning of this *Niphal* participle, נלאה, lies in the preference to the dual meaning of נחלה translated in the OT as "possession/property," or "inheritance" (BDB 635); that is either representing YHWH's relationship with the people of Israel, or the land itself. In which case, נחלה in this context may

PROCLAMATION OF YHWH AS KING IN THE WIND

it with his bounteous rain, and his "flock" (חית), figurative of YHWH's community, finds this a safe haven (v. 11[10]a). Hence, the Psalmist characterizes YHWH's vindication of his people as an act of making provision[408] for the "poor"[409] (v. 11[10]b) in sequel to his redemptive acts at his

---

refer to the people Israel, or to the land given by YHWH as inheritance. In view of the Psalmist's use of contrasts, both meanings here may be deliberately conflated, in order to assert YHWH's theophany in the wind (v. 9[8]) in provision of bounteous rain in satiation of his community (v. 10[9]), and to produce goodness in the land of inheritance (v. 11[10]). The ones benefiting from this divine intervention are referred to as YHWH's people (עם, v. 8[7]), property/inheritance (נחלה, v. 10[9]), community// the poor or afflicted (עני//חית, v. 11[10]), in opposition to the rebellious ones (סררים, v. 7[6]) that YHWH abandons to sterility in a scorched land. This locale indicates utter barrenness, hence a state of deprivation. Therefore, by way of the idea of contrasts, נלאה, emphasized here with a *waw* consecutive as ונלאה, "and (being) weary," may be referring to the famished people of YHWH or the land of promise. But now drenched with YHWH's copious rain; thus conveying a status showing either renewed vitality of the people and/or productivity of the land (see v. 11[10]). It follows, then, that Strawn's suggestion to derive a new meaning for MT נלאה by emendation and repointing of this substantive, along with the prefixed *waw* considered to be vocative, is inappropriate. Strawn proposes to read ונלאה as "O Victorious One" in expression of a divine appellative for YHWH (Strawn, "*wĕnil'āh*," 785-98). Strawn proffers this new meaning based on his discussion on Semitic languages, particularly the dual meanings of the Ugaritic roots *l'y/l'h* and *y*- vocative. He argues that the Ugaritic root *l'h* I, means "to be weak" and is paralleled in Hebrew with לָאָה. However, he argues for a second root, *l'h* II, as attested in Ugaritic *l'y* I, meaning "to be strong," based on evidence from Akkadian, Aramaic, and Phoenician. Following Dahood's philological interpretations, Strawn derives support from Aramaic inscriptions, and Phoenician personal names in order to argue for a possible root לאה II in biblical Hebrew meaning "to be strong," as implied in the personal name Leah (791-92). Therefore, upon analysis of attested roots *l'h* I and *l'h* II in other Semitic languages, and also evidence on these two roots as antonyms in biblical Hebrew, "to be weak" and "to be strong," respectively, Strawn sees the Hebrew *l'h* II in parallel with the Ugaritic *l'y* I, "to be strong, victorious, powerful," and the latter as the root of Ba'al's most notable epithet, *'al'iyn b'l*. Aside from other scholars' views, and in attempt to maintain parallelism, Strawn draws a title for YHWH from the Hebrew root *l'h* II, "to be strong." So, as he reads the *waw* as vocative, Strawn suggests translating *wĕnil'āh* to "O Victorious One" (797-98), as an appellative for YHWH in keeping with its supposed Ugaritic precursor (794). As Strawn further notes in relation to the provenance of Ps 68, he points out that the psalm is thought to contain Ugaritic/ Canaanite motifs and, therefore, assigns it an early date. This presumption is in light of the description of YHWH in Ps 68:5[4] contended to read "rider of the clouds." Hence, Strawn argues for *wĕnil'āh* to derive from the same source, and as another element relating the psalm to Ugaritic/Canaanite motifs or tendencies (Strawn, "*wĕnil'āh*," 794-95). In contrast, however, it is suggested here to maintain the MT *Niphal* feminine participle with *waw* consecutive, ונלאה, as cited in Ps 68:10[9] to read "and (being) weary."

408. See Pss 65:10-12[9-11]; 85:13[12].

409. That the word "poor" (עני) represents all the classifications of those redeemed by YHWH is shown by the terms often appearing in parallel elsewhere:

theophany (vv. 7–9[6–8]). In this regard, the establishing of the heritage and the provision of bounteous rain constitute, as it were, YHWH's act of bringing the distressed "into prosperity." The idea that the Psalmist presents here, therefore, is that of divine presence of YHWH experienced in sustenance, protection and guidance during the wilderness march,[410] and in the granting of fertility following the acquisition of land.

The "Shout" of the King Is in Their Midst

With the theme of divine presence as the focal point, the Psalmist alludes to the role of YHWH in the conquest of land in Ps 68:12[11]. In this verse, YHWH is said to give a "command" (אֹמֶר),[411] which puts hostile kings to flight. Some scholars see in this verse a reference to an oracle[412] of YHWH. In contrast, Mowinckel argues that the word should not be translated "oracle."[413] Instead, he sees here a reference to the "voice" of

---

"poor"//"widow" and "orphan" (עָנִי//אַלְמָנָה and יָתוֹם, Isa 10:2; Zech 7:10; Job 24:9; 29:12–13); "poor"//"solitary" (עָנִי//יָחִיד, Ps 25:16); "prisoner"//"poor" (עָנִי//אָסִיר, Ps 107:10). See Croft, *Identity*, 55, 66–69. He notes that עָנִי can refer to all classes of the afflicted and sometimes to a whole nation (Pss 68:11[10]; 74:19, 21).

410. Mann, *Divine Presence*, 178. In any case, the ideals of sustenance, protection and guidance alluded to here, also echo the role of YHWH as the shepherd in the exodus tradition (see Ps 80:2[1]).

411. The noun אֹמֶר occurs only six times in the Old Testament (Hab 3:9; Pss 19:3, 4; 68:12[11]; 77:9[8]; Job 22:28). This substantive, as much as the verb root אמר from which it is derived, has a variety of nuances in different contexts. See Wagner, who states that the verb אמר has a variety of meanings (Wagner, "אָמַר," 329). Feinberg notes that אֹמֶר has been translated "utterance," "saying," "discourse," "matter," "promise," "plan," "purpose," "decree," "command," and "appointment" to fit various contexts (Feinberg, "'ōmer," 55). However, he assumes that the term אֹמֶר in Hab 3:9 points to the "oaths" or "promises" made to Israel. In regard to Ps 19, a hymn, which deals with the theology of creation, he argues that אֹמֶר refers to the "speech" of the natural creation. In reference to this, Wagner adds that the speech is audible but unintelligible. Accordingly, he sees this speech as audible in the smooth function of YHWH's creative works, which, in a sense, is natural revelation (Wagner, "אָמַר," 342). In Ps 77:9[8], the term is defined by the context as "promise" of YHWH to the righteous. In Job 22:28, the term refers to a stated intention or "matter" that YHWH would establish for Job. In terms of the use in Ps 68, Feinberg adduces that the term אֹמֶר carries a note of command, and is fitting for YHWH's position in vanguard to protect his inheritance. See Feinberg, "'ōmer," 55; cf. Wagner, "אָמַר," 342.

412. Albright, "Catalogue," 37. Mowinckel contends this translation *contra* Olmo Lete, who retains the word "oracle." See Mowinckel, *Achtundsechzigste*, 36; Olmo Lete, "Ps 68," 197, 203.

413. Mowinckel, *Achtundsechzigste*, 35–36. On ideas maintaining the reference to YHWH giving an oracle/order, but with suggested emendations to obliterate the idea

YHWH. He considers it to be the wonder-working word, as in Ps 29, which is directed against YHWH's enemies.[414] Cassuto, on the other hand, thinks that the expression "he gave the command" (יתן אמר) has a counterpart in "he sends forth his voice, his mighty voice" (בקולו קול עז, Ps 68:34[33]b). In view of the juxtaposing of this latter expression with the epithet "rider of the heavens, the ancient heavens" (רכב בשמי שמי קדם, v. 34[33]a), Cassuto sees here a nexus with the idea of salvation for Israel. Thus, in that connection, he views יתן אמר as a parallel expressing YHWH's sentence in favor of salvation.[415] As Feinberg correctly observes, the term אֹמֶר in v. 12[11] relates YHWH's command[416] ahead of the Israelite army[417] giving directions to strike for the ultimate victory,[418] therewith the female hailers herald the tidings. Therefore, אֹמֶר in v. 12[11]a should be read as a metonymy for YHWH's bluster of wind.[419] In essence, YHWH lets out a bluster of wind causing the enemy kings to flee (v. 13[12]a). The latter idea is in keeping with the effect subsumed by the imperative statements in the prelude of the psalm (v. 2[1]): "Let YHWH arise and let his enemies be scattered, and let the ones who hate him flee before him."[420]

Thus, in sequel, is the expression about kings fleeing or dispersing and put to rout as YHWH causes it to snow (תשלג) on Mount Zalmon (Ps

---

of female heralds of good tidings, see Curtis, "Celebrated," 44. Olmo Lete maintains the idea of an oracle, and conflates that with the message of joy the women bring that is strong enough to command or order victory. As he further argues, there is no need for a battle, just victory (Olmo Lete, "Ps 68," 203–4). In fact, the point that is elusive to Olmo Lete's view is the subtlety of YHWH's command, which alludes to his power manifested in the wind causing the hosts of kings to flee (cf. 2 Sam 5:24), and, consequently, the women herald the good tidings.

414. Mowinckel, *Achtundsechzigste*, 36.

415. Cassuto, *Biblical*, 1:261 (see also 244–45).

416. Feinberg, "'ōmer," 55.

417. Gordon notes correctly the idea of YHWH in the vanguard, apart from the intimation of the idea of YHWH's presence in the guise of the wind. See Gordon, *1 & 2 Samuel*, 229.

418. 2 Sam 5:24; cf. Judg 4:14.

419. Weiser points out that this verse refers to YHWH's voice sounding like thunder at his self-manifestation (Weiser, *Psalms*, 486). Since he argues for a cultic tradition of a covenant renewal, he sees this verse as an allusion to YHWH's self-disclosure experienced as a present reality. In contrast to Weiser's view, this verse reflects the victories of YHWH wielded by the power of his wind. Therefore, v. 12[11] should be interpreted as fitting the content of the whole scope of this psalm as a song of victory.

420. See Num 10:35.

68:15[14]). The reference to snow[421] falling on Mount Zalmon corroborates the idea of YHWH's intervention through the phenomenal wind dispersing the meteorological elements, and as arsenal on the battlefield (see Job 38:22–23). This image further amplifies YHWH's theophany in the wind. Here, too, victory is attributed to YHWH, by the jubilant "host of news-bearers" (Ps 68:12[11]b). The idea of women bearing tidings of victory in battle is in harmony with other OT passages involving women reveling in song[422] following successes in routing enemies attributed to the power of Israel's God.[423] The news concerns the scattering of the defeated kings and the dividing of spoils, so great that even the one staying at home apportions a share (Ps 68:13[12]). It is possible that the Psalmist here alludes to the defeat of the Canaanite kings in Judg 5:19, who are ridiculed for not carrying silver or plunder. Again, the graphic image of Sisera's mother in Judg 5:30 expressing apprehension for his delay in returning, and presumed on his participation in dividing the spoil, is mockery to highlight the total victory wielded by YHWH depriving the Canaanite kings of the spoil. Here, YHWH's appearance with the wind brings a downpour[424] causing the Kishon River to flood and confounds the Canaanite kings and their armies to rout.[425] By contrast, YHWH's advocates, as implied in Ps 68:14[13]a, even the noncombatants lying around the campfires divide the spoil.[426] Arguably, the idea refers to the men of the tribe of Reuben, who remain among the campfires, whilst the rest of the tribes risk their lives to encounter the Canaanite kings in battle (Judg 5:15–16). The mention of the confiscation of a dove sheathed with silver and feathers gleaming with gold in Ps 68:14[13]b, is ploy to heighten the triumph attributed to YHWH's intervention,[427] complete subjugation, and plundering of the enemies.

---

421. Snow is mentioned with other meteorological elements at YHWH's bidding (Pss 147:16–17; 148:8; Job 37:6; 38:22–23).

422. Exod 15:20–21; Judg 5:1, 3; 1 Sam 18:6–7.

423. Exod 15:10–12; Judg 4:14–15; 5:19–22; 1 Sam 17:47–50.

424. Judg 5:4cd.

425. Judg 4:7; 14–16; 5:19–22.

426. Judg 5:15d–16b.

427. Undoubtedly, the rest of King David's military campaigns against the surrounding kings meet with success, as YHWH intervenes wherever King David engages in war (2 Sam 8:3–12). King David not only gains the spoils of war, but also receives articles of gold, silver, and bronze as tribute from the kings he subdues. See Gordon, *1 & 2 Samuel*, 242, 245.

Therefore, in spite of all these truncated statements that seem to bear obscure meanings in Ps 68:12–15[11–14]), it is clear that the Psalmist muses over historical events commemorating the victories against Israel's enemies culminating with the establishment of YHWH's inheritance (v. 10[9]b), as noted in Pss 105:10–15; 135:10–12 and 136:17–22.[428] These ideas are also alluded to in Ps 68, and, therefore, underscore the view that the psalm relates the historical incidents associated with the conquest and settlement, and celebrates the victory wielded by the "bluster," or "command" or, rather in keeping with his renown, by the "shout" of YHWH as [the utmost] king in the wind (see Num 23:21cd).

YHWH Ascends to His Mountain-Abode

Following the conquest of the earthly kings, the Psalmist recites how YHWH takes up residence in his earthly abode. It is clear that in Ps 68:16–19[15–18] the Psalmist is at pains to point out YHWH's choice to reside at Mount Zion over and against Mount Bashan.[429] The Psalmist achieves this by setting a contrast between YHWH's abode and that of other gods. The mountain of (the) "gods"[430] (אלהים) is Mount Bashan, the mountain of "many peaks"[431] (גבננים, v. 16[15]b). It is certain, however,

---

428. See Num 21:21–35; Deut 2:24—3:10; Josh 12:1–7; 13:9–12, 29–32. All these various Hebrew texts mention common elements such as the defeat of kings (Num 21:33–35; Deut 3:8; Josh 12:1, 7; Pss 135:10–11; 136:17–18), taking of plunder or booty (שלל, Deut 2:35; 3:7) possession of land—"all of (the) Bashan"—(כל־הבשן, Deut 3:10; Josh 12:5; cf. Pss 135:11b; 136:20) as inheritance (נחלה, Pss 135:12; 136:21–22; cf. Josh 13:32; Num 21:34–35).

429. Curtis maintains that Bashan designates a snake. He attempts to identify Jerusalem with the name Bashan on the basis that the biblical mountain, beneath which the chaos monster is confined, is the temple mount at Jerusalem. He adds that Adonijah's sacrificing at the serpent's stone (אבן הזחלת) near En-rogel (1 Kgs 1:9), the breaking of the bronze serpent called Nehushtan (נחשתן, 2 Kgs 18:4) during Hezekiah's reforms, and the existence of a serpent's spring (עין התנין, Neh 2:13) near Jerusalem during the time of Nehemiah is evidence for Jerusalem's association with a snake (Curtis, "Har-bāšān," 91–92). Olmo Lete points out the association of Mount Bashan with the Canaanite gods (Olmo Lete, "Ps 68," 205).

430. Day, *God's Conflict*, 116. It is proper to read here אלהים as plural for "gods" as attested elsewhere in the Hebrew Bible (Pss 96:4b; 97:7c), *contra* Emerton, who argues that אלהים in Ps 68:16[15] has a singular sense that refers to YHWH, but objects any treatment of אלהים as a superlative (Emerton, "Mountain," 29, 34).

431. The meaning of this term, which is only found here, is uncertain. Most scholars have associated it with "hunchback" (גבן) in Lev 21:20 (see Anderson, *Psalms 1–72*, 490; Emerton, "Mountain," 27). Olmo Lete rejects use of this term to refer to "many peaked mountain" or "rugged" as irrelevant applied to mountains (Olmo Lete, "Ps 68,"

YHWH IN THE WIND(S)

that the mention of the "many peaked mountain" in v. 17[16] still refers to Mount Bashan and the whole range of mountains northeast of the Jordan including Mount Hermon,[432] also known as Sirion,[433] located in the far north of that region.[434]

However, the reference to the many peaks, or the grandiose range, seems to be scorn on Mount Bashan, as implied by the subsequent statements. Here, again, the Psalmist uses another biblical *hapax legomenon*, תרצדון (Ps 68:17[16]a), that is often translated "look at/watch with envy,"[435] in view of the possible Arabic cognate, *raṣada*, meaning "to watch." However, it is clear that, even though the nuance to "look at with envy" or simply to "watch" is adduced for Mount Bashan or the mountain of (the) gods in opposition[436] to the mountain that YHWH chooses as his abode, the Psalmist intends to emphasize that the chosen mount is exclusive to YHWH.[437] Therefore, Mount Bashan is personified and watches the mountain where YHWH chooses to dwell with envy. But, the Psalmist, mindful of the endemic state of worship of other gods in this region,[438] and the association of the mountains thereof, emphasizes that YHWH chooses the insignificant Mount Zion as his dwelling, rendering it impregnable.[439] At the same time, the Psalmist throws into bold relief the idea of YHWH's abiding presence at his mountain (Ps 68:17[16]b).

205n46). But the relevance here is perhaps in the use of contrasts the Psalmist uses throughout the psalm: Mount Bashan is not only a mountain of many peaks but also of many gods compared to the mountain YHWH chooses to indwell.

432. Day states that Mount Bashan is identified with Mount Hermon. He notes evidence adduced by Lipiński that in both Canaanite and Babylonian traditions, Mount Hermon was a dwelling place of the gods (Day, *God's Conflict*, 115–18).

433. The Amorites referred to the same mountain as Senir; Deut 3:9.

434. Deut 3:8–10; 4:47–48; cf. Josh 12:4–5; 1 Chr 5:23.

435. Anderson, *Psalms 1–72*, 490–91; Emerton argues for the uncertainty of this theory of ascribing the nuance "look at/watch with envy" to Ps 68:17[16], whereas the Arabic cognate only means "watch" (Emerton, "Mountain," 28–29).

436. It is necessary to point out here that the contrast in Ps 68:16–17[15–16] is in conformity with the Psalmist's style of presenting his ideas. As highlighted in this discussion, the Psalmist contrasts the salvation of the righteous with the destruction of the wicked (vv. 2–4[1–3]); YHWH's people are brought into prosperity, while the wicked dwell in a desert, or scorched land (v. 7[6]), YHWH instills power in his people, but devastates the ones who delight in war (see vv. 29–31[28–30]). Therefore, the choice of Mount Zion, which is limited or exclusive to YHWH, in antithesis to Mount Bashan or other mountains indwelt by many gods, fits this pattern of contrasts.

437. Cassuto, *Biblical*, 1:264; Emerton, "Mountain," 33.

438. Deut 7:3–4, 16; cf. Judg 3:3–7.

439. Ps 48:2b–3[1b–2], 9[8], 13–14[12–13]; cf. Isa 2:2.

PROCLAMATION OF YHWH AS KING IN THE WIND

He underscores the point by recalling the "ascent" (עלה, v. 19[18]; see Ps 47:6[5]) of YHWH to his abode to heighten YHWH's occupation and possession of it.

YHWH comes with his "chariots" (רֶכֶב) to his chosen abode (Ps 68:18[17]). As in other texts discussed, the mention of YHWH's chariots[440] expresses the idea of YHWH appearing in the sonorous wind. Therefore, with the term בקדש in v. 18[17]b, the Psalmist relates the "grandeur" of YHWH displayed at his phenomenal appearance at Sinai. Subsequently, YHWH is claimed to "ascend" (עלה, v. 19a) to his mountain abode in his luminous and sonorous wind, with his captives in tow. As already stated in connection with Ps 47, the Psalmist echoes the procession to Zion, the city of King David narrated in 2 Sam 6:12–19.[441] But in Ps 68, the Psalmist muses on YHWH's ascent to his earthly abode with a mythical aspect unparalleled in any of the other biblical texts mentioning this aspect. However, the reference to taking tribute from the rebellious at YHWH's ascent restated in Ps 68:19[18]bc), links up with vv. 13b–14[12b–13]),[442] and recalls the victories experienced on the march from Mount Sinai to Mount Zion, showing that YHWH is among his people. In other words, the deity who appears in majesty and subjects his enemies to servitude seals the triumph by taking permanent abode among his people (Ps 68:17[16], 19[18]cd). So, YHWH's people find refuge in him, as their salvation (מושעות, v. 21[20]aβ). Thus, the blessing formula employed here on YHWH suggests praise of him from "day to day"[443] as the victor and protector. Hence, the idea of the enshrined glory of the divine presence in the wind, coupled with the thought of historical victories, makes possible their escape from death (vv. 20–21[19–20]).

---

440. Hab 3:8; Ps 18:11[10]=2 Sam 22:11; cf. Isa 66:15 the chariots of YHWH represent YHWH's *modus operandi* in the wind also associated with "fire" (see 2 Kgs 6:17). That רֶכֶב is collective and synonymous with מרכבת is indicated by the parallelism in Judg 5:28. The term רֶכֶב is also used to refer to multiple chariots in Exod 14:7; 2 Kgs 6:17; 7:6. Therefore the Hebrew idiom "thousands upon thousands" רבתים אלפי שנאן, should be understood as a superlative expression emphasizing YHWH's invisible wind but with a roaring sound comparable to innumerable fast-moving chariots.

441. See discussion on Ps 47, particularly pp. 237–41.

442. Ps 68:32[31].

443. V. 20[19]a; see Ps 96:2; 1 Chr 16:23. The intonation on blessing YHWH from day to day indicates that the Psalmist, again King David, compels worship that is more regular in recognition of YHWH's saving deeds and abiding presence. This also shows that this psalm is not intended for a cultic enthronement of YHWH but a celebration of him, who is recognized as present in the power of the wind.

God among Us

In language that is paralleled in Hab 3:13, the Psalmist in Ps 68 repeats the motif of the salvation of the righteous (Ps 68:20–21[19–20]) in antithesis to the destruction of the wicked (vv. 22–24[21–23]). By contrast, the head of the wicked is crushed, and the people of YHWH also enjoy a share in the victory. The crushing of the head[444] of the wicked, executed by YHWH, in a context where natural phenomena are part of the scheme, recalls the destruction of Pharaoh as the head of the wicked, as noted in Hab 3:13–14. But the battle waged by YHWH as described in Ps 68 is not entirely in mythical terms. YHWH claims that he will bring "them,"—probably his enemies—from "Bashan" and from the "depths of the sea" (Ps 68:23[22]). Here, "Bashan" and the "depths of the sea" are used figuratively as locatives[445] from which YHWH captures his enemies. Day suggests that Bashan in Ps 68:23[22] should be read in reference to the meaning already implied in v. 16[15], that is, as a mountain. He adds that there is nowhere in the Hebrew tradition where Bashan is used as a name for a serpent.[446]

---

444. For the parallelism of ראש and קדקד in describing the destruction of the wicked see Ps 7:17[16]; cf. KTU 1.16.VI:56–57 [CTA 16.vi:56–57]: Keret curses his son, Yaṣṣib, who reprimands him for failing to judge the cause of the widow and protect the poor. He, therefore, calls on the god Horon to break Yaṣṣib's "head" (*rʾiš*) and Asherah his "skull" (*qdqd*).

445. See Ps 18; the Psalmist praises YHWH for drawing him from the depths of the sea (see Cassuto, *Biblical*, 1:269). Again, it is possible that another contrast, as in Ps 68:16–17[15–16], is set up in v. 23[22] with Bashan and sea representing a high and low locations, respectively (see Day, *God's Conflict*, 115–16, 118; Emerton, "Mountain," 31).

446. Day argues that the Hebrew *ptn* is cognate with the Ugaritic *bṯn*, therefore Hebrew *bāšān* may not be viewed as cognate with Ugaritic *bṯn* (Day, *God's Conflict*, 115). Hence, Day points out that Cross and Freedman's translation of *bāšān* "serpent" in Deut 33:22 is unconvincing: "Dan is a lion's whelp / who shies away from a viper" (Cross and Freedman, "Blessing," 195, 208). Instead, Day claims that the reference in Deut 33:22 is simply a comparison: "Dan is a lion's whelp that leaps forth from Bashan" (Day, *God's Conflict*, 115n106). In contrast, Curtis maintains that there is a mythological use of Bashan in this verse but accepts that the precise meaning is not clear, as he translates: "Dan is a lion's whelp, who has sprung forth from the serpent" (Curtis, "Har-bāšān," 91). Nonetheless, he further argues that, for reasons no longer clear to us, Dan is considered to descend from both the lion and the mythical serpent. He adds that the serpentine nature of Dan is clear in Gen 49:17: "Dan will be a snake beside the way, a viper beside the path, who bites the heels of the horse, so that the rider falls backwards." Again, Curtis admits that it is not certain whether these allusions are complimentary or critical. It is clear, as Emerton argues, that the geographic sense of Bashan is well attested in the Hebrew Bible. Hence any conjectural interpretation of *bāšān* to mean serpent without any contextual support is disingenuous (see Emerton, "Mountain," 32);

PROCLAMATION OF YHWH AS KING IN THE WIND

For most scholars the identification of Bashan with the mythical primeval serpent also derives from the fact that "Bashan" appears here in parallel with the "depths of the sea" (מצלות ים). Consequently, this verse has been interpreted in reference to either YHWH's battle with the primeval chaos, that is, the vanquishing of the dragon,[447] or his rescue of Israel from the forces that overpowered them.[448] Yet, a reasonable sense is still maintained for this verse without introducing any mythological import. As Day suggests, "Bashan" and the "depths of the sea" should be read in antithetical parallelism as representing the highest and lowest locations at which YHWH would smite the enemies mentioned in Ps 68:22[21], if they escaped there.[449] Moreover, the extremities of the mountaintops and depths of the sea cannot confine the boundless power of YHWH in the wind (see Amos 9:1–3).[450] As already pointed out,

---

cf. Goldingay, who identifies Mount Bashan with the majestic peaks of Mount Hermon (Goldingay, *Psalms*, 323–24). Longman cites Mount Bashan as the mountain range in the Transjordan located along the north and northeast of the Sea of Galilee (Longman, *Psalms*, 259, 260).

447. Scholars have suggested either, to rearrange, revocalize or emend this verse, in keeping with the battle of Ba'al against Yam. Albright changes the *Hiphil* אשב to *Qal* אשב, supplies the verb מחץ, detaches the initial *mem* in ממצלות and adds it at the end of his conjectural *Qal* to read אשבם. He changes ל to מ in מצלות and introduces another verb צמת to read מצמת in his attempt to establish a parallel with the Ugaritic passage (KTU 1.3.III:36–44 [CTA 3.iii:33–41]). Thus he translates, "YHWH said: From smiting the serpent I return, I return from destroying the sea" (Albright, "Catalogue," 14, 27–28, 38). We should note, however, that the verb צמת in the Ugaritic passage is used to express the silencing of one of Yam's attendants, but Albright proposes to employ this verb in the Hebrew verse to describe the vanquishing of the sea. In the same vein, Dahood emends and revocalizes Ps 68:23[22] and reads: "I stifled the serpent, muzzled the deep sea" (Dahood, *Psalms*, 2:131, 145–46); cf. Miller: "I muzzled the serpent, I muzzled the deep sea" (Miller, *Divine Warrior*, 110). Gray assumes a showdown of YHWH with the arch-enemy and translates: "My lord declared, 'I shall assuredly bring back the serpent, I shall bring back sea from the abyss'" (Gray, "Cantata," 10). See also Day, *God's Conflict*, 114–15. Olmo Lete sees in מצלות ים a term referring to Ba'al's primeval enemy Yam, and he claims that Israel's libretto attests to YHWH's fight and vanquishing of this enemy and his assistants (Olmo Lete, "Ps 68," 206–7).

448. In view of Israel's rescue, Mowinckel reads: "YHWH speaks: 'I bring back (personally) from the snake, from the depths of the sea, I bring back'" (Mowinckel, *Achtundsechzigste*, 48). Fensham translates: "The lord said: 'From the hole of the snake (or Bashan) I will bring back, I will bring back from the depths of the sea (or Yam)'" (Fensham, "Ps 68:23," 293).

449. Day, *God's Conflict*, 115; cf. Longman, who sees a merism expressing the high—low range of YHWH's reach to bring his enemies from the heights of Bashan and out of the depths of the sea (Longman, *Psalms*, 260).

450. Day, *God's Conflict*, 118; cf. Anderson, *Psalms 1–72*, 494; Kraus, *Psalms 60–150*, 55.

YHWH IN THE WIND(S)

YHWH's overpowering roaring wind churns the waters, and causes the mountains to tremble or shake. His domain reaches far and beyond any confines of the feral and infernal regions. Therefore, YHWH's power in the wind is inescapable. As indicated in Ps 68:24[23], total carnage is foreshadowed for this act of vengeance. The participants will bathe[451] their feet in blood, while dogs lap up the blood of the wicked, as a symbol of total destruction.[452]

Subsequent to the description of the utter annihilation of the wicked, the Psalmist relates the victory and theophanic progress, or march "in holiness"[453] (בְּקֹדֶשׁ, Ps 68:25[24]) of YHWH as warrior-king. Here, too, by the expression "your ways" (הליכותיך) the Psalmist throws into bold relief YHWH's age-old *modus operandi* of the wind manifesting his great might. This plausible interpretation undermines biblical scholars' view on Ps 68:25[24] as alluding to the procession of YHWH to his sanctuary in favor of the theory of an enthronement festival of YHWH.[454] Even major advocates of an enthronement hypothesis cannot argue with certainty about the existence of this festival in Israel, despite allocating this verse to an enthronement procession. But also running counter to this view are the numerous examples of the root הלך in reference to the divine presence and guidance in the wilderness tradition.

The people of YHWH experience victory when YHWH, as the vanguard—ההלך—, goes before his people and fights for them and provides ardent protection.[455] We should also note that the root הלך occurs frequently in descriptions of YHWH's theophany either expressing the

---

451. As with other versions, the reading "wash" (תרחץ) is proposed as yielding a clearer meaning. The idea of washing feet in blood as symbolic of complete destruction of the wicked is also expressed in Ps 58:11[10] (cf. Isa 63:2–6 on garments splattered with blood on YHWH's day of vengeance involving use of his arm [v. 5c], that is his wind working salvation, while the wicked reel, as though drunk from YHWH's wind, as YHWH tramples the wicked in battle [v. 6]).

452. YHWH causes panic in the Philistine camp, as the ground shakes from his manifestation in the wind (1 Sam 14:15). Therefore, the Philistines raiding the Israelites in confusion turn swords on each other, and, perhaps, create their own bloodbath (1 Sam 14:20–23; 1 Kgs 21:19; 22:38).

453. In Ps 77:14[13] "sacredness" or "holiness" is associated with YHWH's "ways," given expression by his great deeds of deliverance in the past; see Exod 15:11.

454. Mowinckel, *Achtundsechzigste*, 17, 19–20; Gaster, *Myth*, 759–60; see Jeremias, who maintains that vv. 25–28[24–27] describe the actions of the participants in the procession culminating with YHWH's enthronement (Jeremias, *Königtum Gottes*, 77; Halpern, *Constitution*, 80, 82, 85–86). Olmo Lete considers this as a cultic procession of a well-known performance (Olmo Lete, "Ps 68," 208).

455. Deut 1:30–31; 20:4; 31:6, 8; cf. 2 Sam 7:6–7; Wilson, "Divine," 403–6.

PROCLAMATION OF YHWH AS KING IN THE WIND

release of YHWH's "glistening" or luminous wind as seen in Hab 3:11b and Ps 77:18[17]c,[456] or describing YHWH going about in the wind in Ps 104:3c, or as he traverses the vaulted heavens overshadowed by the clouds.[457] In view of these references, unquestionably the term הלך in these contexts relates YHWH's presence and guidance during the wilderness march, as much as his conventional self-manifestation in the wind. Hence, the substantive הליכות,[458] which occurs in both Hab 3:6e and Ps 68:25[24] with YHWH as subject refers to YHWH's theophany in the phenomenal wind.

As Avishur correctly observes, the expression הליכות אל in both psalms in Ps 68 and Hab 3 implies YHWH's martial activities as a warrior. Avishur further states that this expression in Hebrew, as also its equivalent in Akkadian, originally referred to the deity's marching forth, but later also implied conduct and behavior.[459] It is apparent in Ps 68:25[24] and Hab 3:6 that both meanings are in view. As observed in Hab 3:6e, the expression הליכות אל in Ps 68:25:[24] appears in a context where the focus is on the deeds of YHWH, as he discloses himself in the wind and marches before his people in victory. It is not coincidental, therefore, that the Psalmist in Ps 68, as much as the poet-prophet of Hab 3, describes the marching forth of YHWH in personification of YHWH's disclosure in the phenomenal winds. Once again the image relates YHWH's martial activities, referred to as "eternal ways"[460] (הליכות עולם) in Hab 3:6e. Thus, in concurrence with, and elaboration of Avishur's view,[461] הליכות אלהים in Ps 68:25[24] refers to the manifestation of YHWH's heroic deeds in the guise of the wind in assertion of his warrior traits mentioned in the previous verses (vv. 21–24[20–23]).

The subsequent verses, therefore, refer to the singers and musicians, who recount and celebrate the victory of YHWH's martial deeds.[462] Again, here, as noted for Ps 98, the fascination with the ensemble of

---

456. See Exod 9:23.

457. Job 22:14; cf. Ps 18:11–12[10–11].

458. Of the six occurrences of this substantive in the Hebrew Bible (see also Nah 2:6[5]; Job 6:19; Prov 31:27), only Hab 3:6 and Ps 68:25[24] (twice) relate to YHWH.

459. Avishur, *Studies*, 169–70. As a point of interest, the Akkadian cognate *alakti* ("ways/deeds") is also used to proclaim Marduk's acts of salvation for the gods (EE VI:122; see VII:98).

460. On YHWH's age-old ways in the wind, see pp. 183, 200 above.

461. Avishur, *Studies*, 170.

462. Judg 5:9–18; 1 Sam 18:6.

YHWH IN THE WIND(S)

musical instruments in this theophanic progress recalls the musical din surrounding the transfer of the ark to the city of King David (1 Chr 16:5–6; Ps 98:5–6). Here in Ps 68 there is specificity about the tribes involved in worshiping before YHWH's assembly. As stated, the tribe of Benjamin is in the lead, and the tribe of Judah among the multitude (v. 28[27]). It is significant that the princes of the tribes mentioned—Benjamin, Judah, Zebulun and Naphtali—are commended for their distinct involvement in YHWH's battle against the Canaanite kings in the Song of Deborah (Judg 5). In particular, the tribes of Benjamin, Zebulun, and Naphtali are mentioned for their participation in the battle of YHWH for risking their lives (Judg 5:14, 18). But the tribe of Judah is not mentioned in the Song of Deborah. Perhaps, the reference to Judah in Ps 68:28[27]b, as being among "their throng" (רגמתם), simply reflects not only Judahite propaganda on participating in this melodious procession, but also implicates authorship, or provenance with links to the line of King David (1 Sam 17:12ab). Be that as it may, these verses, again, allude to provenance in the period of King David, and preserve the melodramatic celebration of YHWH's victories, in acknowledgement of him as the prime mover, or source (מקור) of Israel (Ps 68:27[26]).

There is a deliberate shift of address in Ps 68:29[28]a on the community's strength deriving from YHWH to emphasize that the victory of the celebrating community belongs to YHWH. This address in v. 29[28] directed to the celebrating community is the sequel to the divine decree in vv. 23–24[22–23], in which YHWH promises his people that they will participate in acts of victory. It follows, then, that the decree (vv. 23–24[22–23]) of YHWH's vindication is realized. YHWH summons his people and empowers them to discomfit the enemy. Hence, in v. 29[28] a the Psalmist declares that "your God summons (צוה) your strength."[463] So the idea of YHWH empowering his people by his presence in the wind (see עז/גאות),[464] as stated in the concluding verses of the psalm (Ps 68:35–36[34–35]) is paralleled here. Indeed, the Psalmist's imperative on YHWH to disclose his power in the wind to empower them,[465] bodes

---

463. There is no need to read this statement as an imperative. It is not uncommon diction in the Hebrew tradition for an affirmative (preterit) statement to be paralleled with a petition or imperative (see Hab 3:2; Ps 28:8).

464. On the figurative meaning of "strength" (עז) and "majesty" (גאות) for wind, as represented in Ps 93:1, see the discussion on pp. 246–49 above.

465. Exod 15:2; Pss 28:8a; 29:11.

PROCLAMATION OF YHWH AS KING IN THE WIND

well with the view of YHWH's victories in the past (68:29[28]b).[466] Thus, the celebrating community expects the overpowered kings[467] to bring tribute to YHWH's temple at Jerusalem (v. 30[29]).

Furthermore, YHWH is entreated to subdue the hostile powers that the Psalmist ridicules as "beast/community of the reeds" (חית קנה) and "assembly of bulls/mighty ones among the calves of the people" (עדה אבירים בעגלי עמים, Ps 68:31[30]).[468] Undoubtedly, these images refer to Egypt. As in other Hebrew texts, Egypt is dismissed as a futile source of military strength, and ridiculed as a "splintered staff of the reed" by the king of Assyria (משענת הקנה, 2 Kgs 18:21).[469] Therefore, the futility of the king of Judah, Hezekiah, to rely on Egypt for political fealty is exposed, and compared to a man, who leans on a splintered staff of the reed and it pierces his palm. Nonetheless, this חית קנה, meaning the animal or community of the reeds, as a symbol of Egypt that YHWH is petitioned to thwart, is consigned to a very different destiny from that of YHWH's "community" (חית) in Ps 68:11[10].

Again, the reference to "bulls" (אבירים, v. 31[30]aβ) further indicates rancor towards Egypt as a nation. Kapelrud observes that אבירים in Ps 22:13[12] is in parallel to פרים ("bulls") and is used figuratively for enemies.[470] Moreover, Miller's study of the use of animal names supports this explanation.[471] He observes that the figurative use of animal names in Hebrew, to convey different images, is paralleled in Ugaritic literature. He points out, however, that אבירים in Hebrew means either bulls or horses, but is also used metaphorically to designate soldiers, princes, or leaders. He sees the "bulls" in Ps 68:31[30] as representing Egypt or Pharaoh, and "the wild beasts of the reeds,"[472] in line with other interpreters' views, as referring to the latter. However, Miller finds the meaning of

---

466. See Hab 3:2.

467. See 2 Sam 8:2–14. It is possible that here King David has in mind the kings he defeats, who bring articles of silver and gold as tribute.

468. See Day, *God's Conflict*, 119–20.

469. The same as Isa 36:6; cf. Ezek 29:6.

470. Kapelrud, "אָבִיר," 43.

471. See Miller, "Animal Names," 177–86. He notes that animal names are used to convey images of "swiftness, fierceness, hostility, tenderness," and frequently employed metaphorically as designations or titles representing leadership or for warriors (Miller, 177; see Day, *God's Conflict*, 120).

472. Miller, "Animal Names," 180n19. Caquot also suggests that the term refers to the Egyptians, or any such historical enemy with similar characteristics. (Caquot, "גער," 51).

YHWH IN THE WIND(S)

"calves" in בעגלי עמים problematic.[473] Undeniably, however, בעגלי עמים refers to Cush, and not Egypt, based on the juxtaposing of the two nations in v. 32[31], and in Isa 20:3–5.[474] These nations, Cush and Egypt, which delight in war and trample down pieces of silver (Ps 68:31[30]) are destined for YHWH's wrath (see Isa 18:1 and 19:1, respectively). As a case in point, the oracles of Isaiah concerning Cush and Egypt conform to the language characteristic of YHWH's theophany in the wind for judgment.

The prophet Isaiah shows familiarity with the diction of YHWH's appearance in the wind for judgment against Cush and Egypt. He employs language predictive of YHWH's intention to summon his strength against Cush in Isa 18:3. Here the prophet refers to a militaristic gambit of raising a signal in connection with the sound of the ram's horn (שׁופר) signaling YHWH's disclosure and involvement by the power of his wind. But upon judgment, the people of Cush will bring tribute to Mount Zion, the place of the name of YHWH Ṣebā'ôth (v. 7). On the other hand, in the oracle on Egypt in Isa 19:1a, prophet Isaiah uses an expression similar to Ps 68:5[4]: יהוה רכב על־עב (YHWH rides on a swift cloud), again signaling the force of the wind stirring the cloud, which will cause the idols to tremble, and the hearts of the Egyptians to "melt" with fear at YHWH's disclosure with the wind (Isa 19:1bc). Although the prophet expresses this idea in prosaic form, upon judgment Egypt will know YHWH, and worship him with sacrificial offerings (v. 22). In the same manner, the Psalmist in Ps 68 draws from the same tradition of YHWH's disclosure in the wind. Thus, with the term גער in the imperative in Ps 68:31[30], King David impels for the melodramatic outburst of YHWH's ghastly wind, and reminisces on YHWH's primeval battle with the sea. Hence, he recalls the *Chaoskampf.* Therefore, he entreats YHWH to roar[475] and scatter by his wind[476] the "beast/community of the reeds," and "the assembly of bulls/mighty ones among the calves of the peoples" alluding to Egypt and Cush. In essence, as in the prologue of the psalm, he calls on YHWH to scatter [by his wind] these nations who delight in war,[477] and satisfy themselves with tributes of silver. Like in the oracles of Isaiah,

---

473. Miller, "Animal Names," 180–81.

474. See also Ezek 30:9.

475. See the prophet Amos in Amos 1:2 declares that YHWH roars from Zion with reference to YHWH's outburst of wind against Israel, Judah, and the surrounding rebellious nations.

476. Cf. Isa 17:12–13.

477. Cf. Cassuto, *Biblical*, 1:274; Macintosh, "Consideration," 475.

PROCLAMATION OF YHWH AS KING IN THE WIND

the desired effect of the bluster of wind is the despoiling of the nations bringing them into servitude. The notion of submission of both Egypt and Cush is envisaged in envoys bringing tributes[478] of silver to YHWH (Ps 68:32[31]).[479] Just as Ps 76,[480] a Zion song, recalls YHWH's ultimate victory over the Egyptians at the *Yam Suph*, as a consequence of his blustery wind that subdues the horse[, its rider] and chariot,[481] so does Ps 68:31–32[30–31] envision YHWH subduing Egypt, including Cush.

Here, too, the reference to the nobles of Egypt coming out, and Cush stretching out hands to YHWH in v. 32[31]), is in keeping with YHWH establishing his abode in Zion,[482] as the center for all kingdoms to worship and pay homage to YHWH, as noted in other psalms discussed. In a sense, apart from alluding to YHWH's universal dominion, the idea of YHWH's divine presence among the people is reasserted. Thus, with Jerusalem as YHWH's seat of judgment for all the earth (Ps 68:30[29]),[483] the survivors of his judgment,[484] represented here in Ps 68 by the nobles of Egypt and the peoples of Cush, will "bear along gifts" (יוֹבִילוּ שַׁי) to YHWH in Zion (vv. 30[29], 32[31]).[485] Again, YHWH's universal kingship is in view (Ps 68:33[32]).[486]

Whereas with the epithet "rider of the steppes" the call to praise is justified in light of Israel's historical experiences in the wilderness, the epithet "rider of the ancient heavens" expresses YHWH's universal reign and presence, as already implied by Psalmist's bid to the "kingdoms of the earth" to pay homage to YHWH (v. 33[32]; see Ps 76:12[11]b). At this point in Ps 68:33[32], the Psalmist throws into bold relief the

---

478. See Isa 45:14–15, a prophecy expressing Egypt and Cush bringing products in an act of submission, and acknowledgement of the incomparability of the God of Israel as savior.

479. Ps 76:12[11]b; Isa 18:7; 2 Chr 9:24.

480. This psalm is replete with images relating the appearance of YHWH with the wind. The leonine imagery reflected in the use of lair and den for Zion in v. 2[1] echoes the idea of YHWH emerging as a lion from its habitat, and roaring to symbolize YHWH's sonorous wind (Amos 1:2; Jer 25:38; see v. 30). Again, in Ps 76:5[4] YHWH is said to be resplendent with light alluding to his luminous wind, and the idea of his rebuke, confounding horse and rider in v. 7[6], represents his devastating blustery wind.

481. Ps 76:7–8[6–7]; see Exod 15:1, 4, 10.

482. See Ps 68:18–19[17–18]; 76:3[2].

483. See Ps 76:3–4[2–3], 10[9].

484. Ps 76:11[10], 13[12].

485. See Ps 76:12[11]; Isa 18:7.

486. See Pss 47:8–10[7–9]; 76:13[12].

sovereign rule of YHWH over all the nations, as all the kings of the earth are claimed as belonging to YHWH (47:10[9]). Thus, with the designation "rider of the ancient heavens," in depiction of YHWH's discharge of the thunderous wind in Ps 68:34[33], the scope of YHWH's sovereignty could not have been better expressed. His "power" and "majesty" are demonstrated in the "clouds" (שחקים, v. 35[34]), from where he roars with his "mighty voice" (קול עז, v. 34[33]) personifying his mighty wind, by which he scatters the clouds, and also wields his verdicts for the salvation of his (afflicted) people.[487] Undoubtedly, YHWH's majestic wind that dispenses this cosmic rule over all the kingdoms of the earth (see Ps 68:33[32]) is central to the ideas that the Psalmist presents. The Psalmist shows confidence in this empowering deity, as sustained in the tension about the concept of the *Deus praesens* and *Deus absconditus*. The Psalmist can only marvel in this God, whose manifestation at his sanctuary evokes reverential fear over Israel. Yet, YHWH's power in the wind is also demonstrated in the skies as an assertion of YHWH's cosmic governance. But, ultimately, the Psalmist emphasizes YHWH's immanence in the holy place, and, therewith, the people derive their strength and "abundant might"[488] (תעצמות, v. 36[35]).[489]

In summary, Ps 68 is an ode of victory describing the effect of YHWH's ineffable presence in the phenomenal winds. The tenor of the psalm from beginning to end ricochets YHWH's age-old *modus operandi* in the phenomenal wind. The Psalmist employs appropriate terms to emphasize the idea of divine presence and ensuing victorious acts. Hence, YHWH arises as the "rider of the steppes" to discomfit and save. The earth shaking, heavens drooping and releasing copious rain signify YHWH's discharge of the phenomenal winds, as he marches through the desert before his people. As the divine warrior, YHWH's "command" by the bluster of wind confounds the Canaanite kings, causes a snowfall, and the kings scatter. In his "chariots," figurative of the wind roiling the clouds, YHWH "comes" from Sinai in holiness, and rises up to his chosen abode in Jerusalem. YHWH's elected people give homage to YHWH from day to day for their salvation, as YHWH reaches to the farthest extremities to annihilate their enemies. To that end, YHWH's theophanic deeds, in his age-old *modus operandi* in the wind, come into view. In recollection of YHWH's show of strength through his deeds in the past,

---

487. See Ps 76:8–10[7–9].
488. BDB 783.
489. See Ps 68:29[28]a; 28:8; 29:11.

the Psalmist bids YHWH to demonstrate his might; so that all the kings pay homage to YHWH and assimilate into the centralized worship at Jerusalem. Therefore, the Psalmist compels YHWH to roar [with his wind] against the nations who take glee in war. These nations fall into submission to YHWH. With joyful expectation, the Psalmist ends the psalm with an exhortatory call to all the kingdoms of the earth to extol YHWH, who demonstrates his power in the skies by his phenomenal wind. Yet, he empowers his people Israel, and manifests his presence amid them in his earthly sanctuary.

In particular, the Psalmist's cosmic depiction of YHWH in the concluding section substantiates the overarching theme of YHWH's divine presence in Ps 68. YHWH "rides" (רכב, v. 34[33]a) the ancient heavens and, with his wind, he issues his majestic "loud sound" (יתן בקולו קול עז, v. 34[33]b). At the same time, YHWH is "awe-inspiring/fearful" (נורא) from his sanctuary, and "gives" (נתן, v. 36[35]) "power," "strength" and "abundant might" to Israel. The ideas of transcendence and immanence in this final strophe are in tension, when it is read that YHWH is present both in his celestial and terrestrial temples (vv. 34[33]a; 36[35]a), respectively. This idea emphasizes YHWH's omnipresence and relativizes YHWH's age-old *modus operandi* in the wind embodying his enduring presence among his elect. Moreover, the content of the psalm is not consistent with a festal or cultic procession or enthronement such as some scholars suggest. Neither is the Psalmist concerned so much with details of historical incidents or cultic events, as he is with presenting the great deeds of YHWH, and his abiding presence in the guise of the wind. Thus, YHWH is depicted in this melodramatic psalm as savior, judge, prime mover and warrior-king. In essence, the Psalmist could sum up his melodious thoughts with the lyrical statement: "God is with us" (אל עמנו).

In conclusion, the kingship psalms (Pss 29, 47, 68, 93, 96–99, and related texts) discussed in this chapter inform on the celebration of YHWH as king among his people wielding his power for their salvation in the same manner YHWH vanquishes primal chaos. With Israel as YHWH's chosen nation at the center of his divine rule, a universalistic aspect on YHWH's dominion is brought to bear by the call to the nations, inclusive of the subdued nations, to participate in worship in deference to YHWH's sights and sounds revealed in the gaze of the nations.

Final Reflection

The power of YHWH displayed in the phenomenal wind, in assertion of YHWH's purposes in all creation presented in the psalms discussed, is made more concise in the words of the poet of Job in Job 36:29—37:13:

> 29Who can understand the spreading of the clouds,[490] the noises (תשאות) of his booth?
> 30Behold, he spreads his light around him; and covers the roots of the sea.
> 31For he judges people by them,[491] (and) he gives food in abundance.
> 32His light covers his palms, and he commands it to strike the mark.[492]
> 33His roar declares about him, [and] {raging?}wrath[493] of anger concerning [the] one coming up.[494]
> 1Also, at this my heart "trembles"[495] and springs from its place.
> 2Listen to the raging (רגז) of his "voice" [=wind] and the rumbling (הגה) going forth from his mouth;[496]

---

490. See Job 37:15a, 16a; Elihu challenges Job if he understands how YHWH controls the clouds, or how they hang poised.

491. No doubt this is referring to the effect of the meteorological elements that YHWH's wind disperses, and, in particular rain in this verse, as implied in the adjacent phrase.

492. BDB 496 offers the meaning "hollow or flat of the hand"/"palm" for the Hebrew term כף and translates this phrase to imply YHWH's hands filled with light. As presented in this monograph, the hand or arm is personification of YHWH's wind. Therefore, YHWH is pictured here as a warrior poised with his luminous wind as a weapon.

493. It is inappropriate to read the MT "cattle" in this context. Some critics propose that the reading "cattle" should be retained (e.g., Delitzsch and Dhorme, Pope, Habel). This is due to the fact that "cattle" are thought to signal an approaching thunderstorm. "Anger" is one of the elements that herald YHWH when he exercises divine justice (see Job 40:9–11; Isa 30:27–30). Combinations of synonymous words for anger are not unusual in the Hebrew tradition: "Raging anger" (זעף אף, Isa 30:30), "wrath and heat of anger" (עברה וחרון אף, Isa 13:9), "heat of his anger" (חרון אפו, Isa 13:13; cf. Ps 78:49; Johnson, "אנף," 356–60). Gordis suggests the translation "wrath of indignation" (Gordis, *Book of Job*, 424). As noted by Vicchio, there is a plethora of interpretations for this verse (Vicchio, *Book of Job*, 251).

494. In contrast to Gordis, who reads על-עולה "storm, whirlwind" (Gordis, *Book of Job*, 424), it is suggested retaining the MT עולה meaning the "one coming up" (Isa 24:18). In other theophany texts, relating YHWH's power in the wind, אף, "anger," signals the approaching (i.e., one coming up) deity (see Hab 3:8; Ps 76:8[7]).

495. Here the poet of Job is consistent and in keeping with the idea of fear inflicted by YHWH's disclosure in the roaring winds (see Jer 4:19).

496. Again, the wind originates from YHWH. As in Exod 15:8a (see v. 10a), the wind is associated with the blast of breath from YHWH's nostrils (see Vicchio, *Book of*

> 3under all the heavens he lets it go and his light to the corners of the earth!
> 4After it his "voice (wind)" roars (שׁאג), he thunders (רעם) with his majestic "voice (wind)," and he does not restrain them when his "voice (wind)" is heard.
> 5God roars (רעם) with his "voice (wind)" marvelously, doing great things we cannot comprehend.
> 6For to snow (שׁלג) he says "fall to the ground,"[497] and to showers of rains "be a mighty downpour"!...
> 9From the chambers comes out the whirlwind (סופה), and cold from scattering winds.
> 10By the breath [wind] of God ice is given, and broad waters frozen (hard).
> 11Indeed with moisture he loads the cloud, and he scatters [by his wind] the cloud of his light(ning);[498]
> 12and he, from all directions, turns it by his guidance to accomplish all that he commands upon [the world of] the earth;
> 13whether for [the] rod or for his land, or for love, he causes it to happen[499]
> (Job 36:29—37:13).

All in all, this description of YHWH's *modus operandi* in the wind in Job 36:29—37:13, illuminates the purposes of this phenomenal element that attends the manifestation of YHWH as he acts in judgment. Job 37:13 provides the thematic climax: "Whether for the rod (i.e., for correction), or for his land or for his love, he causes it to happen." Indeed, the bluster of wind announces YHWH's presence to chastise or bless. The Psalmists in Pss 29 and 68 preserve the same basic thought evidenced by the idea of the destruction of the "wicked" mentioned in antithesis to the salvation of the "righteous." It is primarily YHWH's might demonstrated in the phenomenal wind at primal creation seen at work again wielding deeds of salvation for the people of Israel *vis-à-vis* other nations. Yet, as noted for all the kingship psalms analyzed, YHWH's overarching divine presence is depicted in the guise of the phenomenal wind, as the warrior,

---

Job, 253). Cf. the god Amma said to puff out the wind.

497. Snow and hail are often elements dispersed by YHWH's wind in expression of his wrath (see Isa 30:30; Ps 78:47–48).

498. In Job 37:11–16, Elihu describes YHWH's wondrous work on how the wind causes evaporation and distillation of moisture, and how the light or luminous flash emanates from his cloud, and the purposes of all these elements dispersed by the wind.

499. As with all other texts in this monograph, the translation of the MT is the author's.

YHWH IN THE WIND(S)

savior and king of Israel, as much as the universal judge and ruler of all the kingdoms of the earth. Thus, YHWH subdues the nations who worship idols or delight in war in deference to his sovereign rule of justice and righteousness. But Israel as the chosen nation declares YHWH's creative works, salvation deeds, and "glory" among the nations, as it extends the invitation to other nations to participate in that revelation. Hence, the defeated nations are incorporated into Israel's God-story with the invocation to pay homage and give praise to YHWH, as the sovereign king at the focal center of worship, that is, Zion, where YHWH dwells among his people.

As alluded to in these kingship psalms discussed, the idea of subduing inimical forces for the establishment of YHWH's choice of Zion, as his abode, is oriented towards YHWH's founding of the earth by his age-old *modus operandi* in the wind to guarantee social organization. Hence, echoing the language recalling the model of subduing primal chaos, the psalmists invoke YHWH to roar with his thunderous wind, and bring the nations (pointedly the Egyptians [Cush included] and Canaanites) to submission and worship of YHWH in Zion. Indeed, when YHWH vanquishes chaos, a quasi-holy kingdom is created for social organization, which embraces all the nations and people of every tribe and tongue. Here, too, Eliade's view on the sociological relevance of the idea of how the cosmos emerged from chaos to order, and all its permutations, is affirmed as charter for social organization for a world order centered on YHWH's rule of equity and justice. So much so that even nature, and all its constituents, is enjoined to sway to the rhythm of the phenomenal winds, and resound the melodic presence of the universal king in the ecological interconnectedness ushered in by YHWH's sovereign governance.

5
Conclusions

YHWH's Potent Wind(s) Churning Chaos to Cosmos

THIS MONOGRAPH PRESENTS YHWH appearing with the wind at creation and subduing chaos to establish cosmic order. By the same means, YHWH breaks into the historical arena to destroy any chaotic forces antithetical to his intended cosmic design and world/social order. As shown in the main, scholars have overlooked parallels from the epistemologies of the Global South by overemphasizing ideas on creation and the characterization of YHWH as borrowing from the ANE traditions of the Global North. A close analysis of the Dogon creation myth of Mali, Africa, proffers conceptual ideas and themes on creation enabling a review of the depiction of YHWH in the biblical Hebrew texts dealing with creation and the manifestation of YHWH in the wind showing affinity with the whirlwind deity, Amma. Although Amma manifests his creative works in the form of the smallest seed, po, his nature is embedded with this seed, and esoterically apprehended as the wind or whirlwind, which releases all the elements of the Dogon cosmogony with a luminous and sonorous motion. The explosive nature in releasing matter,[1] comparable to a birth, is also an expression of Amma's spoken word or voice. This is reenacted by the blowing of the Hogon's horn. The sound produced by the horn is in recollection of Amma's creative works released with a loud sound in the form of a whirlwind.

---

1. Perhaps this idea reflects the convergence of science and religion on the notion of the "big bang," resulting in the creation of the universe.

YHWH IN THE WIND(S)

This critical analysis of the Dogon creation myth in chapter 1 shows that cosmic order evolves from "nothing—creatio ex nihilo—then chaos" ensues in the interim caused by one of the first four creatures, Ogo in Amma's womb before maturity is reached. With an obsession to take over Amma's creative works, and overcome with incessant restlessness, Ogo breaks out of the placenta and causes disruption in Amma's creative works. Ogo is overtaken by the desire to possess Amma's creative works, and attempts to obtain the sene seed. Ogo's aggression causes a fight to erupt between him and the god Amma. However, Ogo's premature egression from the placenta not only breaches his maturity and that of the created first beings in the womb, but also causes disorder in Amma's design of the Dogon universe. Amma's reorganization of his creative works is sequel to this fight with the rebellious creature, Ogo, representing the African version of the *Chaoskampf* myth. The subsequent reordering of the chaos Ogo initiates in Amma's cosmic order, though it takes the form of a sacrifice, in principle Amma transforms chaos into cosmos. This interdisciplinary, intertextual, and comparative analysis of the biblical texts in light of this observation shows that the priestly narrative in Gen 1:1–2, though truncated, is a synopsis on YHWH creating *ex nihilo* by the power of his wind with chaos *in medias res* to cosmos.

As in the case of Amma, whose cosmos emerges from his whirling motion, YHWH appears in the wind, and subdues the chaotic waters in breach of YHWH's intended cosmic order (Job 38:8–9). Examples of Egyptian deities, showing distinctive characteristics of the creative potentiality of the winds comparable to the nature of the Dogon Amma, shed light on the biblical Hebrew statement *rûaḥ ʾĕlōhîm mĕraḥepet ʿal-penê hammayim* ("the wind of God hovered over the waters") in Gen 1:2, as alluding to YHWH's creative tendencies by the phenomenal wind. Unquestionably, in the broader context of Gen 1:1–2, and associated texts, the conflation of the terms "breath," "word" and "voice" recalling elements representing Amma's whirling wind, throws into broad relief the wind(s) as the primary agency at creation in the biblical tradition. Also, in the various texts referring to YHWH's creative deeds, the wind is alluded to in different metaphoric terms in personification of YHWH's battle with the chaotic waters or monsters at creation. The notion of YHWH wielding his "arm" or "right hand" is synecdoche for his manifestation in the wind(s). The image that YHWH "rebukes/roars" against the mythical "deep," "sea," "(many) waters," or monsters by his "thunderous voice" or "loud sound" relates the superiority of the bluster of his wind over the chaotic primal forces. Analogously, the destruction of any chaotic forces and the "wicked" in YHWH's maintenance of cosmic order borrows from, and supersedes, YHWH's initial acts at subduing chaos at primal creation.

The Images of YHWH in the Wind(s) at Creation

The subsequent discussions in the remaining chapters follow from this rationality of thought expressing YHWH's disclosure in the wind(s), either for "creation," or "destruction" and "restoration" in exercise of his various socio-political roles. As stated in chapter 2, previous scholarship on Ps 104 has overstated parallels between this psalm with Ugaritic, Babylonian, and Egyptian antecedents. In particular, scholars still follow the link established by James Breasted claiming that Ps 104 developed from Akhenaton's composition of the Egyptian "Hymn to Aten." But it is noted that Ps 104 presents similarities with the luminous and sonorous motion of the god Amma, again of the epistemologies of the Global South, in its depiction of YHWH appearing with the incandescent and loud winds to subdue the chaotic waters at his establishment of cosmic order. In light of this comparative analysis, the figurative language describing YHWH as the one "who sets clouds (as) his chariot" (השם עבים רכובו), and "who walks on the wings of the wind" (המהלך על־כנפי־רוח) is conferred new meaning, as relating YHWH's theophany in the phenomenal winds.

This new meaning is further illuminated in view of similar expressions in Ps 18. Here, the description of YHWH flying and riding on the "cherub" paralleled by a similar phrase expressing YHWH darting swiftly on the wings of the wind is elucidated by Scott B. Noegel's study. Noegel's observation on iconographic winged creatures associated with the winds, and cardinal directions in the ANE makes lucid the significance of the "cherub" as representing the wind in the depiction of YHWH's theophany in this psalm. Therefore, images of YHWH "riding" on the cherub/cherubim and the "wings of the wind" allude to nothing other than YHWH's disclosure in the wind in keeping with the nature of the Dogon wind deity, Amma.

Moreover, it is noted in discussion of Ps 104 that the figurative expressions "splendor and majesty" (הוד והדר) and YHWH covered in "light" (אור) bear similarity to the picture of the luminous motion of Amma at creation. The same conceptual idea obtains on YHWH's majesty and splendor, characteristic of the luminous nature of Amma, observed in other biblical Hebrew texts reviewed, which alludes to YHWH's theophany in the phenomenal winds at creation. Also, as discussed, the verbs used in describing the reaction of the "waters" (מים), as moving pell-mell to the places assigned to them at YHWH's theophany discharging his "rebuke/roar" (גער), express commotion, and, therefore, suggest a pale reflection of a cosmogonic battle. Arguably, this image of YHWH's appearance with the wind in "splendor and majesty" concurrent with the "roar" is characteristic of, and parallels the luminous and sonorous motion of Amma at the release of all the elements forming the Dogon cosmogony. Hence, it is concluded that in Ps 104, YHWH appears with the phenomenal wind in a luminous and sonorous motion to subdue the primal chaotic waters in the manner of a *Chaoskampf* for the establishment of cosmic order.

Following on from Charles H. Long's view on the integration of the idea of a supreme deity and other themes in the Dogon creation myth, it is evident that Ps 104 as a *de facto* cosmogony in the biblical tradition combines the idea of a creation with wisdom and judgment motifs. The Psalmist in Ps 104 lauds YHWH's wondrous creative order as an expression of his wisdom. Even Leviathan, often apprehended as a mythical monster of chaos in other biblical texts, and, in essence parallels the rebellious creature, Ogo who disrupts Amma's creative order, is mentioned as an element of YHWH's sapiential works.

As the Psalmist declares in Ps 104, all the living things of diverse forms and sizes, and their sustainability depend on YHWH. Thus, the Psalmist underscores that the created order is not independent of YHWH's sovereign will. This idea focuses that as much as YHWH asserts his dominance over primeval chaos by the phenomenal winds associated with his theophany, he also sustains the ecological system. The Psalmist exhorts YHWH to display his glory in creation to eternity, and recalls into tension YHWH's appearance in the wind. As though stating YHWH's theophany in the wind at creation in a reverse form, the Psalmist expresses how YHWH can undo the created order by "looking" and causing the earth to tremble, and by "touching" the mountains and causing them to smoke. By this means, YHWH breaks into his created order that has gone awry. Therefore, the Psalmist is compelled to muse and rejoice in YHWH in harmony with the created order. Here, the Psalmist alludes to "wisdom." Also, intrinsic to the Psalmist's response of praise is the expression of "reverential fear" in submission to the sovereignty of YHWH, as the creator. Through such disposition, the Psalmist expresses his desire for the "wicked" or "sinners" to be annihilated. Although it is not clear how the Psalmist wishes YHWH to expel the wicked, it is argued that the divine discourse in Job 40:6–13 proffers an answer. The poet of Job brings into focus the magnificence and power of YHWH manifested in the wind, and Job is challenged to display and match that potency in an outburst of anger and fury to "scatter," and tread down the proud and wicked in their place. In light of that, the Psalmist's musings in Ps 104 subsume the destruction of the wicked at YHWH's theophany in the phenomenal winds to combat chaos resulting in creation, combined with the wisdom and judgment motifs in depiction of YHWH as the creator.

YHWH in the Wind(s) for "Creation" and "Destruction" in the Book of Job

All the ideas regarding YHWH's disclosure in the wind, creation, wisdom and judgment motifs are topical in the selected texts from Job. Here, the poet of Job combines these themes and motifs in expression of the profound wisdom of YHWH, as the creator of wondrous works by the phenomenal wind. But, at the same time, the poet poses YHWH's dispensation of judgment, or divine justice, ushered by the same means of the creative winds as a paradox. In Job 9:4–10 and 26:7–14, YHWH's manifestation with the phenomenal wind features as the creative agency in these doxologies celebrating YHWH's cosmological activities. His acts of creation by the power of his wind are described as a display of his profound wisdom and might. In these doxologies, YHWH's power in the sonorous wind and his creative deeds are brought together in depiction of him as the creator. Here, too, Job expresses that by the phenomenal winds, YHWH churns the sea, shatters Rahab, "stretches out" the heavens or makes the heavens fair, and pierces the serpent, or dragon. Job says, however, that although YHWH reveals himself through these cosmological activities, his might, manifested by the sonorous sound of his wind, is incomprehensible.

According to Job, this limit on the understanding of YHWH's power by means of the supernatural, also limits the knowledge of the full extent of YHWH's rule. This comes into view in the wider context of these texts with regard to Job's quest for divine justice in ridicule of Bildad's pretentious knowledge of YHWH's design and governance. Nonetheless, Job expresses YHWH's use of the phenomenal wind to manifest his power and purpose. To that effect, it is argued that Job's idea referring to YHWH's command to the luminaries not to give light, alludes to the occurrence of cloud cover brought by the phenomenal winds. But, as Job points out, YHWH's presence in the wind is elusive. Accordingly, Job claims that when YHWH passes by, he cannot discern him. Yet, on the mundane level, Job is aware that YHWH hurls his whirling winds against the wicked. Despite defending his innocence, Job also throws his lot with the wicked. So, Job even suspects that YHWH might crush him with a whirlwind (Job 9:17). He sees YHWH's justice as though now a paradox: both the "blameless" (תם) and "wicked" (רשׁע), YHWH destroys alike (Job 9:22).

At any rate, Job expresses awe at YHWH's incomprehensible deeds at creation, and his continual governance of that order by his phenomenal wind. This idea echoes a statement that only Elihu (Job 37:5) takes up in expression of the enigma surrounding YHWH's cosmological and judicial acts (see vv. 2–6, 9–18, 22–23). Arguably, of significance in this discourse is that the incomprehensible phenomenal wind, symbolizes the self-disclosure of this mysterious deity appearing from the "north" (צפון, Job 26:7) in golden splendor (Job 37:22), though it is impossible to discern his way of establishing "justice" and "righteousness." As seen in Elihu's discourse on YHWH as the creator, the phenomenal wind acts at the divine bidding. According to Elihu, YHWH directs the wind, dispersing the natural meteorological elements to bless and to punish. That means, either for YHWH's benefit to the land to show loving kindness, or punishment of the wicked (Job 36:27–37:1–13).

However, contrary to Job's premonitions, YHWH appears in a whirlwind (Job 38), not for Job's retribution, but encounters Job with a plethora of rhetorical questions on the ingenuity of the mysteries of YHWH's cosmogonic works manifested by the phenomenal wind(s), including the reprisal of the wicked. The ideas on the mystery of divine justice mentioned in the preceding texts are taken up in this long-awaited encounter with the divine, as presented in Job 38. In this context, however, neither are answers proffered in response to Job's concerns on divine justice, nor is the whirlwind unleashed as retributive, in accordance with his angst towards the expected fate of the wicked. In any case, the idea of YHWH wielding the phenomenal wind is also involved in Job 38. It is clear, that in this poem on YHWH's cosmic design, YHWH's theophany in the whirlwind portends his active role in his cosmological acts. The purposes of YHWH's phenomenal wind are made clear in this context, and further substantiated with sustained rhetorical statements in Job 40:6–13. In Job 38, however, the whirlwind functions as the setting from which YHWH communicates the mysteries of his cosmic design. Here, too, his creation of the earth, luminaries, and his control of natural elements by the power of his wind are attributed to his wisdom. The annihilation of the wicked is considered as part of YHWH's creation of cosmic order (Job 38:13). In that respect, Job 38 synthesizes the motifs of creation from chaos by his wind, wisdom and judgment as in the other texts discussed. Therefore, it is concluded that the image of YHWH appearing with the phenomenal winds enriches the depiction of YHWH as the creator who manifests his wisdom in the establishment of cosmic order. In essence, YHWH's use of the phenomenal winds to eliminate the wicked from his cosmic design (Job 40:9–13) supersedes his vanquishing of the primeval chaos at creation.

Hence, not far from the idea of YHWH unleashing judgment on the wicked by using his blustery wind is the reference to YHWH's celestial reserve of snow and hail as arsenal (Job 38:22). Therefore, as alluded to by the rhetoric attributed to the lips of Elihu in Job 37, YHWH boasts of his preservation of these elements for times of trouble and days of war and battle. However, apart from functioning as YHWH's punitive instruments, these elements dispersed by his wind, also fulfill YHWH's providential purposes. So, YHWH has power to dispense these elements accordingly, because, by his wisdom, he begets, or in other words creates, and precipitates rain, dew, ice and hoarfrost (Job 37:28–29). The poet of Job uses Elihu's speech on YHWH's sway over phenomenal elements as foil in anticipation of his disclosure in the whirlwind (Job 38:1). Ironically, the poet employs the whirlwind as the backdrop where YHWH interrogates Job with a series of rhetorical questions. Among them are questions that inquire if Job was present at creation, or comprehends the power of YHWH's winds and understands the wisdom demonstrated at creation and maintenance of that cosmic design. Thus, in Job 38, there is a conflation of elements of creation, wisdom and judgment motifs in the portrait of YHWH as the creator, who asserts his dominance through the agency of his phenomenal wind. The same ideas are employed in prophetic passages expressing the sovereignty of YHWH over the mundane/social realm.

YHWH at "Creation," "Destruction" and "Restoration" in the Guise of the Winds in Amos and Jeremiah

Undoubtedly, the idea of YHWH's cosmological activities, inclusive of his retribution of the wicked by the power of his winds, occurs in the prophetic messages of Amos and Jeremiah. The selected prophetic passages/texts from Amos 1:2, 14; 4:12-13; 5:8-9; 9:5-6 and Jer 10:1-16; 25:15-38; 51:15-19 are often considered by biblical scholars either as erratic blocks, late editorial insertions of no thematic relevance, or inconsistent with the message in their contexts. However, upon identifying the image of YHWH preserved in these texts, it is concluded here that these texts find form and content from the previously discussed biblical texts, and relate YHWH as the creator exercising his prerogative by the power of his wind against wickedness in the form of pervasive idolatry. Although the role of YHWH as the creator is asserted in these prophetic texts, the roaring wind of YHWH is no longer directed against primeval chaos, but against human vice.

In relation to the prophecies of Amos, the "voice" of YHWH personifying the wind, fire, and/or a tempest, is central to the manifestation of YHWH in the predicted imminent judgment (Amos 1:2, 4, 7, 10, 12, 14). YHWH's judgment is presaged with the tempestuous winds manifested against the nations for their perpetrated acts against humanity. At this critical point, Zion/Jerusalem is accorded primacy as YHWH's seat of judgment and appropriate locus for his disclosure. As presented in the discussion on the universal kingship of YHWH expressed in the psalms (see Pss 96:10; 97:9), the holy abode at Zion is considered as a microcosm of its celestial counterpart, therefore fitting for YHWH's manifestation in exercise of his rule and lordship over his chosen people and the nations. It is on the basis of this idea of YHWH's sovereignty, that the prophet Amos employs language relating to creation to give impetus to his judgment oracles.

Although Amos's initial message reaches beyond the confines of Israel and Judah, in order to emphasize YHWH's universal power and hegemony, the remainder of his message focuses on the chastisement of his own people for idolatry, profanity, lack of concern for social responsibility and justice. Amos declares YHWH as the judge of his people, but no less as the creator. Here he brings into view the purposeful function of the message expressed in the doxologies of Amos 4:12-13; 5:8-9 and 9:5-6, often considered to be abrupt, editorial insertions, or irrelevant.

CONCLUSIONS

Thus, as noted, YHWH's sovereignty is emphasized by idioms reminiscent of his battle with primeval chaos (Amos 4:13; cf. Job 9:8),[2] and expressive of his power as the creator of the luminaries (Amos 5:8; cf. Job 9:9) and the upper chambers (Amos 9:6; cf. Ps 104:3). Also, YHWH's ability to manipulate nature at his disclosure with the roaring wind gives expression of his sovereignty. Thus, Amos pronounces and identifies this deity with the appellation YHWH 'ĕlōhê Ṣebā'ôth, meaning YHWH the God of hosts. Arguably, this designation is in purview of the all-comprehensive and limitless power and majesty of YHWH expressing his martial nature by his potent winds, and breaking into both the cosmic and social arena, as the sovereign creator. YHWH has the power to roar and dry up the pastures (Amos 1:2), and no less interrupts daylight with his phenomenal wind, as he "passes by" (עבר, Amos 5:17; cf. Job 9:11, 17; Prov 10:25) to mete out judgment on the ones contravening his rule of "justice" and "righteousness." He calls on the waters of the sea, causing an overwhelming scourge of floodwaters; thus, also featuring as the creator-god, "the one who bursts forth" (המבליג, 5:9) by his bluster of wind against the perverts of his divine order.

As also characteristic of YHWH's appearance with the wind, he touches the mountains and causes them to melt (Amos 9:5; see Ps 46:7[6]b). Hence, it is suggested that this latter outcome, is a metaphorical expression on the effect of YHWH's luminous or fiery wind (Ps 97:3–5) affecting the stable and durable cosmic order. In that purview, YHWH's cosmic activities are predestined against those perverting justice. In essence, YHWH, as the creator, will "turn" nature to accomplish his purposes against those who "turn" "justice" into bitterness and thrust "righteousness" to the ground by defecting to idols. But, they—who neglect YHWH's law and precepts—will experience the full force of YHWH's wrath through his phenomenal winds. So, here, too, the natural phenomenal elements are imbued with divine wisdom, and work in accordance with YHWH's divine will.

However, Amos does not mention the attribute of wisdom in his depiction of YHWH as creator. But, the similarity of terms and ideas with those in Ps 104 and Job indicates wisdom influence. In keeping with the wisdom tradition, Amos's message contained in the doxologies expresses the idea of YHWH's potentiality to manipulate the elements within his creative order for punitive purposes, in order to reinstitute his rule of

---

2. See discussion on Amos 4:12–13; Job 9:4–10, esp. v. 8, in chapter 2.

"justice" and "righteousness." Also, Amos lauds YHWH as "the builder" (הבונה) of his upper chambers in the heavens (see Ps 104:3) and the founder of its vaults (אגדתו) over the earth (Amos 9:6; Job 22:14). In that manner, he alludes to YHWH's creative acts in display of his profound wisdom. On that basis, YHWH has the prerogative to dispense with nature at will. In harking back to creation, YHWH's punitive act on the perverts of his rule is also predicted in terms of YHWH "calling" (הקורא) on the waters of the sea (Amos 5:8c=9:6c) and "pouring" it out on the surface of the earth; thus implying the revoking of the statute or boundary applied to the sea at creation (Ps 104:9; Jer 5:22; Job 38:8–11; Prov 8:29). This rhapsodic integration of the traditions of YHWH's theophany with the phenomenal winds, wisdom, creation, and judgment motifs in the doxologies of Amos enhances the picture of YHWH as the creator and judge.

Similarly, in the prophecies of Jeremiah, elements from creation, wisdom and theophany traditions are part of the language expressing the idea of YHWH as creator-king and judge. It is noted that Jeremiah expresses the wickedness of the people by using wisdom terms: the people are "the wise ones" in doing evil, yet "they do not know how to do good." Jeremiah casts this situation incurred by the people turning to the worship of idols, thus demanding YHWH's judgment. Therefore, Jeremiah predicts YHWH's retribution as though creation has reverted to chaos, as he sets forth images of YHWH's disclosure with the phenomenal winds for judicial purposes. The people's apostasy that provokes divine intervention is marked by idolatry, prostitution/adultery, robbery, deceit and infringement of the law on protecting the poor, widows and fatherless. In light of that, as Jeremiah pronounces in wisdom terms, this is due to the lack of "fear" of YHWH. Hence, in antithesis to nature, which obeys YHWH's statutes set at creation, his people show no reverential fear of YHWH, who is the benefactor of rain (הנתן גשם, Jer 5:24) in its season. This latter aspect throws into bold relief the idea of YHWH roiling the winds as the bestower of rain (Jer 14:22), a characteristic that makes him distinct from idols. The idols are essentially nonentities, over and above which YHWH's universal kingship supersedes (see Zech 14:16–17). It is within this context that Jeremiah inserts passages replete with the themes in discussion, as he also relates the nature of Israel's disobedience, in particular Judah in succumbing to idols, and the predicted judgment thereof. Hence, it is cited that even though the provenance and relevance of Jer 10:1–16 is often questioned; this text is a crucible of the related

CONCLUSIONS

themes and motifs: theophany in the winds, wisdom, creation, and judgment. Therefore, Jer 10:1–16 combines elements of wisdom thought with creation in assertion of YHWH's potentiality to appear with the winds for retributive purposes.

Undoubtedly, in Jer 10:1–16 YHWH is portrayed as the sole creator, who has the capability to manipulate the blustery wind for his own purposes. On that basis alone, Jeremiah casts YHWH as the supreme judge, whose prerogative is to restore his rule against the injustice perpetrated by idolatry. But, as the problem of idolatry also involves other nations, the message of Jeremiah reflects its universalistic orientation in accordance with his divine commissioning to pronounce judgment on all the nations (Jer 1:5, 10). As in the case of Amos, although Jeremiah's message is centered on the chosen people, with Judah as the primary focus, the message also involves pronouncing punishment on the neighboring wicked (הרעים, Jer 12:14) and the surrounding nations (Jer 25:11–26). YHWH intends to reprimand them through his agent, Babylon for their deeds and worshiping the "work of their hands"—idolatry! From that broad context, Jeremiah appeals to creation theology, in order to draw attention to the sovereignty of YHWH exercising his prerogative, as the judge of all the nations. That perspective, then, focuses the relevance and importance of the message in Jer 10:12–16=51:15–19 and Jer 25:30–32, 38 often considered erratic blocks, but significant in depicting YHWH, as also identified by the prophet Amos, with the name YHWH Ṣebāʾôth to amplify his appearance with the winds for judicial purposes.

It is pointed out that Jer 10:12–16=51:15–19 and Jer 25:30–32, in their respective contexts (Jer 10:1–16; 25:15–38; 50–51), expose the intersection of elements from wisdom and creation motifs to underscore YHWH's appearance with the wind, as the creator-king and judge. Here, Jeremiah emphasizes the incomparability of YHWH, and extols his unparalleled prominence. Jeremiah contrasts YHWH with the idols in that the former is said to be superior among the "wise ones of the nations" (חכמי הגוים) and to embody "truth" as the living and "eternal king" (מלך עולם, Jer 10:10). This idea not only bolsters YHWH's authority over the earth, but also anticipates the emphasis on YHWH as the sole creator, as expressed in the statements framing the doxologies (Jer 10:12–16=51:15–19), and by this means points to the inevitability of YHWH's manifestation of his wrath against idolatry. Thus, as in other creation traditions, Jeremiah depicts YHWH as the creator, who establishes the world by his wisdom; an idea that echoes his appearance with roaring winds (cf.

Ps 104:6–9, 24; Job 9:4–10; 26:7–14). It is suggested that the mention of the "sound of his utterance" (קול תתו, Jer 10:13=51:16) not only alludes to YHWH's sonorous winds, causing the "tumult of the waters" in the heavens, but also implies two meanings. The sound causing the tumult of waters in the heavens relates the stirring of YHWH's winds, and underscores his rainmaking act (as emphasized in Jer 5:24 and 14:22; see Zech 14:16–17), and thus, indicates that the rain originates from YHWH over and against the inertness of worthless idols of other nations. At the same time, the idea of winds as the mode of YHWH's disclosure is also thrown into bold relief. The emphasis on YHWH's appearance with the roaring winds may not be denied in view of the expression in Jer 10:10 on the earthshaking experience; a characteristic of his theophany in this melodramatic phenomenon. In that view, YHWH is depicted as the eternal king, who supersedes all the wise ones of the nations. Moreover, YHWH's establishment of the heavens and the earth is proof of his might, profound wisdom, and understanding as the creator (Jer 10:12=51:15). He is the maker of all things including the phenomenal winds. By that means, either in his rainmaking or earthshaking experiences depicting his appearance, YHWH emerges to dispense his divine will, and, at the same time, abolish idolatry and wickedness.

Therefore, it is in light of these theophanic aspects that Jeremiah finds form and content to emphasize YHWH's universal rule, in that he imposes his judgment through the supernatural winds over all the rulers of the earth (Jer 25:30–32). In the broader context of Jer 25:15–38, Jeremiah employs figurative terms: the "voice," a young lion emerging from its lair, and the cup of YHWH's wrath to personify, animate, and picture the roaring, or whirling winds directed against human wickedness. Thus, as in the book of Amos, Jeremiah also appeals to the idea of YHWH breaking out with the winds to judge, and quell forces militating against his divine will and purpose amongst the nations. And, by this means, Jeremiah enhances his message of doom in portrait of YHWH as the creator-king.

Jeremiah's prophecy against Babylon expressed in the wider context of Jer 50–51 is no exception from appealing to YHWH's theophany with the phenomenal winds. Upon Babylon's completion of the divine task in serving YHWH's judicial purposes in creation, divine retribution is turned on this nation. The destruction of Babylon is in no uncertain terms, as YHWH has sworn by himself to carry out his judgment. Again,

CONCLUSIONS

YHWH's identity, as YHWH Ṣebā'ôth is made explicit as the creator,[3] in order to throw sharp contrast from Babylon's breathless molten images. So, Jeremiah bolsters the image of this deity, who threatens Babylon with its ultimate nemesis. Hence, Jeremiah portrays YHWH as the creator of the heavens and earth by his wisdom; and, as such, indicates his sway over all creation (Jer 51:15, 19). As noted, YHWH is able to let the sea deluge Babylon, implying the repeal of the boundary set at creation. Again, in this context, the land "shaking" (Jer 51:29; see Judg 5:4; Pss 18:8[7]; 68:9[8]; 77:19[18]) and the earth "whirling" (חול, see Pss 29:8; 97:4) indicate the effects of YHWH's sonorous winds. These convulsions throw into stark relief YHWH's appearance with the potent winds in assertion of his sovereign rule. Therefore, the same phenomenal elements are represented in the prediction of Babylon's demise, suggesting evidence of YHWH's intervention and undeniable involvement of his bluster of wind at Babylon's downfall (Jer 51:29).

Again, in making a stark contrast between YHWH and the idols of Babylon, Jeremiah espouses YHWH as the sole creator, who dispenses with nature at will. In predicting YHWH's acts of vengeance on Babylon for its wickedness, Jeremiah inflects his message with comic satire. Jeremiah forecasts YHWH drying up Babylon's seas and closing its springs. In essence, this indicates YHWH's potentiality to reverse Marduk's cosmological activities, as (in the Babylonian creation epic) he is attributed with the opening up of sources to provide water in prolific abundance. Also, in contrast, the reference to the prediction on the sea rising up and covering Babylon stands as a polemical statement to show that YHWH has absolute power to reverse the order in creation to its primordial state. This statement is derisive on the ingeniousness of Marduk, in the face of YHWH exercising his unrivalled might and showing the wherewithal to unleash the chaotic sea (=Tiamat), that Marduk is said to have subjugated and put under confinement. In that view, Jeremiah predicts YHWH punishing the nations and their idols. In particular, he focuses on Babylon and its iconic chief god, Bel-Marduk. So, the prophet draws images from the tradition of the battle with chaos, in order to give form and content to his message in portrayal of YHWH's final destruction of Babylon. With a note of irony, and mythic flavor, Jeremiah foretells YHWH punishing Bel(-Marduk) by making him disgorge all that he ingested (Jer 51:44); in

---

3. See Jer 51:15–19—YHWH Ṣebā'ôth: The Creator-King and Judge against Babylon.

YHWH IN THE WIND(S)

a symbolic gesture of releasing Israel and its treasures taken from Zion/Jerusalem.[4]

Arguably, in view of the oracles on Babylon (Jer 50–51), Babylon's nemesis is further predicted in terms borrowing from the creation tradition and transposed to a historical plane. Accordingly, there is a note that even if Babylon tries to fortify a stronghold reaching up to the heavens, there would be no escape from the reach of YHWH's inescapable judgment (Jer 51:53; cf. Amos 9:3–4, 6a; Ps 139:8). The idea recalls the declaration of YHWH as the creator of the heavens (and earth). Therefore, in exercise of his unrivalled dominion, YHWH will silence Babylon's din and put an end to its great sound, comparable to the subjugation of the primal "many waters" (מים רבים, Jer 51:55). This image marks the finality of Babylon's demise. At this point, YHWH's collateral identity, his nature and character as YHWH Ṣebā'ôth, the creator, is also disclosed. He is the "king" (המלך, v. 57d; cf. Ps 97:9), who recompenses Babylon in full as the God of retribution (Jer 51:56). Therefore, all of Babylon's officials and wise men are not exempt from YHWH's sovereign rule. They are destined to experience the wrath of YHWH's whirling wind, figuratively pictured as being made drunk (Jer 51:57; see 25:15–29) and causing them to fall, comparable to sinking to inebriety and death. With this idealistic mental vision, Jeremiah augments the image of YHWH's sovereignty. His unrivalled might and unparalleled wisdom, demonstrated through his creative order, underscore his universal rule. Hence, YHWH has the prerogative to manipulate the phenomenal winds for his own purposes and assert his judicial power in the historical arena against Babylon.

Here, too, Jeremiah, as in the case of Amos' prophecies, interrelates his message on Babylon's nemesis with a note of hope on the redemption of its captives (Jer 51:45; see v. 6). In keeping with that idea, Jeremiah's message postures YHWH as the "redeemer" (גאל) who will avail himself to his people, amid the "trembling" (רגז) of the inhabitants of Babylon (Jer 50:34; cf. 30:23–24). In view of this broad context of the devastation of Babylon, Marduk's guardianship of land as the shepherd is ridiculed, as YHWH, in rhetoric, appears with the winds, and is pictured as the lion coming out of the majesty of the Jordan, and championed as the prime shepherd (Jer 50:44–46). This epithet will be made manifest with the redemption of YHWH's flock, and its restoration to its "pastures" in Carmel and Bashan (Jer 50:19; see 31:10–13; 33:6–13). Yet, in contrast,

---

4. See p. 148.

CONCLUSIONS

the predestined total desolation of Babylon's pastures, and the land as a whole, is also defined showing that YHWH's power in the wind prevails over Babylon. It is concluded that this tension in Jeremiah's message on the "destruction" of Babylon and "restoration" of Israel with YHWH's bluster of wind(s) as the agency, resonates with Jeremiah's divine commission: "To uproot, and to tear down, to destroy, and to throw down, but also to build and to plant" (Jer 1:10), respectively.

It is noted that the book of Amos corresponds with the message of Jeremiah at crucial points. The final chapter of the book of Amos (Amos 9), counterbalances this message of destruction with a note of hope for the restoration of Israel, even though the latter aspect is often considered a late interpolation to Amos's prophetic message. However, Amos's prophecies present messages in anticipation of the destruction of the idolaters and perverts of social justice, but end with a final note of hope on the restoration of Israel, as the counterpoint in Amos 9:11–15. Like Jeremiah, Amos's note of restoration predicts YHWH gathering the people in exile and bringing them to "(re)build" the cities in ruins and "plant" vineyards and gardens. It is clear that this message of restoration echoes and counterpoises Jeremiah's message at key points. Here, YHWH solemnly promises in antithesis to the destructive nature of his winds, which pluck up, or uproot, that he will plant, and not uproot his people but enable them to build in restoration of the remnant of David (Amos 9:14b–15). Apart from the notion of YHWH appearing with the winds, correlated with elements from the creation, wisdom and judgment motifs, to highlight YHWH's unrivalled role in asserting order in the cosmic and social realm, this note of restoration inadvertently alludes to another aspect of YHWH's intervention as savior, which forms the scope of the subsequent chapter.

Sights, Sounds and melodramatic Images of YHWH as Savior

The content of chapter 3 draws on key features highlighted in the first two chapters. The keynote to Pss 18, 77, 144 (in affinity with 18) and Hab 3 emphasized in chapter 3, is the description of YHWH's appearance with the distinctive "sights and sounds" of the wind, and the theological intentionality of this image in these biblical Hebrew hymns previously identified by scholars as fitting the literary form and style of the so-called "storm" theophany hymns. As pointed out, most scholars see in these psalms storm elements associated with the storm gods Baʻal and Marduk. But as argued, these hymns employ figurative language relating the appearance of YHWH with the phenomenal winds in expression of his power and feats as savior. The idea is quite explicit in Ps 18, which serves in this study as the paradigm for the literary features reflected in Pss 77, 144 and Hab 3. Undoubtedly, in these texts the victories of YHWH, through his power manifested with the winds on the historical plane, are explained in terms of the mythological battle against the sea, rivers or many waters. Even though the sea/rivers, and many waters are mentioned as YHWH's mythical foes in these texts, the emphasis is on the "many waters" as the main symbol of chaos. As noted, the origin of the expression "many waters" in the Hebrew tradition cannot be identified with precision. But, as argued, the mythological term ʾil rbm, used for Yam ("god Sea") in the Ugaritic tradition,[5] suggests the possibility of the occurrence of this expression in the Hebrew tradition. However, the identification of the "many waters" with human foes, as equivalent to primeval chaos, against which YHWH directs his phenomenal wind, is evident in Pss 18 and 144. Unquestionably, in relation to Ps 18, and 144 in affinity, the term "many waters" refers to historical enemies. But, in Ps 77 and Hab 3, the mythical symbolism in the term "many waters" is retained wholesale as the chaotic primal waters at creation. Here, the Psalmist and poet-prophet, respectively, allude to the historical event of the exodus and the "many waters" represent the pacified waters of the *Yam Suph*/Red Sea through which YHWH guides his redeemed people.

In these texts, Pss 18, 77, 144 and Hab 3 depicting YHWH as the savior-god, the luminous and sonorous nature of YHWH in the wind, echoing the image of the creator and wind god Amma, characterizes YHWH's divine intervention for his elected people. Also, the use of mythological language in the recital of the historical victories of YHWH in these texts, seeks to enrich the biblical Hebrew thought and belief on YHWH, rather than preserve elements wholesale relating to a mythical battle. The critical analysis of these texts in discussion shows that there is an amalgamation of elements from the creation and exodus/wilderness traditions, particularly features from the Red Sea crossing, and theophany at the Sinai. These elements occur in collation and throw into stark relief YHWH's theophany in the wind as savior. To that effect, the idea of YHWH "rending the heavens" (Pss 18:10[9]; 144:5; cf. Isa 63:19[64:1])

---

5. KTU 1.3.III:39[=CTA 3.iii:36].

previously seen in scholarship as echoes of Ba'al's insertion of a "rift in the clouds," and compared to the imperative on Marduk to "rend the heavens with his thunder," is given new meaning here in light of a closer parallel with the god Amma, the whirlwind deity, who releases his entire work of creation through an opening in the sky.

Furthermore, Noegel's observation on the pervasive association of hybrid creatures with wings and winds (including the cardinal directions) in the ANE, compels a reinterpretation of the well-known image of YHWH "riding on the cherub" in Ps 18:11[10]). In view of Noegel's study, it is suggested here that this image, often paralleled with Ba'al as the "rider of the clouds," depicts nothing other than the graphic appearance of YHWH with the phenomenal wind to manifest his deeds of salvation. Therefore, the latter image has more affinity with Amma's whirling wind at creation. Hence, whether YHWH "rends" the heavens, or "descends" on his cherub from on high to combat the "many waters," this artistry of fusing mythical imagery from different sources with historical elements, focuses YHWH's divine intervention, but, at the same time, enriches the depiction of YHWH as savior breaking onto a historical scene with the phenomenal winds.

Undoubtedly, there is a conflation of elements from different traditions creating this image of the sight and sound of YHWH in the wind in Ps 18. The idea of YHWH bending down the heavens and descending with the winds, and, also with the clouds as his covering, borrows from the creation tradition.[6] In this theophanic unit, as a response to King David's plea, the image of YHWH appearing with the bluster of wind directed against the many waters replicates YHWH's wind roaring to subdue the chaotic waters at primal creation. Yet, on the one hand, the combination of the luminous, but also dark clouds recalls the events at the exodus, at which YHWH's cloud created darkness for the oppressor in pursuit of the escapees, to whom the fiery cloud lit the path to redemption. On the other hand, the seismic trembling and shaking of the cosmic elements echo YHWH's revelation by the power of his winds at Mount Sinai. Arguably, this histrionic outburst of the sight and sound of YHWH in the wind brings into tension the idea of a *Deus praesens* and *Deus absconditus* at the deliverance of his elect from historical foes. The element of light shed or sight of the luminous clouds spells deliverance for King David. But the darkness, or thicket of clouds surrounding

---

6. See discussions on Ps 104 and Job 9:4–10; 26:7–14 in chapter 2.

YHWH IN THE WIND(S)

YHWH, forebodes doom for his enemies; identified with a note of irony, as the "sons of foreigners." As suggested here, the term "sons of foreigners" implied as the many waters refers to the band of kings and the nations King David defeats at YHWH's intervention, possibly as narrated in 2 Sam 8:5–15. No wonder, as described in Ps 18, King David attributes his victories to YHWH, who empowers him in battle at his theophany in the wind. To this point, King David sees himself as a force to contend with at YHWH's divine intervention. Hence, as much as he acclaims the feats of his savior-god manifested in the potent winds, King David even describes his involvement in destroying and crushing his enemies like dust before the (divine) wind,[7] as he evinces his traits as an invincible warrior empowered by YHWH.

Similarly, images of YHWH appearing with the wind occur in Ps 77. As pointed out, scholars agree that the Psalmist in this psalm recalls YHWH's past wondrous deeds comparable to YHWH's cosmogonic activities noted in Job 9:10, as a basis for hope that YHWH will renew his acts of salvation. Therefore, the Psalmist in Ps 77 recalls YHWH's exploits at creation by the power of his wind in the ancient days to give form and content to his musings. Here, the Psalmist employs figurative language in representation of YHWH's appearance with the phenomenal wind. In this manner, he meditates on YHWH's deeds wielded by his ancient "right hand," symbolizing the wind, as the hallmark of the holiness of his ways. Hence, the Psalmist focuses YHWH performing wonders and displaying his might among the people. At this point, he also identifies YHWH's phenomenal wind with another synonymous synecdoche, the "arm" as instrumental to the redemption of the sons of Jacob and Joseph at the exodus. The Psalmist muses over the events at the exodus with a mythic flavor, and alludes to the *Chaoskampf* myth relating YHWH subduing the chaotic "waters," or the "deep" with the power of his wind at primal creation. But, here, the Psalmist identifies YHWH's potent sonorous sound as lodged in the "whirlwind,"[8] which roils the waters. Also, the Psalmist employs the same terms occurring in texts alluding to YHWH subduing the chaotic waters,[9] and conflates the "voice" (קול) with the "sound of thunder" (קול רעם) in expression of YHWH's power manifested in the whirlwind.

---

7. See pp. 202–5.
8. See Ps 81:8[7].
9. See Pss 18, 104.

CONCLUSIONS

As argued, in keeping with other texts depicting YHWH's theophany in the wind, the Psalmist in Ps 77 describes the clouds dripping, waters writhing, deeps quaking, and the earth shaking in reaction to the luminous and sonorous whirlwind. The Psalmist makes a subtle allusion to YHWH's confrontation of the waters of chaos implied by the waters writhing and the deep(s) quaking. However, the Psalmist reverts to the historic incident of the redemption at the Red Sea by referring to YHWH leading the people, comparable to a flock, by the hand of Moses and Aaron. It is argued, here, too, that there is a subtle reference to YHWH's shepherd[10] epithet, as he guides his people like a flock through the "many waters."[11] This idea recalls the image of YHWH as a shepherd depicted in Ps 80:2[1], when the Psalmist implores YHWH, "who dwells (between) the cherubim" (ישב הכרובים), to "shine forth" (הופיע) reminiscent of YHWH's majestic representation from the Sinai tradition.[12] Unquestionably, this appellative in Ps 80, evinces that the appeal directed to YHWH to shine forth, evokes nothing other than the sight and sound of YHWH's manifestation with the "luminous" and "sonorous" winds described in Ps 18. In the same manner, the luminous and sonorous sound of YHWH associated with the whirlwind in Ps 77 sets in tension the notion of YHWH as *Deus praesens* and *Deus absconditus*. Hence, the Psalmist also retains the mythical by highlighting this numinous experience of YHWH carving a path by his whirlwind in the many waters, even though his footprints are not seen, but he delivers his people.

Similar ideas on YHWH's appearance in the wind occur in the mytho-historical recital of YHWH's past deeds in the theophanic unit in Hab 3:3–15. All the natural elements the poet-prophet mentions in attendance of YHWH's theophany, and considered by scholars as parallels to mythic attendants, or minor divinities belonging to either Ba'al's or Marduk's entourage, have a historic component in the poetic hymn of Hab 3. It is argued that the terms "pestilence" and "fire" relate to events involving YHWH's manifestation in the wind in the exodus tradition. In particular the element of fire not only features at the crossing of the Red Sea and the revelation at Mount Sinai, but also occurs with the luminous and sonorous wind at creation. No wonder the poet-prophet mentions fire as issuing at YHWH's feet or footsteps in sequel to the description on the character and nature of YHWH disclosed in the natural elements.

10. See pp. 178–79, 179n118.
11. Ps 77:20–21[19–20]; see Hab 3:13a, 15
12. See p. 179.

Hence, the reference to YHWH's incandescence comparable to light, and associated with "horns," figuratively refer to the splendor and power lodged in his "hand" representing YHWH's wind, as the "secret" or "hiding place" (חביון) of his might.

YHWH's display of his might for deliverance at the exodus is presented in graphic and elaborate mythic terms in the theophanic unit in Hab 3:3–15. Undoubtedly, here, although scholars see elements resonant with literary features relating to the battles of Ba'al and Marduk as storm gods, the poet-prophet employs images from the ancient conflict to reinterpret YHWH's involvement in his age-old *modus operandi* in the wind for the salvation of his people. Therefore, the poet-prophet appeals to ideas associated with the concept of creation from chaos to represent the image of YHWH subduing the chaotic waters. With a series of rhetorical statements, the poet-prophet recites in mythic terms YHWH subjecting the "sea," "rivers," and "many waters" to his wrath and fury. So, in unparalleled poetic hyperbole, the poet-prophet animates YHWH's wrath manifested in the graphic movement of the wind, as riding on his horses and chariots to vent his fury against the waters. However, the poet-prophet intentionally employs these images for poetic emphasis in allusion to the historic events on YHWH's past deeds wielded by the roiling winds at the exodus. It is noted here that the pluralism in "rivers," in contrast to "river," as often thought by scholars to echo the Ugaritic archenemy of Ba'al, Yam, also known as Judge River, is accounted for by the extraordinary historical events in the biblical tradition. So, the point at issue is that, YHWH appears with the potent winds at both the Jordan and Kishon rivers. YHWH's wind cleaves the waters and stops them from flowing for the people to cross the Jordan, as at the Red Sea. Again, YHWH's winds cause the heavens to droop with a downpour over the age-old Kishon, causing a flood to raze the enemy for the redemption of his people.[13] YHWH's "creation" of one nation is through the "destruction" of the other(s) by the power of his wind.

In the remainder of the unit describing YHWH's theophany in Hab 3, the poet-prophet recites YHWH's deeds in the past poised with mythological weapons to represent YHWH's potent wind. The poet-prophet's use of terms familiar from the *Chaoskampf* myth pales off to his description of the cataclysmic reactions in nature indicating YHWH's presence in the phenomenal wind. However, the poet-prophet relates images

---

13. See p. 184.

borrowing from a mythical conflict to the idea of YHWH hewing salvation for the anointed, but destruction of the wicked. It is pointed out that scholars see here images relating YHWH's fight with the dragon echoing the ancient conflict myth. Instead, Habakkuk employs these mythic features to focus YHWH's appearance with the wind, as though poised with mythological weapons: "Bow" and "shafts" for the destruction of the enemy. In the poet-prophet's musings, these mythological weapons are subsumed under YHWH's age-old *modus operandi* in the winds. By this means, the poet-prophet throws into bold relief YHWH's warrior traits manifested in the raging winds to raze the wicked. Hence, the same outcome, as though armed with the bow and shaft, is achieved. Thus, by referring to the idea of shattering the "head of the wicked" and "laying bare the fundament up to neck," the poet-prophet alludes to nothing other than the destruction of Pharaoh, the head of the wicked, who lays slain with bared buttocks from frocks twirled to the neck by the waters churned by YHWH's whirling winds (Ps 77:19[18]a).

Overall, as argued in this third chapter, there is a fusion of elements from the concept of creation-out-of-chaos with the idea of YHWH appearing with the phenomenal winds to subdue the primal chaotic waters, as explored in Pss 18 (with 144 in affinity), 77 and Hab 3. As presented, the ideas consisting of the theophanic units are not merely recitals of the mythical conflict but graphic representations of YHWH's appearance in his age-old *modus operandi* in the wind to raze chaos for the deliverance and establishment of his people. The cataclysmic reactions in the natural elements portend YHWH's disclosure in the winds to subdue the chaotic waters, that is, the "many waters" as specified in all the texts in discussion. However, YHWH's winds are directed against the many waters in Ps 18 (cf. 144), as in the creation out of chaos tradition but the historical element is retained in that the many waters represent the Psalmist's human opponents. But, in Ps 77 and Hab 3, the "many waters" retain the mythic connotations and remain subject to YHWH's disclosure of his might in the phenomenal wind. Yet, in all cases, YHWH's deeds of salvation are accomplished. The Psalmist is delivered from the many waters, meaning historical foes (Ps 18; cf. 144), and the elect people are delivered through the many waters (Ps 77; Hab 3).

Furthermore, it is clear from the thematic literary features employed in the texts in discussion, that there is a pattern to YHWH's dealings with the entities involved at his disclosure implying the "righteous" (צדיק) *vis-à-vis* the "wicked" (רשע). YHWH proffers divine rescue to the "righteous," but is tortuous with the perverts or "wicked." In fact, the theme of salvation is developed along these two opposing terms. In Ps 18, the contrast between these two parties is emphasized by the use of different terms. The Psalmist, King David, claims that his righteousness is procured from reverential fear in compliance with YHWH's ways; that is by observing YHWH's commandments, and earning him deliverance. He also identifies himself as YHWH's "anointed" (משיח). But, in contrast, he variously refers to his opponents as "my enemy" (איבי), "the ones hating me" (משנאי), or "men of violence" (איש חמס), and, specifically, the "sons of foreigners" (בני־נכר), who utter an unavailing plea to YHWH for deliverance. In essence, the Psalmist distinctively implies that they are the "wicked," whom YHWH spoils with his phenomenal winds.

Similarly, the theophanic text in Hab 3 displays the same interaction of YHWH with his "anointed" in antithesis to the destruction of the "wicked," as part of its literary masterpiece. However, the interpretation of these literary features in Hab 3 also hinges on the literary composition of the entire book of Habakkuk, as these two opposing terms are referred to in the national crisis presented in Hab 1–2. Nonetheless, in contrast to Ps 18, where the Psalmist's plea for YHWH to intervene receives a response, the situation of suffering in Habakkuk is unabated. Instead, the divine judgment on the wicked is envisioned and expressed in the form of woe oracles in Hab 2:6–17. Yet, overall, the essence of the message in Hab 2:2–20 is that it sets the tone for the interpretation of Hab 3 in anticipation of the reversal of fortunes between the "righteous" and the "wicked." Thus as in Ps 18, the poet-prophet in Hab 3 harks back to the exodus and conquest traditions in language fused with mythical elements from the *Chaoskampf*, as he contemplates YHWH's disclosure with the phenomenal wind against the wicked. From it, the poet-prophet, Habakkuk, derives confidence and trust, so much so that he envisions a future divine intervention by YHWH, as at the exodus, in his guise as savior. Thereupon, the national crisis existing in his own days would be resolved by YHWH finally silencing the "wicked."

King YHWH Dispensing Divine Rule by His Bluster of Winds

The function of YHWH saving the righteous and judging the wicked merge with the conceptual idea of YHWH dispensing his rule as the sovereign king, who manifests his power in the wind, as discussed in

CONCLUSIONS

chapter 4. Here, it is argued that the YHWH *mālak* psalms, and other related texts scholars posit for an enthronement festival of YHWH, and/or eschatologically oriented, blend themes and motifs discussed in the previous chapters in celebration of YHWH as king. Hence, the idea of YHWH appearing with the wind as at the primal creation is transposed on the historical arena for the destruction of the wicked. As implied in this exposition, YHWH's disclosure with the potent winds simultaneously results in the shaming of the gods of the (wicked) nations but the salvation of the righteous; that is essentially Israel accorded that divine favor, as YHWH's elect. Thus, the whole world is summoned to join in the celebration of YHWH's historical victories as the sovereign king.

As observed, Ps 97 shows affinity in the depiction of YHWH's appearance in the wind with the characterization of Amma. YHWH's candescence in the phenomenal wind and use of fire for destruction recalls Amma's motion at creation, morphology, and his reserve of fire for destruction at will. But other elements relating to YHWH's theophany in the biblical tradition are blended to give a graphic image of YHWH intervening for the righteous, and annihilating all the forces antithetical to his purposes. In essence, Ps 97 describes YHWH appearing with the luminous and sonorous wind to conquer the worshipers of idols, shame their gods, and institute his rule of justice, that is in conformity with the elements of "righteousness" and "justice" forming the basis of his throne (Ps 97:2). From that perspective, it becomes clear that all the elements the proponents (and advocates) espouse for a hypothetical enthronement festival of YHWH are better understood from this biblical view of YHWH's disclosure with the bluster of winds and his function as king. Here, too, the three functions of YHWH of saving, ruling and judging, that are corollary to his role as the divine warrior, as suggested by Miller for other Hebrew texts, come into view in this theophanic psalm. From this analysis of Ps 97 as the paradigm for the selected texts with similar themes and motifs, the theological intentionality of the image of YHWH appearing in the wind as sovereign king, and the historical purpose of these psalms is in view.

The theological element in the other selected texts, thought to embody the cultic theme of an enthronement of YHWH, is also illustrated in this final chapter. The terms in Ps 47:2[1], 6[5], and 9[8] held to suggest cultic acts at an enthronement festival of YHWH in essence relate to YHWH's historical deeds in consummation of his election of his people, and his occupation of Zion. As pointed out, the shout of the saved community resonates with the "sound of the *shôfār*" echoing, and resonating with the "shout" of the king amid them, meaning YHWH's presence in the sonorous wind, as experienced at their victories in battle. Therefore, the idea of YHWH ascending to his throne alludes to YHWH, whose presence in the wind is symbolized by the ark going up to occupy his choice of abode. Both prosaic (2 Sam 5–8) and poetic (Pss 24, 132) texts relate to these historical events.

Furthermore, the notion of Zion as YHWH's "resting place" (מנוחה, Ps 132:8, 14) conclusively supports the idea of YHWH's occupation of Zion, as his rightful place without any implications of a royal investment or enthronement. Yet, as also pointed out, the universal dimension of YHWH's kingship is brought into view in Ps 47. This idea is emphasized by the references to the gathering of "the princes of the nations" in acknowledgement of YHWH's sovereignty, as the one who is "highly exalted" (נעלה, v. 10b). Both ideas expose YHWH's title *'elyôn* ("Most High"), who is the king over all the earth (v. 3[2]), and the deity who subdues nations (v. 4[3]). However, as averred, the idea of YHWH as "highly exalted" in Ps 47:10b is also in correspondence with Ps 97:9. But, in Ps 97:9 the title "Most High" (*'elyôn*) is mentioned in conjunction with the idea of his elevated position—"highly exalted"—over all the earth and gods, and therewith, emphasizing the heavenly perspective of his theophany. Within that purview presented in Ps 97, it shows that the idea of YHWH's "ascent" expressed in Ps 47:6[5], 9[8] implies, not only YHWH's occupation of his royal seat in Zion, but also his "ascending to" and "sitting down" on his celestial throne, which is supported by "justice and righteousness" (see Ps 97:2). YHWH's celestial and earthly thrones are symbiotic in the biblical Hebrew tradition, with one reflecting the other. In any case, this close association of YHWH's celestial and earthly abode evinces the notion of YHWH's "ascent" and "sitting down" in Ps 47:6[5], 9[8], and does not retain an element relating a cultic enactment of YHWH's enthronement. Instead, the Psalmist employs these terms to present a dramatic scene relating the tradition of YHWH's conquest wielded by his phenomenal winds for the establishment and occupation of his throne at Zion. This overarching conceptual idea of YHWH's presence in the guise of the wind depicted in Ps 47, pervades the theme of YHWH's kingship celebrated in the rest of the kingship psalms.

It is not amiss, therefore, to say that, the Israelite faith focuses on the centrality of YHWH as the divine warrior and creator-king appearing with the winds in assertion of his sovereignty. This characterization of YHWH is formulated in language that combines myth and history. Therefore, the superiority of YHWH over all chaotic forces, and the establishment of his governance of the world are expressed in terms of a mythical battle leading to victory in assertion of his eternal kingship. As pointed out in Ps 93, the metaphorical expressions of "clothe" and "gird," often thought to imply enthronement regalia, characterize YHWH's strength and power in the guise of the wind, and directed against chaos. So it is the case in the poetic terms ים, מים רבים and נהרות, of Ps 93 representing the forms of mythological chaos. Here, YHWH's kingship is said to hold up continuously in the face of potentially threatening forces of chaos since primeval times.

In contrast with other ancient traditions, as in the case of Baʿal and Marduk, YHWH's kingship is not determined by his conquest of mythological foes, but his power holds up from primeval time. Therefore, Ps 93 and other related texts emphasize the unrivalled power of YHWH over any rebellious forces or mythical symbols of chaos. YHWH's eternal kingship is asserted by the roar of his potent wind over and above the symbols of chaotic forces. The stability of YHWH's lordship is decisive for the universal order, upon which the stability of his throne and the world order derive. As mentioned in this discussion, spatial dimensions are surpassed with reference to YHWH's presence in his celestial temple, or holy abode, and concurrently, in the terrestrial realm. Thus, in Ps 93, YHWH, by the nature of his numinous presence, is broadly conceived as in his "high locale" (v. 4c) or eternal celestial throne (v. 2) marking his perpetual lordship. Yet, his indivisible presence as embodied in the wind, is also apprehended as palpable in his earthly temple or house and befitting "holiness" (v. 5b); hence, indicating YHWH's limitless scope of dominion over his created order.

Moreover, YHWH's stable kingship and secure world order are seen as the basis for the reliability of his "testimonies" (עדות), that offer guidance to his people (Ps 93:5). In which case, this transcendent and eternal king is conceived coming close to humanity through his revealed will—testimonies—in order to give governance on the moral structure. As pointed out, this further confirms the essence of YHWH's whole being and the totality of his control of the created world order. Therefore, Ps 93 has neither features to support an eschatological interpretation of YHWH's end-time kingship, nor a basis for an enthronement festival of YHWH, as suggested by some biblical scholars, who continue to uphold,

YHWH IN THE WIND(S)

and purport to find in this psalm, a reenactment of the enthronement of YHWH as king.

As in the other psalms discussed in chapter 4, YHWH's potency as the creator and YHWH's victorious deeds manifested among the nations are spoken of as aspects of the same divine rule. In Ps 96 the two are brought into perspective through the lenses of the worthlessness of the gods of the enemy nations. It is by virtue of YHWH's creation of the world, and precisely through the victories of YHWH against enemies and their gods that his kingship is emphasized. YHWH's victorious deeds resulting in the salvation of his people throw into bold relief his power manifested in the wind. And, the establishment of his righteous rule affirms his presence.

There are elements in Ps 96 that put limits on the arguments for the possibility of the Psalmist's borrowing from or depending on the prophecies of Deutero-Isaiah. Features such as the ark, alluded to in Ps 96:6b (see Ps 78:60–61; 1 Sam 4:4–11; Ps 132:8=2 Chr 6:41), and expressions such as the "writhing" or "whirling" (חיל, Ps 96:9b) of the whole earth, suggesting a traditional reaction resulting from YHWH's whirling winds, find parallels in preexilic texts (Pss 29:8b; 77:17[16]b; 97:4b; Hab 3:10a). Also, in parallel with older traditions, Ps 96:10 retains a declaration on YHWH's kingship in concomitance with the acknowledgement of his creation and firm establishment of the world, which is in affinity with the statement in Ps 93:1. Here, again, the Psalmist alludes to the phenomenal winds in attendance at the establishment of the world (Ps 104:6–7). Moreover, in contrast with Deutero-Isaiah where the salvation from YHWH is anticipated, in Ps 96 YHWH's acts of salvation are already experienced. So, YHWH's people are called to declare his deeds among the nations. Therefore, the idea of singing a "new song," and bringing good tidings resonate with both poetic and prosaic evidence from the Davidic era. Ps 96 also mentions the fearsomeness of YHWH in comparison to other gods implying their existence in contrast to Deutero-Isaiah's monotheism.

The Psalmist in Ps 96 alludes to the traditions associated with the ark enshrined in the temple to symbolize the presence of YHWH amid his people. Even the appositional phrases "strength and glory" (עז ותפארת), "splendor and majesty" (הוד והדר) in Ps 96:6, "the splendor of (his) holiness" (בהדרת־קדש) in v. 9a employed to refer to the ark, allude to YHWH's grandiose appearance in the luminous and sonorous wind. These terms are familiar from other texts mentioning YHWH's appearance in the phenomenal wind. In particular, the reference to YHWH's "splendor and majesty" in Ps 96:6a echoes the same term representing YHWH's potent winds as cited in Ps 104:1c; Job 40:10b. It is also noted that the nominal phrase "the splendor of (his) holiness" in Ps 96:9a, occurring verbatim in Ps 29:2b, also appears in the Chronicler's citation of a psalm of King David celebrating the installation of the ark in Zion (1 Chr 16). Undoubtedly, all these terms are employed to assert the trappings of YHWH's presence in the winds as he ushers his righteous rule in the face of the debased gods of other nations.

Furthermore, it is noted that the Psalmist, King David sustains the use of terms alluding to YHWH's presence manifested in the wind. Both in Ps 96:9 and 1 Chr 16:29–30 the nominal phrase, "the splendor of (his) holiness" occurs in juxtaposition with the summons on the earth to tremble. This invoked response resonates with the conventional reactions to YHWH's appearance with the phenomenal winds. Although the verses are not in sequence, both psalms link the declaration of YHWH's kingship to his establishment of the world and the security of its foundation. The idea recalls the power of YHWH's winds at subduing chaos at creation for the firm founding of the world order. However, there is also a note of irony in Ps 96 in that the same God, who establishes the earth and causes the earth to shake to its foundation by the power of his winds, is also the one who ensures the stability of the world, as he ushers in his rule of equity to safeguard the (universal) social order. Hence, in one breath, the certainty of YHWH's kingship compels for all of creation to burst out in jubilation and resound YHWH's presence in the bluster of winds; such that the heavens and earth whistle, the sea and its fullness roar, and the fields and trees rustle at YHWH's prevailing sonorous winds.

It is evident that Ps 96 shows correspondence with the themes in Ps 97 at a few points. The exhortation for worldwide jubilation in acknowledgement of YHWH instituting his just rule of equity is expressed with similar verbs in Pss 96:11 and 97:1. YHWH's intervention by his phenomenal wind, as alluded to in the execution of marvelous deeds in the eyes of the nation, indicates judgment on the idol worshippers, but, at the same time, the salvation of YHWH's people is achieved. Hence, the idea of YHWH performing his judicial acts for the salvation of his people in Ps 96, not only echoes the characteristic features of "justice" and "righteousness," which form the basis of YHWH's throne as mentioned in Ps 97:2b, but also marks the inaugural state of YHWH's universal and just order calling for this worldwide jubilation in acknowledgement of his sovereignty.

Psalm 98 continues the recurrent theme on YHWH's deeds of salvation wielded by the power of his phenomenal bluster of wind, figuratively personified as his "arm" and "right hand." Like Ps 96, this psalm is an imperative hymn to sing a "new song" to YHWH for the accomplished deeds of salvation. However, there are elements in Ps 98 calling for a different interpretation of this psalm. There is no comparison of YHWH with other deities, no definitive terms alluding to ark, or language conventional to theophanies as noted for the other psalms in discussion. Also, the declaration of YHWH's kingship is expressed by the phrase המלך יהוה ("the king [who is] YHWH"), and not the familiar term יהוה מלך ("YHWH reigns/YHWH is king") as in the nuclei of the YHWH *mālāk* psalms. But the theme on YHWH's appearance with the wind in association with his deeds of salvation links Ps 98 with this group of kingship psalms. It is argued here that YHWH's deeds of salvation are performed in the sight of the whole earth. As noted, it is probably the most contemporaneous events in which King David experienced the power of YHWH in the wind that prompted this outburst to sing a new song resonating with the "shout" of King-YHWH, who bursts out with the wind for the salvation of Israel. Therefore, all of nature is compelled to echo the aeolian movement of the wind in jubilation at YHWH's appearance to institute his rule of fairness and justice.

In Ps 99 there is no longer emphasis on the proclamation of YHWH's deeds of salvation among the nations, as much as on the reign of YHWH, who is enthroned at Zion, not only as king of Israel, but as ruler of the nations. YHWH is declared as the king who loves "justice." This ethical sense of governance is established through the House of Jacob, that is, the acts of "justice" and "righteousness" YHWH performs on behalf of Israel (v. 4). However, as noted, the thrust of this psalm is on Israel's personal encounter with YHWH in various modes. Therefore, this psalm yields a range of symbolic representations of YHWH's contemporaneous involvement with Israel.

As discussed, although the connection of the first part of the psalm (vv. 1–5) and the latter (vv. 6–9) is not immediately apparent, the link is forged by the use of different symbols representing YHWH's presence. This is marked by the cherubim (v. 1), Zion (v. 2) and the footstool(=ark; v. 5; see Ps 132:7), all traditionally associated with the Zion tradition. Then, there is also the idea of YHWH's revelation mediated through the

CONCLUSIONS

intercessory role of Moses, Aaron, and Samuel, as presented in the latter part of the psalm. The idea of YHWH seated on the cherubim not only alludes to the ark, thus pointing to the preexilic period, but also, as averred, embodies YHWH's immanence in the winds. Consequently, the imperative on the nations to tremble and the earth to shake in awe of the presence of YHWH, seated on his cherubim, implies the conventional reactions to YHWH's phenomenal winds.

In relating to the priestly/prophetic narratives on Moses, Aaron, and Samuel and the tradition of YHWH's presence in the "pillar of cloud" (עמוד ענן), it is also suggested that YHWH's appearance is asserted in much more than the "pillar of cloud." With this idea, the Psalmist recalls past traditions of YHWH's manifestation in the wind. This idea is summed up in YHWH's response to Moses, Aaron, and Samuel's intercessions, as indicated by the reference to their "calling" and YHWH "answering" them. By this statement on "calling" and YHWH "answering," the Psalmist reaches beyond the image of YHWH availing himself in the "pillar of cloud." So, Moses (along with Aaron) and Samuel, as advocates of the covenantal relationship, call on YHWH and he appears in the phenomenal winds (Exod 19:16-18; 20:18, 20; 1 Sam 12:14-18, respectively). Furthermore, in view of other related texts, it is clear that Moses (along with Aaron) and Samuel, in their intercessory roles, invoke divine blessing and protection on Israel. Thus Moses, as the promulgator of the law, declares YHWH as king of Jeshurun(=Israel) and as the "one riding the heavens" and the "cloud" to Israel's help (Deut 26:26, 29) to evince the visual force of the winds demonstrated in the movements of the clouds. Likewise, Samuel declares YHWH as Israel's source of help following YHWH's response with the sonorous wind burst in vindication from the threat of annihilation by the Philistines, who are sent helter-skelter by YHWH's bluster of wind (1 Sam 7:5-13). Unquestionably, these related traditions, and the terminology common to YHWH's theophany in the wind mentioned in Ps 99:1, bring to bear that YHWH's age-old *modus operandi* in the wind is also involved in this psalm.

At any rate, by emphasizing the idea of YHWH's enduring presence in Ps 99:1, the exercise and establishment of divine justice, and the allusion to YHWH's grace and judgment in Israel's salvation history in accordance with the Deuteronomistic interpretation (vv. 6-8), the Psalmist proclaims the righteous deeds of YHWH in covenantal faithfulness. YHWH loves justice, and dispenses his rule of equity amid his people (v. 4). Therefore, YHWH's indomitable holy presence is featured in his age-old *modus operandi* in the wind embedded with the "cherubim," Zion, ark, "pillar of cloud" and the "holy mountain." These are all symbolic features of YHWH's close communion with his people as he metes out "justice" and "righteousness" in his roles as the sovereign king and judge.

As concluded, therefore, in view of this analysis, it is evident that the contents of Pss 47, 93, 96–99, and the related texts, normally deployed for the reconstruction of a cultic enthronement of YHWH as king, portray his deeds of salvation manifested by his presence in the phenomenal winds that occasions the celebration of his kingship among his people. As discussed, the emphasis is on the involvement of YHWH in the religio-historical tradition of Israel and the saving deeds performed by the power of his winds in covenantal faithfulness. This divine liberation also entails that the defeated nations are called to express reverence to YHWH, as the king of the whole earth. Invariably, Zion is the locus (Amos 1:2), where YHWH "shines forth," and institutes his ethical governance based on justice and righteousness dispensed to the surrounding nations.

Despite various interpretations by scholars on the literary content of Ps 29, ranging from the adaptation of a hymn originally ascribed to the Ugaritic Ba'al to elements drawn from the tradition of El to Babylonian Marduk, it is demonstrated here that there are discernible elements showing an Israelite provenance of the psalm. In particular, Ps 29, though the shortest of these kingship psalms, is replete with themes and motifs similar to the group of the YHWH *mālāk* hymns. It is argued that Ps 29 blends various elements from the biblical Hebrew tradition related with the ark, and its composition fits the liturgical worship instituted by king David as related in the Chronicler's account (1 Chr 16). As discussed, the elements: "Glory" (כבוד), sonorous "sound/voice" (קול), and "fire" (אש), cloud and deep darkness are mentioned as representing the phenomenon experienced at Mount Sinai when YHWH decrees the ten commandments. Subsequently, Moses demands YHWH to reveal himself as guarantee for his presence in the wilderness. It is noted that, at YHWH's disclosure, the term "glory" sums up all these elements associated with the ark, which bears YHWH's name, and represents his presence among his people. Therefore, the idea of ascribing "glory" to YHWH in Ps 29 reflects tendencies typical of the biblical Hebrew religio-historical tradition.

In the context of the theophany proper depicted in Ps 29, it is clear that the elements traced to extra-biblical traditions do not compromise the Hebrew characterization of YHWH. It has been maintained for a long time that the kingship of YHWH in Ps 29 is patterned after that of El and Baʿal in the Ugaritic traditions. However, as noted, the Hebrew tradition used forms and expressions current in its religious and cultural environment. The idea of an assembly consisting of the "sons of gods" is also attested in the Babylonian context. Even though this idea of the court of the gods common to the Ugaritic and Babylonian traditions is drawn upon, it seems to be dismissed in the depiction of YHWH as the transcendent deity to whom alone "honor," "strength" and "glory" are due. In particular, the idea of ascribing "glory" to YHWH is unparalleled in the extra-biblical material. But, it is apparent that the same poetic tenor and relegation of the gods to a status of paying homage to YHWH also echoes the idea expressed in a context of YHWH's disclosure with the fiery winds in Ps 97. Similarly, in Ps 29, emphasis is on summons for obeisance to the one who demonstrates these attributes of strength and glory in his phenomenal winds. Moreover, the content of Ps 29:3 and 10, supposed to derive from Baʿalistic motifs, reflects Hebrew tendencies. From the survey in chapter 2 on the use of the term "many waters" (מים רבים) for human foes (see Pss 18:17 [16]; 144:5), it is suggested a similar meaning entails for this term in Ps 29:3. The term figuratively represents the human opponents, in an equivalent relation to primordial chaos that YHWH subjugates with his bluster of wind.

In view of the centrality of the salvation of the people to YHWH's kingship, it is plausible to proclaim YHWH's kingship in connection with historical events. Thus, it is proposed that the term למבול, interpreted by some biblical critics as a locative "over the flood" to imply YHWH's enthronement following victory over chaos, should be read in the temporal sense "at the flood" (Ps 29:10a). This implies that YHWH's kingship prevailed even at that epoch as in Genesis 6–11, and in particular, the involvement of YHWH's wind at the deluge of Noah. Therefore, the temporal meaning "at the flood" is more in keeping with the subsequent statement expressing the eternal kingship of YHWH (Ps 29:10b), than is the suggested locative "over the flood," in expression of the conceptual *Chaoskampf* myth and cultic enthronement of YHWH. Nonetheless, the chief importance attaches to his warrior characteristics displayed through the phenomenal winds against human opponents (Ps 29:3), in order to bring strength and peace to his people (v. 11), as their eternal king (v. 10). This soteriological orientation of the psalm is consequent to the Psalmist's use of a plethora of melodramatic images and ideas that may seem unrelated, but put together to enhance meaning in this biblical Hebrew psalm. Hence, the Psalmist depicts YHWH manifesting himself with the whirling or roaring wind, personified as the "voice," causing convulsions in the most durable and stable elements of his cosmic order, as he asserts his universal kingship. With that purview, Ps 29 bears features integral with YHWH's age-old *modus operandi* in the wind, kingship and the welfare of YHWH's people as its dominant motifs, as also seen in the analysis of Ps 97.

The divine presence of the sovereign king YHWH is the subject of Ps 68. This ode of victory alludes to different symbolic representations of the presence of YHWH from the wilderness, conquest and settlement traditions. In all these three Israelite traditions alluded to in this psalm, symbols of YHWH's presence in the form of the phenomenal winds are mentioned in close attendance. It is apparent in this psalm that YHWH's age-old *modus operandi* in the winds serves two purposes: he intervenes for the redemption and establishment of his elected people, and, at the same time, brings the existence of the rebellious, or wicked,[14] to an end. All the more so, it appears that the Psalmist, in enriching his ideas, intentionally appeals to earlier OT traditions (Ps 68:2–3[1–2]; see Num 10:35; v. 9[8]; Judg 5:4–5). These traditions are associated with the idea of the indisputable presence of YHWH, in order to emphasize YHWH's acts in redeeming Israel at the destruction of its enemies. Thus, as attested in Ps 68, there is a clear reference to the sacramental "shout" associated with the ark taken out for battle (Num 10:35) in the verses recalling the wilderness "march" and deliverance of Israel (Ps 68:2–9[1–8]). Hence, one of YHWH's distinguishing epithets, "rider of the steppes" (v. 5[4]), echoes this tradition and denotes YHWH's aeolian movements in the wind. YHWH's manifestation in this triumphant march is signaled by the showers of rain and the shaking of the earth (see Judg 5:4), often mistaken for an earthquake,[15] but conventional to YHWH's age-old *modus operandi* in the wind from primal creation. In that manner, YHWH intervenes for the deliverance and establishment of his elected people: that is, the "solitary" (יחידים) and "prisoners" (אסירים), but, conversely, terminates the existence of the "rebellious" (סוררים) or wicked. Therefore, the Psalmist connects "the march of victory" through the wilderness with the unleashing of the phenomenal meteorological elements as

---

14. See pp. 292–93.
15. See p. 294, 294n394.

symbolic of YHWH meting out divine justice for the orphans, widows and the poor *vis-à-vis* the rebellious ones.

This idea of a bipartite nature of YHWH's appearance with the winds may be further understood within the background of the discourses in the book of Job, expressing the purposes of YHWH's natural elements. By these elements, YHWH either blesses, or punishes (Job 36:29–37:13).[16] However, although the Psalmist uses a biblical *hapax legomenon* (בכושרות), the conditions that YHWH occasions at his appearance are easily interpreted within the context of the psalm. Hence, as presented in Ps 68, the giving of abundant or copious rain, not only suggests YHWH's sway over the cloud-bearing winds at his rainmaking act in his role as the fertility-giver, but also constitutes his redeeming act of bringing prisoners or the distressed "into prosperity" (בכושרות). His gift of bounteous rain also anticipates and relates YHWH's act of establishing and sustaining the "'weary' (נלאה) property or inheritance" (נחלה). In contrast, however, the rebellious or insolent are abandoned in "scorched land" (צחיחה). So, in view of these features, the roles of YHWH as the divine warrior, fertility-giver and judge[17] shine through in sequel to his theophany with the phenomenal winds.

Again, in keeping with the theme of YHWH's divine presence focused in Ps 68, YHWH's bluster of wind is also present in the verses referring to the conquest of kings (Ps 68:12[11]). Here, it is argued that אֹמֶר in verse 12[11]a should be read as a metonymy for a bluster of wind, that causes the enemy kings to flee (v. 13[12]a). This idea is understood, if it is considered to be the implied effect of YHWH's phenomenal wind causing this consternation. This eventual upshot corresponds with the possible consequence evoked by the imperative statements at the beginning of the psalm: YHWH arises (קום) and his enemies scatter and flee "from his presence" (מפניו, v. 2[1]). Furthermore, in sequel, this idea is paralleled by the image of kings fleeing, as YHWH unleashes snow on Mount Zalmon (v. 15[14]). This discharge of snow, is yet another representation of YHWH intervening in a battlefield (Job 38:22–23) with meteorological elements familiar from the tradition of his scourge released by his winds (see Job 36:29–37:13).

Furthermore, subsequent to the conquest of kings, the Psalmist describes YHWH's theophanic progress to the choice of abode on Mount

---

16. See p. 316.
17. See pp. 295–96.

Zion. Although insignificant, Mount Zion is set apart as an exclusive abode for YHWH to reside. As pointed out, the Psalmist focuses on this idea through contrasts, by characterizing Mount Bashan as the mountain of (the) "gods" and "many peaks" (Ps 68:16[15]b). Here, yet again, the Psalmist uses another biblical *hapax legomenon*, תרצדון (17[16]a) meaning "look at/watch with envy" seemingly as if to scorn Mount Bashan for YHWH's preference to choosing and taking up residence at Mount Zion and making it impregnable. Even the celebration of YHWH's "ascent" (Ps 47) to his mountain of abode is couched in his age-old *modus operandi* in the winds. This view is supported by the idea of YHWH revealing himself with the aeolian movements of the winds implied in the reference to YHWH's chariotry[18] representing YHWH's theophanic progress. The reference to the chariotry with the superlative "thousands upon thousands" in Ps 68:18[17]a, implying a countless number, means the idea of YHWH's appearance in the indivisible blustery winds is involved. The idea is derived from observing all the texts referring to YHWH's chariots representing the wind comparable to the roar of fast-moving chariots. Therefore, the complimentary term "in holiness" (בַּקֹּדֶשׁ) in Ps 68:18[17]b expresses YHWH's "grandeur" as he ascends to his abode in his luminous and sonorous winds.

The Ode of Victory: God among Us

In view of the nature of this self-disclosure of YHWH, it is concluded that the expression הליכות אל in Ps 68:25[24] represents the theophanic march of the triumphant warrior-king after his defeat of the wicked. The idea runs counter to the theory of an enthronement procession of YHWH. The root הלך in the expression הליכות אל refers to the divine presence in the wilderness traditions and also occurs in the depictions of YHWH's ancient *modus operandi* in the winds. Avishur's observation that the expression הליכות אל, in light of its Akkadian equivalent, could reflect an earlier meaning "marching forth" or, better, a later one implying conduct or behavior, supports this view. Similarly, in Ps 68:25[24] the heroic deeds manifested by YHWH's phenomenal winds as divine warrior are in view, and his victories are celebrated in acknowledgement of him as the prime mover (מקור) of Israel (v. 27[26]).

---

18. See discussion on Ps 68:18[17] on p. 304, 304n440 above.

CONCLUSIONS

It is little wonder, therefore, that YHWH's people have the confidence to bid him to renew his deeds of salvation (Ps 68:29[28], 31[30]) and subdue the nations who delight in war. By appealing to YHWH to "rebuke/roar" (גער, v. 31[30]a), the Psalmist reminisces on the *Chaoskampf* myth and YHWH's subjugation of the sea by his potent winds at creation (see Ps 104:7), and transposes the same concept onto the historical plane. The Psalmist's mention of the corollary act of bringing tribute to the king (YHWH) at Jerusalem (Ps 68:30[29]) indicates the potentiality of YHWH's sonorous sound in the wind confounding the nations to submission. So, Zion/Jerusalem functions as YHWH's terrestrial locale from where he performs his juridical acts, and also will cause the nobles of Egypt and the people of Cush to "bear along gifts" to him in Zion (v. 32[31]; cf. 30[29]; Ps 76:2–3[1–2], 12[11]). Nonetheless, as in other psalms celebrating YHWH's universal kingship, spatial dimensions are surpassed in relation to his presence both on Mount Zion/Jerusalem and in his celestial abode. In that view, YHWH's cosmic rule is enhanced by his majestic sonorous voice from his celestial temple. From the same perspective, his other designation "rider of the ancient heavens" emphasizes his universal dominance in demonstration of the power and majesty of his sonorous sound in the clouds (Ps 68:34–35[33–34]). Yet, at the same time, this melodramatic image throws into bold relief YHWH's enduring presence in his ancient *modus operandi* in the phenomenal winds among his elect people as he empowers them (v. 36[35]; see v. 29[28]),[19] and their victory is guaranteed. All these varied lyrical images of YHWH are found in this ode of victory in Ps 68 depicting YHWH's indomitable presence manifested through the grandiose phenomenal winds in fulfillment of his roles as savior, judge, fertility-giver, prime mover, and, ultimately, warrior-king.

All in all, however, as expressed in this monograph, the Psalmists/poets and poet-prophets employed ideas and formulations common to their religio-cultural milieu, in enhancing the portrait of YHWH without compromising his prominent character, which is unique to the biblical Hebrew tradition. YHWH is seen therein, not as one originally without power, or as one needing to align the conquest of inimical forces with the rise to power through a display of wits. Instead, he is acclaimed as the creator, who exerts his power through the phenomenal winds, as the means to vanquish primordial chaos and, consequently, establish

---

19. See pp. 309, 313.

his cosmic order. By the same phenomenal winds, however, he breaks into the historical arena to quell any forces antithetical to his divine will and cosmic design, as he asserts his universal rule as the sovereign king. With Zion/Jerusalem as the locus of YHWH's sovereign rule over his elect people and all the (subdued) nations, who are called to acknowledge YHWH as the king, the Psalmist/s augur well the idea of a quasi-holy kingdom, incorporating all the nations to live as one entity under YHWH's rule of "justice" and "righteousness."

A Final Thought

Creation myths provide the basis for understanding that human beings have a common descent. As noted by Malinowski on myths of beginnings, such accounts have sociological relevance in that human beings need to grasp the realization of common origin and descent from the deity who created the universe. By bestowing his image on human beings the creator god designed a charter for the global community to function with one common purpose: to be stewards and guardians of what God created. In this realm, God's glory is revealed in the sacredness of his creation. In this realm, as Eliade averred, human beings should function as mortal, sexed and cultural/societal beings according to divine rules of governance, that is, "justice" and "righteousness," as declared in the psalms and prophetic texts discussed. Until human beings recognize this as the codifier and charter for social organization, the world through hostility, wars, and acts of social injustice teeters at the brink of facing the full wrath of the divine creator by the power of his phenomenal winds, as though creation has returned to chaos. All the forms of religious pretentiousness, licentiousness, and social injustice represent chaos, and infringe upon YHWH's ethical governance, causing YHWH to break out with his potent wind(s) to assert his sovereign rule in all its facets. Accordingly, as both the prophets Amos and Jeremiah inflect their messages with a note of hope, YHWH does not abhor, abandon, or completely scatter and destroy his people. With the same potent winds YHWH employ to "create," and "destroy," YHWH will garner his scattered people from the four corners of the earth, in order for them to (re-)build and to plant in restoration of his world and social order as he, YHWH, the sole creator, originally intended.

CONCLUSIONS

In a nutshell, the portrait of YHWH in the guise of the wind(s), emerging from the biblical texts analyzed, shows the contextual, theological and sociological relevance of this image in exposing new meaning in these biblical texts. Therefore, the theological and sociological import of this book is the contemporaneousness of the phenomena depicting YHWH's involvement in controlling all the forms of chaos, and establishing a world/social order founded on YHWH's ethical rule of divine justice and righteousness. This new reading of biblical texts offers the readers a compelling message for reflections that nurture reactionary responses to contextualize, and motivate extemporaneous participation in establishing world/social order, or a quasi-holy kingdom in keeping with YHWH's intended cosmic design, lest YHWH breaks out with his dramaturgical bluster of wind(s) to restore, and maintain his cosmic order.

Bibliography

Aalen, Sverre. "אוֹר." In *TDOT* 1:147–67.
Ackerman, Robert. "Frazer on Myth and Ritual." *Journal of the History of Ideas* 36 (1975) 115–34.
———. *J. G. Frazer: His Life and Work.* Cambridge: Cambridge University Press, 1987.
———. *Selected Letters of Sir J. G. Frazer.* Edited by Robert Ackerman. Oxford: Oxford University Press, 2005.
Ackroyd, P. R. "Notes and Studies: Some Notes on the Psalms." *Journal of Theological Studies* 17.2 (1966) 392–99.
Albright, William F. "A Catalogue of Early Hebrew Lyric Poems (Psalm LXVIII)." *Hebrew Union College Annual* 23 (1950–51) 1–39.
Allen, Douglas. *Myth and Religion in Mircea Eliade.* New York: Routledge, 2002.
Allen, Leslie C. *Jeremiah: A Commentary.* Louisville: Westminster John Knox, 2008.
Amzallag, Nissim. *Psalm 29: A Canaanite Hymn to YHWH in the Psalter.* Etudes bibliques n.s. 89. Leuven: Peeters, 2021.
Andersen, Francis I. *Habakkuk: A New Translation with Introduction and Commentary.* AB 25. New York: Doubleday, 2001.
———. *Job: An Introduction and Commentary.* Tyndale Old Testament Commentaries 14. Downers Grove, IL: InterVarsity, 2008.
Andersen, Francis I., and David Noel Freedman. *Amos: A New Translation with Introduction and Commentary.* AB. Garden City, NY: Doubleday, 1989.
Anderson, Arnold Albert. *Psalms 1–72.* NCBC. 1972. Reprint, Grand Rapids: Eerdmans, 1989.
———. *Psalms 73–150.* NCBC. 1972. Reprint, Grand Rapids: Eerdmans, 1995.
Anderson, Bernhard W. *From Creation to New Creation.* 1994. Reprint, Eugene, OR: Wipf & Stock, 2005.
———. "Introduction: Mythopoeic and Theological Dimensions of Biblical Creation Faith." In *Creation in the Old Testament*, edited by Bernhard W. Anderson, 1–24. Issues in Religion and Theology. Philadelphia: Fortress, 1984.
Anderson, Gary A. "*Creatio ex nihilo* and the Bible." In *Creation ex nihilo: Origins, Development, Contemporary Challenges*, edited by Gary A. Anderson and Markus Bockmuehl, 15–35. Notre Dame: University of Notre Dame Press, 2018.
Andrew, M. E. "The Authorship of Jer 10:1–16." *ZAW* 94 (1982) 128–30.
Ansell, Nicholas. "Fantastic Beasts Where to Find The(ir Wisdo)m." In *Playing with Leviathan: Interpretation and Reception of Monsters from the Biblical World*, edited

by Koert van Bekkum et al., 90–114. Themes in Biblical Narrative 21. Leiden: Brill, 2017.

Arnold, Bill T., and John H. Choi. *A Guide to Biblical Hebrew Syntax*. Cambridge: Cambridge University Press, 2003.

Arnold, Bill T., and Brent A. Strawn. "Beyāh šemô in Psalm 68,5: A Hebrew Gloss to an Ugaritic Epithet?" *ZAW* 115 (2003) 428–32.

Avishur, Yitzhak. *Studies in Hebrew and Ugaritic Psalms*. Jerusalem: Hebrew University, Magnes, 1994.

Ballentine, Scoggins Debra. *The Conflict Myth and Biblical Tradition*. Oxford: Oxford University Press, 2015.

Barbiero, Gianni. "The Two Structures of Psalm 29." *VT* 66 (2016) 378–92.

Barth, C. "יפע." In *TDOT* 6:220–25.

Becking, Bob, and Marjo C. A. Korpel. "To Create, to Separate or to Construct: An Alternative to a Recent Proposal as to the Interpretation of ברא in Gen 1:1–2:4a." *Journal of Hebrew Scriptures* 10.3 (2010) 1–21.

Beek, Walter E. A. van. *Dogon: Africa's People of the Cliffs*. New York: Abrams, 2001.

———. "Dogon Restudied: A Field Evaluation of the work of Marcel Griaule." *Current Anthropology* 32.2 (1991) 139–67.

———. "Haunting Griaule: Experiences From the Restudy of the Dogon." *History in Africa* 31 (2004) 43–68.

Begg, Christopher T. "The Ark Narratives." In *The Chronicler as Theologian: Essays in Honor of Ralph W. Klein*, edited by M. Patrick Graham et al., 133–45. JSOTSup 371. London: T. & T. Clark, 2003.

Bekkum, Koert van. "'Is Your Rage Against the Rivers, Your Wrath Against the Sea?' Storm God Imagery in Habakkuk 3." In *Playing with Leviathan: Interpretation and Reception of Monsters from the Biblical World*, edited by Koert van Bekkum et al., 55–76. Themes in Biblical Narrative 21. Leiden: Brill, 2017.

Bellis, Alice Ogden. *The Structure and Composition of Jeremiah 50:2—51:58*. Lewiston, NY: Mellen Biblical, 1995.

Benz, Brendon C. "Yamm as the Personification of Chaos? A Linguistic and Literary Argument for a Case of Mistaken Identity." In *Creation and Chaos: A Reconsideration of Hermann Gunkel's Chaoskampf Hypothesis*, edited by JoAnn Scurlock et al., 127–46. Winona Lake, IN: Eisenbrauns, 2013.

Berry, Donald K. *The Psalms and Their Readers: Interpretive Strategies for Psalm 18*. JSOTSup 153. Sheffield: JSOT Press, 1993.

Black, Jeremy, et al. *The Literature of Ancient Sumer*. Oxford: Oxford University Press 2004.

Block, Daniel I. *The Book of Ezekiel, Chapters 1–24*. NICOT. Grand Rapids: Eerdmans, 1997.

Bockmuehl, Mark. "Introduction." In *Creatio ex nihilo: Origins, Development, Contemporary Challenges*, edited by Gary A. Anderson et al., 1–14. Notre Dame: University of Notre Dame Press, 2018.

Brettler, Marc Zvi. *God Is King: Understanding an Israelite Metaphor*. JSOTSup 76. Sheffield: JSOT Press, 1989.

Bright, John. *Jeremiah: A New Translation with Introduction and Commentary*. AB 21. Garden City, NY: Doubleday, 1965.

Brueggemann, Walter. "Amos 4:4–13 and Israel's Covenant Worship." *VT* 15 (1965) 1–15.

———. *From Whom No Secrets Are Hid: Introducing the Psalms*. Louisville: Westminster John Knox, 2014.

———. *To Pluck Up, to Tear Down: A Commentary on the Book of Jeremiah 1–25*. Grand Rapids: Eerdmans, 1988.

Brueggemann, Walter, and William H. Bellinger Jr. *Psalms*. NCBC. Cambridge: Cambridge University Press, 2014.

Bullock, C. Hassell. *Encountering the Book of Psalms: A Literary and Theological Introduction*. Grand Rapids: Baker Academic, 2018.

Buren, Douglas van. "Concerning the Horned Cap of the Mesopotamian Gods." *Orientalia* 12 (1943) 318–27.

Buttenwieser, Moses. *The Psalms: Chronologically Treated with a New Translation*. Chicago: University of Chicago Press, 1938.

Caquot, A. "געד." In *TDOT* 3:49–53.

Carroll, Robert P. *Jeremiah: A Commentary*. London: T. & T. Clark, 2004.

Carroll R., M. Daniel. *The Book of Amos*. NICOT. Grand Rapids: Eerdmans, 2020.

Cassuto, Umberto. *Biblical and Oriental Studies*. Translated by Israel Abrahams. 2 vols. Bible and Ancient Oriental Texts. Jerusalem: Magnes, 1973, 1975.

Chisholm, Robert Bruce. "An Exegetical and Theological Study of Psalm 18/2 Samuel 22." PhD diss., Dallas Theological Seminary, 1983.

Chiswa Gandiya, Violet. "Storm-Theophany and the Portrayal of Yahweh as Creator-King in Psalm 104 and in Prophetic and Wisdom Literature." *Journal of the Interdenominational Theological Center* 38 (2012) 107–32.

———. "Storm Theophany in the Hebrew Psalms, Prophetic and Wisdom Literature and the Attribution of Socio-Political Roles to YAHWEH in Ancient Israel." PhD diss., University of Cambridge, 1997.

Clements, Ronald E. *Ezekiel*. Westminster Bible Companion. Louisville: Westminster John Knox, 1996.

Clifford, Richard J. "Cosmogonies in the Ugaritic Texts and in the Bible." *Orientalia* 53 (1984) 183–201.

———. *Creation Accounts in the Ancient Near East and in the Bible*. CBQ Monograph 26. Washington, DC: Catholic Biblical Association of America, 1994.

———. "Creation ex nihilo in the Old Testament/Hebrew Bible." In *Creation ex nihilo: Origins, Development, Contemporary Challenges*, edited by Gary A. Anderson et al., 55–76. Notre Dame: University of Notre Dame Press, 2018.

Clifford, Richard J., and John Joseph Collins, eds. *Creation in the Biblical Traditions*. CBQ Monograph 24. Washington, DC: Catholic Biblical Association of America, 1992.

Coudert, Allison. "Horns." In *Encyclopedia of Religion*, edited by Lindsay Jones, 6:4130–31. Detroit: Macmillan Reference USA, 2005.

Craigie, Peter C. "The Comparison of Hebrew Poetry: Psalm 104 in Light of Egyptian and Ugaritic Poetry." *Semitics* 4 (1974) 10–21.

———. *Psalms 1–50*. WBC 19. Waco, TX: Word, 1983.

Crenshaw, James L. "Amos and the Theophanic Tradition." *ZAW* 80 (1968) 203–15.

———. *Hymnic Affirmation of Divine Justice*. Missoula, MT: Scholars, 1975.

———. *Old Testament Wisdom: An Introduction*. 3rd ed. Louisville: Westminster John Knox, 2010.

———. "Prolegomenon." In *Studies in Ancient Israelite Wisdom*, edited by Harry M. Orlinsky, 1–60. Library of Biblical Studies. New York: Ktav, 1976.

Croft, Steven J. L. *The Identity of the Individual in the Psalms*. JSOTSup 44. Sheffield: JSOT Press, 1987.
Cross, Frank Moore. *Canaanite Myth and Hebrew Epic: Essays in the History and Religion of Israel*. Cambridge: Harvard University Press, 1973.
———. "Notes on a Canaanite Psalm in the Old Testament." *BASOR* 117 (1950) 19–21.
———. *Studies in Ancient Yahwistic Poetry*. Missoula, MT: Scholars, 1975.
Cross, Frank Moore, and David Noel Freedman. "The Blessing of Moses." *JBL* 67.3 (1948) 191–210.
———. "A Royal Psalm of Thanksgiving: 2 Samuel 22 = Psalm 18." *JBL* 72.1 (1953) 15–34.
Curtis, John B. "The Celebrated Victory at Zalmon (Psalm 68:12–15)." *PEGLMBS* 7 (1987) 39–47.
———. "*har-bāšān*, the Mountain of God (Ps 68:16[15])." *PEGLMBS* 6 (1986) 85–95.
Dahood, Mitchell, SJ. *Psalms: Introduction, Translation, and Notes*. AB 16–17A. 3 vols. New York: Doubleday, 1965–1970.
Dalley, Stephanie. *Myths from Mesopotamia: Creation, the Flood, Gilgamesh and Others*. Rev. ed. Oxford: Oxford University Press, 2008.
Day, John. "The Ark and the Cherubim." In *Psalms and Prayers: Papers Read at the Joint Meeting of the Society of Old Testament Studies*, edited by Eric Peels and Bob Becking, 65–78. OTS 55. Leiden: Brill, 2007.
———. "Echoes of Baal's Seven Thunders and Lightnings in Psalm xxix and Habakkuk iii 9 and the Identity of the Seraphim in Isaiah vi." *VT* 29.2 (1979) 143–51.
———. *From Creation to Babel: Studies in Genesis 1–11*. Library of Hebrew Bible / Old Testament 592. London: Bloomsbury Academic, 2013.
———. *God's Conflict with the Dragon and the Sea: Echoes of a Canaanite Myth in the Old Testament*. University of Cambridge Oriental Publications 35. Cambridge: Cambridge University Press, 1985.
———. "Psalm 104 and Akhenaten's Hymn to the Sun." In *Jewish and Christian Approaches to the Psalms: Conflict and Convergence*, edited by Susan Gillingham, 211–28. Oxford: Oxford University Press, 2013.
———. *Psalms*. Old Testament Guides. Sheffield: JSOT Press, 1990.
DeClaissé-Walford, Nancy L. "Psalm 47: Clap Hands and Shout to God." In *The Book of Psalms*, edited by Nancy L. DeClaissé-Walford et al., 956–68. Grand Rapids: Eerdmans, 2014.
———. "Psalm 48: Walk around Zion." In *The Book of Psalms*, edited by Nancy L. DeClaissé-Walford et al., 969–81. Grand Rapids: Eerdmans, 2014.
———. *Psalms Books 4–5*. Wisdom Commentary 22. Collegeville, MN: Liturgical, 2020.
Dhorme, Edouard. *A Commentary on the Book of Job*. London: Nelson, 1967.
Dion, Paul E. "YHWH as Storm-God and Sun-God. The Double Legacy of Egypt and Canaan as Reflected in Psalm 104." *ZAW* 103.1 (1991) 43–71.
Diop, Cheikh Anta. *The African Origin of Civilization: Myth or Reality*. Chicago: Hill, 1974.
Douny, Lawrence. *Living in a Landscape of Scarcity: Materiality and Cosmology in West Africa*. Institute of Archaeology 63. Walnut Creek, CA: Left Coast, 2014.
Durkheim, Emile. *The Elementary Forms of the Religious Life*. Translated by Joseph Ward Swain. New York: Free Press, 1965.
Eaton, John H. "The Origin and Meaning of Habakkuk 3." *ZAW* 76 (1964) 144–71.

———. *Psalms of the Way and the Kingdom: A Conference with the Commentators.* Sheffield: Sheffield Academic, 1995.

Eliade, Mircea. *Myth and Reality.* New York: Harper & Row, 1963.

———. *The Myth of the Eternal Return: Cosmos and History.* Translated by William R. Trask. Princeton: Princeton University Press, 2005.

Emerton, John A. "The Biblical High Place in Light of Recent Study." *Palestinian Exploration Quarterly* 129 (1997) 116–32.

———. "The Interpretation of Proverbs 21:28." *ZAW* 100 (1988) 161–70.

———. "Leviathan and *Ltn*: The Vocalization of the Ugaritic Word for the Dragon." *VT* 32.3 (1982) 327–31.

———. "The 'Mountain of God' in Psalm 68:16." In *History and Traditions of Early Israel: Studies Presented to Eduard Nielsen*, edited by André Lemaire and Benedikt Otzen, 24–37. VTSup 50. Leiden: Brill, 1993.

———. "The Textual and Linguistic Problems of Habakkuk II. 4–5." *Journal of Theological Studies* 28 (1977) 1–18.

Eslinger, Lyle. *Into the Hands of the Living God.* JSOTSup 84. Sheffield: Almond, 1989.

Farr, George. "The Language of Amos, Popular or Cultic." *VT* 16 (1966) 312–24.

Feinberg, Charles L. "' ōmer." In *Theological Word Book of the Old Testament*, edited by R. Laird Harris et al., 55. Chicago: Moody, 1980.

Feldman, Susan. *African Myths and Tales.* New York: Dell, 1963.

Fensham, F. Charles. "Ps 68:23 in the Light of the Recently Discovered Ugaritic Tablets." *JNES* 19 (1960) 292–93.

———. "Psalm 29 and Ugarit." In *Studies on the Psalms: Papers Read at 6th Meeting Held at the Potchefstroom University for CHE, 29–31 January 1963*, edited by A. H. van Zyl, 84–99. Potchefstroom: Pro Rege-Pers Beperk, 1963.

———. "Widow, Orphan and the Poor in Ancient Near Eastern Legal and Wisdom Literature." *JNES* 21 (1962) 129–39.

Fisher, Loren R. "Creation at Ugarit and in the Old Testament." *VT* 15 (1965) 313–24.

Fitzgerald, Aloysius. "A Note on Psalm 29." *BASOR* 215 (1974) 61–63.

Flynn, Shawn W. *YHWH Is King: The Development of Divine Kingship in Ancient Israel.* VTSup 159. Leiden: Brill, 2014.

Foster, Benjamin R. *Before the Muses: An Anthology of Akkadian Literature.* Bethesda, MD: CDL, 2005.

Frankfort, H., and H. A. Frankfort. "Myth and Reality." In *The Intellectual Adventure of Ancient Man: An Essay on Speculative Thought in the Ancient Near East*, edited by H. Frankfort et al., 3–27. Chicago: University of Chicago Press, 1977.

Frazer, James George. *Apollodorus: The Library.* 2 vols. London: Heinemann, 1921.

———. *The Golden Bough.* Vol. 4. London: Macmillan, 1915.

———. *The Golden Bough: A Study in Magic and Religion.* Vol. 1. 3rd ed. New York: Macmillan, 1917.

———. *The Golden Bough: A Study of Magic and Religion.* Vol. 1.3. 1st ed. 1911. Reprint, London: Macmillan, 1923.

Freedman, David Noel, and C. Franke Hyland. "Psalm 29: A Structural Analysis." *Harvard Theological Review* 66.2 (1973) 237–56.

Fuhs, H. F. "עָלָה." In *TDOT* 9:76–95.

Gaster, Theodore H. *Myth, Legend, and Custom in the Old Testament.* New York: Harper & Row, 1969.

———. "Psalm 29." *Jewish Quarterly Review* 37 (1946) 55–65.

———. *Thespis: Ritual, Myth, and Drama in the Ancient Near East.* Garden City, NY: Doubleday, 1961.
Geller, Steven A. "God, Humanity, and Nature in the Pentateuch." In *Gazing on the Deep: Near Eastern and Other Studies in Honor of Tzvi Abusch*, edited by Jeffrey Stackert et al., 421–65. Bethesda, MD: CDL, 2010.
Gerstenberger, Erhard S. *Psalms, Part I with an Introduction to Cultic Poetry.* Forms of the Old Testament Literature 14. Grand Rapids: Eerdmans, 1988.
———. *Psalms, Part 2 and Lamentations.* Forms of Old Testament Literature 15. Grand Rapids: Eerdmans, 2001.
Gibson, John C. L. *Canaanite Myths and Legends.* 2nd ed. London: T. & T. Clark, 2004.
Gile, Jason. *Ezekiel and the World of Deuteronomy.* London: Bloomsbury T. & T. Clark, 2021.
Ginsberg, H. L. "A Phoenician Hymn in the Psalter." In *Atti Del XIX Congresso Internazionale Degli Orientalisti, Roma, 23–29 Settembre 1935–XIII*, 472–76. Roma: Tipografia del Senato G. Bardi, 1935.
———. "Poems about Baal and Anat." In *Ancient Near Eastern Texts Relating to the Old Testament*, edited by James B. Pritchard, 129–42. 3rd ed. Princeton: Princeton University Press, 1969.
———. "The Ugaritic Texts and Textual Criticism." *JBL* 62 (1943) 109–15.
Goedicke, Hans. "Unity and Diversity in the Oldest Religion of Egypt." In *Unity and Diversity: Essays in the History, Literature, and Religion of the Ancient Near East*, edited by Goedicke Hans and J. J. M. Roberts, 201–18. Baltimore: Johns Hopkins University Press, 1975.
Goldingay, John. *Psalms 42–89.* Grand Rapids: Baker Academic, 2007.
Gordis, Robert. *The Book of Job: Commentary, New Translation, and Special Studies.* New York: Jewish Theological Seminary of Studies of America, 1978.
Gordon, Robert P. *1 & 2 Samuel: A Commentary.* Exeter, UK: Paternoster, 1986.
Gray, Alison Ruth. *Psalm 18 in Word and Pictures: A Reading through Metaphor.* Biblical Interpretation Series 127. Leiden: Brill, 2014.
Gray, John. *The Biblical Doctrine of the Reign of God.* Edinburgh: T. & T. Clark, 1979.
———. "A Cantata of the Autumn Festival: Psalm LXVIII." *Journal of Semitic Studies* 22 (1977) 2–26.
Grayson, A. K. "Additions to Tablet V." In *The Ancient Near East: An Anthology of Texts and Pictures*, edited by James B. Pritchard, 36–39. Princeton: Princeton University Press, 2011.
———. "The Creation Epic, Additions to Tablet V–VII." In *Ancient Near Eastern Texts Relating to the Old Testament*, edited by James B. Pritchard, 501–3. 3rd ed. Princeton: Princeton University Press, 1969.
Green, Alberto R. W. *The Storm-God in the Ancient Near East.* Biblical and Judaic Studies 8. Winona Lake, IN: Eisenbrauns, 2003.
Greenberg, Moshe. *Ezekiel 1–20: A New Translation, Introduction, and Commentary.* AB 22. Garden City, NY: Doubleday, 1983.
Griaule, Marcel. *Conversations with Ogotemmêli: An Introduction to Dogon Religious Ideas.* London: Oxford University Press, 1965.
Griaule, Marcel, and Germaine Dieterlen. "The Dogon of the French Sudan." In *African Worlds: Studies in the Cosmological Ideas and Social Values of the African People*, edited by Daryll Forde, 83–110. 1954. Reprint, London: Oxford University Press, 1968.

———. *The Pale Fox*. Translated by Stephen C. Infantino. Chino Valley, AZ: Continuum Foundation, 1986.

Gunkel, Hermann. *Creation and Chaos in the Primeval Era and the Eschaton: A Religio-Historical Study of Genesis 1 and Revelation 12*. Translated by William Whitney Jr. 1895. Grand Rapids: Eerdmans, 2006.

———. *Einleitung in die Psalmen: die Gattungen der reliögisen Lyrik Israels*. 1933. Reprint, Göttingen: Vandenhoeck & Ruprecht, 2011.

———. *Introduction to the Psalms: The Genre of the Religious Lyrics of Israel*. Completed by Joachim Begrich. Translated by James D. Nogalski. 1933. Macon, GA: Mercer University Press, 1998.

———. *Schöpfung und Chaos in Urzeit und Endzeit: Eine religiongeschichtliche Untersuchung über Gen 1 und Ap Joh 12*. Göttingen: Vandenhoeck & Ruprecht, 1895.

Haak, Robert D. *Habakkuk*. VTSup 44. Leiden: Brill, 1992.

Habel, Norman C. *The Book of Job: A Commentary*. OTL. London: SCM, 1985.

———. "He Who Stretches Out the Heavens." *Catholic Biblical Quarterly* 34 (1972) 417–30.

———. "In Defence of God the Sage." In *The Voice from the Whirlwind: Interpreting the Book of Job*, edited by Leo G. Perdue and W. Clark Gilpin, 21–38. Nashville: Abingdon, 1992.

———. *Yahweh versus Baal: A Conflict of Religious Cultures*. New York: Bookman, 1964.

Hadjiev, Tchavdar S. *Joel and Amos: An Introduction and Commentary*. Tyndale Old Testament Commentaries. London: InterVarsity, 2020.

Hallo, William W., and J. J. A. van Dijk. *The Exaltation of Inanna*. New Haven: Yale University Press, 1968.

Halpern, Baruch. *The Constitution of the Monarchy in Israel*. Harvard Semitic Monograph 25. Chico, CA: Scholars, 1981.

Hamilton, Victor P. *The Book of Genesis Chapters 1–17*. NICOT. Grand Rapids: Eerdmans, 1990.

———. "*hādār*." In *Theological Word Book of the Old Testament*, edited by R. Laird Harris et al., 207–8. Chicago: Moody, 1980.

Hartley, John E. *The Book of Job*. NICOT. Grand Rapids: Eerdmans, 1988.

Heidel, Alexander. *The Babylonian Genesis*. Chicago: University of Chicago Press, 1951.

———. "The Meaning of '*mummu*' in Akkadian Literature." *JANES* 7 (1948) 98–105.

Hermission, Hans-Jürgen. "Observations on the Creation Theology in Wisdom." In *Creation in the Old Testament*, edited by Bernard W. Anderson, 118–34. Philadelphia: Fortress, 1984.

Heusch, Luc de. *Sacrifice in Africa: A Structuralist Approach*. Translated by Linda O'Brien and Alice Morton. Bloomington: Indiana University Press, 1985.

Hiebert, Theodore. *God of My Victory: The Ancient Hymn in Habakkuk 3*. Harvard Semitic Monographs 38. Atlanta: Scholars, 1986.

Hoffmeier, James K. "Some Thoughts on Genesis 1 & 2 and Egyptian Cosmology." *JANES* 15 (1983) 39–49.

Holladay, William Lee. *Jeremiah 1: A Commentary on the Book of the Prophet Jeremiah, Chapters 1–25*. Hermeneia. Philadelphia: Fortress, 1986.

Horowitz, Wayne. *Mesopotamian Cosmic Geography*. Mesopotamian Civilizations. Winona Lake, IN: Eisenbrauns, 1998.

Howard, David M., Jr. *The Structure of Psalms 93-100*. Biblical and Judaic Studies 5. Winona Lake, IN: Eisenbrauns, 1997.
Humbert, Paul. "La relation de Genèse 1 et du Psaume 104 avec la liturgie du Nouvel-An Israélite." *Revue d'histoire et de philosophie religieuses* 15.1-2 (1935) 1-27.
Irwin, William A. "The Psalm of Habakkuk." *JNES* 1 (1942) 10-40.
Jacobs, Paul F. "'Cows of Bashan'—A Critical Note on the Interpretation of Amos 4:1." *JBL* 104 (1985) 109-10.
Jacobsen, Thorkild. "The Battle between Marduk and Tiamat." *Journal of American Oriental Society* 88 (1968) 104-8.
Jacobson, Rolf A. "Psalm 29: Ascribe to the Lord." In *The Book of Psalms*, edited by Nancy DeClaissé-Walford et al., 649-64. Grand Rapids: Eerdmans, 2014.
Janowski, Bernd. "Das Königtum Gottes in den Psalmen: Bemerkungen zu einem nuen Gesamtentwurf." *Zeitschrift für Theologie und die Kirche* 86 (1989) 389-454.
Jeremias, Jörg. *The Book of Amos: A Commentary*. Translated by Douglas W. Stott. OTL. Louisville: Westminster John Knox, 1998.
———. *Königtum Gottes in den Psalmen: Israels Begegnung mit dem kanaanäischen Mythos in den Jahweh-König-Psalmen*. Forschungen zur Religion und Literatur des Alten und Neuen Testaments 141. Göttingen: Vandenhoeck & Ruprecht, 1987.
———. *Theophanie: Die Geschichte einer Alttestamentlichen Gattung*. Wissenschaftliche Monographien zum Alten und Neuen Testament. Neukirchen-Vluyn: Neukirchener Verlag des Erziehungsvereins, 1965.
Johnson, Aubrey R. *Sacral Kingship in Ancient Israel*. Cardiff: University of Wales Press, 1955.
Johnson, E. "אנף." In *TDOT* 1:348-60.
Jones, Douglas Rawlinson. *Jeremiah*. NCBC. Grand Rapids: Eerdmans, 1992.
Jong, Matthijs J. de. *Isaiah among the Ancient Near Eastern Prophets: A Comparative Study of the Earliest Stages of the Isaiah Tradition and the Neo-Assyrian Prophecies*. Leiden: Brill, 2007.
Kapelrud, Arvid Schou. "אביר." In *TDOT* 1:42-44.
———. "Creation in the Ras Shamra Texts." *Studia Theologica* 34 (1980) 1-11.
Kautzsch, E., ed. *Gesenius' Hebrew Grammar*. New York: Oxford University Press, 1988.
Kedar-Kopfstein, B. "קרן." In *TDOT* 13:167-74.
Keel, Othmar. *The Symbolism of the Biblical World: Ancient Near Eastern Iconography and the Book of Psalms*. Translated by Timothy J. Hallet. New York: Seabury, 1978.
Kennedy, James M. "The Root *g' r* in the Light of Semantic Analysis." *JBL* 106 (1987) 47-64.
Kessler, Martin. *The Battle of the Gods: The God of Israel versus Marduk of Babylon: A Literary/Theological Interpretation of Jeremiah 50-51*. Assen: Van Gorcum, 2003.
Kidner, Derek. *Psalms 73-150*. 1975. Reprint, Downers Grove, IL: IVP Academic, 2008.
Kinsley, David R. *The Goddesses' Mirror: Visions of the Divine from East and West*. Albany: State University of New York Press, 1989.
Kitts, Margo. "The Near Eastern *Chaoskampf* in the River Battle of Iliad 21." *JANER* 13.1 (2013) 86-112.
Kleinig, John W. *The Lord's Song: The Basis, Function, and Significance of Choral Music in Chronicles*. JSOTSup 156. Sheffield: JSOT Press, 1993.
Kloos, Carola. *Yhwh's Combat with the Sea: A Canaanite Tradition in the Religion of Ancient Israel*. Leiden: Brill, 1986.

BIBLIOGRAPHY

Kraus, Hans-Joachim. *Die Königherrschaft Gottes im Alten Testament: Untersuchungen zu den Liedern von Jahwes Thronbesteigung.* Beiträge zur historischen Theologie 13. Tübingen: Mohr Siebeck, 1951.

———. *Psalms 1–59: A Commentary.* 1978. Translated by Hilton C. Oswald. Continental Commentaries. Minneapolis: Augsburg, 1988.

———. *Psalms 60–150: A Commentary.* 1978. Translated by Hilton C. Oswald. Continental Commentaries. Minneapolis: Augsburg, 1989.

Kravitz, Leonard S., and Kerry M. Olitzk. *The Book of Job: A Modern Translation and Commentary.* Eugene, OR: Wipf & Stock, 2017.

Kselman, John S. "Psalm 77 and the Book of Exodus." *Journal of Ancient Near Eastern Society of Columbia University* 15.3 (1983) 51–58.

Kuntz, John Kenneth. "Psalm 18: A Rhetorical-Critical Analysis." *JSOT* 26 (1983) 3–31.

Kwakkel, Gert. "The Monster as a Toy: Leviathan in Psalm 104:26." In *Playing with Leviathan: Interpretation and Reception of Monsters from the Biblical World*, edited by Koert van Bekkum et al., 77–89. Leiden: Brill, 2017.

Lambert, Wilfred G. *The Babylonian Creation Myths.* Winona Lake, IN: Eisenbrauns, 2013.

———. "Creation in the Bible and the Ancient Near East." In *Creation and Chaos: A Reconsideration of Herman Gunkel's Chaoskampf Hypothesis*, edited by JoAnn Scurlock et al., 44–47. Winona Lake, IN: Eisenbrauns, 2013.

———. "The Gula Hymn of Bullutṣa-rabi." *Orientalia* 36 (1967) 105–32.

———. "Mesopotamian Creation Stories." In *Imagining Creation*, edited by Markham J. Geller and Mineke Schipper, 15–59. Leiden: Brill, 2010.

Lambert, Wilfred G., and Alan Ralph Millard. *Atraḥasīs: The Babylonian Story of the Flood.* Oxford: Clarendon, 1969.

Levenson, Jon Douglas. *Creation and the Persistence of Evil: The Jewish Drama of Divine Omnipotence.* San Francisco: Harper & Row, 1988.

———. *Sinai and Zion: An Entry into the Jewish Bible.* Minneapolis: Winston, 1985.

Lévêque, Jean. "L'Argument de la Création dans le Livre de Job." In *La création dans l'Orient ancien*, edited by Louis Derousseaux, 261–99. Paris: Latour-Maubourg, 1987.

Lillas-Schuil, Rosmari. "A Survey of Syntagms in the Hebrew Bible Classified as Hendiadys." In *Current Issues in the Analysis of Semitic Grammar and Lexicon II*, edited by Lutz Edzard and Jan Retsö, 79–100. Wiesbaden: Harrassowitz, 2006.

Linville, James R. *Amos and the Cosmic Imagination.* Society for Old Testament Studies Series. Aldershot, UK: Ashgate, 2008.

Lipiński, Édouard. *La Royauté de Yahwé dans la Poésie et la Culte de l' Ancien Israël.* Brussels: Paleis der Academiën, 1965.

Lohfink, Norbert. "חרם." In *TDOT* 5:180–99.

Long, Charles H. *Alpha: The Myths of Creation.* Chico, CA: Scholars, 1983.

———. "Creation Myth." *Encyclopedia Britannica*, September 6, 2022. https://www.britannica.com/topic/creation-myth.

Longman, Tremper, III. "Psalm 98: A Divine Warrior Victory Song." *Journal of Evangelical Theological Society* 27 (1984) 267–74.

———. *Psalms: An Introduction and Commentary.* Tyndale Old Testament Commentaries. Downers Grove, IL: InterVarsity, 2014.

Loretz, Oswald. "Der ugaritisch-hebräische Parallelismus *rkb ʿrpt*//*rkb bʿrbwt* in Psalm 68,5." *Ugarit-Forschungen* 34 (2002) 521–26.

———. *Ugarit-Texte und Thronbesteigungspsalmen: Die Metamorphose des Regenspenders Baal-Jahwe (Ps 24, 7–10; 29; 47; 93; 95–100 sowie Ps 77, 17–20; 114)*. Ugaritisch-biblische Literatur 7. Münster: Ugarit-Verlag, 1988.

Lundbom, Jack R. *Jeremiah 37–52: A New Translation with Introduction and Commentary*. AB 21C. New York: Doubleday, 2004.

Luyster, Robert. "Wind and Water: Cosmogonic Symbolism in the Old Testament." *ZAW* 93 (1981) 1–10.

Macintosh, Andrew A. "A Consideration of the Hebrew גער." *VT* 19 (1969) 471–79.

Mafico, Temba J. "Judge, Judging." In *Anchor Bible Dictionary*, edited by David Noel Freedman, 6:1104–6. New York: Doubleday, 1992.

Magonet, Jonathan. "On Reading the Psalms as Liturgy: Psalms 96–99." In *The Shape and Shaping of the Book of Psalms: The Current State of Scholarship*, edited by Nancy L. DeClaissé-Walford, 161–77. Atlanta: SBL, 2014.

Malinowski, Bronislaw. *Magic, Science and Religion and Other Essays*. Garden City, NY: Doubleday, 1948.

Mann, Thomas W. *Divine Presence and Guidance in the Israelite Traditions: The Typology of Exaltation*. Baltimore: Johns Hopkins University Press, 1977.

Margulis, B. "The Canaanite Origin of Psalm 29 Reconsidered." *Biblica* 51 (1970) 332–48.

Markl, Dominik. "Hab 3 in intertextueller und kontextueller Sicht." *Biblia* 85 (2004) 99–108.

Martin, Denise. "Nature, Maat and Myth in Ancient Egyptian and Dogon Cosmology." PhD diss., Temple University Proquest Dissertations, 2001.

May, Herbert G. "Some Cosmic Connotations of *Mayim Rabbîm*, 'Many Waters.'" *JBL* 74.1 (1955) 9–21.

Mays, James Luther. *Amos: A Commentary*. OTL. Philadelphia: Westminster, 1969.

Mbiti, J. S. *New Testament Eschatology in an African Background*. London: Oxford University Press, 1971.

McComiskey, Thomas Edward. "Amos." In *The Expositor's Bible Commentary*, edited by Frank E. Gaebelein et al., 7:269–331. Grand Rapids: Zondervan, 1985.

———. "The Hymnic Elements of the Prophecy of Amos: A Study of Form-Critical Methodology." *Journal of Evangelical Theological Society* 30 (1987) 139–57.

McKane, William. *A Critical and Exegetical Commentary on Jeremiah*. International Critical Commentary 1. Edinburgh: T. & T. Clark, 1986.

McLaughlin, John I. "Is Amos (Still) among the Wise?" *JBL* 133.2 (2014) 281–303.

Mettinger, Tryggve N. D. *The Dethronement of Sebaoth: Studies in the Shem and Kabod Theologies*. Translated by Frederick H. Cryer. Lund: Gleerup, 1982.

———. *In Search of God: The Meaning and Message of the Everlasting Names*. Translated by Frederick H. Cryer. Philadelphia: Fortress, 1987.

———. *Reports from a Scholar's Life: Select Papers on the Hebrew Bible*. Winona Lake, IN: Eisenbrauns, 2015.

———. "YHWH Sabaoth: The Heavenly King on the Cherubim Throne." In *Studies in the Period of David and Solomon and Other Essays*, edited by T. Ishida, 109–38. Winona Lake, IN: Eisenbrauns, 1982.

Miller, Patrick D. "Animal Names as Designations in Ugaritic and Hebrew." *Ugarit-Forschungen* 2 (1970) 177–86.

———. *The Divine Warrior in Early Israel*. Harvard Semitic Monographs 5. Atlanta: SBL, 2006.

Mowinckel, Sigmund. *Der Achtundsechzigste Psalm*. Avhandlinger Utgitt av det Norske. Oslo: Dybwad, 1953.

———. *Psalm Studies*. Translated by Mark E. Biddle. 2 vols. History of Biblical Studies 2. Atlanta: SBL, 2014.

———. *Psalmenstudien II: Das Thronbesteigungsfest Jahwäs und der Ursprung der Eschatologie*. Kristiania: Dybwad, 1922.

———. *The Psalms in Israel's Worship*. Translated by D. R. Ap-Thomas. 1962. Reprint, Grand Rapids: Eerdmans, 2004.

Murphy, Kelly J. "Myth, Reality, and the Goddess Anat: Anat's Violence and Independence in the Baal Cycle." *Ugarit-Forschungen* 41 (2009) 525–41.

Nicholson, Ernest W. *The Book of the Prophet Jeremiah: Chapters 1–25*. Cambridge Bible Commentary. Cambridge: Cambridge University Press, 1973.

Niditch, Susan. *Judges: A Commentary*. OTL. Louisville: Westminster John Knox, 2008.

Nielsen, Kirsten. "Whose Song of Praise? Reflections on the Purpose of the Psalm in 1 Chronicles 16." In *The Chronicler as Author: Studies in Text and Texture*, edited by M. Partick Graham and Steven L. McKenzie, 327–36. JSOTSup 263. Sheffield: Sheffield Academic, 1999.

Noegel, Scott B. *Janus Parallelism in the Book of Job*. JSOTSup 223. Sheffield: Sheffield Academic, 1996.

———. "On the Wings of the Winds: Towards an Understanding of Winged Mischwesen in the Ancient Near East." *KASKAL* 14 (2017) 15–54.

Nwaoru, Emmanuel O. "A Fresh Look at Amos 4:1–3 and Its Imagery." *VT* 59.3 (2009) 460–74.

Okpewho, Isidore. *Myth in Africa: A Study of its Aesthetics and Cultural Relevance*. Cambridge: Cambridge University Press, 1983.

Ollenburger, Ben C. *Zion the City of the Great King: A Theological Symbol of the Jerusalem Cult*. JSOTSup 41. Sheffield: JSOT Press, 1987.

Olmo Lete, Gregorio del. *Mitos y leyendes de Canaan: Según la Tradición de Ugarit*. Madrid: Ediciones Cristianadad, 1981.

———. "Ps 68: A Composite Canaanite-Yahwistic Celebration of Israel's God: A New Reading." In *Zwischen Zion und Zaphon: Studien in Gedenken an den Theologen Oswald Loretz (14.01.1928–12.04.2014)*, edited by Ludger Hiepel und Marie-Theres Wacker, 191–216. Alter Orient und Altes Testament 438. Müster: Ugarit-Verlag, 2016.

Olmo Lete, Gregorio del, and Joaquín Sanmartín. *A Dictionary of the Ugaritic Language in the Alphabetic Tradition*. Translated by Wilfred G. E. Watson. Handbook of Oriental Studies 112. Leiden: Brill, 2003.

Ortlund, Eric N. "An Intertextual Reading of the Theophany of Psalm 97." *Scandinavian Journal of the Old Testament* 20.2 (2006) 273–85.

———. *Piercing Leviathan: God's Defeat of Evil in the Book of Job*. Downers Grove, IL: InterVarsity, 2021.

Otto, Rudolf. *The Idea of the Holy: An Inquiry into the Non-Rational Factor in the Idea of the Divine and Its Relation to the Rational*. Translated by John W. Harvey. Oxford: Oxford University Press, 1923.

Otzen, B. "*běliyya' al*." In *TDOT* 2:133–36.

Paas, Stefan. *Creation and Judgement: Creation Texts in Some Eighth Century Prophets*. Leiden: Brill, 2003.

Pardee, Dennis, and Nancy Pardee. "Gods of Glory Ought to Thunder: The Matrix of Psalm 29." In *Psalm 29 through Time and Tradition*, edited by Lowell K. Handy, 115-25. Princeton Theological Monograph Series 110. Eugene, OR: Pickwick Publications, 2009.
Parker, Simon B., ed. *Ugaritic Narrative Poetry*. Translated by Mark S. Smith et al.. Writings from the Ancient World 9. Atlanta: Scholars, 1997.
Parpola, Simo. *Assyrian Prophecies*. Finland: Helsinki University Press, 1997.
Parrinder, Geoffrey. "Foreword." In *Pears Encyclopaedia of Myths and Legends, Western and Northern Europe, Southern and Central Africa*, edited by Sheila Savill et al., 12. London: Pelham, 1977.
Patterson, Richard D. "The Psalm of Habakkuk." *Grace Theological Journal* 8.2 (1987) 163-94.
Patton, John Hastings. *Canaanite Parallels in the Book of Psalms*. Baltimore: Johns Hopkins University Press, 1944.
Paul, Shalom M. *Amos: A Commentary on the Book of Amos*. Hermeneia. Minneapolis: Fortress, 1991.
Perdue, Leo G. *Wisdom in Revolt: Metaphorical Theology in the Book of Job*. JSOTSup 112. Sheffield: Almond, 1991.
Petersen, Allan Rosengren. *The Royal God: Enthronement Festivals in Ancient Israel and Ugarit?* JSOTSup 259. Sheffield: Sheffield Academic, 1998.
Pettazzoni, Raffaele. *Essays on the History of Religions*. Studies in the History of Religions 1. Leiden: Brill, 1954.
Pfeiffer, Henrik. *Jahwes Kommen von Süden: Jdc 5; Hab 3; Dtn 33 und Ps 68 in ihrem literature- und theologiegeschichtlichen Umfeld*. Forschungen zur Religion und Literatur des Alten und Neuen Testaments 211. Göttingen: Vandenhoeck & Ruprecht, 2005.
Pitard, Wayne T. "The Binding of Yamm: A New Edition of the Ugaritic Text KTU 1.83." *JNES* 57.4 (1998) 261-80.
———. "Just How Many Monsters Did Anat Fight (KTU 1.3.III:38-47)?" In *Ugarit at Seventy-Five*, edited by K. Lawson Younger Jr., 75-88. Winona Lake, IN: Eisenbrauns, 2007.
Pope, Marvin H. *Job*. AB 15. Garden City, NY: Doubleday, 1965.
Prinsloo, Gert T. M. "Reading Habakkuk 3 in the Light of Ancient Unit Delimiters." *HTS Teologiese Studies/Theological Studies* 69.1 (2013) 1-11.
Rad, Gerhard von. *Genesis: A Commentary*. Translated by John H. Marks. OTL. Philadelphia: Westminster, 1972.
———. *Wisdom in Israel*. Translated by James Martin. London: SCM, 1993.
Radine, Jason. *The Book of Amos in Emergent Judah*. Forschungen zum Alten Testament 2/45. Tübingen: Mohr Siebeck, 2010.
Rahmouni, Aicha. *Divine Epithets in the Ugaritic Alphabet Texts*. Translated by J. N. Ford. Handbuch der Orientalistik 93. Leiden: Brill, 2008.
Ray, Benjamin C. *African Religions: Symbol, Ritual, and Community*. Englewood Cliffs, NJ: Prentice-Hall, 1976.
Reif, Stephan C. "A Note on גער." *VT* 21.2 (1971) 241-44.
———. "Psalm 93: An Historical and Comparative Survey of its Jewish Interpretation." In *Genesis, Isaiah, and Psalms: A Festschrift to Honour Professor John Emerton for His Eightieth Birthday*, edited by Katherine Dell et al., 193-214. Leiden: Brill, 2010.

———. "Some Comments on the Connotations of the Stem גער in Early Rabbinic Texts." In *Leshon Limmudim: Essays on the Language and Literature of the Hebrew Bible in Honour of A. A. Macintosh*, edited by David A. Baer et al., 253–67. London: Bloomsbury, 2013.

Reiner, Erica, ed. *The Assyrian Dictionary of the Oriental Institute of the University of Chicago*. Vol. 13. Chicago: Oriental Institute, 1982.

Renz, Thomas. *The Books of Nahum, Habakkuk, and Zephania*. NICOT. Grand Rapids: Eerdmans, 2021.

Ringgren, Helmer. "חָקַק." In *TDOT* 5:139–47.

———. "עָשָׂה." In *TDOT* 11:387–403.

Roberts, Jimmy Jack McBee. "Mowinckel's Enthronement Festival: A Review." In *The Book of the Psalms: Composition and Reception*, edited by Peter W. Flint and Patrick D. Miller, 97–115. Leiden: Brill, 2005.

———. "Zion in the Theology of the Davidic-Solomonic Empire." In *The Bible and the Ancient Near East: Collected Essays*, edited by J. J. M. Roberts, 331–47. Winona Lake, IN: Eisenbrauns, 2002.

Robertson, O. Palmer. *The Books of Nahum, Habakkuk, and Zephania*. Grand Rapids: Eerdmans, 1990.

Robinson, A. "Zion and Ṣāphôn in Psalm xlviii 3." *VT* 24.1 (1974) 118–23.

Rosenbaum, Stanley Ned. *Amos of Israel: A New Interpretation*. Macon, Georgia: Mercer University Press, 1990.

Ross, Allen P. *A Commentary on the Psalms*. 3 vols. Grand Rapids, MI: Kregel, 2016.

Routledge, Robin. "Did God Create Chaos? Unresolved Tension in Genesis 1:1–2." *Tyndale Bulletin* 61.1 (2010) 71–88.

Sagan, Carl. *Broca's Brain: Reflections of the Romance of Science*. 1979. Reprint, New York: Random House, 2011.

Sandoval, Timothy J. "Prophetic and Proverbial Justice: Amos, Proverbs, and Intertextuality." In *Second Wave Intertextuality and the Hebrew Bible*, edited by Marianne Grohmann and Hyun Chul Paul Kim, 131–52. Resources for Biblical Study 93. Atlanta: SBL, 2019.

Sarna, Nahum M. *Genesis: The Traditional Hebrew Text with the New JPS Translation Commentary*. Philadelphia: Jewish Publication Society, 1989.

Schaper, von Joachim. "Psalm 47 und sein *Sitz im Leben*." *ZAW* 106 (1994) 262–75.

Schmidt, Hans. *Die Psalmen*. Handbuch zum Alten Testament 15. Tubingen: Mohr Siebeck, 1934.

Schmidt, Werner H. *Königtum Gottes in Ugarit und Israel: Zur Herkunft der Königsprädikation Jahwes*. BZAW 80. Berlin: Töpelmann, 1966.

Schmuttermayr, Georg. *Psalm 18 und 2 Samuel 22: Studien zu einem Doppeltext*. Munich: Kösel, 1971.

Schwemer, Daniel. "The Storm-Gods of the Ancient Near East: Summary, Synthesis, Recent Studies: Part I." *JANER* 7.2 (2007) 121–68.

———. "The Storm-Gods of the Ancient Near East: Summary, Synthesis, Recent Studies: Part II." *JANER* 8.1 (2008) 1–44.

Scranton, Laird. *The Cosmological Origins of Myth and Symbol: From the Dogon and Ancient Egypt to India, Tibet, and China*. Rochester, VT: Inner Traditions, 2010.

———. *The Science of the Dogon: Decoding the African Mystery Tradition*. Rochester, VT: Inner Traditions, 2006.

Scurlock, JoAnn. "Searching for Meaning in Genesis 1:2: Purposeful Creation out of Chaos without *Kampf*." In *Creation and Chaos: A Reconsideration of Hermann Gunkel's Chaoskampf Hypothesis*, edited by JoAnn Scurlock et al., 48–61. Winona Lake, IN: Eisenbrauns, 2013.

Segal, Robert A. *The Religion of the Semites: The Fundamental Institutions*. New York: Routledge, 2002.

Seow, Choon Leung. *Myth, Drama, and the Politics of David's Dance*. Harvard Semitics Monographs 44. Atlanta: Scholars, 1989.

Shenkel, James Donald. "An Interpretation of Psalm 93,5." *Biblica* 46 (1965) 401–16.

Shveka, Avi. "For a Pair of Shoes: A New Light on an Obscure Verse in Amos' Prophecy." *VT* 62.1 (2012) 95–114.

Simkins, Ronald A. *Creator and Creation: Nature in the Worldview of Ancient Israel*. Peabody, MA: Hendrickson, 1994.

Skinner, John. *A Critical and Exegetical Commentary on Genesis*. New York: Scribner, 1910.

Smick, Elmer B. "Job." In *The Expositor's Bible Commentary*, edited by Frank E. Gaebelein et al., 4:843–1060. Grand Rapids: Zondervan, 1988.

Smith, Mark S. *The Carlsberg Papyri 5: On The Primaeval Ocean*. CNI Publications 26. Copenhagen: Museum Tusculanum Press, 2002.

———. *The Origins of Biblical Monotheism: Israel's Polytheistic Background and the Ugaritic Texts*. Oxford: Oxford University Press, 2001.

———. *The Ugaritic Baal Cycle: Introduction with Text, Translation, and Commentary of KTU 1.1–1.2*. Vol. 1. Leiden: Brill, 1994.

Smith, Mark S., and Wayne T. Pitard. *The Ugaritic Baal Cycle: Introduction with Text, Translation, and Commentary of KTU/CTA 1.3–1.4*. Vol. 2. Leiden: Brill, 2009.

Smith, W. Robertson. *Lectures in the Religion of the Semites: The Fundamental Institutions*. New York: Appleton, 1894.

Sonik, Karen. "From Hesiod's Abyss to Ovid's *rudis indigestaque moles*: Chaos and Cosmos in the Babylonian 'Epic of Creation.'" In *Creation and Chaos: A Reconsideration of Herman Gunkel's Chaoskampf Hypothesis*, edited by JoAnn Scurlock et al., 1–25. Winona Lake, IN: Eisenbrauns, 2013.

Soskice, Janet. "Why *Creatio ex nihilo* for Theology Today?" In *Creation ex nihilo: Origins, Development, Contemporary Challenges*, edited by Gary A. Anderson et al., 37–54. Notre Dame: University of Notre Dame Press, 2018.

Speiser, Ephraim A. "The Creation Epic (Enuma Elish)." In *Ancient Near Eastern Texts Relating to the Old Testament*, edited by James B. Pritchard, 60–72. 3rd ed. Princeton: Princeton University Press, 1992.

Strawn, Brent A. "*kwšrwt* in Ps 68:7 Again. A (Small) Test Case in Relating Ugarit to the Hebrew Bible." *Ugarit-Forschungen* 41 (2009) 631–48.

———. "*wĕnil'āh*, 'O Victorious One,' in Ps 68,10." *Ugarit-Forschungen* 34 (2002) 785–98.

———. *What Is Stronger Than a Lion: Leonine Image and Metaphor in the Hebrew Bible and Ancient Near East*. Fribourg: Academic, 2005.

Strenski, Ivan. *Malinowski and the Work of Myth*. Princeton: Princeton University Press, 2014.

Sutcliffe, Edmund F. "A Note on Psalm CIV 8." *VT* 2.2 (1952) 177–79.

Sweeney, Marvin A. "Structure, Genre, and Intent in the Book of Habakkuk." *VT* 41.1 (1991) 63–83.

Sylva, Dennis. "The Rising נהרות of Psalm 93: Chaotic Order." *JSOT* 36.4 (2012) 471–82.

Talon, Phillipe. *The Standard Babylonian Creation Myth: Enūma Eliš*. State Archives of Assyria Cuneiform Texts 4. Helsinki: Neo-Assyrian Text Corpus Project, 2005.

Tarazi, Paul Nadim. "An Exegesis of Psalm 93." *St. Vladimir's Theological Quarterly* 35.2–3 (1991) 137–48.

Tate, Marvin E. *Psalms 51–100*. WBC 20. Dallas, TX: Word, 1990.

Tengströme, S. "חָלַף." In *TDOT* 4:432–35.

Terrien, Samuel. "Amos and Wisdom." In *Studies in Ancient Israelite Wisdom*, edited by Harry M. Orlinsky, 448–55. New York: Ktav, 1976.

Thomas, Heath A. *Habakkuk*. Two Horizons Old Testament Commentary. Grand Rapids: Eerdmans, 2018.

Thompson, J. A. *The Book of Jeremiah*. NICOT. Grand Rapids: Eerdmans, 1980.

Thury, Eva, and Margaret K Devinney. *Introduction to Mythology: Contemporary Approaches to Classical and World Myths*. Oxford: Oxford University Press, 2009.

Tsumura, David Toshio. "Chaos and *Chaoskampf* in the Bible: Is 'Chaos' a Suitable Term to Describe Creation or Conflict in the Bible?" In *Conversations on Canaanite and Biblical Themes: Creation, Chaos, and Monotheism*, edited by Rebecca S. Watson and Adrian H. W. Curtis, 253–84. Berlin: de Gruyter, 2022.

———. *Creation and Destruction: A Reappraisal of the Chaoskampf Theory in the Old Testament*. Winona Lake, IN: Eisenbrauns, 2005.

———. *The Earth and the Waters in Genesis 1 and 2: A Linguistic Investigation*. JSOTSup 83. Sheffield: Sheffield Academic, 1989.

———. "Ugaritic Poetry and Habakkuk 3." *Tyndale Bulletin* 40.1 (1989) 24–48.

Ulrichsen, Jarl H. "Jhwh mālāḵ: einige sprachliche Beobachtungen." *VT* 27.3 (1977) 361–74.

Uehlinger, C. "Leviathan לויתן." In *Dictionary of Deities and Demons*, edited by Karel van der Toorn et al., 511–15. Leiden: Brill, 1999.

Vesco, Jean-Luc. "Le Psaume 18, Lecture Davidique." *Revue Biblique* 94.1 (1987) 5–62.

Vicchio, Stephen J. *The Book of Job: A History of Interpretation and a Commentary*. Eugene, OR: Wipf & Stock, 2020.

Von Hendy, Andrew. *The Modern Construction of Myth*. Bloomington: Indiana University Press, 2001.

Wagner, Siegfried. "אָמַר." In *TDOT* 1:328–45.

Wallis, G. "רָעָה." In *TDOT* 13:544–53.

Walls, Neal H. *The Goddess Anat in Ugaritic Myth*. SBL Dissertation Series 135. Atlanta: Scholars, 1992.

Waltke, Bruce K., and James M. Houston. *The Psalms as Christian Praise: A Historical Commentary*. Grand Rapids: Eerdmans, 2019.

Waltke, Bruce K., and M. O'Connor. *An Introduction to Biblical Hebrew Syntax*. Winona Lake, IN: Eisenbrauns, 1990.

Walton, John. *Genesis 1 as Ancient Cosmology*. Winona Lake, IN: Eisenbrauns, 2011.

Wardlaw, Terence Randall. "The Meaning of ברא in Genesis 1:1–2:3." *VT* 64.3 (2014) 502–13.

Warmuth, G. "הָדָר." In *TDOT* 3:335–41.

Watson, Rebecca S. *Chaos Uncreated: A Reassessment of the Theme of "Chaos" in the Hebrew Bible*. BZAW 341. Berlin: de Gruyter, 2005.

Watson, Rebecca S., and Adrian H. W. Curtis. *Conversations on Canaanite and Biblical Themes: Creation, Chaos, and Monotheism.* Berlin: de Gruyter, 2022.

Weinfeld, Moshe. "Divine Intervention in War in Ancient Israel and in the Ancient Near East." In *History, Historiography, and Interpretation: Studies in Biblical and Cuneiform Literatures*, edited by Hayim Tadmor et al., 121–47. Jerusalem: Hebrew University, 1983.

Weiser, Artur. *The Psalms: A Commentary.* Translated by Herbert Hartwell. OTL. London: SCM, 1962.

Wenham, Gordon J. *Genesis 1–15.* WBC 1. Grand Rapids: Zondervan, 1987.

Westermann, Claus. *Praise and Lament in the Psalms.* Translated by Keith R. Crim and Richard N. Soulen. Atlanta: John Knox, 1981.

Whitley, John B. "עיפה in Amos 4:13: New Evidence for the Yahwistic Incorporation of Ancient Near Eastern Solar Imagery." *JBL* 134.1 (2015) 127–38.

Wiggermann, Frans A. M. "The Four Winds and the Origins of Pazuzu." In *Das geistige Erfassen der Welt im Alten Orient: Beitrage zu Sprache, Religion, Kultur und Gesellschaft*, edited by Claus Wilcke, 125–65. Wiesbaden: Harrassowitz, 2007.

Wilkinson, Richard H. "The Horus Names and the Forms and Significance of the Serekh in the Royal Egyptian Inscriptions." *Journal of the Society for the Study of Egyptian Antiquities* 15 (1987) 98–104.

Wilson, Ian. "Divine Presence in Deuteronomy." *Tyndale Bulletin* 43.2 (1992) 403–6.

Wilson, John A. "Egypt: The Nature of the Universe." In *The Intellectual Adventure of Ancient Man: An Essay on Speculative Thought in the Ancient Near East*, edited by H. Frankfort et al., 31–61. Chicago: University of Chicago Press, 1977.

———. "The Hymn to the Aton." In *The Ancient Near East: An Anthology of Texts and Pictures*, edited by James B. Pritchard, 324–28. Princeton: Princeton University Press, 2011.

———. "The Instruction for King Meri-Ka-Re." In *Ancient Near Eastern Texts Relating to the Old Testament*, edited by James B. Pritchard, 414–18. 3rd ed. Princeton: Princeton University Press, 1969.

Wolde, Ellen van. *Reframing Biblical Studies: When Language and Text Meet Culture, Cognition, and Context.* Winona Lake, IN: Eisenbrauns, 2009.

———. "Why the Verb ברא Does Not Mean 'To Create' in Genesis 1:1—2:4a" *JSOT* 34.1 (2009) 3–23.

Wolff, Hans Walter. *Amos the Prophet: The Man and His Background.* Edited by John Henry Paul Reumann. Translated by Foster R. McCurley. Philadelphia: Fortress, 1973.

———. *Joel and Amos: A Commentary on the Books of the Prophets.* Edited by S. Dean McBride Jr. Translated by Waldemar Janzen et al. Hermeneia. Philadelphia: Fortress, 1977.

Wolkstein, Diana, and Samuel Noah Kramer. *Inanna: Queen of Heaven and Earth.* New York: Harper & Row, 1983.

Wood, Alice. *Of Wings and Wheels: A Synthetic Study of the Biblical Cherubim.* BZAW 385. Berlin: de Gruyter, 2008.

Wood, Leon J. "חרם." In *Theological Word Book of the Old Testament*, edited by R. Laird Harris et al., 324–25. Chicago: Moody, 1980.

Wright, Christopher J. H. *The Message of Ezekiel: A New Heart and a New Spirit.* Downers Grove, IL: InterVarsity, 2001.

Wyatt, Nicolas. "Arms and the King: The Earliest Allusions of the Chaoskampf Motif and the Implications for the Interpretation of the Ugaritic and Biblical Traditions." In *There's Such Divinity Doth Hedge a King: Selected Essays of Nicholas Wyatt on Royal Ideology in Ugaritic and Old Testament Literature*, edited by Nicolas Wyatt, 151–89. Society for Old Testament Study Monographs. London: Routledge, 2016.

———. "Distinguishing Wood and Trees in the Waters: Creation in Biblical Thought." In *Conversations on Canaanite and Biblical Themes: Creation, Chaos, and Monotheism*, edited by Rebecca S. Watson and Adrian H. W. Curtis, 203–52. Berlin: de Gruyter, 2022.

———. *Religious Texts from Ugarit: The Words of Ilimilku and His Colleagues*. Biblical Seminar 53. Sheffield: Sheffield Academic, 1998.

Xella, P. "HABY חבי." In *Dictionary of Deities and Demons*, edited by Karel van der Toorn et al., 377. Leiden: Brill, 1999.

Yoder, Tyler R. *Fishers of Fish and Fishers of Men: Fishing Imagery in the Hebrew Bible and the Ancient Near East*. Winona Lake, IN: Eisenbrauns, 2016.

Zobel, H. J. "צְבָאוֹת." In *TDOT* 12:215–32.

www.ingramcontent.com/pod-product-compliance
Lightning Source LLC
Chambersburg PA
CBHW071231290426
44108CB00013B/1375